Paul McFedries

Microsoft® Windows 7

UNLEASHED

SAMS | 800 East 96th Street, Indianapolis, Indiana 46240 USA

Microsoft Windows 7 Unleashed

ISBN-13: 978-0-6723-3069-8

ISBN-10: 0-672-33069-5

Library of Congress Cataloging-in-Publication Data:

McFedries, Paul.

  Microsoft Windows 7 unleashed / Paul McFedries.

    p. cm.

  ISBN 978-0-672-33069-8

  1. Microsoft Windows (Computer file) 2. Operating systems (Computers) I. Title.

  QA76.76.O63M398163 2010

  005.4'46—dc22

                       2009024027

Printed in the United States of America

Third Printing: August 2009

Trademarks

All terms mentioned in this book that are known to be trademarks or service marks have been appropriately capitalized. Pearson Education, Inc. cannot attest to the accuracy of this information. Use of a term in this book should not be regarded as affecting the validity of any trademark or service mark.

Warning and Disclaimer

Every effort has been made to make this book as complete and as accurate as possible, but no warranty or fitness is implied. The information provided is on an "as is" basis. The author and the publisher shall have neither liability nor responsibility to any person or entity with respect to any loss or damages arising from the information contained in this book.

Bulk Sales

Pearson offers excellent discounts on this book when ordered in quantity for bulk purchases or special sales. For more information, please contact:

  U.S. Corporate and Government Sales
  1-800-382-3419
  corpsales@pearsontechgroup.com

For sales outside of the U.S., please contact:

  International Sales
  +1-317-581-3793
  international@pearsontechgroup.com

Associate Publisher
Greg Wiegand

Acquisitions Editor
Rick Kughen

Development Editor
Rick Kughen

Managing Editor
Patrick Kanouse

Project Editor
Jennifer Gallant

Copy Editor
Keith Cline

Indexer
Tim Wright

Proofreader
Sheri Cain

Technical Editor
Mark Reddin

Publishing Coordinator
Cindy Teeters

Interior Designer
Gary Adair

Cover Designer
Gary Adair

Compositor
Mark Shirar

Contents at a Glance

Table of Contents

About the Author

Paul McFedries is a full-time technical author who has worked with computers in one form or another since 1975 and has used Windows since version 1. He is the author of more than 60 computer books that have sold over three million copies worldwide. His recent titles include the Sams Publishing book *Microsoft Windows Home Server Unleashed* and the Que Publishing books *Tweak It and Freak It: A Killer Guide to Making Windows Run Your Way, Networking with Microsoft Windows Vista,* and *Build It. Fix It. Own It: A Beginner's Guide to Building and Upgrading a PC.* Paul is also the proprietor of Word Spy (www.wordspy.com), a website devoted to tracking new words and phrases as they enter the English language. Please visit Paul's personal website at www.mcfedries.com or follow him on Twitter at twitter.com/paulmcf and twitter.com/wordspy.

Dedication

For Karen, of course, and for Gypsy, the Dog Unleashed!

Acknowledgments

I've been writing computer books for more than 18 years now (ouch!), which is a long time to do *anything*, much less something that exercises the old noodle the way researching and writing a computer book does. Despite that, however, I still leap out of bed most mornings and can't wait to get my hands on the keyboard once again and start tapping away.

Maintaining enthusiasm for your job is never easy, but it sure helps when you get to work with some amazingly smart, talented, and nice people. I speak, of course, of the bright lights who populate the Que editorial department, who are as awesome a collection of Hoosiers as you're ever likely to meet (assuming you come across Hoosier collections regularly). In particular, I'd like to extend my heartfelt and profuse thanks to the editors I worked with directly on this book, including Acquisitions Editor and Development Editor Rick Kughen; Project Editor Jennifer Gallant; Copy Editor Keith Cline; and Technical Editor Mark Reddin. Thanks to all of you for the excellent work.

We Want to Hear from You!

As the reader of this book, *you* are our most important critic and commentator. We value your opinion and want to know what we're doing right, what we could do better, what areas you'd like to see us publish in, and any other words of wisdom you're willing to pass our way.

As an associate publisher for Sams Publishing, I welcome your comments. You can email or write me directly to let me know what you did or didn't like about this book—as well as what we can do to make our books better.

Please note that I cannot help you with technical problems related to the topic of this book. We do have a User Services group, however, where I will forward specific technical questions related to the book.

When you write, please be sure to include this book's title and author as well as your name, email address, and phone number. I will carefully review your comments and share them with the author and editors who worked on the book.

Email: feedback@samspublishing.com

Mail: Greg Wiegand
         Associate Publisher
         Sams Publishing
         800 East 96th Street
         Indianapolis, IN 46240 USA

Reader Services

Visit our website and register this book at informit.com/register for convenient access to any updates, downloads, or errata that might be available for this book.

Introduction

We shall not cease from exploration
And the end of all our exploring
Will be to arrive where we started
And know the place for the first time.
—T. S. Eliot

W ell, *that* was easy. After the "two steps forward, one step back" development process of Windows Vista, after the interminable Vista beta releases, and after the hype and hoopla that accompanied the Vista release, Windows 7 seemed to arrive on our digital doorsteps fully formed, like a kind of electronic Athena from the skull of some programming Zeus (or something like that).

The development and release of Microsoft's latest bouncing-baby operating system was nothing like its older sibling, but does that mean that Windows 7 itself is nothing like Windows Vista? Actually, in many ways, that's true. Sure, if you're familiar with Windows Vista, you'll have a relatively benign learning curve with Windows 7. But Microsoft didn't spend the past 3 years working on new desktop backgrounds! Windows 7 is loaded with new and changed features; some of them are almost too subtle to notice, whereas others represent veritable system sea changes.

Coincidentally (or not, depending on where you fall in the conspiracy theory spectrum), my approach to Windows has also changed in this edition of the book. Unlike in previous editions, *Windows 7 Unleashed* is *not* my attempt to cover all the features of Windows from Aero Glass to AutoPlay. Windows has simply become too big for that kind of book, and most Windows users know (or can figure out) the basics of most features. So in this edition of the book, I've changed the focus from components (Internet Explorer, Mail, and so on) to subjects: customization, performance, power tools, security, troubleshooting, and networking, and scripting. You get in-depth and useful coverage of these seven areas that will help you unleash the full potential of Windows 7.

Who Should Read This Book

All writers write with an audience in mind. Actually, I'm not sure whether that's true for novelists and poets and the like, but it *should* be true for any technical writer who wants to create a useful and comprehensible book. Here are the members of my own imagined audience:

- **IT professionals**—These brave souls must decide whether to move to Windows 7, work out deployment issues, and support the new Windows 7 desktops. The whole book has information related to your job and Windows 7.

- **Power users**—These elite users get their power via knowledge. With that in mind, this book extends the Windows power user's know-how by offering scripts, Registry tweaks, group policy configurations, and other power tools.

- **Business users**—If your company is thinking of or has already committed to moving to Windows 7, you need to know what you, your colleagues, and your staff are getting into. You also want to know what Windows 7 will do to improve your productivity and make your life at the office easier. You learn all of this and more in this book.

- **Small business owners**—If you run a small or home business, you probably want to know whether Windows 7 will give you a good return on investment. Will it make it easier to set up and maintain a network? Will Windows 7 computers be more stable? Will your employees be able to collaborate easier? The answer turns out to be "yes" for all of these questions, and I'll show you why.

- **Home users**—If you use Windows 7 at home, you probably want to maximize performance, keep your system running smoothly, max out security, and perform customizations that make Windows 7 conform to your style. Check, check, check, check. This book's got your covered in all these areas.

Also, to keep the chapters uncluttered, I've made a few assumptions about what you know and what you don't know:

- I assume that you have knowledge of rudimentary computer concepts, such as files and folders.

- I assume that you're familiar with the basic Windows skills: mouse maneuvering, dialog box negotiation, pull-down menu jockeying, and so on.

- I assume that you can operate peripherals attached to your computer, such as the keyboard and printer.

- ► I assume that you've used Windows for a while and are comfortable with concepts such as toolbars, scrollbars, and, of course, windows.

- ► I assume that you have a brain that you're willing to use and a good supply of innate curiosity.

How This Book Is Organized

As I mentioned earlier, I've completely revamped the structure and coverage in this edition, so the next few sections offer a summary of what you'll find in each part.

Part I: Unleashing Windows 7 Customization

Your purchase of this book (a sound and savvy investment on your part, if I do say so myself) indicates that you're not interested in using Windows 7 in its out-of-the-box configuration. If you're looking to make Windows 7 your own, begin at the beginning with the five chapters in Part I. You learn how to customize Windows Explorer (Chapter 1), Internet Explorer (Chapter 2), the file system (Chapter 3), startup and shutdown (Chapter 4), and the Start menu and taskbar (Chapter 5).

Part II: Unleashing Windows 7 Performance and Maintenance

Everybody wants Windows to run faster, so you'll no doubt be pleased that I devote an entire chapter to this important topic (Chapter 6). Everybody wants Windows to run smoother, so you'll also no doubt be pleased that I devote yet another chapter to *that* important topic (Chapter 7).

Part III: Unleashing Windows 7 Power User Tools

The chapters in Part III kick your advanced Windows 7 education into high gear by covering the ins and outs of a half dozen important Windows 7 power tools: Control Panel (Chapter 8), Local Group Policy Editor (Chapter 9), Microsoft Management Console (Chapter 10), the Services snap-in (Chapter 11), the Registry Editor (Chapter 12), and Command Prompt (Chapter 13).

Part IV: Unleashing Windows 7 Security

With threats to our digital lives coming at us from all sides these days, security may just be the most vital topic in technology. So perhaps that's why Part IV is the biggest section in the book, with no less than seven chapters devoted to various aspects of Windows 7 security. Your first learn some general techniques for locking down Windows 7 (Chapter 14), and you then learn how to configure web security (Chapter 15), email security (Chapter 16), file system security (Chapter 17), user security (Chapter 18), wired network security (Chapter 19), and wireless network security (Chapter 20).

Part V: Unleashing Windows 7 Troubleshooting

Windows 7 may represent the state of Microsoft's operating system art, but it *is* still Windows, which means problems, bugs, and glitches are pretty much inevitable. The four chapters in Part V can help when the Windows demons strike. You learn general troubleshooting techniques (Chapter 21), and how to troubleshoot device (Chapter 22), startup (Chapter 23), and networking (Chapter 24).

Part VI: Unleashing Windows 7 Networking

It's a rare home or small office that doesn't have (or doesn't want to have) a network, and Part VI is a reflection of this fact (that I just made up). You learn how to set up a small network (Chapter 25), how to access and use that network (Chapter 26), how to access your network from remote locations (Chapter 27), how to use Windows 7 as a web server (Chapter 28), and how to incorporate Macs into your network (Chapter 29).

Part VII: Unleashing Windows 7 Scripting

To close out the main part of this book, Part VII takes an in-depth look at two methods for automating Windows tasks with scripts: Windows Scripting Host (Chapter 30) and Windows PowerShell (Chapter 31).

Part VIII: Appendixes

To further your Windows 7 education, Part VIII presents two appendixes that contain extra goodies. You'll find a complete list of Windows 7 shortcut keys (Appendix A), and a detailed look at the TCP/IP protocols that underlie Windows 7 networking (Appendix B).

Conventions Used in This Book

To make your life easier, this book includes various features and conventions that help you get the most out of this book and Windows 7 itself:

Steps	Throughout the book, I've broken many Windows 7 tasks into easy-to-follow step-by-step procedures.
Things you type	Whenever I suggest that you type something, what you type appears in a **bold monospace** font.
Filenames, folder names, and code	These things appear in a `monospace` font.
Commands	Commands and their syntax use the `monospace` font, too. Command placeholders (which stand for what you actually type) appear in an *italic monospace* font.
Pull-down menu commands	I use the following style for all application menu commands: *Menu, Command*, where *Menu* is the name of the menu that you pull down and *Command* is the name of the command you select. Here's an example: File, Open. This means that you pull down the File menu and select the Open command.
Code continuation character	When a line of code is too long to fit on only one line of this book, it is broken at a convenient place and continued to the next line. The continuation of the line is preceded by a code continuation character ([➥]). You should type a line of code that has this character as one long line without breaking it.

This book also uses the following boxes to draw your attention to important (or merely interesting) information:

NOTE

The Note box presents asides that give you more information about the current topic. These tidbits provide extra insights that give you a better understanding of the task. In many cases, they refer you to other sections of the book for more information.

TIP

The Tip box tells you about Windows 7 methods that are easier, faster, or more efficient than the standard methods.

CAUTION

The all-important Caution box tells you about potential accidents waiting to happen. There are always ways to mess things up when you're working with computers. These boxes help you avoid at least some of the pitfalls.

How to Contact Me

If you have any comments about this book, or if you want to register a complaint or a compliment (I prefer the latter), please don't hesitate to send a missive my way. The easiest way to do that is to drop by my website, have a look around, and post a message to the forum: www.mcfedries.com/.

If you do the Twitter thing, you can follow my tweets here: http://twitter.com/paulmcf.

CHAPTER 1

Customizing Windows Explorer

Whoso would be a man, must be a nonconformist.
—Ralph Waldo Emerson

Although I'm sure you've got countless more important things to do with your precious time, at least some of your Windows 7 face time will be spent dealing with files, folders, and other Windows "f-words." These file system maintenance chores are the unglamorous side of the digital lifestyle, but they are, regrettably, necessary for the smooth functioning of that lifestyle.

This means that you'll likely be spending a lot of time with Windows Explorer over the years, so customizing it to your liking will make you more efficient and more productive, and setting up Windows Explorer to suit your style should serve to remove just a bit of the drudgery of day-to-day file maintenance. This chapter takes you through a few of my favorite Windows Explorer customizations.

Returning the Menus to Their Rightful Place

Microsoft seems to hate pull-down menus, for some reason. Over the past few years, Microsoft has hidden the menu system in many programs, and gotten rid of it altogether in Office 2007 (although the old menu keystroke combinations still work). In those programs where the menus are merely hidden, you can display them at any time by tapping the Alt key. This works in Windows Explorer, too, and that's a good thing because Windows Explorer's pull-down menus have several useful commands that simply aren't available through the taskbar, keyboard shortcuts, or even by right-clicking.

Still, it sticks in my craw that accessing the Windows Explorer menus requires the extra step of Alt, particularly if I'm in mouse mode. If you feel the same way, follow these steps to force Windows Explorer to display the menu bar full-time:

1. If you have a folder window open, select Organize, Folder and Search Options. (No folder windows open at the moment? Click Start, type **folder**, and then press Enter to select Folder Options in the search results.) The Folder Options dialog box appears.
2. Click the View tab.
3. Click to activate the Always Show Menus check box.
4. Click OK. Windows Explorer (perhaps a tad grudgingly) restores the menu bar to its rightful place.

Changing the View

The icons in Windows Explorer's content area can be viewed in no less than *eight* different ways, which seems a tad excessive, but Windows has never been about restraint when it comes to interface choices. To see a list of these views, either pull down the Views button in the task pane or click View in the menu bar. You get four choices for icon sizes: Extra Large Icons, Large Icons, Medium Icons, and Small Icons. You also get four other choices:

▶ **List**—This view divides the content area into as many rows as will fit vertically, and it displays the folders and files alphabetically down the rows and across the columns. For each object, Windows Explorer shows the object's icon and name.

▶ **Details**—This view displays a vertical list of icons, where each icon shows the data in all the displayed property columns (such as Name, Date Modified, Type, and Size). See "Viewing More Properties," later in this chapter, to learn how to add to these columns.

TIP

The default property columns you see depend on the template that the folder is using. To change the folder template, right-click the folder, click Properties, and then display the Customize tab. In the Optimize This Folder For list, choose the type you want: General Items, Documents, Pictures, Music, or Videos.

▶ **Tiles**—This view divides the content area into as many columns as will fit horizontally, and it displays the folders and files alphabetically across the columns and down the rows. For each object, Windows Explorer shows the object's icon, name, file type, and (for files only) size.

▶ **NEW TO 7** **Content**—This view, new to Windows 7, displays a vertical list of objects, and for each object it displays the object's icon, name, last modified date, size (files only), and any metadata associated with the object, such as author names and tags; the album name, genre, and track length (for music; see Figure 1.1); and the dimensions and date taken (for photos).

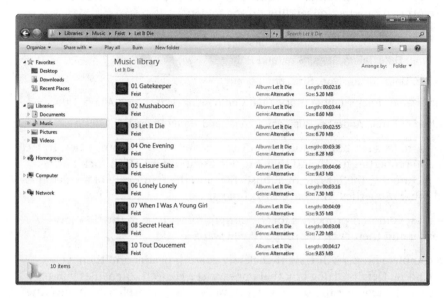

FIGURE 1.1   In Windows 7, Windows Explorer comes with a new Content view.

Viewing More Properties

Explorer's Details view is the preferred choice for power users because it displays a great deal of information in a relatively compact format. (The new Content view also provides lots of information, but each object takes up quite a bit of space, and the object properties that you see aren't customizable.) Details view also gives you a great deal of flexibility. For example, here are some techniques to you can use when working with the Details view:

▶ You can change the order of the property columns by dragging the column headings to the left or right.

▶ You can sort on a column by clicking the column heading.

▶ You can adjust the width of a column by pointing the mouse at the right edge of the column's heading (the pointer changes to a two-headed arrow) and dragging the pointer left or right.

▶ You can adjust the width of a column so that it's as wide as its widest data by double-clicking the right-edge of the column's heading.

TIP

To adjust all the columns so that they're exactly as wide as their widest data, right-click any column header and then click Size All Columns to Fit.

In addition, the Details view is informative because it shows you not only the name of each file, but also other properties, depending on the folder:

Documents—Name, Date Modified, Type, and Size

Pictures—Name, Date Taken, Tags, Size, and Rating

Videos—Name, Date Taken, Type, Size, and Length

Music—Track Name, Track Number, Track Title, Contributing Artists, and Album Title

Contacts—Name, E-mail Address, Business Phone, and Home Phone

These are all useful, to be sure, but Explorer can display many more file properties. In fact, there are nearly 300 properties in all, and they include useful information such as the dimensions of a picture file, the bit rate of a music file, and the frame rate of a video file. To see these and other properties, you have two choices:

▶ To see the most common properties for the current folder type, right-click any column header and then click the property you want to add.

▶ To see the complete property list, right-click any column header and then click More. The Choose Details dialog box that appears (see Figure 1.2) enables you to activate the check boxes for the properties you want to see, as well as rearrange the column order.

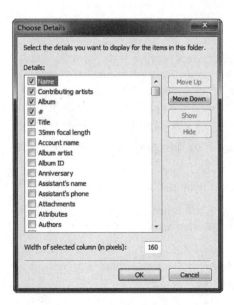

FIGURE 1.2   Use the Choose Details dialog box to add or remove property columns in Windows Explorer.

Turning On File Extensions

Microsoft figures that, crucial or not, the file extension concept is just too hard for new users to grasp. Therefore, right out of the box, Windows Explorer doesn't display file extensions. This may not sound like a big whoop, but not being able to see the extension for each file can be downright confusing. To see why, suppose you have a folder with multiple documents that use the same primary name. This is a not uncommon scenario, but it's also a fiendish one because it's often difficult to tell which file is which.

For example, Figure 1.3 shows a folder with 18 different files, all apparently named Project. Windows unrealistically expects users to tell files apart just by examining their icons. To make matters worse, if the file is an image, Windows 7 shows a thumbnail of the image instead of an icon. (This happens in thumbnail views such as Tiles, Medium Icons, and Large Icons.) The result is that in Figure 1.3 it's impossible to tell at a glance which image is a GIF, which is a JPEG, and so on.

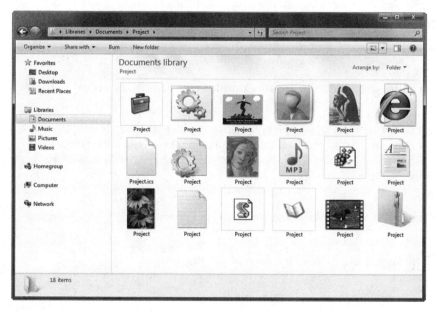

FIGURE 1.3   With file extensions turned off, it's tough to tell one file from another.

The need to become an expert in Windows iconography is bad enough, but it gets worse. Not being able to see file extensions also leads to two other problems:

▶ **You can't rename extensions**—For example, suppose you have a text file named index.txt and you want to rename it to index.html to make it a web page file. Nope, sorry, you can't do it with file extensions hidden. If you try—that is, if you click the file, press F2 to choose the Rename command, and then type **index.html**— you just end up with a text file named **index.html.txt**.

▶ **You can't save a document under an extension of your choice**—Similarly, with file extensions turned off, Windows 7 forces you to save a file using the default extension associated with an application. For example, if you're working in Notepad, every file you save must have a .txt extension. If you create your own web pages, for example, you can't rename these text files with typical web page extensions such as .htm, .html, .asp, and so on.

TIP

There is a way to get around the inability to save a document under an extension of your choice. In the Save As dialog box, use the Save as Type list to select the All Files option, if it exists. You can then use the File Name text box to type the filename with the extension you prefer to use.

You can overcome all these problems by turning on file extensions, as described in the following steps:

1. If you have a folder window open, select Organize, Folder and Search Options (or Tools, Folder Options if you have the menu displayed; otherwise, click Start, type **folder**, and then press Enter to select Folder Options in the search results). The Folder Options dialog box appears.

2. Click the View tab.

3. Deactivate the Hide Extensions for Known File Types check box.

4. Click OK.

Figure 1.4 shows the Project files with extensions in full display.

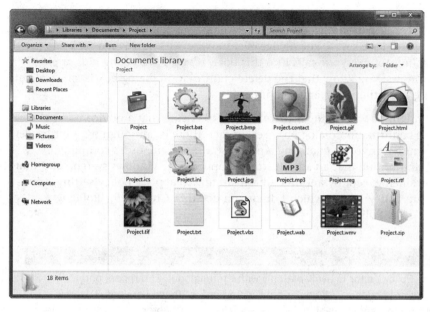

FIGURE 1.4   With file extensions turned on, it's much easier to tell the files apart.

Stopping Delete Confirmations

My biggest Windows pet peeves center around tasks that require you to jump through extra hoops that are totally unnecessary. In Windows XP, for example, clicking the Shut Down command on the Start menu doesn't shut down your computer, at least not right away. Instead, a dialog box shows up and you need to click Shut Down yet again. Dumb!

Another unnecessary dialog box that shows up in all versions of Windows is the "Are you sure you want to move this file to the Recycle Bin?" prompt that pops up when you press Delete. Now you either need to move your hand to the mouse to click Yes, or you can keep your hands on the keyboard by pressing Alt+Y. Either way, it's an extra step that just slows you down.

One way to avoid this confirmation dialog box is to click and drag the file you want to delete and then drop it on the desktop's Recycle Bin icon. That's nice to know, but most of us rarely see our desktops these days, so this method is not very practical.

A much better solution is to configure Recycle Bin to not display the confirmation dialog box at all. Here's how it's done:

1. Right-click the desktop's Recycle Bin icon and then click Properties. Windows 7 displays the Recycle Bin's property sheet.
2. Click to deactivate the Display Delete Confirmation Dialog check box.
3. Click OK to put the new setting into effect.

Now let's consider this tweak from the opposite point of view. The reason Windows displays the delete confirmation dialog box by default is to prevent you from accidentally deleting a file. You and I are savvy, knowledgeable users, so we know when we want to delete something, but not everyone falls into this boat. If you have young kids or elderly folks who use Windows, you know that the delete confirmation dialog box is an excellent safeguard for these and other inexperienced users.

In that case, you might be wondering if there's a way to ensure that a novice user *can't* turn off the delete confirmation dialog box. Yes, in fact, there is, although it's a bit harder to implement because it involves changing a policy setting on the user's computer. A *policy setting* is a kind of rule that an administrator applies to a Windows system, and that rule can't be overridden except by another administrator. To apply a policy setting, you use the Local Group Policy Editor, which I discuss in detail in Chapter 9, "Policing Windows 7 with Group Policies."

> **NOTE**
>
> The Local Group Policy Editor is available only with Professional, Enterprise, and Ultimate versions of Windows 7. If you're not running one of these versions, I'll show you how to perform the same tweak using the Registry (see Chapter 12, "Tweaking the Windows 7 Registry").

You can use two ways to prevent a user from turning off delete confirmations:

- ▶ Disable the Display Delete Confirmation Dialog check box that appears in the Recycle Bin's property sheet.

- ▶ Disable the Recycle Bin's Properties command so that the user can't display the Recycle Bin's property sheet.

Follow these steps to implement one of these policies:

1. On the other user's computer, click Start, type **gpedit.msc**, and then press Enter to select the gpedit program that appears in the search results.
2. Open the User Configuration branch.
3. Open the Administrative Templates branch.
4. Display the property sheet of the policy you want to use, as follows:

   - ▶ If you want to disable the Display Delete Confirmation Dialog check box, open the Windows Components branch and then click Windows Explorer. Double-click the policy named Display Confirmation Dialog When Deleting Files. If you don't have access to the Group Policy Editor, open the Registry Editor and create a DWORD setting named ConfirmFileDelete with the value 1 in the following key:

     HKCU\Software\Microsoft\Windows\CurrentVersion\Policies\Explorer

   - ▶ If you want to disable the Recycle Bin's Properties command, click Desktop and then double-click the Remove Properties from the Recycle Bin Context Menu policy. If you don't have access to the Group Policy Editor, open the Registry Editor and create a DWORD setting named `NoPropertiesRecycleBin` with the value 1 in the following key:

`HKCU\Software\Microsoft\Windows\CurrentVersion\Policies\Explorer`

> **NOTE**
>
> The Remove Properties from the Recycle Bin Context Menu policy has a misleading name because, when enabled, the policy disables some but, strangely, not *all* instances of the Recycle Bin's Properties command. For example, if the user displays the desktop in a folder window and clicks Recycle Bin, the Properties command is disabled in both the Organize menu and the File menu. However, the Properties command is still enabled when you right-click the Recycle Bin icon the desktop, but choosing the command only displays an error message.

5. Click the Enabled option.
6. Click OK to put the policy into effect.

Figure 1.5 shows the Recycle Bin property sheet with the Display Confirmation Dialog When Deleting Files policy in effect. As you can see, the Display Delete Confirmation Dialog check box is activated and disabled, so the setting can't be changed.

FIGURE 1.5   With the Display Confirmation Dialog When Deleting Files policy in effect, the Display Delete Confirmation Dialog check box is activated and disabled.

Running Explorer in Full-Screen Mode

If you want the largest possible screen area for the contents of each folder, you can place Windows Explorer in full-screen mode by pressing F11. (You can also hold down Ctrl and click the Maximize button; if Explorer is already maximized, you first have to click the

Restore button.) This mode takes over the entire screen and hides the title bar, menu bar, status bar, address bar, and search bar. To work with the address bar or search bar, move your mouse pointer to the top of the screen. To restore the window, either press F11 again or display the address bar and search bar and then click the Full Screen button (which is to the right of the Search box).

Exploring the View Options

Windows Explorer's view boasts a large number of customization options that you need to be familiar with. To see these options, you have two choices:

▶ In Windows Explorer, select Organize, Folder and Search Options (or Tools, Folder Options if you have the menu bar displayed).

▶ Click Start, type **folder**, and then press Enter to select the Folder Options item in the search results.

Either way, the view options can be found, appropriately enough, on the View tab of the Folder Options dialog box, as shown in Figure 1.6.

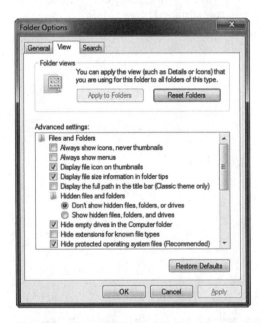

FIGURE 1.6   The View tab has quite a few options for customizing Windows Explorer.

Here's a complete list of the various items in the Advanced Settings list:

▶ **Always Show Icons, Never Thumbnails**—Activate this check box to prevent Windows Explorer from displaying file thumbnails. This can speed up the display of some folders that are heavy on pictures and other "thumbnail-able" file types.

▶ **Always Show Menus**—As you saw earlier (see "Returning the Menus to Their Rightful Place"), you activate this check box to display the menu bar full time in Windows Explorer.

▶ **Display File Icon on Thumbnails**—When this check box is activated, Windows Explorer superimposes the file type icon on the lower-right corner of each file's thumbnail. This is usually a good idea because the extra icon allows you to figure out the file type at a glance. However, if you find the icon getting in the way of the thumbnail image, deactivate this setting.

▶ **Display File Size Information in Folder Tips**—When this setting is activated and you hover your mouse pointer over a folder icon, Windows Explorer calculates the size of the files and subfolders within the folder, and displays the size in a pop-up banner. This is useful information, but if you find that your system takes too long to calculate the file size, consider deactivating this setting.

> **NOTE**
>
> If you activate the Display File Size Information in Folder Tips setting, you must also activate the Show Pop-Up Description for Folder and Desktop Items setting, described later.

▶ **Display the Full Path in the Title Bar**—Activate this setting to place the full pathname of the current folder in the Windows Explorer title bar. The full pathname includes the drive, the names of the parent folders, and the name of the current folder. Note that this only applies to Classic folders, which you activate by clicking the Use Windows Classic Folders option in the General pane.

▶ **Hidden Files and Folders**—Windows 7 hides certain types of files by default. This makes sense for novice users because they could accidentally delete or rename an important file. However, it's a pain for more advanced users who might require access to these files. You can use these options to tell Windows Explorer which files to display:
  Do Not Show Hidden Files, Folders, or Drives—Activate this option to avoid displaying objects that have the hidden attribute set.

  Show Hidden Files, Folders, and Drives—Activate this option to display the hidden files.

> **NOTE**
>
> Files are hidden from view by having their Hidden attribute activated. You can work with this attribute directly by right-clicking a visible file, clicking Properties, and then toggling the Hidden setting on and off.

▶ **Hide Extensions for Known File Types**—As you saw earlier (see "Turning On File Extensions"), you deactivate this setting to display file extensions.

▶ **Hide Protected Operating System Files**—This setting is activated by default, and it tells Windows 7 to hide files that have the System attribute activated. This is not usually a problem because you rarely have to do anything with the Windows system files. However, if you do need to see one of these files, deactivate this setting. When Windows 7 asks whether you're sure, click Yes.

▶ **Launch Folder Windows in a Separate Process**—Activating this setting tells Windows 7 to create a new thread in memory for each folder you open. This makes Windows Explorer more stable because a problem with one thread won't crash the others. However, this also means that Windows Explorer requires far greater amounts of system resources and memory. Activate this option only if your system has plenty of resources and memory.

▶ **Show Drive Letters**—If you deactivate this check box, Windows Explorer hides the drive letters in the Computer folder and in the address bar when you open a drive.

NOTE

If you hide drive letters, Windows Explorer displays drive names such as Local Disk. This isn't particularly useful, so consider renaming your drives. Right-click the drive and then click Rename. Note that you must enter administrator credentials to perform this operation.

▶ **Show Encrypted or Compressed NTFS Files in Color**—When this setting is activated, Windows Explorer shows the names of encrypted files in a green font and the names of compressed files in a blue font. This is a useful way to distinguish these from regular files, but you can deactivate it if you prefer to view all your files in a single color. Note that this only applies to files on NTFS partitions because only NTFS supports file encryption and compression.

▶ **Show Pop-Up Description for Folder and Desktop Items**—Some icons display a pop-up banner when you point the mouse at them. For example, the default desktop icons display a pop-up banner that describes each icon. Use this setting to turn these pop-ups on and off.

▶ **Show Preview Handlers in Preview Pane**—When this check box is activated, Windows Explorer includes controls for previewing certain types of files in the

Reading pane. For example, when you display a video file in the Reading pane, Windows Explorer includes playback controls such as Play, Pause, and Stop.

▶ **Use Check Boxes to Select Items**—Activate this check box to add check boxes beside each folder and file. You can then select objects by activating their check boxes.

▶ **Use Sharing Wizard**—When this check box is activated, Windows 7 uses a simplified file and folder sharing method called the Sharing Wizard. Power users will want to disable the Sharing Wizard (see Chapter 26, "Accessing and Using Your Network").

> ▶ See "Deactivating the Sharing Wizard," **p. 410.**

▶ **When Typing into List View**—These options determine Windows Explorer's behavior when you open a folder and begin typing:

Automatically Type into the Search Box—Activate this option to have your typing appear in the Search box.

Select the Typed Item in the View—Activate this option to jump to the first item in the folder with a name that begins with the letter you type.

Moving User Folders

By default, all your user folders are subfolders of the %USERPROFILE% folder, which is usually the following (where *User* is your username):

`C:\Users\User`

This is not a great location because it means that your documents and Windows 7 are on the same hard disk partition. If you have to wipe that partition to reinstall Windows 7 or some other operating system, you'll need to back up your documents first. Similarly, you might have another partition on your system that has lots of free disk space, so you might prefer to store your documents there. For these and other reasons, moving the location of your user folder is a good idea. Here's how:

1. Create the folder in which you want your user folder to reside.
2. Click Start, type `c:\users\` (replace c with the letter of the drive where your version of Windows 7 is installed), and then click your username in the search results. Windows 7 displays your user profile folders.
3. Right-click the user folder you want to move, and then click Properties. The folder's property sheet appears.
4. In the Location tab, use the text box to enter the full path (drive and folder name) of the folder you created in step 1. (Or click Move to select the folder using a dialog box.)
5. Click OK. If Windows Explorer asks whether you want to create the new folder and then to move your documents to the new location, click Yes in both cases.

> **TIP**
>
> An ideal setup is to have Windows 7 and your programs in one partition and your documents (that is, your user folders) in a separate partition. That way, your documents remain safe if you have to wipe the system partition.

Taking Ownership of Your Files

When you're working in Windows 7, you may have trouble with a folder (or a file) because Windows tells you that you don't have permission to edit (add to, delete, whatever) the folder. You might think the solution is to give your user account Full Control permissions on the folder (see Chapter 17, "Securing the File System"), but it's not as easy as that. Why not? Because you're not the owner of the folder. (If you were, you'd have the permissions you need automatically.) So the solution is to first take ownership of the folder, and then assign your user account Full Control permissions over the folder.

▶ **See** "Setting Security Permissions on Files and Folders," **p. 359.**

Here are the steps to follow:

1. Use Windows Explorer to locate the folder you want to take ownership of.
2. Right-click the folder and then click Properties to open the folder's property sheet.
3. Display the Security tab.
4. Click Advanced to open the Advanced Security Settings dialog box.
5. Display the Owner tab.
6. Click Edit.
7. In the Change Owner To list, click your user account.
8. Activate the Replace Owner on Subcontainers and Objects check box.
9. Click OK. Windows 7 warns you that you need to reopen the property sheet to change the folder's permissions.
10. Click OK in the open dialog boxes.
11. Right-click the folder and then click Properties to open the folder's property sheet.
12. Display the Security tab.
13. If you do not see your user account in the Group or User Names list, click Edit, click Add, type your username, and click OK.
14. Click your username.
15. Click the Full Control check box in the Allow column.
16. Click OK in the open dialog boxes.

Note that, obviously, this is quite a bit of work. If you only have to do it every once in a while, it's not big thing, but if you find you have to take ownership regularly, you'll probably want an easier way to go about it. You've got it! Listing 1.1 shows a Registry Editor file that modifies the Registry in such a way that you end up with a Take Ownership command in the shortcut menu that appears if you right-click any folder and any file.

> **NOTE**
>
> You can find the Registry Editor file (TakeOwnership.reg) on my website at www.mcfedries.com/Windows7Unleashed.

LISTING 1.1   A Registry Editor File That Creates a Take Ownership Command

```
Windows Registry Editor Version 5.00


[HKEY_CLASSES_ROOT\*\shell\runas]
@="Take Ownership"
"NoWorkingDirectory"=""

[HKEY_CLASSES_ROOT\*\shell\runas\command]
@="cmd.exe /c takeown /f \"%1\" && icacls \"%1\" /grant administrators:F"
"IsolatedCommand"="cmd.exe /c takeown /f \"%1\" && icacls \"%1\" /grant administra-
tors:F"

[HKEY_CLASSES_ROOT\Directory\shell\runas]
@="Take Ownership"
"NoWorkingDirectory"=""

[HKEY_CLASSES_ROOT\Directory\shell\runas\command]
@="cmd.exe /c takeown /f \"%1\" /r /d y && icacls \"%1\" /grant administrators:F /t"
"IsolatedCommand"="cmd.exe /c takeown /f \"%1\" /r /d y && icacls \"%1\" /grant
administrators:F /t"
```

To use the file, double-click it and then enter your UAC credentials when prompted. As you can see in Figure 1.7, right-clicking (in this case) a folder displays a shortcut menu with a new Take Ownership command. Click that command, enter your UAC credentials, and sit back as Windows does all the hard work for you!

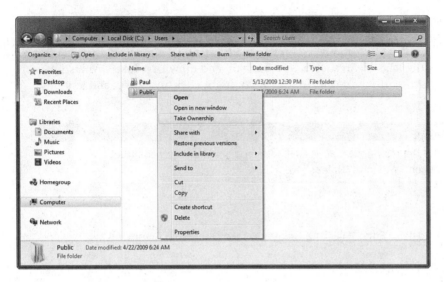

FIGURE 1.7   When you install the Registry mod, you see the Take Ownership command when you right-click a file.

Running Custom Searches

When you open a folder window, you know that you can click inside the Search box, type some text, and you get a list of files and folders that match your text. This worked well in Windows Vista, but it really rocks in Windows 7 because the latest version of the Desktop Search engine is even faster. However, simple text searches aren't going to radically boost anyone's productivity or help you find a file needle in a hard disk haystack. To take searching to the next level, you need to know about two obscure but powerful search features: Advanced Query Syntax and natural language queries.

Using Advanced Query Syntax to Search Properties

When you run a standard text search from any Search box, Windows looks for matches not only in the filename and the file contents, but also in the file metadata: the properties associated with each file. That's cool and all, but what if you want to match only a *particular* property. For example, if you're searching your music collection for albums that include the word *Rock* in the title, a basic search on *rock* will also return music where the artist's name includes *rock* and the album genre is Rock. This is not good.

To fix this kind of thing, you can create powerful and targeted searches by using a special syntax—called Advanced Query Syntax (AQS)—in your search queries.

For file properties, you use the following syntax:

```
property:value
```

Here, *property* is the name of the file property you want to search on, and value is the criteria you want to use. The property can be any of the metadata categories used by Windows. For example, the categories in a music folder include Name, Track, Title, Artists, Album, and Rating. Right-click any column header in Details view to see more properties such as Genre and Length, and you can click More to see the complete list.

Here are a few things to bear in mind:

▶ If the property name is a single word, use that word in your query. For example, the following code matches music where the Artists property is Coldplay:

```
artists:coldplay
```

▶ If the property name uses two or more words, remove the spaces between the words and use the resulting text in your query. For example, the following code matches pictures where the Date Taken property is August 23, 2009:

```
datetaken:8/23/2009
```

▶ If the value uses two or more words and you want to match the exact phrase, surround the phrase with quotation marks. For example, the following code matches music where the Genre property is Alternative & Punk:

```
genre:"alternative & punk"
```

▶ If the value uses two or more words and you want to match both words in any order, surround them with parentheses. For example, the following code matches music where the Album property contains the words Head and Goats in any order:

```
album:(head goats)
```

▶ If you want to match files where a particular property has no value, use empty braces, [], as the value. For example, the following code matches files where the Tags property is empty:

```
tags:[]
```

You can also refine your searches with the following operators and wildcards:

>   Matches files where the specified property is greater than the specified value. For example, the following code matches pictures where the Date Taken property is later than January 1, 2009:

```
datetaken:>1/1/2009
```

>=   Matches files where the specified property is greater than or equal to the specified value. For example, the following code matches files where the Size property is greater than or equal to 10000 bytes:

```
size:>=10000
```

<   Matches files where the specified property is less than the specified value. For example, the following code matches music where the Bit Rate property is less than 128 (bits per second):

```
bitrate:<128
```

<=   Matches files where the specified property is less than or equal to the specified value. For example, the following code matches files where the Size property is less than or equal to 1024 bytes:

```
size:<=1024
```

..   Matches files where the specified property is between (and including) two values. For example, the following code matches files where the Date Modified property is between and including August 1, 2008 and August 31, 2008:

```
datemodified:8/1/2008..8/31/2008
```

*   Substitutes for multiple characters. For example, the following code matches music where the Album property includes the word *Hits*:

```
album:*hits
```

?   Substitutes for a single character. For example, the following code matches music where the Artists property begins with Blu and includes any character in the fourth position:

```
artists:blu?
```

For even more sophisticated searches, you can combine multiple criteria using Boolean operators:

AND (or +)   Use this operator to match files that meet *all* of your criteria. For example, the following code matches pictures where the Date Taken property is later than January 1, 2009 and the Size property is greater than 1000000 bytes:

```
datetaken:>1/1/2009 AND size:>1000000
```

OR   Choose this option to match files that meet *at least one* of your criteria. For example, the following code matches music where the Genre property is either Rock or Blues:

```
genre:rock OR genre:blues
```

NOT   Choose. For example, the following code matches pictures where the Type prop-
(or –)   erty is not JPEG:

```
type:NOT jpeg
```

The Boolean operators AND, OR, and NOT must appear with all-uppercase letters in
your query.

Using Natural Language Queries

In the preceding section, I showed you how to use advanced query syntax to create
powerful search queries. The only problem is that it's a chore having to memorize all
those operators and what they're used for. If you're not up for all that, Windows 7 offers
an alternative. It's called *natural language search*, and it enables you to perform complex
searches without using *any* operators. Sweet!

First, follow these steps to turn on natural language search:

1. If you have a folder window open, select Organize, Folder and Search Options (or
   Tools, Folder Options if you have the menu displayed; otherwise, click Start, type
   folder, and then press Enter to select Folder Options in the search results). The
   Folder Options dialog box appears.
2. Select the Search tab.
3. Activate the Use Natural Language Search check box.
4. Click OK to put the new setting into effect.

Crafting natural language queries is a bit of a black art because Microsoft has no documentation available. Feel free to experiment to get the feel of these queries.

A basic natural language query looks like this:

adjective kind verb value

Here, *adjective* is an optional value that narrows down the search, usually by using a
value from a property (such as a genre for music or a file type for images); *kind* is the type
of file, such as music or images; *verb* is a verb that more or less corresponds to the property
you want to match, such as *modified* (the Date Modified property), *(the Date Created property)*, *from* (the From property in an email), and *by* (the Artist property in a music file);
and *value* is the specific value you want to match.

For example, if you want to return all the pop music done by the band Sloan, you'd enter
the following query:

```
pop music by sloan
```

Similarly, if you want all the JPEG images that were created today, you'd use the following query:

```
jpeg images created today
```

You can keep adding more properties and values to target your searches. For example, if we want our Sloan search to return only those songs rated with five stars, we'd modify the search as follows:

```
pop music by sloan rating *****
```

You can still perform Boolean searches in natural language queries. For example, if you want documents where the Author property includes *Paul* or *Karen*, you'd use the following query:

```
documents by paul or karen
```

Similarly, if you want to return all your videos except those in the QuickTime format, you'd use the following:

```
videos not quicktime
```

> **NOTE**
>
> Unlike with AQS, the Boolean operators or and not can appear in lowercase letters. (The Boolean operator and is implied in all multiterm natural language queries, so you never have to use it.)

Finally, note that when you're working with dates, there are several keywords you can use in your natural language queries, including the following: yesterday, today, tomorrow, week, month, year, last, this, and next. For example, if you want to see all the TIFF images created this week, you'd use the following:

```
jpeg images created this week
```

CHAPTER 2

Customizing Internet Explorer

The great challenge which faces us is to assure that, in our society of big-ness, we do not strangle the voice of creativity, that the rules of the game do not come to overshadow its purpose, that the grand orchestration of society leaves ample room for the man who marches to the music of another drummer.

—Hubert H. Humphrey

As I write this, Internet Explorer is by far the most dominant web browser with, depending on which source you use, anywhere from 70% to 75% of the market. (This is down about 20% since the release of the Firefox browser in late 2004.) And because most computer-savvy people have also been on the Internet for a number of years, it's safe to say that Internet Explorer is probably one of the most familiar applications available today.

Or perhaps I should say that the *basics* of Internet Explorer are familiar to most people. However, as with any complex program, there are hidden pockets of the browser that most people don't know about. Significantly, many of these seldom-seen areas are not as obscure as you might think. You can put many of these features to good use immediately to make your web surfing easier, more efficient, and more productive. In this chapter, I take you on a tour of a few of my favorite Internet Explorer nooks and crannies, and I show you how they can improve your web experience. You'll see that Internet Explorer is chock full of customization options that enable you to set up the program for the way you work and surf.

Displaying the Internet Options

Most of the customizations you learn about in this chapter take place in the occasionally friendly confines of the Internet Options dialog box. As usual, Windows 7 gives you too many choices for getting to this dialog box, but here are two that you might find to be the most useful:

▶ If you've currently got Internet Explorer open, click Tools and then click Internet Options.

▶ Click Start, type **internet op**, and then press Enter to select the Internet Options item in the search results.

Controlling the Web Page Cache

In the same way that a disk cache stores frequently used data for faster performance, Internet Explorer also keeps a cache of files from web pages you've visited recently. The cache is maintained on a per-user basis and is located in the following folder:

```
%UserProfile%\AppData\Local\Microsoft\Windows\Temporary Internet Files
```

Internet Explorer uses these saved files to display web pages quickly the next time you ask to see them or while you are offline.

To control the cache, open the Internet Options dialog box and display the General tab. Use the following buttons in the Browsing History group:

▶ **Delete**—Clicking this button displays the Delete Browsing History dialog box. (You can also display the dialog box by selecting Safety, Delete Browsing History, or by pressing Ctrl+Shift+Delete.) Activate the Temporary Internet Files check box and then click Delete to clean out the Temporary Internet Files folder.

▶ **Settings**—Clicking this button displays the Temporary Internet Files and History Settings dialog box, shown in Figure 2.1.

You have the following options:

▶ **Check for Newer Versions of Stored Pages**—Activate an option in this group to determine when Internet Explorer checks for updated versions of cache files. If you have a fast connection and you want to be certain that you're always seeing the most current data, activate the Every Time I Visit the Webpage option.

NOTE

No matter which cache update option you choose, you can view the most up-to-date version of a page at any time by pressing F5 or by clicking the Refresh button.

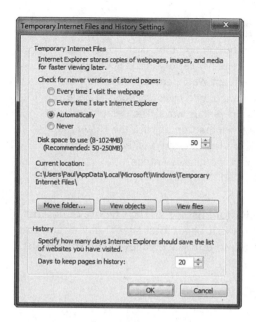

FIGURE 2.1   Use this dialog box to control how the Internet Explorer cache works.

▶ **Disk Space to Use**—Use this spin box to set the size of the cache as a percentage of the hard disk's capacity. A larger cache speeds up website browsing but also uses more hard drive space.

▶ **Move Folder**—Click this button to change the folder used for the cache. For example, you could move the cache to a partition with more free space so that you can increase the cache size, or to a faster hard drive to improve cache performance. Note that you must restart your computer if you move the cache folder.

▶ **View Objects**—Click this button to display the Downloaded Program Files folder, which holds the Java applets and ActiveX controls that have been downloaded and installed on your system.

▶ **View Files**—Click this button to display the Temporary Internet Files folder.

Configuring the Page History

You can improve the efficiency of your web surfing by increasing the number of days that Internet Explorer maintains a record of the sites you've visited. When you navigate to a web page, Internet Explorer adds the page's title and address to the History list, which is part of the Favorites Center. The History list is an important Internet Explorer feature because it enables you to easily and quickly return to a page that you have previously visited. The History list also enables you to view the pages that you have visited most often, so it gives you an easy way to see which pages are your favorites.

NOTE

To work with the History list, you click the Favorites button and then click History, but the fastest way to get there is to press Ctrl+H. The History list organizes your visited sites into date categories such as Today, Yesterday, Last Week, and Last Month. Click a category, click the site with which you want to work, and then click the specific page you want to visit. You can also sort the History list in various ways. The default sort order is View by Date. To change this, display the Favorites Center, click the History tab, and then click View by Site, View by Most Visited, or View by Order Visited Today. You can also click Search History to perform a search on the history entries.

By default, Internet Explorer keeps a page in the History list for 20 days before removing it. However, you may find that you often want to revisit pages after the 20-day period has expired. In that case, you can configure Internet Explorer to save pages in the History list for a longer period. Here's how:

1. Display the Internet Options dialog box.
2. Click the General tab.
3. In the Browsing History group, click Settings. The Temporary Internet Files and History Settings dialog box appears.
4. Use the Days to Keep Pages in History spin box to type or click the number of days you want websites saved. Specify a value between 1 and 999. If you don't want Internet Explorer to keep any pages in the History folder, enter 0.
5. Click OK in the open dialog box to put the new setting into effect.

Adding More Search Engines to Internet Explorer

Besides dealing with a search engine site directly, Internet Explorer also lets you run searches from the Search box, which appears to the right of the address bar. Type your search term in the Search box and then press Enter or click Search. (You can also press Alt+Enter to open the results in a new tab.)

TIP

You can press Ctrl+E to activate the Search box.

By default, Internet Explorer initially submits the search text to the Windows Live search engine. If you want access to other search engines—or *search providers*, as Internet Explorer insists on calling them—via the Search box, follow these steps:

1. Click the drop-down arrow to the right of the Search box.
2. Click Find More Providers. Internet Explorer displays a web page with links to various search engines, as shown in Figure 2.2.

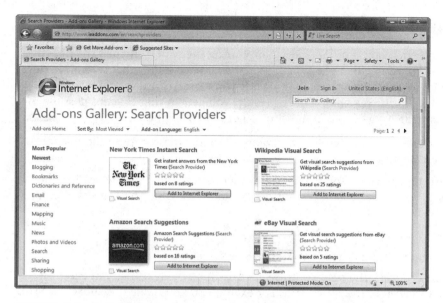

FIGURE 2.2   Internet Explorer offers a list of search providers that you can add to the Search box.

3. Click the Add to Internet Explorer button for the search engine you want to add. The Add Search Provider dialog box appears.

4. If you want Internet Explorer to use this search engine as the default, activate the Make This My Default Search Provider check box.

5. Click Add.

To use the new search engine (assuming you didn't make it the default), drop down the Search box list to see a list of the search engines, and then click the one you want to use.

TIP

You can change the default search engine at any time. Drop down the Search box list and then click Manage Search Providers. In the Manage Add-ons dialog box, click the search engine you want to use and then click Set as Default. Click Close to put the new setting into effect.

TIP

One of the more annoying traits exhibited by some programs is that they insist on suggesting that you change your default search engine to some site they own or sponsor. Boo! To shut down such antisocial behavior, drop down the Search box list and then click Manage Search Providers. In the Manage Add-ons dialog box, activate the Prevent Programs from Suggesting Changes to My Default Search Provider check box. Click Close to put the new setting into effect.

Using Any Search Engine from the Address Bar

Searching via the Search box is often easier than visiting the search engine's site directly, but you're limited to using either the default search engine or some other search provider that you've added to Internet Explorer. But what if you regularly use several search engines, depending on the search text or the results you get? In that case, it's possible to set up address bar searching for any number of other search engines.

To see how this works, let's run through an example. Follow these steps to set up address bar searching for Google:

1. Select Start, type **regedit**, press Enter, and then enter your UAC credentials. (In Windows XP, select Start, Run, type **regedit**, and click OK.) The Registry Editor appears.

2. Navigate to the following key:

   `HKCU\Software\Microsoft\Internet Explore\SearchURL`

3. Create a new subkey. The name of this subkey will be the text that you enter into the address bar before the search text. For example, if you name this subkey `google`, you'll initiate an address bar search by typing **google***text,* where **text** is your *search* **text**.

TIP

I suggest using subkey names that are as short as possible to minimize typing. For example, I use the name g for my Google key (meaning that I can search by typing **gtext** into the address bar).

---

4. Select the new subkey and double-click its (`Default`) value for editing.

5. Type the URL that initiates a search for the search engine, and specify **%s** as a placeholder for the search text. For Google, the URL looks like this:

   http://www.google.com/search?q=%s

6. You also have to specify the characters or hexadecimal values that Internet Explorer substitutes for characters that have special meaning within a query string: space, pound sign (#), percent (%), ampersand (&), plus (+), equal (=), and question mark (?). To do this, add the following settings to the new subkey. Note that these values work with all search engines.

Name	Type	Data
<space>	REG_SZ	+
#	REG_SZ	%23
%	REG_SZ	%25
&	REG_SZ	%26
+	REG_SZ	%2B

Name	Type	Data
=	REG_SZ	%3D
?	REG_SZ	%3F

Figure 2.3 shows a completed example. The text that you type into the address bar before the search string—that is, the name of the new subkey—is called the *search prefix*.

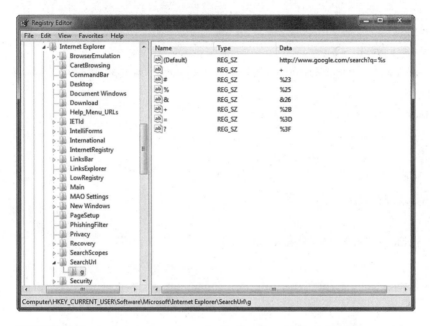

FIGURE 2.3   A sample search prefix for the Google search engine.

How do you know the proper URL to use for a search engine? Go to the search engine site and run a search with a single word. When the results appear, examine the URL in the address bar, which usually takes the following general form:

ScriptURL?QueryString

Here, *ScriptURL* is the address of the site's search script, and *QueryString* is the data sent to the script. In most cases, you can just copy the URL and substitute **%s** for your search text when you set up your search prefix. I often experiment with reducing the query string to the minimum necessary for the search to execute properly. For example, a typical Google search might produce a URL such as the following:

http://www.google.com/search?rls=ig&hl=en&q=mcfedries&btnG=Search

In the query string, each item is separated by an ampersand (&), so I delete one item at a time until either the search breaks or I'm down to the search text (q=mcfedries in the earlier query string). To save you some legwork, the following are the minimal search URLs for a number of search sites:

All the Web:

http://www.alltheweb.com/search?query=%s&cat=web

AltaVista:

http://www.altavista.com/web/results?q=%s

AOL Search:

http://search.aol.com/aolcom/search?query=%s

Ask.com:

http://www.ask.com/web?q=%s

Encarta (Dictionary only):

http://encarta.msn.com/encnet/features/dictionary/DictionaryResults.aspx?search=%s

Encarta (General):

http://encarta.msn.com/encnet/refpages/search.aspx?q=%s

Excite:

http://msxml.excite.com/info.xcite/search/web/%s

Live.com:

http://www.live.com/?q=%s

Lycos:

http://search.lycos.com/default.asp?query=%s

Technorati:

http://www.technorati.com/search/%s

Yahoo!:

http://search.yahoo.com/bin/search?p=%s

Make Tabs More Efficient

Like Firefox, Opera, Safari, and quite a few other browsers, Internet Explorer 7 finally brought tabbed browsing to Microsoft's flagship browser and, of course, the tab tradition continues in Internet Explorer 8. You can open up to about 50 tabs in each window, which ought to be enough for anybody. One of the nicest features of tabs is that Internet Explorer supplies each tab with its own execution thread, which means that you can start a page loading in one tab while reading downloaded page text in another tab. You can also specify multiple home pages that load in their own tabs when you start Internet Explorer, as described a bit later in this chapter (see "Loading Multiple Home Pages at Startup").

Tabs are only as useful as they are easy to use, and Internet Explorer does a good job of smoothing the transition to tabbed browsing. One way that it does this is by giving you a satisfying variety of methods to use for opening a page in a new tab. There are six in all:

- ▶ **Hold down Ctrl and click a link in a web page**—This creates a new tab and loads the linked page in the background.

- ▶ **Use the middle mouse button (if you have one) to click a link in a web page**—This creates a new tab and loads the linked page in the background.

- ▶ **Type the page URL into the address bar and then press Alt+Enter**—This creates a new tab and loads the page in the foreground.

- ▶ **Click the New Tab button (or press Ctrl+T) to display a blank tab**—Type the page URL into the address bar and then press the Enter key. This loads the page in the foreground.

- ▶ **Click and drag a web page link or the current address bar icon and drop it onto the New Tab button**—This creates a new tab and loads the page in the foreground.

- ▶ **Click a link in another program**—This creates a new tab and loads the linked page in the foreground.

Opening a page in the background in a new tab when you Ctrl+click a link is useful if you want to keep reading the current page. However, I find that most of the time I want to read the new page right away. If you have a fast connection, the page loads quickly enough that the delay between clicking and reading is usually minimal.

In such cases, you can tell Internet Explorer to switch to the new tab automatically when you Ctrl+click a link:

1. Select Tools, Internet Options to open the Internet Options dialog box.
2. Display the General tab.
3. Click Settings in the Tabs group to open the Tabbed Browsing Settings dialog box.
4. Activate the Always Switch to New Tabs When They Are Created check box.
5. Click OK in each open dialog box to put the new setting into effect.

Loading Multiple Home Pages at Startup

As you know, a website's home page is the main page of the site, and it's the page where you often begin your exploration of that site. (Although these days, with so many people accessing sites via search engines, blogs, and RSS feeds, you're just as likely to start your site surfing on an inside page rather than the home page. For example, it's been several years since I've seen Microsoft's home page.)

A bit confusingly, Internet Explorer also defines a home page: It's the page that Internet Explorer displays automatically when you first start the program. The default Internet Explorer home page is MSN.com, but most people change that to a page that they use regularly.

With the latest versions of Internet Explorer (7 and later), the home page idea gets a boost because of the new tabbed browsing feature, which lets you open multiple pages in the same window. It makes sense, then, that if you can work with multiple tabs during a browser session, you might also want to work with multiple tabs right off the bat when you start the program. And that's exactly what Internet Explorer enables you do to. You can define two or more home pages, and Internet Explorer dutifully loads those pages into separate tabs when you launch the program.

This feature isn't a big deal if you open just a couple of sites at startup, but it pays big dividends if you regularly open several sites right off. For example, you may open a portal page such as MSN or Yahoo!, a search page such as Google, your company's external or internal website, a news page, one or more blogger pages, and so on. Even if you have all those sites set up as favorites, it would still take a bit of time to create a new tab, load the site, and then repeat for every page you want to open. With multiple home pages defined, Internet Explorer handles opening all your home pages, so you just sit back and let everything happen automatically.

CAUTION

When it comes to opening pages at startup, I'm afraid there's no such thing as a free browser lunch. The more home pages you define, the longer it takes Internet Explorer to start. Note, too, that if you have a home page that requires a login and you've set up that site to remember your login data, that login might fail if the page loads at startup.

Follow these steps to set up multiple home pages in Internet Explorer:

1. Surf to a page you want to load at startup.
2. Click the drop-down arrow beside the Home button and then click Add or Change Home Page. The Add or Change Home Page dialog box appears.
3. Click the Add This Webpage to Your Home Page Tabs option.

TIP

If you're planning to add several pages to your home page tabs, there's an easy way to go about it. First, for each page you want to add, open a new tab and use that tab to surf to the page. If you have any tabs open with pages that you don't want to include, close those tabs. Click the drop-down arrow beside the Home button, click Add or Change Home Page, activate the Use the Current Tab Set as Your Home Page, and then click Yes.

---

4. Click Yes.
5. Repeat steps 1 to 4 to add other pages to your home page tabs.
6. If there are any home page tabs you want to get rid of, click the drop-down arrow beside the Home button, click Remove, click the page, and then click Yes to confirm.

2

Understanding Internet Explorer's Advanced Options

Internet Explorer has a huge list of customization features found in the Advanced tab of the Internet Options dialog box (see Figure 2.4). Many of these settings are obscure, but many others are extremely useful for surfers of all stripes. This section runs through all of these settings.

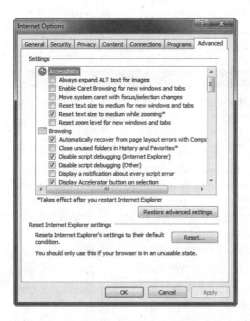

FIGURE 2.4   In the Internet Options dialog box, the Advanced tab contains a long list of Internet Explorer customization settings.

The Accessibility group has six options:

▶ **Always Expand Alt Text for Images**—Most webmasters define a text description for each image they include on a page. If you tell Internet Explorer not to show images (see the later discussion of the Show Pictures check box), all you see are boxes where the images should be, and each box contains the text description (known as *alt text*, where *alt* is short for *alternate*). Activating this check box tells Internet Explorer to expand the image box horizontally so that the alt text appears on a single line.

▶ NEW TO 7 **Enable Caret Browsing for New Windows and Tabs**—Activate this check box to switch Internet Explorer 8 into caret browsing mode. You normally navigate a web page using the mouse to click links and scroll the screen. The keyboard comes into play occasionally for scrolling (with Page Down and Page Up keys) and rarely for selecting links (with the Tab key). However, many people find the mouse difficult to use and would prefer to navigate a web page the same way they navigate a word processing document: using the left- and right-arrow keys to navigate characters, the up and down arrow keys to navigate lines, and Ctrl+arrow key to navigate words (with the left and right keys) or paragraphs (with the up and down keys), and so on. This is called *caret browsing* (where *caret* is a fancy term for a vertical cursor), and it's a new feature in Internet Explorer 8.

NOTE

To activate a link when caret browsing, navigate the cursor inside the link text (Internet Explorer 8 adds a box around the link text), and then press Enter.

▶ **Move System Caret with Focus/Selection Changes**—Activating this check box tells Internet Explorer to move the system caret whenever you change the focus. (The *system caret* is a visual indication of what part of the screen currently has the focus. If a text box has the focus, the system caret is a blinking, vertical bar; if a check box or option button has the focus, the system caret is a dotted outline of the control name.) This is useful if you have a screen reader or screen magnifier that uses the position of the system caret to determine what part of the screen to read or magnify.

▶ **Reset Text Size to Medium for New Windows and Tabs**—Activating this check box tells Internet Explorer to return the Text Size value to Medium when you open a new window or tab. This is useful if you find that you only have to enlarge the text size for a few sites.

▶ **Reset Text Size to Medium While Zooming**—Activating this check box tells Internet Explorer to return the Text Size value to Medium when you use the Zoom feature (select Page, Zoom). This is helpful because it gives you a more consistent zooming experience—you're always starting the zoom from the same text size.

▶ **Reset Zoom Level for New Windows and Tabs**—Activating this check box tells Internet Explorer to return the Zoom value to 100% when you open a new window or tab. This is useful if you find that you have to zoom in on only a few sites.

Here are the options in the Browsing group:

▶ **NEW TO 7** **Automatically Recover from Page Layout Errors with Compatibility View**—If you leave this check box activated, Internet Explorer automatically fixes any page layout problems that occur by switching to Compatibility mode.

▶ **Close Unused Folders in History and Favorites**—When you activate this check box, Internet Explorer keeps unused folders closed when you display the History list and the Favorites list. That is, if you open a folder and then open a second folder, Internet Explorer automatically closes the first folder. This makes the History and Favorites lists easier to navigate, so it's usually best to leave this option activated. You need to restart Internet Explorer if you change this setting.

▶ **Disable Script Debugging (Internet Explorer)**—This check box toggles the script debugger (if one is installed) on and off within Internet Explorer only. You should have to activate this option only if you're a page designer and you have scripts in your pages that you need to debug before uploading them to the Web.

▶ **Disable Script Debugging (Other)**—This is similar to the Disable Script Debugging (Internet Explorer) option, except that it toggles the script debugger (again, if one is installed) on and off within any application other than Internet Explorer that can display web content (such as Windows Mail).

▶ **Display a Notification About Every Script Error**—If you activate this check box, Internet Explorer displays a dialog box to alert you to JavaScript or VBScript errors on a page. If you leave this option deactivated, Internet Explorer displays an error message in the status bar. To see the full error message, double-click the status bar message. Only script programmers will need to enable this option and, even then, only when they're debugging scripts. Many websites are poorly programmed and contain script errors. Therefore, enabling this option means that you'll have to deal with lots of annoying dialog boxes as you surf.

▶ **Display Accelerator Button on Selection**—With this check box is activated, when you select text in a web page, Internet Explorer 8 displays an Accelerator button above the selected text. Click that button to see the installed accelerators (such as Blog with Windows Live and Define with Encarta).

▶ **Enable Automatic Crash Recovery**—When this check box is activated, Internet Explorer 8 attempts to reopen the current tab set if the program crashes. This is welcome behavior, particularly if you regularly have a large bunch of tabs on the go.

▶ **Enable FTP Folder View (Outside of Internet Explorer)**—When you activate this option and you access an FTP (File Transfer Protocol) site, Internet Explorer displays the contents of the site using the familiar Windows folder view. This makes it easy to drag and drop files from the FTP site to your hard disk, and possibly to perform other file maintenance chores, depending on what permissions you have at the site.

▶ **Enable Page Transitions**—This check box toggles Internet Explorer's support for page transitions on and off—websites that use a server that supports FrontPage extensions can define various page transitions (such as wipes and fades). However, these transitions often slow down your browsing, so I recommend turning them off.

▶ **Enable Suggested Sites**—When you enable this check box, you can click Internet Explorer 8's Suggested Sites button to see a list of what Internet Explorer 8 thinks are sites that are similar to the current site (and so might interest you).

▶ **Enable Third-Party Browser Extensions**—With this check box activated, Internet Explorer supports third-party extensions to its interface. For example, the Google toolbar is a third-party extension that integrates the Google search engine into Internet Explorer as a toolbar. If you deactivate this check box, third-party extensions don't appear and can't display. Deactivating this check box is a good way to turn off some (but, unfortunately, not all) of those annoying third-party toolbars that install themselves without permission. You need to restart Internet Explorer if you change this setting.

▶ **Enable Visual Styles on Buttons and Controls in Webpages**—With this check box activated, Internet Explorer applies the current Windows Vista visual style to all web pages for objects such as form buttons. If you deactivate this check box, Internet Explorer applies its default visual style to all page elements.

▶ **Enable Websites to Use the Search Pane**—When you enable this check box, you allow websites to display content using the old Search pane, which has been disabled since Internet Explorer 7. I have no idea why anyone would want to do this.

▶ **Force Offscreen Compositing Even Under Terminal Server**—If you activate this check box, Internet Explorer performs all *compositing*—the combining of two or more images—in memory before displaying the result onscreen. This avoids the image flashing that can occur when running Internet Explorer under Terminal Services, but it can reduce performance significantly. I recommend leaving this option unchecked. You have to restart Internet Explorer if you change this setting.

▶ **Notify When Downloads Complete**—If you leave this check box activated, Internet Explorer leaves its download progress dialog box onscreen after the download finishes (see Figure 2.5). This enables you to click either Open to launch the downloaded file or Open Folder to display the file's destination folder. If you deactivate this check box, Internet Explorer closes this dialog box as soon as the download is complete.

TIP

You can also force Internet Explorer to close the Download Complete dialog box automatically by activating the Close This Dialog Box When Download Completes check box.

▶ **Reuse Windows for Launching Shortcuts**—With this check box enabled and tabbed browsing turned off, Windows looks for an already-open Internet Explorer window when you click a web page shortcut (such as a web address in a Windows Mail email message). If a window is open, the web page loads there. This is a good idea because it prevents Internet Explorer windows from multiplying unnecessarily. If you deactivate this option, Windows always loads the page into a new Internet Explorer window.

FIGURE 2.5   When Internet Explorer completes a file download, it leaves this dialog box onscreen to help you deal with the file.

▶ **Show Friendly HTTP Error Messages**—With this check box enabled, Internet Explorer intercepts the error messages (for, say, pages not found) generated by web servers and replaces them with its own messages that offer more information as well as possible solutions to the problem. If you deactivate this option, Internet Explorer displays the error message generated by the web server. However, I recommend deactivating this option because webmasters often customize the web server error messages to be more helpful than the generic messages reported by Internet Explorer.

▶ **Underline Links**—Use these options to specify when Internet Explorer should format web page links with an underline. The Hover option means that the underline appears only when you position the mouse pointer over the link. Many websites use colored text, so it's often difficult to recognize a link without the underlining. Therefore, I recommend that you activate the Always option.

▶ **Use Inline AutoComplete**—This check box toggles the address bar's inline AutoComplete feature on and off. When Inline AutoComplete is on, Internet Explorer monitors the text that you type in the address bar. If your text matches a previously typed URL, Internet Explorer automatically completes the address by displaying the matching URL in the address bar. It also displays a drop-down list of other matching URLs. When Inline AutoComplete is off, Internet Explorer displays only the drop-down list of matching URLs.

NOTE

If you want to prevent Internet Explorer from displaying the drop-down list of matching URLs, display the Content tab and click the Settings button in the AutoComplete group to display the AutoComplete Settings dialog box. Deactivate the Web Addresses check box. Note that Internet Explorer's AutoComplete feature also applies to web forms. That is, AutoComplete can remember data that you type into a form—including usernames and passwords—and automatically enter that data when you use the form again. You can control the web form portion of AutoComplete by using the other check boxes in the Use AutoComplete For section of the AutoComplete Settings dialog box.

▶ **Use Most Recent Order When Switching Tags with Ctrl+Tab**—If you activate this check box, press Ctrl+Tab (and Ctrl+Shift+Tab) switches between tabs in the order you most recently viewed them.

▶ **Use Passive FTP (for Firewall and DSL Modem Compatibility)**—In a normal FTP session, Internet Explorer opens a connection to the FTP server (for commands), and then the FTP server opens a second connection back to the browser (for data). If you're on a network with a firewall, however, it will not allow incoming connections from a server. With passive FTP, the browser establishes the second (data) connection itself. Therefore, if you're on a firewalled network or are using a DSL modem and you can't establish an FTP connection, activate this check box.

▶ **Use Smooth Scrolling**—This check box toggles a feature called *smooth scrolling* on and off. When you activate this check box to enable smooth scrolling, pressing the Page Down or Page Up key causes the page to scroll down or up at a preset speed. If you deactivate this check box, pressing the Page Down or Page Up key causes the page to jump instantly down or up.

TIP

When reading a web page, you can scroll down one screen by pressing the spacebar. To scroll up one screen, press Shift+spacebar.

The check boxes in the HTTP 1.1 Settings branch determine whether Internet Explorer uses the HTTP 1.1 protocol:

▶ **Use HTTP 1.1**—This check box toggles Internet Explorer's use of HTTP 1.1 to communicate with web servers. (HTTP 1.1 is the standard protocol used on the Web today.) You should deactivate this check box only if you're having trouble connecting to a website. This tells Internet Explorer to use HTTP 1.0, which might solve the problem.

▶ **Use HTTP 1.1 Through Proxy Connections**—This check box toggles on and off the use of HTTP 1.1 only when connecting through a proxy server.

The options in the International group relate to security, so see Chapter 15, "Configuring Web Security," for a discussion about them.

▶ **See** "Understand Internet Explorer's Advanced Security Options," **p. 337.**

The options in the Multimedia branch toggle various multimedia effects on and off:

▶ **Always Use ClearType for HTML**—When this check box is activated, Internet Explorer displays HTML text using ClearType, which gives text a sharper look on LCD monitors. If you don't have an LCD monitor, you might not like how ClearType renders text, so you should deactivate this check box. You need to restart Internet Explorer if you change this setting.

▶ **Enable Automatic Image Resizing**—If you activate this check box, Internet Explorer automatically shrinks large images so that they fit inside the browser window. This is useful if you're running Windows Vista with a small monitor or at a relatively low resolution and you're finding that many website images don't fit entirely into the browser window.

▶ **Play Animations in Webpages**—This check box toggles animated GIF images on and off. Most animated GIFs are unwelcome annoyances, so you'll probably greatly improve your surfing experience by clearing this check box. If you turn this option off and you want to view an animation, right-click the box and then click Show Picture.

▶ **Play Sounds in Webpages**—This check box toggles web page sound effects on and off. Because the vast majority of web page sounds are extremely bad MIDI renditions of popular tunes, turning off sounds will save your ears.

▶ **Show Image Download Placeholders**—If you activate this check box, Internet Explorer displays a box that is the same size and shape as the image it is downloading.

▶ **Show Pictures**—This check box toggles web page images on and off. If you're using a slow connection, turn off this option and Internet Explorer will show only a box where the image would normally appear. (If the designer has included alt text, that text will appear inside the box.) If you want to view a picture when you've toggled images off, right-click the box and select the Show Picture option.

▶ **Smart Image Dithering**—This check box toggles image dithering on and off. *Dithering* is a technique that slightly alters an image to make jagged edges appear smooth.

In the Printing group, the Print Background Colors and Images check box determines whether Internet Explorer includes the page's background when you print the page. Many web pages use solid colors or fancy images as backgrounds, so you'll print these pages faster if you leave this setting deactivated.

The options in the Search from the Address Bar group control Internet Explorer's Address bar searching:

▶ **Do Not Submit Unknown Addresses to Your Auto-Search Provider**—Activate this option to disable address bar searching for terms that are not known to Internet Explorer.

▶ **Just Display the Results in the Main Window**—Activate this option to display, in the main browser window, a list of the sites that the search engine found.

The Security branch has many options related to Internet Explorer security. I discuss these options in Chapter 15.

▶ **See** "Understand Internet Explorer's Advanced Security Options," **p. 337.**

CHAPTER 3

Customizing the File System

Form and function are a unity, two sides of one coin. In order to enhance function, appropriate form must exist or be created.

—Ida P. Rolf

Amazingly, a long list of useful and powerful Windows 7 features are either ignored or given short shrift in the official Microsoft documentation. Whether it's Microsoft Management Console snap-ins, group policies, or the Registry (to name just three that I discuss in this book), Microsoft prefers that curious users figure these things out for themselves (with, of course, the help of their favorite computer book).

The subject of this chapter is a prime example. The idea of the *file type* can be described, without hyperbole, as the very foundation of the Windows 7 file system. Not only does Microsoft offer scant documentation and tools for working with file types, but it also seems to have gone out of its way to hide the whole file type concept. As usual, the reason is to block out this aspect of Windows 7's innards from the sensitive eyes of the novice user. Ironically, however, this just creates a completely new set of problems for beginners and more hassles for experienced users.

This chapter brings file types out into the open. You'll learn the basics of file types and then see a number of powerful techniques for using file types to take charge of the Windows 7 file system.

Understanding File Types

To get the most out of this chapter, you need to understand some background about what a file type is and how Windows 7 determines and works with file types. The next couple of sections tell you everything you need to know to get you through the rest of the chapter.

File Types and File Extensions

One of the fictions that Microsoft has tried to foist on the computer-using public is that we live in a "document-centric" world. That is, that people care only about the documents they create and not about the applications they use to create those documents. This is pure hokum. The reality is that applications are still too difficult to use and the capability to share documents between applications is still too problematic. In other words, you can't create documents unless you learn the ins and outs of an application, and you can't share documents with others unless you use compatible applications.

Unfortunately, we're stuck with Microsoft's worship of the document and all the problems that this worship creates. A good example is the hiding of file extensions. As you learned in Chapter 1, "Customizing Windows Explorer," Windows 7 turns off file extensions by default, and this creates a whole host of problems, from the confusion of trying to determine a file type based on a teensy icon, to not being able to edit extensions, to not being able to save a file under an extension of your choice. You can overcome all these problems by turning on file extensions, as I show in Chapter 1.

> **See** "Turning on File Extensions," **p. 11**.

Why does the lack of file extensions cause such a fuss? Because file extensions determine the file type of a document. In other words, if Windows 7 sees that a file has a .txt extension, it concludes the file uses the Text Document file type. Similarly, a file with the extension .bmp uses the Bitmap Image file type.

The file type, in turn, determines the application that's associated with the extension. If a file has a .txt extension, Windows 7 associates that extension with Notepad, so the file will always open in Notepad. Nothing else inherent in the file determines the file type so, at least from the point of view of the user, the entire Windows 7 file system rests on the scrawny shoulders of the humble file extension.

This method of determining file types is, no doubt, a poor design decision. For example, there is some danger that a novice user could render a file useless by imprudently renaming its extension. Interestingly, Microsoft seems to have recognized this danger and programmed a subtle behavior change into recent versions of Windows (Vista and 7): When file extensions are turned on and you activate the Rename command (click the file and then press F2), Windows displays the usual text box around the entire filename, but it selects *only* the file's primary name (the part to the left of the dot), as shown in Figure 3.1. Pressing any character obliterates the primary name, but leaves the extension intact.

Despite the drawbacks that come with file extensions, they lead to some powerful methods for manipulating and controlling the Windows 7 file system, as you see in the rest of this chapter.

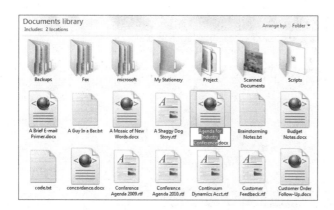

3

FIGURE 3.1 When you activate the Rename command with file extensions turned on, Windows selects just the file's primary name.

File Types and the Registry

As you might expect, everything Windows 7 knows about file types is defined in the Registry. (See Chapter 12, "Tweaking the Windows 7 Registry," for the details on understanding and using the Registry.) You use the Registry to work with file types throughout this chapter, so let's see how things work. Open the Registry Editor (click Start, type **regedit**, press Enter, and enter your UAC credentials) and examine the HKEY_CLASSES_ROOT key. Notice that it's divided into two sections:

▶ The first part of HKEY_CLASSES_ROOT consists of dozens of file extension subkeys (such as .bmp and .txt). There are well over 400 such subkeys in a basic Windows 7 installation, and there could easily be two or three times that number on a system with many applications installed.

▶ The second part of HKEY_CLASSES_ROOT lists the various file types that are associated with the registered extensions. When an extension is associated with a particular file type, the extension is said to be *registered* with Windows 7.

> **NOTE**
>
> HKEY_CLASSES_ROOT also stores information on ActiveX controls in its CLSID subkey. Many of these controls also have corresponding subkeys in the second half of HKEY_CLASSES_ROOT.

To see what this all means, take a look at Figure 3.2. Here, I've selected the .txt key, which has txtfile as its Default value.

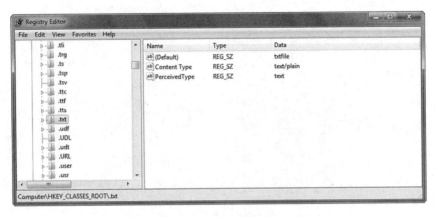

FIGURE 3.2   The first part of the HKEY_CLASSES_ROOT key contains subkeys for all the registered file extensions.

That Default value is a pointer to the extension's associated file type subkey in the second half of HKEY_CLASSES_ROOT. Figure 3.3 shows the txtfile subkey associated with the .txt extension. Here are some notes about this file type subkey:

▶ The Default value is a description of the file type (Text Document, in this case).

▶ The DefaultIcon subkey defines the icon that's displayed with any file that uses this type.

▶ The shell subkey determines the actions that can be performed with this file type. These actions vary depending on the file type, but Open and Print are common. The Open action determines the application that's associated with the file type. For example, the Open action for a Text Document file type is the following:

```
%SystemRoot%\system32\NOTEPAD.EXE %1
```

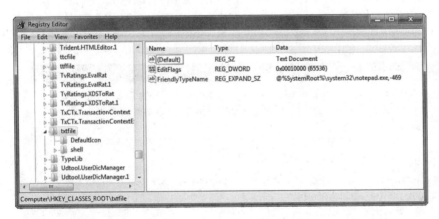

FIGURE 3.3   The second part of HKEY_CLASSES_ROOT contains the file type data associated with each extension.

NOTE

The %1 at the end of the command is a placeholder that refers to the document being opened (if any). If you double-click a file named memo.txt, for example, the %1 place-holder is replaced by memo.txt, which tells Windows to run Notepad and open that file.

Working with Existing File Types

In this section, you'll learn how to work with Windows 7's existing file types. I'll show you how to change the file type description, modify the file type's actions, associate an extension with another file type, and disassociate a file type and an extension. Note that earlier versions of Windows had a decent front-end for these types of hacks: the File Types tab in the Folder Options dialog box. Alas, that tab is nowhere in sight in Windows 7, so you must use the Registry directly for some of what follows.

Setting the Default Action

Many file types have a default action that Windows 7 runs when you double-click a document of that file type. You can see the default action by right-clicking a document and examining the shortcut menu for the command that appears in bold type. You can edit the Registry to change the default action for a file type. Why would you want to do this? Here are some examples:

► For HTML documents (.htm or .html extension), the default action is Open, which opens the document in Internet Explorer. If you hand-code HTML pages, you might prefer the default action to be Edit so that you can quickly load the documents in your text editor.

► For images, the default action is Preview, which opens images in the Photo Gallery Viewer. Again, if you work with images frequently (creating them, cropping them, converting them, and so on), you might prefer that Edit be the default action.

► For Windows Scripting Host file types, such as VBScript Script File (.vbs extension) and JScript Script File (.js extension), the default action is Open, which runs the script. However, these scripts can contain malicious code, so you can boost the security of your system by changing the default action for these file types to Edit.

To change the default action for a file type, follow these steps:

1. Open the Registry Editor.
2. Navigate to the key associated with the file type you want to work with.
3. Open the key and click the Shell branch.
4. Double-click the Default value to open the Edit String dialog box.
5. Type the name of the action that you want to be the default. For example, if you want the Edit action to be the default, type **Edit**.
6. Click OK.

Figure 3.4 shows the VBSFile file type (VBScript Script File) with the Shell branch's Default setting changed to Edit.

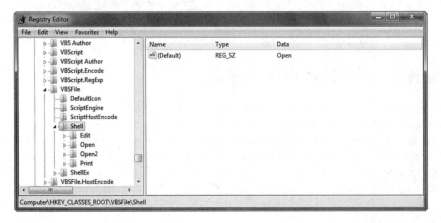

FIGURE 3.4   To change a file type's default action, change the value of the Shell branch's Default setting.

TIP

When you want to open a folder window in the two-paned Explorer view, you have to right-click the folder and then click Explore. To make the latter the default action for a folder, edit the Folder file type, select Explore in the Actions list, and then click Set Default.

Creating a New File Type Action

You're not stuck with just the actions that Windows 7 has defined for a file type. You can add as many new actions that you can think of. For example, if you work with HTML documents, you could keep the default Edit action as it is (this opens the file for editing in Notepad) and create a new action—called, for example, Open in HTML Editor—that opens the file in an HTML editor that you have installed. When you right-click an HTML file, the menu that appears will show both commands: Edit (for Notepad) and Open in HTML Editor (for the other editor; note that, for simplicity's sake, I'm assuming here that when you installed the HTML editor, it didn't modify the Edit action to point to itself).

To create a new action for an existing file type, follow these steps:

1. Open the Registry Editor.
2. Navigate to the key associated with the file type you want to work with.
3. Open the key and click the Shell branch.
4. Select Edit, New, Key, type the name of the new action, and press Enter.
5. Select Edit, New, Key, type **command**, and press Enter.

6. In the command branch, double-click the Default value to open the Edit String dialog box.

7. Type the full pathname of the application you want to use for the action. Here are some notes to bear in mind:

   ► If the pathname of the executable file contains a space, be sure to enclose the path in quotation marks, like so:

   ```
   "C:\Program Files\My Program\program.exe"
   ```

   ► If you'll be using documents that have spaces in their filenames, add the %1 parameter after the pathname:

   ```
   "C:\Program Files\My Program\program.exe" "%1"
   ```

   The %1 part tells the application to load the specified file (such as a filename you click), and the quotation marks ensure that no problems occur with multiple-word filenames.

   ► If you're adding a Print action, be sure to include the /p switch after the application's pathname, like this:

   ```
   "C:\Program Files\My Program\program.exe" /p
   ```

TIP

You can define an accelerator key for the new action. Click the branch that holds the action name, and then double-click the Default value. In the Edit String dialog box, type the action name and precede a letter with an ampersand (&). That letter will be the menu accelerator key. For example, entering **Open in &HTML Editor** defines H as the accelerator key. When you right-click a file of this type, you can then press H to select the command in the shortcut menu.

---

8. Click OK.

Example: Opening the Command Prompt in the Current Folder

When you're working in Windows Explorer, you might occasionally find that you need to do some work at the Command Prompt. For example, the current folder might contain multiple files that need to be renamed—a task that's most easily done within a command-line session. Selecting Start, All Programs, Accessories, Command Prompt starts the session in the %UserProfile% folder, so you have to use one or more CD commands to get to the folder you want to work in.

An easier way would be to create a new action for the Folder file type that launches the Command Prompt and automatically displays the current Windows Explorer folder. To do this, follow these steps:

1. Open the Registry Editor.

2. Navigate to the Folder key.

3. Open the key and click the shell branch.

4. Select Edit, New, Key, type **Open with Command Prompt**, and press Enter.

5. Select Edit, New, Key, type **command**, and press Enter.

6. In the command branch, double-click the Default value to open the Edit String dialog box.

7. Type the following:

   cmd.exe /k cd "%L"

NOTE

The cmd.exe file is the Command Prompt executable file. The /k switch tells Windows 7 to keep the Command Prompt window open after the CD (change directory) command completes. The %L placeholder represents the full pathname of the current folder.

---

8. Click OK. Figure 3.5 shows the Registry Editor with the new Open with Command Prompt action added to the HKCR\Folder\shell key.

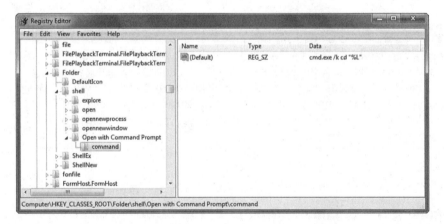

FIGURE 3.5   Modify the HKCR\Folder\shell key to define a new action for the Folder file type.

In Figure 3.6, I right-clicked a folder, and you can see that the new action appears in the shortcut menu.

Hiding a File Type's Extension

A *shortcut* is a file that points to another object: a document, folder, drive, printer, and so on. Shortcuts use the .lnk extension, which is associated with the lnkfile file type. Strangely, if you turn on file extensions, you still never see the .lnk extension when you view a shortcut file. Presumably, Windows 7 hides the extension because we're not supposed to think of the shortcut as an actual file, just a pointer to a file. That's fine with me, but how does Windows 7 accomplish the trick of always hiding a shortcut's file extension?

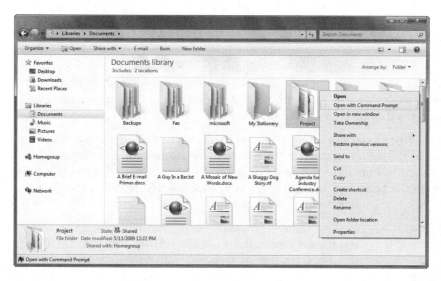

FIGURE 3.6   After you add the new action to the file type's `shell` key, the action appears in the file type's shortcut menu.

The secret is that the Registry's lnkfile (shortcut) key has an empty string setting named NeverShowExt. When Windows 7 comes across this setting, it always hides the file type's extension.

You might want to duplicate this effect for another file type. If you have multiple users on your computer, for example, you might want to turn on file extensions, but hide the extensions of an important file type to ensure that users can't change it. Follow these steps to always hide a file type's extension:

1. Open the Registry Editor.
2. Navigate to the key of the file type you want to work with.
3. Select Edit, New, String Value.
4. Type **NeverShowExt** and press Enter.

Associating an Extension with a Different Application

There are many reasons you might want to override Windows 7's default associations and use a different program to open an extension. For example, you might prefer to open text files in WordPad instead of Notepad. Similarly, you might want to open HTML files in Notepad or some other text editor rather than Internet Explorer.

In those cases, you need to associate the extension with the application you want to use instead of the Windows default association. In Windows 7, you use the Open With dialog box to change the associated application, and Windows 7 gives you many different ways to display this dialog box:

▶ **Right-click**—With this method, right-click any file that uses the extension and then click Open With. If the file type already has multiple programs associated with it, you'll see a menu of those programs. In this case, click the Choose Default Program command from the menu that appears.

▶ **Task pane**—When you click a file, Windows Explorer's task pane displays a button that represents the default action for the file type. For example, if you click an image, a Preview button appears in the task pane; if you click an audio file, you see a Play button in the task pane. In most cases, this default action button also doubles as a drop-down list. Display the list and click Choose Default Program.

▶ **Set associations**—Select Start, Default Programs, Associate a File Type or Protocol with a Program. This opens the Set Associations window, shown in Figure 3.7, which displays a list of file extensions. Click the file type you want to work with and then click Change Program.

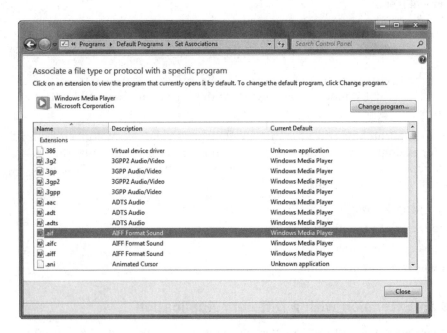

FIGURE 3.7   Use the Set Associations dialog box to change the application associated with any of the displayed file extensions.

No matter which method you use, you end up in the Open With dialog box, shown in Figure 3.8. From here, you follow these steps:

1. Select the program you want to associate with the file type. (If you don't see the program, click Browse, use the new Open With dialog box to select the program's executable file, and then click Open.)

2. Make sure that the Always Use the Selected Program to Open This Kind of File check box is activated. (If you arrived at the Open With dialog box via the Set Associations window, this check box is always activated and disabled.)

3. Click OK.

FIGURE 3.8   Use the Open With dialog box to associate a file type with a different application.

TIP

What if you want only a single file to open with a different application? For example, you might want to always edit a particular HTML file in Notepad, but still open all other HTML files with Internet Explorer. You can set this up by pinning the other application (such as Notepad) to the taskbar as described in Chapter 2, "Customizing the File System." You then pin the file to that taskbar icon (again, as described in Chapter 2). Windows 7 automatically associates just that file with the different application, so whether you open the file via the jump list or by double-clicking it, it will always default to the new application.

Associating an Application with Multiple File Types

Many applications can work with multiple file types. For example, Media Player can play more than 30 file types, including Windows Media Audio (.wma), MP3 (.mp3), CD Audio Track (.cda), and AVI (.avi). Windows 7 has a Set Default Programs window that enables you to specify which file types are associated with a particular application. Here's how to use it:

1. Select Start, Default Programs to display the Default Programs window.

2. Select Set Your Default Programs to display the Set Default Programs window.

3. Use the Programs list to select the application you want to work with.

4. You now have two choices:

   ▶ If you want to associate with the program all the file types that the program is capable of handling, click the Set This Program as Default button.

   ▶ If you want to associate with the program only some of the file types that is can handle, click Choose Defaults for This Program to display the Set Program Associations window. Activate the check box for each file type you want to associate with the program, and then click Save.

5. Click OK.

Creating a New File Type

Windows 7 comes with a long list of registered file types, but it can't account for every extension you'll face in your computing career. For rare extensions, it's best just to use the Open With dialog box. However, if you have an unregistered extension that you encounter frequently, you should register that extension by creating a new file type for it.

> **TIP**
>
> Text files, in particular, seem to come with all kinds of nonstandard (that is, unregistered) extensions. Rather than constantly setting up file types for these extensions or using the Open With dialog box, I created a shortcut for Notepad in my %UserProfile\SendTo folder. That way, I can open any text file by right-clicking it and then selecting Send To, Notepad.

Our old friend the Open With dialog box provides a quick-and-dirty method for creating a simple file type for an unregistered extension:

1. In Windows Explorer, select the file you want to work with.

2. Click Open. (For unregistered file types, Windows 7 doesn't display the Open With command.) Windows 7 displays a dialog box telling you that it cannot open the file.

3. Activate the Select a Program from a List of Installed Programs option and then click OK. The Open With dialog box appears.

4. Select the application you want to use to open the file or click Browse to choose the program from a dialog box.

5. Use the Type a Description That You Want to Use for this Kind of File text box to enter a description for the new file type.

6. Make sure that the Always Use the Selected Program to Open This Kind of File check box is activated.

7. Click OK.

This method creates a new file type with the following properties:

▶ The number of actions Windows 7 creates for the file type depends on the application you selected. If you can use the application to both display and edit the file, Windows 7 creates Open and Edit actions; if you can use the application only to display the file, Windows 7 creates just the Open action.

▶ The icon associated with the file is the same as the one used by the associated application.

▶ In the Registry, you see the extension in HKEY_CLASSES_ROOT and the associated file type name is ext_auto_file, where *ext* is the file's extension.

Associating Two or More Extensions with a Single File Type

The problem with creating a new file type is that you often have to reinvent the wheel. For example, let's say you want to set up a new file type that uses the .1st extension. These are usually text files (such as readme.1st) that provide preinstallation instructions, so you probably want to associate them with Notepad. However, this means repeating some or all of the existing Text Document file types. To avoid this, it's possible to tell Windows 7 to associate a second extension with an existing file type. Here are the steps to follow:

1. Open the Registry Editor.
2. Select the HKEY_CLASSES_ROOT key.
3. Select Edit, New, Key.
4. Type the file extension used with the new file type (such as .1st), and press Enter.
5. In the new file extension key, double-click Default.
6. Type the name of the existing file type key that you want to associate with the new file type. For example, if you want the new file type to be associated with the Text Document (.txt) file type, enter **txtfile.**
7. Click OK.

Customizing the New Menu

One of Windows 7's handiest features is the New menu, which enables you to create a new file without working within an application. In Windows Explorer (or on the desktop), right-click an empty part of the folder and then select New. In the submenu that appears, you'll see items that create new documents of various file types, including a folder, shortcut, bitmap image, WordPad document, text document, compressed folder, and possibly many others, depending on your system configuration and the applications you have installed.

What mechanism determines whether a file type appears on the New menu? The Registry, of course. To see how this works, start the Registry Editor and open the HKEY_CLASSES_ROOT key. As you've seen, most of the extension subkeys have only a Default setting that's either blank (if the extension isn't associated with a registered file type) or a string that points to the extension's associated file type.

However, many of these extension keys also have subkeys, and a few of them have a subkey named ShellNew, in particular. For example, open the .bmp key and you see that it has a subkey named ShellNew. This subkey is what determines whether a file type appears on the New menu. Specifically, if the extension is registered with Windows 7 and it has a ShellNew subkey, the New menu sprouts a command for the associated file type.

The ShellNew subkey always contains a setting that determines how Windows 7 creates the new file. Four settings are possible:

NullFile   This setting, the value of which is always set to a null string (""), tells Windows 7 to create an empty file of the associated type. Of the file types that appear on the default New menu, three use the NullFile setting: Text Document (.txt), Bitmap Image (.bmp), and Shortcut (.lnk).

Directory   This setting tells Windows 7 to create a folder. The New menu's Briefcase (see the Briefcase\ShellNew key in the Registry) command uses this setting.

Command   This setting tells Windows 7 to create the new file by executing a specific command. This command usually invokes an executable file with a few parameters. Two of the New menu's commands use this setting:

- **Contact**—The .contact\ShellNew key contains the following value for the Command setting:

    "%ProgramFiles%\Windows Mail\Wab.exe" /CreateContact "%1"

- **Journal Document**—In the .jnt\jntfile\ShellNew key, you'll see the following value for the Command setting:

    "%ProgramFiles%\Windows Journal\Journal.exe" /n 0

Data   This setting contains a value, and when Windows 7 creates the new file, it copies this value into the file. The New menu's Rich Text Document (.rtf) and Compressed (Zipped) Folder (.zip) commands use this setting.

Adding File Types to the New Menu

To make the New menu even more convenient, you can add new file types for documents you work with regularly. For any file type that's registered with Windows 7, you follow a simple three-step process:

1. Add a ShellNew subkey to the appropriate extension key in HKEY_CLASSES_ROOT.

2. Add one of the four settings discussed in the preceding section (`NullFile`, `Directory`, `Command`, or `Data`).

3. Type a value for the setting.

In most cases, the easiest way to go is to use `NullFile` to create an empty file.

Deleting File Types from the New Menu

Many Windows 7 applications (such as Microsoft Office) like to add their file types to the New menu. If you find that your New menu is getting overcrowded, you can delete some commands to keep things manageable. To do this, you need to find the appropriate extension in the Registry and delete its `ShellNew` subkey.

CAUTION

Instead of permanently deleting a `ShellNew` subkey, you can tread a more cautious path by simply renaming the key (to, for example, `ShellNewOld`). This still prevents Windows 7 from adding the item to the New menu, but it also means that you can restore the item just by restoring the original key name. Note, however, that some third-party Registry cleanup programs flag such renamed keys for deletion or restoration. The better programs—such as Registry Mechanic (www.pctools.com)—enable you to specify keys that the program should ignore.

Customizing Windows 7's Open With List

You've used the Open With dialog box a couple of times so far in this chapter. This is a truly useful dialog box, but you can make it even more useful by customizing it. The rest of this chapter takes you through various Open With customizations.

Opening a Document with an Unassociated Application

From what you've learned in this chapter, you can see the process that Windows 7 goes through when you double-click a document:

1. Look up the document's extension in `HKEY_CLASSES_ROOT`.

2. Examine the `Default` value to get the name of the file type subkey.

3. Look up the file type subkey in `HKEY_CLASSES_ROOT`.

4. Get the `Default` value in the `shell\open\command` subkey to get the command line for the associated application.

5. Run the application and open the document.

What do you do if you want to bypass this process and have Windows 7 open a document in an *unassociated* application? (That is, an application other than the one with which the document is associated.) For example, what if you want to open a text file in WordPad?

One possibility would be to launch the unassociated application and open the document from there. To do so, you'd run the File, Open command (or whatever) and, in the Open dialog box, select All Files in the Files of Type list.

That will work, but it defeats the convenience of being able to launch a file directly from Windows Explorer. Here's how to work around this:

1. In Windows Explorer, select the document with which you want to work.

2. Select File, Open With. (Alternatively, right-click the document, and then click Open With in the shortcut menu.)

3. The next step depends on the file you're working with:

   ▶ For most files, Windows 7 goes directly to the Open With dialog box. In this case, skip to step 4.

   ▶ For a system file, Windows asks whether you're sure that you want to open the file. In this case, click Open With.

   ▶ For some file types, Windows 7 displays a submenu of suggested programs. In this case, if you see the alternative program you want, select it. Otherwise, select Choose Default Program.

4. Select the unassociated application in which you want to open the document. (If the application you want to use isn't listed, click Browse and then select the program's executable file from the dialog box that appears.)

5. To prevent Windows 7 from changing the file type to the unassociated application, make sure that the Always Use the Selected Program to Open this Kind of File check box is deactivated.

6. Click OK to open the document in the selected application.

Note that Windows 7 remembers the unassociated applications that you choose in the Open With dialog box. When you next select the Open With command for the file type, Windows 7 displays a menu that includes both the associated program and the unassociated program you chose earlier.

How the Open With Feature Works

Before you learn about the more advanced Open With customizations, you need to know how Windows 7 compiles the list of applications that appear on the Open With list:

▶ Windows 7 checks HKEY_CLASSES_ROOT\.*ext* (where .*ext* is the extension that defines the file type). If it finds an OpenWith subkey, the applications listed under that subkey are added to the Open With menu, and they appear in the Open With dialog box in the Recommended Programs section.

▶ Windows 7 checks HKEY_CLASSES_ROOT\.*ext* to see whether the file type has a PerceivedType setting. If so, it means the file type also has an associated *perceived type*. This is a broader type that groups related file types into a single category. For example, the Image perceived type includes files of type BMP, GIF, and JPEG, whereas the Text perceived type includes the files of type TXT, HTM, and XML. Windows 7 then checks the following:

HKEY_CLASSES_ROOT\SystemFileAssociations*PerceivedType*\OpenWithList

Here, *PerceivedType* is value of the file type's `PerceivedType` setting. The application keys listed under the `OpenWithList` key are added to the file type's Open With menu and dialog box.

▶ Windows 7 checks `HKEY_CLASSES_ROOT\Applications`, which contains subkeys named after application executable files. If an application subkey has a `\shell\open\command` subkey, and if that subkey's `Default` value is set to the path name of the application's executable file, the application is added to the Open With dialog box.

▶ Windows 7 checks the following key:

`HKEY_CURRENT_USER\Software\Microsoft\Windows\CurrentVersion\Explorer\`
➥`FileExts\.ext\OpenWithList`

Here, *ext* is the file type's extension. This key contains settings for each application that the current user has used to open the file type via Open With. These settings are named a, b, c, and so on, and there's an `MRUList` setting that lists these letters in the order in which the applications have been used. These applications are added to the file type's Open With menu.

Removing an Application from a File Type's Open With Menu

When you use the Open With dialog box to choose an alternative application to open a particular file type, that application appears on the file type's Open With menu (that is, the menu that appears when you select the File, Open With command). To remove the application from this menu, open the following Registry key (where *ext* is the file type's extension):

`HKEY_CURRENT_USER\Software\Microsoft\Windows\CurrentVersion\Explorer\`
➥`FileExts\.ext\OpenWithList`

Delete the setting for the application you want removed from the menu. Also, edit the `MRUList` setting to remove the letter of the application you just deleted. For example, if the application setting you deleted was named b, delete the letter b from the `MRUList` setting.

Removing a Program from the Open With List

Instead of customizing only a single file type's Open With menu, you might need to customize the Open With dialog box for all file types. To prevent a program from appearing in the Open With list, open the Registry Editor and navigate to the following key:

`HKEY_CLASSES_ROOT/Applications`

Here, you'll find a number of subkeys, each of which represents an application installed on your system. The names of these subkeys are the names of each application's executable file (such as `notepad.exe` for Notepad). To prevent Windows 7 from displaying an application in the Open With list, highlight the application's subkey, and create a new string value named `NoOpenWith`. (You don't have to supply a value for this setting.) To restore the application to the Open With list, delete the `NoOpenWith` setting.

> **NOTE**
>
> The NoOpenWith setting works only for applications that are not the default for opening
> a particular file type. For example, if you add NoOpenWith to the notepad.exe subkey,
> Notepad will still appear in the Open With list for text documents, but it won't appear
> for other file types, such as HTML files.

Adding a Program to the Open With List

You can also add an application to the Open With dialog box for all file types. Again, you
head for the following Registry key:

```
HKEY_CLASSES_ROOT/Applications
```

Display the subkey named after the application's executable file. (If the subkey doesn't
exist, create it.) Now add the \shell\open\command subkey and set the Default value to
the pathname of the application's executable file.

Disabling the Open With Check Box

The Open With dialog box enables you to change the application associated with a file
type's Open action by activating the Always Use the Selected Program to Open This Kind
of File check box. If you share your computer with other people, you might not want
them changing this association, either accidentally or purposefully. In that case, you can
disable the check box by adjusting the following Registry key:

```
HKEY_CLASSES_ROOT\Unknown\shell\opendlg\command
```

The Default value of this key is the following:

```
%SystemRoot%\system32\rundll32.exe %SystemRoot%\system32\shell32.dll,OpenAs_RunDLL %1
```

To disable the check box in the Open With dialog box, append %2 to the end of the
Default value:

```
%SystemRoot%\system32\rundll32.exe %SystemRoot%\system32\shell32.dll,
➡OpenAs_RunDLL %1 %2
```

Customizing Startup and Shutdown

The White Rabbit put on his spectacles. "Where shall I begin, your Majesty?" he asked.
"Begin at the beginning," the King said, very gravely, "and go on till you come to the end: then stop."

—Lewis Carroll, *Alice's Adventures in Wonderland*

At first blush, this might seem like a surprising topic for an entire chapter. After all, the Windows 7 startup procedure gives new meaning to the term no-brainer: You turn on your system, and a short while later, Windows 7 reports for duty. What's to write about?

You'd be surprised. The progress of a typical boot appears uneventful only because Windows 7 uses a whole host of default options for startup. By changing these defaults, you can take control of the startup process and make Windows 7 start your way. This chapter takes you through the entire startup process, from go to whoa, and shows you the options you can use to customize it and to troubleshoot it should things go awry.

Customizing Startups Using the Boot Configuration Data

NEW TO 7 If your system can boot to one or more operating systems other than Windows 7, or to multiple installations of Windows 7, you'll see a menu similar to the following during startup:

```
Choose the operating system or tool you want to start:
(Use the arrow keys to highlight your choice.)
```

```
Earlier version of Windows
Windows 7
```

```
To specify an advanced option for this choice, press F8.
Seconds until highlighted choice will be started automatically: 30
```

```
Tools:
    Windows Memory Diagnostic
```

If you do nothing at this point, Windows 7 will boot automatically after 30 seconds. Otherwise, you select the operating system you want and then press the Enter key to boot it. (To switch between the operating system menu and the Tools menu, press the Tab key.) The specifics of this menu are determined by the *Boot Configuration Data* (BCD), a new data store that replaces the BOOT.INI file used in earlier versions of Windows. BOOT.INI still exists, but it's used only for loading the legacy operating systems in multiboot setups. Why the change? There are three main reasons:

▶ It didn't make sense to have two different types of boot information stores: one for BIOS-based systems and another for EFI-based systems. BCD creates a common store for both types of operating systems.

▶ The need to support *boot applications*, which refers to any process that runs in the boot environment that the Windows Boot Manager creates. The main types of boot applications are Windows 7 partitions, legacy installations of Windows, and startup tools, such as the Windows Memory Diagnostic that appears in the Windows Boot Manager menu. In this sense, Windows Boot Manager is a kind of miniature operating system that displays an interface (the Windows Boot Manager menu) that lets you select which application you want to run.

▶ The need to make boot options scriptable. The BCD exposes a scripting interface via a Windows Management Instrumentation (WMI) provider. This enables you to create scripts that modify all aspects of the BCD.

Windows 7 gives you four methods to modify some or all the data in the BCD store:

▶ The Startup and Recovery feature

▶ The System Configuration utility

▶ The BCDEDIT command-line utility

▶ The BCD WMI provider

NOTE

I don't discuss the BCD WMI provider in this chapter. To get more information, see the following page:

msdn2.microsoft.com/en-us/library/aa362677.aspx

Using Startup and Recovery to Modify the BCD

You can modify a limited set of BCD options using the Startup and Recovery dialog box: the default operating system, the maximum time the Windows Boot Manager menu is displayed, and the maximum time the Windows 7 startup recovery options are displayed. Here are the steps to follow:

1. Select Start, right-click Computer, and then click Properties. Windows 7 displays Control Panel's System window.

2. Click Advanced System Settings. The System Properties dialog box appears.

TIP

Another way to get to the System Properties dialog box is to select Start, type **systempropertiesadvanced**, and then press Enter.

---

3. In the Advanced tab, click the Settings button in the Startup and Recovery group. Windows 7 displays the Startup and Recovery dialog box, shown in Figure 4.1.

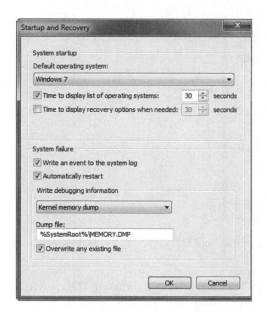

FIGURE 4.1   Use the Startup and Recovery dialog box to modify some aspects of the BCD.

4. Use the Default Operating System list to click the operating system that Windows Boot Manager highlights by default at startup. (In other words, this is the operating system that runs automatically if you do not make a choice in the Windows Boot Manager menu.)

5. Use the Time to Display List of Operating Systems spin box to set the interval after which Windows Boot Manager launches the default operating system. If you don't want Windows Boot Manager to select an operating system automatically, deactivate the Time to Display List of Operating Systems check box.

6. If Windows 7 is not shut down properly, Windows Boot Manager displays a menu of recovery options at startup. If you want the default options selected automatically after a time interval, activate the Time to Display Recovery Options When Needed check box and use the associated spin box to set the interval.

7. Click OK in all open dialog boxes to put the new settings into effect.

Using the System Configuration Utility to Modify the BCD

For more detailed control over the BCD store, you can modify the data by using the System Configuration Utility. To start this program, follow these steps:

1. Select Start, type **msconfig**, and then press Enter. The System Configuration Utility window appears.

2. Select the Boot tab, shown in Figure 4.2.

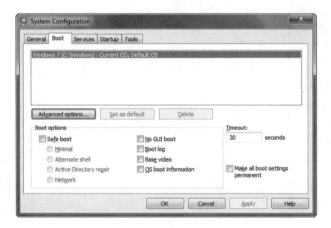

FIGURE 4.2   In the System Configuration Utility, use the Boot tab to modify the BCD store.

The large box near the top of the tab displays the Windows 7 installations on the current computer. You see Current OS beside the Windows 7 installation you are running now; you see Default OS beside the Windows 7 installation that is set up as the default. There are four main tasks you can perform:

▶ Click the Set as Default button to set the highlighted Windows 7 install as the default for the Windows Boot Manager menu.

▶ Use the Timeout text box to set the maximum time that Windows Boot Manager waits before selecting the default OS.

► Use the check boxes in the Boot Options group to set the following startup options for the currently highlighted Windows 7 install:

Safe Boot: Minimal—Boots Windows 7 in *Safe mode*, which uses only a minimal set of device drivers. Use this switch if Windows 7 won't start, if a device or program is causing Windows 7 to crash, or if you can't uninstall a program while Windows 7 is running normally.

Safe Boot: Minimal (Alternate Shell)—Boots Windows 7 in Safe mode but also bypasses the Windows 7 GUI and boots to the Command Prompt instead. Use this switch if the programs you need to repair a problem can be run from the Command Prompt or if you can't load the Windows 7 GUI.

NOTE

The shell loaded by the `/safeboot:minimal(`*alternateshell)* switch is determined by the value in the following Registry key:

`HKEY_LOCAL_MACHINE\SYSTEM\CurrentControlSet\SafeBoot\AlternateShell`

The default value is `cmd.exe` (the Command Prompt).

Safe Boot: Active Directory Repair—Boots Windows 7 in Safe mode and restores a backup of the Active Directory service. (This option applies only to domain controllers.)

Safe Boot: Network—Boots Windows 7 in Safe mode but also includes networking drivers. Use this switch if the drivers or programs you need to repair a problem exist on a shared network resource, if you need access to email or other network-based communications for technical support, or if your computer is running a shared Windows 7 installation.

No GUI Boot—Tells Windows 7 not to load the VGA display driver that is normally used to display the progress bar during startup. Use this switch if Windows 7 hangs while switching video modes for the progress bar, or if the display of the progress bar is garbled.

Boot Log—Boots Windows 7 and logs the boot process to a text file named `ntbtlog.txt` that resides in the `%SystemRoot%` folder. Move to the end of the file and you might see a message telling you which device driver failed. You probably need to reinstall or roll back the driver (see Chapter 22, "Troubleshooting Devices"). Use this switch if the Windows 7 startup hangs, if you need a detailed record of the startup process, or if you suspect (after using one of the other Startup menu options) that a driver is causing Windows 7 startup to fail.

► **See** "Rolling Back a Device Driver," **p. 466**.

NOTE

`%SystemRoot%` refers to the folder into which Windows 7 was installed. This is usually `C:\Windows`.

Base Video—Boots Windows 7 using the standard VGA mode: 640×480 with 256 colors. This is useful for troubleshooting video display driver problems. Use this switch if Windows 7 fails to start using any of the Safe mode options, if you recently installed a new video card device driver and the screen is garbled, the driver is balking at a resolution or color depth setting that's too high, or if you can't load the Windows 7 GUI. After Windows 7 has loaded, you can reinstall or roll back the driver, or you can adjust the display settings to values that the driver can handle.

OS Boot Information—Displays the path and location of each device driver as it loads, as well as the operating system version and build number, the number of processors, the system memory, and the process type.

▶ Click the Advanced Options button to display the BOOT Advanced Options dialog box shown in Figure 4.3. You can set the following options:

Number of Processors—In a multiprocessor system, specifies the maximum of processors that Windows 7 can use. Activate this check box if you suspect that using multiple processors is causing a program to hang.

Maximum Memory—Specifies the maximum amount of memory, in megabytes, that Windows 7 can use. Use this value when you suspect a faulty memory chip might be causing *problems.*

PCI Lock—Activate this check box to tell Windows 7 not to dynamically assign hardware resources for PCI devices during startup. The resources assigned by the BIOS during the POST are locked in place. Use this switch if installing a PCI device causes the system to hang during startup.

Detect HAL—Activate this check box to force Windows 7 to detect the computer's *hardware abstraction layer (HAL)* at startup. The HAL is a software layer that resides between the computer's hardware and the operating system kernel, and its job is to hide hardware differences so that the kernel can run on a variety of hardware. If you force Windows 7 to detect the HAL, it can use the HAL to interact with the computer's hardware at startup. This is useful if dealing with the hardware directly is causing startup problems.

Debug—Enables remote debugging of the Windows 7 kernel. This sends debugging information to a remote computer via one of your computer's ports. If you use this switch, you can use the Debug Port list to specify a serial port, IEEE 1394 port, or USB port. If you use a serial port, you can specify the transmission speed of the debugging information using the Baud Rate list; if you use an IEEE 1394 connection, activate Channel and specify a channel value; if you use a USB port, type the device name in the USB Target Name text box.

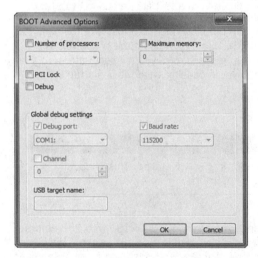

FIGURE 4.3   In the Boot tab, click Advanced Options to display the dialog box shown here.

Using BCDEDIT to Customize the Startup Options

The System Configuration utility makes it easy to modify BCD store items, but it doesn't give you access to the entire BCD store. For example, the Boot tab doesn't list any legacy boot items on your system, and there are no options for renaming boot items or for changing the order in which the boot items are displayed in the Windows Boot Manager menu. For these tasks, and indeed for every possible BCD task, you need to use the BCDEDIT command-line tool.

Note that BCDEDIT is an administrator-only tool, so you must run it under the Administrator account (not just any account in the Administrators group). The easiest way to do this is to elevate your privileges when running the Command Prompt, as described in the following steps:

1. Select Start and type **command** in the Search box. Command Prompt appears at the top of the search results.

2. Right-click Command Prompt and then click Run as Administrator. The User Account Control dialog box appears.

3. Either click Continue or type an administrator password and click Submit. The Command Prompt window appears

See Chapter 18, "Setting Up User Security," to learn more about elevating privileges in Windows 7.

▶ **See** "Elevating Privileges," **p. 375**.

Table 4.1 summarizes the switches you can use with BCDEDIT.

TABLE 4.1   Switches Available for the **BCDEDIT** Command-Line Tool

Switch	Description
/bootdebug	Toggles boot debugging for a boot application on and off
/bootems	Toggles Emergency Management Services for a boot application on and off
/bootsequence	Sets the one-time boot sequence for the boot manager
/copy	Makes a copy of an entry
/create	Creates a new entry
/createstore	Creates a new and empty BCD store
/dbgsettings	Sets the global debugger settings
/debug	Toggles kernel debugging for an operating system entry
/default	Sets the default entry
/delete	Deletes an entry
/deletevalue	Deletes an entry value
/displayorder	Sets the order in which Boot Manager displays the operating system entries

TABLE 4.1   Continued

Switch	Description
/ems	Enables or disables Emergency Management Services for an operating system entry
/emssettings	Sets the global Emergency Management Services settings
/enum	Lists the entries in the BCD store
/export	Exports the contents of the BCD store to a file
/import	Restores the BCD store from a backup file created with the /export switch
/mirror	Creates a mirror of an entry
/set	Sets an option value for an entry
/store	Specifies the BCD store to use
/timeout	Sets the Boot Manager timeout value
/toolsdisplayorder	Sets the order in which Boot Manager displays the Tools menu
/types	Displays the data types required by the /set and /deletevalue commands
/v	Displays all entry identifiers in full, instead of using well-known identifiers

To help you understand how BCDEDIT works, let's examine the output that appears when you run BCDEDIT with the /enum switch:

```
Windows Boot Manager
--------------------
identifier              {bootmgr}
device                  partition=\Device\HarddiskVolume1
description             Windows Boot Manager
locale                  en-US
inherit                 {globalsettings}
default                 {current}
resumeobject            {53c701aa-e1c3-11dd-9af1-8cfcc639165e}
displayorder            {ntldr}
                        {current}
toolsdisplayorder       {memdiag}
timeout                 30
```

```
Windows Legacy OS Loader
------------------------
identifier              {ntldr}
device                  partition=\Device\HarddiskVolume1
path                    \ntldr
description             Earlier Version of Windows

Windows Boot Loader
-------------------
identifier              {current}
device                  partition=C:
path                    \Windows\system32\winload.exe
description             Windows 7
locale                  en-US
inherit                 {bootloadersettings}
recoverysequence        {53c701ac-e1c3-11dd-9af1-8cfcc639165e}
recoveryenabled         Yes
osdevice                partition=C:
systemroot              \Windows
resumeobject            {53c701aa-e1c3-11dd-9af1-8cfcc639165e}
nx                      OptIn
```

As you can see, this BCD store has three entries: one for Windows Boot Manager, one for a legacy Windows install, and one for a Windows 7 install. Notice that each entry has an Identifier setting, and these IDs are unique to each entry. All IDs are actually 32-digit *globally unique identifiers* (GUIDs), but by default BCDEDIT works with a collection of *well-known identifiers*, including the following (type **bcdedit id /?** to see the complete list):

bootmgr	The Windows Boot Manager entry
ntldr	An entry that uses a legacy operating system loader (NTLDR) to boot earlier versions of Windows
current	The entry that corresponds to the operating system that is currently running
default	The entry that corresponds to the Windows Boot Manager default operating system
memdiag	The Windows Memory Diagnostics entry

If you want to see the full GUIDs for every entry, add the /v (verbose) switch:

```
bcdedit /enum /v
```

It would take dozens of pages to run through all the BCDEDIT switches, so I'll just give you a few examples so you can get a taste of how this powerful utility operates.

Making a Backup Copy of the BCD Store

Before you do any work on the BCD store, you should make a backup copy. That way, if you make an error when you change something in the BCD, you can always restore the backup copy to get your system back to its original state.

You create a backup copy using the /export switch. For example, the following command backs up the BCD store to a file named bcd_backup in the root folder of the C: drive:

```
bcdedit /export c:\bcd_backup
```

If you need to restore the backup, use the /import switch, as in this example:

```
bcdedit /import c:\bcd_backup
```

Renaming an Entry

The names that Windows Boot Manager assigns to the boot applications leave a lot to be desired. For a legacy operating system entry, for example, the default Earlier Version of Windows is not particularly descriptive. A simpler name such as Windows XP Pro would be much more useful. Similarly, all Windows 7 installs get the same name: Windows 7, which can be quite confusing. Names such as Windows 7 Home Premium and Windows 7 Ultimate would be much more understandable.

To rename an entry using BCDEDIT, use the following syntax:

```
bcdedit /set {id} description "name"
```

Here, replace *id* with the entry identifier (the GUID or the well-known identifier, if applicable) and replace *name* with the new name you want to use. For example, the following command replaces the current name of the legacy operating system entry (ntldr) with Windows XP Pro:

```
bcdedit /set {ntldr} description "Windows XP Pro"
```

TIP

GUIDs are 32-character values, so typing them by hand is both time-consuming and error-prone. To avoid this, first run the `bcdedit /enum` command to enumerate the BCD entries, and then scroll up until you see the GUID of the entry with which you want to work. Pull down the system menu (click the upper-left corner of the window or press Alt+spacebar), select Edit, Mark, click-and-drag over the GUID to select it, and then press the Enter key to copy it. Begin typing your BCDEDIT command, and when you get to the part where the identifier is required, pull down the system menu again and select Edit, Paste.

Changing the Order of the Entries

If you'd prefer that the Boot Manager menu entries appear in a different order, you can use BCDEDIT's /displayorder switch to change the order. In the simplest case, you might want to move an entry to either the beginning or the end of the menu. To send an entry to the beginning, include the /addfirst switch. Here's an example:

```
bcdedit /displayorder {a8ef3a39-a0a4-11da-bedf-97d9bf80e36c} /addfirst
```

To send an entry to the end of the menu, include the /addlast switch instead, as in this example:

```
bcdedit /displayorder {current} /addfirst
```

To set the overall order, include each identifier in the order you want, separated by spaces:

```
bcdedit /displayorder {current} {a8ef3a39-a0a4-11da-bedf-97d9bf80e36c} {ntldr}
```

Customizing Startups with the Advanced Options Menu

When the Windows Boot Manager menu appears at startup, you see the following message when you highlight a Windows 7 install:

```
To specify an advanced option for this choice, press F8.
```

If you press F8, you get to the Advanced Boot Options menu, which looks like this:

```
        Advanced Boot Options


Choose Advanced Options for: Microsoft Windows 7
(use the arrow keys to highlight your choice.)

    Repair Your Computer

    Safe Mode
    Safe Mode with Networking
    Safe Mode with Command Prompt

    Enable Boot Logging
    Enable low-resolution video (640×480)
    Last Known Good Configuration (advanced)
    Directory Services Restore Mode
    Debugging Mode
    Disable automatic restart on system failure
    Disable Driver Signature Enforcement

    Start Windows Normally
```

TIP

If your system doesn't automatically display the Windows Boot Manager menu at start-up, you can display it manually. After you start your computer, wait until the POST is complete, and then press F8 to display the Windows Boot Manager menu. If your computer is set up to "fast boot," it might not be obvious when the POST ends. In that case, just turn on your computer and press F8 repeatedly until you see the Windows Boot Manager menu. Note, however, that if your system picks up two separate F8 presses, you might end up directly in the Advanced Boot Options menu.

The Start Windows Normally option loads Windows 7 in the usual fashion. You can use the other options to control the rest of the startup procedure:

▶ **Repair Your Computer**—This option (it's new with Windows 7) opens the System Recovery Options, which enable you to perform a startup repair or system restore, recover your PC from a system image, and more. I discuss this option in detail in Chapter 23, "Troubleshooting Startup."

  ▶ **See** "Recovering Using the System Recovery Options," **p. 485.**

▶ **Safe Mode**—If you're having trouble with Windows 7—for example, if a corrupt or incorrect video driver is mangling your display, or if Windows 7 won't start—you can use the Safe Mode option to run a stripped-down version of Windows 7 that includes only the minimal set of device drivers that Windows 7 requires to load. You could reinstall or roll back the offending device driver and then load Windows 7 normally. Starting in Safe mode displays the Administrator account in the Welcome screen, which is the account to use when troubleshooting problems. When Windows 7 finally loads, the desktop reminds you that you're in Safe mode by displaying Safe Mode in each corner. (Also, Windows Help and Support appears with Safe mode–related information and links.)

NOTE

If you're curious to know which drivers are loaded during a Safe mode boot, see the subkeys in the following Registry key:

HKEY_LOCAL_MACHINE\SYSTEM\CurrentControlSet\Control\SafeBoot\Minimal\

▶ **Safe Mode with Networking**—This option is identical to plain Safe mode, except that Windows 7's networking drivers are also loaded at startup. This enables you to log on to your network, which is handy if you need to access the network to load a device driver, run a troubleshooting utility, or send a tech support request. This option also gives you Internet access if you connect via a gateway on your network. This is useful if you need to download drivers or contact online tech support.

▶ **Safe Mode with Command Prompt**—This option is the same as plain Safe mode, except that it doesn't load the Windows 7 GUI. Instead, it runs cmd.exe to load a Command Prompt session.

▶ **Enable Boot Logging**—This option is the same as the Boot Normally option, except that Windows 7 logs the boot process in a text file named ntbtlog.txt that resides in the system root.

▶ **Enable Low-Resolution Video (640×480)**—This option loads Windows 7 with the video display set to 640×480 and 256 colors. This is useful if your video output is garbled when you start Windows 7. For example, if your display settings are configured at a resolution that your video card can't handle, boot in the low-resolution mode and then switch to a setting supported by your video card.

▶ **Last Known Good Configuration**—This option boots Windows 7 using the last hardware configuration that produced a successful boot.

▶ **Directory Services Restore Mode**—Boots Windows 7 in Safe mode and restores a backup of the Active Directory service. (This option applies only to domain controllers.)

▶ **Debugging Mode**—Enables remote debugging of the Windows 7 kernel.

▶ **Disable Automatic Restart on System Failure**—Prevents Windows 7 from restarting automatically when the system crashes. Choose this option if you want to prevent your system from restarting so that you can read an error message or deduce other information that can help you troubleshoot the problem.

▶ **Disable Driver Signature Enforcement**—Prevents Windows 7 from checking whether devices drivers have digital signatures. Choose this option to ensure that Windows 7 loads an unsigned driver, if failing to load that driver is causing system problems.

For more information about these options, see Chapter 23.

▶ **See** "When to Use the Various Advanced Startup Options," **p. 482**.

Useful Windows 7 Logon Strategies

The default Windows 7 logon is fine for most users, but there are many ways to change Windows 7's logon behavior. This section offers up a few tips and techniques for altering the way you log on to Windows 7.

Logging On to a Domain

In versions of Windows prior to Vista, when you logged on to a domain you always used the Classic Windows logon, which consisted of pressing Ctrl+Alt+Delete and then typing your username and password in the Log On to Windows dialog box. (You also had the option of specifying a different domain.) However, the Classic Windows logon was removed from Vista and remains gone from Windows 7. To log on to a domain in Windows 7, you must specify the domain as part of the username. You have two choices:

▶ **NetBIOSName\UserName**—Here, replace *NetBIOSName* with the NetBIOS name of the domain, and replace *UserName* with your network username (for example, logophilia\paulm).

▶ **UserName@Domain**—Here, replace *Domain* with the domain name, and replace *UserName* with your network username (for example, paulm@logophilia.com).

Enabling the Administrator Account

One of the confusing aspects about Windows 7 is that the Administrator account seems to disappear after the setup is complete. That's because, for security reasons, Windows 7 doesn't give you access to this all-powerful account. I should say it doesn't give you *easy* access to this account. The Welcome screen doesn't include an option to choose the Administrator, and no option exists anywhere in the Control Panel's user account windows to enable this account to log on.

That's probably just as well because it keeps most users much safer, but it's annoying for those of us who might occasionally require the Administrator account. For example, tools such as the Windows Automated Installation Kit require that you be logged on with the Administrator account.

Fortunately, you can activate the Administrator account in several ways. Here's a quick look at two of them:

- **Using the Local Security Policy Editor**—Select Start, type `secpol.msc`, press Enter, and then enter your UAC credentials. In the Local Security Policy Editor, open the Local Policies, Security Options branch, and then double-click the Accounts: Administrator Account Status policy. Click Enabled, and then click OK.

- **Using the Local Users and Groups snap-in**—Select Start, type `lusrmgr.msc`, press Enter, and then enter your UAC credentials. In the Local Users and Groups snap-in, click Users and then double-click Administrator. In the Administrator Properties dialog box, deactivate the Account Is Disabled check box, as shown in Figure 4.4, and then click OK.

FIGURE 4.4   One way to activate the Administrator account is to use the Local Users and Groups snap-in to open the Administrator Properties dialog box.

These methods suffer from a serious drawback: They don't work in all versions of Windows 7, in particular Windows 7 Home Basic and Windows 7 Home Premium.

Fortunately, we haven't exhausted all the ways to activate Windows 7's Administrator account. Here's a method that works with *all* versions of Vista:

1. Select Start, type **command**, right-click Command Prompt, and then click Run as Administrator. The User Account Control dialog box appears.
2. Enter your UAC credentials to continue.
3. At the command line, enter the following command:

```
net user Administrator /active:yes
```

That's it! Log off and you now see the Administrator account in the logon screen, as shown in Figure 4.5.

FIGURE 4.5   When you activate the Administrator account, an icon for that account appears in the logon screen.

CAUTION

Right now, your freshly activated Administrator account has *no* password! Log on as the administrator and immediately use the Control Panel to give the account a strong password.

> **NOTE**
>
> When you're done with the Administrator account, be sure to disable it again for security. At an Administrator Command Prompt, enter the follow command:
>
> ```
> net user Administrator /active:no
> ```
>
> With the Administrator account active, it's a good idea to rename it; **see** "Renaming Built-In Accounts for Better Security," **p. 405**.

Setting Up an Automatic Logon

If you're using a standalone computer that no one else has access to (or that will be used by people you trust), you can save some time at startup by not having to type a username and password. In this scenario, the easiest way to do this is to set up Windows 7 with just a single user account without a password, which means Windows 7 logs on that user automatically at startup. If you have multiple user accounts (for testing purposes, for example) or if you want the Administrator account to be logged on automatically, you need to set up Windows 7 for automatic logons.

> **CAUTION**
>
> Setting up an automatic logon is generally not a good idea for notebook computers because they're easily lost or stolen. By leaving the logon prompt in place, the person who finds or steals your notebook will at least be unlikely to get past the logon, so your data won't be compromised.

Follow these steps:

1. Select Start, type **control userpasswords2**, press Enter, and then enter your UAC credentials. The User Accounts dialog box appears.
2. Display the Users tab.
3. Click your username (or the name of whichever user you want to automatically log on).
4. Deactivate the Users Must Enter a User Name and Password to Use this Computer check box, as shown in Figure 4.6.
5. Click OK. The Automatically Log On dialog box appears. The username you clicked in step 3 is filled in automatically.
6. Type the user's password into the Password and Confirm Password text boxes.
7. Click OK.

The next time you start your PC, Windows logs on your account automatically.

FIGURE 4.6   Use the User Accounts dialog box to configure an automatic logon.

TIP

If you have other accounts on your system, you can still log on one of them at startup if need be. Restart your computer and, after the various BIOS messages are done, press and hold the Shift key. This tells Windows to bypass the automatic logon and display the logon screen.

Disabling Automatic Logon Override

As you saw in the Tip sidebar in the preceding section, you can hold down the Shift key to override an automatic logon. In some situations, this is not preferable. For example, you might have a computer set up for a particular user and you want only that user to log on. In that case, you don't want the user overriding the automatic logon.

To prevent the override of an automatic logon using the Shift key, open the Registry Editor once again and navigate to the following key:

```
HKLM\Software\Microsoft\Windows NT\CurrentVersion\Winlogon\
```

Create a new String value named IgnoreShiftOverride and set its value to 1.

Setting Up One-Click Restarts and Shutdowns

My admittedly obsessive quest to minimize clicks and keystrokes is a quirk, I know, but it's a defensible one (I keep telling myself). After all, the fewer mouse and keyboard moves you have to make—particularly when you're doing day-to-day system drudgery—the more time you have for being a productive member of society.

Unfortunately, the technique I'm about to show you isn't a great example of this because I'm talking here about reducing the number of clicks it takes to restart and shut down Windows 7, and how often does anyone do that in the course of a day? Still, I really like this tip because it just bugs me that I have to display the *Start* menu to *stop* Windows 7 (which is just senseless), and it takes two clicks to do it. Bah! In this section, you learn how to restart and shut down Windows with just one measly click.

At the heart of this technique is the SHUTDOWN command, which you can use to restart or shut down your computer (or, as you see a bit later in the "Turn Off Your Windows Computer from Anywhere" section, a remote computer on your network). Here's the full syntax:

```
SHUTDOWN [[/R] | [/S] | [/L] | [/H] | [/I] | [/P] | [/E] | [/A]] [/F] | [/T seconds]
➥[/D [P:]xx:yy] [/M \\ComputerName] [/C "comment"]
```

/R	Restarts the computer.
/S	Shuts down the computer.
/L	Logs off the current user immediately.
/H	Puts the computer into hibernation, if the computer supports hibernation mode.
/I	Displays the Remote Shutdown dialog box, which enables you to specify many of the options provided by these switches.
/P	Turns off the local computer immediately (that is, without the usual warning interval).
/E	Enables you to document the reason for an unexpected shutdown.
/A	Cancels the pending restart or shutdown.
/F	Forces all running programs on the target computer to shut down without warning. This, obviously, is dangerous and should be used only as a last resort.
/D [P:]*major:minor*	Specifies the reason for the shutdown. Include P: to indicate the shutdown is planned. Use values between 0 and 255 for *major* and between 0 and 65535 for *minor*. Windows also defines a number of predefined values for the *major* and *minor* parameters:

major	minor	Reason
0	0	Other (Planned)
0	5	Other Failure: System Unresponsive
1	1	Hardware: Maintenance (Unplanned)
1	1	Hardware: Maintenance (Planned)
1	2	Hardware: Installation (Unplanned)
1	2	Hardware: Installation (Planned)
2	3	Operating System: Upgrade (Planned)
2	4	Operating System: Reconfiguration (Unplanned)
2	4	Operating System: Reconfiguration (Planned)
2	16	Operating System: Service Pack (Planned)
2	17	Operating System: Hot Fix (Unplanned)
2	17	Operating System: Hot Fix (Planned)
2	18	Operating System: Security Fix (Unplanned)
2	18	Operating System: Security Fix (Planned)
4	1	Application: Maintenance (Unplanned)
4	1	Application: Maintenance (Planned)
4	2	Application: Installation (Planned)
4	5	Application: Unresponsive
4	6	Application: Unstable
5	15	System Failure: Stop Error
5	19	Security Issue
5	19	Security Issue
5	19	Security Issue
5	20	Loss of Network Connectivity (Unplanned)
6	11	Power Failure: Cord Unplugged
6	12	Power Failure: Environment
7	0	Legacy API Shutdown

/M \\ComputerName	Specifies the remote computer you want to shut down.

/T seconds	Specifies the number of seconds after which the computer is shut down. The default is 30 seconds, and you can specify any number up to 600.
/C "comment"	The *comment* text (which can be a maximum of 127 characters) appears in the dialog box and warns the user of the pending shutdown. This *comment* text also appears in the shutdown event that is added to the System log in Event Viewer. (Look for an Event ID of 1074.)

For example, to restart your computer immediately, use the following command:

```
shutdown /r /t 0
```

If you've launched a restart or shutdown using some nonzero value for /T, and you need to cancel the pending shutdown, run SHUTDOWN with the /A switch before the timeout interval is over:

```
shutdown /a
```

Create a Restart Shortcut

Okay, let's use our newfound knowledge of the SHUTDOWN command to set up Windows 7 with one-click restarts:

1. Right-click an empty section of the desktop, and then select New, Shortcut. The Create Shortcut Wizard appears.
2. In the text box, type **shutdown /r /t 0**, as shown in Figure 4.7.

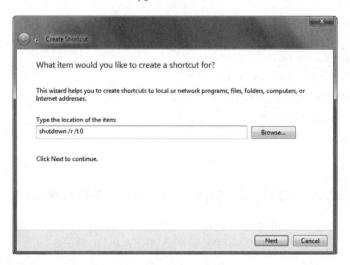

FIGURE 4.7   Use shutdown /r /t 0 as the command for your restart shortcut.

3. Click Next. The Create Shortcut wizard prompts you to enter a name for the shortcut.

4. Type a name (such as **The Amazing One-Click Restart Thingy**) and then click Finish.

5. Right-click the new shortcut and then click Properties. The shortcut's property sheet appears.

6. In the Shortcut tab, click Change Icon. Windows tells you that `shutdown.exe` contains no icons.

7. Click OK. The Change Icon dialog box appears.

8. Click an icon that looks "restart-y" and then click OK.

9. Click OK. Windows applies the new icon to the shortcut.

10. Right-click the shortcut and then click Pin to Taskbar. Windows 7 adds your icon to the taskbar, and restarts are now just a click away.

Create a Shutdown Shortcut

I think you know what comes next, right? Follow these very similar steps to add a shutdown shortcut to the Quick Launch toolbar:

1. Right-click an empty section of the desktop, and then select New, Shortcut. The Create Shortcut Wizard appears.

2. In the text box, type **shutdown /s /t 0**.

3. Click Next. The Create Shortcut wizard prompts you to enter a name for the shortcut.

4. Type a name (such as **The Amazing One-Click Shutdown Whatsit**) and then click Finish.

5. Right-click the new shortcut and then click Properties. The shortcut's property sheet appears.

6. In the Shortcut tab, click Change Icon. Windows tells you that `shutdown.exe` contains no icons.

7. Click OK. The Change Icon dialog box appears.

8. Click an icon that looks "shutdown-y" and then click OK.

9. Click OK. Windows applies the new icon to the shortcut.

10. Right-click the shortcut and then click Pin to Taskbar. Windows 7 adds your icon to the taskbar, and restarts are now just a click away.

Turning Off Your Windows 7 Computer from Anywhere

If you're working at a network computer and you decide you need to shut down or restart your own PC, you can actually do it from your remote location on the network.

NOTE

The technique in this section works with Windows 7, but *only* if the Windows 7 PC has User Account Control turned off. Personally, I think the security of UAC immensely outweighs the convenience of a remote shutdown, so I highly recommend leaving UAC alone and skipping this tweak for your Windows 7 PC. As a workaround, set up your Windows 7 machine as a Remote Desktop host (assuming your version of Windows 7 supports this—see Chapter 27, "Making Remote Network Connections"), which enables you to connect to the PC over the network and shut it down manually from there.

To shut down a remote computer, you must run SHUTDOWN using an account that has administrator privileges on the remote computer. If the logged on user account on your local machine also exists on the remote machine and is a member of the Administrators group, you automatically have sufficient privileges to shut down the remote PC.

You do this by running SHUTDOWN with the following general syntax:

```
shutdown /s /m \\ComputerName
```

Here, *ComputerName* is the name of the remote PC. For example, the following command shuts down a remote PC named GAMINGPC:

```
shutdown /s /m \\gamingpc
```

If the local account you're logged on with does *not* exist on the remote computer, or if it does exist but doesn't have administrator rights, you need to run the SHUTDOWN command using a remote administrator account. This requires you to use the RUNAS command-line tool:

```
RUNAS /user:ComputerName\UserName cmd
```

ComputerName	The name of the remote computer
UserName	The name of the account under which you want to run cmd
cmd	The command you want to run

For a remote shutdown, *UserName* will be a remote administrator-level account, and *cmd* will be the SHUTDOWN command, enclosed in quotation marks. Here's an example that uses an account named Paul to shut down a remote computer named OFFICEPC in 120 seconds:

```
runas /user:officepc\paul "shutdown /s /m \\officepc /t 120"
```

When you enter the RUNAS command, Windows prompts you for the account password:

```
Enter the password for officepc\paul:
```

Type the password (it doesn't appear onscreen) and press Enter.

TIP

If you need to embed a quotation mark in the *cmd* portion of RUNAS, precede it with a backslash (\). Here's an example:

```
runas /user:officepc\paul "shutdown /s /m \\officepc /c \"Comment\""
```

If you need to cancel a pending shutdown on a remote computer, run SHUTDOWN with the /A switch before the timeout interval is over:

```
runas /user:officepc\paul "shutdown /a /m \\officepc"
```

Customizing the Start Menu's Power Button

I criticized the Windows 7 shut down procedure earlier, but I'll admit it's a bit of an improvement over Vista (which required three clicks to shut down) and it's a lot better than XP (which required as many as four clicks). However, what if you rarely shut down your PC? For example, many people prefer to put their computer into sleep mode rather than shutting it down altogether. Similarly, you may find that you lock your computer or switch users far more often than you shut down.

Unfortunately, choosing the Sleep, Lock, and Switch User commands in Windows 7 requires three annoying clicks (click Start, click the arrow beside Shut Down, and then click your command). Fortunately, the Windows 7 programmers have taken pity on us and made the power button (the Start menu button that says Shut Down by default) fully customizable, meaning that you can replace the Shut Down command with any of the following: Lock, Log Off, Restart, Sleep, or Switch User. Nice!

Here are the steps to follow:

1. Click Start.
2. Right-click the power button and then click Properties. Windows 7 displays the Taskbar and Start Menu Properties dialog box with the Start Menu tab displayed.
3. Use the Power Button Action list to choose the command you want to see on the power button.
4. Click OK.

Figure 4.8 shows the Windows 7 Start customized to run the Sleep command when the power button is clicked.

FIGURE 4.8   You can customize the Windows 7 Start menu's power button command.

Customizing Your Notebook's Power and Sleep Buttons

Most newer notebooks enable you to configure three "power buttons" closing the lid, using the on/off button, and using the sleep button. When you activate these buttons, they put your system into sleep mode, hibernate mode, or turn it off altogether. On some notebooks, there isn't a separate sleep button; you simply tap the on/off button quickly.

To configure these buttons for power management in Windows 7, follow these steps:

1. Click Start, type **power options**, and then press Enter. The Power Options window appears.
2. Click the Choose What the Power Buttons Do link to see the System Settings window, shown in Figure 4.9.
3. Use the lists to configure the power button, sleep button, and lid switch for battery power and AC power.
4. Click Save Changes.

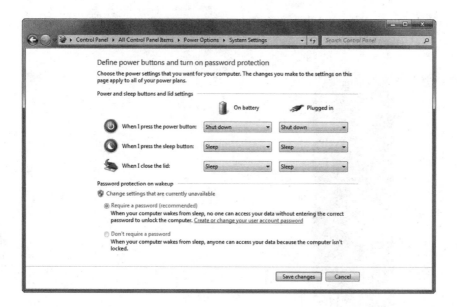

FIGURE 4.9   Use this window to configure what Vista does when you press the power button, the sleep button, or close the notebook lid.

TIP

By default, Windows 7 disables the options in the Password Protection on Wakeup group. This means that you always have to enter your user account password when Windows 7 wakes from sleep mode. If you prefer not to enter your password each time, you can enable these options by clicking the Change Settings That Are Currently Unavailable link, and then clicking the Don't Require a Password option.

CHAPTER 5

Customizing the Start Menu and Taskbar

The mark of our time is its revulsion against imposed patterns.

—Marshall McLuhan

Microsoft spent countless hours and untold millions of dollars testing and retesting the Windows 7 *user interface* (UI) in its usability labs. It's important, however, to remember that Windows 7 is an operating system designed for the masses. With an installed base running in the hundreds of millions, it's only natural that the Windows UI would incorporate lots of lowest common denominator thinking. So in the end, you have an interface that most people find easy to use most of the time; an interface that skews toward accommodating neophytes and the newly digital; an interface designed for a typical computer user, whoever the heck that is.

In other words, unless you consider yourself a typical user (and your purchase of this book proves otherwise), Windows 7 in its right-out-of-the-box getup won't be right for you. Fortunately, you'll find no shortage of options and programs that will help you remake Windows 7 in your own image, and that's just what the chapters here in Part I are all about. After all, you weren't produced by a cookie cutter, so why should your operating system look like it was?

Having said that, I should also point out that it's my philosophy that the litmus test of any interface customization is a simple question: Does it improve productivity? I've seen far too many tweaks that fiddle uselessly with some obscure setting, resulting in little or no improvement to the user's day-to-day Windows experience. This may be fine for people with lots of time to kill, but most of us don't have that luxury, so efficiency and productivity must be the goals of the customization process. (Note that this does not preclude aesthetic improvements to the Windows 7 interface. A better-looking Windows provides a happier computing experience, and a happier worker is a more productive worker.)

To that end, I devote this chapter to one of the most common of computing tasks: launching programs and documents. I packed this chapter with useful tips and techniques for rearranging the Windows 7 Start menu and taskbar to help you get your programs and documents up and running as quickly and as easily as possible.

Customizing the Start Menu for Easier Program and Document Launching

The whole purpose of the Start menu is, as its name implies, to start things, particularly programs and documents. Yes, you can also launch these objects via shortcut icons on the desktop, but that's not a great alternative because windows cover the desktop most of the time. Yes, Windows 7's enhanced taskbar enables you to launch stuff with the click of an icon, but there's only so much room on the taskbar, so that handy technique should be saved for your most often used program (more on this later; see "Pinning a Favorite Program to the Taskbar").

So, if you want to get something going in Windows 7, the vast majority of the time you're going to have to do it via the Start menu. The good news is that Windows 7's Start menu is wonderfully flexible and geared, in fact, to launching objects with as few mouse clicks or keystrokes as possible. To get to that state, however, you have to work with a few relatively obscure options and settings, which you'll learn about in the next few sections.

Getting More Favorite Programs on the Start Menu

The Start menu is divided vertically into two sections, as shown in Figure 5.1:

 ▶ **Favorite programs**—This is the left side of the Start menu, which appears by default with a white background. This side includes shortcut icons for the 10 programs that you've used most frequently. You can also "pin" programs to the top of this list, which I show you how to do in the next section.

> **NOTE**
>
> If you're coming to Windows 7 from Vista or XP, note that Windows 7 does away with the permanent Internet and E-mail icons at the top of the Start menu. Why would they do such a thing? For starters, there's no email client in Windows 7 (although you can install Windows Live Mail from the Windows Live Essentials site, downloads.live.com); for seconds, an icon for Internet Explorer is just a click away on the new taskbar. So that chunk of Start menu real estate is better used either for displaying more programs or for pinning your own favorite programs.

 ▶ **Built-in features**—This is the right side of the Start menu, which appears by default with a black or gray background. It contains icons for various Windows 7 folders and features.

Most Used Programs

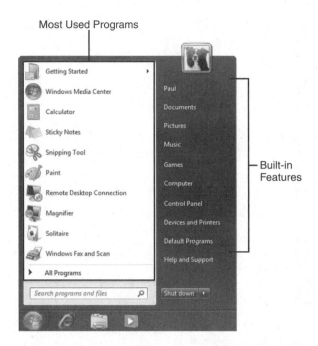

Built-in
Features

FIGURE 5.1   The Start menu lists favorite programs on the left and built-in icons for Windows 7 features on the right.

The list of favorite programs is one of the best features in Windows 7 because it ensures that the programs you use most often are always just a couple of mouse clicks away. If there's a downside to this feature, it's that it displays only 10 icons, so the list omits many frequently used programs. However, if you have enough room, you can tell Windows 7 to display up to 30 icons in this area. Here's how:

1. Right-click the Start button and then click Properties. The Taskbar and Start Menu Properties dialog box appears with the Start Menu tab displayed.

2. Click Customize. The Customize Start Menu dialog box appears, as shown in Figure 5.2.

3. Use the Number of Recent Programs to Display spin box to specify the number of favorite programs you want to display.

4. If you don't think you have enough screen space to display all the icons, deactivate the Large Icons option (which is near the bottom of the list of Start menu features). This significantly reduces the amount of space each icon takes up on the Start menu.

5. Click OK in the open dialog boxes.

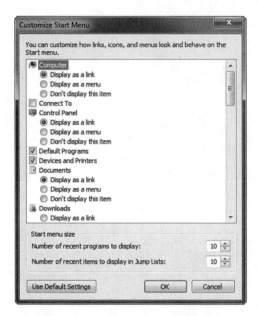

FIGURE 5.2   Use the Customize Start Menu dialog box to set the maximum number of short-cut icons that appear in the Start menu's list of favorite programs.

TIP

To prevent a program from appearing on the Start menu's favorite programs list, open the Registry Editor (see Chapter 12, "Tweaking the Windows 7 Registry") and display the following key:

        HKCR\Applications*program.exe*

Here, *program.exe* is the name of the program's executable file. (If the key doesn't exist, create it.) Create a string value called *NoStartPage*. (You don't need to assign a value to it.) Restart Windows 7 to put the new setting into effect.

Pinning a Favorite Program Permanently to the Start Menu

The Start menu's list of favorite programs is such a time-saving feature that it can be frustrating if a program drops off the list. Another aggravation is that the icons often change position because Windows 7 displays the programs in order of popularity. When you display the Start menu, this constant shifting of icons can result in a slight hesitation while you look for the icon you want. (This is particularly true if you've expanded the maximum number of icons as I described in the previous section.)

Wouldn't it be nice if you could tell Windows 7 to keep a particular icon in a particular place for all time? Well, you can! Specifically, you can *pin* them to the Start menu, which means that Windows 7 moves the icon above the favorite programs list and keeps it there no matter what.

To do this, first open the Start menu and find the shortcut you want to work with. Then you have two choices:

▶ Right-click the shortcut and then click Pin to Start Menu.

▶ Drag the shortcut to the top edge of the Start menu and then drop it.

Figure 5.3 shows the Start menu with two pinned icons: Windows Live Mail and Command Prompt.

Permanently Pinned Icons

FIGURE 5.3   You can pin icons so that they reside permanently at the top of the Start menu.

You can also use this technique to pin shortcuts residing on the desktop to the pinned programs lists. If you decide later that you no longer want a shortcut pinned to the Start menu, right-click the shortcut and then click Unpin from Start Menu.

TIP

When you display the Start menu, you can select an item quickly by pressing the first letter of the item's name. If you add several shortcuts to the pinned programs list, however, you might end up with more than one item that begins with the same letter. To avoid conflicts, rename each of these items so that they begin with a number. For example, renaming "Backup" to "1 Backup" means you can select this item by pressing 1 when the Start menu is displayed. (To rename a Start menu item, right-click the item and then click Rename.)

Clearing the Recent Programs List

Windows 7 allows you to clear the Start menu list of recent programs. Why would you want to do this? You might want to start over with an empty list of frequent programs so that you can populate it with the programs you will use over the next few days. Alternatively, you might want to keep the list cleared for privacy reasons if other people have access to your computer. Follow these steps to clear the list:

1. Right-click the Start button and then click Properties. The Taskbar and Start Menu Properties dialog box appears with the Start Menu tab displayed.
2. Deactivate the Store and Display Recently Opened Programs in the Start Menu check box.
3. Click Apply. Windows 7 clears the list.
4. If you want to start a new list, activate the Store and Display Recently Opened Programs in the Start Menu check box.
5. Click OK.

TIP

If you need to get rid of only one or two icons from the Start menu's favorite programs list, click Start, right-click an icon you want to delete, and then click Remove from This List.

Setting Program Access and Defaults

You can modify Windows 7 to use other programs as the default for activities such as web browsing, email, instant messaging, and media playing. This enables you to have your favorite programs available in more convenient locations and to have those programs launch automatically in certain situations.

Your version of Windows 7 is most likely set up to use Internet Explorer, Windows Mail, Windows Messenger, and Windows Media Player as the default programs for web browsing, email, instant messaging, and media playing, respectively. This means that these programs launch automatically in response to certain events. For example, when you right-click a media file and then click Play, the media plays in Windows Media Player.

You can set up as defaults any other programs you have installed for web browsing, email, instant messaging, and media playing. You can also disable access to programs so that other users cannot launch them on your computer. Here are the steps to follow:

1. Select Start, Default Programs to display the Default Programs window.
2. Click Set Program Access and Computer Defaults. Windows 7 displays the Set Program Access and Computer Defaults dialog box.
3. Click the configuration you want to start with:
   - ▶ **Computer Manufacturer**—This configuration appears only if your computer vendor defined its own program defaults.

▶ **Microsoft Windows**—This configuration is the Windows default as defined by Microsoft.

▶ **Non-Microsoft**—This configuration is generated by Windows 7 if you have one or more non-Microsoft programs available in any of the categories (such as a web browser or email program).

▶ **Custom**—Use this item to configure your own default programs.

4. If you activated the Custom configuration, you see options similar to those shown in Figure 5.4. You can do two things with this configuration:

▶ Activate the option buttons of the programs you prefer to use as the system defaults.

▶ Deactivate the Enable Access to This Program check box for any program that you don't want other users to have access to.

5. Click OK to put the new defaults into effect.

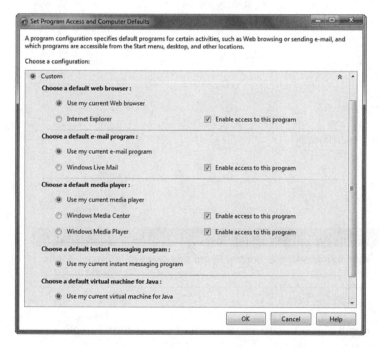

FIGURE 5.4   Use the Set Program Access and Computer Defaults feature to set up a custom program configuration for your system.

Streamlining the Start Menu by Converting Links to Menus

The right side of the Start menu contains a number of built-in Windows 7 features, which are set up as links. That is, you click an item and a window or a program runs in response. That's fine for items such as Search or Default Programs, but it's not very efficient for an item such as the Control Panel, where you're usually looking to launch a specific icon. It seems wasteful to have to open the Control Panel window, launch the icon, and then close the Control Panel.

A better approach is to convert a link into a menu of items that would normally display in a separate window. For example, the Control Panel item could display a menu of its icons. One of the nicer features in Windows 7 is that it's easy to convert many of the Start menu links into menus. Here are the required steps:

1. Right-click the Start button and then click Properties. The Taskbar and Start Menu Properties dialog box appears with the Start Menu tab displayed.

2. Click Customize to open the Customize Start Menu dialog box.

3. In the list of Start menu items, find the following items and activate the Display as a Menu option:

Computer

Control Panel

Documents

Games

Music

Personal Libraries (your username)

Pictures

Recorded TV

Videos

NOTE

To see an example of the Start menu with the Control Panel displayed as a menu, see Figure 8.3 on page 176.

---

4. Activate the Favorites Menu check box to add a menu of your Internet Explorer favorites to the Start menu.

5. Activate the Recent Items check box. This adds the Recent Items menu to the Start menu, which displays the last 15 documents that you've worked with.

6. In the Start Menu Items group, find the System Administrative Tools item and activate the Display on the All Programs Menu and the Start Menu option. This gives you an Administrative Tools menu that offers shortcuts to features such as Computer Management, Device Manager, System Configuration, and the Local Security Policy editor.

7. Click OK to return to the Taskbar and Start Menu Properties dialog box.

8. Make sure that the Store and Display a List of Recently Opened Files check box is activated. This ensures that Windows 7 populates the Recent Items list.

9. Click OK.

Adding, Moving, and Removing Other Start Menu Icons

Besides the main Start menu, you can also customize the icons on the All Programs menu and submenus to suit the way you work. Using the techniques I discuss in this section, you can perform the following Start menu productivity boosts:

▶ Move important features closer to the beginning of the All Programs menu hierarchy.

▶ Remove features you don't use.

▶ Add new commands for features not currently available on the All Programs menu (such as the Registry Editor).

Windows 7 offers three methods for adding and removing Start menu shortcuts, and I explain each of them in the next three sections.

Dragging and Dropping onto the Start Button

The quickest way to add a shortcut is to drag an executable file from Windows Explorer and then do either of the following:

▶ **Drop it on the Start button**—This pins the shortcut to the Start menu.

▶ **Hover over the Start button**—After a second or two, the main Start menu appears. Now hover the file over All Programs until the menu appears, and then drop the file where you want the shortcut to appear.

Working with the Start Menu Folder

The All Programs shortcuts are stored in two places:

▶ `%AppData%\Microsoft\Windows\Start Menu\Programs`—Shortcuts in this subfolder appear only in the current user's Start menu. Here, `%AppData%` is `%SystemDrive%\Users\`*user*`\AppData\Roaming,` where *user* is the name of the current user.

▶ `%AllUsersProfile%\Microsoft\Windows\Start Menu\Programs`—The All Users\Start Menu\Programs subfolder. Shortcuts in this folder appear to all user accounts defined on the computer. Here, `%AllUsersProfile%` is `%SystemDrive%\ProgramData.`

TIP

A quick way to get to the current user's Start Menu folder is to right-click the Start button and then click Explore.

By working with these folders, you get the most control over not only where your Start menu shortcuts appear, but also the names of those shortcuts. Here's a summary of the techniques you can use:

► Within the Programs folder and its subfolders, you can drag existing shortcuts from one folder to another.

► To create a new shortcut, drag the executable file and drop it inside the folder you want to use. Remember that if you want to create a shortcut for a document or other nonexecutable file, right-drag the file and then select Create Shortcuts Here when you drop the file.

► You can create your own folders within the Programs folder hierarchy and they'll appear as submenus within the All Programs menu.

► You can rename a shortcut the same way you rename any file.

► You can delete a shortcut the same way you delete any file.

Working with All Programs Menu Shortcuts Directly

Many of the chores listed in the previous section are more easily performed by working directly within the All Programs menu itself. That is, you open the All Programs menu, find the shortcut you want to work with, and then use any of these techniques:

► Drag the shortcut to another section of its current menu.

► Drag the shortcut to another menu or to the Recycle Bin.

► Right-click the shortcut and then select a command (such as Delete) from the context menu.

Customizing the Taskbar for Easier Program and Document Launching

In Windows 7, the taskbar acts somewhat like a mini-application. The purpose of this "application" is to launch other programs, display a button for each running program, and to enable you to switch from one program to another. Like most applications these days, the taskbar also has its own toolbars that, in this case, enable you to launch programs and documents.

Improving Productivity by Setting Taskbar Options

The taskbar comes with a few options that can help you be more productive either by saving a few mouse clicks or by giving you more screen room to display your applications, so let's start there. Follow these steps to set these taskbar options:

1. Right-click the taskbar and then click Properties. The Taskbar and Start Menu Properties dialog box appears with the Taskbar tab displayed, as shown in Figure 5.5.

FIGURE 5.5   Use the Taskbar tab to set up the taskbar for improved productivity.

2. Activate or deactivate the following options, as required to boost your productivity:

   ▶ **Lock the Taskbar**—When this check box is activated, you can't resize the taskbar and you can't resize or move any taskbar toolbars. This is useful if you share your computer with other users and you don't want to waste time resetting the taskbar if it's changed by someone else.

TIP

You can also toggle taskbar locking on and off by right-clicking an empty section of the taskbar and then clicking Lock the Taskbar.

   ▶ **Auto-Hide the Taskbar**—When this check box is activated, Windows 7 reduces the taskbar to a thin, blue line at the bottom of the screen when you're not using it. This is useful if you want a bit more screen room for your applications. To redisplay the taskbar, move the mouse pointer to the bottom of the screen. Note, however, that you should consider leaving this option deactivated if you use the taskbar frequently; otherwise, auto-hiding it will slow you down because it takes Windows 7 a second or two to restore the taskbar when you hover the mouse pointer over it.

   ▶ **Use Small Icons**—Activate this check box to shrink the taskbar's program icons. This not only reduces the overall height of the taskbar (so you get more room for the desktop and your programs), but it also allow you to populate the taskbar with more icons.

3. Use the Taskbar Location on Screen list to choose where you want to situate the taskbar: Bottom, Left, Right, or Top. For example, if you want to maximize the available screen height, move the taskbar to one side or the other.

4. Use the Taskbar Buttons list to choose how you want Windows 7 to group taskbar buttons when an application has multiple windows open (or an application such as Internet Explorer has multiple tabs open):

   ▸ **Always Combine, Hide Labels**—Choose this option to have Windows 7 always group similar taskbar buttons.

   ▸ **Combine When Taskbar is Full**—Choose this option to have Windows 7 only group similar taskbar buttons when the taskbar has no more open space to displays buttons.

   ▸ **Never Combine**—Choose this option to have Windows 7 never group similar taskbar buttons.

5. Click Customize to configure the notification area to your liking. (See "Taking Control of the Notification Area," later in this chapter, for more information.)

6. NEW TO **7** If you don't want to use Windows 7's new Aero Peek feature, for some reason, deactivate the Use Aero Peek to Preview the Desktop check box.

7. Click OK.

NOTE

Aero Peek is Windows 7's answer to the perennial question, "Why should I put anything on my desktop if I can't see it?" This question is particularly urgent in Windows 7 because all gadgets now reside on the desktop itself (the Sidebar that was introduced in Windows Vista is history). If you have Aero Peek activated, hover your mouse pointer over the Show Desktop button on the right edge of the taskbar, and Windows 7 temporarily turns your open windows transparent so that you can see the desktop. Slip the mouse pointer off the Show Desktop button and your windows rematerialize. Nice!

Pinning a Favorite Program to the Taskbar

NEW TO **7** Earlier you saw that you can pin an icon for your favorite program to the Start menu, which is nice. But we live in a "two clicks bad, one click good" world, so even the apparent benefit of having a favorite application a mere two clicks away pales when you've got icons for Internet Explorer, Windows Explorer, and Media Player a mere one click away on the default Windows 7 taskbar.

Vista and XP refugees may think of these icons as being glorified Quick Launch toolbar icons, but there's a big difference: In Windows 7, when you click one of these icons, it turns into its own running program icon! In other words, a separate icon doesn't show up on the taskbar; instead, Windows 7 puts a frame around the icon to indicate that its program is running.

So how can you get in on this one-click action for your own programs? You can pin those program to the taskbar. You have three choices:

▶ Right-click a program's icon or a program's shortcut and then click Pin to Taskbar.

▶ If the program is already running, right-click its taskbar icon and then click Pin This Program to Taskbar.

▶ Drag a program's icon or a program's shortcut to an empty section of the taskbar and then drop it.

If you decide later that you longer want a program pinned to the taskbar, right-click the program's taskbar icon and then click Unpin This Program from Taskbar.

TIP

Once you've pinned a program to the taskbar, you can use that icon to open documents that aren't normally associated with the program. You normally do this by right-clicking the document, clicking Open With, and then selecting the other program. In Windows 7, however, you can hold down Shift, click and drag the document, and drop it on the program's taskbar icon.

Pinning a Destination to a Program's Jump List

NEW TO 7 A new feature in Windows 7 is the *jump list*, which is a menu of program commands, the 10 most recently used files, and other features that appears when you right-click a program's taskbar icon. For example, the Internet Explorer jump list includes a History list of recently viewed sites, and the Media Player jump list includes a list of frequently played music and a command to Play All Music Shuffled.

TIP

By default, the jump lists only show the 10 most recently used destinations. If you'd like to see more (or, I guess, fewer) recent items, you can customize that number. To do this right-click Start, click Properties, and then click Customize. Use the Number of Recent Items to Display in Jump Lists spin button to set the number of items you prefer (the maximum is 60), and then click OK.

Most jump lists also include a hidden section that enables you to pin your favorite destinations to the jump list. Here, "destinations" depends on the application: For Internet Explorer, it's websites; for Windows Explorer, it's folders; for Media Player, it's media (a song, an artist, or whatever); for just about any other application, it's documents you create in that application.

Pinning a destination to its program's jump list is a handy way to launch that destination because all you have to do is right-click the taskbar icon and then click the pinned icon at the top of the jump list. Windows 7 offers a couple of ways to pin a destination to its program's jump list:

▶ If the destination already appears in the program's jump list, right-click the destination and then click Pin to This List.

▶ Drag the destination to its program's taskbar icon (or to an empty section of the taskbar) and then drop it.

Figure 5.6 shows the Internet Explorer jump list with a few sites pinned at the top.

FIGURE 5.6   Each program jump list includes a Pinned area where you can tack up your favorite program destinations.

TIP

To add a website to Internet Explorer's jump list, either drag an item from the Favorites list and drop it on the Internet Explorer taskbar icon, or navigate to the site, drag the address bar icon, and drop it on the Internet Explorer taskbar icon.

If you decide later that you no longer want a destination pinned to the program's jump list, click the program's taskbar icon, right-click the pinned destination, and then click Unpin from This List.

Using the Windows Key to Start Taskbar Programs

I'm a big fan of the new super-duper Windows 7 taskbar because it offers the easiest way to launch my favorite programs: Just click the icon. However, even that easy-as-pie method is ever-so-slightly inconvenient when your hands are busy typing. It would be a tad more efficient if you could launch taskbar icons from the comfort of your keyboard.

But wait, you can! In Windows 7, you can use the Windows Logo key and the numbers across the top of your keyboard (*not* the ones on the numeric keypad) to press taskbar icons into service without having to reach all the way over to the mouse.

The trick here is that Windows 7 numbers the pinned taskbar icons starting at 1 for the leftmost icon, 2 for the icon to its right, and so on. The first nine icons are numbered from 1 to 9 (again, left to right), and if there's a tenth icon it's numbered as 0. To select a particular pinned taskbar icon from the keyboard, hold down the Windows Logo key and press the corresponding icon number on the top row of the keyboard. For example, on most Windows 7 systems, Windows Explorer is the third pinned taskbar icon from the left, so you can start it by pressing Windows Logo+3.

NOTE

Bear in mind that when Windows 7 numbers the taskbar icons, it only looks at the pinned icons. For example, suppose you start a program, and then decide later to pin some other program to the taskbar. That pinned icon will be the fifth icon on the taskbar, but it will be the fourth *pinned* icon, so you'd launch it by pressing Windows Logo+4.

Taking Control of the Notification Area

NEW TO 7 The notification area (sometimes called by its old name, the *system tray*) on the right side of the taskbar has been a fixture on the Windows landscape since Windows 95, and for most people it's either really useful or it's a complete waste of otherwise useful taskbar space. You're more likely to fall into the latter camp if your notification area in earlier versions of Windows was bristling with icons, as shown in Figure 5.7.

FIGURE 5.7   An out-of-control notification area.

Horror stories of notification areas threatening to take over the taskbar must have inspired Microsoft to finally rein in the bloat. Now, in Windows 7, no matter how many of your installed programs try to run roughshod over the notification area, you'll always see *only* the following icons: Volume, Network, Action Center, and (if you have a notebook PC) Power. Bliss!

That doesn't mean all your other notification area icons are gone for good, they're just permanently hidden, although in two different ways:

▶ Some icons are visible, but to see them you have to click the upward-pointing arrow on the left side of the notification area (see Figure 5.8).

FIGURE 5.8   In Windows 7, you have to click the arrow to see your other notification area icons.

▶ Some icons are completely hidden, but you do see any notification messages displayed by those icons.

This new setup simplifies things considerably and gives you more taskbar breathing room, but there are times when it's not so convenient. For example, if you frequently control a program by right-clicking its tray icon, you either have that extra click to get at the icon, or you can't get at it at all. Fortunately, you can customize the notification area to show an icon right in the tray, hide it in the extra menu, or remove it completely and see just its notifications. Here's how:

1. Click the notification area arrow and then click Customize. (You can also right-click the taskbar, click Properties, and then click Customize.) The Notification Area Icons window appears, as shown in Figure 5.9.

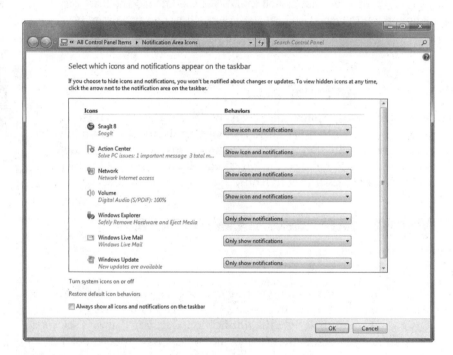

FIGURE 5.9   Use the Notification Area Icons window to customize the notification area.

2. For each icon, use the Behaviors list to choose one of the following options:

▶ **Show Icon and Notifications**—Choose this option to add the icon to the main notification area.

▶ **Hide Icon and Notifications**—Choose this option to shuffle the icon off to the notification area's extra menu.

▶ **Only Show Notifications**—Choose this option to completely remove the icon from the main notification area. Windows 7 will still display the icon's notifications, however.

3. Click the Turn System Icons On or Off link. The System Icons window appears, as shown in Figure 5.10.

FIGURE 5.10   Use the System Icons window to specify with system icons appear in the notification area.

4. Deactivate the check box for each system icon you don't use.
5. Click OK in each open window.

If you have zero use for the notification area, you can disable it entirely by following these steps:

NOTE

These steps require the Group Policy Editor, which is available only with Windows 7 Professional, Windows 7 Enterprise, and Windows 7 Ultimate. If you're not running one of these versions, I'll show you how to perform the same tweak using the Registry.

1. Select Start, type and press Enter. The local Group Policy Editor appears.
2. Open the User Configuration branch.
3. Open the Administrative Templates branch.
4. Click the Start Menu and Taskbar branch.
5. Double-click the Hide the Notification Area policy, click Enabled, and then click OK.

6. Double-click the Remove Clock from the System Notification Area policy, click Enabled, and then click OK.

7. Log off and then log back on to put the policy into effect.

If you prefer (or need) to implement this policy via the Registry, first open the Registry Editor (click Start, type **regedit**, press Enter, and enter your UAC credentials). Navigate to the following key:

```
HKCU\Software\Microsoft\Windows\CurrentVersion\Policies\Explorer
```

(If you don't see the Explorer key, click the Policies key, select Edit, New, Key, type **Explorer**, and press Enter.)

Now follow these steps:

1. Select Edit, New, DWORD (32-bit) Value.

2. Type **NoTrayItemsDisplay** and press Enter.

3. Press Enter to open the NoTrayItemsDisplay setting, type **1**, and then click OK.

4. Select Edit, New, DWORD (32-bit) Value.

5. Type **HideClock** and press Enter.

6. Press Enter to open the HideClock setting, type **1**, and then click OK.

7. Log off and then log back on to put the policies into effect.

Displaying Multiple Clocks for Different Time Zones

If you have colleagues, friends, or family members who work or live in a different time zone, it's often important to know the correct time in that zone. For example, you wouldn't want to call someone at home at 9 a.m. your time if that person lives in a time zone that's three hours behind you. Similarly, if you know that a business colleague leaves work at 5 p.m. and that person works in a time zone that's seven hours ahead of you, you know that any calls you place to that person must occur before 10 a.m. your time.

If you need to be sure about the current time in another time zone, you can customize Windows 7's date and time display to show not only your current time, but also the current time in the other time zone. Follow these steps:

1. Click the Clock icon in the notification area and then click Change Date and Time Settings to display the Date and Time dialog box.

2. Click the Additional Clocks tab. Figure 5.11 shows a completed version of this tab.

3. Activate the first Show This Clock check box.

4. Use the Select Time Zone list to click the time zone you want to display in the additional clock.

5. Use the Enter Display Name text box to type a name for the clock.

6. Repeat steps 4 and 5 for the second clock.

7. Click OK.

FIGURE 5.11   Use the Additional Clocks tab to add one or two more clocks for different time zones in Windows 7.

To see the clocks, click the time to display a fly-out similar to the one shown in Figure 5.12.

FIGURE 5.12   Click the time to see your additional clocks.

TIP

After you customize Windows 7 with the extra clocks, you normally click the time in the notification area to see the clocks. However, if you just hover the mouse pointer over the time, Windows 7 displays a banner that shows the current date, your current local time, and the current time in the other time zones.

Displaying the Built-In Taskbar Toolbars

Windows 7 taskbar comes with four default toolbars:

▶ **Address**—This toolbar contains a text box into which you can type a local address (such as a folder or file path), a network address (a UNC path), or an Internet address. When you press Enter or click the Go button, Windows 7 loads the address into Windows Explorer (if you entered a local or network folder address), an application (if you entered a file path), or Internet Explorer (if you entered an Internet address). In other words, this toolbar works just like the address bar used by Windows Explorer and Internet Explorer.

▶ **Links**—This toolbar contains several buttons that link to predefined Internet sites. This is the same as the links toolbar that appears in Internet Explorer.

▶ **Tablet PC Input Panel**—This toolbar contains just a single icon: the Tablet PC Input Panel icon, which, when clicked, displays the Tablet PC Input Panel.

▶ **Desktop**—This toolbar contains all the desktop icons, as well as an icon for Internet Explorer and submenus for your user folder and the following folders: Public, Computer, Network, Control Panel, and Recycle Bin.

NOTE

You can adjust the size of a toolbar by clicking and dragging the toolbar's left edge. However, this won't work if the taskbar is locked. To unlock the taskbar, right-click an empty section of the taskbar and then click Lock the Taskbar to deactivate it.

To toggle these toolbars on and off, right-click an empty spot on the taskbar and then use either of the following techniques:

▶ Click Toolbars and then click the toolbar you want to work with.

▶ Click Properties, click the Toolbars tab, activate the check box of the toolbar you want to work with, and then click OK.

Setting Some Taskbar Toolbar Options

After you've displayed a toolbar, there are a number of options you can set to customize the look of the toolbar and to make the toolbars easier to work with. Right-click an empty section of the toolbar and then click one of the following commands:

▶ **View**—This command displays a submenu with two options: Large Icons and Small Icons. These commands determine the size of the toolbar's icons. For example, if a toolbar has more icons than can be shown given its current size, switch to the Small Icons view.

▶ **Show Text**—This command toggles the icon titles on and off. If you turn on the titles, it makes it easier to decipher what each icon does, but you'll see fewer icons in a given space.

▶ **Show Title**—This command toggles the toolbar title (displayed to the left of the icons) on and off.

Creating New Taskbar Toolbars

In addition to the predefined taskbar toolbars, you can create new toolbars that display the contents of any folder on your system. For example, if you have a folder of programs or documents that you launch regularly, you can get one-click access to those items by displaying that folder as a toolbar. Here are the steps to follow:

1. Right-click an empty spot on the toolbar, and then click Toolbars, New Toolbar. Windows 7 displays the New Toolbar dialog box.

2. Select the folder you want to display as a toolbar. (Or click New Folder to create a new subfolder within the currently selected folder.)

3. Click Select Folder. Windows 7 creates the new toolbar.

Modifying the Start Menu and Taskbar with Group Policies

5

You see throughout this book that the group policies offer unprecedented control over the Windows 7 interface without having to modify the Registry directly. This is particularly true of the Start menu and taskbar, which boast more than 60 policies that do everything from removing Start menu links such as Run and Help to hiding the taskbar's notification area. To see these policies, launch the Group Policy Editor (see Chapter 9, "Policing Windows 7 with Group Policies") and select User Configuration, Administrative Templates, Start Menu and Taskbar.

Most of the policies are straightforward: By enabling them, you remove a feature from the Start menu or taskbar. For example, enabling the Remove Run Menu from Start Menu policy prevents the user from adding the Run command to the Start menu (or hides the Run command if the user has already added it) and disables the Windows Logo+R shortcut key. This is handy if you're trying to restrict a user to using only those programs and documents that appear on the Start menu.

Here are a few policies that I think are the most useful:

▶ **Clear History of Recently Opened Documents on Exit**—Enable this policy to remove all documents from the current user's Recent Items list whenever Windows 7 exits.

▶ **Remove Drag-and-Drop Context Menus on the Start Menu**—Enable this policy to prevent the current user from rearranging the Start menu using drag-and-drop techniques.

▶ **Do Not Keep History of Recently Opened Documents**—Enable this policy to prevent Windows 7 from tracking the current user's recently opened documents.

▶ **Prevent Changes to Taskbar and Start Menu Settings**—Enable this policy to prevent the current user from accessing the Taskbar and Start Menu Properties dialog box.

▶ **Remove Access to the Context Menus for the Taskbar**—Enable this policy to prevent the current user from seeing the taskbar's shortcut (also called *context*) menus by right-clicking the taskbar.

▶ **Do Not Display Any Custom Toolbars in the Taskbar**—Enable this policy to prevent the current user from adding custom toolbars to the taskbar.

▶ **Remove User Name from Start Menu**—Enable this policy to prevent the current user's name from appearing at the top of the Start menu. This is a good idea if you need more room on the Start menu for the pinned or favorite programs lists.

▶ **Turn Off All Balloon Notifications**—Enable this policy to prevent the current user from seeing the balloon tips that Windows 7 displays when it prompts you about new hardware being detected, downloading automatic updates, and so on.

CHAPTER 6

Tuning Windows 7's Performance

Now, here, you see, it takes all the running you can do, to stay in the same place. If you want to get somewhere else, you must run at least twice as fast as that!
—Lewis Carroll, *Through the Looking Glass*

We often wonder why our workaday computer chores seem to take just as long as they ever did, despite the fact that hardware is generally more reliable and more powerful than ever. The answer to this apparent riddle comes in the form of McFedries' law of computing codependence: *The increase in software system requirements is directly proportional to the increase in hardware system capabilities.* For example, imagine that a slick new chip is released that promises a 10% speed boost; software designers, seeing the new chip gain wide acceptance, add 10% more features to their already bloated code to take advantage of the higher perfor-mance level. Then another new chip is released, followed by another software upgrade—and the cycle continues *ad nauseum* as these twin engines of computer progress lurch codependently into the future.

So, how do you break out of the performance deadlock created by the immovable object of software code bloat meeting the irresistible force of hardware advancement? By optimizing your system to minimize the effects of over-grown applications and to maximize the native capabilities of your hardware. Of course, it helps if your operating system gives you a good set of tools to improve and monitor performance, diagnose problems, and keep your data safe. Windows XP came with a decent set of client tools, Vista improved on them (although not with anything radically new or earth shattering), and Windows 7 stays the course.

Monitoring Performance

Performance optimization is a bit of a black art in that every user has different needs, every configuration has different operating parameters, and every system can react in a unique and unpredictable way to performance tweaks. That means if you want to optimize your system, you have to get to know how it works, what it needs, and how it reacts to changes. You can do this by just using the system and paying attention to how things look and feel, but a more rigorous approach is often called for. To that end, the next few sections take you on a brief tour of Windows 7's performance monitoring capabilities.

Viewing Your Computer's Performance Rating

Like Windows Vista, Windows 7 tailors certain aspects of itself to the capabilities of the system on which you're installing it. For example, the Windows 7 interface changes depending on the graphics hardware on the machine, with low-end machines getting the Windows 7 Basic theme, and high-end GPUs getting the full Aero treatment.

But Windows 7 also scales other aspects up or down to suit its hardware home. With games, for example, Windows 7 enables certain features only if the hardware can support them. Other features scaled for the computer's hardware are TV recording (for example, how many channels can it record at once?) and video playback (for example, what is the optimal playback size and frame rate that doesn't result in dropped frames?).

The tool that handles all of this, not only for Windows 7 itself but also for third-party programs, is the Windows System Assessment Tool, or *WinSAT*. This tool runs during setup, and again whenever you make major performance-related hardware changes to your system. It focuses on four aspects of your system performance: graphics, memory, processor, and storage. For each of these subsystems, WinSAT maintains a set of metrics stored as an *assessment* in XML format. Windows 7 needs to examine only the latest assessment to see what features the computer can support. Note, too, that third-party programs can use an application programming interface that gives them access to the assessments, so developers can tune program features depending on the WinSAT metrics.

Five metrics are used:

- ▶ **Processor**—This metric determines how fast the system can process data. The Processor metric measures calculations per second processed.

- ▶ **Memory (RAM)**—This metric determines how quickly the system can move large objects through memory. The Memory metric measures memory operations per second.

- ▶ **Graphics**—This metric determines the computer's capability to run a composited desktop like the one created by the Desktop Window Manager. The Graphics metric expresses frames per second.

- ▶ **Gaming Graphics**—This metric determines the computer's capability to render 3D graphics, particularly those used in gaming. The Gaming Graphics metric expresses effective frames per second.

▶ **Primary Hard Disk**—This metric determines how fast the computer can write to and read from the hard disk. The Primary Hard Disk storage metric measures megabytes per second.

In addition to WinSAT, Windows 7 comes with the Performance Rating tool that rates your system based on its processor, RAM, hard disk, regular graphics, and gaming graphics. The result is the Windows Experience Index base score.

To launch this tool, select Start, type **performance,** and then click Performance Information and Tools in the search results. In the Performance Information and Tools window, if you see a button named Rate this Computer, click that button to run the initial assessment.

As you can see in Figure 6.1, Windows 7 supplies a subscore for each of the five categories and calculates an overall base score. You can get a new rating (for example, if you change performance-related hardware) by clicking the Re-run the Assessment link.

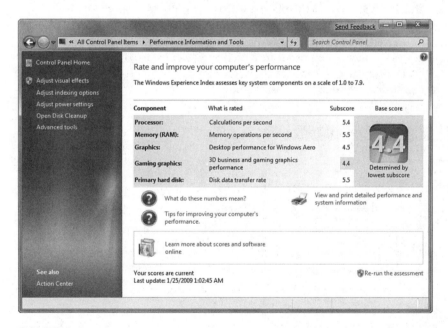

FIGURE 6.1   Windows 7 calculates a Windows System Performance Rating based on five categories.

Interpreting the ratings is a bit of a black art, but I can tell you the following:

▶ In general, the higher the rating, the better the performance.

▶ The lowest possible value is 1.0.

▶ The highest possible value is 7.9 (up from 5.9 in Windows Vista, which is a reflection of hardware improvements over the past few years).

▶ The base score takes a weakest-link-in-the-chain approach. That is, you could have nothing but 5.0 scores for everything else, but if you get just 1.0 because your notebook can't do gaming graphics, your base score will be 1.0.

Monitoring Performance with Task Manager

The Task Manager utility is excellent for getting a quick overview of the current state of the system. To get it onscreen, press Ctrl+Alt+Delete to open the Windows Security screen and then click the Start Task Manager link.

TIP

To bypass the Windows Security screen, either press Ctrl+Shift+Esc, or right-click an empty section of the taskbar and click Start Task Manager.

The Processes tab, shown in Figure 6.2, displays a list of the programs, services, and system components currently running on your system. (By default, Windows 7 shows just the process you have started. To see all the running processes, click Show Processes from All Users.) The processes display in the order in which they were started, but you can change the order by clicking the column headings. (To return to the original, chronological order, you must shut down and restart Task Manager.)

FIGURE 6.2   The Processes tab lists your system's running programs and services.

In addition to the image name of each process, the user who started the process, and a description of the process, you see two performance measures:

▶ **CPU**—The values in this column tell you the percentage of CPU resources that each process is using. If your system seems sluggish, look for a process consuming all or nearly all the resources of the CPU. Most programs will monopolize the CPU occasionally for short periods, but a program that is stuck at 100 (percent) for a long time most likely has some kind of problem. In that case, try shutting down the program. If that doesn't work, click the program's process and then click End Process. Click the Yes button when Windows 7 asks whether you're sure that you want to do this.

▶ **Memory**—This value tells you approximately how much memory a process is using. This value is less useful because a process might genuinely require a lot of memory to operate. However, if this value is steadily increasing for a process that you're not using, it could indicate a problem and you should shut down the process.

TIP

The four default columns in the Processes tab aren't the only data available to you. Select the View, Select Columns command to see a list of more than two dozen items that you can add to the Processes tab.

The Performance tab, shown in Figure 6.3, offers a more substantial collection of performance data, particularly for that all-important component, your system's memory.

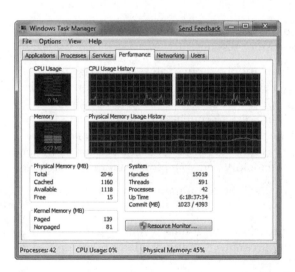

FIGURE 6.3   The Performance tab lists various numbers related to your system's memory components.

The graphs show you both the current value and the values over time for the CPU usage (the total percentage of CPU resources that your running processes are using) and the physical memory usage. Below the graphs are various numbers. Here's what they mean:

▶ **Physical Memory Total**—The total amount of physical RAM in your system.

▶ **Physical Memory Cached**—The amount of physical RAM that Windows 7 has set aside to store recently used programs and documents.

▶ **Physical Memory Free**—The amount of physical RAM that Windows 7 has available for your programs. Note that Windows 7 does not include the system cache (refer to the previous item) in this total.

▶ **Kernel Memory Paged**—The amount of kernel memory mapped to pages in virtual memory.

▶ **Kernel Memory Nonpaged**—The amount of kernel memory that cannot map to pages in virtual memory.

▶ **System Handles**—The number of object handles used by all running processes. A *handle* is a pointer to a resource. For example, if a process wants to use a particular service offered by a particular object, the process asks the object for a handle to that service.

▶ **System Threads**—The number of threads used by all running processes. A *thread* is a single processor task executed by a process, and most processes can use two or more threads at the same time to speed up execution.

▶ **System Processes**—The number of processes currently running (that is, the number of items you see in the Processes tab if you activate the Show Processes from All Users control).

▶ **System Up Time**—The number of days, hours, minutes, and seconds that you have been logged on to Windows 7 in the current session.

▶ **System Commit (MB)**—The minimum and maximum values of the page file. What is a page file? Your computer can address memory beyond the amount physically installed on the system. This nonphysical memory is *virtual memory* implemented by setting up a piece of your hard disk to emulate physical memory. This hard disk storage is actually a single file called a *page file* (or sometimes a *paging file* or a *swap file*). When physical memory is full, Windows 7 makes room for new data by taking some data that's currently in memory and swapping it out to the page file.

Here are two notes related to these values that will help you monitor memory-related performance issues:

▶ If the Physical Memory Free value approaches zero, it means your system is starving for memory. You might have too many programs running or a large program is using lots of memory.

▶ If the Physical Memory Cached value is much less than half the Physical Memory Total value, it means your system isn't operating as efficiently as it could because Windows 7 can't store enough recently used data in memory. Because Windows 7 gives up some of the system cache when it needs RAM, close down programs you don't need.

In all of these situations, the quickest solution is to reduce the system's memory footprint by closing either documents or applications. For the latter, use the Processes tab to determine which applications are using the most memory and shut down the ones you can live without for now. The better, but more expensive, solution is to add more physical RAM to your system. This decreases the likelihood that Windows 7 will need to use the paging file, and it enables Windows 7 to increase the size of the system cache, which greatly improves performance.

TIP

If you're not sure which process corresponds to which program, display the Applications tab, right-click a program, and then click Go to Process. Task Manager displays the Processes tab and selects the process that corresponds to the program.

Using the Resource Monitor

Windows 7 comes with a new tool for monitoring your system yourself: the Resource Monitor. (It's actually a standalone (and revamped) version of the Resource Monitor from Windows Vista.) You load this tool by selecting Start, typing **monitor**, and then clicking Resource Monitor in the search results. Figure 6.4 shows the window that appears.

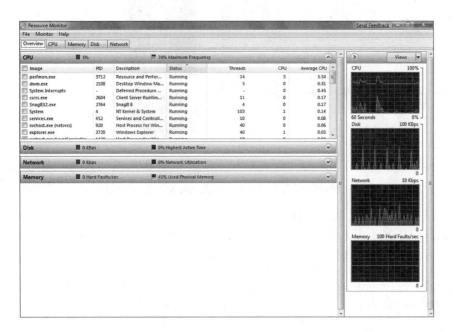

FIGURE 6.4   The new Resource Monitor enables you to monitor various aspects of your system.

The Resource Monitor is divided into five tabs:

▶ **Overview**—This section shows a couple of basic metrics in four categories: CPU, Disk, Network, and Memory, as well as graphs that show current activity in each of these categories. To see more data about a category (as with the CPU category in Figure 6.4), click the downward-pointing arrow on the right side of the category header.

▶ **CPU**—This section (see Figure 6.5) shows the CPU resources that your system is using. In two lists named Processes and Services, you see for each item the current status (such as Running), the number of threads used, the CPU percentage currently being used, and the average CPU percentage. You also get graphs for overall CPU usage, service CPU usage, and CPU usage by processor (or by core).

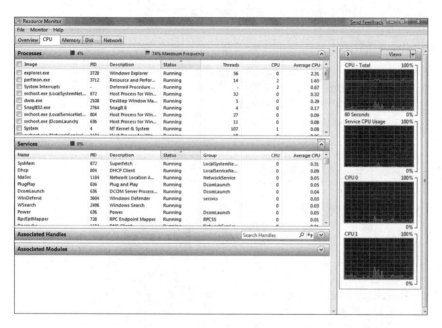

FIGURE 6.5   The CPU tab breaks down CPU usage by processes and by services.

▶ **Memory**—This tab displays a list of processes and for each one it shows the average number of hard memory faults per minute, the total memory committed to the process, the *working set* (the number of kilobytes resident in memory), the amount of *shareable* memory (memory that other processes can use if needed), and the amount of *private* memory (memory that is dedicated to the process and cannot be shared).

NOTE

A memory fault does not refer to a physical problem. Instead, it means that the system could not find the data it needed in the file system cache. If it finds the data elsewhere in memory, it is a *soft fault*; if the system has to go to the hard disk to retrieve the data, it is a *hard fault*.

▶ **Disk**—This tab shows the total hard disk I/O transfer rate (disk reads and writes in bytes per minute), as well as separate read and write transfer rates.

▶ **Network**—This tab shows the total network *data transfer rate* (data sent and received in bytes per minute).

Using the Performance Monitor

The Performance Monitor provides you with real-time reports on how various system settings and components are performing. You load it by selecting Start, typing **performance**, and then pressing Enter to choose Performance Monitor in the search results. In the Performance Monitor window, open the Monitoring Tools branch and click Performance Monitor.

Performance Monitor displays real-time data using *performance counters*, which are measurements of system activity or the current system state. For each counter, Performance Monitor displays a graph of recent values over a time space (the default time space is 100 seconds), as well as statistics such as the average, maximum, and minimum values over that span.

By default, Performance Monitor doesn't show any counters. To add one to the Performance Monitor window, follow these steps:

1. Right-click anywhere inside the Performance Monitor and then click Add Counters. The Add Counters dialog box appears.
2. To use the Available Counters list, click the downward-pointing arrow beside a counter category (such as Memory, Paging File, or Processor). A list of available counters appears.
3. Select the counter you want to use. (If you need more information about the item, activate the Show Description check box.)
4. If the counter has multiple instances, they appear in the Instances of Selected Object list. Click the instance you want to use.
5. Click Add.
6. Repeat steps 2–5 to add any other counters you want to monitor.
7. Click OK.

The counter appears at the bottom of the window (see Figure 6.6). A different-colored line represents each counter, and that color corresponds to the colored lines shown in the graph. Note, too, that you can get specific numbers for a counter—the most recent value, the average, the minimum, and the maximum—by clicking a counter and reading the boxes just below the graphs. The idea is that you should configure Performance Monitor to show the processes you're interested in (page file size, free memory, and so on) and then keep it running while you perform your normal chores. By examining the Performance Monitor readouts from time to time, you gain an appreciation of what is typical on your system. If you run into performance problems, you can check Performance Monitor to see whether you've run into any bottlenecks or anomalies.

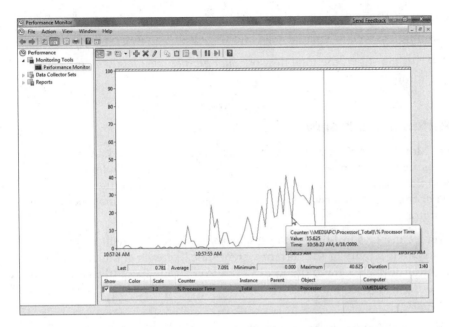

FIGURE 6.6   Use Performance Monitor to keep an eye on various system settings and components.

Performance Monitor has a few new features that make it easier to use and a more powerful diagnostics tool:

▶ If you're using a counter with a significantly different scale, you can scale the output so that the counter appears within the graph. For example, the graph's vertical axis runs from 0 to 100; if you're displaying a percentage counter, the Scale value is 1.0, which means the graph numbers correspond directly to the percentages (50 on the graph corresponds to 50%). If you're also showing, say, the Commit Limit counter, which shows values in bytes, the numbers can run in the billions. The Commit Limit counter's Scale value is 0.00000001, so the value 20 on the graph corresponds to 2 billion bytes.

▶ You can save the current graph as a GIF image file: right-click the graph and then click Save Image As.

▶ You can toggle the display of individual counters on and off. You do this by toggling the check boxes in the Show column.

▶ You can change the duration of the sample (the number of seconds of data that appear on the chart). Right-click the chart, click Properties, click the General tab, and then modify the Duration value. You can specify a value between 2 and 1,000 seconds.

▶ You can see individual data points by hovering the mouse over a counter. After a second or two, Performance Monitor displays the counter name, the time and date of the sample, and the counter value at that time (refer to Figure 6.6).

Data Collector Sets

A *data collector* is a custom set of performance counters, event traces, and system-configuration data that you define and save so that you can run and view the results any time you need them. You can configure a data collector set to run for a preset length of time or until the set reaches a specified size. You can also configure a data collector to run on a schedule. For example, you could run the data collector every hour for 15 minutes from 9 a.m. to 5 p.m. This enables you to benchmark performance and analyze the results not only intraday (to compare performance at different times of the day) but also interday (to see whether performance is slowing over time).

Reports

This section holds the reports created by each data collector set. These are `.blg` files, and you can see the results by clicking the report and then switching to Sysmon view (click the Chart icon in the toolbar). Alternatively, open the folder that contains the report file in Windows Explorer (the default save location is `%SystemDrive%\perflogs`) and double-click the report file.

Optimizing Startup

One of the longest-running debates in computer circles involves the question of whether to turn off the computer when you're not using it. The "off" camp believes that shutting down the computer reduces hard disk wear and tear (because the disk's platters spin full time, even when the computer is idle), prevents damage from power surges or power failures that occur while the machine is off, and saves energy. The "on" camp believes that cold starts are hard on many computer components, that energy can be saved by taking advantage of power-saving features, and that leaving the computer running is more productive because it avoids the lengthy startup process.

In the end, I believe the overall boot time is what usually determines which of these camps you belong to. If your startup time is unbearably long, you'll certainly be more inclined to leave your computer running all the time. Fortunately, Windows 7 has made great strides on improving startup times, which now routinely clock in at well under a minute (instead of the multiminute startups of yesteryear). However, if you're convinced that turning off the computer is a sensible move but you hate waiting even for Windows 7's faster startup process, the next few sections provide a few tips for improving startup performance even more.

Reducing or Eliminating BIOS Checks

Many computers run through one or more diagnostic checks at system startup. For example, it's common for machines to check the integrity of the system memory chips. That seems like a good idea, but it can take an interminable amount of time to complete on a system with a great deal of memory. Access your system's BIOS settings and turn off these checks to reduce the overall time of the computer's *power-on self test* (POST).

NOTE

How you access your computer's BIOS settings (also called the *CMOS setup*) depends on the manufacturer. You usually have to press a function key (normally F1, F2, or F10), a key such as Delete or Esc, or a key combination. During the POST, you should see some text on the screen that tells you what key or key combination to press.

Reducing the OS Choices Menu Timeout

If you have two or more operating systems on your computer, you see Windows 7's OS Choices menu at startup. If you're paying attention to the startup, you can press the Enter key as soon as this menu appears and your system will boot the default operating system. If your mind is elsewhere, however, the startup process waits 30 seconds until it automatically selects the default choice. If this happens to you frequently, you can reduce that 30-second timeout to speed up the startup. There are three ways to do this:

▶ Select Start, type **system**, and then press Enter to select System Configuration in the search results. In the System Configuration window, display the Boot tab and then modify the value in the Timeout text box.

▶ Select Start, type **advanced system**, and then press Enter to select View Advanced System Settings in the search results. This opens the System Properties dialog box and displays the Advanced tab. In the Startup and Recovery group, click Settings and then adjust the value of the Time to Display List of Operating Systems spin box.

▶ Select Start, type **command**, right-click Command Prompt in the search results, click Run as Administrator, and then enter your UAC credentials. At the Command Prompt, enter the following command (replace **ss** with the number of seconds you want to use for the timeout):

```
BCDEDIT /timeout ss
```

Turning Off the Startup Splash Screen

You can prevent the Windows 7 splash screen from appearing, which will shave a small amount of time from the startup. Select Start, type **system**, and then press Enter to select System Configuration in the search results. In the System Configuration window, display the Boot tab and then activate the No GUI Boot check box.

CAUTION

Activating the No GUI Boot option means that you won't see any startup blue-screen errors. In other words, if a problem occurs, all you'll know for sure is that your system has hung, but you won't know why. For this reason, the small performance improvement represented by activating the No GUI Boot option is likely not enough to offset the lack of startup error messages.

Upgrading Your Device Drivers

Device drivers designed to work with Windows 7 will generally load faster than older drivers. Therefore, you should check each of your device drivers to see whether a Windows 7–compatible version exists. If one is available, upgrade to that driver as described in Chapter 22, "Troubleshooting Devices."

▶ **See** "Updating a Device Driver," **p. 466**.

Using an Automatic Logon

One of the best ways to reduce startup time frustration is to ignore the startup altogether by doing something else (such as getting a cup of coffee) while the boot chores occur. However, this strategy fails if the logon process interrupts the startup. If you're the only person who uses your computer, you can overcome this problem by setting up Windows 7 to log you on automatically. I discussed this in Chapter 4, "Customizing Startup and Shutdown."

▶ **See** "Setting Up an Automatic Logon," **p. 79**.

Configuring the Prefetcher

Prefetching is a Windows 7 performance feature that analyzes disk usage and then reads into memory the data that you or your system accesses most frequently. The prefetcher can speed up booting, application launching, or both. You configure the prefetcher using the following Registry setting (open the Registry Editor by selecting Start, typing **regedit,** and then pressing Enter; see Chapter 12, "Tweaking the Windows 7 Registry," for more information):

```
HKLM\SYSTEM\CurrentControlSet\Control\SessionManager\Memory Management\
➥PrefetchParameters\EnablePrefetcher
```

There's also a SuperFetch setting:

```
HKLM\SYSTEM\CurrentControlSet\Control\SessionManager\Memory Management\
➥PrefetchParameters\EnableSuperfetch
```

In both cases, set the value to 1 for application-only fetching, 2 for boot-only fetching, or 3 for both application and boot fetching (this is the default for both settings). You can try experimenting with boot-only fetching to see whether it improves your startup times, but my own testing shows only minimal startup improvements. The more programs you run at startup, the more your startup performance should improve with boot-only fetching.

Optimizing Applications

Running applications is the reason we use Windows 7, so it's a rare user who doesn't want his applications to run as fast as possible. The next few sections offer some pointers for improving the performance of applications under Windows 7.

Adding More Memory

All applications run in RAM, of course, so the more RAM you have, the less likely it is that Windows 7 will have to store excess program or document data in the page file on the hard disk, which is a real performance killer. Use one of the following Windows 7 monitoring tools to watch the available memory value:

▶ **Task Manager**—Display the Performance tab and watch the Physical Memory: Available value.

▶ **Resource Monitor**—Display the Memory tab and watch the Available to Programs value.

▶ **Performance Monitor**—Start a new counter, open the Memory category, and then select the Available Mbytes counter.

If the amount of available memory starts to get low, you should consider adding RAM to your system.

Installing to the Fastest Hard Drive

If your system has multiple hard drives that have different performance ratings, install your applications on the fastest drive. (See "Examining Hard Drive Performance Specifications" later in this chapter.) This enables Windows 7 to access the application's data and documents faster.

Optimizing Application Launching

As I mentioned earlier in this chapter (see "Configuring the Prefetcher"), Windows 7's fetching components can optimize disk files for booting, application launching, or both. It probably won't make much difference, but experiment with setting the Registry's EnablePrefetcher and EnableSuperfetch values to 1 to optimize application launching.

Getting the Latest Device Drivers

If your application works with a device, check with the manufacturer or Windows Update to see whether a newer version of the device driver is available. In general, the newer the driver, the faster its performance. I show you how to update device drivers in Chapter 22.

▶ **See** "Updating a Device Driver," **p. 466**.

Optimizing Windows 7 for Programs

You can set up Windows 7 so that it's optimized to run programs. This involves adjusting the *processor scheduling*, which determines how much time the processor allocates to the computer's activities. In particular, processor scheduling differentiates between the *foreground program* (the program in which you are currently working) and *background programs* (programs that perform tasks, such as printing or backing up, while you work in another program).

Optimizing programs means configuring Windows 7 so that it gives more CPU time to your programs. This is the default in Windows 7, but it's worth your time to make sure that this default configuration is still the case on your system. Here are the steps to follow:

1. Select Start, type **advanced system**, and then press Enter to select View Advanced System Settings in the search results. This opens the System Properties dialog box with the Advanced tab displayed.

2. In the Performance group, click Settings to display the Performance Options dialog box.

3. Display the Advanced tab, shown in Figure 6.7.

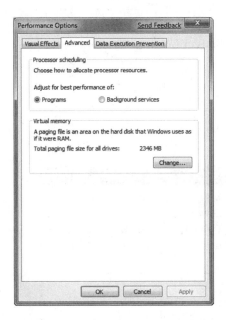

FIGURE 6.7   In the Performance Options dialog box, use the Advanced tab to optimize Windows 7 for programs.

4. In the Processor Scheduling group, activate the Programs option.

5. Click OK.

6. When Windows 7 tells you the changes require a restart, click OK to return to the System Properties dialog box.

7. Click OK. Windows 7 asks whether you want to restart your system.

8. Click Yes.

Setting the Program Priority in Task Manager

You can improve the performance of a program by adjusting the priority given to the program by your computer's processor. The processor enables programs to run by doling out thin slivers of its computing time to each program. These time slivers are called *cycles* because they are given to programs cyclically. For example, if you have three programs running—A, B, and C—the processor gives a cycle to A, one to B, another to C, and then another to A again. This cycling happens quickly, appearing seamless when you work with each program.

The *base priority* is the ranking that determines the relative frequency with which a program gets processor cycles. A program given a higher frequency gets more cycles, which improves the program's performance. For example, suppose that you raise the priority of program A. The processor might give a cycle to A, one to B, another to A, one to C, another to A, and so on.

Follow these steps to change a program's priority:

1. Launch the program you want to work with.
2. Open Task Manager, as described earlier in this chapter (refer to "Monitoring Performance with Task Manager").
3. Display the Processes tab.
4. Right-click your application's process to display its shortcut menu.
5. Click Set Priority, and then click (from highest priority to lowest) Realtime, High, or AboveNormal.

TIP

After you've changed the priority of one or more programs, you might forget the values that you have assigned to each one. To help, you can view the priority for all the items in the Processes tab. Click View and then click Select Columns to display the Select Columns dialog box. Activate the Base Priority check box and click OK. This adds a Base Priority column to the Processes list.

Optimizing the Hard Disk

Windows 7 uses the hard disk to fetch application data and documents as well as to store data in the page file temporarily. Therefore, optimizing your hard disk can greatly improve Windows 7's overall performance, as described in the next few sections.

Examining Hard Drive Performance Specifications

If you're looking to add another drive to your system, your starting point should be the drive itself: specifically, its theoretical performance specifications. There are three things to consider: the hard drive speed, the size of the hard drive cache, and the hard drive seek time.

The Hard Drive Speed

The hard drive *speed* is a measure of how fast the drive's internal platters spin, measured in revolutions per minute (rpm). In general, the higher the rpm value, the better the drive's performance. Most hard drives spin at 7,200rpm, although some older drives spin at 5,400rpm. You should avoid these older drives because the performance hit is substantial, and they're not that much cheaper than the equivalent 7,200rpm drive. If money is no object, drives are available that spin at 10,000rpm, which offers a substantial performance boost.

The Hard Drive Cache

The hard drive *cache* refers to a RAM memory area embedded in the hard drive. This memory is used as a holding place for frequently used bits of data. If the CPU finds the data it needs in the hard drive cache, it saves time because it can load that data directly into memory instead of asking the hard drive to fetch it from the disk. The bigger the hard drive cache, the more data it can hold, so the more likely the CPU is to find the data it needs, and thus the better the overall performance of the hard drive.

Inexpensive hard drives usually come with just a 2MB cache, whereas most mainstream drives come with either an 8MB or a 16MB cache. Some high-end drives come with a whopping 32MB cache.

The Hard Drive Seek Time

There are four measures of hard disk read/write performance:

- ▶ **Seek time**—The time it takes the hard drive's actuator arm to move the read/write head over the track that contains the sector that will be read or written to.

- ▶ **Latency**—The time it takes the hard drive to rotate the disk so that the sector is directly under the read/write head (so this value is sometimes called the *rotational latency*).

- ▶ **Write time**—The time it takes the writing mechanism on the read/write head to write data to the sector.

- ▶ **Read time**—The time it takes the reading mechanism on the read/write head to read data from the sector.

In all cases, the lower the time, the faster the drive's performance.

Of these, the seek time is the most important—or, at least, it's the one that's most often quoted in hard drive ads and descriptions. The seek time is usually an average because sometimes the read/write head has to travel a relatively long distance along the arm and sometimes a relatively short distance. The seek time, similar to the latency, write, and read time, is measured in milliseconds. For a low-end drive, the average seek time is usually 12ms or higher; for a mainstream drive, the average seek time is usually around 10ms; and for a high-end drive, the average seek time is usually under 9ms. (For comparison, note that most of the 10,000rpm drives on the market now boast average seek times around 4.6ms, which is blazingly fast.)

Performing Hard Drive Maintenance

For an existing drive, optimization is the same as maintenance, so you should implement the maintenance plan I discuss in Chapter 7, "Maintaining Your Windows 7 System." For a hard disk, this means doing the following:

- ▶ Keeping an eye on the disk's free space to make sure that it doesn't get too low
- ▶ Periodically cleaning out any unnecessary files on the disk
- ▶ Uninstalling any programs or devices you no longer use
- ▶ Checking all partitions for errors frequently
- ▶ Defragmenting partitions on a regular schedule

Disabling Compression and Encryption

If you use NTFS on a partition, Windows 7 enables you to compress files to save space, as well as to encrypt files for security. (See "Converting FAT16 and FAT32 Partitions to NTFS" later in this chapter.) From a performance point of view, however, you shouldn't use compression and encryption on a partition if you don't have to. Both technologies slow down disk accesses because of the overhead involved in the compression/decompression and encryption/decryption processes.

Turning Off the Content Indexing

The Indexer is a Windows 7 background process that indexes the contents of a drive on-the-fly as you add or delete data. This greatly speeds up Windows 7's search features (including Instant Search) because Windows 7 knows the contents of each file. However, you should consider turning off content indexing to improve overall performance, particularly on any drive where you don't do much file searching. (You can still search based on file properties.) To do this, follow these steps:

1. Select Start, Computer.
2. Right-click the drive you want to work with and then click Properties. Windows 7 display's the drive's property sheet.
3. On the General tab, deactivate the Allow Files on This Drive to Have Contents Indexed in Addition to File Properties check box.
4. Click OK.

Enabling Write Caching

You should also make sure that your hard disk has write caching enabled. *Write caching* means that Windows 7 doesn't flush changed data to the disk until the system is idle, which improves performance. The downside of write caching is that a power outage or system crash means that the data never gets written, so the changes are lost. The chances of this happening are minimal, so I recommend leaving write caching enabled, which is the Windows 7 default. To make sure, follow these steps:

1. Select Start, type **device**, and then click Device Manager in the search results.
2. Open the Disk Drives branch.
3. Double-click your hard disk to display its property sheet.

4. In the Policies tab, make sure that the Enable Write Caching on the Device check box is activated.

5. For maximum performance, activate the Turn Off Windows Write-Cache Buffer Flushing on the Device check box. (Note that this option is available only with certain hard drives that support it.)

6. Click OK.

CAUTION

Activating the Turn Off Windows Write-Cache Buffer Flushing on the Device option tells Windows 7 to use an even more aggressive write-caching algorithm. However, an unscheduled power shutdown means you will almost certainly lose some data. Activate this option only if your system is running off an uninterruptible power supply (UPS).

Converting FAT16 and FAT32 Partitions to NTFS

The NTFS file system is your best choice if you want optimal hard disk performance because, in most cases, NTFS outperforms both FAT16 and FAT32. (This is particularly true with large partitions and with partitions that that have lots of files.) Note, however, that for best NTFS performance you should format a partition as NTFS and then add files to it. If this isn't possible, Windows 7 offers the CONVERT utility for converting a FAT16 or FAT32 drive to NTFS:

```
CONVERT volume /FS:NTFS [/V] [/CvtArea:filename] [/NoSecurity] [/X]
```

volume	Specifies the drive letter (followed by a colon) or volume name you want to convert.
/FS:NTFS	Specifies that the file system is to be converted to NTFS.
/V	Uses verbose mode, which gives detailed information during the conversion.
/CvtArea:*filename*	Specifies a contiguous placeholder file in the root directory that will be used to store the NTFS system files.
/NoSecurity	Specifies that the default NTFS permissions are not to be applied to this volume. All the converted files and folders will be accessible by everyone.
/X	Forces the volume to dismount first if it currently has open files.

For example, running the following command at the Command Prompt converts the D: drive to NTFS:

```
convert d: /FS:NTFS
```

In some cases, you may see the following message:

Convert cannot gain exclusive access to the D: drive, so it cannot
convert it now. Would you like to schedule it to be converted the
next time the system restarts? <Y/N>

In this case, press Y to schedule the conversion.

If you make the move to NTFS, either via formatting a partition during setup or by using
the CONVERT utility, you can implement a couple of other tweaks to maximize NTFS performance. I cover these tweaks in the next two sections.

Turning Off 8.3 Filename Creation

To support legacy applications that don't understand long filenames, for each file, NTFS
keeps track of a shorter name that conforms to the old 8.3 standard used by the original
DOS file systems. The overhead involved in tracking two names for one file isn't much for
a small number of files, but it can become onerous if a folder has a huge number of files
(300,000 or more).

To disable the tracking of an 8.3 name for each file, enter the following statement at the
Command Prompt:

```
fsutil behavior set disable8dot3 1
```

Note, too, that you can do the same thing by changing the value of the following Registry
setting to 1. (Note that the default value is 2.)

```
HKLM\SYSTEM\CurrentControlSet\Control\FileSystem\NtfsDisable8dot3NameCreation
```

> **NOTE**
>
> The FSUTIL program requires Administrator account privileges. Click Start, type
> **command,** right-click Command Prompt in the search results, click Run as Administrator,
> and then enter your UAC credentials.

Disabling Last Access Timestamp

For each folder and file, NTFS stores an attribute called Last Access Time that tells you
when the user last accessed the folder or file. If you have folders that contain a large
number of files and if you use programs that frequently access those files, writing the Last
Access Time data can slow down NTFS. To disable writing of the Last Access Time
attribute, enter the following statement at the Command Prompt:

```
fsutil behavior set disablelastaccess 1
```

You can achieve the same effect by changing the value of the following Registry setting to
1 (although this now seems to be the default value in Windows 7):

```
HKLM\SYSTEM\CurrentControlSet\Control\FileSystem\NtfsDisableLastAccessUpdate
```

Optimizing Virtual Memory

No matter how much main memory your system boasts, Windows 7 still creates and uses a page file for virtual memory. To maximize page file performance, you should make sure that Windows 7 is working optimally with the page file. The next few sections present some techniques that help you do just that.

Storing the Page File Optimally

The location of the page file can have a major impact on its performance. There are three things you should consider:

- **If you have multiple physical hard disks, store the page file on the hard disk that has the fastest access time**—You'll see later in this section that you can tell Windows 7 which hard disk to use for the page file.

- **Store the page file on an uncompressed partition**—Windows 7 is happy to store the page file on a compressed NTFS partition. However, as with all file operations on a compressed partition, the performance of page file operations suffers because of the compression and decompression required. Therefore, you should store the page file on an uncompressed partition.

- **If you have multiple hard disks, store the page file on the hard disk that has the most free space**—Windows 7 expands and contracts the page file dynamically depending on the system's needs. Storing the page file on the disk with the most space gives Windows 7 the most flexibility.

See "Changing the Paging File's Location and Size," later in this chapter, for the information about moving the page file.

Splitting the Page File

If you have two or more physical drives (not just two or more partitions on a single physical drive), splitting the page file over each drive can improve performance because it means that Windows 7 can extract data from each drive's page file simultaneously. For example, if your current initial page file size is 384MB, you'd set up a page file on a drive with a 192MB initial size, and another page file on a second drive with a 192MB initial size.

See "Changing the Paging File's Location and Size" to learn how to split the page file.

Customizing the Page File Size

By default, Windows 7 sets the initial size of the page file to 1.5 times the amount of RAM in your system, and it sets the maximum size of the page file to 3 times the amount of RAM. For example, on a system with 1GB RAM, the page file's initial size will be 1.5GB and its maximum size will be 3GB. The default values work well on most systems, but you might want to customize these sizes to suit your own configuration. Here are some notes about custom page file sizes:

▶ The less RAM you have, the more likely it is that Windows 7 will use the page file, so the Windows 7 default page file sizes make sense. If your computer has less than 1GB RAM, you should leave the page file sizes as is.

▶ The more RAM you have, the less likely it is that Windows 7 will use the page file. Therefore, the default initial page file size is too large and the disk space reserved by Windows 7 is wasted. On systems with 2GB RAM or more, you should set the initial page file size to half the RAM size, but leave the maximum size at three times the amount of RAM, just in case.

▶ If disk space is at a premium and you can't move the page file to a drive with more free space, set the initial page file size to 16MB (the minimum size supported by Windows 7). This should eventually result in the smallest possible page file, but you'll see a bit of a performance drop because Windows 7 will often have to increase the size the page file dynamically as you work with your programs.

▶ You might think that setting the initial size and the maximum size to the same relatively large value (say, two or three times RAM) would improve performance because it would mean that Windows 7 would never resize the page file. In practice, however, it has been shown that this trick does *not* improve performance, and in some cases actually decreases performance.

▶ If you have a large amount of RAM (at least 2GB), you might think that Windows 7 would never need virtual memory, so it would be okay to turn off the page file. This won't work, however, because Windows 7 needs the page file anyway, and some programs might crash if no virtual memory is present.

See "Changing the Paging File's Location and Size" to learn how to customize the page file size.

Watching the Page File Size

Monitor the page file performance to get a feel for how it works under normal conditions, where *normal* means while running your usual collection of applications and your usual number of open windows and documents.

Start up all the programs you normally use (and perhaps a few extra, for good measure) and then watch Performance Monitor's Process\Page File Bytes and Process\Page File Bytes Peak counters.

Changing the Paging File's Location and Size

The page file is named Pagefile.sys and it's stored in the root folder of the %SystemDrive%. Here's how to change the hard disk that Windows 7 uses to store the page file as well as the page file sizes:

> **NOTE**
>
> The Pagefile.sys file is a hidden system file. To see it, open any folder window and select Organize, Folder and Search Options. In the Folder Options dialog box, click the View tab, activate the Show Hidden Files and Folders option, and deactivate the Hide Protected Operating System Files check box. When Windows 7 asks you to confirm the display of protected operating system files, click Yes, and then click OK.

1. If necessary, defragment the hard disk that you'll be using for the page file, as described in Chapter 7.

   ▶ **See** "Defragmenting Your Hard Disk," **p. 145**.

2. Select Start, type **advanced system**, and then press Enter to select View Advanced System Settings in the search results. This opens the System Properties dialog box with the Advanced tab displayed.

3. In the Performance group, click Settings to display the Performance Options dialog box.

4. In the Advanced tab's Virtual Memory group, click Change. Windows 7 displays the Virtual Memory dialog box.

5. Deactivate the Automatically Manage Paging File Size for All Drives check box. Windows 7 enables the rest of the dialog box controls, as shown in Figure 6.8.

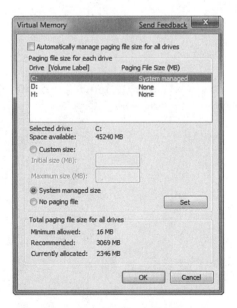

FIGURE 6.8   Use the Virtual Memory dialog box to select a different hard disk to store the page file.

6. Use the Drive list to select the hard drive you want to use.

7. Select a page file size option:

   ▸ **Custom Size**—Activate this option to set your own page file sizes using the Initial Size (MB) and Maximum Size (MB) text boxes. Ensure that Windows 7 is able to resize the page file dynamically, as needed, by entering a maximum size that's larger than the initial size.

   ▸ **System Managed Size**—Activate this option to let Windows 7 manage the page file sizes for you.

   ▸ **No Paging File**—Activate this option to disable the page file on the selected drive.

TIP

If you want to move the page file to another drive, first select the original drive and then activate the No Paging File option to remove the page file from that drive. Select the other drive and choose either Custom Size or System Managed Size to add a new page file to that drive.

TIP

If you want to split the page file over a second drive, leave the original drive as is, select the second drive, and choose either Custom Size or System Managed Size to create a second page file on that drive.

8. Click Set.

Exit all the dialog boxes. If you changed the drive or decreased either the initial size or the maximum size, you need to restart your computer to put the changes into effect.

CHAPTER 7

Maintaining Your Windows 7 System

He is safe from danger who is on guard even when safe.
—Publilius Syrus

Computer problems, like the proverbial death and taxes, seem to be one of those constants in life. Whether it's a hard disk giving up the ghost, a power failure that trashes your files, or a virus that invades your system, the issue isn't *whether* something will go wrong, but rather *when* it will happen. Instead of waiting to deal with these difficulties after they've occurred (what I call *pound-of-cure mode*), you need to become proactive and perform maintenance on your system in advance (*ounce-of-prevention mode*). This not only reduces the chances that something will go wrong, but it also sets up your system to recover more easily from any problems that do occur. This chapter shows you various Windows 7 utilities and techniques that can help you do just that. At the end of the chapter, I give you a step-by-step plan for maintaining your system and checking for the first signs of problems.

Checking Your Hard Disk for Errors

Our hard disks store our programs and, most important, our precious data, so they have a special place in the computing firmament. They ought to be pampered and coddled to ensure a long and trouble-free existence, but that's rarely the case, unfortunately. Just consider everything that a modern hard disk has to put up with:

▶ **General wear and tear**—If your computer is running right now, its hard disk is spinning away at probably 7,200 revolutions per minute. That's right, even though you're not doing anything, the hard disk is hard at work. Because of this constant activity, most hard disks simply wear out after a few years.

> **NOTE**
>
> I should say that your hard disk is *probably* spinning away as I speak. Windows 7 is actually configured out of the box to put your hard disk to sleep after 20 minutes of inactivity, so your hard disk may be resting. If you want to change the hard disk sleep interval (personally, I turn it off on my machines to improve performance), select Start, type **power**, and then click Change Power-Saving Options in the search results. Select the power plan you want to use, click Change Plan Settings, and then click Change Advanced Power Settings, Open the Hard Disk branch, open the Turn Off Hard Disk After branch, and then set the interval you prefer.

▶ **The old bump-and-grind**—Your hard disk includes *read/write heads* that are used to read data from and write data to the disk. These heads float on a cushion of air just above the spinning hard disk platters. A bump or jolt of sufficient intensity can send them crashing onto the surface of the disk, which could easily result in trashed data. If the heads happen to hit a particularly sensitive area, the entire hard disk could crash. Notebook computers are particularly prone to this problem.

▶ **Power surges**—The current supplied to your PC is, under normal conditions, relatively constant. It's possible, however, for massive power surges to assail your computer (for example, during a lightning storm). These surges can wreak havoc on a carefully arranged hard disk.

So, what can you do about it? Windows 7 comes with a program called Check Disk that can check your hard disk for problems and repair them automatically. It might not be able to recover a totally trashed hard disk, but it can at least let you know when a hard disk might be heading for trouble.

Check Disk performs a battery of tests on a hard disk, including looking for invalid filenames, invalid file dates and times, bad sectors, and invalid compression structures. In the hard disk's file system, Check Disk also looks for the following errors:

▶ Lost clusters

▶ Invalid clusters

▶ Cross-linked clusters

▶ File system cycles

The next few sections explain these errors in more detail.

Understanding Clusters

Large hard disks are inherently inefficient. Formatting a disk divides the disk's magnetic medium into small storage areas called *sectors*, which usually hold up to 512 bytes of data. A large hard disk can contain tens of millions of sectors, so it would be too inefficient for Windows 7 to deal with individual sectors. Instead, Windows 7 groups sectors into *clusters*, the size of which depends on the file system and the size of the partition, as shown in Table 7.1.

TABLE 7.1   Default Cluster Sizes for Various File Systems and Partition Sizes

Partition Size	FAT16 Cluster Size	FAT32 Cluster Size	NTFS Cluster Size
7MB–16MB	2KB	N/A	512 bytes
17MB–32MB	512 bytes	N/A	512 bytes
33MB–64MB	1KB	512 bytes	512 bytes
65MB–128MB	2KB	1KB	512 bytes
129MB–256MB	4KB	2KB	512 bytes
257MB–512MB	8KB	4KB	512 bytes
513MB–1,024MB	16KB	4KB	1KB
1025MB–2GB	32KB	4KB	2KB
2GB–4GB	64KB	4KB	4KB
4GB–8GB	N/A	4KB	4KB
8GB–16GB	N/A	8KB	4KB
16GB–32GB	N/A	16KB	4KB
32GB–2TB	N/A	N/A	4KB

Still, each hard disk has many thousands of clusters, so it's the job of the file system to keep track of everything. In particular, for each file on the disk, the file system maintains an entry in a *file directory*, a sort of table of contents for your files. (On an NTFS partition, this is the *Master File Table*, or MFT.)

Understanding Lost Clusters

A *lost cluster* (also sometimes called an *orphaned cluster*) is a cluster that, according to the file system, is associated with a file, but that has no link to any entry in the file directory. Program crashes, power surges, or power outages are some typical causes of lost clusters.

If Check Disk comes across lost clusters, it offers to convert them to files in either the file's original folder (if Check Disk can determine the proper folder) or in a new folder named Folder.000 in the root of the %SystemDrive%. (If that folder already exists, Check Disk creates a new folder named Folder.001 instead.) In that folder, Check Disk converts the lost clusters to files with names such as File0000.chk and File0001.chk.

You can look at these files (using a text editor) to see whether they contain any useful data and then try to salvage it. Most often, however, these files are unusable and most people just delete them.

Understanding Invalid Clusters

An *invalid cluster* is one that falls under one of the following three categories:

▶ A file system entry with an illegal value. (In the FAT16 file system, for example, an entry that refers to cluster 1 is illegal because a disk's cluster numbers start at 2.)

▶ A file system entry that refers to a cluster number larger than the total number of clusters on the disk.

▶ A file system entry that is marked as unused, but is part of a cluster chain.

In this case, Check Disk asks whether you want to convert these lost file fragments to files. If you say yes, Check Disk truncates the file by replacing the invalid cluster with an *EOF* (*end of file*) marker and then converts the lost file fragments to files. These are probably the truncated portion of the file, so you can examine them and try to piece everything back together. More likely, however, you just have to trash these files.

Understanding Cross-Linked Clusters

A *cross-linked cluster* is a cluster assigned to two different files (or twice in the same file). Check Disk offers to delete the affected files, copy the cross-linked cluster to each affected file, or ignore the cross-linked files altogether. In most cases, the safest bet is to copy the cross-linked cluster to each affected file. That way, at least one of the affected files should be usable.

Understanding Cycles

In an NTFS partition, a *cycle* is a corruption in the file system whereby a subfolder's parent folder is listed as the subfolder itself. For example, a folder named C:\Data should have C:\ as its parent; if C:\Data is a cycle, C:\Data—the same folder—is listed as the parent instead. This creates a kind of loop in the file system that can cause the cycled folder to "disappear."

Running the Check Disk GUI

Check Disk has two versions: a GUI version and a command-line version. See the next section to learn how to use the command-line version. Here are the steps to follow to run the GUI version of Check Disk:

1. Select Start, Computer, right-click the drive you want to check, and then click Properties. The drive's property sheet appears.

2. Display the Tools tab.

3. Click the Check Now button. The Check Disk window appears, as shown in Figure 7.1.

FIGURE 7.1   Use Check Disk to scan a hard disk partition for errors.

4. Activate one or both of the following options, if desired:

   ▶ **Automatically Fix File System Errors**—If you activate this check box, Check Disk automatically repairs any file system errors that it finds. If you leave this option deactivated, Check Disk just reports on any errors it finds.

   ▶ **Scan for and Attempt Recovery of Bad Sectors**—If you activate this check box, Check Disk performs a sector-by-sector surface check of the hard disk surface. If Check Disk finds a bad sector, it automatically attempts to recover any information stored in the sector and it marks the sector as defective so that no information can be stored there in the future.

5. Click Start.

6. If you activated the Automatically Fix File System Errors check box and are checking a partition that has open system files, Check Disk will tell you that it can't continue because it requires exclusive access to the disk. It will then ask whether you want to schedule the scan to occur the next time you boot the computer. Click Schedule Disk Check.

7. When the scan is complete, Check Disk displays a message letting you know and a report on the errors it found, if any.

The AUTOCHK Utility

If you click Schedule Disk Check when Check Disk asks whether you want to schedule the scan for the next boot, the program adds the AUTOCHK utility to the following Registry setting:

```
HKLM\SYSTEM\CurrentControlSet\Control\Session Manager\BootExecute
```

This setting specifies the programs that Windows 7 should run at boot time when the Session Manager is loading. AUTOCHK is the automatic version of Check Disk that runs at system startup. If you want the option of skipping the disk check, you need to specify a timeout value for AUTOCHK. You change the timeout value by adding the AutoChkTimeOut setting as a DWORD value in the same Registry key:

```
HKLM\SYSTEM\CurrentControlSet\Control\Session Manager\
```

Set this to the number of seconds that you want to use for the timeout. Another way to set the timeout value is to use the CHKNTFS /T:[*time*] command, where *time* is the number of seconds to use for the timeout. (If you exclude *time*, *CHKNTFS* returns the current timeout setting.) For example, the following command sets the timeout to 60 seconds:

```
CHKNTFS /T:60
```

When AUTOCHK is scheduled with a timeout value greater than 0, you see the following the next time you restart the computer:

```
A disk check has been scheduled.
```

```
To skip disk checking, press any key within 60 second(s).
```

You can bypass the check by pressing a key before the timeout expires.

Checking Free Disk Space

Hard disks with capacities measured in the hundreds of gigabytes are commonplace even in low-end systems nowadays, so disk space is much less of a problem than it used to be. Still, you need to keep track of how much free space you have on your disk drives, particularly the %SystemDrive% (usually the C: drive), which usually stores the virtual memory page file.

One way to check disk free space is to view the Computer folder using either the Tiles or Content views, which include the free space and total disk space with each drive icon, or the Details view, which includes columns for Total Size and Free Space, as shown in Figure 7.2. Alternatively, right-click the drive in Windows Explorer and then click Properties. The disk's total capacity, as well as its current used and free space, appear in the General tab of the disk's property sheet.

TIP

To see the File System and Percent Full columns shown in Figure 7.2, right-click any column header and then click the File System property, then repeat and click the Percent Full property.

Listing 7.1 presents a VBScript procedure that displays the status and free space for each drive on your system.

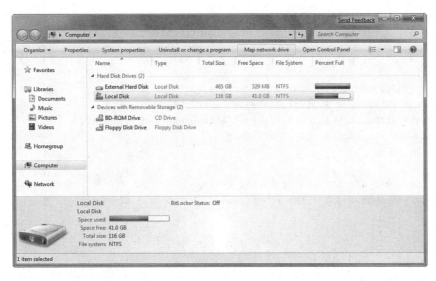

FIGURE 7.2   Display the Computer folder in Details view to see the total size and free space on your system's disks.

> **NOTE**
>
> To get the file with the Listing 7.1 code—it's called `DriveStatusAndSpace.vbs`—see my website: www.mcfedries.com/Windows7Unleashed.

LISTING 7.1   A VBScript Example That Displays the Status and Free Space for Your System's Drives

```
Option Explicit
Dim objFSO, colDiskDrives, objDiskDrive, strMessage

' Create the File System Object
Set objFSO = CreateObject("Scripting.FileSystemObject")

' Get the collection of disk drives
Set colDiskDrives = objFSO.Drives

' Run through the collection
strMessage = "Disk Drive Status Report" & vbCrLf & vbCrLf
For Each objDiskDrive in colDiskDrives

    ' Add the drive letter to the message
    strMessage = strMessage & "Drive: " & objDiskDrive.DriveLetter & vbCrLf
```

LISTING 7.1   Continued

```
    ' Check the drive status
    If objDiskDrive.IsReady = True Then

        ' If it's ready, add the status and the free space to the message
        strMessage = strMessage & "Status: Ready" & vbCrLf
        strMessage = strMessage & "Free space: " & objDiskDrive.FreeSpace
        strMessage = strMessage & vbCrLf & vbCrLf
    Else

        ' Otherwise, just add the status to the message
        strMessage = strMessage & "Status: Not Ready" & vbCrLf & vbCrLf
    End If
Next

' Display the message
Wscript.Echo strMessage
```

This script creates a `FileSystemObject` and then uses its `Drives` property to return the system's collection of disk drives. Then a `For Each...Next` loop runs through the collection, gathering the drive letter, the status, and, if the disk is ready, the free space. It then displays the drive data as shown in Figure 7.3.

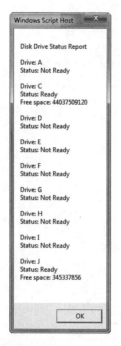

FIGURE 7.3   The script displays the status and free space for each drive on your system.

Deleting Unnecessary Files

If you find that a hard disk partition is getting low on free space, you should delete any unneeded files and programs. Windows 7 comes with a Disk Cleanup utility that enables you to remove certain types of files quickly and easily. Before discussing this utility, let's look at a few methods you can use to perform a spring cleaning on your hard disk by hand:

▸ **Uninstall programs you don't use**—If you have an Internet connection, you know it's easier than ever to download new software for a trial run. Unfortunately, that also means it's easier than ever to have unused programs cluttering your hard disk. Use the Control Panel's Add or Remove Programs icon to uninstall these and other rejected applications.

▸ **Delete downloaded program archives**—Speaking of program downloads, your hard disk is also probably littered with ZIP files or other downloaded archives. For those programs you use, you should consider moving the archive files to a removable medium for storage. For programs you don't use, you should delete the archive files.

▸ **Archive documents you don't need very often**—Our hard drives are stuffed with ancient documents that we use only rarely, if at all: old projects, business records from days gone by, photos and videos from occasions held long ago, and so on. You probably don't want to delete any of this, but you can free up hard disk space by archiving those old documents to removable media such as recordable CD or DVD disks, or a flash drive.

▸ **Delete application backup files**—Applications often create backup copies of existing files and name the backups using either the `.bak` or `.old` extension. Use Windows Explorer's Search utility to locate these files and delete them.

After you've performed these tasks, you should next run the Disk Cleanup utility, which can automatically remove some of the preceding file categories, as well as several other types of files, including downloaded programs, Internet Explorer cache files, the hibernation files, Recycle Bin deletions, temporary files, file system thumbnails, and offline files. Here's how it works:

1. Select Start, Computer, right-click the drive you want to clean up, and then click Properties. The drive's property sheet appears.
2. Click Disk Cleanup. Disk Cleanup scans the drive to see which files can be deleted, and then displays a window similar to the one in Figure 7.4.

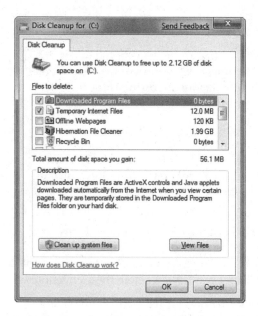

FIGURE 7.4   Disk Cleanup can automatically and safely remove certain types of files from a disk drive.

TIP

Windows 7 offers a faster route to the Disk Cleanup window. Select Start, type `cleanmgr /d`*drive*, **where** *drive* is the letter of the drive you want to work with (for example, `cleanmgr /dc`), and then press Enter.

---

3. Click Clean Up System Files. Disk Cleanup displays an expanded list of file types.

4. In the Files to Delete list, activate the check box beside each category of file you want to remove. If you're not sure what an item represents, select it and read the text in the Description box. Note, too, that for most of these items you can click View Files to see what you'll be deleting.

5. Click OK. Disk Cleanup asks whether you're sure that you want to delete the files.

6. Click Yes. Disk Cleanup deletes the selected files.

SAVING DISK CLEANUP SETTINGS

It's possible to save your Disk Cleanup settings and run them again at any time. This is handy if, for example, you want to delete all your downloaded program files and temporary Internet files at shutdown. Select Start, type the following command, and then press Enter:

`cleanmgr /sageset:1`

Note that the number 1 in the command is arbitrary: You can enter any number between 0 and 65535. This launches Disk Cleanup with an expanded set of file types to delete. Make your choices and click OK. What this does is save your settings to the Registry; it doesn't delete the files. To delete the files, select Start, type the following command, and then press Enter:

```
cleanmgr /sagerun:1
```

You can also create a shortcut for this command, add it to a batch file, or schedule it with the Task Scheduler.

Defragmenting Your Hard Disk

Windows 7 comes with a utility called Disk Defragmenter that's an essential tool for tuning your hard disk. Disk Defragmenter's job is to rid your hard disk of file fragmentation.

File fragmentation is one of those terms that sounds scarier than it actually is. It simply means that a file is stored on your hard disk in scattered, noncontiguous bits. This is a performance drag because it means that when Windows 7 tries to open such a file, it must make several stops to collect the various pieces. If a lot of files are fragmented, it can slow even the fastest hard disk to a crawl.

Why doesn't Windows 7 just store files contiguously? Recall that Windows 7 stores files on disk in clusters, and that these clusters have a fixed size, depending on the disk's capacity. Recall, too, that Windows 7 uses a file directory to keep track of each file's whereabouts. When you delete a file, Windows 7 doesn't actually clean out the clusters associated with the file. Instead, it just marks the deleted file's clusters as unused.

To see how fragmentation occurs, let's look at an example. Suppose that three files—FIRST.TXT, SECOND.TXT, and THIRD.TXT—are stored on a disk and that they use up four, three, and five clusters, respectively. Figure 7.5 shows how they might look on the disk.

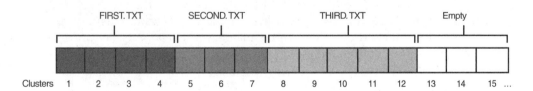

FIGURE 7.5 Three files before fragmentation.

If you now delete SECOND.TXT, clusters 5, 6, and 7 become available. But suppose that the next file you save—call it FOURTH.TXT—takes up five clusters. What happens? Well, Windows 7 looks for the first available clusters. It finds that 5, 6, and 7 are free, so it uses them for the first three clusters of FOURTH.TXT. Windows continues and finds that clusters 13 and 14 are free, so it uses them for the final two clusters of FOURTH.TXT. Figure 7.6 shows how things look now.

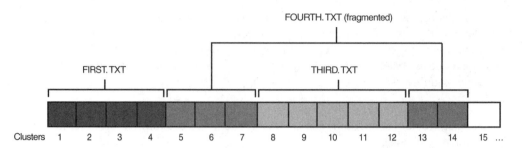

FIGURE 7.6   A fragmented file.

As you can see, FOURTH.TXT is stored noncontiguously—in other words, it's fragmented. Although a file fragmented in two pieces isn't that bad, it's possible for large files to split into dozens of blocks.

Running the Disk Defragmenter Tool

The good news with Windows 7 is that it configures Disk Defragmenter to run automatically—the default schedule is weekly: every Wednesday at 1:00 a.m. This means that you should never need to defragment your system manually. However, you might want to run a defragment before loading a particularly large software program.

Before using Disk Defragmenter, you should perform a couple of housekeeping chores:

▶ Delete any files from your hard disk that you don't need, as described in the previous section. Defragmenting junk files only slows down the whole process.

▶ Check for file system errors by running Check Disk as described earlier in this chapter (refer to "Checking Your Hard Disk for Errors").

Follow these steps to use Disk Defragmenter:

1. Select Start, type **defrag**, and then click Disk Defragmenter in the search results. Alternatively, in Windows Explorer, right-click the drive you want to defragment, click Properties, display the Tools tab in the dialog box that appears, and then click the Defragment Now button. Either way, the Disk Defragmenter window appears, as shown in Figure 7.7.

2. Click the disk you want to defragment.

3. Click Defragment Disk. Windows 7 defragments your hard drives.

4. When the defragment is complete, click Close.

TIP

In some cases, you can defragment a drive even further by running Disk Defragmenter on the drive twice in a row. (That is, run the defragment, and when it's done immediately run a second defragment.)

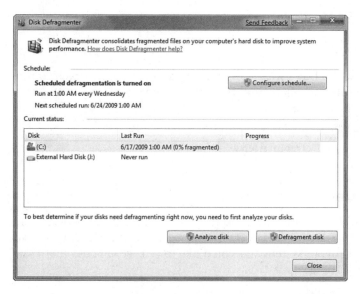

FIGURE 7.7   Use Disk Defragmenter to eliminate file fragmentation and improve hard disk performance.

Changing the Disk Defragmenter Schedule

If you want to run Disk Defragmenter on a different day, at a different time, more often or less often, follow these steps to change the default schedule:

1. Select Start, type **defrag**, and then click Disk Defragmenter in the search results.
2. Click Configure Schedule to display the Disk Defragmenter: Modify Schedule dialog box, shown in Figure 7.8.

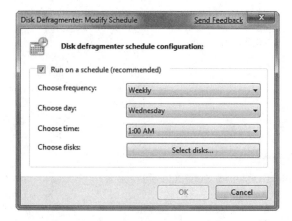

FIGURE 7.8   Use Disk Defragmenter: Modify Schedule dialog box to set up a custom defrag schedule.

3. Make sure that the Run on a Schedule check box is activated.

4. Use the Frequency list to select the defragment frequency: Daily, Weekly, or Monthly.

5. For a Weekly schedule, use the Day list to select the day of the week on which to run the defragment; for a Monthly schedule, use the Day list to select the day of the month on which to run the defragment.

6. Use the Time list to select the time of day to run the defragment.

7. Click OK to return to the Disk Defragmenter window.

8. Click Close.

Changing Which Disks Get Defragmented

Disk Defragmenter also has a feature that enables you to select which disks get worked on when the program performs its weekly (or whatever) defragment. This is useful if you have many hard drives or partitions on your system and you'd like to restrict the ones that Disk Defragmenter works on to speed things up.

Follow these steps to specify which disks get defragmented:

1. Select Start, type **defrag**, and then click Disk Defragmenter in the search results.

2. Click Configure Schedule to display the Disk Defragmenter: Modify Schedule dialog box.

3. Click Select Disks to display the Disk Defragmenter: Select Disks for Schedule dialog box, shown in Figure 7.9.

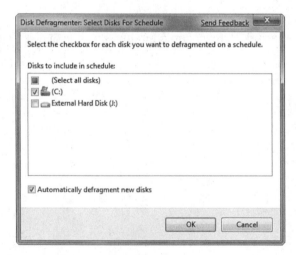

FIGURE 7.9   Use the Disk Defragmenter: Select Disks for Schedule dialog box to choose which disks get defragmented.

4. Deactivate the check box beside any disk that you don't want defragmented.

5. If you want Disk Defragmenter to stop adding new disks to the defragment list, deactivate the Automatically Defragment New Disks check box.

6. Click OK to return to the Disk Defragmenter: Modify Schedule dialog box.

7. Click OK.

Preparing for Trouble

A big part of the ounce-of-prevention mode that I talked about at the top of the chapter is the unwavering belief that someday something *will* go wrong with your computer. That might sound unduly pessimistic, but hey this is a *PC* we're talking about here, and it's never a question of *if* the thing will go belly up one day, but rather *when* that day will come.

With that gloomy mindset, the only sensible thing to do is prepare for that dire day so that you're ready to get your system back on its feet. So part of your Windows 7 maintenance chores should be getting a few things ready that will serve you well on the day your PC decides to go haywire on you. Besides performing a system image backup (which I describe a bit later), you should be setting system restore points and creating a system recovery disc. The next two sections cover these last two techniques.

Setting System Restore Points

One of the biggest causes of Windows instability in the past was the tendency of some newly installed programs simply to not get along with Windows. The problem could be an executable file that didn't mesh with the Windows system or a Registry change that caused havoc on other programs or on Windows. Similarly, hardware installs often caused problems by adding faulty device drivers to the system or by corrupting the Registry.

To help guard against software or hardware installations that bring down the system, Windows 7 offers the System Restore feature. Its job is straightforward, yet clever: to take periodic snapshots—called *restore points* or *protection points*—of your system, each of which includes the currently installed program files, Registry settings, and other crucial system data. The idea is that if a program or device installation causes problems on your system, you use System Restore to revert your system to the most recent restore point before the installation.

System Restore automatically creates restore points under the following conditions:

▶ **Every 24 hours**—This is called a *system checkpoint*, and it's set once a day as long as your computer is running. If your computer isn't running, the system checkpoint is created the next time you start your computer, assuming that it has been at least 24 hours since that previous system checkpoint was set.

> **NOTE**
>
> The system checkpoint interval is governed by a task in the Task Scheduler (select Start, type **scheduler**, and then click Task Scheduler in the search results). Open the Task Scheduler Library, Microsoft, Windows branch, and then click the SystemRestore task. To make changes to the task, click Properties in the Action pane to display the SR Properties dialog box. To change the schedule that Windows 7 uses to create system checkpoints, display the Triggers tab, click the trigger you want to change (Daily or At Startup), and then click Edit.

▶ **Before installing certain applications**—Some newer applications (notably Office 2000 and later) are aware of System Restore and will ask it to create a restore point prior to installation.

▶ **Before installing a Windows Update patch**—System Restore creates a restore point before you install a patch either by hand via the Windows Update site or via the Automatic Updates feature.

▶ **Before installing an unsigned device driver**—Windows 7 warns you about installing unsigned drivers. If you choose to go ahead, the system creates a restore point before installing the driver.

▶ **Before restoring backed-up files**—When you use the Windows 7 Backup program to restore one or more backed-up files, System Restore creates a restore point just in case the restore causes problems with system files.

▶ **Before reverting to a previous configuration using System Restore**— Sometimes reverting to an earlier configuration doesn't fix the current problem or it creates its own set of problems. In these cases, System Restore creates a restore point before reverting so that you can undo the restoration.

It's also possible to create a restore point manually using the System Protection feature. Here are the steps to follow:

1. Select Start, type **restore point**, and then click Create a Restore Point in the search results. This opens the System Properties dialog box with the System Protection tab displayed, as shown in Figure 7.10.

2. By default, Windows 7 creates automatic restore points for just the system drive. If you have other drives on your system and you want to create automatic restore points for them, as well, click the drive in the Protection Settings list, click Configure, activate the Restore System Settings and Previous Versions of Files option, and then click OK.

3. Click Create to display the Create a Restore Point dialog box.

4. Type a description for the new restore point and then click Create. System Restore creates the restore point and displays a dialog box to let you know.

5. Click Close to return to the System Properties dialog box.

6. Click OK.

FIGURE 7.10   Use the System Protection tab to set a restore point.

TIP

To change how much disk space System Restore uses to store checkpoints on a drive, click the drive in the Protection Settings list, click Configure, use the Max Usage slider to set the amount of disk space you want. If the hard disk is getting low on free space, you can also click the Delete button to remove all the restore points from the hard disk.

If you find yourself setting restore points frequently, it can be a pain to go through those steps every time. A much faster way to go about this is to use a script that creates a restore point instantly. Listing 7.2 shows just such a script.

NOTE

To get the file with the Listing 7.2 code—it's called `InstantRestorePoint.vbs`—see my website: www.mcfedries.com/Windows7Unleashed.

LISTING 7.2   A Script That Creates a Restore Point

```
Option Explicit
Dim strComputer, objWMI, objSR, strDesc, intResult
'
' Get the SystemRestore object
'
strComputer = "."
Set objWMI = GetObject("winmgmts:\\" & strComputer & "\root\default")
```

LISTING 7.2   Continued

```
Set objSR = objWMI.Get("SystemRestore")
'
' Ask for a restore point description
'
strDesc = InputBox ("Enter a description for the restore point:", , _
                    "Instant Restore Point")
'
' Create the restore point
'
intResult = objSR.CreateRestorePoint (strDesc, 0, 100)
'
' Check the result
'
If intResult = 0 Then
    '
    ' Success!
    '
    WScript.Echo "Instant restore point '" & strDesc & "' created!"
Else
    '
    ' Failure!
    '
    WScript.Echo "Instant restore point '" & strDesc & "' failed!" & _
                vbCrLf & "Error code: " & intResult
End If
'
' Release the objects
'
Set objWMI = Nothing
Set objSR = Nothing
```

Note that you must run this script under the Administrator account, as described in Chapter 30, "Programming the Windows Scripting Host."

▶ **See** "Running a Script as the Administrator," **p. 664**.

This script uses Windows Management Instrumentation (WMI) to return the SystemRestore class. The script displays a dialog box so that you can type a description of the restore point, and it then uses that description when it runs the CreateRestorePoint method. The script checks the result and displays a dialog box letting you know whether the restore point was created successfully.

Creating a System Repair Disc

In Windows Vista, you could attempt to get a badly behaving machine up and running again by booting to the Vista install disc and then accessing the system recovery options. That was a nice feature, but only if you could find your install disc (or if you ever had one in the first place)! Windows 7 fixes that problem by giving you the option of creating your own system repair disc. Here's how you go about this:

1. Select Start, type **recovery disc**, and then click Create a System Repair Disc in the search results. The Create a System Repair Disc dialog box appears, as shown in Figure 7.11.

FIGURE 7.11   Windows 7 thoughtfully enables you to create your own system repair disc.

2. Insert a blank recordable CD or DVD into your burner. If the AutoPlay dialog box shows up, close it.

3. If you have multiple burners, use the Drive list to select the one you want to use

4. Click Create Disc. Windows 7 creates the disk (it takes a minute or two), and then displays a particularly unhelpful dialog box.

5. Click Close and then click OK.

Eject the disc, label it, and then put it someplace where you'll be able to find it later on. To learn how to use the system repair disc in the event of a real emergency, see Chapter 21, "Troubleshooting and Recovering from Problems."

▶ **See** "Recovering Using the System Recovery Options," **p. 457**.

Backing Up Your Files

In theory, theory and practice are the same thing; in practice, they're not. That old saw applies perfectly to data backups. In theory, backing up data is an important part of everyday computing life. After all, we know that our data is valuable to the point of being irreplaceable, and you saw earlier that there's no shortage of causes that can result in a hard disk crashing: power surges, rogue applications, virus programs, or just simple wear and tear. In practice, however, backing up our data always seems to be one of those chores we'll get to "tomorrow." After all, that old hard disk seems to be humming along just fine, thank you.

When it comes to backups, theory and practice don't usually converge until that day you start your system and you get an ugly Invalid system configuration or Hard disk failure message. Believe me: Losing a hard disk that's crammed with unarchived (and now lost) data brings the importance of backing up into focus real quick. To avoid this sorry fate, you have to find a way to take some of the pain out of the practice of backing up.

In versions of Windows prior to Vista, backing up files was never as easy as it should have been. The old Microsoft Backup program seemed, at best, an afterthought, a token thrown in because an operating system should have *some* kind of backup program. Most users who were serious about backups immediately replaced Microsoft Backup with a more robust third-party alternative.

The Windows Backup that debuted in Vista was an improvement on its predecessors:

▶ You could back up to a writeable optical disc, USB flash drive, external hard disk, or other removable medium.

▶ You could back up to a network share.

▶ After you set up the program, backing up was completely automated, particularly if you backed up to a resource that has plenty of room to hold your files (such as a hard disk or roomy network share).

▶ You could create a system image backup that saves the exact state of your computer and thus enables you to completely restore your system if your computer dies or is stolen.

The downside was that Windows Backup was not very friendly to power users: It was completely wizard driven, and there was no way to configure a backup manually.

NEW TO 7 The version of Windows Backup that comes with Windows 7 improves upon the Vista version by giving you quite a bit more control over what gets backed up. Also, the lame Backup and Restore Center is gone, and the revamped Backup and Restore window is a big improvement.

You launch Windows Backup by selecting Start, typing **backup**, and then clicking Backup and Restore in the search results. Figure 7.12 shows the initial version of the window.

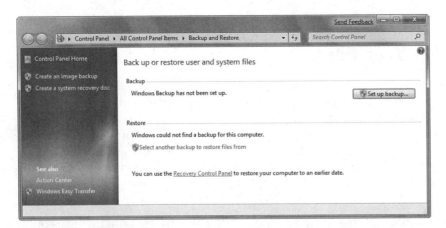

FIGURE 7.12   When you first launch Windows Backup, you see this version of the Backup and Restore window.

Configuring Automatic File Backups

Follow these steps to configure and activate Windows 7's automatic file backup feature:

1. Click Set Up Backup to start the Set Up Backup Wizard.

2. The wizard first wants to know the backup destination. You have two choices. (Click Next when you're ready to continue.)

   ▶ **Local hard disk or optical drive**—The Save Backup On list shows the available drives on your system, and you use this list to select the drive you want to use.

   ▶ **Network share**—This is the way to go if you want to use a shared network folder to store the backup. Click Save On a Network, then either type the UNC address of the share or click Browse to use the Browse for Folder dialog box to select the shared network folder. Type a username and password for accessing the share, and then click OK. Make sure the network share is selected in the Save Backup On list.

3. In the What Do You Want to Back Up dialog box, you have two choices. (Click Next when you've made your choice.)

   ▶ **Let Windows Choose**—Select this option to leave it up to Windows 7 to select what gets backed up. This includes everything in your user profile, including your documents, pictures, videos, and email.

   ▶ **Let Me Choose**—This is the way to go if you want more control over what gets backed up (and who wouldn't want more control over such a crucial procedure?). This is a big improvement over the Windows Vista backup program, which gave you very little control. When you click Next, you see the dialog box shown in Figure 7.13. The folders in your user profile are all selected by default. If you want to include any other folder, open the Computer branch, drill down to the folder, and then activate its check box. Click Next when you're done.

4. In the Review Your Backup Settings dialog box, click Change Schedule to open up the How Often Do You Want to Back Up dialog box.

5. Make sure the Run Backup On a Schedule check box is activated, and then set up your preferred backup schedule. (Click OK when you're done.)

   ▶ **How Often**—Select Daily, Weekly, or Monthly.

   ▶ **What Day**—If you chose Weekly, select the day of the week you want the backups to occur; if you chose Monthly, select the day of the month you want the backups to occur.

   ▶ **What Time**—Select the time of day you want the backup to run. (Choose a time when you won't be using your computer.)

6. Click Save Settings and Run Backup to save your configuration and launch the backup. Windows 7 returns you to the Backup and Restore and shows the progress of the backup.

FIGURE 7.13   Activate the check box beside each folder on your system that you want to include in the backup.

When the backup is done, the Backup and Restore window looks something like the one shown in Figure 7.14. As you can see, there's now all kinds of useful information here, including the backup size, the free space on the backup drive, the previous and next backup dates, and the schedule. The window also sprouts three new options:

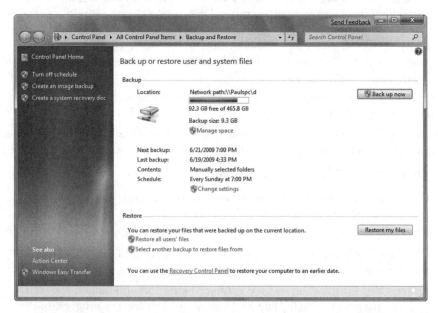

FIGURE 7.14   The Backup and Restore window after performing at least one backup.

▸ **Back Up Now**—Click this option to rerun the entire backup.

▸ **Change Settings**—Click this option to change your backup configuration by running through the Configure Backup Wizard's dialog boxes again.

▸ **Turn Off Schedule**—Click this link to disable the automatic backup feature. (Click the Turn On Schedule link to reinstate automatic backups.)

Creating a System Image Backup

The worst-case scenario for PC problems is a system crash that renders your hard disk or system files unusable. Your only recourse in such a case is to start from scratch with either a reformatted hard disk or a new hard disk. This usually means that you have to reinstall Windows 7 and then reinstall and reconfigure all your applications. In other words, you're looking at the better part of a day or, more likely, a few days, to recover your system. However, Windows 7 has a feature that takes most of the pain out of recovering your system. It's called a *system image* backup, and it's part of the system recovery options that I discuss in Chapter 22, "Troubleshooting Devices."

▸ **See** "Recovering Using the System Recovery Options," **p. 485.**

The system image backup is actually a complete backup of your Windows 7 installation. It takes a long time to create a system image (at least several hours, depending on how much stuff you have), but it's worth it for the peace of mind. Here are the steps to follow to create the system image:

1. Select Start, type **backup**, and then click Backup and Restore in the search results.

2. Click Create an Image. The Create a System Image Wizard appears.

3. The wizard asks you to specify a backup destination. You have three choices. (Click Next when you're ready to continue.)

   ▸ **On a Hard Disk**—Select this option if you want to use a disk drive on your computer. If you have multiple drives, use the list to select the one you want to use.

   ▸ **On One or More DVDs**—Select this option if you want to use DVDs to hold the backup.

   ▸ **On a Network**—Select this option if you want to use a shared network folder. Either type the UNC address of the share or click Select, and then either type the UNC address of the share or click Browse to use the Browse for Folder dialog box to select the shared network folder. Type a username and password for accessing the share, and then click OK.

4. The system image backup automatically includes your internal hard disk in the system image, and you can't change that. However, if you also have external hard drives, you can add them to the backup by activating their check boxes. Click Next. Windows Backup asks you to confirm your backup settings.

5. Click Start Backup. Windows Backup creates the system image.

6. When the backup is complete, click Close.

Checking for Updates and Security Patches

Microsoft is constantly working to improve Windows 7 with bug fixes, security patches, new program versions, and device driver updates. All of these new and improved components are available online, so you should check for updates and patches often.

The main online site for Windows 7 updates is the Windows Update website, which you load into Internet Explorer by selecting Start, All Programs, Windows Update. You should visit this site regularly to look for crucial new components that can make Windows 7 more reliable and more secure.

Windows 7 also comes with an automatic updating feature, which can download and install updates automatically. If you prefer to know what's happening with your computer, it's possible to control the automatic updating by following these steps:

1. Select Start, type **windows update**, and then click Windows Update in the search results. This displays the Windows Update window, which shows you the current update status and enables you to view installed updates.

NOTE

To view the updates installed on your computer, click the View Update History link.

2. Click the Change Settings link to display the Change Settings window, shown in Figure 7.15.

FIGURE 7.15   Use the Change Settings window to configure Windows 7's automatic updating.

3. Activate one of the following options to determine how Windows 7 performs the updating:

   ▶ **Install Updates Automatically**—This option tells Windows 7 to download and install updates automatically. Windows 7 checks for new updates on the date (such as Every Day or Every Sunday) and time you specify. For example, you might prefer to choose a time when you won't be using your computer.

CAUTION

To go into effect, some updates require your computer to reboot. In such cases, if you activate the Install Updates Automatically option, Windows 7 will automatically reboot your system. This could lead to problems if you have open documents with unsaved changes or if you need a particular program to be running at all times. You can work around these problems by saving your work constantly, by setting up an automatic logon (refer to "Setting Up an Automatic Logon" in Chapter 4, "Customizing Startup and Shutdown"), and by putting any program you need running in your Start menu's Startup folder.

   ▶ **Download Updates, but Let Me Choose Whether to Install Them**—If you activate this option, Windows 7 checks for new updates and then automatically downloads any updates that are available. Windows 7 then displays an icon in the notification area to let you know that the updates are ready to install. Click the icon to see the list of updates. If you see an update that you don't want to install, deactivate its check box.

TIP

An update that you choose not to install still appears in the View Available Updates window. If you'd prefer not to see that update, right-click the update, click Hide Update, and then click Cancel. If you later want to unhide the update, display the Windows Update window and click the Restore Hidden Updates link. In the Restore Hidden Updates window, activate the update's check box and then click Restore.

   ▶ **Check for Updates but Let Me Choose Whether to Download and Install Them**—If you activate this option, Windows 7 checks for new updates and then, if any available, displays an icon in the notification area to let you know that the updates are ready to download. Click the icon to see the list of updates. If you see an update that you don't want to download, deactivate its check box. Click Start Download to initiate the download. When the download is complete, Windows 7 displays an icon in the notification area to let you know that the updates are ready to install. Click the icon and then click Install to install the updates.

▶ **Never Check for Updates**—Activate this option to prevent Windows 7 from checking for new updates.

4. Click OK to put the new settings into effect.

Reviewing Event Viewer Logs

Windows 7 constantly monitors your system for unusual or noteworthy occurrences. It might be a service that doesn't start, the installation of a device, or an application error. Windows 7 tracks these occurrences, called *events*, in several different event logs. For example, the Application log stores events related to applications, including Windows 7 programs and third-party applications. The System log stores events generated by Windows 7 and components such as system services and device drivers.

To examine these logs, you use the Event Viewer snap-in. Select Start, type **eventvwr**, and then press Enter. Figure 7.16 shows the home page of the Event Viewer, which offers a summary of events, recent views, and available actions.

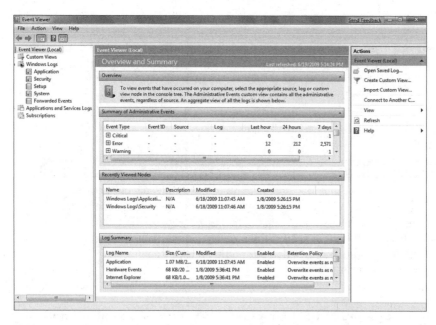

FIGURE 7.16   Use the Event Viewer to monitor events in Windows 7.

The scope pane offers three branches: Custom Views, Windows Logs, and Applications and Services Logs.

The Custom Views branch lists the event views defined on your system (as described later). If you filter an event log or create a new event view, the new view is stored in the Custom Views branch.

The Windows Logs branch displays several sub-branches, four of which represent the main logs that the system tracks (see Figure 7.17):

▶ **Application**—Stores events related to applications, including Windows 7 programs and third-party applications

▶ **Security**—Stores events related to system security, including logons, user accounts, and user privileges

▶ **Setup**—Stores events related to Windows setup

▶ **System**—Stores events generated by Windows 7 and components such as system services and device drivers

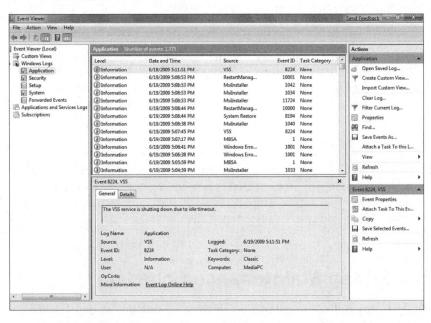

FIGURE 7.17   Click a log to see a list of the events in that log.

You should scroll through the Application and System event logs regularly to look for existing problems or for warnings that could portend future problems. The Security log isn't as important for day-to-day maintenance. You need to use it only if you suspect a security issue with your machine; for example, if you want to keep track of who logs on to the computer.

> **NOTE**
>
> The System log catalogs device driver errors, but Windows 7 has other tools that make it easier to see device problems. As you'll see in Chapter 22, Device Manager displays an icon on devices that have problems, and you can view a device's property sheet to see a description of the problem. Also, the System Information utility (Msinfo32.exe) reports hardware woes in the System Summary, Hardware Resources, Conflicts/Sharing branch and the System Summary, Components, Problem Devices branch.

When you select a log, the middle pane displays the available events, including the event's date, time, and source; its type (Information, Warning, or Error); and other data. Here's a summary of the major interface changes and new features that you get when viewing a log in Windows 7's Event Viewer:

▶ The Preview pane shows you the basic event data in the General tab, and more specific data in the Details tab. You can toggle the Preview pane on and off by selecting View, Preview Pane.

▶ Event data is now stored in XML format. To see the schema, click XML View in the Preview pane's Details tab.

▶ The Filter command now generates queries in XML format.

▶ You can click Create Custom View to create a new event view based on the event log, event type, event ID, and so on.

▶ You can attach tasks to events. Click the event you want to work with and then click Attach Task to This Event in the Action pane. This launches the Scheduled Tasks Wizard, which enables you to either run a program or script or have an email sent to you each time the event fires.

▶ You can save selected events to a file using the Event File (.elf) format.

The Applications and Services Logs branch lists the programs, components, and services that support the standard event-logging format that is new to Windows 7. All the items in this branch formerly stored their logs in separate text files that were unavailable in older versions of Event Viewer unless you specifically opened the log file.

Setting Up a 9-Step Maintenance Schedule

Maintenance is effective only if it's done regularly, but there's a fine line to be navigated. If maintenance is performed too often, it can become a burden and interfere with more interesting tasks; if it's performed too seldom, it becomes ineffective. Here's a 9-step maintenance plan:

1. Check your hard disk for errors. Run a basic scan about once a week. Run a more thorough disk surface scan once a month. The surface scan takes a long time, so run it when you won't be using your computer for a while.

2. Check free disk space. Do this once about once a month. If the free space is getting low on a drive, check it approximately once a week.

3. Delete unnecessary files. If free disk space isn't a problem, run this chore once every two or three months.

4. Defragment your hard disk. How often you defragment your hard disk depends on how often you use your computer. If you use it every day, you should run Disk Defragmenter about once a week. If your computer doesn't get heavy use, you probably need to run Disk Defragmenter only once a month or so.

5. Set restore points. Windows 7 already sets regular system checkpoints, so you need create your own restore points only when you're installing a program or device or making some other major change to your system.

6. Back up your files. If you use your computer frequently and generate a lot of data each day, use the Daily automatic backup. For a computer you use infrequently, a Monthly backup is sufficient.

7. Create a system image backup. You should create a system image backup once a month or any time you make major changes to your system.

8. Check Windows Update. If you've turned off automatic updating, you should check in with the Windows Update website about once a week.

9. Review Event Viewer logs. If your system appears to be working fine, you need only check the Application and System log files weekly or every couple of weeks. If the system has a problem, check the logs daily to look for warning or error events.

Remember that Windows 7 offers a couple of options for running most of these maintenance steps automatically:

▶ If you want to run a task every day, set it up to launch automatically at startup.

▶ Use the Task Scheduler (Start, All Programs, Accessories, System Tools, Task Scheduler) to set up a program on a regular schedule.

CHAPTER 8

Controlling Windows 7 with Control Panel

A little knowledge that acts is worth infinitely more than much knowledge that is idle.

—Kahlil Gibran

My goal in this book is to help you unleash the true power of Windows 7, and my premise is that this goal can't be met by toeing the line and doing only what the Help system tells you. Rather, I believe you can reach this goal only by taking various off-the-beaten track routes that go beyond Windows orthodoxy.

The chapters here in Part III illustrate this approach quite nicely, I think. The tools I discuss—Control Panel, Group Policy Editor, Microsoft Management Console, Services, Registry Editor, and Command Prompt—aren't difficult to use, but they put an amazing amount of power and flexibility into your hands. I discuss them in depth because you'll be using these important tools throughout the book. However, you can scour the Windows 7 Help system all day long and you'll find only a few scant references to these tools. To be sure, Microsoft is just being cautious because these *are* powerful tools, and the average user can wreak all kinds of havoc if these features are used incorrectly. However, your purchase of this book is proof that you are not an average user. So, by following the instructions in these next few chapters, I'm sure you'll have no trouble at all using these tools.

We begin here in Chapter 8 with an in-depth look at Control Panel: understanding it, navigating it, and customizing it to suit your needs.

Touring the Control Panel Window

Control Panel is a folder that contains a large number of icons—there are nearly 60 icons in the Classic view (depending on your version of Windows 7) of a default Windows 7 setup, but depending on your system configuration, even more icons could be available. Each of these icons deals with a specific area of the Windows 7 configuration: hardware, applications, fonts, printers, multimedia, and much more.

Opening an icon displays a window or dialog box containing various properties related to that area of Windows. For example, launching the Programs and Features icon enables you to install or uninstall third-party applications and to activate or deactivate Windows 7 components.

To display the Control Panel folder, select Start, Control Panel.

TIP

To learn how to convert the Start menu's Control Panel link to a menu of Control Panel icons, see "Putting Control Panel on the Start Menu" later in this chapter.

By default, Windows 7 displays the Control Panel Category view, shown in Figure 8.1, which displays icons for eight different categories (System and Security, Network and Internet, and so on), as well as two or three links to common tasks under each category icon. Windows XP's version of Control Panel offered a similar Category view, which was designed to help novice users, but it just delayed the rest of us unnecessarily and I always counseled my students to switch to Classic View as soon as possible.

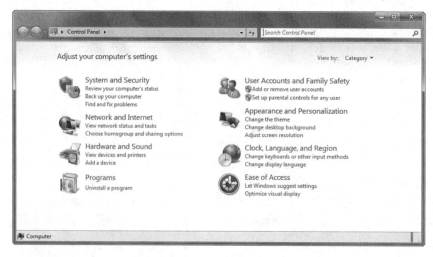

FIGURE 8.1   Control Panel's default home page view displays icons for eight categories.

I didn't do that with Windows Vista, and I don't do it with Windows 7, either. After I got used to the layout of the home page and its offshoots, I can find what I want quite quickly. However, when I switch to the Small Icons view (by selecting Small Icons in the View By list), I find that trying to pick out the one icon I want out of the nearly five dozen plus icons (see Figure 8.2) is frustrating and time-consuming.

FIGURE 8.2   Switch Control Panel to the Small Icons view to see all the icons in one window.

TIP

If you prefer the All Control Panel Items window, but you find that the Small Icons view makes the icons too small, you can make it a tad easier to manage by switching to the Large Icons view, which still enables you to see every icon if you enlarge or maximize the Control Panel window. In the View By list, click Large Icons.

Reviewing the Control Panel Icons

To help you familiarize yourself with what's available in Control Panel, this section offers summary descriptions of the Control Panel icons found in a standard Windows 7 installation. Note that your system might have extra icons, depending on your computer's configuration and the programs you have installed.

▶ **NEW TO 7** **Action Center**—Displays a list of your computer's current security issues and hardware and software problems.

▶ **Administrative Tools**—Displays a window with more icons, each of which enables you to administer a particular aspect of Windows 7:

NEW TO 7 **Component Services**—Displays the Component Services window, which you can use to investigate Component Object Model (COM) and Distributed COM (DCOM) applications and services.

Computer Management—Enables you to manage a local or remote computer. You can examine hidden and visible shared folders, set group policies, access Device Manager, manage hard disks, and much more.

Data Sources (ODBC)—Enables you to create and work with *data source names*, which are connection strings that you use to connect to local or remote databases.

Event Viewer—Enables you to examine Windows 7's list of *events*, which are unusual or noteworthy occurrences on your system, such as a service that doesn't start, the installation of a device, or an application error. See "Reviewing Event Viewer Logs" in Chapter 7, "Maintaining Your Windows 7 System."

iSCSI Initiator—Displays the iSCSI Initiator property sheet, which enables you to manage connections to iSCSI devices such as tape drives.

Local Security Policy—Displays the Local Security Settings snap-in, which enables you to set up security policies on your system. See Chapter 9, "Policing Windows 7 with Group Policies."

Performance Monitor—Runs the Performance Monitor, which enables you to monitor various aspects of your system. See "Using the Performance Monitor" in Chapter 6, "Tuning Windows 7's Performance."

Print Management—Displays the Print Management console, which enables you to manage, share, and deploy printers and print servers.

Services—Displays a list of the system services available with Windows 7. System services are background routines that enable the system to perform tasks such as network logon, disk management, Plug and Play, Internet connection sharing, and much more. You can pause, stop, and start services, as well as configure how service load at startup. For the details, see Chapter 11, "Controlling Services."

System Configuration—Opens the System Configuration utility. In Chapter 4, "Customizing Startup and Shutdown," see the "Using the System Configuration Utility to Modify the BCD" section, and in Chapter 23, "Troubleshooting Startup," see the "Troubleshooting Startup Using the System Configuration Utility" section.

Task Scheduler—Runs the Task Scheduler console, which enables you to runs programs or scripts on a schedule.

Windows Firewall with Advanced Security—Enables you to control every aspect of Windows 7's bidirectional firewall. See "Managing Windows Firewall" in Chapter 14, "Securing Windows 7."

Windows Memory Diagnostic—Runs the Windows Memory Diagnostics Tool, which checks your computer's memory chips for problems. See "Running the Memory Diagnostics Tool" in Chapter 21, "Troubleshooting and Recovering from Problems."

Windows PowerShell Modules—Loads Windows PowerShell and installs whatever PowerShell modules are on your system. To learn about PowerShell, see Chapter 31, "Scripting Windows with PowerShell."

▶ **AutoPlay**—Opens the AutoPlay window, which enables you to configure AutoPlay defaults for various media.

▶ **Backup and Restore**—Operates as a front-end for Windows Backup (see Backing Up Your Files" in Chapter 7).

▶ NEW TO **7** **Biometric Devices**—Enables you to configure biometric tools such as a fingerprint reader.

▶ **BitLocker Drive Encryption**—Turns on and configures BitLocker, which encrypts your Windows 7 system drive to protect it from unauthorized viewing. In Chapter 17, "Securing the File System," see "Encrypting a Disk with BitLocker."

▶ **Color Management**—Enables you to configure the colors of your monitor and printer to optimize color output.

▶ NEW TO **7** **Credential Manager**—This new tool enables you to store and work with usernames and passwords for servers, websites, network shares, and other secure resources.

▶ **Date and Time**—Enables you to set the current date and time, select your time zone, and set up an Internet time server to synchronize your system time. You can also display extra clocks to monitor other time zones (see "Displaying Multiple Clocks for Different Time Zones" in Chapter 5, "Customizing the Start Menu and Taskbar").

▶ **Default Programs**—Displays the Default Programs window, which enables you to change the programs that are associated with Windows 7's file types (in Chapter 3, see "Associating an Extension with a Different Application").

▶ NEW TO **7** **Desktop Gadgets**—Enables you to add and remove gadgets to and from the Windows 7 desktop. (In Windows 7, the Sidebar is gone and you just deal with gadgets directly on the desktop.)

▶ **Device Manager**—Launches Device Manager, which enables you to view and work with your system devices and their drivers. See Chapter 22, "Troubleshooting Devices," for more information.

▶ NEW TO **7** **Devices and Printers**—Displays a list of the major devices connected to your computer. This is the same as selecting Start, Devices and Printers.

▶ NEW TO **7** **Display**—Enables you to change the size of the screen text and perform other display-related tasks.

▶ **Ease of Access Center**—Enables you to customize input (the keyboard and mouse) and output (sound and display for users with special mobility, hearing, or vision requirements.

▶ **Folder Options**—Enables you to customize the display of Windows 7's folders, set up whether Windows 7 uses single- or double-clicking, work with file types, and configure offline files.

▶ **Fonts**—Displays the Fonts folder, from which you can view, install, and remove fonts.

▶ NEW TO 7 **Getting Started**—Displays general information about your computer and icons to common Windows 7 tasks. This replaces the Welcome Center introduced with Windows Vista.

▶ NEW TO 7 **HomeGroup**—Enables you to join a home group, which is Windows 7's new user account-free networking technology. In Chapter 25, "Setting Up a Small Network," see "Creating a Home Group."

▶ **Indexing Options**—Enables you to configure the index used by Windows 7's new search engine.

▶ **Internet Options**—Displays a large collection of settings for modifying Internet properties (how you connect, the Internet Explorer interface, and so on).

▶ **Keyboard**—Enables you to customize your keyboard, work with keyboard languages, and change the keyboard driver.

▶ NEW TO 7 **Location and Other Sensors**—Displays a list of the sensors attached to your computer. You use sensors to detect your current location (for GPS-enabled programs) and the current spatial orientation of your PC.

▶ **Mouse**—Enables you to set various mouse options and to install a different mouse device driver.

▶ **Network and Sharing Center**—Displays general information about your network connections and sharing settings. See "Displaying the Network and Sharing Center" in Chapter 25.

▶ NEW TO 7 **Notification Area Icons**—Gives you access to notification area customization options. In Chapter 5, see the section "Taking Control of the Notification Area."

▶ **Parental Controls**—Enables you to restrict computer usage for other users of the computer. In Chapter 14, "Securing Windows 7," see "Implementing Parental Controls."

▶ **Pen and Touch**—Displays the Pen and Input Devices dialog box, which enables you to configure your Tablet PC's digital pen.

▶ **Performance Information and Tools**—Displays the performance rating for your computer (see "Viewing Your Computer's Performance Rating" in Chapter 6).

▶ **Personalization**—Offers a large number of customization options for the current Windows 7 theme: glass effects, colors, desktop background, screensaver, sounds, mouse pointers, and display settings.

- **Phone and Modem**—Enables you to configure telephone dialing rules (see "Working with Different Dialing Locations" in Chapter 27, "Making Remote Network Connections") and to install and configure modems.

- **Power Options**—Enables you to configure power management properties for powering down system components (such as the monitor and hard drive), defining low-power alarms for notebook batteries, enabling sleep and hibernation modes, and configuring notebook power buttons.

- **Programs and Features**—Enables you to install and uninstall applications, add and remove Windows 7 components, and view installed updates.

- NEW TO **7** **Recovery**—Enables you to recover your system by restoring it to an earlier working configuration. In Chapter 21, see "Recovering Using System Restore."

- **Region and Language**—Enables you to configure international settings for country-dependent items such as numbers, currencies, times, and dates.

- NEW TO **7** **RemoteApp and Desktop Connections**—Enables you to create a work with remote programs and desktops.

- **Sound**—Enables you to control the system volume, map sounds to specific Windows 7 events (such as closing a program or minimizing a window), specify settings for audio, voice, and other multimedia devices.

- **Speech Recognition**—Enables you to configure Windows 7's speech recognition feature.

- **Sync Center**—Enables you to set up and maintain synchronization with other devices and with offline files.

- **System**—Displays basic information about your system including the Windows 7 edition, system rating, processor type, memory size, computer and workgroup names, and whether Windows 7 is activated. Also gives you access to Device Manager and settings related to performance, startup, System Protection, Remote Assistance, and the Remote Desktop.

- **Tablet PC Settings**—Displays settings for configuring handwriting and other aspects of your Tablet PC.

- **Taskbar and Start Menu**—Enables you to customize the taskbar and Start menu. See Chapter 5 for more information.

- NEW TO **7** **Troubleshooting**—Displays a collection of tasks related to troubleshooting various aspects of your system.

- **User Accounts**—Enables you to set up and configure user accounts.

- **Windows CardSpace**—Enables you to use Microsoft's new CardSpace system to manage your personal online data.

▶ **Windows Defender**—Launches Windows Defender, Windows 7's antispyware program. See "Thwarting Spyware with Windows Defender" in Chapter 14.

▶ **Windows Firewall**—Enables you to configure Windows Firewall. See "Managing Windows Firewall" in Chapter 14.

▶ **Windows Mobility Center**—Displays Windows 7's Mobility Center for notebooks.

▶ **Windows Update**—Enables you to configure Windows 7's Windows Update feature, check for updates, view update history, and set up a schedule for the download and installation of updates.

NOTE

You'd think that with nearly 50 icons in a default Control Panel, Microsoft isn't in the business of *removing* icons. However, there are a few that have been relegated to the dustbin of Windows history. The following Vista icons are gone from the Windows 7 version of Control Panel: Add Hardware, Bluetooth Devices, Game Controllers, Infrared, iSCSI Initiator, Offline Files, People Near Me (although see Table 8.1, later), Printers (replaced by Devices and Printers), Problem Reports and Solutions (replaced by Action Center), Text to Speech, Scanners and Cameras, Security Center (replaced by Action Center), Welcome Center (replaced by Getting Started), Windows Sidebar (replaced by Desktop Gadgets) and Windows SideShow.

Understanding Control Panel Files

Many of the Control Panel icons represent *Control Panel extension* files, which use the .cpl extension. These files reside in the %SystemRoot%\System32 folder. When you open Control Panel, Windows 7 scans the System32 folder looking for CPL files, and then displays an icon for each one.

The CPL files offer an alternative method for launching individual Control Panel dialog boxes. The idea is that you run control.exe and specify the name of a CPL file as a parameter. This bypasses the Control Panel folder and opens the icon directly. Here's the syntax:

```
control CPLfile [,option1 [, option2]]
```

CPLfile—The name of the file that corresponds to the Control Panel icon you want to open (see Table 8.1 later in this chapter).

option1—This option is obsolete and is included only for backward compatibility with batch files and scripts that use Control.exe for opening Control Panel icons.

option2—The tab number of a multitabbed dialog box. Many Control Panel icons open a dialog that has two or more tabs. If you know the specific tab you want to work with, you can use the *option2* parameter to specify an integer that corresponds to the tab's relative position from the left side of the dialog box. The first (leftmost) tab is 0, the next tab is 1, and so on.

For example, to open Control Panel's System icon with the Hardware tab displayed, run the following command (using the Start menu's Search box or the Run command):

```
control sysdm.cpl,,2
```

Table 8.1 lists the various Control Panel icons and the appropriate command line to use. (Note, however, that some Control Panel icons—such as Taskbar and Start Menu—can't be accessed by running Control.exe.)

TABLE 8.1   Command Lines for Launching Individual Control Panel Icons

Control Panel Icon	Command	Dialog Box Tabs
Action Center	control wscui.cpl	N/A
Administrative Tools	control admintools	N/A
Date and Time	control timedate.cpl	3
Personalization	control desk.cpl	1
Ease of Access Center	control access.cpl	N/A
Folder Options	control folders	N/A

TABLE 8.1   Continued

Control Panel Icon	Command	Dialog Box Tabs
Fonts	control fonts	N/A
Game Controllers	control joy.cpl	N/A
Internet Options	control inetcpl.cpl	7
Keyboard	control keyboard	N/A
Mouse	control mouse	N/A
Network Connections	control ncpa.cpl	N/A
People Near Me	control collab.cpl	2
Pen and Touch	control tabletpc.cpl	N/A
Phone and Modem	control telephon.cpl	N/A
Power Options	control powercfg.cpl	N/A
Printers	control printers	N/A
Programs and Features	control appwiz.cpl	N/A
Regional and Language	control intl.cpl	4
Scanners and Cameras	control scannercamera	N/A
Sound	control mmsys.cpl	3
System	control sysdm.cpl	5
Table PC Settings	control tabletpc.cpl	3
User Accounts	control nusrmgr.cpl	N/A
Windows CardSpace	control infocardcpl.cpl	N/A
Windows Firewall	control firewall.cpl	N/A

NOTE

If you find your Control Panel folder is bursting at the seams, you can trim it down to size by removing those icons you never use. There are a number of ways you can do this in Windows 7, but the easiest is probably via group policies. See "Removing an Icon from Control Panel" later in this chapter.

Easier Access to Control Panel

Control Panel is certainly a useful and important piece of the Windows 7 package. It's even more useful if you can get to it easily. In this section, I show you a few methods for gaining quick access to individual icons and the entire folder.

Alternative Methods for Opening Control Panel Icons

Access to many Control Panel icons is scattered throughout the Windows 7 interface, meaning that there's more than one way to launch an icon. Many of these alternative methods are faster and more direct than using the Control Panel folder. Here's a summary:

▶ **Action Center**—Click (or right-click) the Action Center icon in the notification area and then click Open Action Center.

▶ **Administrative Tools**—You can display these tools as a menu on the main Start menu. To learn how, see "Streamlining the Start Menu by Converting Links to Menus" in Chapter 5.

▶ **Date and Time**—Right-click the clock in the notification area and then click Adjust Date/Time.

▶ **Desktop Gadgets**—Click Start, All Programs, Desktop Gadget Gallery.

▶ **Devices and Printers**—Click Start, Devices and Printers.

▶ **Personalization**—Right-click the desktop and then click Personalize.

▶ **Folder Options**—In Windows Explorer, select Organize, Folder and Search Options.

▶ **Fonts**—In Windows Explorer, open the %SystemRoot%\Fonts folder.

▶ **Internet Options**—In Internet Explorer, select Tools, Internet Options.

▶ **Network and Sharing Center**—Click (or right-click) the Network icon in the notification area and then click Open Network and Sharing Center.

▶ **Notification Area Icons**—Right-click an empty section of the notification area and then click Custom Notification Area.

▶ **Power Options**—Click the Power icon in the notification area and then click More Power Options.

▶ **Default Programs**—Select Start, Default Programs.

▶ **Sound**—Right-click the Volume icon in the notification area and then click Sounds.

▶ **System**—Click Start, right-click Computer, and then click Properties.

▶ **Taskbar and Start Menu**—Right-click the Start button or an empty section of the taskbar, and then click Properties.

8

▶ **Troubleshooting**—Right-click the Action Center icon in the notification area and then click Troubleshoot a Problem.

▶ **Windows Update**—Click Start, All Programs, Windows Update, or right-click the Action Center icon in the notification area and then click Open Windows Update.

Another relatively easy way to get at a Control Panel icon is to use the powerful Windows 7 search engine, which indexes the Control Panel. (I'm assuming here that you didn't turn off the indexer, as I suggested in Chapter 6.) Select Start, type some or all of the Control Panel icon name, and then click the icon that appears in the Control Panel section of the search results. For example, in Figure 8.3, I typed **clear** in the Search box, and you can see that ClearType Text Tuner shows up at the top of the results.

FIGURE 8.3   You can use the Start menu's Search box to search for Control Panel icons.

Putting Control Panel on the Start Menu

You can turn the Start menu's Control Panel command into a menu that displays the Control Panel icons by following these steps:

1. Right-click the Start button and then click Properties. The Taskbar and Start Menu Properties dialog box appears with the Start Menu tab displayed.
2. Click Customize. The Customize Start Menu dialog box appears.
3. In the list of Start menu items, find the Control Panel item and activate the Display as a Menu option.
4. Click OK.

Figure 8.4 shows the Start menu with the Control Panel item configured as a menu. Depending on the screen resolution you are using, not all the Control Panel icons might fit on the screen. In that case, hover the mouse pointer over the downward-pointing arrow at the bottom of the menu to scroll through the rest of the icons. (To scroll up, hover the pointer over the upward-pointing arrow that appears at the top of the menu.)

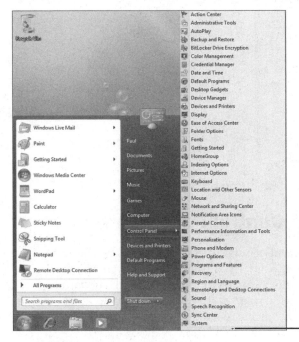

Click the arrow to scroll the menu

FIGURE 8.4   The Start menu's Control Panel item configured as a menu.
Click the arrow to scroll the menu

8

Removing an Icon from Control Panel

You can gain a bit more control over the Control Panel by configuring it not to display icons that you don't ever use or that aren't applicable to your system. This is done with group policies (see Chapter 9), and you follow these steps:

1. Select Start, type **gpedit.msc**, and then click **gpedit** in the results. The Local Group Policy Editor appears.

2. Select the User Configuration, Administrative Templates, Control Panel branch.

3. Double-click the Hide Specified Control Panel Items policy.

4. Click the Enabled Option.

5. Click the Show button. The Show Contents dialog box appears.

6. For each Control Panel icon you want to hide, type the icon name and press Enter. Figure 8.5 shows dialog box with a few Control Panel icons added.

7. Click OK to return to the Hide Specified Control Panel Items dialog box.

8. Click OK. Windows 7 puts the policy into effect.

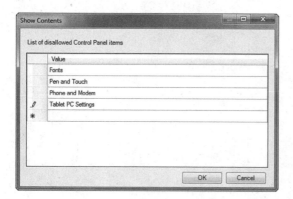

FIGURE 8.5   Type the name of each Control Panel icon you want to hide.

Showing Only Specified Control Panel Icons

Disabling a few Control Panel icons is useful because it reduces a bit of the clutter in the All Control Panel Items window. However, what if you want to set up a computer for a novice user, and you'd like that person to have access to just a few relatively harmless icons, such as Personalization and Getting Started? In that case, it's *way* too much work to disable most of the icons, one at a time. A much easier approach is to specify just those few Control Panel icons you want the user to see. Here's how:

1. Select Start, type **gpedit.msc**, and then click **gpedit** in the results. The Local Group Policy Editor appears.

2. Select the User Configuration, Administrative Templates, Control Panel branch.

3. Double-click the Show Only Specified Control Panel Items policy.

4. Click the Enabled Option.

5. Click the Show button. The Show Contents dialog box appears.

6. For each Control Panel icon you want to show, type the icon name and press Enter.

7. Click OK to return to the Show Only Specified Control Panel Items dialog box.

8. Click OK. Windows 7 puts the policy into effect.

Other Control Panel Policies

While you've got the Local Group Policy Editor up and running, consider the other two Control Panel-related policies that appear in the User Configuration, Administrative Templates, Control Panel branch:

▶ **Always Open All Control Panel Items When Opening Control Panel**—If you enable this policy, Control Panel is always displayed in the All Control Panel Items window, and the user can't change to the Home Page view. If you disable this policy, Control Panel is always displayed in the Home Page view, and the user can't change to the All Control Panel Items window.

▶ **Prohibit Access to the Control Panel**—If you enable this policy, users can't access Control Panel using the Start menu or `control.exe` executable.

Policing Windows 7 with Group Policies

A policy is a temporary creed liable to be changed, but while it holds good it has got to be pursued with apostolic zeal.

—Mahatma Gandhi

You've seen in many places throughout this book that you can perform some pretty amazing things by using a tool that's about as hidden as any Windows power tool can be: the Local Group Policy Editor. That Microsoft has buried this program in a mostly untraveled section of the Windows landscape isn't the least bit surprising, because in the wrong hands, the Local Group Policy Editor can wreak all kinds of havoc on a system. It's a kind of electronic Pandora's box that, if opened by careless or inexperienced hands, can loose all kinds of evil upon the Windows world.

Of course, none of this doom-and-gloom applies to you, dear reader, because you're a cautious and prudent wielder of all the Windows power tools. This means that you'll use the Local Group Policy Editor in a safe, prudent manner, and that you'll create a system restore point if you plan to make any major changes. I knew I could count on you.

As you see in this chapter, the Local Group Policy Editor isn't even remotely hard to use. However, it's such a powerful tool that it's important for you to know exactly how it works, which will help ensure that nothing goes awry when you're making your changes.

Understanding Group Policies

Put simply, *group policies* are settings that control how Windows works. You can use them to customize the Windows 7 interface, restrict access to certain areas, specify security settings, and much more.

Group policies are mostly used by system administrators who want to make sure that novice users don't have access to dangerous tools (such as the Registry Editor) or who want to ensure a consistent computing experience across multiple machines. Group policies are also ideally suited to situations in which multiple users share a single computer. However, group policies are also useful on single-user standalone machines, as you've seen throughout this book.

Local Group Policy Editor and Windows Versions

The power of the Local Group Policy Editor is aptly illustrated not only by the fact that Microsoft hides the program deep in the bowels of the system, but most tellingly by the fact that Microsoft doesn't even offer Local Group Policy Editor in the following Windows versions:

- ▶ Windows 7 Home Basic
- ▶ Windows 7 Home Premium

In earlier versions of Windows, this tool was also removed from Windows XP Home, Windows Vista Home Basic, and Windows Vista Home Premium. In other words, those Windows versions that Microsoft expects novices to be using are the same Windows versions where Microsoft doesn't even include the Local Group Policy Editor, just to be safe.

Of course, plenty of experienced users use these Windows versions, mostly because they're cheaper than high-end versions such as Windows 7 Ultimate. So what's a would-be policy editor to do when faced with having no Local Group Policy Editor?

The short answer is: Don't sweat it. That is, although the Local Group Policy Editor does provide an easy-to-use interface for many powerful settings, it's not the only way to put those settings into effect. Most group policies correspond to settings in the Windows Registry, so you can get the identical tweak on any Windows 7 Home system by modifying the appropriate Registry setting, instead. Throughout this book, I've tried to augment group policy tweaks with the corresponding Registry tweak, just in case you don't have access to the Local Group Policy Editor.

TIP

Understanding that most group policies have parallel settings in the Registry is all fine and dandy, but how on earth are you supposed to know which of the Registry's thousands upon thousands of settings is the one you want? The old method was to export the Registry to a REG file, make the change in the Local Group Policy Editor, export the Registry again, and then compare the two files. *Way* too much work (and impossible if all you have to work with is a Windows Home version)! You can also try filtering the policies as described later (see "Filtering Policies"). Fortunately, Microsoft has an Excel workbook that lists every single group policy value and gives the corresponding Registry setting. You can download the Group Policy Settings Reference, which covers both Windows Vista and XP (no sign of a Windows 7 version as I write this), here:

www.microsoft.com/downloads/details.aspx?FamilyID=41DC179B-3328-4350-ADE1-
C0D9289F09EF

NOTE

Given a setting that you can tweak using either the Local Group Policy Editor or the Registry Editor (and assuming you're running a version of Windows that comes with the Local Group Policy Editor), which tool should you choose? I highly recommend using the Local Group Policy Editor, because (as you'll see) it offers a simpler and more straight-forward user interface, which means it saves time and you'll be much less likely to make an error.

Launching the Local Group Policy Editor

As I've said, you make changes to group policies using the Local Group Policy Editor, a Microsoft Management Console snap-in. To start the Local Group Policy Editor, follow these steps:

1. Press Start.
2. Type **gpedit.msc**.
3. Press Enter.

Figure 9.1 shows the Local Group Policy Editor window that appears. (The word *Local* refers to the fact that you're editing group policies on your own computer, not on some remote computer.)

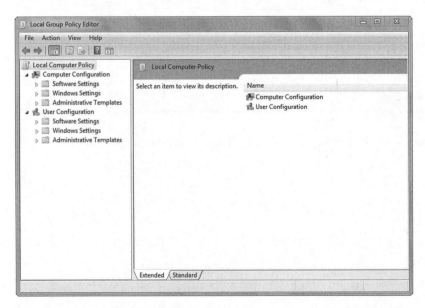

FIGURE 9.1   You use the Local Group Policy Editor to modify group policies on your PC.

Working with Group Policies

The Local Group Policy Editor window is divided into two sections:

▶ **Left pane**—This pane contains a tree-like hierarchy of policy categories, which is divided into two main categories: Computer Configuration and User Configuration. The Computer Configuration policies apply to all users and are implemented before the logon. The User Configuration policies apply only to the current user and, therefore, are not applied until that user logs on.

▶ **Right pane**—This pane contains the policies for whichever category is selected in the left pane.

The idea, then, is to open the tree's branches to find the category you want. When you click the category, its policies appear in the right pane. For example, Figure 9.2 shows the Local Group Policy Editor window with the User Configuration, Administrative Templates, Start Menu and Taskbar category highlighted.

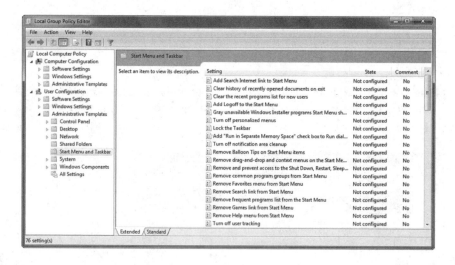

FIGURE 9.2   When you select a category in the left pane, the category's policies appear in the right pane.

> **TIP**
>
> Windows comes with another tool called the Local Security Policy Editor, which displays only the policies found in the Local Group Policy Editor Computer Configuration, Windows Settings, Security Settings branch. To launch the Local Security Policy Editor, select Start, type **secpol.msc**, and press Enter. As you might expect, this snap-in isn't available in the Windows 7 Home editions.

In the right pane, the Setting column tells you the name of the policy, and the State column tells you the current state of the policy. Click a policy to see its description on the left side of the pane, as shown in Figure 9.3. If you don't see the description, click the Extended tab.

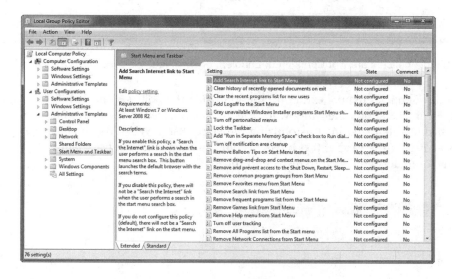

FIGURE 9.3   Click a policy to see its description.

Configuring a Policy

To configure a policy, double-click it. The type of window you see depends on the policy:

▶ For simple policies, you see a window similar to the one shown in Figure 9.4. These kinds of policies take one of three states: Not Configured (the policy is not in effect), Enabled (the policy is in effect and its setting is enabled), and Disabled (the policy is in effect but its setting is disabled).

> **NOTE**
>
> Take note of the Supported On value in the dialog box. This value tells you which versions of Windows support the policy.

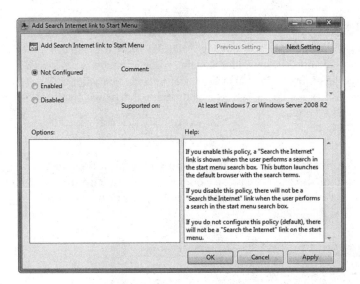

FIGURE 9.4   Simple policies are Not Configured, Enabled, or Disabled.

▶ Other kinds of policies require extra information when the policy is enabled. For example, Figure 9.5 shows the window for the Items Displayed in the Places Bar policy (described in detail later in "Customizing the Places Bar"). When the Enabled option is activated, the various text boxes become enabled, and you use them to type paths for folders you want to display in the Places bar.

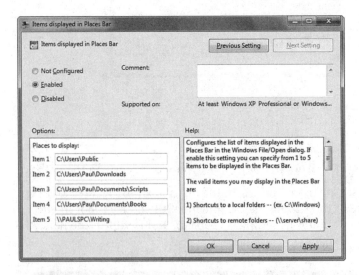

FIGURE 9.5   More complex policies also require extra information, such as a list of folders to display in the Places bar.

Filtering Policies

I've been saying for years that the Local Group Policy Editor desperately needs a search feature. There are nearly 3,000 policies and they're scattered around dozens of folders. Trying to find the policy you need by rooting around in the Local Group Policy Editor is like trying to find a particularly small needle in a particularly large haystack. The Local Group Policy Editor in Windows Vista included a rudimentary filtering feature, but it redefined the word *useless*.

Fortunately, although the Windows 7 version of the Local Group Policy Editor still isn't searchable (unless you export it to a text file by selecting Action, Export List), it does come with two new features that make it quite a bit easier to track down a wayward policy:

▶ The two Administrative Templates branches (one in Computer Configuration and the other in User Configuration) each come with a new sub-branch called All Settings. Selecting this branch displays a complete list of all the policies in that Administrative Templates branch. (Almost all non-security-related policies are in the Administrative Templates branches, so that's why they get singled out for special treatment.)

▶ A beefed-up filtering feature that's actual useful for cutting the vastness of the policy landscape down to size.

In combination, these two features make it much easier to find what you're looking for. The basic idea is that you select the All Settings branch that you want to work with, and then set up a filter that defines what you're looking for. Local Group Policy Editor then displays just those policies that match your filter criteria.

To show you how this works, let's run through an example. Suppose I want to find the Items Displayed in Places Bar policy shown earlier in Figure 9.5. Here's how I'd use a filter to locate it:

1. Select the User Configuration, Administrative Templates, All Settings branch.
2. Select Action, Filter Options to open the Filter Options dialog box.
3. Make sure the Enable Keyword Filters check box is activated.
4. Use the Filter for Word(s) text box to type a word or phrase that should match the policy you're looking for. In our example, we know that "places" is part of the policy name, so I'll use that as the filter text.
5. Use the associated drop-down list to choose how you want the policy text to match your search text:

   ▶ **Any**—Choose this option to match only those policies that include at least one of your search terms.

   ▶ **All**—Choose this option to match only those policies that include all of your search terms in any order.

   ▶ **Exact**—Choose this option to match only those policies that include text that exactly matches your search phrase.

6

6. Use the Within check boxes to specify where you want the filter to look for matches:

   ▶ **Policy Setting Title**—Select this check box to look for matches in the policy name. In our example, "places" is part of the policy name, and it's a relatively unique term, so it should suffice to only filter on the title, as shown in Figure 9.6.

   ▶ **Explain Text**—Select this check box to look for matches in the policy description.

   ▶ **Comment**—Select this check box to look for matches in the Comments text. (Each policy comes with a Comments box that you can use to add your two-cent's worth about any policy.)

7. Click OK.

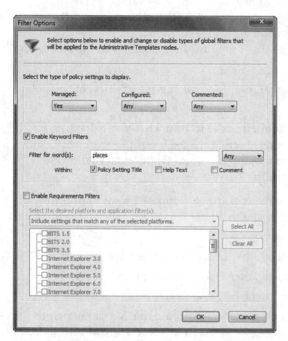

FIGURE 9.6   In the Windows 7 Local Group Policy Editor, you can use the Filter Options dialog box to find the policy you need.

With your filter in place, select Action, Filter On (or click to activate the Filter button in the toolbar). The Local Group Policy Editor displays just those policies that match your filter settings. For example, Figure 9.7 shows the results when the filter in Figure 9.6 is turned on. As you can see, the Items Displayed in Places Bar policy is among the results.

Filter

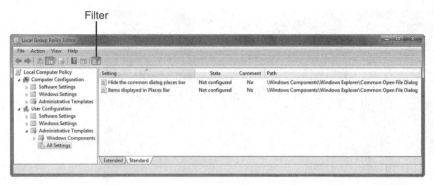

FIGURE 9.7   The results when the filter set up in Figure 9.6 is turned on.

Group Policy Examples

Although there are plenty of examples of group policies in action throughout this book, I'm a firm believer that you can't get enough of this powerful tool. With that in mind, the rest of this chapter takes you through a few of my favorite policies.

Customizing the Windows Security Window

When you press Ctrl+Alt+Delete while logged on to Windows 7, you see the Windows Security window, which contains the following buttons, as shown in Figure 9.8:

- ▶ **Lock This Computer**—Click this button to hide the desktop and display the Locked window. To return to the desktop, you must enter your Windows 7 user account password. This is useful if you're going to leave Windows 7 unattended and don't want another person accessing the desktop. However, Windows 7 offers a faster way to lock the computer: Press Windows Logo+L.

- ▶ **Switch User**—Click this button to switch to a different user account while also leaving your current user account running.

- ▶ **Log Off**—Click this button to display the Welcome screen, which lets you log on using a different user account.

- ▶ **Change a Password**—Click this button to display the Change Password window, which enables you to specify a new password for your account.

- ▶ **Start Task Manager**—Click this button to open Task Manager.

Of these five commands, all but Switch User are customizable using group policies. So if you find that you never use one or more of those commands, or (more likely) if you want to prevent a user from accessing one or more of the commands, you can use group policies to remove them from the Windows Security window. Here are the steps to follow:

9

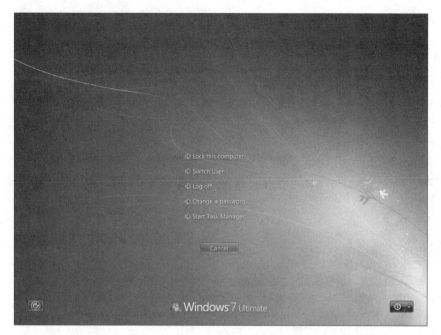

FIGURE 9.8   In Windows 7, press Ctrl+Alt+Delete to display the Windows Security dialog box.

1. Open the Local Group Policy Editor window, as described earlier in this chapter.

2. Open the User Configuration, Administrative Templates, System, Ctrl+Alt+Del Options branch.

3. Double-click one of the following policies:

   ▶ **Remove Change Password**—You can use this policy to disable the Change a Password button in the Windows Security window.

   ▶ **Remove Lock This Computer**—You can use this policy to disable the Lock Computer button in the Windows Security window.

   ▶ **Remove Task Manager**—You can use this policy to disable the Start Task Manager button in the Windows Security window.

   ▶ **Remove Logoff**—You can use this policy to disable the Log Off button in the Windows Security window.

4. In the policy dialog box that appears, click Enabled and then click OK.

5. Repeat steps 3 and 4 to disable all the buttons you don't need.

Figure 9.9 shows the Windows Security window with the four buttons removed.

To perform the same tweak using the Registry (see Chapter 12, "Tweaking the Windows 7 Registry"), open the Registry Editor and open the following key:

`HKCU\Software\Microsoft\Windows\CurrentVersion\Policies\System`

FIGURE 9.9   You can use group policies to remove most of the buttons in the Windows Security dialog box.

Change the value of one or more of the following settings to **1:**

```
DisableChangePassword
DisableLockWorkstation
DisableTaskMgr
```

To remove the Log Off button via the Registry, open the following key:

```
HKCU\Software\Microsoft\Windows\CurrentVersion\Policies\Explorer
```

Change the value of the NoLogoff setting to **1.**

Customizing the Places Bar

The left side of the old-style Save As and Open dialog boxes in Windows 7 include icons for several common locations: Recent Places, Desktop, Libraries, Computer, and Network, as shown in Figure 9.10.

> **NOTE**
>
> If you display the Save As or Open dialog box and you see the Navigation pane instead, it means the application uses the updated dialog boxes. However, you can still customize the Favorites section: To add a folder, drag it from the folder list and drop it on Favorites; to remove a custom shortcut from the Favorites list, right-click it, click Delete, and then click Yes when Windows asks you to confirm.

FIGURE 9.10   The old Save As and Open dialog boxes display icons on the left for common locations.

The area that contains these icons is called the Places bar. If you have two or more folders that you use regularly (for example, you might have several folders for various projects that you have on the go), switching between them can be a hassle. To make this chore easier, you can customize the Places bar to include icons for each of these folders. That way, no matter which location you have displayed in the Save As or Open dialog box, you can switch to one of these regular folders with a single click of the mouse.

The easiest way to do this is via the Local Group Policy Editor, as shown in the following steps:

1. Open the Local Group Policy Editor window, as described earlier in this chapter.

2. Open the following node: User Configuration, Administrative Templates, Windows Components, Windows Explorer, Common Open File Dialog.

3. Double-click the Items Displayed in Places Bar policy.

4. Click Enabled.

5. Use the Item 1 through Item 5 text boxes to type the paths for the folders you want to display. These can be local folders or network folders, as shown earlier in Figure 9.5.

6. Click OK to put the policy into effect. Figure 9.11 shows a dialog box with icons for the folders from Figure 9.5 displayed in the Places bar.

If you don't have access to the Local Group Policy Editor, you can use the Registry Editor to perform the same tweak. Open the Registry Editor and navigate to the following key:

```
HKCU\Software\Microsoft\Windows\CurrentVersion\Policies\
```

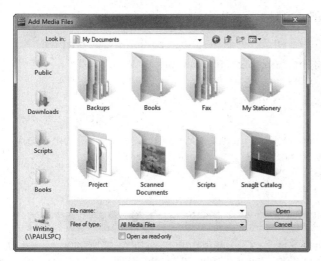

FIGURE 9.11   A dialog box showing the custom Places bar.

Now follow these steps:

1. Select Edit, New, Key, type **comdlg32, and press Enter.**
2. Select Edit, New, Key, type **Placesbar, and press Enter.**
3. Select Edit, New, String Value, type **Place0, and press Enter.**
4. Press Enter to open the new setting, type the folder path, and then click OK.
5. Repeat steps 3 and 4 to add other places (named Place1 through Place4).

> **NOTE**
>
> If you don't use the Places bar at all, you might prefer to hide it to give yourself more room in the old Open and Save As dialog boxes. To do that, open the Local Group Policy Editor and navigate to the User Configuration, Administrative Templates, Windows Components, Windows Explorer, Common Open File Dialog branch. Double-click the Hide the Common Dialog Places Bar, click Enabled, and then click OK.

Increasing the Size of the Recent Documents List

In Chapter 5, "Customizing the Start Menu and Taskbar," I showed you how to customize the Windows 7 Start menu to include the Recent Items menu. Clicking Recent Items displays a list of the 15 documents you worked on most recently. If you find that a document you need often doesn't appear on this list, even though you did use it recently, it's likely that 15 documents isn't enough for you. In that case, you can use a group policy to configure Windows 7 to display a higher number of recent documents.

▶ To learn how to add Recent Items to the Start menu, **see** "Streamlining the Start Menu by Converting Links to Menus," **p. 96.**

Here are the steps to follow to customize the size of the Recent Items list:

1. Open the Local Group Policy Editor window, as described earlier in this chapter.
2. Navigate to the User Configuration, Administrative Templates, Windows Components, Windows Explorer branch.
3. Double-click the Maximum Number of Recent Documents policy.
4. Click Enabled.
5. Use the Maximum Number of Recent Documents spin box to specify the number of documents you want Windows 7 to display.
6. Click OK.

NOTE

You can specify a value between 1 and 9,999 (!) in the Maximum Number of Recent Documents spin box. If you specify more documents than can fit vertically on your screen, Windows 7 adds scroll buttons to the top and bottom of the My Recent Documents list.

Enabling the Shutdown Event Tracker

When you select Start, Shut Down, Windows 7 proceeds to shut down without any more input from you (unless any running programs have documents with unsaved changes). That's usually a good thing, but you might want to keep track of why you shut down or restart Windows 7, or why the system itself initiates a shutdown or restart. To do that, you can enable a feature called Shutdown Event Tracker. With this feature, you can document the shutdown event by specifying whether it is planned or unplanned, selecting a reason for the shutdown, and adding a comment that describes the shutdown.

Here are the steps to follow to use a group policy to enable the Shutdown Event Tracker feature:

1. Open the Local Group Policy Editor window, as described earlier in this chapter.
2. Navigate to the Computer Configuration, Administrative Templates, System branch.
3. Double-click the Display Shutdown Event Tracker policy.
4. Click Enabled.
5. In the Shutdown Event Tracker Should Be Displayed list, select Always.
6. Click OK.

Now when you select Start, Shut Down, you see the Shut Down Windows dialog box shown in Figure 9.12. The Shutdown Event Tracker group gives you three new controls to operate:

FIGURE 9.12 The Shut Down Windows dialog box appears with the Shutdown Event Tracker feature enabled.

▶ **Planned**—Leave this check box activated if this is a planned shutdown. If you didn't plan on shutting down Windows 7 (for example, you're restarting because a program has crashed or because the system appears unstable), deactivate this check box.

▶ **Option**—Use this list to select the reason for the shutdown. (Note that the items you see in this list change depending on the state of the Planned check box.)

▶ **Comment**—Use this text box to describe the shutdown event. If you choose either Other (Planned) or Other (Unplanned) in the Option list, you must add a comment to enable the OK button; for all other items in the Option list, the comment text is optional.

To enable the Shutdown Event Tracker on systems without the Local Group Policy Editor, open the Registry Editor and dig down to the following key:

`HKLM\Software\Policies\Microsoft\Windows NT\Reliability`

Change the value of the following two settings to **1**:

`ShutdownReasonOn`
`ShutdownReasonUI`

CHAPTER 10

Configuring the Microsoft Management Console

There are two essential rules to management. One, the customer is always right; and two, they must be punished for their arrogance.

—Scott Adams

The Microsoft Management Console (MMC) is a system administration program that can act as a host application for a variety of tools. The advantage of MMC is that it displays each tool as a *console*, a two-pane view that has a tree-like hierarchy in the left pane (this is called the *tree pane*) and a *taskpad* in the right pane that shows the contents of each branch (this is called the *results pane*). This gives each tool a similar interface, which makes it easier to use the tools. You can also customize the console view in a number of ways, create custom taskpad views, and save a particular set of tools to reuse later. These tools are called *snap-ins* because you can "snap them in" (that is, attach them) as *nodes* to the console root.

This chapter gives you an overview of the MMC and shows you a few techniques for getting the most out of its often-useful tools.

Reviewing the Windows 7 Snap-Ins

When you work with the MMC interface, what you're really doing is editing a Microsoft Common Console Document, a .msc file that stores one or more snap-ins, the console view, and the taskpad view used by each snap-in branch. You learn how to create custom MSC files in this chapter, but you should know that Windows 7 comes with a large number of predefined MSC snap-ins, and I've summarized them in Table 10.1.

TABLE 10.1   The Default Windows 7 Snap-Ins

Snap-In	File	Description
Active X Control	N/A	Launches the Insert ActiveX Control Wizard, which enables you to choose an ActiveX control to display as a node. I haven't been able to find a good use for this one yet!
Authorization Manager	azman.msc	Used by developers to set permissions on applications.
Certificates	certmgr.msc	Enables you to browse the security certificates on your system.
Component Services	comexp.msc	Enables you to view and work with Component Object Model (COM) services.
Computer Management	compmgmt.msc	Contains a number of snap-ins for managing various aspects of Windows 7. You can examine hidden and visible shared folders, set group policies, access Device Manager, manage hard disks, and much more.
Device Manager	devmgmt.msc	Enables you to add and manage your system hardware. See Chapter 22, "Troubleshooting Devices."
Disk Management	diskmgmt.msc	Enables you to view and manage all the disk drives on your system.
Event Viewer	eventvwr.msc	Enables you to view the Windows 7 event logs. See Chapter 7, "Maintaining Your Windows 7 System."
Folder	N/A	Enables you to add a folder node to the root to help you organize your nodes.
Group Policy Object Editor	gpedit.msc	Enables you to work with group policies. See Chapter 9, "Policing Windows 7 with Group Policies."
IP Security Monitor	N/A	Enables you to monitor Internet Protocol (IP) security settings.
IP Security Policy Management	N/A	Enables you to create IP Security (IPSec) policies.

TABLE 10.1   Continued

Snap-In	File	Description
Link to Web Address	N/A	Adds a node that displays the contents of a specified web page.
Local Users and Groups	`lusrmgr.msc`	Enables you to add, modify, and delete user accounts. See Chapter 18, "Setting Up User Security."
NAP Client Configuration	`napclcfg.msc`	Enables you to configure Network Access Protection (NAP) for a computer.
Performance Monitor	`perfmon.msc`	Enables you to monitor one or more performance counters. See Chapter 6, "Tuning Windows 7's Performance."
Print Management	`printmanagement.msc`	Enables you to view and manage either local printers or network print servers.
Resultant Set of Policy	`rsop.msc`	Shows the applied group policies for the current user.
Security Configuration and Analysis	N/A	Enables you to open an existing security database, or build a new security database based on a security template you create using the Security Templates snap-in.
Security Templates	N/A	Enables you to create a security template where you enable and configure one or more security-related policies.
Services	`services.msc`	Enables you to start, stop, enable, and disable services. See Chapter 11, "Controlling Services."
Shared Folders	`fsmgmt.msc`	Enables you to monitor activity on your shared folders. See Chapter 26, "Accessing and Using Your Network."
Task Scheduler	`taskschd.msc`	Enables you to schedule programs, scripts, and other items to run on a schedule.
TPM Management	`tpm.msc`	Enables you to configure a work with Trusted Platform Module (TPM) security devices.
Windows Firewall with Advanced Security	`wf.msc`	Presents an advanced Windows Firewall interface.
WMI Control	`wmimgmt.msc`	Enables you to configure properties related to Windows Management Instrumentation. See Chapter 30, "Programming the Windows Scripting Host."

10

Launching the MMC

To get the MMC onscreen, you have two choices:

▶ To start with a blank console, select Start, type **mmc**, and then press Enter.

▶ To start with an existing snap-in, select Start, type the name of the .msc file you want to load (see Table 10.1), and then press Enter.

Figure 10.1 shows a blank MMC window. I show you how to add snap-ins to the console in the next section.

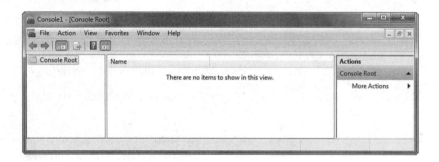

FIGURE 10.1   The Microsoft Management Console ready for customizing.

Adding a Snap-In

You start building your console file by adding one or more snap-ins to the console root, which is the top-level MMC container. (Even if you loaded the MMC by launching an existing snap-in, you can still add more snap-ins to the console.) Here are the steps to follow:

1. Select File, Add/Remove Snap-In (or press Ctrl+M). The MMC displays the Add or Remove Snap-ins dialog box, shown in Figure 10.2.
2. In the Available Snap-ins list, select the snap-in you want to use.
3. Click Add.

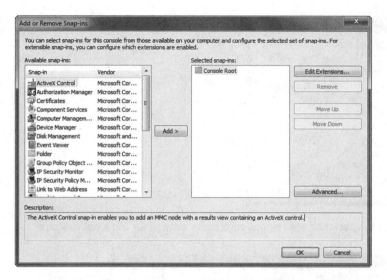

FIGURE 10.2   You use the Add or Remove Snap-ins dialog box to populate the MMC with snap-in nodes.

TIP

You can help organize your snap-ins by adding subfolders to the console root. In the list of snap-ins, select Folder and then click Add. When you return to the MMC, right-click the new subfolder and then click Rename to give the subfolder a useful name. To add a snap-in inside this subfolder, select File, Add/Remove Snap-In (or press Ctrl+M) to open the Add/Remove Snap-In dialog box. Click Advanced, activate the Allow Changing the Parent Snap-in check box, and then click OK. In the new Parent Snap-In list that appears, choose the subfolder you added. See Figure 10.4, later in this chapter, for some example subfolders.

---

4. If the snap-in can work with remote computers, you see a dialog box similar to the one shown in Figure 10.3. To have the snap-in manage a remote machine, select Another Computer, type the computer name in the text box, and then click Finish.

   ▶ To use a snap-in with a remote computer, that machine must have remote administration enabled; **see** "Configuring a Network Computer for Remote Administration," **p. 605**.

5. Repeat steps 2–4 to add other snap-ins to the console.

6. Click OK.

Figure 10.4 shows the MMC with a custom console consisting of several snap-ins and subfolders.

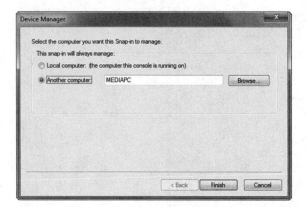

FIGURE 10.3   Some snap-ins can manage remote computers as well as the local machine.

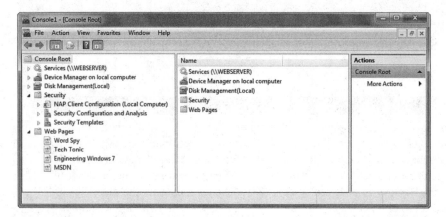

FIGURE 10.4   The MMC with a custom console.

NOTE

In Figure 10.4, the items in the Web Pages subfolder are based on the Link to Web Address snap-in, which is a special snap-in that displays the current version of whatever web page you specify. When you add the snap-in, the MMC runs the Link to Web Address Wizard. Type the web page address (either an Internet URL or a path to a local or network page), click Next, type a name for the snap-in, and then click Finish.

Saving a Console

If you think you want to reuse your custom console later on, you should save it to a .msc file. Here are the steps to follow:

1. Select File, Save (or press Ctrl+S) to open the Save As dialog box.

2. Type a filename for the console.

3. Select a location for the console file.

TIP

By default, MMC assumes you want to save your console file in the Administrative Tools folder. This enables you to launch the console from the Start menu if you've Administrative Tools as a menu, as described in Chapter 5, "Customizing the Start Menu and Taskbar." (Select Start, All Programs, Administrative Tools, and then click the console name.) However, if you want to be able to launch your console file from the Start menu's Search box (or the Run dialog box), you should save it in the %SystemRoot%\System32 folder, along with the predefined snap-ins.

▶ **See** "Streamlining the Start Menu by Converting Links to Menus," **p. 96**.

4. Click Save.

Creating a Custom Taskpad View

A *taskpad view* is a custom configuration of the MMC results (right) pane for a given snap-in. By default, the results pane shows a list of the snap-in's contents—for example, the list of categories and devices in the Device Manager snap-in and the list of installed services in the Services snap-in. However, you can customize this view with one or more tasks that run commands defined by the snap-in, or any program or script that you specify. You can also control the size of the list, whether the list is displayed horizontally or vertically in the results pane, and more.

Here are the steps to follow to create a custom taskpad view:

1. Select a snap-in in the tree pane, as follows:

   ▶ If you want to apply the taskpad view to a specific snap-in, select that snap-in.

   ▶ If you want to apply the taskpad view to a group of snap-ins that use the same snap-in type, specify one snap-in from the group. For example, if you want to customize all the folders, select any folder (such as the Console Root folder); similarly, if you want to customize all the Link to Web Address snap-ins, select one of them.

2. Select Action, New Taskpad View to launch the New Taskpad View Wizard.

3. Click Next to open the Taskpad Style dialog box, shown in Figure 10.5.

10

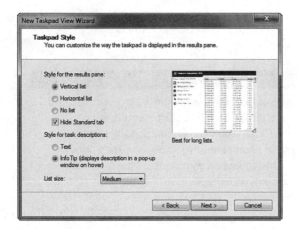

FIGURE 10.5   Use the New Taskpad View Wizard to create your custom taskpad view.

4. Use the following controls to set up the style of taskpad you want:

▶ **Style for Results Pane**—Select an option for displaying the snap-in's results: Vertical List (this is best for lists with a large number of items), Horizontal List (this is best for web pages or lists with a large number of columns), or No List (choose this option if you want only tasks to appear in the results pane).

▶ **Hide Standard Tab**—After you create the new taskpad view, the MMC displays two tabs in the results pane: The Extended tab shows your custom taskpad view, and the Standard tab shows the default view. To keep the option of displaying the default view, deactivate the Hide Standard Tab dialog box.

▶ **Style for Task Descriptions**—When you add descriptions for your tasks later on, you can have the MMC display each description either as text below the task link or as an InfoTip that appears when you hover the mouse over the task link.

▶ **List Size**—Choose the size of the list: Small (good if you add lots of tasks), Medium (this is the default), or Large (good if you have few or no tasks).

5. Click Next. The Taskpad Reuse dialog box appears.

6. The wizard assumes you want to apply the new taskpad view to all snap-ins of the same type. If you only want to apply the taskpad view to the current snap-in, select the Selected Tree Item option.

7. Click Next. The Name and Description dialog box appears.

8. Type a name and optional description for the taskpad view, and then click Next. The final wizard dialog box appears.

9. If you don't want to add tasks to the new view, deactivate the Add New Tasks to This Taskpad After the Wizard Closes check box.

10. Click Finish. If you elected to add tasks to the view, the New Task Wizard appears.

11. Click Next. The Command Type dialog box appears.

12. Select one of the following command types:

   ▶ **Menu Command**—Select this option to create a task that runs an MMC or snap-in menu command.

   ▶ **Shell Command**—Select this option to create a task that runs a program, script, or batch file.

   ▶ **Navigation**—Select this option to create a task that takes you to another snap-in that's in your MMC Favorites list.

> **NOTE**
>
> To add a snap-in to the MMC Favorites list, select the snap-in in the tree pane and then select Favorites, Add to Favorites.

13. Click Next.

14. How you proceed from here depends on the command type you selected in step 12:

   ▶ **Menu Command**—In the Menu Command dialog box, first select an item from the Command Source list: Choose Item Listed in the Results Pane to apply the command to whatever item is currently selected in the results pane; choose Node in the Tree to select a command based on an item in the MMC tree pane.

   ▶ **Shell Command**—In the Command Line dialog box, use the Command text box to specify the path to the program executable, script, or batch file that you want the task to run. You can also specify startup Parameters, the Start In folder, and a Run window type.

   ▶ **Navigation**—In the Navigation dialog box, select the items from the MMC Favorites list.

15. Click Next. The Name and Description dialog box appears.

16. Edit the task name and description, and then click Next. The Task Icon dialog box appears, as shown in Figure 10.6.

17. Click Next. The final New Task Wizard dialog box appears.

18. If you want to add more tasks, activate the When I Click Finish, Run This Wizard Again check box.

19. Click Finish.

20. If you elected to add more tasks, repeat steps 11–19, as needed.

Figure 10.7 shows the MMC with a custom taskpad view applied to a Link to Web Address snap-in.

> **NOTE**
>
> To make changes to a custom taskpad view, right-click the snap-in and then click Edit Taskpad View.

10

FIGURE 10.6   Use the Task Icon dialog box to choose an icon to display with your task.

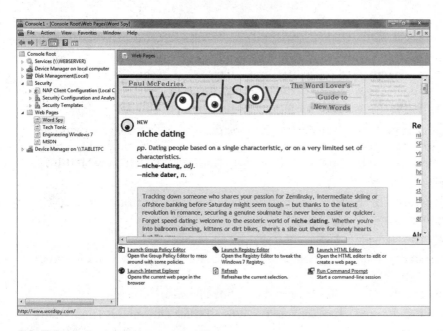

FIGURE 10.7   A custom taskpad view.

Controlling Snap-Ins with Group Policies

If you share Windows 7 with other people, you can control which snap-ins they're allowed to use, and you can even prevent users from adding snap-ins to the MMC.

The latter is the simpler of the two options, so let's begin with that. The MMC has an *author mode* that enables you to add snap-ins to it. If you prevent the MMC from entering author mode, you prevent users from adding snap-ins. You can do this using a group policy. Note, too, that this policy also prevents users from entering author mode for those snap-ins that can be opened directly (from the Start menu Search box, from the Run dialog box, from the command line, from Administrative Tools, and so on). Here are the steps to follow:

1. Open the Local Group Policy Editor, as described in Chapter 9.
2. Navigate to the User Configuration, Administrative Templates, Windows Components, Microsoft Management Console branch.
3. Double-click the Restrict the User from Entering Author Mode policy.
4. Activate the Enabled option.
5. Click OK.

Rather than blocking off the MMC entirely, you might prefer to allow users access only to specific snap-ins. Here are the steps to follow:

1. Open the Local Group Policy Editor, as described in Chapter 9.
2. Navigate to the User Configuration, Administrative Templates, Windows Components, Microsoft Management Console branch.
3. Double-click the Restrict Users to the Explicitly Permitted List of Snap-Ins policy.
4. Activate the Enabled option.
5. Click OK.
6. Navigate to the User Configuration, Administrative Templates, Windows Components, Microsoft Management Console, Restricted/Permitted Snap-Ins branch.
7. Double-click a snap-in that you want users to access.
8. Activate the Enabled option.
9. Click OK.
10. Repeat steps 7–9 for each snap-in that you want users to access.

10

CHAPTER 11

Controlling Services

O who knows what slumbers in the background of the times?

—Johann Christoph Friedrich von Schiller

Windows 7 comes with a long list of programs called *services* that operate behind the scenes and perform essential tasks either on their own or in support of other programs or Windows features. These services are background routines that enable the system to perform tasks such as logging on to the network, managing disks, collecting performance data, and writing event logs. Windows 7 comes with more than 150 installed services, which is a Windows record.

You won't have to interact with services very often, but when they do come up, you'll be glad to have this chapter's tools in your Windows 7 toolbox. For example, although services usually operate behind the scenes, you may need to pause, stop, and start services, as well as configure how service loads at startup. The first few sections in this chapter show you the various methods you can use to perform these service tasks.

Controlling Services with the Services Snap-In

The standard interface for the Windows 7 services is the Services snap-in, which you can load by using any of the following techniques:

▶ Select Start, type **services.msc**, and press Enter.

▶ Select Start, Control Panel, All Control Panel Items, Administrative Tools, Services.

▶ Select Start, right-click Computer, click Manage, and then select the Services and Applications, Services branch.

The Services snap-in that appears displays a list of the installed services, and for each service, it displays the name of the service and a brief description, the current status of the service (Started, Paused, or blank for a stopped service), the service's startup type (such as Automatic or Manual), and the name of the system account that the service uses to logs on at startup. When you select a service, the Extended tab of the taskpad view shows the service name and description and offers links to control the service status (such as Start, Stop, or Restart). Figure 11.1 shows an example.

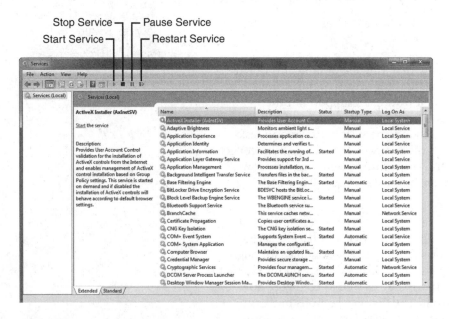

FIGURE 11.1 You can use the Services snap-in to control the Windows 7 services.

To change the status of a service, select it and then use one of the following techniques:

▶ To start a stopped service, either click the Start link in the taskpad or click the Start Service toolbar button.

▶ To stop a running service, either click the Stop link in the taskpad or click the Stop Service toolbar button.

▶ To pause a running service, either click the Pause link in the taskpad or click the Start Service toolbar button. (Note that only a few services support the Pause task.)

▶ To resume a paused service, either click the Restart link in the taskpad or click the Restart Service toolbar button.

NOTE

If a service is started but it has no Stop link and the Stop toolbar button is disabled, it means the service is essential to Windows 7 and can't be stopped. Examples of essential services include DCOM Server Process Launcher, Group Policy Client, Plug and Play, Remote Procedure Call (RPC), and Security Accounts Manager.

CAUTION

It's possible that a service might be dependent on one or more other services, and if those services aren't running, the dependent service will not work properly. If you stop a service that has dependent services, Windows 7 also stops the dependents. However, when you restart the main service, Windows 7 may not start the dependent services as well. You need to start those services by hand. To see which services depend on a particular service, double-click that service to open its property sheet, and then display the Dependencies tab.

To change the way a service starts when you boot Windows 7, follow these steps:

1. Double-click the service you want to work with to open its property sheet. Figure 11.2 shows an example.

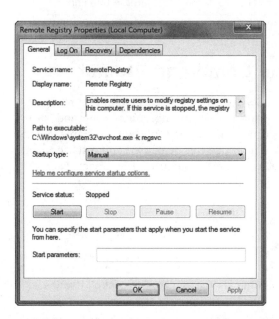

FIGURE 11.2   You use a service's property sheet to control its startup type.

2. In the General tab, use the Startup Type list to select one of the following types:

  ▶ **Automatic**—The service starts automatically when Windows 7 boots. The service is started before the logon screen appears.

  ▶ **Automatic (Delayed Start)**—The service starts automatically when Windows 7 boots. The service does not start until you log on.

  ▶ **Manual**—The service does not start when Windows 7 boots. You must start the service yourself.

  ▶ **Disabled**—The service does not start when Windows 7 boots, and you can't start the service manually.

3. Click OK.

NOTE

If the Startup Type list is disabled, it means the service is essential to Windows 7 and must be started automatically when the system boots.

TIP

If you make changes to service startup types and you find your system is unstable or causing problems, the best thing to do is return each service to its default startup type. If you're not sure of the default for a service, see Table 11.3, later in this chapter.

Controlling Services at the Command Prompt

If you regularly stop and start certain services, loading the Services snap-in and manually stopping and then restarting each service can be time-consuming. A better method is to take advantage of the NET STOP and NET START command-line tools, which enable you to stop and start any service that isn't disabled. If a service can be paused and restarted, you can also use the NET PAUSE and NET CONTINUE commands to control the service. Each of these commands uses the same syntax:

```
NET STOP Service
NET START Service
NET PAUSE Service
NET CONTINUE Service
```

    Service   The name of the service you want to control. Use the same value that appears in the Name column of the Services snap-in. If the name contains a space, surround the name with quotation marks.

Here are some examples:

```
net start Telephony
net stop "Disk Defragmenter"
net pause "World Wide Web Publishing Service"
net continue "Windows Time"
```

You can combine multiple commands in a batch file to easily control several services with a single task.

TIP

To see a list of the currently running services, open a command-line session and enter the command **net start** without the *Service* parameter.

Controlling Services with a Script

If you want to automate service control, but you want to also control the startup type, you need to go beyond the command line and create scripts that manage your services. Windows Management Instrumentation (WMI) has a class called `Win32_Service` that represents a Windows service. You can return an instance of this class to work with a specific service on Windows 7. After you have the service object, you can query its current status with the `State` property; determine whether the service is running with the `Started` property; and return the service's startup type with the `StartMode` property. You can also change the service state using the `StartService`, `StopService`, `PauseService`, and `ResumeService` methods.

▶ For the details on WMI scripting, **see** "Programming the Windows Management Instrumentation Service," **p. 695**.

Listing 11.1 presents a script that uses most of these properties and methods.

NOTE

You can find this script on my website at www.mcfedries.com/Windows7Unleashed.

LISTING 11.1 A WMI Script That Toggles a Service's State Between Started and Stopped

```
Option Explicit
Dim strComputer, strServiceName, intReturn
Dim objWMI, objServices, objService
'
' Get the WMI service
'
```

LISTING 11.1   Continued

```
strComputer = "localhost"
Set objWMI = GetObject("winmgmts:{impersonationLevel=impersonate}!\\" & _
    strComputer & "\root\cimv2")
'
' Specify the service name
'
strServiceName = "Remote Registry"
'
' Get the service instance
'
Set objServices = objWMI.ExecQuery("SELECT * FROM Win32_Service " & _
                    "WHERE DisplayName = '" & strServiceName & "'")
For Each objService In objServices
    '
    ' Save the service name
    '
    strServiceName = objService.DisplayName
    '
    ' Is the service started?
    '
    If objService.Started Then
        '
        ' Can it be stopped?
        '
        If objService.AcceptStop Then
            '
            ' Attempt to stop the service
            '
            intReturn = objService.StopService
            '
            ' Check the return value
            '
            If intReturn <> 0 Then
                '
                ' Display the error message
                '
                WScript.Echo "ERROR: The " & strServiceName & " service " & _
                            "failed to stop. The return code is " & intReturn
            Else
                '
                ' Display the current state
                '
                WScript.Echo "The " & strServiceName & " service is now " & _
                            objService.State
```

LISTING 11.1   Continued

```
            End If
        Else
            '
            ' Display the error message
            '
            WScript.Echo "ERROR: The " & strServiceName & " service " & _
                         "cannot be stopped."
        End If
    Else
        '
        ' Attempt to start the service
        '
        intReturn = objService.StartService
        '
        ' Check the return value
        '
        If intReturn <> 0 Then
            '
            ' Display the error message
            '
            WScript.Echo "ERROR: The " & strServiceName & " service " & _
                         "failed to start. The return code is " & intReturn
        Else
            '
            ' Display the current state
            '
            WScript.Echo "The " & strServiceName & " service is now " & _
                         objService.State
        End If
    End If
Next
'
' Release the objects
'
Set objWMI = Nothing
Set objServices = Nothing
Set objService = Nothing
```

This script gets the WMI service object and uses its ExecQuery method to return an instance of the Win32_Service class by using the WHERE clause to look for a specific service name. That name was earlier stored in the strServiceName variable. In the For Each...Next loop, the script first checks to see whether the service is currently started by checking its Started property:

▶ If the Started property returns True, the service is running, so we want to stop it. The script then checks the service's AcceptStop property, which returns False for essential Windows 7 services that can't be stopped. In this case, the script returns an error message. If AcceptStop returns True, the script attempts to stop the service by running the StopService method.

▶ If the Started property returns False, the service is stopped, so we want to start it. The script attempts to start the service by running the StartService method.

The StopService and StartService methods generate the return codes shown in Table 11.2.

TABLE 11.2   Return Codes Generated by the **StartService** and **StopService** Methods

Return Code	Description
0	Success
1	Not supported
2	Access denied
3	Dependent services running
4	Invalid service control
5	Service cannot accept control
6	Service not active
7	Service request timeout
8	Unknown failure
9	Path not found
10	Service already stopped
11	Service database locked
12	Service dependency deleted
13	Service dependency failure
14	Service disabled
15	Service logon failed
16	Service marked for deletion
17	Service no thread
18	Status circular dependency
19	Status — duplicate name
20	Status — invalid name
21	Status — invalid parameter
22	Status — invalid service account
23	Status — service exists
24	Service already paused

For both the StopService and StartService methods, the script stores the return code in the intReturn variable and then checks to see whether it's a number other than 0. If so, the script displays an error message that includes the return code; otherwise, the script displays the new state of the service (as given by the State property).

Disable Services for Faster Performance

Because services are software, they run in memory and so take up a small chunk of your system's resources. Any one service doesn't affect performance all that much, but load up a bunch of them and your PC slows down noticeably.

Windows understands this, so many services don't run automatically at startup. Instead, the services run only when you or a program requests them. So you can improve Windows performance by doing two things:

▶ Prevent Windows from automatically starting some services at boot time.

▶ Prevent Windows from starting other services that you don't need.

In both cases, you do this by disabling those services that you don't (or *think* you don't) need. First, here are the general steps to follow to disable a service:

1. Select Start, type **services.msc**, and then press Enter. The Services window appears.
2. Double-click the service you want to disable.
3. In the General tab, drop down the Startup Type list and select Disabled.
4. Click OK.

That's easy enough, but the hard part is knowing which services are okay to disable. To help out, Table 11.3 presents a list of the Windows services that you may be able to disable. None of these services are required by other services, so disabling any of these won't break something else. However, I suggest caution: Disable one at a time, reboot, and make sure Windows seems to be operating normally. Also, if your PC is part of a corporate network, you might want to get permission or guidance from your IT department before disabling any services.

NOTE

Whether you see many of the services in Table 11.3 depends on which version of Windows you're running. For example, you don't see many of these services if you're using Windows 7 Home Basic or Windows 7 Home Premium. Also, many third-party programs add their own services, so your version of Windows 7 may many services not listed here.

TABLE 11.3   Windows Services You Might Consider Disabling

Service	Startup Type	Disable If...
Adaptive Brightness	Manual	Your monitor or notebook PC doesn't contain a brightness sensor or you don't want your screen's brightness adjusted automatically.
AppID Service	Manual	You don't deploy application control policies.
Application Experience	Manual	You don't run any programs that aren't designed to work with either Windows Vista or Windows 7.
Application Layer Gateway Service	Manual	You don't use Internet Connection Sharing.
Application Management	Manual	You don't deploy software using Group Policy.
BitLocker Drive Encryption Service	Manual	You don't use BitLocker to encrypt drives.
Block Level Backup Engine Service	Manual	You don't use Windows 7's built-in Backup service.
BranchCache	Manual	You don't use Windows 7 in a corporate setting that has multiple remote offices (branches).
Certificate Propagation	Manual	You don't use smart cards.
Computer Browser	Automatic	You're willing to refresh the Network window by hand (because this service looks for network computers automatically).
Desktop Window Manager Session Manager	Automatic	You don't use Windows 7's Aero theme.
Diagnostic Policy Service	Automatic	You don't need Windows components to access the built-in diagnostic services (problem detection and troubleshooting).
Diagnostic Service Host	Manual	Same as above.
Diagnostic System Host	Manual	Ditto.
Distributed Transaction Coordinator	Manual	You're not running software that requires transaction processing (which is restricted to big-time corporate services such as transactional databases).
Fax	Manual	You don't use your PC for faxing.
Handsfree Headset Service	Automatic	You don't use a Bluetooth headset with Windows 7.
Health Key and Certificate Management	Manual	You don't use any software that requires X.509 cryptographic certificates.
HomeGroup Listener	Manual	You don't use Windows 7's HomeGroup feature to share files over your network.

TABLE 11.3   Continued

Service	Startup Type	Disable If...
HomeGroup Provider	Manual	Ditto.
Human Interface Device Access	Manual	Your keyboards, remote controls, and other input devices have their own drivers to handle their special function buttons (such as the Copy button on a scanner).
IKE and AuthIP IPsec Keying Modules	Automatic	You don't use high-end Internet security protocols.
Internet Connection Sharing (ICS)	Disabled	You don't allow other computers to share your Internet connection.
IP Helper	Automatic	You don't use the latest version of the Internet Protocol (IPv6), which is almost certainly the case (IPv4 still being the standard).
IPsec Policy Agent	Automatic	You don't implement any group policies that require Internet Protocol security (IPSec).
Jumpstart Wifi Protected Setup	Manual	None of your networking devices use WiFi Protected Setup.
KtmRm for Distributed Transaction Coordinator	Automatic	You don't use databases or other resources that require the Microsoft Distributed Transaction Coordinator (which is needed only by corporate systems).
Link-Layer Topology Discovery Mapper	Manual	You never use Window 7's Network Map feature.
Microsoft iSCSI Initiator Service	Manual	You don't use any remote SCSI devices.
Microsoft Software Shadow Copy Provider	Manual	You don't need to access the volume shadow copies (essentially, file and folder snapshots) to revert objects to a previous state.
Net.Tcp Port Sharing Service	Disabled	You don't (or your applications don't) need to share TCP ports.
Netlogon	Manual	You don't use a domain controller.
Network Access Protection Agent	Manual	Your network doesn't have a server that implements Network Access Protection.
Offline Files	Automatic	You never use network files while not connected to the network.
Peer Name Resolution Protocol	Manual	You don't use collaborative applications such as Windows Meeting Space.

11

TABLE 11.3   Continued

Service	Startup Type	Disable If...
Peer Networking Grouping	Manual	Same as above.
Peer Networking Identity Manager	Manual	Ditto.
Performance Logs and Alerts	Manual	You don't use performance logs and alerts.
PnP-X IP Bus Enumerator	Manual	You don't mind that Windows doesn't show external network devices automatically.
PNRP Machine Name Publication Service	Manual	You don't run any programs that require the Peer Name Resolution Protocol.
Pong Service for Wireless USB	Manual	You don't use any wireless USB devices.
Print Spooler	Automatic	You don't print.
Problem Reports and Solutions Control Panel Support	Manual	You don't use Vista's Problem Reports and Solutions feature.
Program Compatibility Assistant Service	Automatic	You don't run applications using compatibility mode.
Quality Windows Audio Video Experience	Manual	You don't stream audio or video on your home network.
Remote Registry	Manual	You don't need to allow network computers to connect to your PC's Registry.
Security Center	Automatic	You don't need to use the Security Center to monitor your PC's security status.
Sensors MTP Monitor Service	Manual	You don't use any devices that use Media Transfer Protocol (MTP) sensors to provide sensor data to your PC.
Smart Card	Manual	You don't use smart cards.
Smart Card Removal Policy	Manual	Same as above.
SNMP Trap	Manual	Your network doesn't use any Simple Network Management Protocol (SNMP) programs.
SuperFetch	Automatic	You don't want Windows to use the SuperFetch cache to improve performance (as described in Chapter 6, "Tuning Windows 7's Performance").

▶   **See** "Configuring the Prefetcher," **p. 123**.

Service	Startup Type	Disable If...
Tablet PC Input Service	Automatic	Your computer isn't a TabletPC.
Task Scheduler	Automatic	You don't use Task Scheduler.

Service	Startup Type	Disable If...
Themes	Automatic	You don't use themes to customize your PC.
TPM Base Services	Manual	You don't use Vista's BitLocker drive encryption.
Windows Backup	Manual	You don't use Windows Backup.
Windows Biometric Service	Manual	You don't use any biometric devices (such as a fingerprint reader).
Windows CardSpace	Manual	You don't use a CardSpace digital ID.
Windows Connect Now - Config Registrar	Manual	None of your networking devices use WiFi Protected Setup.
Windows Defender	Automatic	You use an antispyware program other than Windows Defender.
Windows Error Reporting Service	Automatic	You don't send error data to Microsoft.
Windows Firewall	Automatic	You use a hardware firewall or a software firewall other than Windows Firewall.
Windows Media Center Extender Service	Disabled	You don't use a Media Center Extender device.
Windows Media Center Receiver Service	Manual	You don't use Windows to play TV or radio signals.
Windows Media Center Scheduler Service	Manual	You don't use Media Center to record TV shows.
Windows Media Center Service Launcher	Automatic	You've disabled the previous two services. (This service launches the previous two services at startup if your computer has a TV tuner card.)
Windows Media Player Network Sharing Service	Manual	You don't share your Media Player library.
Windows Search	Automatic	You don't use Vista's desktop search engine (or you use another, such as Google Desktop Search).
Windows Time	Manual	You don't use Windows 7's time synchronization feature.
WMI Performance Adapter	Manual	You don't have any network programs that use Windows Management Instrumentation (WMI) to track performance data.

11

Make Windows Shut Down Services Faster

If it seems to take Windows forever to shut down, the culprit might be all those services that it has running because Windows has to shut down each service one by one before it can shut down the PC. In each case, Windows waits a certain amount of time for the service to close, and if it hasn't closed in that time, Windows kills the service. It's that waiting for services to shut themselves down that can really bring the shutdown process to its knees.

However, most services shut down as soon as they get the command from Windows. So although it's polite of Windows to give some services a bit of extra time, it's really wasted time because in most cases Windows is just going to have to kill those slow services anyway. So in that case, you should configure Windows 7 to tell it to kill services faster. Here's how:

1. Select Start, type **regedit**, and then press Enter. The Registry Editor appears.
2. Navigate to the following key:

    HKLM\SYSTEM\CurrentControlSet\Control

3. Double-click the WaitToKillServiceTimeout setting.
4. Reduce the value from 20000 to **1000.**
5. Click OK.

TIP

You can also reduce the amount of time that Windows 7 waits before killing running applications at shutdown. In the Registry Editor, navigate to the following key:

    HKCU\Control Panel\Desktop

Double-click the WaitToKillAppTimeout setting. (If you don't see this setting, select Edit, New, String Value, type **WaitToKillAppTimeout**, and click OK.) Change the value to 5000, and click OK.

Reset a Broken Service

If Windows 7 is acting erratically (or, I should say, if it's acting more erratically than usual), the problem could be a service that's somehow gotten corrupted. How can you tell? The most obvious clue is an error message that tells you a particular service isn't running or couldn't start. You can also check the Event Viewer for service errors. Finally, if a particular feature of Windows 7 is acting funny and you know that a service is associated with that feature, you might suspect that service is causing the trouble.

To fix the problem (hopefully!), you can reset the broken service, a procedure that involves the following four general steps:

1. Find out the name of the service that is (or that you suspect is) broken.
2. Delete the service.

3. Load a backup copy of the system hive into the Registry.

4. Copy the service from the backup hive copy to service's actual Registry location.

To begin, follow these steps to determine the name of the service:

1. Select Start, type **services.msc**, and press Enter. Windows 7 opens the Services snap-in.

2. Double-click the service you want to reset.

3. In the General tab, locate the Service Name value (see Figure 11.3) and make a note of it.

4. Click OK.

FIGURE 11.3   Open the service you want to reset and make note of the Service Name value.

Next, follow these steps to delete the service:

1. Select Start, type **command**, right-click Command Prompt in the results, click Run as Administrator, and then enter your User Account Control credentials. Windows 7 opens an Administrator Command Prompt session.

2. Type the following (where *service* is the service name that you noted in the previous set of steps):

```
sc delete service
```

3. Press Enter. Windows 7 attempts to delete the service.

If the deletion works properly, you see the following message:

```
[SC] DeleteService SUCCESS
```

Note that you need the Command Prompt again a bit later, so leave the session open for now.

NOTE

If the deletion isn't successful, double-check the service name. If you're sure you have the name right, try deleting the service using the Registry Editor, instead. Open the Registry Editor, navigate to the HKLM\System\CurrentControlSet\Services key, and then locate the service. Right-click the service and then click Delete.

Now follow these steps to load a fresh copy of the system hive:

1. Select Start, type **regedit**, press Enter, and then enter your User Account Control credentials to open the Registry Editor.

2. Select the HKEY_LOCAL_MACHINE key.

3. Select File, Load Hive to open the Load Hive dialog box.

4. Open the system backup file:

    %SystemRoot%\system32\config\RegBack\SYSTEM.OLD

5. Click Open. The Registry Editor prompts you for a key name.

6. Type **reset** and click OK.

You now have the backup copy of the system hive loaded into HKLM\reset key. Now you complete the operation by copying the service from this backup:

1. Return to the Command Prompt.

2. Type the following (where *service* is the service name that you noted in the first set of steps):

    ```
    reg copy
    hklm\reset\controlset001\services\service hklm\system\currentcontrolset\servi
    ➥ces\service /s /f
    ```

3. Press Enter. Windows 7 copies the backup version of the service to the original Registry location.

4. Reboot your PC to put the change into effect.

CHAPTER 12

Tweaking the Windows 7 Registry

It is almost everywhere the case that soon after it is begotten the greater part of human wisdom is laid to rest in repositories.

—G. C. Lichtenberg

When you change the desktop background using Control Panel's Personalization window, the next time you start your computer, how does Windows 7 know which image or color you selected? If you change your video display driver, how does Windows 7 know to use that driver at startup and not the original driver loaded during setup? In other words, how does Windows 7 remember the various settings and options either that you've selected yourself or that are appropriate for your system?

The secret to Windows 7's prodigious memory is the Registry. The Registry is a central repository Windows 7 uses to store anything and everything that applies to the configuration of your system. This includes all the following:

▶ Information about all the hardware installed on your computer

▶ The resources those devices use

▶ A list of the device drivers that Windows 7 loads at startup

▶ Settings that Windows 7 uses internally

▶ File type data that associates a particular type of file with a specific application

▶ Backgrounds, color schemes, and other interface customization settings

▸ Other customization settings for things such as the Start menu and the taskbar

▸ Internet and network connections and passwords

▸ Settings for Windows 7 applications such as Windows Explorer and Internet Explorer

▸ Settings and customization options for many third-party applications

It's all stored in one central location, and, thanks to a handy tool called the Registry Editor, it's yours to play with (carefully!) as you see fit, and that's what this chapter is all about.

Firing Up the Registry Editor

All the direct work you do with the Registry happens inside the reasonably friendly confines of a program called the Registry Editor, which enables you to view, modify, add, and delete Registry settings. It also has a search feature to help you find settings and export and import features that enable you to save settings to and from a text file.

To launch the Registry Editor, select Start, type **regedit** into the Search box, and then press Enter. When the User Account Control dialog box shows up, enter your credentials to continue.

Figure 12.1 shows the Registry Editor window that appears. (Note that your Registry Editor window might look different if someone else has used the program previously. Close all the open branches in the left pane to get the view shown in Figure 12.1.)

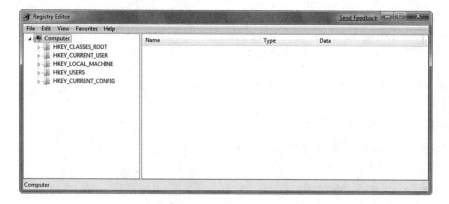

FIGURE 12.1   Run the regedit command to launch the Registry Editor, the program that enables you to work with the Registry's data.

> **CAUTION**
>
> The Registry Editor is arguably the most dangerous tool in the Windows 7 arsenal. The Registry is so crucial to the smooth functioning of Windows 7 that a single imprudent change to a Registry entry can bring your system to its knees. Therefore, now that you have the Registry Editor open, don't start tweaking settings willy-nilly. Instead, read the section titled "Keeping the Registry Safe," later in this chapter, for some advice on protecting this precious and sensitive resource.

Getting to Know the Registry

The Registry may be a dangerous tool, but you can mitigate that danger somewhat by becoming familiar with the layout of the Registry and what it various bits and parts are used for. This will help you avoid sensitive areas and stick to those Registry neighborhoods where it's safe to poke around. The next few sections introduce you to the major parts of the Registry.

Navigating the Keys Pane

The Registry Editor is reminiscent of Windows Explorer, and it works in sort of the same way. The left side of the Registry Editor window is similar to Explorer's Folders pane, except that rather than folders, you see *keys*. For lack of a better phrase, I'll call the left pane the *Keys pane*.

The Keys pane, like Explorer's Folders pane, is organized in a tree-like hierarchy. The five keys that are visible when you first open the Registry Editor are special keys called *handles* (which is why their names all begin with HKEY). These keys are collectively referred to as the Registry's *root keys*. I'll tell you what to expect from each of these keys later (see the section called "Getting to Know the Registry's Root Keys" later in this chapter).

These keys all contain subkeys, which you can display by clicking the arrow to the left of each key, or by highlighting a key and pressing the plus-sign key on your keyboard's numeric keypad. To close a key, click the minus sign or highlight the key and press the minus-sign key on the numeric keypad. Again, this is just like navigating folders in Explorer.

You often have to drill down several levels to get to the key you want. For example, Figure 12.2 shows the Registry Editor after I've opened the HKEY_CURRENT_USER key, and then the Control Panel subkey, and then clicked the Mouse subkey. Notice how the status bar tells you the exact path to the current key, and that this path is structured just like a folder path.

> **NOTE**
>
> To see all the keys properly, you likely will have to increase the size of the Keys pane. To do this, use your mouse to click and drag the split bar to the right. Alternatively, select View, Split, use the right-arrow key to adjust the split bar position, and then press Enter.

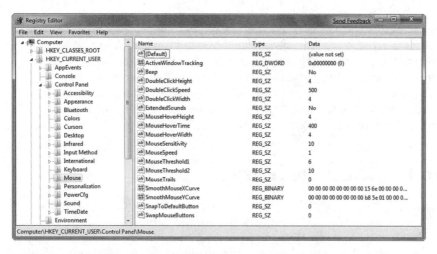

FIGURE 12.2   Open the Registry's keys and subkeys to find the settings you want to work with.

Understanding Registry Settings

If the left side of the Registry Editor window is analogous to Explorer's Folders pane, the right side is analogous to Explorer's Contents pane. In this case, the right side of the Registry Editor window displays the settings contained in each key (so I'll call it the *Settings pane*). The Settings pane is divided into three columns:

▶ **Name**—This column tells you the name of each setting in the currently selected key (analogous to a filename in Explorer).

▶ **Type**—This column tells you the data type of the setting. There are six possible data types:

REG_SZ—This is a string value.

REG_MULTI_SZ—This is a series of strings.

REG_EXPAND_SZ—This is a string value that contains an environment variable name that gets "expanded" into the value of that variable. For example, the %SystemRoot% environment variable holds the folder in which Windows 7 was installed. So, if you see a Registry setting with the value %SystemRoot%\System32\, and Windows 7 is installed in C:\Windows, the setting's expanded value is C:\Windows\System32\.

REG_DWORD—This is a double word value: a 32-bit hexadecimal value arranged as eight digits. For example, 11 hex is 17 decimal, so this number would be represented in DWORD form as 0x00000011 (17). (Why "double word"? A 32-bit value represents four bytes of data, and because a *word* in programming circles is defined as two bytes, a four-byte value is a *double word*.)

REG_QWORD—This is a quadruple word value: a 64-bit hexadecimal value arranged as 16 digits. Note that leading zeros are suppressed for the high 8 digits. Therefore, 11 hex appears as 0x00000011 (17), and 100000000 hex appears as 0x1000000000 (4294967296).

REG_BINARY—This value is a series of hexadecimal digits.

▶ **Data**—This column displays the value of each setting.

Getting to Know the Registry's Root Keys

The root keys are your Registry starting points, so you need to become familiar with what kinds of data each key holds. The next few sections summarize the contents of each key.

HKEY_CLASSES_ROOT

HKEY_CLASSES_ROOT—usually abbreviated as HKCR—contains data related to file extensions and their associated programs, the objects that exist in the Windows 7 system, as well as applications and their automation information. There are also keys related to shortcuts and other interface features.

The top part of this key contains subkeys for various file extensions. You see .bmp for bitmap (Paint) files, .txt for text (Notepad) files, and so on. In each of these subkeys, the Default setting tells you the name of the registered file type associated with the extension. (I discussed file types in more detail in Chapter 3, "Customizing the File System.") For example, the .txt extension is associated with the txtfile file type.

▶ See "Understanding File Types," **p. 46**.

These registered file types appear as subkeys later in the HKEY_CLASSES_ROOT branch, and the Registry keeps track of various settings for each registered file type. In particular, the shell subkey tells you the actions associated with this file type. For example, in the shell\open\command subkey, the Default setting shows the path for the executable file that opens. Figure 12.3 shows this subkey for the txtfile file type.

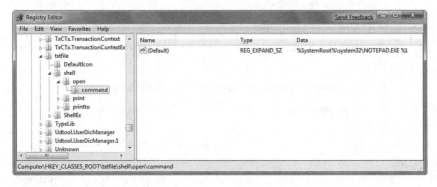

FIGURE 12.3   The registered file type subkeys specify various settings associated with each file type, including its defined actions.

HKEY_CLASSES_ROOT is actually a copy (or an *alias*, as these copied keys are called) of the following HKEY_LOCAL_MACHINE key:

HKEY_LOCAL_MACHINE\Software\Classes

The Registry creates an alias for HKEY_CLASSES_ROOT to make these keys easier for applications to access and to improve compatibility with legacy programs.

HKEY_CURRENT_USER

HKEY_CURRENT_USER—usually abbreviated as HKCU—contains data that applies to the user that's currently logged on. It contains user-specific settings for Control Panel options, network connections, applications, and more. Note that if a user has group policies set on his account, his settings are stored in the HKEY_USERS*sid* subkey (where *sid* is the user's security ID). When that user logs on, these settings are copied to *HKEY_CURRENT_USER*. For all other users, HKEY_CURRENT_USER is built from the user's profile file, ntuser.dat (located in %UserProfile%).

TIP

How do you find out each user's SID? First, open the following Registry key:

HKLM\SOFTWARE\Microsoft\Windows NT\CurrentVersion\ProfileList\

Here you'll find a list of SIDs. The ones that begin S-1-5-21 are the user SIDs. Highlight one of these SIDs and then examine the ProfileImagePath setting, which will be of the form %SystemDrive%\Users*user*, where *user* is the username associated with the SID.

Here's a summary of the most important HKEY_CURRENT_USER subkeys:

AppEvents	Contains sound files that play when particular system events occur (such as maximizing of a window)
Control Panel	Contains settings related to certain Control Panel icons
Keyboard Layout	Contains the keyboard layout as selected via Control Panel's Keyboard icon
Network	Contains settings related to mapped network drives
Software	Contains user-specific settings related to installed applications and Windows

HKEY_LOCAL_MACHINE

HKEY_LOCAL_MACHINE (HKLM) contains non-user-specific configuration data for your system's hardware and applications. You'll use the following three subkeys most often:

Hardware	Contains subkeys related to serial ports and modems, as well as the floating-point processor.

Software	Contains computer-specific settings related to installed applications. The Classes subkey is aliased by HKEY_CLASSES_ROOT. The Microsoft subkey contains settings related to Windows (as well as any other Microsoft products you have installed on your computer).
System	Contains subkeys and settings related to Windows startup.

HKEY_USERS

HKEY_USERS (HKU) contains settings that are similar to those in HKEY_CURRENT_USER. HKEY_USERS is used to store the settings for users with group policies defined, as well as the default settings (in the .DEFAULT subkey) which get mapped to a new user's profile.

HKEY_CURRENT_CONFIG

HKEY_CURRENT_CONFIG (HKCC) contains settings for the current hardware profile. If your machine uses only one hardware profile, HKEY_CURRENT_CONFIG is an alias for HKEY_LOCAL_MACHINE\SYSTEM\ControlSet001. If your machine uses multiple hardware profiles, HKEY_CURRENT_CONFIG is an alias for HKEY_LOCAL_MACHINE\SYSTEM\ControlSet*nnn*, where *nnn* is the numeric identifier of the current hardware profile. This identifier is given by the CurrentConfig setting in the following key:

HKLM\SYSTEM\CurrentControlSet\Control\IDConfigDB

Understanding Hives and Registry Files

The Registry database actually consists of a number of files that contain a subset of the Registry called a *hive*. A hive consists of one or more Registry keys, subkeys, and settings. Each hive is supported by several files that use the extensions listed in Table 12.1.

TABLE 12.1   Extensions Used by Hive Supporting Files

Extension	Descriptions
None	A complete copy of the hive data.
.log1	A log of the changes made to the hive data.
.log, .log2	These files are created during the Windows 7 setup, but remain unchanged as you work with the system.

> **NOTE**
>
> To see all of these files, you must display hidden files on your system. In Windows Explorer, select Organize, Folder and Search Options, select the View tab, and then activate the Show Hidden Files, Folder, and Drives option. While you're here, you can also deactivate the Hide Extensions for Known File Types check box. Click OK.

Table 12.2 shows the supporting files for each hive. (Note that not all of these files might appear on your system.)

TABLE 12.2   Supporting Files Used by Each Hive

Hive	Files
HKLM\BCD00000000	%SystemRoot%\System32\config\BCD-Template
	%SystemRoot%\System32\config\BCD-Template.LOG
HKLM\COMPONENTS	%SystemRoot%\System32\config\COMPONENTS
	%SystemRoot%\System32\config\COMPONENTS.LOG
	%SystemRoot%\System32\config\COMPONENTS.LOG1
	%SystemRoot%\System32\config\COMPONENTS.LOG2
HKLM\SAM	%SystemRoot%\System32\config\SAM
	%SystemRoot%\System32\config\SAM.LOG
	%SystemRoot%\System32\config\SAM.LOG1
	%SystemRoot%\System32\config\SAM.LOG2
HKLM\SECURITY	%SystemRoot%\System32\config\SECURITY
	%SystemRoot%\System32\config\SECURITY.LOG
	%SystemRoot%\System32\config\SECURITY.LOG1
	%SystemRoot%\System32\config\SECURITY.LOG2
HKLM\SOFTWARE	%SystemRoot%\System32\config\SOFTWARE
	%SystemRoot%\System32\config\SOFTWARE.LOG
	%SystemRoot%\System32\config\SOFTWARE.LOG1
	%SystemRoot%\System32\config\SOFTWARE.LOG2
HKLM\SYSTEM	%SystemRoot%\System32\config\SYSTEM
	%SystemRoot%\System32\config\SYSTEM.LOG
	%SystemRoot%\System32\config\SYSTEM.LOG1
	%SystemRoot%\System32\config\SYSTEM.LOG2
HKU\.DEFAULT	%SystemRoot%\System32\config\DEFAULT
	%SystemRoot%\System32\config\DEFAULT.LOG
	%SystemRoot%\System32\config\DEFAULT.LOG1
	%SystemRoot%\System32\config\DEFAULT.LOG2

Also, each user has his or her own hive, which maps to HKEY_CURRENT_USER during logon. The supporting files for each user hive are stored in \Users*user,* where *user* is the username.

In each case, the `ntuser.dat` file contains the hive data, and the `ntuser.dat.log1` file tracks the hive changes. (If a user has group policies set on her account, the user data is stored in an `HKEY_USERS` subkey.)

Keeping the Registry Safe

The sheer wealth of data stored in one place makes the Registry convenient, but it also makes it very precious. If your Registry went missing somehow, or if it got corrupted, Windows 7 simply would not work. With that scary thought in mind, let's take a moment to run through several protective measures. The techniques in this section should ensure that Windows 7 never goes down for the count because you made a mistake while editing the Registry.

Preventing Other Folks from Messing with the Registry

Do you share your computer with other people? How brave! In that case, there's a pretty good chance that you don't want them to have access to the Registry Editor. In Windows 7, User Account Control automatically blocks Standard users unless they know an administrator's password. For other administrators, you can prevent any user from using the Registry Editor by setting a group policy:

1. Select Start, type **gpedit.msc**, and then press Enter.
2. Open the User Configuration, Administrative Templates, System branch.
3. Double-click the Prevent Access to Registry Editing Tools policy.
4. Click Enabled.
5. In the Disable Regedit from Running Silently? list, click Yes.
6. Click OK.

Note that *you* won't be able to use the Registry Editor, either. However, you can overcome that by temporarily disabling this policy prior to running the Registry Editor. Even better, you can run the following script, which toggles the Registry Editor between enabled and disabled:

> **NOTE**
>
> The file that contains the code for this script (`ToggleRegistryEditing.vbs`) is available on my website at www.mcfedries.com/Windows7Unleashed.

```
Set objWshShell = WScript.CreateObject("WScript.Shell")
'
' Get the current setting
'
intDisableRegistryTools = Int(objWshShell.RegRead("HKCU\Software\Microsoft\
➥Windows\CurrentVersion\Policies\System\DisableRegistryTools"))
'
' Toggle the current setting
'
If intDisableRegistryTools = 0 Then
    objWshShell.RegWrite "HKCU\Software\Microsoft\Windows\CurrentVersion\
➥Policies\System\DisableRegistryTools", 2, "REG_DWORD"
    WScript.Echo "The Registry Editor is disabled."
Else
    objWshShell.RegWrite "HKCU\Software\Microsoft\Windows\CurrentVersion\
➥Policies\System\DisableRegistryTools", 0, "REG_DWORD"
    WScript.Echo "The Registry Editor is enabled."
End If
```

Note that you need to run this script as the administrator. I show you how to do this in Chapter 30, "Programming the Windows Scripting Host."

▶ See "Running a Script as the Administrator," **p. 664.**

Backing Up the Registry

Windows 7 maintains what is known as the *system state*: the crucial system files that Windows 7 requires to operate properly. Included in the system state are the files used during system startup, the Windows 7–protected system files, and, naturally, the Registry files. Windows 7's Backup utility has a feature called a system image backup that enables you to easily back up the current system state, so it's probably the most straightforward way to create a backup copy of the Registry should anything go wrong. See Chapter 7, "Maintaining Your Windows 7 System," for the details.

▶ See "Creating a System Image Backup," **p. 157.**

Saving the Current Registry State with System Restore

Another easy way to save the current Registry configuration is to use Windows 7's System Restore utility. This program takes a snapshot of your system's current state, including the Registry. If anything should go wrong with your system, the program enables you to restore a previous configuration. It's a good idea to set a system restore point before doing any work on the Registry. I show you how to work with System Restore in Chapter 7.

▶ See "Setting System Restore Points," **p. 149.**

> **TIP**
>
> Another way to protect the Registry is to ensure that its keys have the appropriate permissions. By default, Windows 7 gives members of the Administrators group full control over the Registry. A standard user gets Full Control permission only over the HKCU key when that user is logged on and Read permissions over the rest of the Registry. To adjust the permissions, right-click the key in the Registry Editor, and then click Permissions. Make sure that only administrators have the Full Control check box activated.

Protecting Keys by Exporting Them to Disk

If you're just making a small change to the Registry, backing up all of its files might seem like overkill. Another approach is to back up only the part of the Registry that you're working on. For example, if you're about to make changes within the HKEY_CURRENT_USER key, you could back up just that key, or even a subkey within HKCU. You do that by exporting the key's data to a registration file, which is a text file that uses the .reg extension. That way, if the change causes a problem, you can import the .reg file back into the Registry to restore things the way they were.

Exporting the Entire Registry to a .reg File

The easiest way to protect the entire Registry is to export the whole thing to a .reg file on a separate hard drive or network share. Note that the resulting file will be about 150MB on a default Windows 7 system, and possibly twice that size (or more) if you have lots of other programs installed, so make sure the target destination has enough free space.

Here are the steps to follow:

1. Open the Registry Editor.
2. Select File, Export to display the Export Registry File dialog box.
3. Select a location for the file.
4. Use the File Name text box to type a name for the file.
5. Activate the All option.
6. Click Save.

Exporting a Key to a .reg File

Here are the steps to follow to export a key to a registration file:

1. Open the Registry Editor and select the key you want to export.
2. Select File, Export to display the Export Registry File dialog box.
3. Select a location for the file.
4. Use the File Name text box to type a name for the file.
5. Activate the Selected Branch option.
6. Click Save.

Finding Registry Changes

One common Registry scenario is to make a change to Windows 7 using a tool such as the Group Policy Editor, and then try and find which Registry setting (if any) was affected by the change. However, because of the sheer size of the Registry, this is usually a needle-in-a-haystack exercise that ends in frustration. One way around this is to export some or all the Registry before making the change and then export the same key or keys after making the change. You can then use the FC (file compare) utility at the command prompt to find out where the two files differ. Here's the FC syntax to use for this:

```
FC /U pre_edit.reg post-edit.reg > reg_changes.txt
```

Here, change *pre_edit.reg* to the name of the registration file you exported before editing the Registry; change *post_edit.reg* to the name of the registration file you exported after editing the Registry; and change *reg_changes.txt* to the name of a text file to which the FC output is redirected. Note that the */U* switch is required because registration files use the Unicode character set.

Importing a .reg File

If you need to restore the key that you backed up to a registration file, follow these steps:

1. Open the Registry Editor.
2. Select File, Import to display the Import Registry File dialog box.
3. Find and select the file you want to import.
4. Click Open.
5. When Windows 7 tells you the information has been entered into the Registry, click OK.

NOTE

You also can import a .reg file by locating it in Windows Explorer and then double-clicking the file.

CAUTION

Many applications ship with their own .reg files for updating the Registry. Unless you're sure that you want to import these files, avoid double-clicking them. They might end up overwriting existing settings and causing problems with your system.

Working with Registry Entries

Now that you've had a look around, you're ready to start working with the Registry's keys and settings. In this section, I'll give you the general procedures for basic tasks, such as modifying, adding, renaming, deleting, and searching for entries, and more. These techniques will serve you well throughout the rest of the book when I take you through some specific Registry modifications.

Changing the Value of a Registry Entry

Changing the value of a Registry entry is a matter of finding the appropriate key, displaying the setting you want to change, and editing the setting's value. Unfortunately, finding the key you need isn't always a simple matter. Knowing the root keys and their main subkeys, as described earlier, will certainly help, and the Registry Editor has a Find feature that's invaluable. (I'll show you how to use it later.)

To illustrate how this process works, let's work through an example: changing your registered owner name and company name. In earlier versions of Windows, the installation process probably asked you to enter your name and, optionally, your company name. These registered names appear in several places as you work with Windows:

▶ If you select Help, About in most Windows 7 programs, your registered names appear in the About dialog box.

▶ If you install a 32-bit application, the installation program uses your registered names for its own records (although you usually get a chance to make changes).

Unfortunately, if you install a clean version of Windows 7, Setup doesn't ask you for this data, and it takes your username as your registered owner name. (If you upgraded to Windows 7 for Windows XP, the owner name and company name were brought over from your previous version of Windows.) With these names appearing in so many places, it's good to know that you can change either or both names (for example, to put in your proper names if Windows 7 doesn't have them or if you give the computer to another person). The secret lies in the following key:

`HKLM\SOFTWARE\Microsoft\WindowsNT\CurrentVersion`

To get to this key, you open the branches in the Registry Editor's tree pane: `HKEY_LOCAL_MACHINE`, and then `SOFTWARE`, and then `Microsoft`, and then `Windows NT`. Finally, click the `CurrentVersion` subkey to select it. Here, you see a number of settings, but two are of interest to us (see Figure 12.4):

`RegisteredOrganization`	This setting contains your registered company name.
`RegisteredOwner`	This setting contains your registered name.

TIP

If you have keys that you visit often, you can save them as favorites to avoid trudging through endless branches in the keys pane. To do this, navigate to the key and then select Favorites, Add to Favorites. In the Add to Favorites dialog box, edit the Favorite Name text box, if desired, and then click OK. To navigate to a favorite key, pull down the Favorites menu and select the key name from the list that appears at the bottom of the menu.

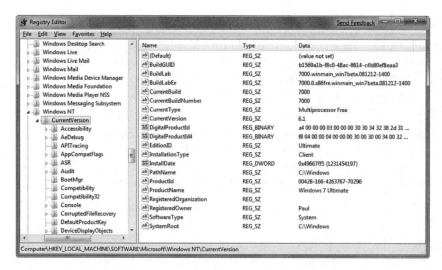

FIGURE 12.4   Navigate to `HKLM\SOFTWARE\Microsoft\Windows NT\CurrentVersion` to see your registered names.

Now you open the setting for editing by using any of the following techniques:

▶ Select the setting name and either select Edit, Modify or press Enter.

▶ Double-click the setting name.

▶ Right-click the setting name and click Modify from the context menu.

The dialog box that appears depends on the value type you're dealing with, as discussed in the next few sections. Note that edited settings are written to the Registry right away, but the changes might not go into effect immediately. In many cases, you need to exit the Registry Editor and then either log off or restart Windows 7.

Editing a String Value

If the setting is a `REG_SZ` value (as it is in our example), a `REG_MULTI_SZ` value, or a `REG_EXPAND_SZ` value, you see the Edit String dialog box, shown in Figure 12.5. Use the Value Data text box to enter a new string or modify the existing string, and then click OK. (For a `REG_MULTI_SZ` multistring value, Value Data is a multiline text box. Type each string value on its own line. That is, after each string, press Enter to start a new line.)

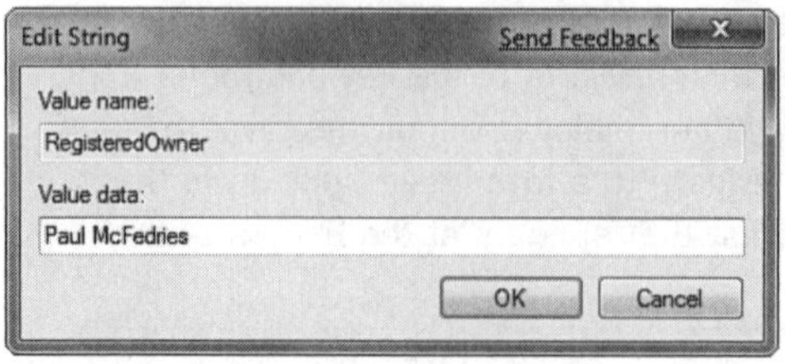

FIGURE 12.5   You see the Edit String dialog box if you're modifying a string value.

Editing a DWORD or QWORD Value

If the setting is a REG_DWORD, you see the Edit DWORD (32-Bit) Value dialog box shown in Figure 12.6. In the Base group, select either Hexadecimal or Decimal, and then use the Value Data text box to enter the new value of the setting. (If you chose the Hexadecimal option, enter a hexadecimal value; if you chose Decimal, enter a decimal value.) Note that editing a QWORD value is identical, except that the dialog box is named Edit QWORD (64-Bit) Value, instead.

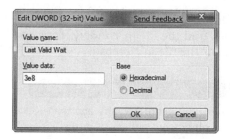

FIGURE 12.6 You see the Edit DWORD Value dialog box if you're modifying a double word value.

Editing a Binary Value

If the setting is a REG_BINARY value, you see an Edit Binary Value dialog box like the one shown in Figure 12.7.

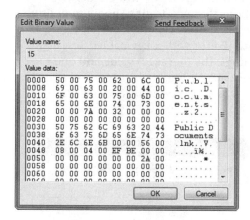

FIGURE 12.7 You see the Edit Binary Value dialog box if you're modifying a binary value.

For binary values, the Value Data box is divided into three vertical sections:

▶ **Starting Byte Number**—The four-digit values on the left of the Value Data box tell you the sequence number of the first byte in each row of hexadecimal numbers. This sequence always begins at 0, so the sequence number of the first byte in the first row is 0000. There are eight bytes in each row, so the sequence number of the first byte in the second row is 0008, and so on. You can't edit these values.

▶ **Hexadecimal Numbers (Bytes)**—The eight columns of two-digit numbers in the middle section display the setting's value, expressed in hexadecimal numbers, where which each two-digit number represents a single byte of information. You can edit these values.

▶ **ANSI Equivalents**—The third section on the right side of the Value Data box shows the ANSI equivalents of the hexadecimal numbers in the middle section. For example, the first byte of the first row is the hexadecimal value 54, which represents the uppercase letter *T*. You can also edit the values in this column.

Editing a `.reg` File

If you exported a key to a registration file, you can edit that file and then import it back into the Registry. To make changes to a registration file, find the file in Windows Explorer, right-click the file, and then click Edit. Windows 7 opens the file in Notepad.

TIP

If you need to make global changes to the Registry, export the entire Registry and then load the resulting registration file into WordPad or some other word processor or text editor. Use the application's Replace feature (carefully!) to make changes throughout the file. If you use a word processor for this, be sure to save the file as a text file when you're done. You can then import the changed file back into the Registry.

Creating a `.reg` File

You can create registration files from scratch and then import them into the Registry. This is a handy technique if you have some customizations that you want to apply to multiple systems. To demonstrate the basic structure of a registration file and its entries, Figure 12.8 shows two windows. The top window is the Registry Editor with a key named Test highlighted. The Settings pane contains six sample settings: the (Default) value and one each of the five types of settings (binary, DWORD, expandable string, multistring, and string). The bottom window shows the Test key in Notepad as an exported registration file (Test.reg).

NOTE

The file that contains the test Registry code (test.reg) is available on my website at www.mcfedries.com/Windows7Unleashed.

Windows 7 registration files always start with the following header:

```
Windows Registry Editor Version 5.00
```

TIP

If you're building a registration file for a Windows 9x, Me, or NT 4 system, change the header to the following:

```
REGEDIT4
```

FIGURE 12.8   The settings in the Test key shown in the Registry Editor correspond to the data shown in Test.reg file shown in Notepad.

Next is an empty line followed by the full path of the Registry key that will hold the settings you're adding, surrounded by square brackets:

```
[HKEY_CURRENT_USER\Test]
```

Below the key are the setting names and values, which use the following general form:

> **TIP**
>
> If you want to add a comment to a .reg file, start a new line and begin the line with a semicolon (;).

```
"SettingName"=identifier:SettingValue
```

SettingName	The name of the setting. Note that you use the @ symbol to represent the key's Default value.
identifier	A code that identifies the type of data. REG_SZ values don't use an identifier, but the other four types do:

dword	Use this identifier for a DWORD value.
hex(b)	Use this identifier for a QWORD value.
hex	Use this identifier for a binary value.

	hex(2)	Use this identifier for an expandable string value.
	hex(7)	Use this identifier for a multistring value.
SettingValue		This is the value of the setting, which you enter as follows:
	String	Surround the value with quotation marks.
	DWORD	Enter an eight-digit DWORD value.
	QWORD	Enter eight two-digit hexadecimal pairs, separated by commas, with the pairs running from highest order to lowest. For example, to enter the QWORD value 123456789abcd, you would use the following value:

cd,ab,89,67,45,23,01,00

	Binary	Enter the binary value as a series of two-digit hexadecimal numbers, separating each number with a comma.
	Expandable string	Convert each character to its hexadecimal equivalent and then enter the value as a series of two-digit hexadecimal numbers, separating each number with a comma, and separating each character with 00.
	Multistring	Convert each character to its hexadecimal equivalent and then enter the value as a series of two-digit hexadecimal numbers, separating each number with a comma, and separating each character with 00, and separating each string with space (00 hex).

TIP

To delete a setting using a `.reg` file, set its value to a hyphen (-), as in this example:
Windows Registry Editor Version 5.00

[HKEY_CURRENT_USER\Test]
"BinarySetting"=-

To delete a key, add a hyphen to the start of the key name, as in this example:
Windows Registry Editor Version 5.00

[-HKEY_CURRENT_USER\Test]

Renaming a Key or Setting

You won't often need to rename existing keys or settings. Just in case, though, here are the steps to follow:

1. In the Registry Editor, find the key or setting you want to work with, and then highlight it.
2. Select Edit, Rename, or press F2.
3. Edit the name and then press Enter.

> **CAUTION**
>
> Rename only those keys or settings that you created yourself. If you rename any other key or setting, Windows 7 might not work properly.

Creating a New Key or Setting

Many Registry-based customizations don't involve editing an existing setting or key. Instead, you have to create a new setting or key. Here's how you do it:

1. In the Registry Editor, select the key in which you want to create the new subkey or setting.
2. Select Edit, New. (Alternatively, right-click an empty section of the Settings pane and then click New.) A submenu appears.
3. If you're creating a new key, select the Key command. Otherwise, select the command that corresponds to the type of setting you want: String Value, Binary Value, DWORD Value, Multi-String Value, or Expandable String Value.
4. Type a name for the new key or setting.
5. Press Enter.

Deleting a Key or Setting

Here are the steps to follow to delete a key or setting:

1. In the Registry Editor, select the key or setting that you want to delete.
2. Select Edit, Delete, or press Delete. The Registry Editor asks whether you're sure.
3. Click Yes.

> **CAUTION**
>
> Again, to avoid problems, you should delete only those keys or settings that you created yourself. If you're not sure about deleting a setting, try renaming it instead. If a problem arises, you can also return the setting back to its original name.

Finding Registry Entries

The Registry contains only five root keys, but they contain hundreds of subkeys. The fact that some root keys are aliases for subkeys in a different branch only adds to the confusion. If you know exactly where you're going, the Registry Editor's tree-like hierarchy is a reasonable way to get there. If you're not sure where a particular subkey or setting resides, however, you could spend all day poking around in the Registry's labyrinthine nooks and crannies.

To help you get where you want to go, the Registry Editor has a Find feature that enables you to search for keys, settings, or values. Here's how it works:

1. In the Keys pane, select Computer at the top of the pane (unless you're certain of which root key contains the value you want to find; in this case, you can highlight the appropriate root key instead).

2. Select Edit, Find or press Ctrl+F. The Registry Editor displays the Find dialog box, shown in Figure 12.9.

FIGURE 12.9   Use the Find dialog box to search for Registry keys, settings, or values.

3. Use the Find What text box to enter your search string. You can enter partial words or phrases to increase your chances of finding a match.

4. In the Look At group, activate the check boxes for the elements you want to search. For most searches, you want to leave all three check boxes activated.

5. If you want to find only those entries that exactly match your search text, activate the Match Whole String Only check box.

6. Click the Find Next button. The Registry Editor highlights the first match.

7. If this isn't the item you want, select Edit, Find Next (or press F3) until you find the setting or key you want.

When the Registry Editor finds a match, it displays the appropriate key or setting. Note that if the matched value is a setting name or data value, Find doesn't highlight the current key. This is a bit confusing, but remember that the current key always appears at the bottom of the Keys pane.

CHAPTER 13

Controlling Windows 7 from the Command Line

When you can do the common things of life in an uncommon way, you will command the attention of the world.

—George Washington Carver

All versions of Windows have at their core a basic premise: that it's easier, faster, and more intuitive to work and play using a graphical user interface (GUI) than using an old-fashioned command-line interface of the kind we saw way back in the days when MS-DOS and its variants ruled the PC world. Few, if any, people today would dispute that premise; the last of the Windows versus MS-DOS battles was fought a long time ago.

However, that doesn't mean that a GUI is the *only* way to operate a PC. All versions of Windows still come with a Command Prompt utility that gives you access to the command line. That's not surprising, but what *is* surprising is that the command line is a source of tremendous power and flexibility. After you have that blinking cursor in front of you, a huge and potent arsenal of commands, tools, and utilities becomes available. With these features at your disposal, you can perform amazing tricks in the areas of disk and file management, performance monitoring, network administration, system maintenance, and much more. This chapter introduces you to the Windows 7 command line and takes you through quite a few of the available command-line tools.

Getting to the Command Line

To take advantage of the command line and all its many useful commands, you need to start a Command Prompt session. Windows 7 offers a number of different ways to do this, but perhaps the easiest is to select Start, type **command**, and then click Command Prompt in the search results. (It's even faster to type just **cmd** in the Search box and then press Enter.) Windows 7 opens a Command Prompt window like the one shown in Figure 13.1.

FIGURE 13.1   Use the Command Prompt window for your Windows 7 command-line adventures.

> ▶ It's also possible to configure Windows 7's Folder file type to open the Command Prompt in Windows Explorer's current folder. To learn how, **see** "Example: Opening the Command Prompt in the Current Folder," **p. 51.**

Running Command Prompt as the Administrator

Once in a while, you not only need to start a Command Prompt session, but you need to start an *elevated* session. That's because there are certain Windows commands and utilities that require administrator-level permission. This is normally handled by User Account Control, which prompts you for administrator credentials before letting you continue with the operation. However, this is usually not the case with operations launched from the Command Prompt.

For example, in Chapter 4, "Customizing Startup and Shutdown," you learn how to use the BCDEDIT tool to edit the Windows 7's Boot Manager. This tool requires administrator permissions, but you run it from the Command Prompt, so UAC doesn't come into play. To use BCDEDIT (or any Command Prompt utility or command that requires elevation) successfully, you need to run it within a Command Prompt session that has been elevated to administrator status. Here's how it's done:

1. Select Start and type **command** in the Search box. The Command Prompt icon appears in the search results.

2. Right-click Command Prompt and then click Run as Administrator. UAC prompts you for your credentials.

3. Enter your administrator credentials to continue.

In this case, the Command Prompt window still appears, but the title bar reads `Administrator: Command Prompt` to remind you that you're in an elevated session (see Figure 13.2).

FIGURE 13.2   When you launch an elevated Command Prompt session, Windows includes *Administrator:* in the window title bar.

> **NOTE**
>
> When you start your computer using the Safe Mode with Command Prompt startup option (see Chapter 4), the Command Prompt session you get is an administrator session.

Running CMD

You can also launch Command Prompt using the CMD executable, which enables you to specify extra switches after the cmd.exe filename. Most of these switches aren't particularly useful, so let's start with the simplest syntax that you'll use most often:

CMD [[/S] [/C | /K] *command*]

/S   Strips out the first and last quotation marks from the *command*, provided that the first quotation mark is the first character in *command*

/C   Executes the *command* and then terminates

/K   Executes the *command* and remains running

command The command to run

For example, if your ISP provides you with a dynamic IP address, you can often solve some connection problems by asking the IP for a fresh address. You do that by running the command ipconfig /renew at the command line. In this case, you don't need the

Command Prompt window to remain open, so you can specify the /C switch to shut down the command-line session automatically after the IPCONFIG utility finishes:

```
cmd /c ipconfig /renew
```

On the other hand, you often either want to see the results of the command, or you want to leave the Command Prompt window open so that you can run other commands. In those cases, use the /K switch. For example, the following command runs the SET utility (which displays the current values of the Windows 7 environment variables) and then leaves the command-line session running:

```
cmd /k set
```

Here's the full syntax of cmd.exe:

```
CMD [/A | /U] [/Q] [/D] [/T:bf] [/E:ON | /E:OFF] [/F:ON | /F:OFF] [/V:ON | /V:OFF]
➥[[/S] [/C | /K] command]
```

/Q   Turns command echoing off. If *command* is a batch file, you won't see any of the batch file commands as they're executed. This is the same as adding the statement @ECHO OFF at the beginning of a batch file.

/D   Disables the execution of AutoRun commands from the Registry. These commands run automatically when you start any command-line session. You can find the settings here:

HKLM\Software\Microsoft\Command Processor\AutoRun
HKCU\Software\Microsoft\Command Processor\AutoRun

TIP

If you do not see an AutoRun setting in one or both keys, select the key, select File, New, String Value, type **AutoRun**, and press Enter.

TIP

The AutoRun Registry settings are handy if you always run a particular command at the beginning of each command-line session. If you run multiple commands to launch a session, you can add those commands to either AutoRun setting. In that case, you must separate each command with the command separator string: &&. For example, to run the IPCONFIG and SET utilities at the start of each command-line session, change the value of an AutoRun setting to the following:

ipconfig&&set

/A   Converts the output of internal commands to a pipe or file to the ANSI character set.

/U   Converts the output of internal commands to a pipe or file to the Unicode character set.

/T:*bf*   Sets the foreground and background colors of the Command Prompt window, where *f* is the foreground color and *b* is the background color. Both *f* and *b* are hexadecimal digits that specify the color as follows:

0	Black	8	Gray
1	Blue	9	Light blue
2	Green	A	Light green
3	Aqua	B	Light aqua
4	Red	C	Light red
5	Purple	D	Light purple
6	Yellow	E	Light yellow
7	White	F	Bright white

TIP

You can also set the foreground and background colors during a command-line session by using the COLOR *bf* command, where *b* and *f* are hexadecimal digits specifying the colors you want. To revert to the default Command Prompt colors, run COLOR without the *bf* parameter.

/E:ON   Enables *command extensions*, which are extra features added to the following commands. (At the command line, type the command name followed by a space and /? to see the extensions.)

ASSOC	IF
CALL	MD or MKDIR
CD or CHDIR	POPD
COLOR	PROMPT
DEL or ERASE	PUSHD
ENDLOCAL	SET
FOR	SETLOCAL
FTYPE	SHIFT
GOTO	START

/E:OFF   Disables command extensions.

/F:ON   Turns on file and directory name completion, which enables you to press special key combinations to scroll through a list of files or subdirectories in the current directory that match the characters you've already typed. For example, suppose that the current directory contains files named budget2006.doc, budget2007.doc, and budget2008.doc. If you type **start budget** in a command-line session started with /F:ON, pressing Ctrl+F tells Windows 7 to display the first file (or subfolder) in the current folder with a name that starts with budget. Pressing Ctrl+F again displays the next file with a name that starts with budget, and so on. You can do the same thing with just subfolder names by pressing Ctrl+D instead.

TIP

You don't need to start the Command Prompt with the /F:ON switch to use file and directory name completion. The Command Prompt offers a similar feature called *AutoComplete* that's turned on by default. At the prompt, type the first letter or two of a file or subfolder name, and then press the Tab key to see the first object that matches your text in the current folder. Keep pressing Tab to see other matching objects. If, for some reason, you prefer to turn off AutoComplete, pull down the Command Prompt window's control menu (right-click the title bar), select Defaults, and then deactivate the AutoComplete check box in the Options tab.

/F:OFF   Turns off file and directory name completion.

/V:ON   Enables delayed environment variable expansion using ! as the delimiter: !*var*!, where *var* is an environment variable. This is useful for batch files in which you want to delay the expansion of an environment variable. Normally, Windows 7 expands all environment variables to their current values when it reads the contents of a batch file. With delayed expansion enabled, Windows 7 doesn't expand a particular environment variable within a batch file until it executes the statement containing that variable.

/V:OFF   Disables delayed environment expansion.

/S   Strips out the first and last quotation marks from *command*, provided the first quotation mark is the first character in *command*.

/C   Executes the *command* and then terminates.

/K   Executes the *command* and remains running.

command   The command to run.

Working at the Command Line

When you have your command-line session up and running, you can run commands and programs, create and launch batch files, perform file maintenance, and so on. If you haven't used the Command Prompt since the days of DOS, you'll find that the Windows 7 Command Prompt offers a few extra command-line goodies. The next few sections highlight some of the more useful ones.

> **CAUTION**
>
> When you're working in the Command Prompt, be warned that any files you delete aren't sent to the Recycle Bin but are purged from your system.

Running Commands

Although many of the Windows 7 accessories provide more powerful and easier-to-use replacements for nearly all commands, a few commands still have no Windows 7 peer. These include the REN command, as well as the many Command Prompt–specific commands, such as CLS, DOSKEY, and PROMPT.

> **NOTE**
>
> Command-line commands that exist as separate executable files—such as CHKDSK, DEFRAG, and XCOPY—are called *external commands*; all other command-line commands—such as DIR, CD, and CLS—are part of the CMD shell and are known as *internal commands*.

How you run a command depends on whether it's an internal or external command and on what you want Windows 7 to do after the command is finished. For an internal command, you have two choices: You can either enter the command at the Command Prompt, or you can include it as a parameter with CMD. As you saw earlier, you can run internal commands with CMD by specifying either the /C switch or the /K switch. If you use the /C switch, the command executes, and then the command-line session shuts down. This is fine if you're running a command for which you don't need to see the results. For example, if you want to redirect the contents of your user profile folder to the text file profile.txt, entering the following command in the Run dialog box (for example, press Windows Logo+R to open Run) will do the job:

```
cmd /c dir %userprofile% > %userprofile%\profile.txt
```

On the other hand, you might want to examine the output of a command before the Command Prompt window closes. In that case, you need to use the /K switch. The following command runs DIR on your user profile folder and then drops you off in the Command Prompt:

```
cmd /k dir %userprofile%
```

For an external command, you have three choices: Enter the command at the Command Prompt, enter the command by itself from within Windows 7, or include it as a parameter with CMD.

Entering a command by itself from within Windows 7 means launching the command's file in Explorer, entering the command in the Run dialog box, or creating a shortcut for the command. For the latter two methods, you can embellish the command by adding parameters and switches.

Working with Long Filenames

If you want to use long filenames in a command, you need to be careful. If the long filename contains a space or any other character that's illegal in an 8.3 filename, you need to surround the long name with quotation marks. For example, if you run the following command, Windows 7 tells you this: The syntax of the command is incorrect:

```
copy Fiscal Year 2009.doc Fiscal Year 2010.doc
```

Instead, you need to enter this command as follows:

```
copy "Fiscal Year 2009.doc" "Fiscal Year 2010.doc"
```

Long filenames are, of course, long, so they tend to be a pain to type in the Command Prompt. Fortunately, Windows 7 offers a few methods for knocking long names down to size:

▶ In Explorer, drag a folder or file and drop it inside the Command Prompt window. Windows 7 pastes the full pathname of the folder or file to the end of the prompt.

▶ In Windows Explorer, navigate to the folder you want to work with and then select and copy the folder path in the address bar. (To see the address instead of the folder breadcrumb path, click an empty section of the address bar.) Return to the Command Prompt window, type the command up to the point where you want the path to appear, right-click the tile bar, and then select Edit, Paste.

▶ If you're trying to run a program that resides in a folder with a long name, add the folder to the PATH. This technique enables you to run programs from the folder without having to specify the full pathname.

> **TIP**
>
> To edit the PATH environment variable, you have two choices. At the command line, enter the following command (where *folder* is the path of the folder you want to add to the PATH variable):
>
>   path %path%;*folder*
>
> Alternatively, select Start, right-click Computer, click Properties, and then click Advanced System Settings. In the Advanced tab, click Environment Variables. In the System Variables list, click Path, click Edit, and then append the folder to the end of the Variable Value string. Be sure to separate each folder path with a semicolon (;).

▶ Use the SUBST command to substitute a virtual drive letter for a long pathname. For example, the following command substitutes the S: drive for the Start menu's System Tools folder:

    subst s: "%AllUsersProfile%\Start Menu\Programs\Accessories\System Tools"

Changing Folders Faster

At the command line, you use the CD command to change to a different folder on the current drive. However, the Command Prompt has a few short forms you can use to save time.

You might know that both the Command Prompt and Windows 7 use the dot symbol (.) to represent the current folder, and the double-dot symbol (..) to represent its parent folder. You can combine the CD command and the dot notation to jump immediately to a folder's parent folder, or even higher.

To make this more concrete, suppose that the current folder is D:\Animal\Mammal\Dolphin. Table 13.1 demonstrates the techniques you can use to navigate to this folder's parent, grandparent (two levels up), and great grandparent (three levels up) folders.

TABLE 13.1 Combining the **CD** Command with Dot Notation

Current Folder	Command	New Folder
D:\Animal\Mammal\Dolphin	Cd..	D:\Animal\Mammal
D:\Animal\Mammal\Dolphin	Cd..\..	D:\Animal
D:\Animal\Mammal\Dolphin	Cd..\..\..	D:\
D:\Animal\Mammal\Dolphin	Cd..\Baboon	D:\Animal\Mammal\Baboon

> **TIP**
>
> If you want to return to the root folder of any drive, type **cd** and press Enter.

Taking Advantage of DOSKEY

Windows 7 loads the DOSKEY utility by default when you start any command-line session. This useful little program brings a number of advantages to your command-line work:

▶ You can recall previously entered commands with just a keystroke or two.

▶ You can enter multiple commands on a single line.

▶ You can edit commands instead of retyping them.

The next few sections take you through the specifics.

Recalling Command Lines

The simplest DOSKEY feature is command recall. DOSKEY maintains a *command history buffer* that keeps a list of the commands you enter. To scroll through your previously entered commands in reverse order, press the up-arrow key; when you've done that at least once, you can change direction and run through the commands in the order you entered them by pressing the down-arrow key. To rerun a command, use the arrow keys to find it and then press Enter.

> **TIP**
>
> If you don't want to enter commands from the history buffer, press Esc to get a clean command line.

Table 13.2 lists all the command-recall keys you can use.

TABLE 13.2   **DOSKEY** Command-Recall Keys

Press	To
Up arrow	Recall the previous command in the buffer.
Down arrow	Recall the next command in the buffer.
Page Up	Recall the oldest command in the buffer.
Page Down	Recall the newest command in the buffer.
F7	Display the entire command buffer.
Alt+F7	Delete all commands from the buffer.
F8	Have DOSKEY recall a command that begins with the letter or letters you've typed on the command line.
F9	Have DOSKEY prompt you for a command list number. (You can see the numbers with the F7 key.) Type the number and press Enter to recall the command.

TIP

The command history buffer holds 50 commands by default. If you need a larger buffer, run DOSKEY with the /LISTSIZE=*buffers* switch, where *buffers* is the number of commands you want to store. You also need to include the /REINSTALL switch to install a new copy of DOSKEY, which puts the new history buffer setting into effect. For example, to change the buffer size to 100, enter the following command:

```
doskey /listize=100 /reinstall
```

Entering Multiple Commands on a Single Line

DOSKEY enables you to run multiple commands on a single line. To do this, insert the characters && between commands. For example, a common task is to change to a different drive and then run a directory listing. Normally, you'd do this with two separate commands:

```
e:
dir
```

With DOSKEY, however, you can do it on one line, like so:

```
e:&&dir
```

TIP

You can enter as many commands as you like on a single line, but just remember that the total length of the line can't be more than 8,191 characters (which should be plenty!).

Editing Command Lines

Instead of simply rerunning a previously typed command, you might need to run the command again with slightly different switches or parameters. Rather than retyping the whole thing, DOSKEY enables you to edit any recalled command line. You use various keys to move the cursor to the offending letters and replace them. Table 13.3 summarizes DOSKEY's command-line editing keys.

TABLE 13.3   **DOSKEY** Command-Line Editing Keys

Press	To
Left arrow	Move the cursor one character to the left.
Right arrow	Move the cursor one character to the right.
Ctrl+left arrow	Move the cursor one word to the left.
Ctrl+right arrow	Move the cursor one word to the right.

TABLE 13.3   Continued

Home	Move the cursor to the beginning of the line.
End	Move the cursor to the end of the line.
Delete	Delete the character over the cursor.
Backspace	Delete the character to the left of the cursor.
Ctrl+Home	Delete from the cursor to the beginning of the line.
Ctrl+End	Delete from the cursor to the end of the line.
Insert	Toggle DOSKEY between Insert mode (your typing is inserted between existing letters on the command line) and Overstrike mode (your typing replaces existing letters on the command line).

Redirecting Command Output and Input

Windows 7 is always directing things here and there. This generally falls into two categories:

▶ Directing data into its commands from a device called *standard input*

▶ Directing data out of its commands to a device called *standard output*

A device called *CON* (*console*) normally handles standard input and standard output, which is your keyboard and monitor. Windows 7 assumes that all command input comes from the keyboard and that all command output (such as a DIR listing or a system message) goes to the screen. Redirection is just a way of specifying different input and output devices.

Redirecting Command Output

To send command output to somewhere other than the screen, you use the *output redirection operator* (>). One of the most common uses for output redirection is to capture the results of a command in a text file. For example, you might want to use the report produced by the SYSTEMINFO command as part of a word processing document. (For the details on this command, see "SYSTEMINFO: Returning System Configuration Data," later in this chapter.) You could use the following command to first capture the report as the file systeminfo.csv:

```
systeminfo /fo csv > %userprofile%\systeminfo.csv
```

When you run this command, the usual SYSTEMINFO data doesn't appear onscreen. That's because you directed it away from the screen and into the systeminfo.csv file.

You can use this technique to capture DIR listings, CHKDSK reports, and more. One caveat: If the file you specify as the output destination already exists, Windows 7 overwrites it without warning. To avoid this, you can use the *double output redirection symbol* (>>). This tells Windows 7 to append the output to the end of the file if the file exists. For example, suppose you used the following command to output the results of the CHKDSK C: command to chkdsk.txt:

```
chkdsk c: > %userprofile%\chkdsk.txt
```

If you then want to append the results of the CHKDSK D: command to chkdsk.txt, you enter the following command:

```
chkdsk d: >> %userprofile%\chkdsk.txt
```

You can also redirect output to different devices. Table 13.4 lists the various devices that Windows 7 installs each time you start your system.

TABLE 13.4   Devices Installed by Windows 7 When You Start Your System

Device Name	Device
AUX	Auxiliary device (usually COM1)
CLOCK$	Real-time clock
COM*n*	Serial port (COM1, COM2, COM3, or COM4)
CON	Console (keyboard and screen)
LPT*n*	Parallel port (LPT1, LPT2, or LPT3)
NUL	NUL device (nothing)
PRN	Printer (usually LPT1)

For example, you can send a DIR listing to the printer with the following command. (Of course, you need to be sure that your printer is on before doing this. Also note that this only works for a printer attached to a parallel port; it doesn't work for USB printers.)

```
dir > prn
```

The NUL device usually throws people for a loop when they first see it. This device (affectionately known as the *bit bucket*) is, literally, nothing. Batch files normally use it to suppress the usual messages Windows 7 displays when it completes a command. For example, Windows 7 normally says 1 file(s) copied when you copy a file. However, the following command sends that message to *NUL*, so you wouldn't see it onscreen:

```
copy somefile.doc \\server\users\paul\ > nul
```

> **TIP**
>
> Unfortunately, Windows 7 gives you no way to redirect output to a USB port. However, there's a workaround you can use if you're trying to redirect output to a USB printer. Assuming the printer is shared and that no other device is using the port LPT2, run the following command:
>
> NET USE LPT2 *server**printer*

Here, replace *server* with the name of your Windows 7 computer and *printer* with the share name of the USB printer. Now, when you redirect output to LPT2, Windows 7 sends the output to the USB printer.

Redirecting Input

The *input redirection operator* (<) handles getting input to a Windows 7 command from somewhere other than the keyboard. Input redirection is almost always used to send the contents of a text file to a Windows 7 command. The most common example is the MORE command, which displays one screen of information at a time. If you have a large text file that scrolls off the screen when you use TYPE, the following command, which sends the contents of BIGFILE.TXT to the MORE command, solves the problem:

```
more < bigfile.txt
```

When you run this command, the first screen of text appears, and the following line shows up at the bottom of the screen:

```
-- More --
```

Just press any key, and MORE displays the next screen. (Whatever you do, don't mix up < and > when using MORE. The command more > bigfile.txt erases BIGFILE.TXT!) MORE is an example of a *filter* command. Filters process whatever text is sent through them. The other Windows 7 filters are SORT and FIND, which I discuss in a moment.

Another handy use for input redirection is to send keystrokes to Windows 7 commands. For example, create a text file called enter.txt that consists of a single press of the Enter key, and then try this command:

```
date < enter.txt
```

Windows 7 displays the current date, and instead of waiting for you to either type in a new date or press Enter, it just reads enter.txt and uses its single carriage return as input. (For an even easier way to input the Enter key to a command, check out the next section.)

One common recipient of redirected input is the SORT command. SORT, as you might guess from its name, sorts the data sent to it and displays the results onscreen. So, for example, here's how you would sort a file called JUMBLED.TXT:

```
sort < jumbled.txt
```

Instead of merely displaying the results of the sort onscreen, you can use > to redirect them to another file.

TIP

SORT normally starts with the first column and works across. To start with any other column, use the */+n switch*, where *n* is the number of the column you want to use. To sort a file in reverse order (that is, a descending sort—Z to A, then 9 to 0—instead of an ascending sort —0 to 9, then A to Z), use the /R switch.

Piping Commands

Piping is a technique that combines both input and output redirection. Using the pipe operator (|), the output of one command is captured and sent as input to another command. For example, the SYSTEMINFO command displays about five screens of data, so you usually need to scroll back to see the data you're looking for. However, you can pause the output by piping it to the MORE command:

```
systeminfo | more
```

The pipe operator captures the SYSTEMINFO output and sends it as input to MORE, which then displays the SYSTEMINFO results one screen at a time.

> **NOTE**
>
> Piping works by first redirecting the output of a command to a temporary file. It then takes this temporary file and redirects it as input to the second command. A command such as SYSTEMINFO | MORE is approximately equivalent to the following two commands:
>
> ```
> SYSTEMINFO > tempfile
> MORE tempfile
> ```

I showed you in the preceding section how to use input redirection to send keystrokes to a Windows 7 command. But if you have to send only a single key, piping offers a much nicer solution. The secret is to use the ECHO command to echo the character you need and then pipe it to the Windows 7 command.

For example, if you use the command DEL *.*, Windows 7 always asks whether you're sure that you want to delete all the files in the current directory. This is a sensible precaution, but you can override it if you do things this way:

```
echo y | del *.*
```

Here, the y that would normally be echoed to the screen is sent to DEL instead, which interprets it as a response to its prompt. This is a handy technique for batch files in which you want to reduce or even eliminate user interaction.

> **TIP**
>
> You can even use this technique to send an Enter keypress to a command. The command ECHO. (that's ECHO followed by a period) is equivalent to pressing Enter. So, for example, you could use the following command in a batch file to display the time without user input:
>
> ```
> ECHO. | TIME
> ```

Understanding Batch File Basics

As you've seen so far, the command line is still an often useful and occasionally indispensable part of computing life, and most power users will find themselves doing at least a little work in the Command Prompt window. Part of that work might involve writing short batch file programs to automate routine chores, such as performing simple file backups and deleting unneeded files. And if you throw in any of the commands that enhance batch files, you can do many other interesting and useful things.

When you run a command in a command-line session, the Command Prompt executes the command or program and returns to the prompt to await further orders. If you tell the Command Prompt to execute a batch file, however, things are a little different. The Command Prompt goes into *Batch mode*, where it takes all its input from the individual lines of a batch file. These lines are just commands that (in most cases) you otherwise have to type in yourself. The Command Prompt repeats the following four-step procedure until it has processed each line in the batch file:

1. It reads a line from the batch file.
2. It closes the batch file.
3. It executes the command.
4. It reopens the batch file and reads the next line.

The main advantage of Batch mode is that you can lump several commands together in a single batch file and tell the Command Prompt to execute them all simply by typing the name of the batch file. This is great for automating routine tasks such as backing up the Registry files or deleting leftover .tmp files at startup.

Creating Batch Files

Before getting started with some concrete batch file examples, you need to know how to create them. Here are a few things to bear in mind:

▶ Batch files are simple text files, so using Notepad (or some other text editor) is probably your best choice.

▶ If you decide to use WordPad or another word processor, make sure that the file you create is a text-only file.

▶ Save your batch files using the .bat extension.

▶ When naming your batch files, don't use the same name as a Command Prompt command. For example, if you create a batch file that deletes some files, don't name it Del.bat. If you do, the batch file will never run! Here's why: When you enter something at the prompt, CMD first checks to see whether the command is an internal command. If it's not, CMD then checks for (in order) a .com, .exe, .bat, or .cmd file with a matching name. Because all external commands use a .com or .exe extension, CMD never bothers to check whether your batch file even exists!

After you've created the batch file, the rest is easy. Just enter any commands exactly as you would at the command line, and include whatever batch instructions you need.

> **TIP**
>
> If you find yourself creating and using a number of batch files, things can get confusing if you have the files scattered all over your hard disk. To remedy this, it makes sense to create a new folder to hold all your batch files. To make this strategy effective, however, you have to tell the Command Prompt to look in the batch file folder to find these files. To do that, you need to add the batch file folder to the PATH variable, as described earlier (see "Working with Long Filenames").

REM: Adding Comments to a Batch File

The first of the batch file–specific commands is REM (which stands for *remark*). This simple command tells the Command Prompt to ignore everything else on the current line. Batch file mavens use it almost exclusively to add short comments to their files:

```
REM This batch file changes to drive C
REM folder and starts CHKDSK in automatic mode.
C:
CHKDSK /F
```

Why would anyone want to do this? Well, it's probably not all that necessary with short, easy-to-understand batch files, but some of the more complex programs you'll be seeing later in this chapter can appear incomprehensible at first glance. A few pithy REM statements can help clear things up (not only for other people, but even for you if you haven't looked at the file in a couple of months).

> **CAUTION**
>
> It's best not to go overboard with REM statements. Having too many slows a batch file to a crawl. You really need only a few REM statements at the beginning to outline the purpose of the file and one or two to explain each of your more cryptic commands.

ECHO: Displaying Messages from a Batch File

When it's processing a batch file, Windows 7 normally lets you know what's going on by displaying each command before executing it. That's fine, but it's often better to include more expansive descriptions, especially if other people will be using your batch files. The ECHO batch file command makes it possible for you to do just that.

For example, here's a simple batch file that deletes all the text files in the current user's Cookies and Recent folders and courteously tells the user what's about to happen:

```
ECHO This batch file will now delete your Internet Explorer cache files
DEL "%localappdata%\microsoft\windows\temporary internet files\*.*"
ECHO This batch file will now delete your recent documents list
DEL "%appdata%\microsoft\windows\recent items\*.lnk"
```

The idea here is that when Windows 7 stumbles on the ECHO command, it simply displays the rest of the line onscreen. Sounds pretty simple, right? Well, here's what the output looks like when you run the batch file:

```
C:\>ECHO This batch file will now delete your Internet Explorer cache files
This batch file will now delete your Internet Explorer cache files
C:\>DEL "%localappdata%\microsoft\windows\temporary internet files\*.*"
C:\>ECHO This batch file will now delete your recent documents list
This batch file will now delete your recent documents list
C:\>DEL "%appdata%\microsoft\windows\recent items\*.lnk"
```

What a mess! The problem is that Windows 7 is displaying the command and ECHOing the line. Fortunately, Windows 7 provides two solutions:

▶ To prevent Windows 7 from displaying a command as it executes, precede the command with the @ symbol:

```
@ECHO This batch file will now delete your Internet Explorer cache files
```

▶ To prevent Windows 7 from displaying any commands, place the following at the beginning of the batch file:

```
@ECHO OFF
```

Here's what the output looks like with the commands hidden:

```
This batch file will now delete your Internet Explorer cache files
This batch file will now delete your recent documents list
```

TIP

You might think that you can display a blank line simply by using ECHO by itself. That would be nice, but it doesn't work. (Windows 7 just tells you the current state of ECHO: on or off.) Instead, use ECHO. (that's ECHO followed by a dot).

PAUSE: Temporarily Halting Batch File Execution

Sometimes you want to see something that a batch file displays (such as a folder listing produced by the DIR command) before continuing. Or, you might want to alert users that something important is about to happen so that they can consider the possible ramifications (and bail out if they get cold feet). In both cases, you can use the PAUSE command to halt the execution of a batch file temporarily. When Windows 7 comes across PAUSE in a batch file, it displays the following:

```
Press any key to continue . . .
```

To continue processing the rest of the batch file, press any key. If you don't want to continue, you can cancel processing by pressing Ctrl+C or Ctrl+Break. Windows 7 then asks you to confirm:

```
Terminate batch job (Y/N)?
```

Either press Y to return to the prompt or N to continue the batch file.

Using Batch File Parameters

Most command-line utilities require extra information such as a filename (for example, when you use COPY or DEL) or a folder path (such as when you use CD or MD). These extra pieces of information—they're called *parameters*—give you the flexibility to specify exactly how you want a command to work. You can add the same level of flexibility to your batch files. To understand how this works, first look at the following example:

```
@ECHO OFF
ECHO.
ECHO The first parameter is %1
ECHO The second parameter is %2
ECHO The third parameter is %3
```

As you can see, this batch file doesn't do much except ECHO four lines to the screen (the first of which is just a blank line). Curiously, however, each ECHO command ends with a percent sign (%) and a number. Type in and save this batch file as Parameters.bat. Then, to see what these unusual symbols mean, enter the following at the command line:

parameters A B C

This produces the following output:

```
C:\>parameters A B C


The first parameter is A
The second parameter is B
The third parameter is C
```

The following ECHO command in Parameters.bat produces the first line in the output (after the blank line):

```
ECHO The first parameter is %1
```

When Windows sees the %1 symbol in a batch file, it examines the original command, looks for the first item after the batch filename, and then replaces %1 with that item. In the example, the first item after parameters is A, so Windows uses that to replace %1. Only when it has done this does it proceed to ECHO the line to the screen.

NOTE

If your batch file command has more parameters than the batch file is looking for, it ignores the extras. For example, adding a fourth parameter to the parameters command line has no effect on the file's operation. Note, too, that you can't use more than nine replaceable parameters in a batch file (%1 through %9). However, a tenth replaceable parameter (%0) holds the name of the batch file.

TIP

If the replaceable parameter is a string that includes one or more spaces, surround the parameter with quotations marks (for example, "%1").

FOR: Looping in a Batch File

The FOR command is a batch file's way of looping through an instruction:

FOR %%parameter IN (set) DO command

%%parameter   This is the parameter that changes each time through the loop. You can use any single character after the two % signs (except 0 through 9). There are two % signs because Windows deletes single ones as it processes the batch file.

IN (set)   This is the list (it's officially called the set) of choices for %%parameter. You can use spaces, commas, or semicolons to separate the items in the set, and you must enclose them in parentheses.

DO command   For each item in the set, the batch file performs whatever instruction is given by command. The %%parameter is normally found somewhere in command.

Here's an example of the FOR command in a simple batch file that might help clear things up:

```
@ECHO OFF
FOR %%B IN (A B C) DO ECHO %%B
```

This batch file (call it Parameters.bat) produces the following output:

```
D:\BATCH>parameters2
A
B
C
```

All this does is loop through the three items in the set (A, B, and C) and substitute each one for %%B in the command ECHO %%B.

GOTO: Jumping to a Line in a Batch File

Your basic batch file lives a simple, linear existence. The first command is processed, and then the second, the third, and so on to the end of the file. It's boring, but that's all you need most of the time.

However, sometimes the batch file's usual one-command-after-the-other approach breaks down. For example, depending on a parameter or the result of a previous command, you might need to skip over a line or two. How do you do this? With the GOTO batch command:

```
...
... (the opening batch commands)
...
GOTO NEXT
...
... (the batch commands that get skipped)
...
:NEXT
...
... (the rest of the batch commands)
...
```

Here, the GOTO command is telling the batch file to look for a line that begins with a colon and the word NEXT (this is called a *label*) and to ignore any commands in between.

GOTO is useful for processing different batch commands depending on a parameter. Here's a simple example:

```
@ECHO OFF
CLS
GOTO %1
:A
ECHO This part of the batch file runs if A is the parameter.
GOTO END
:B
ECHO This part of the batch file runs if B is the parameter.
:END
```

Suppose that this file is named GOTOTest.BAT and you enter the following command:

gototest a

In the batch file, the line GOTO %1 becomes GOTO A. That makes the batch file skip down to the :A label, where it then runs the commands (in this example, just an ECHO statement) and skips to :END to avoid the rest of the batch file commands.

NOTE

Many of the batch file examples in this chapter are available for download from my website at www.mcfedries.com/Windows7Unleashed.

IF: Handling Batch File Conditions

Batch files sometimes have to make decisions before proceeding. Here are a few examples of what a batch file might have to decide:

▶ If the %2 parameter equals /Q, jump to the QuickFormat section. Otherwise, do a regular format.

▶ If the user forgets to enter a parameter, cancel the program. Otherwise, continue processing the batch file.

▶ If the file that the user wants to move already exists in the new folder, display a warning. Otherwise, proceed with the move.

▶ If the last command failed, display an error message and cancel the program. Otherwise, continue.

For these types of decisions, you need to use the IF batch command. IF has the following general form:

IF *condition command*

condition   This is a test that evaluates to a yes or no answer ("Did the user forget a parameter?").

command   This is what is executed if the *condition* produces a positive response ("Cancel the batch file").

For example, one of the most common uses of the IF command is to check the parameters that the user entered and proceed accordingly. From the previous section, the simple batch file that used GOTO can be rewritten with IF as follows:

```
@ECHO OFF
CLS
IF "%1"=="A" ECHO This part of the batch file runs if A is the parameter.
IF "%1"=="B" ECHO This part of the batch file runs if B is the parameter.
```

The condition part of an IF statement is a bit tricky. Let's look at the first one: "%1"=="A". Remember that the condition is always a question with a yes or no answer. In this case, the question boils down to the following:

Is the first parameter (%1) equal to A?

The double equal sign (==) looks weird, but that's just how you compare two strings of characters in a batch file. If the answer is yes, the command executes. If the answer is no, the batch file moves on to the next IF, which checks to see whether the parameter is "B".

> **NOTE**
>
> Strictly speaking, you don't need to include the quotation marks ("). Using %1==A accomplishes the same thing. However, I prefer to use them for two reasons: First, it makes it clearer that the IF condition is comparing strings; second, as you'll see in the next section, the quotation marks enable you to check whether the user forgot to enter a parameter at all.

> **CAUTION**
>
> This batch file has a serious flaw that will prevent it from working under certain condi-
> tions. Specifically, if you use the lowercase "a" or "b" as a parameter, nothing
> happens because, to the IF command, "a" is different from "A". The solution is to
> add extra IF commands to handle this situation:
>
> ```
> IF "%1"=="a" ECHO This part of the batch file runs if a is the parameter
> ```

Proper batch file techniques require you to check to see not only what a parameter is, but also whether one exists. This can be vital because a missing parameter can cause a batch file to crash and burn. For example, here's a batch file called DontCopy.bat designed to copy all files in the current folder to a new destination (given by the second parameter) except those you specified (given by the first parameter):

```
@ECHO OFF
CLS
ATTRIB +H %1
ECHO.
ECHO Copying all files to %2 except %1:
ECHO.
XCOPY *.* %2
ATTRIB -H %1
```

What happens if the user forgets to add the destination parameter (%2)? Well, the XCOPY command becomes XCOPY *.*, which terminates the batch file with the following error:

```
File cannot be copied onto itself
```

The solution is to add an IF command that checks to see whether %2 exists:

```
@ECHO OFF
CLS
```

```
IF "%2"=="" GOTO ERROR
ATTRIB +H %1
ECHO.
ECHO Copying all files to %2 except %1:
ECHO.
XCOPY32 *.* %2
ATTRIB -H %1
GOTO END
:ERROR
ECHO You didn't enter a destination!
ECHO Please try again...
:END
```

The condition "%2"=="" is literally comparing %2 to nothing (""). If this proves to be true, the program jumps (using GOTO) to the :ERROR label, and a message is displayed to admonish the user. Notice, too, that if everything is okay (that is, the user entered a second parameter), the batch file executes normally and jumps to the :END label to avoid displaying the error message.

Another variation of IF is the IF EXIST command, which checks for the existence of a file. This is handy, for example, when you're using COPY or MOVE. First, you can check whether the file you want to copy or move exists. Second, you can check whether a file with the same name already exists in the target folder. (As you probably know, a file that has been copied over by another of the same name is downright impossible to recover.) Here's a batch file called SafeMove.bat, which uses the MOVE command to move a file but first checks the file and then the target folder:

```
@ECHO OFF
CLS
IF EXIST %1 GOTO SO_FAR_SO_GOOD
ECHO The file %1 doesn't exist!
GOTO END
:SO_FAR_SO_GOOD
IF NOT EXIST %2 GOTO MOVE_IT
ECHO The file %1 exists on the target folder!
ECHO Press Ctrl+C to bail out or, to keep going,
PAUSE
:MOVE_IT
MOVE %1 %2
:END
```

To explain what's happening, I'll use a sample command:

```
safemove moveme.txt "%userprofile%\documents\moveme.txt"
```

The first IF tests for the existence of %1 (MOVEME.TXT in the example). If there is such a file, the program skips to the :SO_FAR_SO_GOOD label. Otherwise, it tells the user that the file doesn't exist and then jumps down to :END.

The second IF differs slightly. In this case, I want to continue only if MOVEME.TXT doesn't exist in the current user's My Documents folder, so I add NOT to the condition. (You can include NOT in any IF condition.) If this proves true (that is, the file given by %2 doesn't exist), the file skips to :MOVE_IT and performs the move. Otherwise, the user is warned and given an opportunity to cancel.

Working with the Command-Line Tools

The real power of the command line shines through when you combine the techniques you've learned so far with any of Windows 7's dozens of command-line tools. I don't have enough space to cover every tool (that would require a book in itself), so the rest of this chapter takes you through the most useful and powerful command-line tools in three categories: disk management, file management, and system management.

Working with Disk Management Tools

Windows 7 comes with a large collection of command-line disk management tools that enable you to check disks or partitions for errors, as well as defragment, format, partition, and convert disks. Table 13.5 lists the disk management tools that you can use with Windows 7.

TABLE 13.5   Windows 7's Command-Line Disk Management Tools

Tool	Description
CHKDSK	Checks a specified volume for errors.
CHKNTFS	Configures automatic disk checking.
CONVERT	Converts a specified volume to a different file system.
DEFRAG	Defragments a specified volume.
DISKCOMP	Compares the contents of two floppy disks. (This tool does not compare hard disks or other types of removable media, such as memory cards.)
DISKCOPY	Copies the contents of one floppy disk to another. (This tool does not copy hard disks or other types of removable media, such as memory cards.)
DISKPART	Enables you to list, create, select, delete, and extend disk partitions.
EXPAND	Extracts one or more files from a compressed file such as a .cab file found on some installation discs.

TABLE 13.5 Continued

Tool	Description
FORMAT	Formats the specified volume.
FSUTIL	Performs a number of file system tasks.
LABEL	Changes or deletes the name of a specified volume.
MOUNTVOL	Creates, displays, or deletes a mount point.
VOL	Displays the name and serial number of a specified volume.

NOTE

In this section, I use the word *volume* to refer to any disk, partition, or mount point.

The next four sections give you more detailed coverage of the CHKDKS, CHKNTFS, and DEFRAG tools.

CHKDSK: Checking for Hard Disk Errors

In Chapter 7, "Maintaining Your Windows 7 System," you learned how to use the Check Disk utility to check a hard disk for errors. Check Disk also comes with a command-line version called CHKDSK that you can run in a Command Prompt window.

▶ For information on Check Disk and the types of errors it looks for, **see** "Checking Your Hard Disk for Errors," **p. 135**.

Here's the syntax for CHKDSK:

CHKDSK [*volume* [*filename*]] [/F] [/V] [/R] [/B] [/X] [/I] [/C] [/L:[*size*]]

volume	The drive letter (followed by a colon) or mount point.
filename	On FAT16 and FAT32 disks, the name of the file to check. Include the path if the file isn't in the current folder.
/F	Tells CHKDSK to automatically fix errors. This is the same as running the Check Disk GUI with the Automatically Fix File System Errors option activated.
/V	Runs CHKDSK in verbose mode. On FAT16 and FAT32 drives, CHKDSK displays the path and name of every file on the disk; on NTFS drives, CHKDSK displays cleanup messages, if any.
/R	Tells CHKDSK to scan the disk surface for bad sectors and recover data from the bad sectors, if possible. (The /F switch is implied.) This is the same as running the Check Disk GUI with the Scan for and Attempt Recovery of Bad Sectors option activated.
/B	Tells CHKDSK to clear the list of bad sectors on the disk and then recheck the entire disk. Including this parameter is the same as also including the /R parameter.

/X	On NTFS nonsystem disks that have open files, forces the volume to dismount, invalidates the open file handles, and then runs the scan. (The /F switch is implied.)
/I	On NTFS disks, tells CHKDSK to check only the file system's index entries.
/C	On NTFS disks, tells CHKDSK to skip the checking of cycles within the folder structure. This is a rare error, so using /C to skip the cycle check can speed up the disk check.
/L:[size]	On NTFS disks, tells CHKDSK to set the size of its log file to the specified number of kilobytes. The default size is 65,536, which is plenty big enough for most systems, so you should never need to change the size. Note that if you include this switch without the size parameter, Check Disk tells you the current size of the log file.

For example, to run a read-only check—that is, a check that doesn't repair errors—on the C: drive, you enter the following command:

```
chkdsk c:
```

Note that when you use the /F switch to fix errors, CHKDSK must lock the volume to prevent running processes from using the volume during the check. If you use the /F switch on the %SystemDrive%, which is the drive where Windows 7 is installed (usually drive C:), CHKDSK can't lock the drive, and you see the following message:

```
Cannot lock current drive.
```

```
Chkdsk cannot run because the volume is in use by another
process. Would you like to schedule this volume to be
checked the next time the system restarts? (Y/N)
```

If you press Y and Enter, CHKDSK schedules a check for drive C: to run the next time you reboot Windows 7.

CHKNTFS: Scheduling Automatic Disk Checks

You saw in the preceding section that CHKDSK prompts you to schedule an automatic disk check during the next reboot if you run CHKDSK /F on the system drive (usually drive C: in Windows 7).

If you press Y and Enter at these prompts, CHKDSK adds the AUTOCHK utility to the following Registry setting:

```
HKLM\SYSTEM\CurrentControlSet\Control\Session Manager\BootExecute
```

This setting specifies the programs that Windows 7 should run at boot time when the Session Manager is loading. AUTOCHK is the automatic version of CHKDSK that runs at system startup.

Windows 7 also comes with a command-line tool named CHKNTFS that enables you to cancel pending automatic disk checks, schedule boot-time disk checks without using CHKDSK, and set the time that AUTOCHK counts down before running the automatic disk checks.

Here's the syntax for CHKNTFS:

```
CHKNTFS [volume ][/C volume:] [/X volume:] [/D] [/T:[time]]
```

volume	A drive letter (followed by a colon) or mount point.
/C volume	Tells CHKNTFS to schedule an automatic startup disk check for the specified volume. You can specify multiple volumes (separated by spaces).
/X volume	Tells CHKNTFS to exclude the specified volume from an automatic startup disk check. You can specify multiple volumes (separated by spaces).
/D	Tells CHKNTFS to exclude all volumes from an automatic startup disk check.
/T:[time]	Specifies the time that AUTOCHK counts down before starting the automatic disk checks.

When you run CHKNTFS with just a volume name, you see one of the following:

▶ If the volume is not scheduled for a startup disk check, you see the volume's file system:

```
The type of the file system is NTFS.
```

▶ If the volume is scheduled for a startup disk check, you see the following message:

```
Chkdsk has been scheduled manually to run on next reboot.
```

▶ If Windows 7's Storage Manager has detected an error on the volume, it marks the volume as *dirty*, so in this case, you see the following message (using drive C: as an example):

```
C: is dirty. You may use the /C option to schedule chkdsk for this drive.
```

This last message is confusing because Windows 7 *always* performs an automatic startup disk check of any volume that's marked as dirty. What you can do with CHKNTFS is bypass the automatic startup disk check of any volume that is marked as dirty. To do that, run CHKNTFS with the /X switch, as in this example:

```
chkntfs /x c:
```

NOTE

To manually mark a volume as dirty, use the FSUTIL DIRTY SET *volume* command, where *volume* is the drive you want to work with. For example, the following command marks drive C: as dirty:

```
fsutil dirty set c:
```

If you're not sure whether a drive is dirty, either run CHKNTFS *volume* or run FSUTIL DIRTY QUERY *volume*, as in this example:

```
fsutil dirty query c:
```

Note, however, that FSUTIL doesn't give you any way to unmark a drive as dirty.

If a volume isn't already marked as dirty, you can force CHKDSK to check a volume at startup by running CHKNTFS with the /C switch. For example, the following command sets up an automatic start check for the D: drive:

```
chkntfs /c d:
```

Note that the /C switch is cumulative, meaning that if you run it multiple times and specify a different volume each time, CHKNTFS adds each new volume to the list of volumes to check at startup. Instead of running multiple commands, however, you can specify multiple volumes in a single command, like so:

```
chkntfs /c c: d:
```

If you know a volume has been scheduled for a startup check, but you want to cancel that check, run CHKNTFS with the /X switch, as in this example:

```
chkntfs /x d:
```

You can also specify multiple volumes, if needed:

```
chkntfs /x c: d:
```

If you know that multiple volumes are scheduled for automatic startup checks, you can cancel all the checks by running CHKNTFS with the /D switch:

```
chkntfs /d
```

If you've scheduled a startup check for one or more volumes, or if a volume is marked as dirty, the next time you reboot Windows 7, you see a message similar to the following (which uses drive C: as an example):

```
Checking file system on C:
The type of the file system is NTFS.
Volume label is SYS.

One of your disks needs to be checked for consistency. You
may cancel the disk check, but it is strong recommended
that you continue.
To skip disk checking, press any key within 10 second(s).
```

13

The number of seconds in the last line counts down to 0: If you press a key before the countdown ends, Windows 7 skips the disk check; otherwise, it continues with CHKDSK.

CAUTION

Pressing any key to skip the disk check usually only works with wired keyboards. On most wireless keyboards, pressing a key has no effect.

You can change the initial countdown value by running CHKNTFS with the /T switch, followed by the number of seconds you want to use for the countdown. For example, the following command sets the countdown to 30 seconds:

```
chkntfs /t:30
```

Note that if you run the command CHKNTFS /T (that is, you don't specify a countdown value), CHKNTFS returns the current countdown value.

DEFRAG: Defragmenting the System Drive

In Chapter 7, you learned how to defragment a volume using Windows 7's Disk Defragmenter program. If you want to schedule a defragment or perform this chore from a batch file, you have to use the DEFRAG command-line tool. Here's the syntax:

```
DEFRAG disks[/a] [/c] [/e] [/f] [/h] [/r] [/t] [/u] [/v]
```

disks	Specifies the drive letter (followed by a colon) of each disk you want to defragment (separate multiple drives with a space).
/a	Tells DEFRAG only to analyze the disk.
/c	Tells DEFRAG to defragment all the system's drives.
/e	Tells DEFRAG to defragment all the system's drives except those specified with the *disks* parameter.
/f	Forces DEFRAG to defragment the disk, even if it doesn't need defragmenting or if the disk has less than 7% free space. (DEFRAG normally requires at least that much free space because it needs an area in which to sort the files.)
/h	Runs DEFRAG with a higher program priority for better performance.
/r	Tells DEFRAG to defragment all the specified drives at the same time (in parallel).
/t	Tells DEFRAG to show the progress of an already running defrag.
/u	Tells DEFRAG to show the progress of the defrag.
/v	Runs DEFRAG in verbose mode, which displays both the analysis report and the defragmentation report.

> **NOTE**
>
> To run the DEFRAG utility, you must use an administrator Command Prompt session, as described earlier (see "Running Command Prompt as the Administrator").

> **CAUTION**
>
> The DEFRAG switches are case sensitive. So, for example, the following command will work properly:
>
> defrag c: -a
>
> However, this command will not:
>
> defrag c: -A

For example, to get an analysis report of the fragmentation of drive C:, enter the following command:

defrag c: -a

If the volume isn't too fragmented, you see a report similar to this:

```
Post Defragmentation Report:


        Volume Information:
                Volume size             = 116.49 GB
                Free space              = 106.89 GB
                Total fragmented space  = 1%
                Largest free space size = 56.49 GB


        Note: File fragments larger than 64MB are not
        included in the fragmentation statistics.


        You do not need to defragment this volume.
```

However, if the drive is quite fragmented, you see a report similar to the following:

```
Post Defragmentation Report:


        Volume Information:
                Volume size             = 397.12 GB
                Free space              = 198.32 GB
                Total fragmented space  = 9%
                Largest free space size = 158.43 GB
```

13

```
Note: File fragments larger than 64MB are not
included in the fragmentation statistics.
```

You should defragment this volume.

If you try to defragment a volume that is running low on disk space, DEFRAG displays the following message:

```
Volume DATA has only 9% free space available for use by Disk Defragmenter.
To run effectively, Disk Defragmenter requires at least 15% usable free space.
There is not enough disk space to properly complete the operation.
Delete some unneeded files on your hard disk, and then try again.
```

If you can't delete files from the volume (for example, if this is a Windows 7 data partition), you can try running DEFRAG with the -f switch to force the operation:

```
defrag d: -f
```

NOTE

Forcing the defrag operation shouldn't cause problems in most cases. With less free space in which to work, DEFRAG just takes quite a bit longer to defragment the volume, and there may be parts of the volume that it simply can't defragment.

Working with File and Folder Management Tools

Windows Explorer is the GUI tool of choice for most file and folder operations. However, Windows 7 comes with an impressive collection of command-line file and folder tools that let you perform all the standard operations such as renaming, copying, moving, and deleting, as well as more interesting chores such as changing file attributes and comparing the contents of two files. Table 13.6 lists the file management tools that you can use with Windows 7.

TABLE 13.6   Windows 7's Command-Line File and Folder Management Tools

Tool	Description
ATTRIB	Displays, applies, or removes attributes for the specified file or folder.
CD	Changes to the specified folder.
COMP	Compares the contents of two specified files byte by byte.
COMPACT	Displays or modifies the compression settings for the specified file or folder (which must be located on an NTFS partition).
COPY	Creates a copy of the specified file or folder in another location.
DEL	Deletes the specified file or folder.
DIR	Displays a directory listing for the current folder or for the specified file or folder.

TABLE 13.6   Continued

Tool	Description
FC	Compares the content of two specified files.
FIND	Searches for and displays all the instances of a specified string in a file.
FINDSTR	Uses a regular expression to search for and display all the instances of a specified string in a file.
MKDIR	Creates the specified folder.
MOVE	Moves the specified file or folder to another location.
REN	Changes the name of the specified file or folder.
REPLACE	Replaces files in the destination folder with files in the source folder that have the same name.
RMDIR	Deletes the specified folder.
SORT	Sorts the specified file and then displays the results.
SFC	Runs the System File Checker, which scans and verifies the protected Windows 7 files.
TAKEOWN	Enables an administrator to take ownership of the specified file.
TREE	Displays a graphical tree diagram showing the subfolder hierarchy of the current folder or the specified folder.
WHERE	Searches for and displays all the files that match a specified pattern in the current folder and in the PATH folders.
XCOPY	Creates a copy of the specified file or folder in another location. This tool offers many more options than the COPY command.

The next few sections take a closer look at a half dozen of these tools: ATTRIB, FIND, REN, REPLACE, SORT, and XCOPY.

Before getting to the tools, I should mention that most of the file and folder management tools work with the standard wildcard characters: ? and *. In a file or folder specification, you use ? to substitute for a single character, and you use * to substitute for multiple characters. Here are some examples:

File Specification	Matches
Budget200?.xlsx	Budget2009.xlsx, Budget2008.xlsx, and so on
Memo.doc?	Memo.doc, Memo.docx, Memo.docm, and so on
*.txt	ReadMe.txt, log.txt, to-do.txt, and so on
*200?.pptx	Report2009.pptx, Budget2007.pptx, Conference2008.pptx, and so on
.	Every file

ATTRIB: Modifying File and Folder Attributes

A file's *attributes* are special codes that indicate the status of the file. There are four attributes you can work with:

▶ **Archive**—When this attribute is turned on, it means the file has been modified since it was last backed up.

▶ **Hidden**—When this attribute is turned on, it means the file doesn't show up in a DIR listing and isn't included when you run most command-line tools. For example, if you run DEL *.* in a folder, Windows 7 deletes all the files in that folder, except the hidden files.

▶ **Read-only**—When this attribute is turned on, it means the file can't be modified or erased.

▶ **System**—When this attribute is turned on, it means the file is an operating system file (that is, a file that was installed with Windows 7).

The ATTRIB command lets you turn these attributes on or off. Here's the syntax:

```
ATTRIB [+A | -A] [+H | -H] [+R | -R] [+S | -S] filename [/S [/D]]
```

+A	Sets the archive attribute
-A	Clears the archive attribute
+H	Sets the hidden attribute
-H	Clears the hidden attribute
+R	Sets the read-only attribute
-R	Clears the read-only attribute
+S	Sets the system attribute
-S	Clears the system attribute
filename	The file or files you want to work with
/S	Applies the attribute change to the matching files in the current folder and all of its subfolders
/D	Applies the attribute change only to the current folder's subfolders. You must use this switch in conjunction with /S

For example, if you want to hide all the DOC files in the current directory, use the following command:

```
attrib +h *.doc
```

As another example, if you've ever tried to delete or edit a file and got the message Access denied, the file is likely read-only. You can turn off the read-only attribute by running ATTRIB with the -R switch, as in this example:

```
attrib -r readonly.txt
```

> **NOTE**
>
> If you want to check out a file's attributes, use the DIR command's /A switch. Use /AA to see files with their archive attribute set, /AH for hidden files, /AR for read-only, and /AS for system files.

You can also use ATTRIB for protecting important or sensitive files. When you hide a file, it doesn't show up in a listing produced by the DIR command. Out of sight is out of mind, so someone taking a casual glance at your files won't see the hidden ones and, therefore, won't be tempted to display or erase them.

Although a hidden file is invisible, it's not totally safe. Someone who knows the name of the file can attempt to modify the file by opening it with the appropriate program. As an added measure of safety, you can also set the file's read-only attribute. When you do this, the file can't be modified. You can set both attributes with a single command:

```
attrib +h +r payroll.xlsx
```

FIND: Locating a Text String in a File

You use the FIND command to search for a string inside a file. Here's the syntax:

```
FIND [/C] [/I] [/N] [/V] "string" filename
```

/C	Displays the number of times that *string* appears in *filename.*
/I	Performs a case-insensitive search.
/N	Displays each match of *string* in *filename* with the line number in *filename* where each match occurs.
/V	Displays the lines in *filename* that don't contain *string.*
string	The string you want to search for.
filename	The file you want to search in. (Note that you can't use wildcards with the FIND command.) If the filename contains one or more spaces, surround it with double quotation marks.

NOTE

The FIND command doesn't work with the new Office 2007 file formats. However, it works fine with most documents created in earlier versions of Office.

For example, to find the string *DVD* in a file named WishList.txt, you use the following command:

```
find "DVD" WishList.txt
```

If the string you want to find contains double quotation marks, you need to place two quotation marks in the search string. For example, to find the phrase *Dave "The Hammer" Schultz* in the file players.doc, use the following command:

```
find "Dave ""The Hammer"" Schultz" players.doc
```

TIP

The FIND command doesn't accept wildcard characters in the *filename* parameter. That's too bad, because it's often useful to search multiple files for a string. Fortunately, you can work around this limitation by using a FOR loop where the command you run on each file is FIND. Here's the general syntax to use:

```
FOR %f IN (filespec) DO FIND "string" %f
```

Replace *filespec* with the file specification you want to use, and *string* with the string you want to search for. For example, the following command runs through all the .doc files in the current folder and searches each file for the string *Thanksgiving*:

```
FOR %f IN (*.doc) DO FIND "Thanksgiving" %f
```

If the file specification will match files with spaces in their names, you need to surround the last %f parameter with quotation marks, like so:

```
FOR %f IN (*.doc) DO FIND "Thanksgiving" "%f"
```

One of the most common uses of the FIND command is as a filter in pipe operations (see "Piping Commands," earlier in this chapter). In this case, instead of a filename, you pipe the output of another command through FIND. In this case, FIND searches this input for a specified string and, if it finds a match, it displays the line that contains the string.

For example, the last line of a DIR listing tells you the number of bytes free on the current drive. Rather than wade through the entire DIR output just to get this information, use this command instead:

```
dir | find "free"
```

You'll see something like the following:

```
2 Dir(s) 28,903,331,184 bytes free
```

FIND scours the DIR listing piped to it and looks for the word *free*. You can use this technique to display specific lines from, say, a CHKDSK report. For example, searching for *bad* finds the number of bad sectors on the disk.

REN: Renaming a File or Folder

You use the REN (or RENAME) command to change the name of one or more files and folders. Here's the syntax:

```
REN old_filename1 new_filename
```

old_filename	The original filename
new_filename	The new filename

For example, the following command renamed Budget 2007.xlsx to Budget 2008.xlsx:

```
ren "Budget 2007.xlsx" "Budget 2008.xlsx"
```

A simple file or folder rename such as this probably isn't something you'll ever fire up a command-line session to do because renaming a single object is faster and easier in Windows Explorer. However, the real power of the REN command is that it accepts wildcards in the file specifications. This enables you to rename several files at once, something you can't do in Windows Explorer.

For example, suppose you have a folder full of files, many of which contain 2009 somewhere in the filename. To rename all those files by changing 2009 to 2010, you'd use the following command:

```
ren *2009* *2010*
```

Similarly, if you have a folder full of files that use the .htm extension and you want to change each extension to .asp, you use the following command:

```
ren *.htm *.asp
```

Note that for these multiple-file renames to work, in most cases the original filename text and the new filename text must be the same length. For example, digital cameras often supply photos with names such as img_1234.jpg and img_5678.jpg. If you have a number of related photos in a folder, you might want to give them more meaningful names. If the photos are from a vacation in Rome, you might prefer names such as Rome_Vacation_1234.jpg and Rome_Vacation_5678.jpg. Unfortunately, the REN command can't handle this. However, it can rename the files to Rome_1234.jpg and Rome_5678.jpg:

```
ren img_* Rome*
```

13

The exception to the same length rule is if the replacement occurs at the end of the file-names. For example, the following command renames all files with the `.jpeg` extension to `.jpg`:

```
ren *.jpeg *.jpg
```

REPLACE: Smarter File Copying

If there was such a thing as a Most Underrated Command award, REPLACE would win it hands down. This command, which you almost never hear about, can do three *very* useful (and very different) things:

- ▶ It copies files, but only if their names match those in the target directory.

- ▶ It copies files, but only if their names don't exist in the target directory.

- ▶ It copies files, but only if their names match those in the target directory and the matching files in the target directory are older than the files being copied.

Here's the syntax:

```
REPLACE source_files target /A /U /P /R /S /W
```

`source_files`	The path and file specification of the files you want to copy.
`target`	The folder to which you want to copy the files.
`/A`	Copies only new files to the `target` folder. You can't use this switch in conjunction with `/S` or `/U`.
`/U`	Copies files that have the same name in the `target` folder and that are newer than the matching files in the `target` folder. You can't use this switch in conjunction with `/A`.
`/P`	Prompts you for confirmation before replacing files.
`/R`	Replaces read-only files.
`/S`	Replaces files in the `target` folder's subfolders. You can't use this switch in conjunction with `/A`.
`/W`	Waits for you to insert a disk before starting.

If you don't specify switches, REPLACE copies a file from the source folder to the target folder if and only if it finds a file with a matching name in the target.

More useful is the REPLACE command's updating mode, where it copies a file from the source folder to the target folder if and only if it finds a file with a matching name in the target and that target file is older than the source file. A good example where updating comes in handy is when you copy some files to a disk or memory card so that you can use them on another machine (such as taking files from your computer at work to use them at home). When you need to copy the files back to the first machine, the following REPLACE command does the job. (This assumes the disk or memory card is in the G: drive.)

```
replace g:*.* %UserProfile% /s /u
```

For each file on the G: drive, REPLACE looks for matching filenames anywhere in the %UserProfile% folder and its subfolders (thanks to the /S switch) and replaces only the ones that are newer (the /U switch).

What if you created some new files on the other computer? To copy those to the first machine, use the /A switch, as follows:

```
replace g:*.* %UserProfile%\Documents /a
```

In this case, REPLACE only copies a file from the G: drive if it doesn't exist in the %UserProfile%\Documents folder. (You have to specify a target folder because you can't use the /S switch with /A.)

SORT: Sorting the Contents of a File

When you obtain a file from the Internet or some other source, the data in the file may not appear in the order you want. What I usually do in such cases is import the file into Word or Excel and then use the program's Sort feature. This sometimes involves extra steps (such as converting text to a table in Word), so it's not always an efficient way to work.

If the file is text, it's often easier and faster to run the SORT command-line tool. By default, SORT takes the content of the file, sorts it in ascending alphanumeric order (0 to 9, then a to z, and then A to Z) starting at the beginning of each line in the file, and then displays the sorted results. You can also run descending order sorts, write the results to the same file or another file, and more. Here's the syntax:

```
SORT [input_file] [/+n] [/R] [/L locale] [/M kilobytes] [/REC characters]
➥[/T temp_folder] [/O output_file]
```

input_file	The file you want to sort.
/+n	Specifies the starting character position (*n*) of the sort. The default is 1 (that is, the first character on each line in the file).
/R	Sorts the file in descending order (Z to A, then z to a, and then 9 to 0).
/L locale	Specifies a *locale* for sorting other than the default system locale. Your only choice here is to use "C" to sort the file using the binary values for each character.
/M kilobytes	Specifies the amount of memory, in kilobytes, that SORT uses during the operation. If you don't specify this value, SORT uses a minimum of 160KB and a maximum of 90% of available memory.

13

/REC *characters*	Specifies the maximum length, in characters, of each line in the file. The default value is 4,096 characters, and the maximum value is 65,535 characters.
/T *temp_folder*	Specifies the folder that SORT should use to hold the temporary files it uses during the sort.
/O *output_file*	Specifies the file that SORT should create to store the results of the sort. You can specify a different file or the *input file*.

For example, the following SORT command sorts the data in records.txt and stores the results in sorted_records.txt:

```
sort records.txt sorted_records.txt
```

XCOPY: Advanced File Copying

The XCOPY command is one of the most powerful of the file management command-line tools, and you can use it for some fairly sophisticated file copying operations. Here's the syntax for XCOPY:

```
XCOPY source destination [/A | /M] [/C] [/D[:mm-dd-yyyy]]
➥[/EXCLUDE:file1[+file2[+file3]]] [/F] [/G] [/H] [/I] [/K] [/L] [/N] [/O] [/P] [/Q]
➥[/R] [/S [/E]] [/T] [/U] [/V] [/W] [/X] [/Y | -Y] [/Z]
```

source	The path and names of the files you want to copy.
destination	The location where you want the *source* files copied.
[/A]	Tells XCOPY to only copy those *source* files that have their archive attribute turned on. The archive attribute is not changed. If you use /A, you can't also use /M.
[/M]	Tells XCOPY to only copy those *source* files that have their archive attribute turned on. The archive attribute is turned off. If you use /M, you can't also use /A.
[/C]	Tells XCOPY to ignore any errors that occur during the copy operation. Otherwise, XCOPY aborts the operation if an error occurs.
[/D[:*mm-dd-yyyy*]]	Copies only those *source* files that changed on or after the date specified by *mm-dd-yyyy*. If you don't specify a date, using /D tells XCOPY to copy those *source* files that are newer than *destination* files that have the same name.
[/EXCLUDE:*file1*[+*file2*[+*file3*]]]	Tells XCOPY to not copy the files or file specification given by *file1*, *file2*, *file3*, and so on.
[/F]	Displays the *source* and *destination* filename during the copy operation.

[/G]	Creates decrypted copies of encrypted *source* files.
[/H]	Tells XCOPY to include in the copy operation any hidden and system files in the *source* folder.
[/I]	Tells XCOPY to create the *destination* folder. For this to work, the *source* value must be a folder or a file specification with wildcards.
[/K]	For each *source* file that has its read-only attribute set, tells XCOPY to maintain the read-only attribute on the corresponding *destination* file.
[/L]	Displays a list of the files that XCOPY will copy. (No files are copied if you use /L.)
[/N]	Tells XCOPY to use 8.3 filenames in the *destination* folder. Use this switch if the *destination* folder is a FAT partition that doesn't support long filenames.
[/O]	Tells XCOPY to also copy ownership and discretionary access control list data to the *destination*.
[/P]	Prompts you to confirm each file copy.
[/Q]	Tells XCOPY not to display messages during the copy.
[/R]	Includes read-only files in the copy.
[/S]	Tells XCOPY to also include the *source* folder's subfolders in the copy.
[/E]	Tells XCOPY to include empty subfolders in the copy if you specify the /S or /T switch.
[/T]	Tells XCOPY to copy the *source* folder subfolder structure. (No files are copied, just the subfolders.)
[/U]	Only copies those *source* files that exist in the *destination* folder.
[/V]	Tells XCOPY to verify that each *destination* copy is identical to the original *source* file.
[/W]	Displays the message Press any key to begin copying file(s) before copying. You must press a key to launch the copy (or press Ctrl+C to cancel).
[/X]	Tells XCOPY to also copy file audit settings and system access control list data to the *destination*. (This switch implies /O.)
[/Y]	Tells XCOPY not to ask you whether you want to overwrite existing files in the *destination*.

13

| [/ -Y] | Tells XCOPY to ask you whether you want to overwrite existing files in the *destination*. Use this switch if you've set the %COPYCMD% environment variable to /Y, which suppresses overwrite prompts for XCOPY, COPY, and MOVE. |
| [/Z] | If you're copying to a network *destination*, this switch tells XCOPY to restart to the copy if the network connection goes down during the operation. |

In its basic form, XCOPY works just like COPY. So, for example, to copy all the .doc files in the current folder to a folder called Documents in the G: drive, use the following command:

```
xcopy *.doc g:\documents
```

Besides being faster, XCOPY also contains a number of features not found in the puny COPY command. Think of it as COPY on steroids. (The X in XCOPY means that it's an extended COPY command.) For example, suppose you want to copy all the .doc files in the current folder and all the .doc files in any attached subfolders to G:\Documents. With COPY, you first have to create the appropriate folders on the destination partition and then perform separate COPY commands for each folder, which is not very efficient, to say the least. With XCOPY, all you do is add a single switch:

```
xcopy *.doc g:\documents /s
xcopy *.bat d:\batch /s
```

The /S switch tells XCOPY to copy the current folder and all nonempty subfolders, and to create the appropriate folders in the destination, as needed. (If you want XCOPY to copy empty subfolders, include the /E switch, as well.)

Another useful feature of XCOPY is the ability to copy files by date. This is handy for performing incremental backups of files that you modified on or after a specific date. For example, suppose you keep your word processing documents in %UserProfile%\Documents and you want to make backup copies in your Windows 7 user share of all the .doc files that have changed since August 23, 2007. You can do this with the following command:

```
xcopy %userprofile%\documents\*.doc \\server\users\%Username%\ /d:08-23-2007
```

It's common to use XCOPY in batch files, but take care to handle errors. For example, what if a batch file tries to use XCOPY, but there's not enough memory? Or what if the user presses Ctrl+C during the copy? It might seem impossible to check for these kinds of errors; yet it is not only possible, it's really quite easy.

When certain commands finish, they always file a report on the progress of the operation. This report, or *exit code*, is a number that specifies how the operation went. For example, Table 13.7 lists the exit codes that the XCOPY command uses.

TABLE 13.7 **XCOPY** Exit Codes

Exit Code	What It Means
0	Everything's okay; the files were copied.
1	Nothing happened because no files were found to copy.
2	The user pressed Ctrl+C to abort the copy.
4	The command failed because there wasn't enough memory or disk space or because there was something wrong with the command's syntax.
5	The command failed because of a disk error.

What does all this mean for your batch files? You can use a variation of the IF command—IF ERRORLEVEL—to test for these exit codes. For example, here's a batch file called CheckCopy.bat, which uses some of the XCOPY exit codes to check for errors:

```
@ECHO OFF
XCOPY %1 %2
IF ERRORLEVEL 4 GOTO ERROR
IF ERRORLEVEL 2 GOTO CTRL+C
IF ERRORLEVEL 1 GOTO NO_FILES
GOTO DONE
:ERROR
ECHO Bad news! The copy failed because there wasn't
ECHO enough memory or disk space or because there was
ECHO something wrong with your file specs . . .
GOTO DONE
:CTRL+C
ECHO Hey, what gives? You pressed Ctrl+C to abort . . .
GOTO DONE
:NO_FILES
ECHO Bad news! No files were found to copy . . .
:DONE
```

As you can see, the ERRORLEVEL conditions check for the individual exit codes and then use GOTO to jump to the appropriate label.

NOTE

How does a batch file know what a command's exit code was? When Windows 7 gets an exit code from a command, it stores it in a special data area set aside for exit code information. When Windows 7 sees the IF ERRORLEVEL command in a batch file, it retrieves the exit code from the data area so that it can be compared to whatever is in the IF condition.

One of the most important things to know about the IF ERRORLEVEL test is how Windows 7 interprets it. For example, consider the following IF command:

```
IF ERRORLEVEL 2 GOTO CTRL+C
```

Windows 7 interprets this command as "If the exit code from the last command is equal to or greater than 2, jump to the CTRL+C label." This has two important consequences for your batch files:

▶ The test IF ERRORLEVEL 0 doesn't tell you much because it's always true. If you just want to find out whether the command failed, use the test IF NOT ERRORLEVEL 0.

▶ To get the correct results, always test the *highest* ERRORLEVEL first and then work your way down.

Working with System Management Tools

System management is one of those catch-all terms that encompasses a wide range of tasks, from simple adjustments such as changing the system date and time to more complex tweaks such as modifying the Registry. Windows 7's command-line system management tools also enable you to monitor system performance, shut down or restart the computer, and even modify the huge Windows Management Instrumentation (WMI) interface. Table 13.8 lists the system management command-line tools that apply to Windows 7.

TABLE 13.8   Windows 7's Command-Line System Management Tools

Tool	Description
BCDEDIT	Displays or modifies the Boot Manager startup parameters
CHCP	Displays or changes the number of active console code pages
DATE	Displays or sets the system date
EVENTCREATE	Creates a custom event in an event log
REG	Adds, modifies, displays, and deletes Registry keys and settings
REGSVR32	Registers dynamic link library (DLL) files as command components in the Registry
SHUTDOWN	Shuts down or restarts Windows 7 or a remote computer
SYSTEMINFO	Displays a wide range of detailed configuration information about the computer
TIME	Displays or sets the system time

TABLE 13.8   Conitnued

Tool	Description
TYPEPERF	Monitors a performance counter
WHOAMI	Displays information about the current user, including the domain name (not applicable to Windows 7), computer name, username, security group member-ship, and security privileges
WMIC	Operates the Windows Management Instrumentation command-line tool that provides command-line access to the WMI interface

The next few sections take more detailed looks at five of these command-line tools: REG, SYSTEMINFO, TYPEPERF, and WHOAMI.

> ▶ I covered the SHUTDOWN tool in Chapter 4; **see** "Setting Up One-Click Restarts and Shutdowns," **p. 81.**

REG: Working with Registry Keys and Settings

In Chapter 12, "Tweaking the Windows 7 Registry," you learned how to view, add, and modify Registry keys and settings using the Registry Editor. That's the easiest and safest way to make Registry changes. However, there may be some settings that you change quite often. In such cases, it can become burdensome to be frequently launching the Registry Editor and changing the settings. A better idea is to create a shortcut or batch file that uses the REG command-line tool to make your Registry changes for you.

REG actually consists of 11 subcommands, each of which enables you to perform different Registry tasks:

REG ADD	Adds new keys or settings to the Registry. You can also use this command to modify existing settings.
REG QUERY	Displays the current values of one or more settings in one or more keys.
REG COMPARE	Compares the values of two Registry keys or settings.
REG COPY	Copies Registry keys or settings to another part of the Registry.
REG DELETE	Deletes a key or setting.
REG EXPORT	Exports a key to a .reg file.
REG IMPORT	Imports the contents of a .reg file.
REG SAVE	Copies Registry keys or settings to a hive (.hiv) file.
REG RESTORE	Writes a hive file into an existing Registry key. The hive file must be created using REG SAVE.
REG LOAD	Loads a hive file into a new Registry key. The hive file must be created using REG SAVE.
REG UNLOAD	Unloads a hive file that was loaded using REG LOAD.

13

I won't go through all of these commands. Instead, I'll focus on the three most common Registry tasks: viewing, adding, and modifying Registry data.

To view the current value of the Registry setting, you use the REG QUERY command:

```
REG QUERY KeyName [/V SettingName | /VE] [/C] [/D] [/E] [/F data] [/K | [/S]
➡[/SE separator] [/T type] [/Z]
```

KeyName	The Registry key that contains the setting or settings that you want to view. The KeyName must include a root key value: HKCR, HKCU, HKLM, HKU, or HKCC. Place quotation marks around key names that include spaces.
/V ValueName	The Registry setting in KeyName that you want to view.
/VE	Tells REG to look for empty settings (that is, settings with a null value).
/F data	Specifies the data that REG should match in the KeyName settings.
/C	Runs a case-sensitive query.
/E	Returns only exact matches.
/K	Queries only key names, not settings.
/S	Tells REG to query the subkeys of KeyName.
/SE separator	Defines the separator to search for in REG_MULTI_SZ settings.
/T type	Specifies the setting type or types to search: REG_SZ, REG_MULTI_SZ, REG_EXPAND_SZ, REG_DWORD, REG_BINARY, or REG_NONE.
/Z	Tells REG to include the numeric equivalent of the setting type in the query results.

For example, if you want to know the current value of the RegisteredOwner setting in HKLM\Software\Microsoft\Windows NT\CurrentVersion, run the following command:

```
reg query "hklm\software\microsoft\windows nt\currentversion" registeredowner
```

The Registry Editor has a Find command that enables you to look for text within the Registry. However, it would occasionally be useful to see a list of the Registry keys and settings that contains a particular bit of text. You can do this using the /F switch. For example, suppose you want to see a list of all the HKLM keys and settings that contain the text *Windows Defender*. Here's a command that will do this:

```
reg query hklm /f "Windows Defender" /s
```

To add a key or setting to the Registry, use the REG ADD command:

```
REG ADD KeyName [/V SettingName | /VE] [/D data] [/F | [/S separator] [/T type]
```

KeyName	The Registry key that you want to add or to which you want to add a setting. The KeyName must include a root key value: HKCR, HKCU, HKLM, HKU, or HKCC. Place quotation marks around key names that include spaces.
/V ValueName	The setting that you want to add to KeyName.
/VE	Tells REG to add an empty setting.
/D data	Specifies the data that REG should use as the value for the new setting.
/F	Modifies an existing key or setting without prompting to confirm the change.
/S separator	Defines the separator to use between multiple instances of data in a new REG_MULTI_SZ setting.
/T type	Specifies the setting type: REG_SZ, REG_MULTI_SZ, REG_EXPAND_SZ, REG_DWORD, REG_DWORD_BIG_ENDIAN, REG_DWORD_LITTLE_ENDIAN, REG_BINARY, or REG_LINK.

For example, the following command adds a key named MySettings to the HKCU root key:

```
reg add hkcu\MySettings
```

Here's another example that adds a setting named CurrentProject to the new MySettings key and sets the value of the new setting to Win7 Unleashed:

```
reg add hkcu\MySettings /v CurrentProject /d "Win7 Unleashed"
```

If you want to make changes to an existing setting, run REG ADD on the setting. For example, to change the HKCU\MySettings\CurrentProject setting to Windows 7 Unleashed, you run the following command:

```
reg add hkcu\MySettings /v CurrentProject /d "Windows 7 Unleashed"
```

Windows 7 responds with the following prompt:

```
Value CurrentProject exists, overwrite (Yes/No)?
```

To change the existing value, press Y and press Enter.

TIP

To avoid being prompted when changing existing settings, add the /F switch to the REG ADD command.

SYSTEMINFO: Returning System Configuration Data

If you want to get information about various aspects of your computer, a good place to start is the SYSTEMINFO command-line tool, which displays data about the following aspects of your system:

▶ The operating system name, version, and configuration type

▶ The registered owner and organization

▶ The original install date

▶ The system boot time

▶ The computer manufacturer, make, and model

▶ The system processors

▶ The BIOS version

▶ The total and available physical memory

▶ The paging file's maximum size, available size, in-use value, and location

▶ The installed hotfixes

▶ The network interface card data, such as the name, connection, DHCP status, and IP address (or addresses)

You can see all this data (and more), as well as control the output, by running SYSTEMINFO with the following syntax:

SYSTEMINFO [/S computer] [/U [domain]\username] [/P password] [/FO format] [/NH]

/S *computer*	The name of the remote computer for which you want to view the system configuration.
/U [*domain*]*username*	The *username* and, optionally, the *domain*, of the account under which you want to run the SYSTEMINFO command.
/P *password*	The *password* of the account you specified with /U.
/FO *format*	The output format, where *format* is one of the following values:

	table	The output is displayed in a row-and-column format, with headers in the first row and values in subsequent rows.
	list	The output is displayed in a two-column list, with the headers in the first column and values in the second column.
	csv	The output is displayed with headers and values separated by commas. The headers appear on the first line.

/NH	Tells SYSTEMINFO not to include column headers when you use the /FO switch with either table or csv.

The output of SYSTEMINFO is quite long, so pipe it through the MORE command to see the output one screen at a time:

```
systeminfo | more
```

If you want to examine the output in another program or import the results into Excel or Access, redirect the output to a file and use the appropriate format. For example, Excel can read .csv files, so you can redirect the SYSTEMINFO output to a .csv file while using csv as the output format:

```
systeminfo /fo csv > systeminfo.csv
```

TYPEPERF: Monitoring Performance

In Chapter 6, "Tuning Windows 7's Performance," you learned how to use the Performance Monitor utility to track the real-time performance of counters in various categories such as processor and memory.

> ▶ See "Using the Performance Monitor," **p. 119**.

You can get the same benefit without the Performance Monitor GUI by using the powerful TYPEPERF command-line tool. Here's the syntax:

```
TYPEPERF [counter1 [counter2 ...]] [-CF file] [-O file] [-F format] [-SI interval]
➡[-SC samples] [-Q [object]] [-QX [object]] [-CONFIG file] [-S computer]
```

counter1 [counter2 ...]	Specifies the path of the performance counter to monitor. If you want to track multiple counters, separate each counter path with a space. If any path includes spaces, surround the path with quotation marks.
-CF file	Loads the counters from file, where file is a text file that lists the counter paths on separate lines.
-O file	Specifies the path and name of the file that will store the performance data.
-F format	Specifies the format for the output file format given by the /O switch, where format is one of the following values:

	csv	The output is displayed with each counter separated by a comma and each sample on its own line. This is the default output format.
	tsv	The output is displayed with each counter separated by a tab and each sample on its own line.
	bin	The output is displayed in binary format.

13

-SI *interval*	Specifies the time interval between samples. The *interval* parameter uses the form [mm:] ss. The default interval is 1 second.
-SC *samples*	Specifies the number of samples to collect. If you omit this switch, TYPEPERF samples continuously until you press Ctrl+C to cancel.
-Q [*object*]	Lists the available counters for *object* without instances.
-QX [*object*]	Lists the available counters for *object* with instances.
-CONFIG *file*	Specifies the pathname of the settings file that contains the TYPEPERF parameters you want to run.
-S *computer*	Specifies that the performance counters should be monitored on the PC named *computer* if no computer name is specified in the counter path.
-Y	Answers yes to any prompts generated by TYPEPERF.

The official syntax of a counter path looks like this:

[*Computer*]*Object*([*Parent*/][*Instance*][#*Index*])*Counter*

Computer	The computer on which the counter is to be monitored. If you omit a computer name, TYPEPERF monitors the counter on the local computer.
Object	The performance object—such as Processor, Memory, or PhysicalDisk—that contains the counter.
Parent	The container instance of the specified *Instance*.
Instance	The instance of the *Object*, if it has multiple instances. For example, in a two- (or dual-core) processor system, the instances are 0 (for the first processor), 1 (for the second processor), or Total (for both processors combined). You can also using an asterisk (*) to represent all the instances in *Object*.
Index	The index number of the specified *Instance*.
Counter	The name of the performance counter. You can also use an asterisk (*) to represent all the counter in *Object(Instance)*.

In practice, however, you rarely use the *Computer, Parent,* and *Index* parts of the path, so most counter paths use one of the following two formats:

*Object**Counter*
Object(*Instance*)*Counter*

For example, here's the path for the Memory object's Available MBytes counter:

\Memory\Available MBytes

Here's a TYPEPERF command that displays five samples of this counter:

```
typeperf "\Memory\Available Mbytes" -sc 5
```

Similarly, here's the path for the Processor object's % Processor Time counter, using the first processor instance:

```
\Processor(0)\% Processor Time
```

Here's a TYPEPERF command that displays 10 samples of this counter every 3 seconds, and saves the results to a file named ProcessorTime.txt:

```
typeperf "\Processor(0)\% Processor Time" -sc 10 -si 3 -o ProcessorTime.txt
```

To use the -CONFIG parameter with TYPEPERF, you need to create a text file that stores the command line parameters you want to use. This configuration file consists of a series of parameter/value pairs that use the following general format:

```
[Parameter]
Value
```

Here, *Parameter* is text that specifies a TYPEPERF parameter—such as F for the -F parameter and S for the -S parameter. Use C to specify one or more counter paths—and *Value* is the value you want to assign to the parameter.

For example, consider the following command:

```
typeperf "\PhysicalDisk(_Total)\% Idle Time" -si 5 -sc 10 -o idletime.txt
```

To run the same command using the -CONFIG parameter, you first need to create a file with the following text:

```
[c]
\PhysicalDisk(_Total)\% Idle Time
[si]
5
[sc]
10
[o]
idletime.txt
```

If this file is named IdleTimeCounter.txt, you can run it at any time with the following command (assuming IdleTimeCounter.txt resides in the current folder):

```
typeperf -config IdleTimeCounter.txt
```

WHOAMI: Getting Information About the Current User

The WHOAMI command gives you information about the user who is currently logged on to the computer:

WHOAMI [/UPN | /FQDN | LOGONID] [/USER | /GROUPS | /PRIV] [/ALL] [/FO *Format*]

/UPN	(Domains only) Returns the current user's name using the user principal name (UPN) format.
/FQDN	(Domains only) Returns the current user's name using the fully qualified domain name (FQDN) format.
/LOGONID	Returns the current user's security identifier (SID).
/USER	Returns the current username using the *computer\user* format.
/GROUPS	Returns the groups of which the current user is a member.
/PRIV	Returns the current user's privileges.
/ALL	Returns the current user's SID, username, groups, and privileges.
/FO *format*	The output format, where *format* is one of the following values:

table The output is displayed in a row-and-column format, with headers in the first row and values in subsequent rows.

list The output is displayed in a two-column list, with the headers in the first column and values in the second column.

csv The output is displayed with headers and values separated by commas. The headers appear on the first line.

You probably won't use this command often on the Windows 7 computer because you'll almost always be logged on as administrator. However, WHOAMI is useful when you're working on a client computer and you're not sure who is currently logged on.

For example, the following command redirects the current user's SID, username, groups, and privileges to a file named whoami.txt using the list format:

```
whoami /all /fo list > whoami.txt
```

CHAPTER 14

Securing Windows 7

Uncertainty is the only certainty there is, and knowing how to live with insecurity is the only security.
—John Allen Paulos

Some folks claim that you can never be too thin or too rich. Other folks might give you an argument about one or both assertions, but I doubt anyone would take you to task if you added a third item to the list: Your Windows PC can never be too secure. There are just too many threats out there, and too many ways that the defenses in Windows can be breached.

With that in mind, this book gives you no less than *seven* chapters that cover various aspects of Windows 7 security, including web security, email security, file system security, user security, wired network security, and wireless network security.

In this chapter, I focus on general PC security, including basic precautions that everyone should take, a review of your computer's security settings, and instructions for managing your first line of Windows 7 defense: Windows Firewall.

Thwarting Snoops and Crackers

Let's begin with a look at protecting your PC from direct attacks: that is, when an unauthorized *cracker* (which I define as a hacker who has succumbed to the Dark Side of the Force) sits down at your keyboard and tries to gain access to your system. Sure, it may be unlikely that a malicious user would gain physical access to the computer in your home or office, but it's not impossible.

Crackers specialize in breaking into systems ("cracking" system security, hence the name), and at any given time, hundreds, perhaps even thousands, of crackers roam cyberspace looking for potential targets. If you're online right now, the restless and far-seeing eyes of the crackers are bound to find you eventually.

Sounds unlikely, you say? You wish. Crackers are armed with programs that automatically search through millions of IP addresses (the addresses that uniquely identify any computer or device connected to the Internet). Crackers specifically look for computers that aren't secure, and if they find one, they'll pounce on it and crack their way into the system.

Again, if all this sounds unlikely or that it would take them forever to find you, think again. Tests have shown that new and completely unprotected systems routinely get cracked within 20 minutes of connecting to the Internet!

First, Some Basic Precautions

So how do your thwart the world's crackers? I often joke that it's easy if you follow a simple four-prong plan:

- ▶ Don't connect to the Internet. Ever.

- ▶ Don't install programs on your computer. No, not even that one.

- ▶ Don't let anyone else work with, touch, glance at, talk about, or come with 20 feet of your computer.

- ▶ Burglar-proof your home or office.

The point here is that if you use your computer (and live your life) in an even remotely normal way, you open up your machine to security risks. That's a bleak assessment, for sure, but fortunately it doesn't take a lot of effort on your part to turn your computer into a maximum security area. The security techniques in this chapter (and the next half dozen chapters) will get to that goal, but first make sure you've nailed down the basics:

- ▶ **Leave User Account Control turned on**—Yes, I know UAC is a hassle, but it's *way* better in Windows 7 because it doesn't get in your face nearly as often. UAC is the best thing that's happened to Windows security in a long time, and it's a fact of life that your computer is much more secure when UAC has got your back. See "Making Sure User Account Control is Turned On," later in this chapter.

- ▶ **Be paranoid**—The belief that everyone's out to get you may be a sign of trouble in the real world, but it's just common sense in the computer world. Assume someone will sit down at your desk when you're not around; assume someone will try to log on to your computer when you leave for the night; assume all uninvited email attachments are viruses; assume unknown websites are malicious; assume any offer that sounds too good to be true probably is.

- ▶ **Keep to yourself**—We all share lots of personal info online these days, but there's sharing and then there's asking-for-trouble sharing. Don't tell anybody any of your passwords. Don't put your email address online unless it's disguised in some way (for example, by writing it as username at yourdomain dot com). Don't give out sensitive personal data such as your social security number, bank account number, or even your address and phone number (unless making a purchase with a reputable vendor). Only give your credit card data to online vendors that you trust implicitly or, even better, get a secure PayPal account and use that instead.

▶ **Test the firewall**—A firewall's not much good if it leaves your computer vulnerable to attack, so you should test the firewall to make sure it's doing its job. I show you several ways to do this, later in this chapter (see "Making Sure the Firewall Is Up to Snuff").

▶ **Take advantage of your router's firewall, too**—Why have one line of defense when in all probability you can have two! If your network has a router and that router connects to the Internet, then it, too, has an IP address that crackers can scan for vulnerabilities, particularly holes that expose your network. To prevent this, most routers come with built-in hardware firewalls that provide robust security. Access your router's setup pages, locate the firewall settings (see Figure 14.1 for an example), and then make sure the firewall is turned on.

14

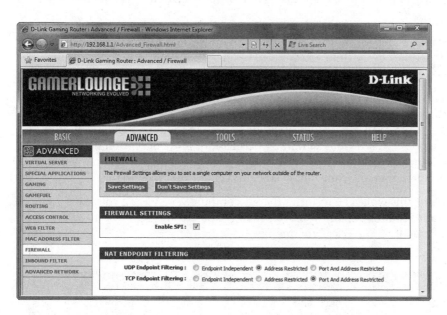

FIGURE 14.1   If your network has a router, make sure its firewall is turned on.

NOTE

To access the router setup pages, open a web browser, type the router address, and then press Enter. See your device documentation for the correct URL, but for most routers the address is either http://192.168.1.1 or http://192.168.0.1. In most cases, you have to log in with a username and password, so, again, see your documentation.

▶ **Update, update, update**—Many crackers take advantage of known Windows vulnerabilities to compromise a system. To avoid this, keep your PC updated with the latest patches, fixes, and service packs, many of which are designed to plug security leaks.

> ▶ See "Checking for Updates and Security Patches," **p. 158.**

▶ **Assume the worst**—Back up your data regularly, keep your receipts, keep all email correspondence, and read the fine print.

Locking Your Computer

In Chapter 17, "Securing the File System," you learn a few more security tweaks, including important measures such as advanced file permissions and encryption. These two features are great, but they each have one small flaw: They rely on the assumption that after you've entered a legitimate username and password to log on to your Windows user account, only *you* will use your computer. This means that after you log on, you become a "trusted" user and you have full access to your files, even if they're protected by permissions and encryption.

This is certainly reasonable on the surface. After all, you wouldn't want to have to enter your account credentials every time you want to open, edit, create, or delete a document. So while you're logged on and at your desk, you get full access to your stuff.

But what happens when you leave your desk? If you remain logged on to Windows, any other person who sits down at your computer can take advantage of your trusted-user status to view and work with secure files (including copying them to a USB flash drive inserted by the snoop). This is what I mean by permissions and encryption having a flaw, and it's a potentially significant security hole in large offices where it wouldn't be hard for someone to pull up your chair while you're stuck in yet another meeting.

One way to prevent this would be to turn off your computer every time you leave your desk. That way, any would-be snoop would have to get past your login to get to your files. This, obviously, is wildly impractical and inefficient.

CAUTION

I'm assuming that because you have files worthy of being protected by permissions or encryption, you haven't set up Windows to automatically log on, as I described in Chapter 4, "Customizing Startup and Shutdown."

Is there a better solution? You bet: You can lock your system before leaving your desk. Anyone who tries to use your computer must enter your password to access the Windows desktop.

Locking Your Computer Manually

Windows 7 gives you three ways to lock your computer before heading off:

▶ Select Start, Shut Down, Lock.

   ▶ If you lock your PC regularly, consider changing the Shut Down button to a Lock button; **see** "Customizing the Start Menu's Power Button," **p. 86**.

▶ Press Windows Logo+L.

▶ Press Ctrl+Alt+Delete and then click Lock This Computer.

Whichever method you use, you end up at the Windows logon screen, shown in Figure 14.2. Note that it says Locked under the username.

FIGURE 14.2   You see a screen similar to this when you lock your Windows 7 computer.

Locking Your Computer Automatically

The locking techniques from the previous section are easy enough to do, but the hard part is *remembering* to do them. If you're late for a meeting or a rendezvous, locking up your machine is probably the last thing on your mind as you dash out the door. The usual course of events in these situations is that just as you arrive at your destination, you remember that you forgot to lock your PC, and you then spend the whole time fretting about your defenseless computer.

To avoid the fretting (not to mention the possible intrusion), you can configure your computer to lock automatically after a period of inactivity. Earlier versions of Windows required a screen saver to do this, but not Windows 7. Here's how it's done:

1. Right-click the desktop and then click Personalize to open the Personalization windows.
2. Click Screen Saver.
3. If you want to have a screensaver kick in after your PC is inactive for a while, choose one from the Screen Saver list.
4. Use the Wait spin box to set the interval (in minutes) of idle time that Windows 7 waits before locking your PC.
5. Activate the On Resume, Display Logon Screen check box.
6. Click OK.

Requiring Ctrl+Alt+Delete at Startup

Protecting your Windows 7 user account with a password (as described in Chapter 18), though an excellent idea, is not foolproof. Hackers are an endlessly resourceful bunch, and some of the smarter ones figured out a way to defeat the user account password system. The trick is that they install a virus or Trojan horse program—usually via an infected email message or malicious website—that loads itself when you start your computer. This program then displays a *fake* version of the Windows 7 Welcome screen. When you type your user name and password into this dialog box, the program records it and your system security is compromised.

To thwart this clever ruse, Windows 7 enables you to configure your system so that you must press Ctrl+Alt+Delete before you can log on. This key combination ensures that the authentic Welcome screen appears.

To require that users must press Ctrl+Alt+Delete before they can log on, follow these steps:

1. Press Windows Logo+R to display the Run dialog box.
2. Type **control userpasswords2** and then click OK. The User Accounts dialog box appears.
3. Display the Advanced tab.
4. Activate the Require Users to Press Ctrl+Alt+Delete check box.
5. Click OK.

Checking Your Computer's Security Settings

Windows 7 comes with four security features enabled by default:

- ▶ Windows Firewall is turned on.

- ▶ Windows Defender protects your computer against spyware in real time and by scanning your PC on a schedule.

- ▶ User Account Control is turned on.

- ▶ The Administrator account is disabled.

However, even though these are the default settings, they're important enough not to be left to chance. The next four sections show you how to check that these crucial security settings really are enabled on your PC.

Making Sure Windows Firewall Is Turned On

By far, the most important thing you need to do to thwart crackers is to have a software firewall running on your computer. A *firewall* is a security feature that blocks unauthorized attempts to send data to your computer. The best firewalls completely hide your computer from the Internet, so those dastardly crackers don't even know you're there! Windows Firewall is turned on by default, but you should check this, just to be safe:

1. Select Start.
2. Type `firewall` and then click Windows Firewall in the search results. The Windows Firewall window appears. Check the Windows Firewall State value. If it says On, you're fine; otherwise, continue to step 3.
3. Click Turns Windows Firewall On or Off. The Customize Settings window appears.
4. In the Home or Work (Private) Network Location Settings section, activate the Turn On Windows Firewall option.
5. In the Public Network Location Settings section, activate the Turn On Windows Firewall option.
6. Click OK.

Making Sure Windows Defender Is Turned On

I've been troubleshooting Windows PCs for many years. It used to be that users accidentally deleting system files or making ill-advised attempts to edit the Registry or some other important configuration file caused most problems. Recent versions of Windows (particularly XP) could either prevent these kinds of PEBCAK (*problem exists between chair and keyboard*) issues or recover from them without a lot of trouble. However, I think we're all too well aware of the latest menace to rise in the past few years, and it has taken over as the top cause of desperate troubleshooting calls I receive: *malware*, the generic term for malicious software such as viruses and Trojan horses. The worst malware offender by far these days is *spyware*, a plague upon the earth that threatens to deprive a significant portion of the online world of its sanity. As often happens with new concepts, the term *spyware* has become encrusted with multiple meanings as people attach similar ideas to a convenient and popular label. However, spyware is generally defined as any program that surreptitiously monitors a user's computer activities—particularly the typing of passwords, PINs, and credit card numbers—or harvests sensitive data on the user's computer, and then sends that information to an individual or a company via the user's Internet connection (the so-called *back channel*) without the user's consent.

You might think that having a robust firewall between you and the bad guys would make malware a problem of the past. Unfortunately, that's not true. These programs piggyback on other legitimate programs that users actually *want* to download, such as file sharing programs, download managers, and screensavers. A *drive-by download* is the download and installation of a program without a user's knowledge or consent. This relates closely to a *pop-up download*—the download and installation of a program after the user clicks an option in a pop-up browser window, particularly when the option's intent is vaguely or misleadingly worded.

To make matters even worse, most spyware embeds itself deep into a system, and removing it is a delicate and time-consuming operation beyond the abilities of even experienced users. Some programs actually come with an Uninstall option, but it's nothing but a ruse, of course. The program appears to remove itself from the system, but what it actually does is a *covert reinstall*—it reinstalls a fresh version of itself when the computer is idle.

All this means that you need to buttress your firewall with an antispyware program that can watch out for these unwanted programs and prevent them from getting their hooks into your system. In versions of Windows prior to Vista, you needed to install a third-party program. However, Windows Vista came with an antispyware program named Windows Defender, and that tool remains part of Windows 7.

TIP

Many security experts recommend installing multiple antispyware programs on the premise that one program may miss one or two examples of spyware, but two or three programs are highly unlikely to miss any. So, in addition to Windows Defender, you might also consider installing antispyware programs such as Lavasoft Ad-Aware (www.lavasoft.com) and PC Tools Spyware Doctor (www.pctools.com).

Windows Defender protects your computer from spyware in two ways. It can scan your system for evidence of installed spyware programs (and remove or disable those programs, if necessary), and it can monitor your system in real time to watch for activities that indicate the presence of spyware (such as a drive-by download or data being sent via a back channel).

If the real-time protection feature of Windows Defender is turned off, you usually see the Action Center message shown in Figure 14.3. Click that message to launch Windows

Defender and turn on real-time protection. Otherwise, select Start, type **defender**, and then press Enter.

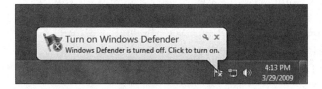

FIGURE 14.3   The Windows 7 Action Center will let you know if Windows Defender isn't monitoring your system in real-time for spyware.

In the Windows Defender Status area, check the following values:

▶ **Scan Schedule**—If you see Do Not Auto Scan, it means that Windows Defender isn't set up to scan your system for spyware automatically.

▶ **Real-Time Protection**—If you see Off here, it means that Windows Defender is actively guarding against spyware activity.

Follow these steps to ensure not only that Windows Defender is set up to automatically scan your system for spyware regularly, but that it's also actively monitoring your system for suspicious activity:

1. Click Tools.
2. Click Options.
3. Click Automatic Scanning.
4. Activate the Automatically Scan My Computer check box.
5. Click Real-Time Protection.
6. Activate the Use Real-Time Protection check box.
7. Click OK.

Spyware Scanning
For the scanning portion of its defenses, Windows Defender supports three different scan types:

▶ **Quick Scan**—This scan checks just those areas of your system where it is likely to find evidence of spyware. This scan usually takes just a couple of minutes. This scan is the default, and you can initiate one at any time by clicking the Scan link.

▶ **Full Scan**—This scan checks for evidence of spyware in system memory, all running processes, and the system drive (usually drive C:), and it performs a deep scan on all folders. This scan might take 30 minutes or more, depending on your system. To run this scan, pull down the Scan menu and click Full Scan.

▶ **Custom Scan**—This scan checks just the drives and folders that you select. The length of the scan depends on the number of locations you select and the number of objects in those locations. To run this scan, pull down the Scan menu and click Custom Scan, which displays the Select Scan Options page shown in Figure 21.6. Click Select, activate the check boxes for the drives you want scanned, and then click OK. Click Scan Now to start the scan.

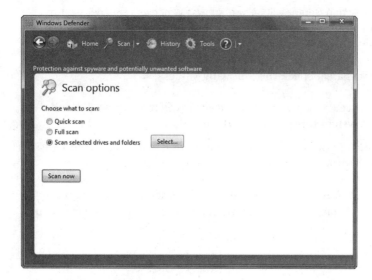

FIGURE 14.4   In the Scan menu, select Custom Scan to see the Select Scan Options page.

Windows Defender Settings

By default, Windows Defender is set up to perform a Quick Scan of your system every morning at 2:00 a.m. To change this, select Tools, Options, Automatic Scanning, and then use the controls to specify the scan frequency time and type.

The rest of the Options page offers options for customizing Windows Defender. There are six more groups:

▶ **Default Actions**—Set the action that Windows Defender should take if it finds alert items (potential spyware) in the Severe, High, Medium, and Low categories: Recommended Action Based on Definitions (Windows Defender's default action for the detected spyware), Ignore, Quarantine (disables the threat without removing it), Remove, or Allow.

▶ **Real-Time Protection**—Besides toggling real-time protection on and off, you can also toggle security agents on and off. *Security agents* monitor Windows components that are frequent targets of spyware activity.

> **TIP**
>
> Windows Defender will often warn you that a program might be spyware and ask whether you want to allow the program to operate normally or to block it. If you accidentally allow an unsafe program, click Tools, Allowed Items; select the program in the Allowed Items list, and then click Remove from List. Similarly, if you accidentally blocked a safe program, click Tools, Quarantined Items; select the program in the Quarantined Items list, and then click Remove.

▶ **Excluded Files and Folders**—Use this section to specify files or folders that you don't want Windows Defender to scan.

▶ **Excluded File Type**—Use this section to specify file extensions that you don't want Windows Defender to scan.

▶ **Advanced**—Use these options to enable scanning inside archive files, email messages, and removable drives.

▶ **Administrator**—This section has a check box that toggles Windows Defender on and off, and another that, when activated, allows you to see Windows Defenders items (such as allowed programs) for all users accounts on the computer.

Making Sure User Account Control Is Turned On

I'll be talking about User Account Control in detail in Chapter 18. For now, let's just make sure it's enabled on your system:

1. Select Start, type **user**, and then click Change User Account Control Settings in the search results. The User Account Control Settings dialog box appears.

2. Make sure the slider is set to anything other than Never Notify at the bottom. See Chapter 18 to learn about the different settings. If you're not sure what to go with, for now choose Default (second from the top).

   ▶ See "Configuring User Account Control," **p. 377**.

3. Click OK.

4. Restart your computer to put the new setting into effect.

Making Sure the Administrator Account Is Disabled

One of the confusing aspects about Windows 7 is that the Administrator account seems to disappear after the setup is complete. That's because, for security reasons, Windows 7 doesn't give you access to this all-powerful account. However, there are ways to activate this account, so it pays to take a second and make sure it's still in its disabled state.

You can so this in several ways, but here's a quick look at two of them:

▶ **Using the Local Security Policy Editor**—Select Start, type **secpol.msc**, and then press Enter. In the Local Security Policy Editor, open the Local Policies, Security

Options branch, and then double-click the Accounts: Administrator Account Status policy. Click Disabled, and then click OK.

▶ **Using the Local Users and Groups snap-in**—Select Start, type `lusrmgr.msc`, and then press Enter. In the Local Users and Groups snap-in, click Users and then double-click Administrator. In the Administrator Properties dialog box, activate the Account Is Disabled check box, and then click OK.

These methods suffer from a serious drawback: They don't work in all versions of Windows 7, in particular Windows 7 Home Basic and Windows 7 Home Premium. Fortunately, we haven't exhausted all the ways to activate Windows 7's Administrator account. Here's a method that works with *all* versions of Windows 7:

1. Select Start, type **command**, right-click Command Prompt, and then click Run as Administrator. The User Account Control dialog box appears.

2. Enter your UAC credentials to continue.

3. At the command line, enter the following command:

   ```
   net user Administrator /active:no
   ```

Managing Windows Firewall

If you access the Internet using a broadband—cable modem or DSL—service, chances are that you have an always-on connection, which means there's a much greater chance that a malicious hacker could find your computer and have his way with it. You might think that with millions of people connected to the Internet at any given moment, there would be little chance of a "script kiddy" finding you in the herd. Unfortunately, one of the most common weapons in a black-hat hacker's arsenal is a program that runs through millions of IP addresses automatically, looking for live connections. The fact that many cable systems and some DSL systems use IP addresses in a narrow range compounds the problem by making it easier to find always-on connections.

When a cracker finds your address, he has many avenues from which to access your computer. Specifically, your connection uses many different ports for sending and receiving data. For example, the File Transfer Protocol (FTP) uses ports 20 and 21, web data and commands typically use port 80, email uses ports 25 and 110, the domain name system (DNS) uses port 53, and so on. In all, there are dozens of these ports, and each one is an opening through which a clever cracker can gain access to your computer.

As if that weren't enough, attackers can check your system for the installation of some kind of Trojan horse or virus. (Malicious email attachments sometimes install these programs on your machine.) If the hacker finds one, he can effectively take control of your machine (turning it into a *zombie computer*) and either wreck its contents or use your computer to attack other systems.

Again, if you think your computer is too obscure or worthless for someone else to bother with, think again. For a typical computer connected to the Internet all day long, hackers probe for vulnerable ports or installed Trojan horses at least a few times every day.

Making Sure the Firewall Is Up to Snuff

If you want to see just how vulnerable your computer is, several good sites on the Web will test your security:

- **Gibson Research (Shields Up)**—grc.com/default.htm

- **DSL Reports**—www.dslreports.com/secureme_go

- **HackerWhacker**—www.hackerwhacker.com

The good news is that Windows includes the Windows Firewall tool, which is a personal firewall that can lock down your ports and prevent unauthorized access to your machine. In effect, your computer becomes invisible to the Internet (although you can still surf the Web and work with email normally). Other firewall programs exist out there, but Windows Firewall does a good job. For example, Figure 14.5 shows the output of the Shields Up tool from Gibson Research after probing a typical Windows 7 computer. As you can see, Windows Firewall held its own.

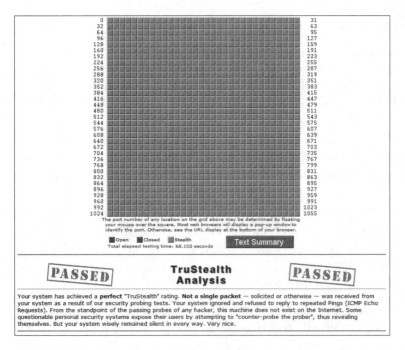

FIGURE 14.5   This standard Windows 7 PC stood up to everything the Shields Up tool threw at it.

Creating a Windows Firewall Exception

I just told you how important a firewall is for a secure computer, so it may seem more than a little strange that I'm now going to show you how to poke holes in that firewall. Actually, this kind of thing is fairly routine, at least behind the scenes, where programs such as Microsoft Office Outlook and iTunes often configure Windows Firewall to allow them to access the Internet. That's fine, but why would *you* want to do something like this? There are many reasons, but they mostly boil down to needing some sort of data to get though the firewall. For example, if you want to perform administrative duties on a computer on your network, that computer's firewall needs to be configured to allow the Remote Assistance service through. Similarly, if you activate Windows 7's built-in web server, you need to configure that PC to allow data through port 80.

These are examples of firewall *exceptions*, and there are actually three types of exceptions you can set up:

▶ **Enable an existing exception**—Windows maintains a list of programs and services that are often used as exceptions, and you can toggle these on and off.

▶ **Add a program or as a new exception**—If the program you want to use isn't in the list, you can add it yourself.

▶ **Add a port as a new exception**—You can also configure a port as an exception, and the firewall will allow data to pass back and forth through the port.

The next three sections show you how to create the three types of firewall exceptions.

Activating an Existing Exception

Windows Firewall maintains a list of programs, services, and sometimes ports that are currently enabled as exceptions, or that are commonly enabled but currently are not. This is the easiest way to set up an exception because all you have to do is activate a check box or two:

1. Select Start, type **firewall**, and then click Allow a Program Through Windows Firewall in the search results. The Allowed Programs window appears.
2. Click Change Settings. Windows Firewall enables the exceptions, as shown in Figure 14.6.
3. Activate the Home/Work (Private) check box beside the exception you want to enable.
4. If you also connect to public networks (such as wireless hotspots) and you also want the exception enabled on those networks, activate the Public check box beside the exception you want to enable
5. Click OK to put the exception into effect.

Adding a Program as a New Exception

If you don't see the program or port you want to work with, you can add it by hand. Here's how:

1. Select Start, type **firewall**, and then click Allow a Program Through Windows Firewall in the search results. The Allowed Programs window appears.
2. Click Change Settings. Windows Firewall enables the exceptions.
3. Click Allow Another Program. The Add a Program dialog box appears.
4. If you see your program in the list, click it. Otherwise, click Browse, use the Browse dialog box to select the program's executable file, and then click Open.

5. Click Add. Windows Firewall adds the program to the list.

6. Activate the Home/Work (Private) check box.

7. If you also connect to public networks (such as wireless hot spots) and you want the program allowed through on those networks, activate the Public check box.

8. Click OK to put the exception into effect.

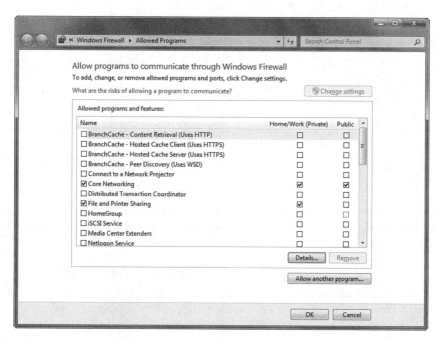

FIGURE 14.6   Windows Firewall's Allowed Programs windows lets you keep track of the Windows Firewall exceptions.

TIP

You can prevent computers on your network from adding program exceptions if you're worried about security. On the other computer, log on as an administrator, open the Group Policy Editor (see Chapter 9, "Policing Windows 7 with Group Policies"), and open the following branch: Computer Configuration, Administrative Templates, Network, Network Connections, Windows Firewall, Standard Profile. Enable the Windows Firewall: Do Not Allow Exceptions policy and the Windows Firewall: Protect All Network Connections policies.

Adding a Port as a New Exception

If you need to open a port on your computer, you can't do it via the Allowed Programs windows. Instead, you need to work with a Microsoft Management Console snap-in called Windows Firewall with Advanced Security (WFAS). To load it, select Start, **wf.msc**, and then press Enter User Account Control credentials. Figure 14.7 shows the WFAS snap-in.

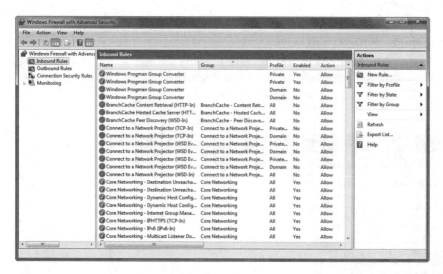

FIGURE 14.7   The Windows Firewall with Advanced Security snap-in offers sophisticated fire-wall-management features.

The home page of the snap-in presents an overview of the current firewall settings, as well as a number of links to configure and learn about WFAS. This snap-in configures the firewall by setting policies and storing them in three profiles. The domain profile is used when your computer is connected to a network domain, the private profile is used when your computer is connected to a private network, and the public profile is used when your computer is connected to a public network. To change the settings for the profiles, click the Windows Firewall Properties link, and then use the Domain Profile, Private Profile, and Public Profile tabs to modify the settings (although the defaults should be fine for most people).

The scope pane contains four main sub-branches:

▶ **Inbound Rules**—This branch presents a list of defined rules for inbound connections. In most cases, the rules aren't enabled. To enable a rule, you right-click it and then click Enable Rule (or you can click the rule and then click Enable Rule in the Action pane). You can create your own rule (as you'll soon see) by right-clicking Inbound Rules and then clicking New Rule (or clicking New Rule in the Action pane). This launches the New Inbound Rule Wizard.

▶ **Outbound Rules**—This branch presents a list of defined rules for outbound connections. As with inbound connections, you can enable the rules you want to use and create your own rules. Note, too, that you can customize any rule by double-clicking it to display its property sheet. With this property sheet, you can change the program executable to which the exception is applied, allow or block a connection, set the computer and user authorization, change the ports and protocols, and specify the interface types and services.

▶ **Connection Security Rules**—This branch is where you create and manage *authentication rules*, which determine the restrictions and requirements that apply to connections with remote computers. Right-click Computer Connection Security and then click New Rule (or click New Rule in the Action pane) to launch the New Connection Security Rule Wizard.

▶ **Monitoring**—This branch shows the enabled firewall settings. For example, the Firewall sub-branch shows the enabled inbound and outbound firewall rules, and the Connection Security Rules sub-branch shows the enabled authentication rules.

Here are the steps to follow to use WFAS to create a port exception:

1. Click Inbound Rules.
2. In the Actions pane, click New Rule to launch the New Inbound Rule Wizard.
3. Click Port and then click Next. The Protocol and Ports dialog box appears.
4. Click the data protocol you want the exception to use: TCP or UDP. (If you're not sure, choose TCP.)
5. Activate the Specific Local Ports option and use the text box to type the port you want to set up as an exception.
6. Click Next. The Action dialog box appears.
7. Click Allow the Connection and then click Next. The Profile dialog box appears.
8. Activate the check box beside each profile you use (Domain, Private, or Public), and then click Next. The Name dialog box appears.
9. Use the Name text box to make up a name for this exception. This is the name that appears in the Exceptions tab, so make it reasonably descriptive (for example, `Port 80 for Web Server`).
10. Click Finish to put the exception into effect.

TIP

If you're worried about someone on your network adding a port as an exception and possibly opening up a security hole (for example, by forgetting to change the scope to something local), you can disable new port exceptions on that computer. Log on as an administrator, open the Group Policy Editor (see Chapter 9), and open the following branch: Computer Configuration, Administrative Templates, Network, Network Connections, Windows Firewall, Standard Profile. Disable the Windows Firewall: Allow Local Port Exceptions policy.

Configuring Internet Explorer Security

The fantastic advances in the field of electronic communication constitute a greater danger to the privacy of the individual.
—Earl Warren

As more people, businesses, and organizations establish a presence online, the world becomes an increasingly connected place. And the more connected the world becomes, the more opportunities arise for communicating with others, doing research, sharing information, and collaborating on projects. The flip side to this new connectedness is the increased risk of connecting with a remote user whose intentions are less than honorable. The person at the other end of the connection could be a fraud artist who sets up a legitimate-looking website to steal your password or credit card number, or a cracker who breaks into your Internet account. It could be a virus programmer who sends a Trojan horse attached to an email, or a website operator who uses web browser security holes to run malicious code on your machine.

While all this was happening, Microsoft's operating systems seemed to become less secure. It's difficult to say whether overall operating system security got worse with each new release, but it's not hard to see that a perfect security storm was brewing:

▶ Thanks to the Internet, news of vulnerabilities spread quickly and efficiently.

▶ An increasing number of malicious users online worked to exploit those vulnerabilities.

▶ An increasing number of Windows users got online, most of whom didn't keep up with the latest security patches from Microsoft.

▶ An increasing number of online users had always-on broadband connections, which give malicious users more time to locate and break into poorly patched machines.

So, even though it might have been the case that each new version of Windows was no less secure than its predecessors, it *appeared* that Windows was becoming increasingly vulnerable to attack.

To combat not only this perception but also the fundamental design flaws that were causing these security holes, Microsoft began its Trustworthy Computing Initiative (TCI) in 2003. The goal was to make people "as comfortable using devices powered by computers and software as they are today using a device that is powered by electricity." How is Microsoft going about this? It's a broad initiative, but it really comes down to two things:

▶ **Reduce the "attack surface area"**—This means reducing the number of places where an attacker can get a foothold on the system. For example, why run any ActiveX controls that the user or system doesn't require, particularly if that object is potentially exploitable?

▶ **Help the user to avoid making "bad trust decisions"**—If the user lands on a phishing website, why not have the web browser warn the user that the site is probably not trustworthy?

Windows 7 implements many of these ideas, and in this chapter you learn about the Web-related security features in Windows 7.

Enhancing Your Browsing Privacy

You might think that the biggest online privacy risks are sitting out "there" in cyberspace, but that's not true. Your biggest risk is actually sitting right under your nose, so to speak: It's Internet Explorer. That's because Internet Explorer (just like Firefox, Safari, and any other web browser) saves tons of information related to your online activities. So the first step in covering your online tracks is to manage the information that Internet Explorer stores. The next few sections offer some suggestions.

Deleting Your Browsing History

As you surf the Web, Internet Explorer maintains what it calls your *browsing history*, which consists of the following six data types:

▶ **Temporary Internet files**—This is Internet Explorer's cache, and it consists of copies of text, images, media, and other content from the pages you've visited recently. Internet Explorer stores all this data so that the next time you view one of those pages, it can retrieve data from the cache and display the site much more quickly. This is clearly a big-time privacy problem because it means that anyone can examine the cache to learn where you've been surfing.

▶ **Cookies**—This is Internet Explorer's collection of cookie files, which are small text files that sites store on your computer. I discuss cookies in more detail later in this chapter, but for now it's enough to know that although most cookies are benign, they can be used to track your activities online.

▶ **History**—This is a list of addresses of the sites you've visited, as well as each of the pages you visited within those sites. By default, Internet Explorer stores 20 days' worth of history. Again, this is a major privacy accident just waiting to happen, because anyone sitting at your computer can see exactly where you've been online over the page 20 days.

▶ **Form data**—This refers to the AutoComplete feature, which stores the data you type in forms and then uses that saved data to suggest possible matches when you use a similar form in the future. For example, if you use a site's Search box frequently, Internet Explorer remembers your search strings and displays strings that match what you've typed, as shown in Figure 15.1. (Press the down-arrow key to select the one you want, and then press Enter.) This is definitely handy, but it also means that anyone else who uses your computer can see your previously entered form text.

FIGURE 15.1 Internet Explorer's AutoComplete feature suggests previously entered text that matches what you've typed so far.

▶ **Passwords**—This is another aspect of AutoComplete, and Internet Explorer uses it to save form passwords. For example, if you enter a username and a password on a form, Internet Explorer asks if you want to save the password. If you click Yes, Internet Explorer stores the password and enters it automatically the next time you fill in the form (provided you enter the same username). Again, this is nice and convenient, but it's really just asking for trouble because it means that someone sitting down at your computer can log on to a site, a job made all the easier if you activated the site option to save your username!

15

NOTE

If you don't want Internet Explorer to save your form data, passwords, or neither, select Tools, Internet Options, select the Content tab, and then click Settings in the AutoComplete group. In the AutoComplete Settings dialog box, deactivate the Forms check box to stop saving form data. If you no longer want to save form passwords, deactivate the User Name and Passwords on Forms check box. Click OK in all open dialog boxes.

TIP

You can configure Internet Explorer to remove all files from the Temporary Internet Files folder each time you exit the program. Select Tools, Options to open the Internet Options dialog box, display the Advanced tab, and then activate the Empty Temporary Internet Files Folder When Browser Is Closed check box.

▶ **InPrivate Filtering Data**—This is information that Internet Explorer 8 gathers to detect when third-party providers are supplying data to the sites you visit. For more information, see "Total Privacy: InPrivate Browsing and Filtering," later in this chapter.

Fortunately, you can plug any and all of these privacy holes by deleting the data. Here's how it's done in Internet Explorer 8:

1. Select Safety, Delete Browsing History (or press Ctrl+Shift+Delete) to display the Delete Browsing History dialog box shown in Figure 15.2.

2. If you don't want to save the cache and cookie files associated with sites on your Favorites list, deactivate the Preserve Favorites Website Data check box.

3. Leave the Temporary Internet Files check box activated to remove all files from the Internet Explorer cache, located in the following folder:

   `%UserProfile%\AppData\Local\Microsoft\Windows\Temporary Internet Files`

4. Leave the Cookies check box activated to remove all the cookies from the following folder:

   `%UserProfile%\AppData\Roaming\Microsoft\Windows\Cookies`

TIP

If you just want to delete certain cookies—for example, those from advertisers—open the Cookies folder and delete the files individually.

5. Leave the History check box activated to remove the list of websites you've visited, which resides as files in the following folder:

   `%UserProfile%\AppData\Local\Microsoft\Windows\History`

FIGURE 15.2   Use the Delete Browsing History dialog box to delete some or all of your Internet Explorer 8 browsing history.

15

TIP

If you want to delete history from a certain site, day, or week, click Favorites Center (or press Alt+C), and click History to display the History list. If you want to delete just a few sites, open the appropriate History branch, and then, for each site, right-click the site and then click Delete. If you want to delete a number of sites, right-click the appropriate day or week and then click Delete. Click Yes when Internet Explorer asks you to confirm.

---

6. Activate the Form data check box to remove your saved form data.

7. Activate the Passwords check box to remove your saved passwords.

8. Activate the InPrivate Filtering Data check box to remove your saved InPrivate Filtering information.

9. Click Delete. Internet Explorer removes the selected data.

Windows Media Player Privacy Options

When you use Windows Media Player to play content from an Internet site, the program communicates certain information to the site, including the unique ID number of your copy of Windows Media Player. This allows content providers to track the media you play, and they might share this data with other sites. So, although the player ID does not identify you personally, it might result in sites sending you targeted ads based on your media choices. If you do not want such an invasion of privacy, you can instruct Windows Media Player not to send the Player ID. Press Alt+F and then select Tools, Options. In the Options dialog box, display the Privacy tab and make sure that the Send Unique Player ID to Content Providers check box is deactivated. (However, remember that some content sites *require* the player ID before you can play any media. For example, a site might request the ID for billing purposes. In that case, you should read the site's privacy statement to see what uses it makes of the ID.) Also deactivate the I Want to Help Make Microsoft Software and Services Even Better check box to avoid sending your Windows Media Player usage data to Microsoft. You should also deactivate the check boxes in the History group if you don't want other people who use your computer to see the media files and sites that you play and visit.

Clearing the Address Bar List

Another part of Internet Explorer's AutoComplete feature involves the web addresses that you type into the address bar. When you start typing a URL into the address bar, Internet Explorer displays a list of addresses that match what you've typed. If you see the one you want, use the arrow keys to select it, and then press Enter to surf to it.

That's mighty convenient, but not very private because other people who have access to your PC can also see those addresses. So another excellent way to enhance your privacy is to clear the address bar list so that no URLs appear as you type.

One way to clear the address bar list is to clear the history files, as described in the previous section. That is, you select Safety, Delete Browsing History, activate the History check box, deactivate all the other check boxes, and then click Delete.

NOTE

You can configure Internet Explorer to not save the web addresses that you type. Select Tools, Internet Options, select the Content tab, and then click Settings in the AutoComplete group. In the AutoComplete Settings dialog box, deactivate the Address Bar check box to stop saving typed URLs. Click OK in all open dialog boxes.

That works well, but it also means that you lose all your browsing history. That might be exactly what you want, but you may prefer to preserve the history files. In this section, I show you a script that removes the address bar URLs but lets you save your history.

First, note that Internet Explorer stores the last 25 typed URLs in the following Registry key (see Figure 15.3):

```
HKCU\Software\Microsoft\Internet Explorer\TypedURLs
```

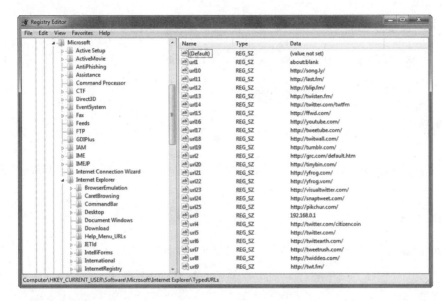

FIGURE 15.3   The last 25 addresses you typed into the address bar are stored in the TypedURLs Registry key.

You can therefore clear the address bar list by closing all Internet Explorer windows and deleting the settings url1 through url25 in this key. Listing 15.1 presents a script that does this for you.

> **NOTE**
>
> See Chapter 30, "Programming the Windows Scripting Host," to learn how to run this script. The file containing the script in Listing 15.1—DeleteTypedURLs.vbs—is available from my website at www.mcfedries.com/Windows7Unleashed/.

LISTING 15.1   A Script That Deletes Internet Explorer's Typed URLs

```
Option Explicit
Dim objWshShell, nTypedURLs, strRegKey, strURL, i
Set objWshShell = WScript.CreateObject("WScript.Shell")
On Error Resume Next
'
' First determine the number of typed URLs in the Registry
'
```

LISTING 15.1   Continued

```
nTypedURLs = 0
strRegKey = "HKCU\Software\Microsoft\Internet Explorer\TypedURLs\"
Do While True
    '
    ' Read the next typed URL
    '
    strURL = objWshShell.RegRead(strRegKey & "url" & nTypedURLs + 1)
    '
    ' If we get an error, it means we've read all
    ' the typed URLs, so exit the loop
    If Err <> 0 Then
        Exit Do
    End If
    nTypedURLs = nTypedURLs + 1
Loop
'
' Run through the typed URLs
'
For i = 1 to nTypedURLs
    '
    ' Delete the Registry setting
    '
    objWshShell.RegDelete strRegKey & "url" & i
Next 'i
objWshShell.Popup "Finished deleting " & nTypedURLs & _
                  " typed URLs", , "Delete Typed URLs"
```

This script begins by running through all the settings in the TypedURLs key, and counts them as it goes. This is necessary because there may not be the full 25 typed URLs in the key, and if you try to delete a nonexistent Registry key, you get an error. With the number of typed URLs in hand, the script then performs a second loop that deletes each Registry setting.

Enhancing Online Privacy by Managing Cookies

A *cookie* is a small text file that's stored on your computer. Websites use them to "remember" information about your session at that site: shopping cart data, page customizations, usernames, passwords, and so on.

No other site can access your cookies, so they're generally safe and private under most—but definitely not all—circumstances. To understand why cookies can sometimes compromise your privacy, you have to understand the different cookie types that exist:

▶ **Temporary cookie**—This type of cookie lives just as long as you have Internet Explorer running. Internet Explorer deletes all temporary cookies when you shut down the program.

▶ **Persistent cookie**—This type of cookie remains on your hard disk through multiple Internet Explorer sessions. The cookie's duration depends on how it's set up, but it can be anything from a few seconds to a few years.

▶ **First-party cookie**—This is a cookie set by the website you're viewing.

▶ **Third-party cookie**—This is a cookie set by a site other than the one you're viewing. Advertisers that have placed an ad on the site you're viewing create and store most third-party cookies.

These cookie types can compromise your privacy in two ways:

▶ A site might store *personally identifiable information*—your name, email address, home address, phone number, and so on—in a persistent first- or third-party cookie and then use that information in some way (such as filling in a form) without your consent.

▶ A site might store information about you in a persistent third-party cookie and then use that cookie to track your online movements and activities. The advertiser can do this because it might have (for example) an ad on dozens or hundreds of websites, and that ad is the mechanism that enables the site to set and read their cookies. Such sites are supposed to come up with *privacy policies* stating that they won't engage in surreptitious monitoring of users, they won't sell user data, and so on.

To help you handle these scenarios, Internet Explorer implements a privacy feature that gives you extra control over whether sites can store cookies on your machine. To check out this feature, select Internet Explorer's Tools, Internet Options command, and then display the Privacy tab, shown in Figure 15.4. You set your cookie privacy level by using the slider in the Settings group.

You set your cookie privacy level by using the slider in the Settings group. First, let's look at the two extreme settings:

▶ **Accept All Cookies**—This setting (at the bottom of the slider) tells Internet Explorer to accept all requests to set and read cookies.

▶ **Block All Cookies**—This setting (at the top of the slider) tells Internet Explorer to reject all requests to set and read cookies.

CAUTION

Blocking all cookies might sound like the easiest way to maximize your online privacy. However, many sites rely on cookies to operate properly, so if you block all cookies you might find that your web surfing isn't as convenient or as smooth as it used to be.

In between are four settings that offer more detailed control. Table 15.1 shows you how each setting affects the three types of privacy issues.

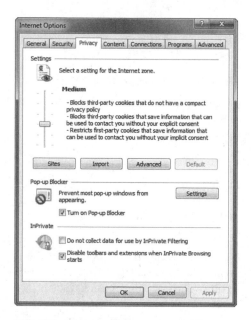

FIGURE 15.4   In the Internet Options dialog box, use the Privacy tab to manage your cookies.

TABLE 15.1   Cookie Settings and Their Effect on Surfing Privacy

	Third-Party Cookies with No Compact Information Privacy Policy	Third-Party Cookies Using Personally Identifiable Information Without the Type of Consent	First-Party Cookies Using Personally Identifiable Information Without the Type of Consent
Low	Restricted	Restricted (implicit)	OK
Medium	Blocked	Blocked (implicit)	Restricted (implicit)
Medium High	Blocked	Blocked (explicit)	Blocked (implicit)
High	Blocked	Blocked (explicit)	Blocked (explicit)

Here are some notes about the terminology in this table:

▶ *Restricted* means that Internet Explorer doesn't allow the site to set a persistent cookie, just a temporary one.

▶ A *compact* privacy policy is a shortened form of a privacy policy that can be sent along with the cookie and that can be read by the browser.

▶ *Implicit consent* means that one or more pages leading up to the cookie warned you that your personally identifiable information would be used and you agreed that it was okay.

▶ *Explicit consent* means that the page that reads the cookie warned you that your personally identifiable information would be used and you agreed that it was okay.

NOTE

If you decide to change the privacy setting, you should first delete all your cookies because the new setting won't apply to any cookies already on your computer. See "Deleting Your Browser History," earlier in this chapter.

That's fine on a broad level, but you can fine-tune your cookie management by preventing specific sites from adding cookies to your computer. For example, you can prevent Google from tracking your search activity by preventing it from adding cookies to your PC. You might also want to block ad sites such as doubleclick.net.

Here are the steps to follow in Internet Explorer to block a site from adding cookies:

1. Select Tools, Internet Options.
2. Display the Privacy tab.
3. Click Sites.
4. Use the Address of Website text box to type the site domain.
5. Click Block.
6. Repeat steps 4 and 5 to add all the sites you want blocked.
7. Click OK in the open dialog boxes.

Total Privacy: InPrivate Browsing and Filtering

NEW TO **7** The privacy techniques you've seen so far suffer from a complete of glaring problems:

▶ **They work after the fact**—For example, if you've visited a site with sensitive data, you delete your browsing history after you leave the site. This is a problem because you might forget to delete your history.

▶ **They're all or nothing**—When you delete format data, passwords, history, cookies, or the cache files, you delete *all* of them (unless you preserve the cookies and cache files for your favorites). This is a problem because you often want to remove the data for only a single site or a few sites.

Fortunately, Internet Explorer 8 implements a single new feature that solves both problems: InPrivate browsing. When you activate this feature, Internet Explorer stops storing private data when you visit websites. It no longer saves temporary Internet files, cookies, browsing history, form data, and passwords. Here's how this solves the privacy problems I mentioned earlier:

▶ **It works before the fact**—By turning on InPrivate browsing before you visit a site, you don't have to worry about deleting data afterward because no data is saved.

▶ **It works only while it's on**—When you activate InPrivate browsing and surf some private sites, no data is stored, but all your other privacy data remains intact. When you then deactivate InPrivate browsing, Internet Explorer resumes saving privacy data.

To use InPrivate browsing, select Safety, InPrivate Browsing (or press Ctrl+Shift+P). Internet Explorer opens a new browser window as shown in Figure 15.5. Notice two things in this window that tell you InPrivate browsing is activated:

▶ You see `InPrivate` in the title bar.

▶ You see the InPrivate icon in the address bar.

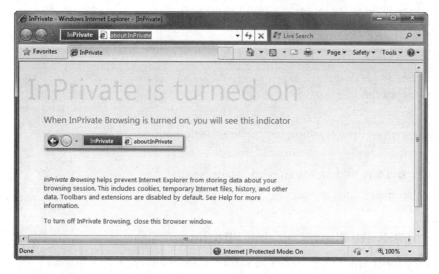

FIGURE 15.5   When you activate InPrivate browsing, Internet Explorer 8 opens a new window and displays indicators in the title bar and address bar.

A similar idea is InPrivate filtering. When you visit a website, it's possible that the site loads some of its content from a third-party provider. It could be an ad, a map, a YouTube video, or an image. That's not a terrible thing once in a while, but if a particular third-party company provides data for many different sites, that company could conceivably build up a profile of your online activity.

What InPrivate filtering does is watch out for these third-party providers and track the data they provide. If the InPrivate feature detects that a third-party site is providing data quite often to the sites you visit, InPrivate will begin blocking that site's content so that it can't build up a profile of your activity.

InPrivate filtering is off by default. To turn it on, select Safety, InPrivate Filtering (or press Ctrl+Shift+F).

Enhancing Your Browsing Security

Surfing the Web may be inherently unsecure, but fortunately Internet Explorer 8 comes with lots of defensive weapons that you can deploy. The next few sections take a look at the most important ones.

Blocking Pop-Up Windows

Among the most annoying things on the Web are those ubiquitous pop-up windows that infest your screen with advertisements when you visit certain sites. (A variation on the theme is the *pop under*, a window that opens under your current browser window, so you don't know it's there until you close the window.) Pop-up windows can also be dangerous because some unscrupulous software makers have figured out ways to use them to install software on your computer without your permission. They're nasty things, any way you look at them.

Fortunately, Microsoft has given us a way to stop most pop-ups before they start. Internet Explorer comes with a feature called the *Pop-up Blocker* that looks for pop-ups and prevents them from opening. It's not perfect (the occasional pop-under still breaks through the defenses), but it make surfing sites much more pleasant. Follow these steps to use and configure the Pop-up Blocker:

1. Select Tools, Pop-up Blocker.
2. If you see the command Turn Off Pop-up Blocker, skip to step 3; otherwise, select Turn On Pop-up Blocker, and then click Yes when Internet Explorer asks you to confirm.
3. Select Tools, Pop-up Blocker, Pop-up Blocker Settings to display the Pop-up Blocker Settings dialog box. You have the following options:

   ▶ **Address of Web Site to Allow**—Use this option when you have a site that displays pop-ups you want to see. Type the address and then click Add.

   ▶ **Play a Sound When a Pop-up Is Blocked**—When this check box is activated, Internet Explorer plays a brief sound each time is blocks a pop-up. If this gets annoying after a while, deactivate this check box.

   ▶ **Show Information Bar When a Pop-up Is Blocked**—When this check box is activated, Internet Explorer displays a yellow bar below the address bar each time it blocks a pop-up so that you know it's working on your behalf.

   ▶ **Blocking Level**—Use this list to choose how aggressively you want it to block pop-ups: High (no pop-ups get through, ever), Medium (the default level), or Low (allows pop-ups from secure sites).

4. Click Close.

With the Pop-Up Blocker on the case, it monitors your surfing and steps in front of any pop-up window that tries to disturb your peace. A yellow information bar appears under the address bar to let you know that Pop-up Blocker thwarted a pop-up. Clicking the information bar displays a menu with the following choices:

▶ **Temporarily Allow Pop-Ups**—Click this command to enable pop-ups on the site only during the current session.

▶ **Always Allow Pop-Ups from This Site**—Click this command to allow future pop-ups for the current domain.

▶ **Settings**—Click this command to see a submenu with three commands: Click Turn Off Pop-Up Blocker to turn off the feature entirely; click Show Information Bar for Pop-Ups to tell Internet Explorer to stop displaying the information bar for each blocked pop-up; and click Settings to display the Pop-Up Blocker Settings dialog box.

Adding and Removing Zone Sites

When implementing security for Internet Explorer, Microsoft realized that different sites have different security needs. For example, it makes sense to have stringent security for Internet sites, but you can probably scale the security back a bit when browsing pages on your corporate intranet.

To handle these different types of sites, Internet Explorer defines various *security zones*, and you can customize the security requirements for each zone. The status bar displays the current zone.

To work with zones, either select Tools, Internet Options in Internet Explorer, or select Start, Control Panel, Security, Internet Options. In the Internet Properties dialog box that appears, select the Security tab, shown in Figure 15.6.

TIP

Another way to get to the Security tab is to double-click the security zone shown in the Internet Explorer status bar.

The list at the top of the dialog box shows icons for the four types of zones available:

▶ **Internet**—Websites that aren't in any of the other three zones. The default security level is Medium.

▶ **Local Intranet**—Web pages on your computer and your network (intranet). The default security level is Medium-Low.

▶ **Trusted Sites**—Websites that implement secure pages and that you're sure have safe content. The default security level is Low.

▶ **Restricted Sites**—Websites that don't implement secure pages or that you don't trust, for whatever reason. The default security level is High.

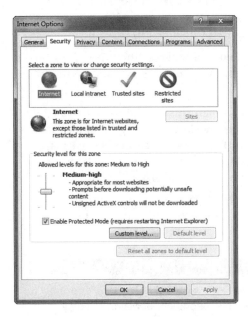

FIGURE 15.6   Use the Security tab to set up security zones and customize the security options for each zone.

15

TIP

You can use the Group Policy Editor to hide the Security and Privacy tabs in the Internet Options dialog box. Select User Configuration, Administrative Templates, Windows Components, Internet Explorer, Internet Control Panel, and then enable the Disable the Privacy Page and Disable the Security Page policies. The Security Page sub-branch enables you to set policies for the settings in each zone.

Three of these zones—Local Intranet, Trusted Sites, and Restricted Sites—enable you to add sites. To do so, follow these steps:

1. Select the zone you want to work with and then click Sites.

2. If you selected Trusted Sites or Restricted Sites, skip to step 4. Otherwise, if you selected the Local Intranet zone, you see a dialog box with four check boxes. The Automatically Detect Intranet Network check box activates by default, and this tells

Windows 7 to detect intranets automatically, which should be fine in most cases. If you want more detailed control, deactivate that check box to enable the other three:

▶ **Include All Local (Intranet) Sites Not Listed in Other Zones**—When activated, this option includes all intranet sites in the zone. If you add specific intranet sites to other zones, those sites aren't included in this zone.

▶ **Include All Sites That Bypass the Proxy Server**—When this check box is activated, sites that you've set up to bypass your proxy server (if you have one) are included in this zone.

▶ **Include All Network Paths (UNCs)**—When this check box is activated, all network paths that use the Universal Naming Convention are included in this zone. (UNC is a standard format used with network addresses. They usually take the form *server**resource*, where *server* is the name of the network server and *resource* is the name of a shared network resource.)

3. To add sites to the Local Intranet zone, click Advanced.

4. Type the site's address in the Add This Website to the Zone text box and then click Add.

NOTE

When typing an address, you can include an asterisk as a wildcard character. For example, the address http://*.microsoft.com adds every microsoft.com domain, including www.microsoft.com, support.microsoft.com, windowsupdate.microsoft.com, and so on.

---

5. If you make a mistake and enter the wrong site, select it in the Websites list and then click Remove.

6. Two of these dialog boxes (Local Intranet and Trusted Sites) have a Require Server Verification (https:) for All Sites In This Zone check box. If you activate this option, each site you enter must use the secure HTTPS protocol.

7. Click OK.

Changing a Zone's Security Level

To change the security level for a zone, select the zone and then use the Security Level for This Zone slider to set the level. To set up your own security settings, click Custom Level. This displays the Security Settings dialog box shown in Figure 15.7.

The Security Settings dialog box provides you with a long list of possible security issues, and your job is to specify how you want Internet Explorer to handle each issue. You usually have three choices:

▶ **Disable**—Security is on. For example, if the issue is whether to run an ActiveX control, the control does not run.

▶ **Enable**—Security is off. For example, if the issue is whether to run an ActiveX control, the control runs automatically.

▶ **Prompt**—Internet Explorer asks how you want to handle the issue (for example, whether you want to accept or reject an ActiveX control).

FIGURE 15.7   Use this dialog box to set up customized security levels for the selected zone.

Protected Mode: Reducing Internet Explorer's Privileges

Because spyware often leeches onto a system through a drive-by or pop-up download, it makes sense to set up the web browser as the first line of defense. Microsoft has done just that by including *protected mode* for Internet Explorer. Protected mode builds on Windows 7's User Account Control feature. User Account Control means that Internet Explorer runs with a privilege level that's high enough to surf the Web, but that's about it. Internet Explorer can't install software without your permission, modify the user's files or settings, add shortcuts to the Startup folder, or even change its own settings for the default home page and search engine. The Internet Explorer code is completely isolated from any other running application or process on your system. In fact, Internet Explorer can write data only to the Temporary Internet Files folder. If it needs to write elsewhere (during a file download, for example), it must get your permission. Therefore, Internet Explorer blocks any add-ons or other malware that attempts a covert install via Internet Explorer before they can even get to Windows Defender.

> **NOTE**
>
> If you don't want to run Internet Explorer in protected mode for some reason, you can turn it off. Select Tools, Internet Options, and then select the Security tab. Click the Enable Protected Mode check box to deactivate it, click OK, and then click OK again in the Warning! dialog box. Internet Explorer displays a message in the information bar telling you that your security settings are putting you at risk.

Thwarting Phishers with the SmartScreen Filter

NEW TO 7 *Phishing* refers to creating a replica of an existing web page to fool a user into submitting personal, financial, or password data. The term comes from the fact that Internet scammers are using increasingly sophisticated lures as they "fish" for users' financial information and password data. The most common ploy is to copy the web page code from a major site—such as AOL or eBay—and use it to set up a replica page that appears to be part of the company's site. (This is why another name for phishing is *spoofing*.) Phishers send out a fake email with a link to this page, which solicits the user's credit card data or password. When a recipient submits the form, it sends the data to the scammer and leaves the user on an actual page from the company's site so that he or she doesn't suspect a thing.

A phishing page looks identical to a legitimate page from the company because the phisher has simply copied the underlying source code from the original page. However, no spoof page can be a perfect replica of the original. Here are five things to look for:

▶ **The URL in the address bar**—A legitimate page will have the correct domain—such as aol.com or ebay.com—whereas a spoofed page will have only something similar—such as aol.whatever.com or blah.com/ebay.

NOTE

With some exceptions (see the following discussion of domain spoofing), the URL in the address bar is usually the easiest way to tell whether a site is trustworthy. For this reason, Internet Explorer 8 makes it impossible to hide the address bar in all browser windows, even simple pop-ups.

▶ **The URLs associated with page links**—Most links on the page probably point to legitimate pages on the original site. However, some links might point to pages on the phisher's site.

▶ **The form-submittal address**—Almost all spoof pages contain a form into which you're supposed to type whatever sensitive data the phisher seeks from you. Select View, Source, and look at the value of the `<form>` tag's `action` attribute—the form submits your data to this address. Clearly, if the form is not sending your data to the legitimate domain, you're dealing with a phisher.

▶ **Text or images that aren't associated with the trustworthy site**—Many phishing sites are housed on free web hosting services. However, many of these services place an advertisement on each page, so look for an ad or other content from the hosting provider.

▶ **Internet Explorer's lock icon in the status bar and Security Report area**—A legitimate site would transmit sensitive financial data only using a secure HTTPS connection, which Internet Explorer indicates by placing a lock icon in the status bar and in the address bar's new Security Report area. If you don't see the lock icon on a page that asks for financial data, the page is almost certainly a spoof.

If you watch for these things, you'll probably never be fooled into giving up sensitive data to a phisher. However, it's often not as easy as it sounds. For example, some phishers employ easily overlooked domain-spoofing tricks such as replacing the lowercase letter *L* with the number 1, or the uppercase letter *O* with the number 0. Still, phishing sites don't fool most experienced users, so this isn't a big problem for them.

Novice users, on the other hand, need all the help they can get. They tend to assume that if everything they see on the Web looks legitimate and trustworthy, it probably is. And even if they're aware that scam sites exist, they don't know how to check for telltale phishing signs. To help these users, Internet Explorer 8 comes with a new tool called the *SmartScreen Filter*. This filter alerts you to potential phishing scams by doing two things each time you visit a site:

▶ Analyzes the site content to look for known phishing techniques (that is, to see whether the site is *phishy*). The most common of these is a check for domain spoofing. This common scam also goes by the names *homograph spoofing* and the *lookalike attack*. Internet Explorer 8 also supports Internationalized Domain Names (IDN), which refers to domain names written in languages other than English, and it checks for *IDN spoofing*, domain name ambiguities in the user's chosen browser language.

▶ Checks a global database of known phishing sites to see whether it lists the site. This database is maintained by a network of providers such as Cyota, Inc., Internet Identity, and MarkMonitor, as well as by reports from users who find phishing sites while surfing. According to Microsoft, this "URL reputation service" updates several times an hour with new data.

Here's how the SmartScreen Filter works:

▶ If you visit a site that Internet Explorer knows is a phishing scam, it changes the background color of the address bar to red and displays a `Phishing Website` message in the Security Report area. It also blocks navigation to the site by displaying a separate page telling you that the site is a known phishing scam. A link is provided to navigate to the site, if you so choose.

NOTE

In the Security Report area, clicking whatever text or icon appears in this area produces a report on the security of the site. For example, if you navigate to a secure site, you see the lock icon in this area. Click the lock to see a report that shows the site's digital certificate information.

▶ If you visit a site that Internet Explorer thinks is a potential phishing scam, it changes the background color of the address bar to yellow and displays a `Suspicious Website` message in the Security Report area.

For a suspected phishing site, click the Suspicious Website text, and Internet Explorer displays a security report. If you're sure that this is a scam site, report it to improve the database of phishing sites and prevent others from giving up sensitive data. You should also send a report if you're sure that the site is *not* being used for phishing, because that improves the database as well. To report a site, either click the Report link in the security report or select Tools, SmartScreen Filter, Report Unsafe Website.

Encoding Addresses to Prevent IDN Spoofing

I mentioned earlier that phishers often resort to IDN spoofing to fool users into thinking an address is legitimate. For example, instead of the address ebay.com, a phisher might use εbáy.com (with the Greek letters ε (epsilon) and α (alphá) in place of e and a). Almost all the world's characters have a Unicode value, but Internet Explorer is usually set up to recognize only a single language (such as English). If it comes across a character it doesn't recognize, it works around the problem by converting all Unicode values into an equivalent value that uses only the ASCII characters supported by the domain name system.

This conversion uses a standard called *Punycode*. If the domain name uses only ASCII characters, the Punycode value and the Unicode value are the same. For a domain such as εbáy.com, the Punycode equivalent is xn--by--c9b0.com. (The xn--prefix always appears; it tells you that the domain name is encoded.) Internet Explorer encodes the domain to this Punycode value and then surfs to the site. For example, in Figure 15.8, you can see that I entered http://εbáy.com in the address bar, but Internet Explorer shows the Punycode value http://xn--by--mia42m.com in the status bar. If you were able to successfully surf to this site (it doesn't exist, of course), you'd also see the Punycode domain in the address bar. (Internet Explorer also displays a message in the information bar telling you that the address contains characters it doesn't recognize.) In other words, an IDN spoofing site is less likely to fool users because the URL that appears in the status bar and the address no longer looks similar to the URL of the legitimate site.

Note that Internet Explorer doesn't always display Punycode. There are actually three instances where you see Punycode instead of Unicode:

▶ The address contains characters that don't appear in any of the languages you've added to Internet Explorer. (To add a language, select Tools, Internet Options, click Languages in the General tab, and then click Add.)

▶ The address contains characters from two or more different languages (for example, it contains a Greek character and an Arabic character).

▶ The address contains one or more characters that don't exist in any language.

With Internet Explorer 8, IDN spoofs can work in only a single language, and will work only if the user has added that single language to Internet Explorer.

Internet Explorer comes with a few options that enable you to control aspects of this encoding process and related features. Select Tools, Internet Options, click the Advanced tab, and scroll down the International section, which contains the following check boxes. (You need to restart Internet Explorer if you change any of these settings.)

Unicode entered

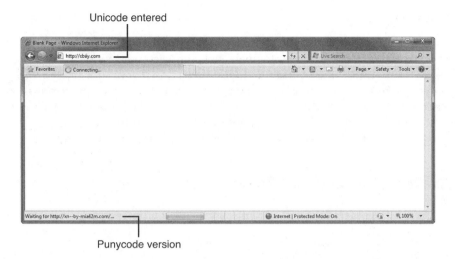

Punycode version

FIGURE 15.8   Internet Explorer encodes IDN domain names to their Punycode equivalents before surfing to the site.

▶ **Always Show Encoded Addresses**—Activate this check box to tell Internet Explorer to display the encoded Punycode web addresses in the status bar and address bar. If you're not worrying about IDN spoofing, you can deactivate this check box to see the Unicode characters instead.

▶ **Send IDN Server Names**—When activated, this check box tells Internet Explorer to encode addresses into Punycode before sending them for domain resolution.

▶ **Send IDN Server Names for Intranet Addresses**—When activated, this check box tells Internet Explorer to encode intranet addresses into Punycode before sending them for resolution. Some intranet sites don't support Punycode, so this setting is off by default.

▶ **Send UTF-8 URLs**—When activated, this check box tells Internet Explorer to send web page addresses using the UTF-8 standard, which is readable in any language. If you're having trouble accessing a page that uses non-English characters in the URL, the server might not be able to handle UTF-8, so deactivate this check box.

▶ **Show Information Bar for Encoded Addresses**—When activated, this check box tells Internet Explorer to display the following information bar message when it encodes an address into Punycode: This Web address contains letters or symbols that cannot be displayed with the current language settings.

▶ **Use UTF-8 for Mailto Links**—When activated, this check box tells Internet Explorer to use UTF-8 for the addresses in mailto links.

Managing Add-Ons

NEW TO 7 Internet Explorer 8 gives you a much better interface for managing all your browser add-ons, including ActiveX controls, toolbars, helper objects, and more. Select Tools, Manage Add-Ons to display the Manage Add-Ons dialog box shown in Figure 15.9. Select the add-on you want to work with and then click Disable (or Enable if you've previously disabled an add-on). If the add-on also has related add-ons installed, Internet Explorer displays the Disable Add-On dialog box, which gives you the opportunity to disable the related objects, as well. Click Close when you're done, and then restart Internet Explorer.

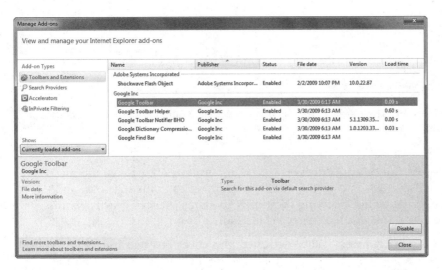

FIGURE 15.9   Use the Manage Add-Ons dialog box to view, disable, and enable Internet Explorer add-ons.

Total Security: Internet Explorer Without Add-Ons

NEW TO 7 For the ultimate in browsing security, Windows 7 ships with an alternative Internet Explorer shortcut that loads the browser without any third-party add-ons, extensions, toolbars, or ActiveX controls. This is useful if you suspect your computer is infected with spyware that has hijacked your browser. This often means not only that the spyware has changed your home page, but in many cases the spyware also prevents you from accessing antispyware or antivirus sites. By running Internet Explorer without any add-ons, you effectively disable the spyware, and you can then surf to whatever site you need. Internet Explorer without add-ons is also completely safe from being infected with spyware, so running this version of Internet Explorer is useful if you'll be surfing in darker areas of the Web where you suspect the possibility of infection is very high.

Select Start, All Programs, Accessories, System Tools, Internet Explorer (No Add-Ons). Internet Explorer starts and displays the Add-Ons Disabled page. Click the Home button or enter an address to continue browsing.

Understand Internet Explorer's Advanced Security Options

To close our look at Windows 7's web security features, this section takes you through Internet Explorer's Advanced security options. Select Tools, Internet Options, display the Advanced tab, and then scroll down to the Security section to see the following options:

- ▶ **Allow Active Content from CDs to Run on My Computer**—Leave this check box deactivated to prevent active content such as scripts and controls located in CD-based web pages to execute on your computer. However, if you have a CD-based program that won't function, you might need to activate this check box to enable the program to work properly.

- ▶ **Allow Active Content to Run in Files on My Computer**—Leave this check box deactivated to prevent active content such as scripts and controls located in local web pages to execute on your computer. If you're testing a web page that includes active content, activate this check box so that you can test the web pages locally.

- ▶ **Allow Software to Run or Install Even If the Signature Is Invalid**—Leave this check box deactivated to avoid running or installing software that doesn't have a valid digital signature. If you can't get a program to run or install, consider activating this check box.

- ▶ **Check for Publisher's Certificate Revocation**—When this option is activated, Internet Explorer examines a site's digital security certificates to see whether they have been revoked.

- ▶ **Check for Server Certificate Revocation**—If you activate this option, Internet Explorer also checks the security certificate for the web page's server.

- ▶ **Check for Signatures on Downloaded Programs**—If you activate this check box, Internet Explorer checks for a digital signature on any program that you download.

- ▶ **Do Not Save Encrypted Pages to Disk**—If you activate this option, Internet Explorer won't store encrypted files in the Temporary Internet Files folder.

- ▶ **Empty Temporary Internet Files Folder When Browser Is Closed**—With this option activated, Internet Explorer removes all files from the Temporary Internet Files folder when you exit the program.

- ▶ **Enable DOM Storage**—When this check box is activated, Internet Explorer 8 stores Document Object Model (DOM) data, which is similar to cookie data, but with a much larger capacity (up to 10MB as opposed to the maximum of 10KB with cookies). Internet Explorer 8 might not be able to save session data if you disable this option. If you're worried about Internet Explorer storing that much personal data, the data actually gets cleared automatically as soon as you close any Internet

15

Explorer tab or window that requires that data. However, deleting cookies (as described earlier) also deletes the DOM storage.

▶ **Enable Integrated Windows Authentication**—With this check box activated, Internet Explorer uses Integrated Windows Authentication (formerly known as Windows NT Challenge/Response Authentication) to attempt to log on to a restricted site. This means the browser attempts to log on using the current credentials from the user's network domain logon. If this doesn't work, Internet Explorer displays a dialog box prompting the user for a username and password.

▶ **Enable Memory Protection to Help Mitigate Online Attacks**—This option (which you can't deactivate) enables Data Execution Prevention for Internet Explorer, which prevents malicious code from running in protected memory locations.

▶ **Enable Native XMLHTTP Support**—With this check box activated, Internet Explorer works properly with sites that use the XMLHTTPRequest API to transfer XML data between the browser and a server. This API is most commonly used in Ajax-powered sites. Ajax (Asynchronous JavaScript and XML) is a web development technique that creates sites that operate much like desktop programs. In particular, the XMLHTTPRequest API enables the browser to request and accept data from the server without reloading the page.

▶ **Enable SmartScreen Filter**—This options toggled the SmartScreen phishing filter on and off.

▶ **Use SSL 2.0**—This check box toggles support for the Secure Sockets Layer Level 2 security protocol on and off. This version of SSL is currently the Web's standard security protocol.

▶ **Use SSL 3.0**—This check box toggles support for SSL Level 3 on and off. SSL 3.0 is more secure than SSL 2.0 (it can authenticate both the client and the server), but isn't currently as popular as SSL 2.0.

▶ **Use TLS 1.0**—This check box toggles support for *Transport Layer Security* (*TLS*) version 1.0 on and off. TLS is the successor to SSL, and is starting to be implemented more widely, which may be why Internet Explorer 8 activates this check box by default.

▶ **Use TLS 1.1**—This check box toggles support for TLS version 1.1. Activate this option if have trouble accessing a secure site (for example, if Internet Explorer displays an error telling you the site's security certificate can't be verified).

▶ **Use TLS 1.2**—This check box toggles support for TLS version 1.2. Activate this option if have trouble accessing a secure site and enabling support for TSL 1.1 didn't help.

▶ **Warn About Certificate Address Mismatch**—When activated, this option tells Internet Explorer to display a warning dialog box if a site is using an invalid digital security certificate.

- ▶ **Warn If Changing Between Secure and Not Secure Mode**—When activated, this option tells Internet Explorer to display a warning dialog box whenever you enter and leave a secure site.

- ▶ **Warn If POST Submittal Is Redirected to a Zone That Does Not Permit Posts**—When activated, this option tells Internet Explorer to display a warning dialog box if a form submission is sent to a site other than the one hosting the form.

15

Implementing Email Security

Email—when it absolutely positively has to get lost at the speed of light.

—Anonymous

Although people are increasingly communicating via instant messaging and social networking, email remains the default mode of message exchange if for no other reason than almost everyone who can get online has at least one email account. In fact, many of us rely utterly on email for business and for keeping in touch with far-flung friends and family members.

It's this day-to-day dependence on email that makes it all the more vexing that the email system is often so frustrating in terms of security and privacy. Email viruses are legion; spam gets worse every day; and messages that should be secret are really about as secure as if they were written on the back of a postcard. Fortunately, it doesn't take much to remedy these and other email problems, as you see in this chapter.

Protecting Yourself Against Email Viruses

Computing veterans will remember that way back when the primary method that computer viruses used to propagate themselves was the floppy disk. A user with an infected machine would copy some files to a floppy, and the virus would surreptitiously add itself to the disk. When the recipient inserted the disk, the virus copy came to life and infected yet another computer.

Most of us haven't even *seen* a floppy disk in years, but that didn't stop the spread of viruses. On the contrary, the Internet's now firm foothold in the mainstream has been a boon to virus writers everywhere, who happily adapted to the new reality and soon began propagating their malware either via malicious websites or via infected program files downloaded to users' machines.

However, by far the most productive method for viruses to replicate has been the humble email message: Melissa, I Love You, BadTrans, Sircam, Klez. The list of email viruses and Trojan horses is a long one, but they all operate more or less the same way: They arrive as a message attachment, usually from someone you know. When you open the attachment, the virus infects your computer and then, without your knowledge, uses your email client and your address book to ship out messages with more copies of itself attached. The nastier versions also mess with your computer by deleting data or corrupting files.

You can avoid infection by one of these viruses by implementing a few commonsense procedures:

▶ Never open an attachment that comes from someone you don't know.

▶ Even if you know the sender, if the attachment isn't something you're expecting, assume that the sender's system is infected. Write back and confirm that the sender emailed the message.

▶ Some viruses come packaged as scripts hidden within messages that use the HTML format. This means that the virus can run just by viewing the message! If a message looks suspicious, don't open it; just delete it. (Note that you'll need to turn off the Windows Live Mail Reading pane before deleting the message. Otherwise, when you highlight the message, it appears in the Reading pane and sets off the virus. Click Menus in the toolbar (or press Alt+M), click Layout, deactivate the Show Reading Pane check box, and click OK.)

CAUTION

It's particularly important to turn off the Reading pane before displaying Windows Live Mail's Junk E-mail folder. Because many junk messages also carry a virus payload, your chances of initiating an infection are highest when working with messages in this folder. Fortunately, Windows Live Mail is sensible enough to turn off the Reading pane by default when you open the Junk E-mail folder.

▶ Install a top-of-the-line antivirus program, particularly one that checks incoming email. In addition, be sure to keep your antivirus program's virus list up-to-date. As you read this, there are probably dozens, maybe even hundreds, of morally challenged scumnerds designing even nastier viruses. Regular updates will help you keep up. Here are some security suites to check out:

Norton Internet Security (www.symantec.com/index.jsp)
McAfee Internet Security Suite (http://mcafee.com/us)

Avast! Antivirus (www.avast.com)

AVG Internet Security (http://free.grisoft.com/)

Besides these general procedures, Windows Live Mail also comes with its own set of virus protection features. Here's how to use them:

1. In Windows Live Mail, click Menus (or press Alt+M) and then click Safety Options. Windows Live Mail opens the Safety Options dialog box.

2. Display the Security tab.

3. In the Virus Protection group, you have the following options:

   ▶ **Select the Internet Explorer Security Zone to Use**—In Chapter 15, "Configuring Web Security," I described the security zone model used by Internet Explorer. From the perspective of Windows Live Mail, you use the security zones to determine whether to allow active content inside an HTML-format message to run:

   Internet Zone—If you choose this zone, active content is allowed to run.

   Restricted Sites Zone—If you choose this option, active content is disabled. This is the default setting and the one I recommend.

   ▶ **Warn Me When Other Applications Try to Send Mail as Me**—As I mentioned earlier, it's possible for programs and scripts to send email messages without your knowledge. This happens by using *Simple MAPI* (*Messaging Application Programming Interface*) calls, which can send messages via your computer's default mail client—and it's all hidden from you. With this check box activated, Windows Live Mail displays a warning dialog box when a program or script attempts to send a message using Simple MAPI.

16

Sending Messages Via CDO

Activating the Warn Me When Other Applications Try to Send Mail as Me option protects you against scripts that attempt to send surreptitious messages using Simple MAPI calls. However, there's another way to send messages behind the scenes. It's *Collaboration Data Objects* (*CDO*), and Windows 7 installs it by default. Here's a sample script that uses CDO to send a message:

```
Dim objMessage

Dim objConfig

strSchema = "http://schemas.microsoft.com/cdo/configuration/"


Set objConfig = CreateObject("CDO.Configuration")

With objConfig.Fields

    .Item(strSchema & "sendusing") = 2

    .Item(strSchema & "smtpserver") = "smpt.yourisp.com"

    .Item(strSchema & "smtpserverport") = 25
```

```
        .Item(strSchema & "smtpauthenticate") = 1

        .Item(strSchema & "sendusername") = "your_user_name"

        .Item(strSchema & "sendpassword") = "your_password"

        .Update

End With


Set objMessage = CreateObject("CDO.Message")

With objMessage

        Set .Configuration = objConfig

        .To = "you@there.com"

        .From = "me@here.com"

        .Subject = "CDO Test"

        .TextBody = "Just testing..."

        .Send

End With

Set objMessage = Nothing

Set objConfig = Nothing
```

The Warn Me When Other Applications Try to Send Mail as Me option does *not* trap this kind of script, so bear in mind that your system is still vulnerable to Trojan horses that send mail via your Windows 7 accounts. However, in the preceding example, I've included code to handle SMTP authentication (just in case you want to try out the script and your ISP requires authentication). In practice, a third-party script wouldn't know your SMTP password, so a CDO script will fail on any account that requires authentication.

▶ **Do Not Allow Attachments to Be Saved or Opened That Could Potentially Be a Virus**—With this check box activated, Windows Live Mail monitors attachments to look for file types that could contain viruses or destructive code. If it detects such a file, it disables your ability to open and save that file, and it displays a note at the top of the message to let you know about the unsafe attachment.

File Types Disabled by Windows Live Mail

Internet Explorer's built-in unsafe-file list defines the file types that Windows Live Mail disables. That list includes file types associated with the following extensions: .ad, .ade, .adp, .bas, .bat, .chm, .cmd, .com, .cpl, .crt, .exe, .hlp, .hta, .inf, .ins, .isp, .js, .jse, .lnk, .mdb, .mde, .msc, .msi, .msp, .mst, .pcd, .pif, .reg, .scr, .sct, .shb, .shs, .url, .vb, .vbe, .vbs, .vsd, .vss, .vst, .vsw, .wsc, .wsf, and .wsh.

> **TIP**
>
> What do you do if you want to send a file that's on the Windows Live Mail unsafe file list and you want to make sure that the recipient will be able to open it? The easiest workaround is to compress the file into a `.zip` file—a file type not blocked by Windows Live Mail, Outlook, or any other mail client that blocks file types.

4. Click OK to put the new settings into effect.

Configuring Windows Defender to Scan Email

The evil known as spyware usually infects a PC by luring an unsuspecting user to a malicious website that either uses a script to infect an unprotected browser, or uses a pop-up window to dupe the user into clicking a button that installs the malware (a so-called *drive-by download*). However, spyware crackers also ship out their wares as email attachments. The Windows Live Mail antivirus settings should thwart this kind of thing, but for an extra line of defense you can also configure Windows Defender to scan email messages. Here's how to set this up:

1. Select Start, type **defend**, and then press Enter to open Windows Defender.
2. Click Tools.
3. Click Options. The Options dialog box appears.
4. Click Advanced.
5. Activate the Scan E-mail check box.
6. Click Save.

Thwarting Spam with Windows Live Mail's Junk Filter

Spam—unsolicited commercial messages—has become a plague upon the earth. Unless you've done a masterful job at keeping your address secret, you probably receive at least a few spam emails every day, and it's more likely that you receive a few dozen. The bad news is that most experts agree that it's only going to get worse. And why not? Spam is one of the few advertising media for which the costs are substantially borne by the users, not the advertisers.

The best way to avoid spam is to avoid getting on a spammer's list of addresses in the first place. That's hard to do these days, but here are some steps you can take:

▶ Never use your actual email address in a newsgroup account. The most common method that spammers use to gather addresses is to harvest them from newsgroup posts. One common tactic you can use is to alter your email address by adding text that invalidates the address but is still obvious for other people to figure out:

```
user@myisp.remove_this_to_email_me.com
```

▶ When you sign up for something online, use a fake address, if possible. If you need or want to receive email from the company and so must use your real address, make sure that you deactivate any options that ask if you want to receive promotional offers. Alternatively, enter the address from an easily disposable free web-based account (such as a Hotmail account) so that any spam you receive will go there instead of to your main address. If your free email account overflows with junk mail, remove it and create a new one. (You can also do this through your ISP if it allows you to create multiple email accounts.)

▶ Never open suspected spam messages. Doing so can sometimes notify the spammer that you've opened the message, thus confirming that your address is legit. For the same reason, you should never display a spam message in the Windows Live Mail Reading pane. Shut off the Reading pane (select View, Layout, deactivate Show Preview Pane, and click OK) before selecting any spam messages that you want to delete.

▶ Never—I repeat, *never*—respond to spam, even to an address within the spam that claims to be a "removal" address. By responding to the spam, all you're doing is proving that your address is legitimate, so you'll just end up getting *more* spam.

TIP

If you create web pages, never put your email address on a page because spammers use *crawlers* that harvest addresses from web pages. If you must put an address on a page, hide it using some simple JavaScript code:

```
<script language="JavaScript" type="text/javascript">
<!--
var add1 = "webmaster"
var add2 = "@"
var add3 = "whatever.com"
document.write(add1 + add2 + add3)
//-->
</script>
```

If you do get spam despite these precautions, the good news is that Windows Live Mail comes with a junk email feature that can help you cope. The junk email feature is a *spam filter*, which means that it examines each incoming message and applies sophisticated tests to determine whether the message is spam. If the tests determine that the message is probably spam, Windows Live Mail exiles the email to a separate Junk E-mail folder. The basis for the Windows Live Mail spam filter is the much-admired filter that comes with Microsoft Outlook. It's not perfect (no spam filter is), but with a bit of fine-tuning as described in the next few sections, it can be a very useful weapon against spam.

Setting the Junk Email Protection Level

Filtering spam is always a trade-off between protection and convenience. That is, the stronger the protection you use, the less convenient the filter becomes, and vice versa. This inverse relationship is the result of a filter phenomenon called a *false positive*—a legitimate message that the filter has pegged as spam and so (in Windows Live Mail's case) moved the message to the Junk E-mail folder. The stronger the protection level, the more likely it is that false positives will occur, so the more time you must spend checking the Junk E-mail folder for legitimate messages that need to be rescued.

Fortunately, Windows Live Mail gives you several junk email levels to choose from, so you can choose a level that gives the blend of protection and convenience that suits you. To set the junk email level, click Menus (or press Alt+M), and then click Safety Options. Windows Live Mail displays Safety Options dialog box. The Options tab gives you four options for the junk email protection level:

- ▶ **No Automatic Filtering**—This option turns off the junk email filter. However, Windows Live Mail still moves messages from blocked senders to the Junk E-mail folder (see "Blocking Senders," later in this chapter). Choose this option only if you use a third-party spam filter or if you handle spam using your own message rules.

- ▶ **Low**—This is the default protection level, and it's designed to move only messages with obvious spam content to the Junk E-mail folder. This is a good level to start with—particularly if you get only a few spams a day—because it catches most spam and has only a minimal risk of false positives.

- ▶ **High**—This level handles spam aggressively and so only rarely misses a junk message. On the downside, the High level also occasionally catches legitimate messages in its nets, so you need to check the Junk E-mail folder regularly to look for false positives. Use this level if you get a lot of spam—a few dozen messages or more each day.

NOTE

If you get a false positive in your Junk E-mail folder, click the message and then click Not Junk in the toolbar. Windows Live Mail moves the messages to the Inbox.

- ▶ **Safe List Only**—This level treats all incoming messages as spam, except for those messages that come from people or domains in your Safe Senders list (see "Specifying Safe Senders," later in this chapter) or that are sent to addresses in your Safe Recipients list. Use this level if your spam problem is out of control (a hundred or more spams each day) and if most of your nonspam email comes from people you know or from mailing lists you subscribe to.

16

If you hate spam so much that you never want to even *see* it, much less deal with it, activate the Permanently Delete Suspected Junk E-mail check box.

CAUTION

Spam is so hair-pullingly frustrating that you might be tempted to activate the Permanently Delete Suspected Junk E-mail check box out of sheer spite. I don't recommend this, however. The danger of false positives is too great, even with the Low level, and it's not worth missing a crucial message.

You can improve the performance of the junk email filter by giving Windows Live Mail a bit more information. Specifically, you can specify safe senders and you can block senders and countries.

Specifying Safe Senders

If you use the Low or High junk email protection level, you can reduce the number of false positives by letting Windows Live Mail know about the people or institutions that regularly send you mail. By designating these addresses as Safe Senders, you tell Windows Live Mail to leave their incoming messages in your Inbox automatically and never redirect them to the Junk E-mail folder. Certainly, if you use the Safe Lists Only protection level, you must specify some Safe Senders because Windows Live Mail treats everyone else as a spammer (unless someone sends mail to an address in your Safe Recipients list—see the next section).

Your Safe Senders list can consist of three types of addresses:

▶ **Individual email addresses of the form** *someone@somewhere.com*—All messages from those addresses are not treated as spam.

▶ **Domain names of the form** *@somewhere.com*—All messages from any address within that domain are not treated as spam.

▶ **Your Contacts list**—You can tell Windows Live Mail to treat everyone in your Contacts list as a Safe Sender, which makes sense because you're unlikely to be spammed by someone you know.

You can specify a Safe Sender contact in two ways:

▶ **Enter the address by hand**—In the Safety Options dialog box, display the Safe Senders tab, click Add, type the address, and then click OK.

▶ **Use an existing message from the sender**—Right-click the message, select Junk E-mail, and then select either Add Sender to Safe Senders List or Add Sender's Domain to Safe Senders List.

Blocking Senders

If you notice that a particular address is the source of much spam or other annoying email, the easiest way to block the spam is to block all incoming messages from that address. You can do this using the Blocked Senders list, which watches for messages from a specific address and relegates them to the Junk E-mail folder.

As with the Safe Senders list, you can specify a Blocked Sender address in two ways:

▶ **Enter the address by hand**—Display the Blocked Senders tab in the Safety Options dialog box, click Add, type the address, and then click OK.

▶ **Use an existing message from the sender**—Right-click the message, select Junk E-mail, and then select either Add Sender to Blocked Senders List or Add Sender's Domain to Blocked Senders List.

Blocking Countries and Languages

Windows Live Mail also has two features that enable you to handle spam with an international flavor:

▶ **Spam that comes from a particular country or region**—If you receive no legitimate messages from that country or region, you can treat all messages from that location as spam. Windows Live Mail does this by using the *top-level domain* (*TLD*), which is the final suffix that appears in a domain name. There are two types: a generic top-level domain, such as com, edu, or net; and a country code top-level domain, such as ca (Canada) and fr (France). Windows Live Mail uses the latter to filter spam that comes from certain countries.

NOTE

According to Spamhaus (www.spamhaus.org), some of the worst spam origin countries (after the United States, which is number 1!), are China, Russia, South Korea, and India.

▶ **Spam that comes in a foreign language**—If you don't understand a language, you can safely treat all messages that appear in that language as spam. The character set of a foreign language always appears using a special encoding unique to that language. (An *encoding* is a set of rules that establishes a relationship between the characters and their representations.) Windows Live Mail uses that encoding to filter spam in a specified language.

With the Safety Options dialog box open, use the following steps to configure these aspects of your spam filter:

1. Display the International tab.
2. To filter spam based on one or more countries, click the Blocked Top-Level Domain List button. You see the Blocked Top-Level Domain dialog box, shown in Figure 16.1.

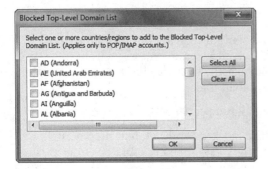

FIGURE 16.1   Use the Blocked Top-Level Domain dialog box to select the country domains that you want to treat as spam.

3. Activate the check box beside each of the countries you want to filter.

4. Click OK.

5. To filter spam based on one or more languages, click the Blocked Encodings List button. You see the Blocked Encodings List dialog box, shown in Figure 16.2.

FIGURE 16.2   Use the Blocked Encodings List dialog box to select the languages that you want to treat as spam.

6. Activate the check box beside each of the languages you want to filter.

7. Click OK.

8. Click to put the new filter settings into effect.

Email Phishing Protection

Internet Explorer's SmartScreen Filter works well if you stumble into a phishing site while surfing the Web. However, most phishing "lures" are email messages that appear to be from legitimate businesses, and they include links that send you to phishing sites where they hope to dupe you into giving up confidential information.

To help prevent you from falling into that trap, Windows Live Mail includes an antiphishing feature of its own: If it detects a potential phishing email, it blocks that message from appearing. The Phishing tab in the Junk E-mail Options dialog box controls this feature. Make sure that you activate the Protect My Inbox from Messages with Potential Phishing Links check box. Note, too, that you can also redirect potential phishing messages to the Junk E-mail folder by activating the Move Phishing E-mail to the Junk Mail Folder check box.

If Windows Live Mail detects a potential phishing message, it displays a message to let you know (see Figure 16.3) and it displays the message header in red text. If you open the suspicious message, Windows Live Mail displays the `Suspected Phishing Message` bar shown in Figure 16.4 and disables the message's images and links. If you're sure that the message is not a phishing attempt, click Unblock Message.

FIGURE 16.3   If Windows Live Mail suspects a message is a phishing attempt, it displays this message to let you know.

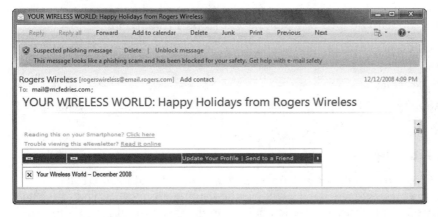

FIGURE 16.4   If you open a suspected phishing message, Windows Live Mail blocks the message's links and images.

Maintaining Your Privacy While Reading Email

You wouldn't think that the simple act of reading an email message would have privacy implications, but you'd be surprised. Two scenarios can compromise your privacy: read receipts and web bugs.

Blocking Read Receipts

A *read receipt* is an email notification that tells the sender that you've opened the message sent to you. If the sender requests a read receipt and you either select the message so that the message text appears in the preview pane, or double-click the message to open it, Windows Live Mail displays the dialog box shown in Figure 16.5. Click Yes to send the receipt, or click No to skip it.

FIGURE 16.5   You see this dialog box when you open a message for which the sender has requested a read receipt.

Many people like asking for read receipts because they offer proof of delivery. It has been my experience, however, that getting a read receipt back starts a kind of internal clock that the sender uses to measure how long it takes you to respond after reading the message. Because of this annoyance, and because I feel it's nobody's business to know when I read a message, I always click No when asked to send a read receipt. (Spammers, too, sometimes request read receipts as a way of validating email addresses.) In fact, you can go one better and tell Windows Live Mail never to send a read receipt:

1. Click Menus (or press Alt+M), and then click Options to display the Options dialog box.
2. Display the Receipts tab.
3. In the Returning Read Receipts group, activate the Never Send a Read Receipt option.
4. Click OK.

Squashing Web Bugs

A *web bug* is an image that resides on a remote server and is included in an HTML-formatted email message by referencing a URL on the remote server. When you open the message, Windows Live Mail uses the URL to download the image for display within the message. That sounds harmless enough, but if the message is junk email, it's likely that the URL will also contain either your email address or a code that points to your email address. When the remote server gets a request for this URL, it knows not only that you've opened the message, but also that your email address is legitimate.

You have three ways to combat web bugs:

► **Don't open a message that you suspect to be spam, and don't preview the message in the Windows Live Mail preview pane**—In fact, before you can delete the message, you have to turn off the preview pane temporarily, as described earlier in this chapter.

▶ **Read your messages in plain text**—In Windows Live Mail, click Menus (or press Alt+M), and then click Options to display the Options dialog box. Choose the Read tab, and then activate the Read All Messages in Plain Text check box. This prevents Windows Live Mail from downloading any web bugs because it displays all messages in plain text, which means that it also thwarts other message formatting, as well.

TIP

If you get a legitimate HTML message, you can tell Windows Live Mail to display the formatting. Select the message, press Alt to display the menu bar, and then select View Message in HTML (or press Alt+Shift+H).

▶ **Block images from displaying**—In Windows Live Mail, click Menus (or press Alt+M), and then click Safety Options to display the Safety Options dialog box. Display the Security tab, and then activate the Block Images and Other External Content in HTML E-mail check box. This prevents Windows Live Mail from downloading web bugs and any other items that would otherwise come from some remote server.

Sending and Receiving Secure Email

When you connect to a website, your browser sets up a direct connection—called a *channel*—between your machine and the web server. Because the channel is a direct link, it's relatively easy to implement security because all you have to do is secure the channel.

However, email security is entirely different and much more difficult to set up. The problem is that email messages don't have a direct link to a Simple Mail Transfer Protocol (SMTP) server. Instead, they must usually hop from server to server until they reach their final destination. Combine this with the open and well-documented email standards used on the Internet, and you end up with three email security issues:

▶ **Privacy**—Because messages often pass through other systems and can even end up on a remote system's hard disk, it isn't that hard for someone with the requisite know-how and access to the remote system to read a message.

▶ **Tampering**—Because a user can read a message passing through a remote server, it comes as no surprise that he can also change the message text.

▶ **Authenticity**—With the Internet email standards an open book, it isn't difficult for a savvy user to forge or *spoof* an email address.

To solve these issues, the Internet's gurus came up with the idea of *encryption*. When you encrypt a message, a complex mathematical formula scrambles the message content to make it unreadable. In particular, the encryption formula incorporates a *key value*. To unscramble the message, the recipient feeds the key into the decryption formula.

Such *single-key encryption* works, but its major drawback is that both the sender and the recipient must have the same key. *Public-key encryption* overcomes that limitation by using two related keys: a *public key* and a *private key*. The public key is available to everyone, either by sending it to them directly or by offering it in an online key database. The private key is secret and is stored on the user's computer. Here's how public-key cryptography solves the issues discussed earlier:

- ▶ **Privacy**—When you send a message, you obtain the recipient's public key and use it to encrypt the message. The encrypted message can now only be decrypted using the recipient's private key, thus assuring privacy.

- ▶ **Tampering**—An encrypted message can still be tampered with, but only randomly because the content of the message can't be seen. This thwarts the most important skill used by tamperers: making the tampered message look legitimate.

- ▶ **Authenticity**—When you send a message, you use your private key to digitally sign the message. The recipient can then use your public key to examine the digital signature to ensure that the message came from you.

If there's a problem with public-key encryption, it is that the recipient of a message must obtain the sender's public key from an online database. (The sender can't just send the public key because the recipient would have no way to prove that the key came from the sender.) Therefore, to make this more convenient, a *digital ID* is used. This is a digital certificate that states a trusted certifying authority authenticates the sender's public key. The sender can then include his or her public key in outgoing messages.

Setting Up an Email Account with a Digital ID

To send secure messages using Windows Live Mail, you first have to obtain a digital ID. Here are the steps to follow:

1. In Windows Live Mail, click Menus (or press Alt+M), and then click Safety Options to display the Safety Options dialog box.
2. Display the Security tab.
3. Click Get Digital ID. Internet Explorer loads and takes you to the Microsoft Office Marketplace digital ID page on the Web.
4. Click a link to the certifying authority (such as VeriSign) you want to use.
5. Follow the authority's instructions for obtaining a digital ID. (Note that digital IDs are not free; they typically cost about $20 per year.)

With your digital ID installed, the next step is to assign it to an email account:

1. In Windows Live Mail, press Alt to display the menu bar, then select Tools, Accounts to open the Internet Accounts dialog box.
2. Select the account you want to work with and then click Properties. The account's property sheet appears.

3. Display the Security tab.

4. In the Signing Certificate group, click Select. Windows Live Mail displays the Select Default Account Digital ID dialog box.

5. Make sure to select the certificate that you installed and then click OK. Your name appears in the Security tab's first Certificate box.

6. Click OK to return to the Internet Accounts dialog box.

7. Click Close.

TIP

To make a backup copy of your digital ID, open Internet Explorer and select Tools, Internet Options. Display the Content tab and click Certificates to see a list of your installed certificates (be sure to use the Personal tab). Click your digital ID and then click Export.

Obtaining Another Person's Public Key

Before you can send an encrypted message to another person, you must obtain his public key. How you do this depends on whether you have a digitally signed message from that person.

If you have a digitally signed message, open the message, as described later in this chapter in the "Receiving a Secure Message" section. Windows Live Mail adds the digital ID to the Contacts list automatically:

▶ If you have one or more contacts whose email addresses match the address associated with the digital ID, Windows Live Mail adds the digital ID to each contact. To see it, click Contacts to open Windows Live Contacts, open the contact, and display the IDs tab.

▶ If there are no existing matches, Windows Live Mail creates a new contact.

TIP

If you don't want Windows Live Mail to add digital IDs automatically, click Menus (or press Alt+M), click Safety Options, display the Security tab, and click Advanced. In the dialog box that appears, deactivate the Add Senders' Certificates to My Windows Live Contacts check box.

If you don't have a digitally signed message for the person you want to work with, you have to visit a certifying authority's website and find the person's digital ID. For example, you can go to the VeriSign site (www.verisign.com) to search for a digital ID and then download it to your computer. After that, follow these steps:

1. Click Contacts to open Windows Live Contacts.

2. Open the person's contact info or create a new contact.

3. Type one or more email addresses and fill in the other data as necessary.

4. Display the IDs tab.

5. In the Select an E-Mail Address list, select the address that corresponds with the digital ID you downloaded.

6. Click the Import button to display the Select Digital ID File to Import dialog box.

7. Find and select the downloaded digital ID file and then click Open.

8. Click OK.

Sending a Secure Message

After installing your digital ID, you can start sending out secure email messages. You have two options:

▶ **Digitally sign a message to prove that you're the sender**—Start a new message, press Alt to display the menu bar, then either select the Tools, Digitally Sign command. A certificate icon appears to the right of the header fields.

▶ **Encrypt a message to avoid snooping and tampering**—In the New Message window, press Alt to display the menu bar, then activate the Tools, Encrypt command. A lock icon appears to the right of the header fields.

TIP

You can tell Windows Live Mail to digitally sign/encrypt all your outgoing messages. Select Menus (or press Alt+M) click Safety Options, and then display the Security tab. To encrypt all your messages, activate the Encrypt Contents and Attachments for All Outgoing Messages check box. To sign all your messages, activate the Digitally Sign All Outgoing Messages check box.

Receiving a Secure Message

The technology and mathematics underlying the digital ID are complex, but there's nothing complex about dealing with incoming secure messages. Windows Live Mail handles everything behind the scenes, including the authentication of the sender (for a digitally signed message) and the decryption of the message (for an encrypted message). In the latter case, a dialog box tells you that Windows Live Mail decrypted the message with your private key.

Windows Live Mail gives you a few visual indications that you're dealing with a secure message:

▶ The message displays with a certificate icon.

▶ The message text doesn't appear in the preview pane.

▶ The preview pane title is Security Help and the subtitle tells you the type of security used: Digitally Signed and/or Encrypted.

▶ The preview pane text describes the security used in the message.

To read the message, click the Continue button at the bottom. If you don't want to see this security preview in the future, activate the Don't Show Me This Help Screen Again check box.

TIP

If you change your mind and decide you want to see the preview screen, you have to edit the Registry. Open the Registry Editor and head for the following key:

`HKCU\Software\Microsoft\Windows Live Mail\Dont Show Dialogs`

Open the `Digital Signature Help` setting and change its value to 0.

CHAPTER 17

Securing the File System

I have six locks on my door all in a row. When I go out, I lock every other one. I figure no matter how long somebody stands there picking the locks, they are always locking three.

—Elayne Boosler

With the exception of "on-the-fly" items, such as typed passwords and security keys, most of the information we want to keep out of the wrong hands resides in a file somewhere. It might be salary numbers in a spreadsheet, private financial info in a personal finance program data file, or sensitive company secrets in a word processing document. Whatever the data and wherever on your computer it's stored, keeping the wrong sets of eyes off that data comes down to securing some part of your computer's the file system.

Windows 7 offers a limited set of options here, but you can do three things to keep your files secure: Set security permissions on files and folders, encrypt files and folders, and encrypt an entire hard disk. This chapter takes you through all three techniques.

Setting Security Permissions on Files and Folders

At the file system level, security for Windows 7 is most often handled by assigning *permissions* to a file or folder. Permissions specify whether a user or group is allowed to access a file or folder and, if access is allowed, they also specify what the user or group is allowed to do with the file or folder. For example, a user may be allowed only to read the contents of a file or folder, while another may be allowed to make changes to the file or folder.

Windows 7 offers a basic set of six permissions for folders, and five permissions for files:

▶ **Full Control**—A user or group can perform any of the actions listed. A user or group can also change permissions.

▶ **Modify**—A user or group can view the file or folder contents, open files, edit files, create new files and subfolders, delete files, and run programs.

▶ **Read and Execute**—A user or group can view the file or folder contents, open files, and run programs.

▶ **List Folder Contents** (folders only)—A user or group can view the folder contents.

▶ **Read**—A user or group can open files, but cannot edit them.

▶ **Write**—A user or group can create new files and subfolders, and open and edit existing files.

There is also a long list of so-called *special permissions* that offers more fine-grained control over file and folder security. (I'll run through these special permissions a bit later; see "Assigning Special Permissions.")

Permissions are often handled most easily by using the built-in security groups. Each security group is defined with a specific set of permissions and rights, and any user added to a group is automatically granted that group's permissions and rights. There are two main security groups:

▶ **Administrators**—Members of this group have complete control over the computer, meaning they can access all folders and files; install and uninstall programs (including legacy programs) and devices; create, modify, and remove user accounts; install Windows updates, service packs, and fixes; use Safe mode; repair Windows; take ownership of objects; and more.

▶ **Users**—Members of this group (also known as standard users) can access files only in their own folders and in the computer's shared folders, change their account's password and picture, and run programs and install programs that don't require administrative-level rights.

In addition to those groups, Windows 7 also defines up to a dozen others that you'll use less often. Note that the permissions assigned to these groups are automatically assigned to members of the Administrators group. This means that if you have an Administrator account, you don't also have to be a member of any other group to perform the task's specific to that group. Here's the list of groups:

▶ **Backup Operators**—Members of this group can access the Backup program and use it to back up and restore folders and files, no matter what permissions are set on those objects.

▶ **Cryptographic Operators**—Members of this group can perform cryptographic tasks.

▶ **Distributed COM Users**—Members of this group can start, activate, and use Distributed COM (DCOM) objects.

▶ **Event Log Readers**—Members of this group can access and read Windows 7's event logs.

▶ **Guests**—Members of this group have the same privileges as those of the Users group. The exception is the default Guest account, which is not allowed to change its account password.

▶ **HomeUsers**—Members of this group have access to resources shared using Windows 7's new Homegroup networking feature.

▶ **IIS_IUSRS**—Members of this group can access an Internet Information Server website installed on the Windows 7 computer.

▶ **Network Configuration Operators**—Members of this group have a subset of the administrator-level rights that enables them to install and configure networking features.

▶ **Performance Log Users**—Members of this group can use the Windows Performance Diagnostic Console snap-in to monitor performance counters, logs, and alerts, both locally and remotely.

▶ **Performance Monitor Users**—Members of this group can use the Windows Performance Diagnostic Console snap-in to monitor performance counters only, both locally and remotely.

▶ **Power Users**—Members of this group have a subset of the Administrators group privileges. Power users can't back up or restore files, replace system files, take ownership of files, or install or remove device drivers. In addition, power users can't install applications that explicitly require the user to be a member of the Administrators group.

▶ **Remote Desktop Users**—Members of this group can log on to the computer from a remote location using the Remote Desktop feature.

▶ **Replicator**—Members of this group can replicate files across a domain.

Assigning a User to a Security Group

The advantage of using security groups to assign permissions is that once you set the group's permissions on a file or folder, you never have to change the security again on that object. Instead, any new users you create you assign to the appropriate security group, and they automatically inherit that group's permissions.

Here are the steps to follow to assign a user to a Windows 7 security group:

1. Press Windows Logo+R (or select Start, All Programs, Accessories, Run) to display the Run dialog box.

2. In the Open text box, type `control userpasswords2`.

3. Click OK. Windows 7 displays the User Accounts dialog box, shown in Figure 17.1.

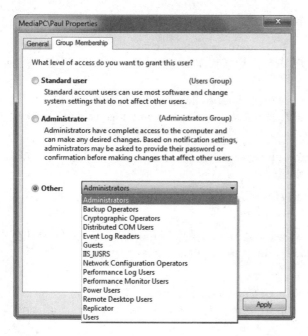

FIGURE 17.1   The User Accounts dialog box enables you to assign users to any Windows 7 security group.

4. Click the user you want to work with, and then click Properties. The user's property sheet appears.

5. Display the Group Membership tab.

6. Click the Other option, and then use the list to select the security group.

7. Click OK. Windows 7 assigns the user to the security group.

Assigning a User to Multiple Security Groups

If you want to assign a user to more than one security group, the User Account dialog box method that I ran through in the preceding section won't work. If you have Windows 7 Ultimate, Enterprise, or Business, you can use the Local Users and Groups snap-in to assign a user to multiple groups. Here's how:

1. Select Start, type `lusrmgr.msc`, and then press Enter. The Local users and Groups snap-in appears.

2. Double-click the user you want to work with. The user's property sheet appears.

3. Display the Member Of tab.

4. Click Add. Windows 7 displays the Select Groups dialog box.

5. If you know the name of the group, type it in the large text box. Otherwise, click Advanced, Find Now, and then double-click the group in the list that appears.

6. Repeat step 5 to assign the user to other groups, as needed.

7. Click OK. The Member Of tab shows the assigned groups, as shown in Figure 17.2.

8. Click OK. Windows 7 assigns the user to the security groups the next time the user logs on.

FIGURE 17.2   Using the Local User and Groups snap-in to assign a user to multiple security groups.

Assigning Standard Permissions

When you're ready to assign any of the standard permissions that I discussed earlier to a user or group, follow these steps:

1. In Windows Explorer, display the file or folder you want to secure.

2. Right-click the file or folder, and then click Properties. (If you have the folder open, you can select Organize, Properties, instead.)

3. Display the Security tab.

4. Click Edit. The Permissions for *Object* dialog box appears, where *Object* is the name of the file or folder.

5. Click Add to open the Select Users or Groups dialog box.

6. If you know the name of the user or group you want to add, type it in the large text box. Otherwise, click Advanced, Find Now, and then double-click the user or group in the list that appears.

7. Click OK. Windows 7 returns you to the Permissions for *Object* dialog box with the new user or group added.

8. Use the check boxes in the Allow and Deny columns to assign the permissions you want for this user or group, as shown in Figure 17.3.

9. Click OK in all the open dialog boxes.

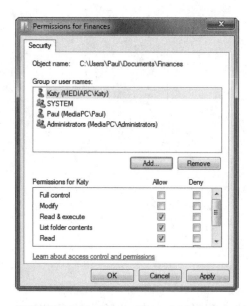

FIGURE 17.3   Use a file or folder's Permissions dialog box to assign standard permissions for a user or security group.

Assigning Special Permissions

In some situations, you might want more fine-tuned control over a user's or group's permissions. For example, you may want to allow a user to add new files to a folder, but not new subfolders. Similarly, you may want to give a user full control over a file or folder, but deny that user the ability to change permissions or take ownership of the object.

For these more specific situations, Windows 7 offers a set of 14 special permissions for folders, and 13 special permissions for files:

▸ **Full Control**—A user or group can perform any of the actions listed below.

▸ **Traverse Folder / Execute File**—A user or group can open the folder to get to another folder, or can execute a program file.

▸ **List Folder / Read Data**—A user or group can view the folder contents or can read the contents of a file.

▶ **Read Attributes**—A user or group can read the folder's or file's attributes, such as Read-Only or Hidden.

To see a file's or folder's attributes, right-click the item, click Properties, and then display the General tab.

▶ **Read Extended Attributes**—A user or group can read the folder's or file's extended attributes. (These are extra attributes assigned by certain programs.)

▶ **Create File / Write Data**—A user or group can create new files within a folder, or can make changes to a file.

▶ **Create Folders / Append Data**—A user or group can create new subfolders within a folder, or can add new data to the end of a file (but can't change any existing file data).

▶ **Write Attributes**—A user or group can change the folder's or file's attributes.

▶ **Write Extended Attributes**—A user or group can change the folder's or file's extended attributes.

▶ **Delete Subfolders and Files** (folders only)—A user or group can delete subfolders and files within the folder.

▶ **Delete**—A user or group can delete the folders or file.

▶ **Read Permissions**—A user or group can read the folder's or file's permissions.

▶ **Change Permissions**—A user or group can edit the folder's or file's permissions.

▶ **Take Ownership**—A user or group can take ownership of the folder or file.

Here are the steps to follow to assign special permissions to a file or folder:

1. In Windows Explorer, display the file or folder you want to secure.
2. Right-click the file or folder, and then click Properties. (If you have the folder open, you can select Organize, Properties, instead.)
3. Display the Security tab.
4. Click Advanced. The Advanced Security Settings for *Object* dialog box appears, where *Object* is the name of the file or folder.
5. In the Permissions tab, click Change Permissions.
6. Click the existing permission you want to edit.

17

7. Click Edit. The Permission Entry for *Object* dialog box appears.

8. Use the check boxes in the Allow and Deny columns to assign the permissions you want for this user or group, as shown in Figure 17.4.

9. Click OK in all the open dialog boxes.

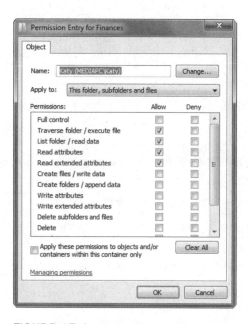

FIGURE 17.4   Use a file or folder's Permission Entry dialog box to assign special permissions for a user or security group.

Encrypting Files and Folders

If a snoop can't log on to your Windows PC, does that mean your data is safe? No, unfortunately, it most certainly does not. If a cracker has physical access to your PC—either by sneaking into your office or by stealing your computer—the cracker can use advanced utilities to view the contents of your hard drive. This means that if your PC contains extremely sensitive or confidential information—personal financial files, medical histories, corporate salary data, trade secrets, business plans, journals or diaries—it wouldn't be hard for the interloper to read and even copy that data.

If you're worried about anyone viewing these or other "for your eyes only" files, Windows 7 enables you to *encrypt* the file information. Encryption encodes the file to make it completely unreadable by anyone unless the person logs on to your Windows 7 account. After you encrypt your files, you work with them exactly as you did before, with no noticeable loss of performance.

> **NOTE**
>
> To use file encryption, your hard drive must use NTFS (New Technology File System). To check the current file system, click Start, and then click Computer. In the Computer window, click the hard drive, and then examine the file system information in the Details pane. If you need to convert a drive to NTFS, click Start, type **command,** right-click Command Prompt, and then click Run as Administrator. Type **convertd: /fs:ntfs, where *d*** is the letter of the hard drive you want to convert, and press Enter. If Windows asks to "dismount the volume," press **Y** and then Enter.

Follow these steps to encrypt important data:

1. Use Windows Explorer to display the icon of the folder containing the data that you want to encrypt.

> **TIP**
>
> Although it's possible to encrypt individual files, encrypting an entire folder is easier because Windows 7 then automatically encrypts new files that you add to the folder.

2. Right-click the folder icon and click Properties to open the folder's property sheet.
3. Click the General tab.
4. Click Advanced. The Advanced Attributes dialog box appears.
5. Click to activate the Encrypt Contents to Secure Data check box.
6. Click OK in each open dialog box. The Confirm Attribute Changes dialog box appears.
7. Click the Apply Changes to This Folder, Subfolders and Files option.
8. Click OK. Windows encrypts the folder's contents.

> **TIP**
>
> By default, Windows displays the names of encrypted files and folders in a green font, which helps you to differentiate these items from unencrypted files and folders. If you'd rather see encrypted filenames and folder names in the regular font, open any folder window, select Organize, Folder and Search Options. Click the View tab, click to deactivate the Show Encrypted or Compressed NTFS Files in Color check box, and then click OK.

Encrypting a Disk with BitLocker

Take Windows 7 security technologies such as the bidirectional Windows Firewall, Windows Defender, and Windows Service Hardening; throw in good patch-management policies (that is, applying security patches as soon as they're available); and add a dash of common sense. If you do so, your computer should never be compromised by malware while Windows 7 is running.

Windows Service Hardening

Windows Service Hardening is an under-the-hood Windows 7 security feature designed to limit the damage that a compromised service can wreak upon a system by implementing the following security techniques:

- ▶ All services run in a lower privilege level.
- ▶ All services have been stripped of permissions that they don't require.
- ▶ All services are assigned a security identifier (SID) that uniquely identifies each service. This enables a system resource to create its own access control list (ACL) that specifies exactly which SIDs can access the resource. If a service that's not on the ACL tries to access the resource, Windows 7 blocks the service.
- ▶ A system resource can restrict which services are allowed write permission to the resource.
- ▶ All services come with network restrictions that prevent services from accessing the network in ways not defined by the service's normal operating parameters.

However, what about when Windows 7 is *not* running? If your computer is stolen or if an attacker breaks into your home or office, your machine can be compromised in a couple of different ways:

- ▶ By booting to a floppy disk and using command-line utilities to reset the administrator password
- ▶ By using a CD-based operating system to access your hard disk and reset folder and file permissions

Either exploit gives the attacker access to the contents of your computer. If you have sensitive data on your machine—financial data, company secrets, and so on—the results could be disastrous.

To help you prevent a malicious user from accessing your sensitive data, Windows 7 comes with a technology called BitLocker that encrypts an entire hard drive. That way, even if a malicious user gains physical access to your computer, he or she won't be able to read the drive contents. BitLocker works by storing the keys that encrypt and decrypt the sectors on a system drive in a Trusted Platform Module (TPM) 1.2 chip, which is a hardware component available on many newer machines.

NOTE

To find out whether your computer has a TPM chip installed, restart the machine and then access the computer's BIOS settings (usually by pressing Delete or some other key; watch for a startup message that tells you how to access the BIOS). In most cases, look for a Security section and see if it lists a TPM entry.

Enabling BitLocker on a System with a TPM

To enable BitLocker on a system that comes with a TPM, select Start, Control Panel, System and Security, BitLocker Drive Encryption. In the BitLocker Drive Encryption window, shown in Figure 17.5, click the Turn On BitLocker link associated with your hard drive.

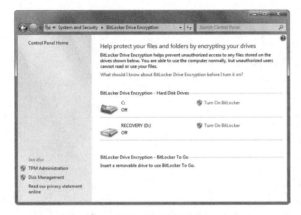

FIGURE 17.5   Use the BitLocker Drive Encryption window to turn BitLocker on and off.

> **NOTE**
>
> You can also use the Trusted Platform Module (TPM) Management snap-in to work with the TPM chip on your computer. Press Windows Logo+R, type **tpm.msc**, and click OK. This snap-in enables you to view the current status of the TPM chip, view information about the chip manufacturer, and perform chip-management functions.

17

Enabling BitLocker on a System Without a TPM

If your PC doesn't have a TPM chip, you can still use BitLocker. In this case, you'll need a USB Flash drive, which is where BitLocker will store the startup key. You'll need to insert this USB Flash drive each time you start your computer to decrypt the drive and work with your computer in the normal way.

First, you need to configure Windows 7 to allow BitLocker on a system without a TPM. Here's how it's done:

1. Select Start, type **gpedit.msc**, and then press Enter to open the Local Group Policy Editor.
2. Open the Computer Configuration, Administrative Templates, Windows Components, BitLocker Drive Encryption, Operating System Drive branch.
3. Double-click the Require Additional Authentication at Startup policy.
4. Select Enabled.

5. Click to activate the Allow BitLocker Without a Compatible TPM check box, as shown in Figure 17.6.

FIGURE 17.6   Use the Require Additional Authentication at Startup policy to configure Windows 7 to use BitLocker without a TPM.

6. Click OK.

7. To ensure that Windows 7 recognizes the new policy right away, select Start, type **gpupdate /force**, and press Enter.

You can now enable BitLocker:

1. Select Start, Control Panel, System and Security, BitLocker Drive Encryption to open the BitLocker Drive Encryption window.

2. Click the Turn On BitLocker link beside your hard drive. The BitLocker Drive Encryption Wizard appears.

3. Click Next. The wizard lets you know that it will use another drive or free space on the system drive to enable BitLocker.

4. Click Next. The wizard prepares your hard drive and then prompts you to restart.

5. Click Restart Now. Your computer restarts, and when you return to Windows, the wizard reappears.

6. Click Next. The Set BitLocker Startup Preferences dialog box appears.

7. Click Require a Startup Key at Every Startup, and then click Next.

8. Insert the USB Flash drive you want to use to hold the Startup key.

9. In the list of drives, select your USB Flash drive, and then click Save. The wizard now asks how you want to store your recovery key.

10. Select one of the following options, and then click Next:

   ▶ **Save the Recovery Key to a USB Flash Drive**—Click this option to save the recovery key to a Flash drive. This is probably the best way to go because it means you can recover your files just by inserting the Flash drive. Insert the Flash drive, select it in the list that appears, and then click Save.

   ▶ **Save the Recovery Key to a File**—Click this option to save the recovery key to a separate hard drive on your system. Use the Save BitLocker Key As dialog box to choose a location, and then click Save.

   ▶ **Print the Recovery Key**—Click this option to print out the recovery key. Choose your printer in the dialog box that appears, and then click Print.

11. Click Continue. BitLocker tells you your system must be restarted.

12. If you chose to save you recovery key on a USB Flash drive, insert that drive (if it's not still inserted), and then click Restart Now.

When your computer restarts, BitLocker starts encrypting the drive, and you see the notification shown in Figure 17.7. You can click the message to watch the progress.

FIGURE 17.7   When you restart, BitLocker starts encrypting your hard drive.

Setting Up User Security

PEBCAK (acronym): Problem Exists Between Chair And Keyboard.

—Anonymous IT wag

If you're the only person who uses your computer, you don't have to worry all that much about the security of your user profile (that is, your files and Windows 7 settings). However, if you share your computer with other people, either at home or at the office, you need to set up some kind of security to ensure that each user has his "own" Windows and can't mess with anyone else's (either purposely or accidentally). Similarly, if you're responsible for setting up users on other computers, you need to keep security in mind from the get go.

Here's a list of security precautions to set up when sharing your computer or setting up users on other computers:

▶ **Create an account for each user**—Everyone who uses the computer, even if only occasionally, should have his own user account. (If a user needs to access the computer rarely, or only once, activate the Guest account and let him use that. You should disable the Guest account after the user finishes his session.)

▶ **Remove unused accounts**—If you have accounts set up for users who no longer require access to the computer, you should delete those accounts.

▶ **Limit the number of administrators**—Members of the Administrators group can do *anything* in Windows 7 simply by clicking Submit in the User Account Control dialog box. These powerful accounts should be kept to a minimum. Ideally, your system should have just one (besides the built-in Administrator account).

▶ **Rename the Administrator account**—Renaming the Administrator account ensures that no other user can be certain of the name of the computer's top-level user.

▶ **Put all other accounts in the Users (Standard Users) group**—Most users can perform almost all of their everyday chores with the permissions and rights assigned to the Users group, so that's the group you should use for all other accounts.

▶ **Use strong passwords on all accounts**—Supply each account with a strong password so that no user can access another's account by logging on with a blank or simple password.

▶ **Set up each account with a screensaver and be sure the screensaver resumes to the Welcome screen**—To do this, right-click the desktop, click Personalize, and then click Screen Saver. Choose an item in the Screen Saver, and then activate the On Resume, Display Welcome Screen check box.

▶ **Lock your computer**—When you leave your desk for any length of time, be sure to lock your computer. Either select Start, Lock or press Windows Logo+L. This displays the Welcome screen, and no one else can use your computer without entering your password.

▶ **Use disk quotas**—To prevent users from taking up an inordinate amount of hard disk space (think MP3 downloads), set up disk quotas for each user. To enable quotas, select Start, Computer, right-click a hard drive, and then click Properties to display the disk's property sheet. Display the Quota tab, click Show Quota Settings, enter your credentials, and then activate the Enable Quota Management check box.

Except where noted, this chapter takes you through all of these techniques and a lot more.

Understanding User Account Control (UAC)

Most (I'm actually tempted to say the vast majority) security-related problems in versions of Windows prior to Vista boiled down to a single root cause: Most users were running Windows with administrator-level permissions. Administrators can do *anything* to a Windows machine, including installing programs, adding devices, updating drivers, installing updates and patches, changing Registry settings, running administrative tools, and creating and modifying user accounts. This is convenient, but it leads to a huge problem: Any malware that insinuates itself onto your system will also be capable of operating with administrative permissions, thus enabling the program to wreak havoc on the computer and just about anything connected to it.

Windows XP tried to solve the problem by creating a second-tier account level called the *limited user*, which had only very basic permissions. Unfortunately, there were three gaping holes in this "solution:"

▶ XP prompted you to create one or more user accounts during setup, but it didn't force you to create one. If you skipped this part, XP started under the Administrator account.

▶ Even if you elected to create users, the setup program didn't give you an option for setting the account security level. Therefore, any account you created during XP's setup was automatically added to the Administrators group.

▶ If you created a limited user account, you probably didn't keep it for long because XP hobbled the account so badly that you couldn't use it to do anything but the most basic computer tasks. You couldn't even install most programs because they generally require write permission for the %SystemRoot% folder and the Registry, and limited users lacked that permission.

Windows Vista tried again to solve this problem, and its solution was called User Account Control (UAC), which used a principle called the *least-privileged user*. The idea behind this is to create an account level that has no more permissions than it requires. Again, such accounts are prevented from editing the Registry and performing other administrative tasks. However, these users can perform other day-to-day tasks:

▶ Install programs and updates

▶ Add printer drivers

▶ Change wireless security options (such as adding a WEP or WPA key)

The least-privileged user concept arrives in the form of a new account type called the standard user. This means that Windows Vista had three basic account levels:

▶ **Administrator account**—This built-in account can do anything to the computer.

▶ **Administrators group**—Members of this group (except the Administrator account) run as standard users but can elevate their privileges when required just by clicking a button in a dialog box (see the next section).

▶ **Standard Users group**—These are the least-privileged users, although they, too, can elevate their privileges when needed. However, they require access to an administrator password to do so.

Windows 7 carries on with UAC, but as you see a bit later, the implementation is much less intrusive.

Elevating Privileges

This idea of elevating privileges is at the heart of the UAC security model. In Windows XP, you could use the Run As command to run a task as a different user (that is, one with higher privileges). In Windows 7 (as with Vista), you usually don't need to do this because Windows 7 prompts you for the elevation automatically.

If you're a member of the Administrators group, you run with the privileges of a standard user for extra security. When you attempt a task that requires administrative privileges, Windows 7 prompts for your consent by displaying a User Account Control dialog box similar to the one shown in Figure 18.1. Click Yes to permit the task to proceed. If this dialog box appears unexpectedly, it's possible that a malware program is trying to perform some task that requires administrative privileges; you can thwart that task by clicking Cancel instead.

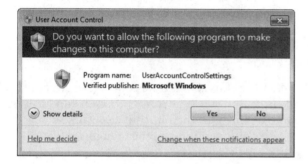

FIGURE 18.1   When an administrator launches a task that requires administrative privileges, Windows 7 displays this dialog box to ask for consent.

If you're running as a standard user and attempt a task that requires administrative privileges, Windows 7 uses an extra level of protection. That is, instead of just prompting you for consent, it prompts you for the credentials of an administrator, as shown in Figure 18.2. If your system has multiple administrator accounts, each one is shown in this dialog box. Type the password for any administrator account shown, and then click Yes. Again, if this dialog box shows up unexpectedly, it might be malware, so you should click Cancel to prevent the task from going through.

Note, too, that in both cases, Windows 7 switches to secure desktop mode, which means that you can't do anything else with Windows 7 until you give your consent or credentials or cancel the operation. Windows 7 indicates the secure desktop by darkening everything on the screen except the User Account Control dialog box.

NOTE

It's also possible to elevate your privileges for any individual program. Do this by right-clicking the program file or shortcut and then clicking Run as Administrator.

FIGURE 18.2   When a standard user launches a task that requires administrative privileges, Windows 7 displays this dialog box to ask for administrative credentials.

File and Registry Virtualization

You might be wondering how secure Windows 7 really is if a standard user can install programs. Doesn't that mean that malware can install, too? No, because in Windows 7, you need administrative privileges to write anything to the %SystemRoot% folder (usually C:\Windows), the %ProgramFiles% folder (usually C:\Program Files), and the Registry. Windows 7 handles this for standard users in two ways:

▶ During a program installation, Windows 7 first prompts the user for credentials (that is, Windows 7 displays one of the Windows Security dialog boxes shown earlier in Figures 18.1 and 18.2). If they are provided, Windows 7 gives permission to the program installer to write to %SystemRoot%, %ProgramFiles%, and the Registry.

▶ If the user cannot provide credentials, Windows 7 uses a technique called *file and Registry virtualization*, which creates virtual %SystemRoot% and %ProgramFiles% folders, and a virtual HKEY_LOCAL_MACHINE Registry key, all of which are stored with the user's files. This enables the installer to proceed without jeopardizing actual system files.

Configuring User Account Control

NEW TO 7   So far, UAC in Windows 7 is the same as it was in Windows Vista. However, if there was a problem with the UAC implementation in Vista, it was that it was a tad, well, *enthusiastic* (to put the best face on it). Any minor setting change (even changing the date or time) required elevation, and if you were a dedicated settings changer, UAC probably caused you to tear out more than few clumps of hair in frustration.

18

The good (some would say great) news in Windows 7 is that Microsoft has done two things to rein in UAC:

▶ It made UAC configurable so that you can tailor the notifications to suit your situation.

▶ It set up the default configuration of UAC so that it now only rarely prompts you for elevation when you change the settings on your PC. Two notable (and excusable) exceptions are when you change the UAC configuration and when you start the Registry Editor.

These are welcome changes, to be sure, although the UAC configuration choices are a bit limited, as you'll soon see. Here's how to configure UAC in Windows 7:

1. Select Start, type **user**, and then click Change User Account Control Settings in the search results. The User Account Control Settings dialog box appears, as shown in Figure 18.3.

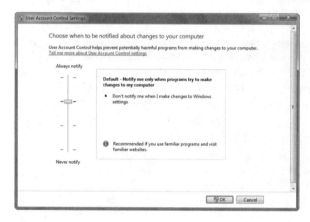

FIGURE 18.3   In Windows 7, you can use the User Account Control Settings dialog box to set up UAC as you see fit.

2. Use the slider to choose one of the following four UAC settings:

▶ **Always Notify**—This is the top level, and it works much like UAC in Windows Vista in that you're prompted for elevation when you change Windows settings, and when programs try to change settings and install software.

▶ **Default**—This is the second highest level, and it prompts you for elevation only when programs try to change settings and install software. This level uses secure desktop mode to display the UAC dialog box.

▶ **No Secure Desktop**—This is the second lowest level, and it's the same as the Default level (that is, it only prompts you for elevation when programs try to change settings and install software), but this level doesn't use secure desktop mode when displaying the UAC dialog box.

> ▶ **Never Notify**—This is the bottom level, and it turns off UAC. Of course you, as a responsible PC user, would never select this setting, right? I figured as much.

3. Click OK. The User Account Control dialog box appears.

4. Enter your UAC credentials to put the new setting into effect.

User Account Control Policies

You can customize User Account Control to a certain extent by using group policies. In the Local Security Settings snap-in (select Start, type **secpol.msc**, and then press Enter), open the Security Settings, Local Policies, Security Options branch. Here you'll find nine policies related to User Account Control (as shown in Figure 18.4).

> ▶ **User Account Control: Admin Approval Mode for the Built-In Administrator Account**—This policy controls whether the Administrator account falls under User Account Control. If you enable this policy, the Administrator account is treated like any other account in the Administrators group and must click Continue in the consent dialog box when Windows 7 requires approval for an action.

> ▶ **User Account Control: Allow UIAccess Applications to Prompt for Elevation Without Using the Secure Desktop**—Use this policy to enable or disable whether Windows 7 allows elevation for accessibility applications that require access to the user interface of another window without using the secure desktop mode.

> ▶ **User Account Control: Behavior of the Elevation Prompt for Administrators in Admin Approval Mode**—This policy controls the prompt that appears when an administrator requires elevated privileges. The default setting is Prompt for Consent, where the user clicks either Continue or Cancel. You can also choose Prompt for Credentials to force the user to type his or her password. If you choose No Prompt, administrators cannot elevate their privileges.

> ▶ **User Account Control: Behavior of the Elevation Prompt for Standard Users**—This policy controls the prompt that appears when a standard user requires elevated privileges. For a more detailed look at this policy, see "Preventing Elevation for All Standard Users," later in this chapter.

> ▶ **User Account Control: Detect Application Installations and Prompt for Elevation**—Use this policy to enable or disable automatic privilege elevation while installing programs.

18

▶ **User Account Control: Only Elevate Executables That Are Signed and Validated**—Use this policy to enable or disable whether Windows 7 checks the security signature of any program that asks for elevated privileges.

▶ **User Account Control: Only Elevate UIAccess Applications That Are Installed in Secure Locations**—Use this policy to enable or disable whether Windows 7 allows elevation for accessibility applications that require access to the user interface of another window only if they are installed in a secure location (such as the %ProgramFiles% folder).

▶ **User Account Control: Run All Administrators in Admin Approval Mode**—Use this policy to enable or disable running administrators (excluding the Administrator account) as standard users.

▶ **User Account Control: Switch to the Secure Desktop When Prompting for Elevation**—Use this policy to enable or disable whether Windows 7 switches to the secure desktop when the elevation prompts appear.

▶ **User Account Control: Virtualize File and Registry Write Failures to Per-User Locations**—Use this policy to enable or disable file and Registry virtualization for standard users.

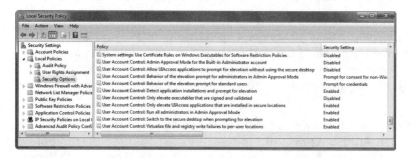

FIGURE 18.4   Windows 7 policies related to User Account Control.

Creating and Enforcing Bulletproof Passwords

Windows 7 sometimes gives the impression that passwords aren't all that important. For example, it's possible to remove the password from the user account you created during setup. Because that account is supplied with administrative-level privileges, this is a dangerous setup, because it means that anyone can start your computer and automatically get administrative rights, and that standard users can elevate permissions without needing a password. However, these problems are easily remedied by supplying a password to *all* local users. This section gives you some pointers for creating strong passwords and runs through Windows 7's password-related options and policies.

Creating a Strong Password

It's not enough to just use any old password. You can improve the security of Windows—and, hence, of your entire network—by making each password robust enough that it is impossible to guess and is impervious to software programs designed to try different password combinations. Such a password is called a *strong* password. Ideally, you want to build a password that provides maximum protection while still being easy to remember.

Lots of books will suggest absurdly fancy password schemes (I've written some of those books myself), but you really need to know only three things to create strong-like-bull passwords:

▶ **Use passwords that are at least 8 characters long**—Shorter passwords are susceptible to programs that just try every letter combination. You can combine the 26 letters of the alphabet into about 12 million 5-letter word combinations, which is no big deal for a fast program. If you bump things up to 8-letter passwords, however, the total number of combinations rises to 200 *billion*, which would take even the fastest computer quite a while. If you use 12-letter passwords, as many experts recommend, the number of combinations goes beyond mind-boggling: 90 *quadrillion*, or 90,000 trillion!

▶ **Mix up your character types**—The secret to a strong password is to include characters from the following categories: lowercase letters, uppercase letters, numbers, and symbols. If you include at least one character from three (or, even better, all four) of these categories, you're well on your way to a strong password.

▶ **Don't be too obvious**—Because forgetting a password is inconvenient, many people use meaningful words or numbers so that their password will be easier to remember. Unfortunately, this means that they often use extremely obvious things such as their name, the name of a family member or colleague, their birth date, their social security number, or even their system username. Being this obvious is just asking for trouble.

TIP

How will you know whether the password you've come up with fits the definition of *strong*? One way to find out is to submit the password to an online password complexity checker. (If you're the least bit paranoid about these things, consider submitting a password that's only similar to the one you want to use to.) I recommend Microsoft's (http://tinyurl.com/cpjh4 or www.microsoft.com/protect/yourself/password/checker. mspx), but a Google search on "password complexity checker" will reveal many others.

User Account Password Options

Each user account has a number of options related to passwords. To view these options, open the Local Users and Groups snap-in (as described later in this chapter; see "Working with the Local Users and Groups Snap-In"), and double-click the user with which you want to work. There are three password-related check boxes in the property sheet that appears:

- ▶ **User Must Change Password at Next Logon**—If you activate this check box, the next time the user logs on, she will see a dialog box with the message that she is required to change her password. When the user clicks OK, the Change Password dialog box appears, and the user enters her new password.

- ▶ **User Cannot Change Password**—Activate this check box to prevent the user from changing the password.

- ▶ **Password Never Expires**—If you deactivate this check box, the user's password will expire. The expiration date is determined by the Maximum Password Age policy, discussed in the next section.

Taking Advantage of Windows 7's Password Policies

Windows 7 maintains a small set of useful password-related policies that govern settings such as when passwords expire and the minimum length of a password. In the Local Security Settings snap-in (select Start, type `secpol.msc`, and then press Enter), select Security Settings, Account Policies, Password Policy, as shown in Figure 18.5.

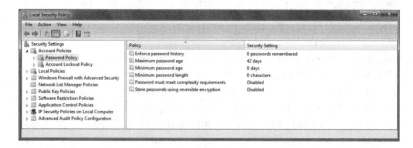

FIGURE 18.5   In the Password Policy branch, use the six policies shown here to enforce strong passwords and other protections.

There are six policies:

- ▶ **Enforce Password History**—This policy determines the number of old passwords that Windows 7 stores for each user. This is to prevent a user from reusing an old password. For example, if you set this value to 10, the user can't reuse a password until he or she has used at least 10 other passwords. Enter a number between 0 and 24.

- ▶ **Maximum Password Age**—This policy sets the number of days after which passwords expire. This applies only to user accounts where the Password Never Expires property has been disabled (refer to the previous section). Enter a number between 1 and 999.

▶ **Minimum Password Age**—This policy sets the numbers of days that a password must be in effect before the user can change it. Enter a number between 1 and 998 (but less than the Maximum Password Age value).

▶ **Minimum Password Length**—This policy sets the minimum number of characters for the password. Enter a number between 0 and 14 (where 0 means no password is required).

▶ **Password Must Meet Complexity Requirements**—If you enable this policy, Windows 7 examines each new password and accepts it only if it meets the following criteria: It doesn't contain all or part of the username; it's at least six characters long; and it contains characters from three of the following four categories: uppercase letters, lowercase letters, digits (0–9), and nonalphanumeric characters (such as $ and #).

▶ **Store Passwords Using Reversible Encryption**—Enabling this policy tells Windows 7 to store user passwords using reversible encryption. Some applications require this, but they're rare and you should never need to enable this policy because it makes your passwords much less secure.

CAUTION

Reversible encryption means that data is encrypted using a particular code as a seed value, and you can then decrypt the data by applying that same code. Unfortunately, this type of encryption has been cracked, and programs to break reversible encryption are easy to find on the Net. This means that hackers with access to your system can easily decrypt your password store and see all your passwords. Therefore, you should never enable the Store Passwords Using Reversible Encryption policy.

Recovering from a Forgotten Password

Few things in life are as frustrating as a forgotten password. To avoid this headache, Windows 7 offers a couple of precautions that you can take now just in case you forget your password.

The first precaution is called the password hint (see "Creating and Managing User Accounts"), which is a word, phrase, or other mnemonic device that can help you remember your password. To see the hint in the Welcome screen, type any password and press Enter. When Windows 7 tells you the password is incorrect, click OK. Windows 7 redisplays the Password text box with the hint below it.

The second precaution you can take is the password reset disk. This is a USB Flash drive that enables you to reset the password on your account without knowing the old password. To create a password reset disk, follow these steps:

1. Log on as the user for whom you want to create the disk.

2. Select Start, Control Panel, User Accounts and Family Safety, User Accounts.

3. In the Tasks pane, click Create a Password Reset Disk. This launches the Forgotten Password Wizard.

4. Insert a USB Flash drive, and then click Next.

5. Choose your USB Flash drive and click Next.

6. Type your user account password and click Next. Windows 7 creates the reset disk.

7. Click Next.

8. Click Finish.

The password reset disk contains a single file named Userkey.psw, which is an encrypted backup version of your password. Be sure to save this disk in a secure location and, just to be safe, don't label the disk. If you need to use this disk, follow these steps:

1. Start Windows 7 normally.

2. When you get to the Welcome screen, leave your password blank and press the Enter key. Windows 7 will then tell you the password is incorrect.

3. Click OK.

4. Click the Reset Password link.

5. In the initial Password Reset Wizard dialog box, click Next.

6. Insert the password reset Flash drive.

7. Select the Flash drive and click Next.

8. Type a new password (twice), type a password hint, and click Next.

9. Click Finish.

Creating and Managing User Accounts

Windows 7 has a number of methods for working with user accounts. The most direct route is to use Control Panel's Manage Accounts window (select Start, Control Panel, Add or Remove User Accounts). You create a new user account by following these steps:

1. Click Create a New Account. The Create New Account window appears.

2. Type the name for the account. The name can be up to 20 characters and must be unique on the system.

3. Activate either Administrator (to add the user to the Administrators group) or Standard User (to add the user to the Users group).

4. Click Create Account.

To modify an existing account, you have two choices:

▶ To modify your own account, click Go to the Main User Accounts Page to open the User Accounts window. Note that the links you see are slightly different from the ones listed next. For example, instead of Change Name, you see Change Your Name.

▶ To modify another user's account, click the account in the Manage Accounts window.

The latter technique opens the Change an Account window, which includes some of or all the following tasks:

▶ **Change the Account Name**—Click this link to change the account's username. In the Rename Account window, type the new name and click Change Name.

▶ **Create a Password**—You see this task only if the user doesn't yet have an account password. Click the link to open the Create Password window, type the password twice, type a password hint, and then click Change Password.

NOTE

A strong password is the first line of defense when it comes to local computer security. Before setting up a password for an account, check out the section "Creating and Enforcing Bulletproof Passwords," earlier in this chapter.

CAUTION

The *password hint* is text that Windows 7 displays in the Welcome screen if you type an incorrect password (see "Recovering from a Forgotten Password," earlier in this chapter). Because the hint is visible to anyone trying to log on to your machine, make the hint as vague as possible but still useful to you if you forget your password.

▶ **Change the Password**—If the user already has a password, click this link to change it. In the Change Password window, type the password twice, type a password hint, and then click Change Password.

▶ **Remove the Password**—If the user already has a password, click this link to delete it. In the Remove Password window, click Remove Password.

▶ **Change the Picture**—Click this link to change the random picture that Windows 7 assigns to each account. In the Choose Picture window, either click one of the displayed images and then click Change Picture, or click Browse for More Pictures to use the Open dialog box to pick out an image from the Pictures folder (or wherever you like).

▶ **Set Up Guest Mode**—Click this link to display the Set Up Guest Mode window shown in Figure 18.6. When guest mode is turned on, any changes the user makes during a session (settings configured, new files created, and so on) are reversed so that the computer returns to the exact state it was in before the user logged on.

▶ **Set Up Parental Controls**—Click this link to apply parental controls to the user. See "Using Parental Controls to Restrict Computer Usage," later in this chapter.

18

▶ **Change the Account Type**—Click this link to open the Change Account Type window. Click either Standard User or Administrator, and then click Change Account Type.

▶ **Delete the Account**—Click this link to delete the user account. In the Delete Account window, click either Delete Files or Keep Files (to delete or keep the user's documents), and then click Delete Account.

FIGURE 18.6   In Windows 7, you can enable guest mode for a standard user.

Working with the User Accounts Dialog Box

Control Panel's User Accounts window has one major limitation: It offers only the Administrator and Standard User account types. If you want to assign a user to one of the other groups, you have to use the User Accounts dialog box. You get there by following these steps:

1. Press Windows Logo+R (or select Start, All Programs, Accessories, Run) to display the Run dialog box.

2. In the Open text box, type `control userpasswords2`.

3. Click OK. Windows 7 displays the User Accounts dialog box, shown in Figure 18.7.

To enable the list of users, make sure that the Users Must Enter a User Name and Password to Use This Computer check box is activated.

Adding a New User

To add a new user via the User Accounts dialog box, follow these steps:

1. Click Add to launch the Add New User Wizard.

2. Type the new user's User Name (no more than 20 characters, and it must be unique). You can also type the user's Full Name and Description, but these are optional. Click Next.

FIGURE 18.7   The User Accounts dialog box enables you to assign users to any Windows 7 security group.

3. Type the user's Password, and then type it again in the Confirm Password text box. Click Next.

4. Activate the option that specifies the user's security group: Standard User (Users group), Administrator (Administrators group), or Other. Activate the latter to assign the user to any of the 14 default Windows 7 groups.

5. Click Finish.

Performing Other User Tasks

Here's a list of the other tasks you can perform in the User Accounts dialog box:

▶ **Delete a user**—Select the user and click Remove. When Windows 7 asks you to confirm, click Yes.

▶ **Change the user's name or group**—Select the user and click Properties to display the user's property sheet. Use the General tab to change the username; use the Group Membership tab to assign the user to a different group. Note that you can only assign the user to a single group using this method. If you need to assign a user to multiple groups, see "Working with the Local Users and Groups Snap-In," next.

▶ **Change the user's password**—Select the user and click Reset Password. Type the password in the New Password and Confirm New Password text boxes and click OK.

18

Working with the Local Users and Groups Snap-In

The most powerful of the Windows 7 tools for working with users is the Local Users and Groups MMC snap-in. To load this snap-in, Windows 7 offers three methods:

▶ In the User Accounts dialog box (refer to the previous section), display the Advanced tab, and then click the Advanced button.

▶ Select Start, type `lusrmgr.msc,` and then press Enter.

▶ Select Start, right-click Computer, and then click Manage. In the Computer Management window, select System Tools, Local Users and Groups.

Whichever method you use, in the snap-in window that appears, select the Users branch to see a list of the users on your system, as shown in Figure 18.8.

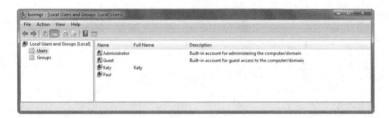

FIGURE 18.8   The Users branch lists all the system's users and enables you to add, modify, and delete users.

From here, you can perform the following tasks:

▶ **Add a new user**—Make sure that no user is selected, and then select Action, New User. In the New User dialog box, type the User Name, Password, and Confirm Password. (I discussed the password-related check boxes in this dialog box earlier in this chapter; see "User Account Password Options.") Click Create.

▶ **Change a user's name**—Right-click the user, and then click Rename.

▶ **Change a user's password**—Right-click the user, and then click Set Password.

▶ **Add a user to a group**—Double-click the user to open the user's property sheet. In the Member Of tab, click Add and use the Enter the Object Names to Select box to enter the group name. If you're not sure of the name, click Advanced to open the Select Groups dialog box, click Find Now to list all the groups, select the group, and then click OK. Click OK to close the property sheet.

> **NOTE**
>
> Another way to add a user to a group is to select the Groups branch in the Local Users and Groups snap-in. Right-click the group you want to work with, and then click Add to Group. Now click Add, type the username in the Enter the Object Names to Select box, and then click OK.

▶ **Remove a user from a group**—Double-click the user to open the user's property sheet. In the Member Of tab, select the group from which you want the user removed, and then click Remove. Click OK to close the property sheet.

▶ **Change a user's profile**—Double-click the user to open the user's property sheet. Use the Profile tab to change the profile path, logon script, and home folder (activate the Local Path option to specify a local folder; or activate Connect to specify a shared network folder).

▶ **Disable an account**—Double-click the user to open the user's property sheet. In the General tab, activate the Account Is Disabled check box.

▶ **Delete a user**—Right-click the user, and then click Delete. When Windows 7 asks you to confirm, click Yes.

Setting Account Policies

Windows 7 offers several sets of policies that affect user accounts. There are three kinds of account policies: security options, user rights, and account lockout policies. The next three sections take you through these policies.

Setting Account Security Policies

To see these policies, launch the Local Security Settings snap-in (select Start, type `secpol.msc`, and press Enter) and select Security Settings, Local Policies, Security Options, as shown in Figure 18.9.

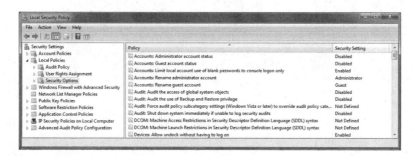

FIGURE 18.9   In the Security Options branch, use the five Accounts policies to configure security for your accounts.

The Accounts grouping has five policies:

▶ **Administrator Account Status**—Use this policy to enable or disable the Administrator account. This is useful if you think someone else might be logging on as the administrator. (A less-drastic solution is to change the administrator password or rename the Administrator account.)

NOTE

The Administrator account is always used during a Safe mode boot, even if you disable the account.

▶ **Guest Account Status**—Use this option to enable or disable the Guest account.

▶ **Limit Local Account Use of Blank Passwords to Console Logon Only**— When this option is enabled, Windows 7 allows users with blank passwords to log on to the system directly only by using the Welcome screen. Such users can't log on via either the RunAs command or remotely over a network. This policy modifies the following Registry setting:

```
HKLM\SYSTEM\CurrentControlSet\Control\Lsa\limitblankpassworduse
```

▶ **Rename Administrator Account**—Use this option to change the name of the Administrator account.

▶ **Rename Guest Account**—Use this option to change the name of the Guest account.

CAUTION

The Administrator account is all-powerful on Windows 7, so the last thing you want is for some malicious user to gain control of the system with administrator access. Fortunately, Windows 7 disables the Administrator account by default. However, it's worth taking a few minutes now to ensure that the Administrator account is disabled on your Windows 7 machine. Open the Local Users and Groups snap-in, as described earlier, double-click the Administrator account to open the Administrator Properties dialog box, and then make sure the Account Is Disabled check box is activated.

> **TIP**
>
> Black-hat hackers have one foot in your digital door already because they know that every Windows 7 machine comes with an account named Administrator. If you've disabled the Administrator account, you almost certainly have no worries. However, you can close the door completely on malicious intruders by taking away the one piece of information they know: the name of the account. By changing the account name from Administrator to something completely unexpected, you add an extra layer of security to Windows 7. The Guest account also has an obvious and well-known name, so if you've enabled the Guest account, be sure to rename it, too.

Setting User Rights Policies

Windows 7 has a long list of policies associated with user rights. To see these policies, launch the Local Security Settings snap-in (select Start, type `secpol.msc`, and press Enter) and select Security Settings, Local Policies, User Rights Assignment, as shown in Figure 18.10.

Each policy is a specific task or action, such as Back Up Files and Directories, Deny Logon Locally, and Shut Down the System. For each task or action, the Security Setting column shows the users and groups who can perform the task or to whom the action applies. To change the setting, double-click the policy. Click Add User or Group to add an object to the policy; or delete an object from the policy by selecting it and clicking Remove.

Setting Account Lockout Policies

Last of all, Windows 7 has a few policies that determine when an account gets *locked out*, which means the user is unable to log on. A lockout occurs when the user fails to log on after a specified number of attempts. This is a good security feature because it prevents an unauthorized user from trying a number of different passwords.

To see these policies, launch the Local Security Settings snap-in (select Start, type `secpol.msc`, and press Enter) and select Security Settings, Local Policies, Account Lockout Policy, as shown in Figure 18.11.

18

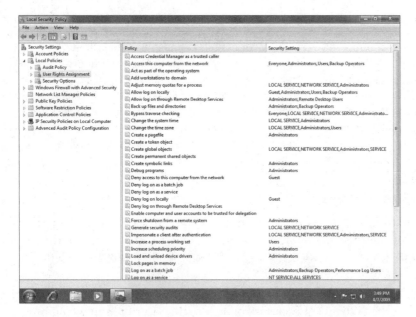

FIGURE 18.10   In the User Rights Assignment branch, use the policies to configure the rights assigned to users or groups.

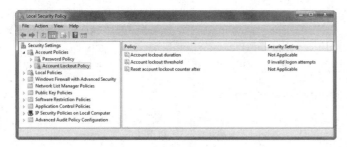

FIGURE 18.11   In the Account Lockout Policy branch, use the policies to configure when an account gets locked out of the system.

There are three policies:

▶ **Account Lockout Duration**—This policy sets the amount of time, in minutes, that the user is locked out. Note that, to change this policy, you must set the Account Lockout Threshold (described next) to a nonzero number.

▶ **Account Lockout Threshold**—This policy sets the maximum number of logons the user can attempt before being locked out. Note that after you change this to a nonzero value, Windows 7 offers to set the other two policies to 30 minutes.

▶ **Reset Account Lockout Counter After**—This policy sets the amount of time, in minutes, after which the counter that tracks the number of invalid logons is reset to zero.

Working with Users and Groups from the Command Line

You can script your user and group chores by taking advantage of the NET USER and NET LOCALGROUP commands. These commands enable you to add users, change passwords, modify accounts, add users to groups, and remove users from groups. Note that you must run these commands under the Administrator account, so first follow these steps to open a command prompt session:

1. Select Start, All Programs, Accessories.
2. Right-click Command Prompt, and then click Run As Administrator.
3. Enter your User Account Control credentials.

The NET USER Command

You use the NET USER command to add users, set account passwords, disable accounts, set account options (such as the times of day the user is allowed to log on), and remove accounts. For local users, the NET USER command has the following syntax:

```
NET USER [username [password | * | /RANDOM] [/ADD] [/DELETE] [options]]
```

username	The name of the user you want to add or work with. If you run NET USER with only the name of an existing user, the command displays the user's account data.
password	The password you want to assign to the user. If you use *, Windows 7 prompts you for the password; if you use the /RANDOM switch, Windows 7 assigns a random password (containing eight characters, consisting of a random mix of letters, numbers, and symbols), and then displays the password on the console.
/ADD	Creates a new user account.
/DELETE	Deletes the specified user account.
options	These are optional switches you can append to the command:
/ACTIVE:{YES | NO}	Specifies whether the account is active or disabled.
/EXPIRES:{*date* | NEVER}	The date (expressed in the system's Short Date format) on which the account expires.
/HOMEDIR:*path*	The home folder for the user, which should be a subfolder within %SystemDrive%\Users (make sure that the folder exists).
/PASSWORDCHG:{YES | NO}	Specifies whether the user is allowed to change his password.
/PASSWORDREQ:{YES | NO}	Specifies whether the user is required to have a password.

18

/PROFILEPATH:*path*	The folder that contains the user's profile.
/SCRIPTPATH:*path*	The folder that contains the user's logon script.
/TIMES:{*times* | ALL}	Specifies the times that the user is allowed to log on to the system. Use single days or day ranges (for example, Sa or M-F). For times, use 24-hour notation or 12-hour notation with am or pm. Separate the day and time with a comma, and separate day/time combinations with semicolons. Here are some examples:

```
M-F,9am-5pm
M,W,F,08:00-13:00
Sa,12pm-6pm;Su,1pm-5pm
```

CAUTION

If you use the /RANDOM switch to create a random password, make a note of the new password so that you can communicate it to the new user.

Note, too, that if you execute NET USER without any parameters, it displays a list of the local user accounts.

TIP

If you want to force a user to log off when his logon hours expire, open the Group Policy Editor and select Computer Configuration, Windows Settings, Security Settings, Local Policies, Security Options. In the Network Security category, enable the Force Logoff When Logon Hours Expire policy.

The NET LOCALGROUP Command

You use the NET LOCALGROUP command to add users to and remove users from a specified security group. NET LOCALGROUP has the following syntax:

```
NET LOCALGROUP [group name1 [name2 ...] {/ADD | /DELETE}
```

group	This is the name of the security group with which you want to work.
name1 [*name2* ...]	One or more usernames that you want to add or delete, separated by spaces.
/ADD	Adds the user or users to the group.
/DELETE	Removes the user or users from the group.

Using Parental Controls to Restrict Computer Usage

If you have children who share your computer, or if you're setting up a computer for the kids' use, take precautions regarding the content and programs that they can access. Locally, this might take the form of blocking access to certain programs (such as your financial software), using ratings to control which games they can play, and setting time limits on when the computer is used.

> **NOTE**
>
> **NEW TO 7** In Windows 7, Microsoft no longer offers Internet-related parental controls, such as allowing (or blocking) specific sites, blocking certain types of content, and preventing file downloads, and it no longer offers activity reporting. These are now handled through third-party parental control service providers, which you must install on your PC to enable them within the Windows 7 Parental Controls window. As I wrote this, it wasn't clear how Microsoft was planning to handle these third-party providers.

All this sounds daunting, but Windows 7's parental controls make things a bit easier by offering an easy-to-use interface that lets you set all the aforementioned options and lots more. (You get parental controls in the Home Basic, Home Premium, and Ultimate editions of Windows 7.)

Before you begin, create a Standard User account for each child who uses the computer. When that's done, you get to parental controls by selecting Start, typing **parent**, and then pressing Enter. In the Parental Controls window, click the user you want to work with to get to the User Controls window.

Activating Parental Controls

With the User Controls window onscreen, click to activate the On, Enforce Current Settings option. This enables the Time Limits, Games, and Allow and Block Specific Programs links in the Windows Settings area, as shown in Figure 18.12.

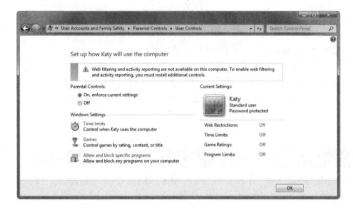

FIGURE 18.12   The User Controls page enables you to set up time, game, and program restrictions for the selected user.

The User Controls window gives you some links to use when setting up the controls for this user:

▶ **Time Limits**—Click this link to display the Time Restrictions page, which shows a grid where each square represents an hour during the day for each day of the week, as shown in Figure 18.13. Click the squares to block computer usage during the selected times.

NOTE

If the user is logged on when a restricted time approaches, an icon appears in the notification area to let that user know. If the user is still logged on when the restricted time occurs, the user is immediately logged off and cannot log back on until the restricted time has passed. Fortunately, Windows 7 is kind enough to restore the user's programs and documents when he or she logs back on.

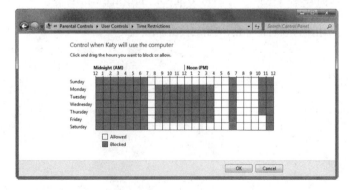

FIGURE 18.13   Use the grid on the Time Restrictions page to block computer access during specified hours.

▶ **Games**—Click this link to display the Game Controls page. Here you can allow or disallow all games, restrict games based on ratings and content, and block or allow specific games. You see how this works in the next section.

▶ **Allow and Block Specific Programs**—Click this link to display the Application Restrictions page, which displays a list of the programs on your computer. Activate the *User* Can Only Use the Programs I Allow option, and then click the check boxes for the programs you want to allow the person to use.

Example: Setting Up Parental Controls for Games

If you have kids, chances are, they have a computer—either their own or one shared with the rest of the family—and, chances are, they play games on that computer. That's not a problem when they are being supervised, but few of us have the time or energy to sit beside our kids for each and every computer session—and the older the kid, the more likely that a hovering adult will be seen as an interloper. In other words, for all but the youngest users, your children will have some unsupervised gaming time at the computer.

To avoid worrying about whether your 8-year-old is playing *Grand Theft Auto* or something equally unsuitable, you can take advantage of the Game Controls section that enables you to control gaming using ratings and content descriptors.

Before setting up the controls, you should select the rating system you want to use. Return to the Parental Controls window and click the Games Ratings Systems link to display the Game Rating Systems window shown in Figure 18.14. Select the rating system you prefer, and then click OK to return to the Parental Controls window.

Click the user you want to work with to display the User Controls window. Activate the On, Enforce Current Settings option (if you haven't done so already), and then click Games to display the Game Controls window, shown in Figure 18.15.

18

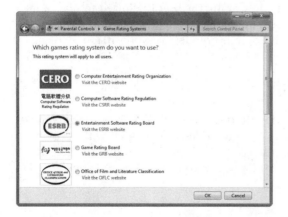

FIGURE 18.14   Use the Game Rating Systems window to choose the rating system you want to use with parental controls.

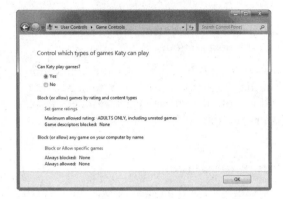

FIGURE 18.15   Use the Game Controls window to set the gaming restrictions for the selected user.

The next three sections run through the three methods you can use to control game play.

Turn Off Game Play

If your kids are too young to play any games, or if you'd prefer that they spend time on the computer working on more constructive pursuits, you can turn off game playing altogether. In the Can *UserName* Play Games? section, select No to prevent the user named *UserName* from launching any games from the Games Explorer. If you select Yes instead, you can use the techniques in the next two sections to control the games the user can play.

Controlling Games via Ratings and Descriptors

Instead of shutting off all game play, you're more likely to want to prevent each user from playing certain types of games. The easiest way to do that is to use game ratings and content descriptors. In the Game Controls window, click Set Game Ratings to display the Game Restrictions window, shown in Figure 18.16.

Click the rating option that represents the highest rating the user is allowed to play. For example, if you're using the ESRB rating system and you select the Teen option, the user will be able to play games rated as Early Childhood, Everyone, Everyone 10+, and Teen. He or she will not be able to play games rated as Mature or Adults Only.

You can also prevent the user from playing unrated games by selecting the Block Games with No Rating option.

You can also block games based on content descriptors. If you scroll down in the Game Restrictions window, you see the complete set of content descriptors, each with its own check box. For each check box you activate, the user will not be able to run any games that include that content description, even if the game has a rating that you allow.

FIGURE 18.16   Use the Game Restrictions window to control game playing using ratings and content descriptors.

Blocking and Allowing Specific Games

You might want to fine-tune your game controls by overriding the restrictions you've set up based on ratings and content descriptors. For example, you might have activated the Block Games with No Rating option, but you have an unrated game on your system that you want to allow the kids to play. Similarly, there might be a game that Windows 7 allows based on the ratings and descriptors, but you'd feel more comfortable blocking access to the game.

In the Game Controls window, click Block or Allow Specific Games to display the Game Overrides window, shown in Figure 18.17. The table displays the title and rating of your installed games, and shows the current control status—Can Play or Cannot Play. To allow the user to play a specific game, click Always Allow; to prevent the user from playing a specific game, click Always Block.

18

FIGURE 18.17   Use the Game Overrides window to allow or block specific games.

More User Security Tricks

User accounts may seem like simple things, but there's a lot more to them than meets the eye. For example, you know that in Windows 7 all standard users must enter administrator credentials to perform actions such as installing certain programs or modifying system settings, but did you know that you can disable all elevation prompts for those users? Did you know that you can disable all user accounts (except your own, of course)? Did you know that you can use the built-in Guest account as an easy way to give someone temporary (and limited) access to your computer? Did you know that it's possible to find out who is logged on to another computer on your network?

All these tasks are very doable, and the sections in the rest of this chapter show you how.

Preventing Elevation for All Standard Users

You saw earlier (see "Elevating Privileges") that when a standard user attempts a task that requires elevation, he or she sees a UAC dialog box that requires an administrator password, and the screen switches to secure desktop mode.

There are two problems with this:

► Standard users almost never have the proper credentials to elevate an action.

► The combination of the sudden appearance of the User Account Control dialog box and the change into secure desktop mode is confusing for many users, particularly the inexperienced.

These two problems mean that in most cases it would be better if a standard user didn't get prompted to elevate their privileges. Instead, it would be better to display an Access Denied message and let the user move on from there.

You can use the Local Security Settings snap-in to set this up. Here are the steps to follow:

> **NOTE**
>
> These steps require the Local Security Settings snap-in, which is available only with Windows 7 Professional, Vista Enterprise, and Vista Ultimate. If you're not running one of these versions, normally I'd show you how to modify the Registry to get the same effect. Unfortunately, the policy value that we tweak here doesn't have a Registry equivalent for security reasons.

1. Select Start, type **secpol.msc** into the Search box, and then press Enter. The Local Security Policy snap-in appears.
2. Open the Local Policies branch.
3. Click the Security Options branch.
4. Double-click the User Account Control: Behavior of the Elevation Prompt for Standard Users policy.
5. In the list, choose Automatically Deny Elevation Requests, as shown in Figure 18.18.
6. Click OK to put the new setting into effect.

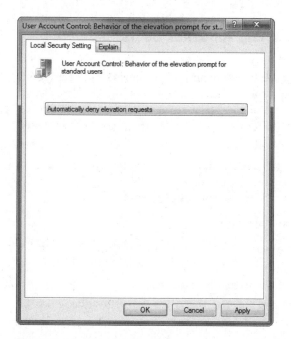

FIGURE 18.18   Open the User Account Control: Behavior of the Elevation Prompt for Standard Users policy and choose Automatically Deny Elevation Requests.

Now when a standard user attempts something that requires elevated privileges, he or she just sees a simple dialog box like the one shown in Figure 18.19. Windows 7 doesn't switch into secure desktop mode, and the user just has to click Close to continue.

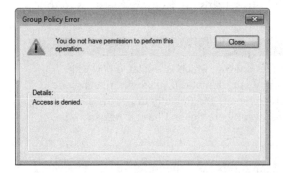

FIGURE 18.19   When standard users are denied elevation requests, they see a simple dialog box when they attempt an administrator-level task.

> **NOTE**
>
> The dialog box the user sees varies depending on the program or service that requires elevation. In each case, however, the user's only choice is to click a button (usually labeled either Close or OK).

Closing Off Your Computer by Disabling All Other Users

If you've got other user accounts on your computer, there may be times when you don't want anyone else to use the computer for a while. For example, perhaps the hard drive is getting full and you don't want anyone using the machine until you add more capacity. Similarly, if you have an account set up for a child and that child violates the rules you've set for using the computer, you might want to temporarily disable the account as punishment.

Whatever the reason, you need some way of disabling all other user accounts. The standard Windows user account tools don't give you any direct way of doing this, but it's possible to make it happen by using the Local Users and Groups snap-in.

Follow these steps to disable one or more user accounts:

1. Select Start, type `lusrmgr.msc` into the Search box, and then press Enter. The Local Users and Groups snap-in appears.
3. Click Users. Windows displays a list of the users on your system.
4. Double-click the account you want to disable. The account's Properties dialog box appears.
5. Activate the Account Is Disabled check box.
6. Click OK to return to the Local Users and Groups window.

> **NOTE**
>
> When you disable an account, Windows indicates this by adding a downward-pointing arrow to the account icon, as shown earlier in Figure 18.8 with the Administrator and Guest accounts (which are disabled by default in Windows 7).

7. Repeat steps 4 to 6 to disable the other accounts you want to block.
8. Select File, Exit to close the Local Users and Groups snap-in.

When an account is disabled, Windows doesn't include an icon for it in the logon screen, so there's no way for the user to log on to his or her account. When you're ready to give others access to the PC, repeat the preceding steps, except deactivate the Account Is Disabled check box for each account.

Hiding Usernames in the Logon Screen

When you start most Windows PCs, you end up at the logon screen so that you can choose your username and log on by entering your password. In Windows 7, the logon screen always displays icons for each user account, and each icon shows the name of the account. Figure 18.20 shows a typical Windows 7 logon screen.

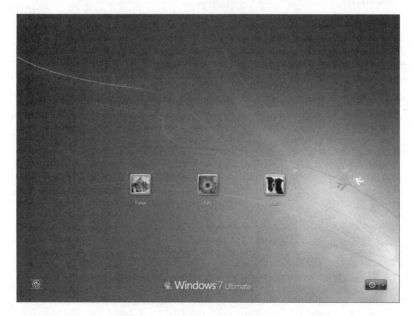

FIGURE 18.20   The Windows 7 logon screen shows the names of the computer's user accounts.

18

This may not seem all that important, but that logon screen is actually helping any would-be cracker a great deal. Why? The nefarious nogoodnik now has an important advantage because he knows the names of all your user accounts (or, in the case of XP Pro, one of your accounts). Yes, the evildoer must still guess an account's password, but you can make things a heckuva lot harder by forcing the snoop to also guess a username on your system. How do you do that? By tweaking Windows so that it doesn't display usernames in the logon screen. Sneaky!

You do that by following these steps:

> **NOTE**
>
> These steps require the Local Security Policy snap-in, which is available only with Windows 7 Professional, Windows 7 Enterprise, Windows 7 Ultimate, and XP Professional. In case you're not running one of these versions, I'll show you how to perform the same tweak using the Registry.

1. Select Start, type **secpol.msc** into the Search box, and then press Enter. The Local Security Policy snap-in appears.
2. Open the Local Policies branch.
3. Click the Security Options branch.
4. Double-click the Interactive Logon: Do Not Display Last User Name policy.
5. Click the Enabled option.
6. Click OK to put the new setting into effect.

If you don't have access to the Local Security Policy snap-in, open the Registry Editor and create (if it's not there already) a DWORD setting named DontDisplayLastUserName with the value 1 in the following key:

HKLM\Software\Microsoft\Windows\CurrentVersion\Policies\System

The next time you start your computer, no usernames appear in the logon screen. Figure 18.21 shows the Windows 7 logon screen without usernames.

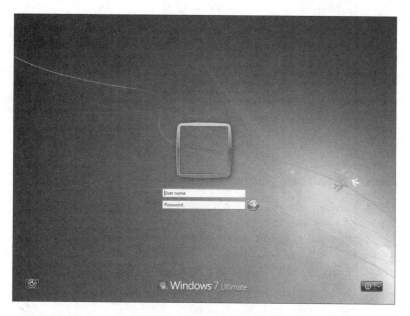

FIGURE 18.21   With the Do Not Display Last User Name policy enabled, the logon screen no longer shows the names of the computer's user accounts.

Renaming Built-In Accounts for Better Security

Windows 7 comes with a built-in Administrator account. This account is all-powerful on Windows, so the last thing you want is for some malicious user to gain control of the system with administrator access. This is why Windows 7 systems come with the Administrator account disabled by default. However, earlier in this book, I showed you how to activate the Administrator account in Windows 7.

▶ **See** "Enabling the Administrator Account," **p. 76**.

Windows 7 also comes with a built-in account called Guest, which you can enable to give people temporary access to your computer, as described in the next section. (The Guest account is disabled by default in Windows 7.)

If the Administrator and Guest accounts are disabled, you have no worries about these accounts. However, if the accounts are enabled, black-hat hackers have one foot in your digital door already because they know the names of two accounts: Administrator and Guest. Now all they have to do is guess the password associated with one of these accounts. If you've protected the Administrator and Guest accounts with strong passwords, you almost certainly have nothing to fret about here.

However, you can close the door completely on malicious intruders by taking away the one piece of information they know: the name of each account. By changing the account names from Administrator and Guest to new names that are completely unobvious, you add an extra layer of security to your Windows system.

18

Here are the steps to follow to change the names of these accounts:

1. Select Start, type `lusrmgr.msc`, and then press Enter. The Local Users and Groups snap-in appears.
2. Right-click the Administrator account, and then click Rename.
3. Type the new account name, and then press Enter.
4. Right-click the Guest account, and then click Rename.
5. Type the new account name, and then press Enter.

Using the Guest Account to Give Folks Temporary Access

What do you do if you have someone visiting your place and that person wants to, for instance, surf the Web or access some media on your computer? You could allow the person to log on using an existing account, but that might not be reasonable because of privacy or security concerns. You could set up a user account for that person, but that seems like overkill, particularly for a person on a short visit.

A better solution is to enable the Guest account and allow your visitor to log on under that account. Follow these steps to enable the Guest account:

CAUTION

You should probably rename the Guest account if you're going to leave it activated for a while. See the previous section for the details.

1. Select Start, type **user**, and click the User Accounts result. The User Accounts window appears.
2. Click the Manage Another Account link. The User Accounts window appears.
3. Click the Guest account icon. Windows asks if you want to turn on the Guest account.
4. Click Turn On. Windows activates the Guest account.

Your guest is now free to use your computer safely: In the Windows 7 logon screen (see Figure 18.22), click the Guest icon.

FIGURE 18.22   With the Guest account enabled, you see an icon for the account in the Windows 7 logon screen.

Determining Who Is Logged On

How do you know who's logged on to a Windows 7 machine? For example, what if you're sitting down at another person's computer and you're not sure who's logged on and what privileges they have?

No problem. The WHOAMI command gives you information about the user who is currently logged on to the computer:

```
WHOAMI [/UPN | /FQDN | LOGONID] [/USER | /GROUPS | /PRIV] [/ALL] [/FO format]
```

This command redirects the current user's SID, username, groups, and privileges to a file named whoami.txt using the list format, and then opens the file.

For example, start a Command Prompt session on the computer (in Windows 7, select Start, type **command** into the Search box, and press Enter), and run the following command:

```
whoami /all /fo list > whoami.txt&&start whoami.txt
```

TIP

My command is actually two commands in one, thanks to the DOSKEY && operator, which lets you run multiple commands on a single line.

/UPN   (Domains only) Returns the current user's name using the user principal name (UPN) format.

/FQDN   (Domains only) Returns the current user's name using the fully qualified domain name (FQDN) format.

/LOGONID   Returns the current user's security identifier (SID).

/USER   Returns the current username using the *computer\user* format.

/GROUPS   Returns the groups of which the current user is a member.

/PRIV   Returns the current user's privileges.

/ALL   Returns the current user's SID, username, groups, and privileges.

/FO *format* The output format, where *format* is one of the following values:

    table   The output is displayed in a row-and-column format, with headers in the first row and values in subsequent rows.

    list   The output is displayed in a two-column list, with the headers in the first column and values in the second column.

    csv   The output is displayed with headers and values separated by commas. The headers appear on the first line.

CHAPTER 19

Implementing Network Security

I always get back to the question, is it really necessary that men should consume so much of their bodily and mental energies in the machinery of civilized life?

—William Allingham

Whenever you string two or more computers together to form a network, security becomes an issue. On the user level, you want to make sure that others can access only those parts of your system you designate as fit for public consumption. No one, whether a colleague or an administrator, should be able to poke around in areas of your system that you deem private. On the network level, administrators need to make sure that computers are set up with appropriate access limitations.

If you want to control not only who has access to your data, but also what those users can do with the data, you need to implement a few network security precautions. Of course, other users inadvertently seeing data they shouldn't is one problem, but an outsider gaining unauthorized access to the network is quite another. Fortunately, you can take steps to minimize this sort of intrusion. This chapter takes you through a few useful techniques for securing your network.

Remember that your network is only as secure as its client computers, so be sure to read the tips and techniques for making Windows 7 more secure that I covered in the previous few chapters. Also, if you have wireless network connections, find out how to secure them in Chapter 20, "Tightening Wireless Network Security."

Configuring Windows 7 for Secure Networking

Windows 7's network security hatches are pretty tightly battened down right out of the box, but you need to do a couple of things to ensure the most secure networking environment: Make sure that password-protected sharing is turned on, and disable the low-end Sharing Wizard so that you can use high-end sharing permissions instead.

Making Sure Password-Protected Sharing Is Enabled

Password-protected sharing means that the only people who can access your shared network resources are those who know the username and password of a user account on your system. This is the most secure way to share resources on a network, which is why Windows 7 comes with password-protected sharing turned on by default. So, unless network security isn't an issue for you at all (in which case I'm not sure why you're reading this!), it pays to take a few seconds to double-check that password-protected sharing is enabled:

1. Click the Network icon in the notification area.

2. Click Open Network and Sharing Center.

3. In the sidebar, click Change Advanced Sharing Settings. Windows 7 opens the Advanced Sharing Settings window.

4. In the Home or Work section of the window, locate the Password Protected Sharing group and click the Turn On Password Protected Sharing option, as shown in Figure 19.1.

5. Click Save Changes.

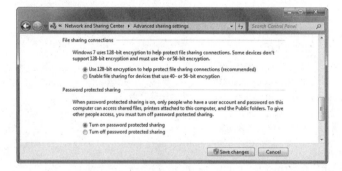

FIGURE 19.1   Activate the Turn On Password Protected Sharing option.

Deactivating the Sharing Wizard

Sharing can be a complex business when you get into file permissions and other minutiae. Windows 7 minutiae are what this book is all about, so sharing holds no terrors for the likes of you and me. However, novice users want sharing to be simple and straightforward, and to that end, Windows 7 offers the Sharing Wizard. This wizard presents the wary with a stripped-down set of sharing options and a method for letting other people know that a shared resource is available.

The Sharing Wizard is activated by default, and in a second I'll show you how to deactivate it. Just so that you know what you're giving up, Figure 19.2 shows the initial wizard dialog box. (To get there, click a folder or file, click Share With, and then click Specific People.) You use the list to select a user account on your computer, and then you assign that user one of two permission levels: Read (read-only) or Read/Write (read and write). When you click Share, the Sharing Wizard shows the address of the share and offers a link to email the share address to other people.

FIGURE 19.2   The Sharing Wizard offers a simple, novice-oriented interface for sharing resources.

The Sharing Wizard is fine for new users. However, the rest of us want the full power of permissions and other sharing goodies. To get at them, you have to deactivate the Sharing Wizard feature by following these steps:

1. Select Start, type **folder**, and then click Folder Options in the search results. (Or, in any folder window, select Organize, Folder and Search Options.)

2. Display the View tab.

3. Deactivate the Use Sharing Wizard check box.

4. Click OK.

Setting Sharing Permissions on Shared Folders

With the File Sharing Wizard no longer active, you can now share a folder with advanced permissions. You use these permissions to decide who has access to the folder and what those users can do with the folder. You can also apply advanced permissions to entire security groups rather than individual users. For example, if you apply permissions to the Administrators group, those permissions automatically apply to each member of that group.

▶ Before continuing, make sure you have a user account set up for each person who will access the share; **see** "Creating and Managing User Accounts," **p. 384**.

Follow these steps to share a folder with advanced permissions:

1. In Windows Explorer, select the folder you want to share. If you want to share a subfolder or file, instead, open its folder and then click the subfolder or file.

2. Click the Share With button in the Task pane, and then click Advanced Sharing. Windows 7 displays the object's Properties sheet with the Sharing tab selected.

TIP

You can also right-click the folder and then click Share With, Advanced Sharing.

3. Click Advanced Sharing. The Advanced Sharing dialog box appears.

4. Activate the Share This Folder check box, as shown in Figure 19.3.

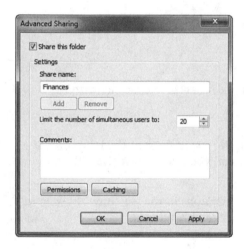

FIGURE 19.3   Activate the Share This Folder check box.

5. By default, Windows 7 uses the folder name as the share name. If you prefer to use a different name, edit the Share Name text box.

6. In a small network, it's unlikely you'll need to restrict the number of users who can access this resource, so you're probably safe to leave the Limit the Number of Simultaneous Users To spin box value at 20.

7. Click Permissions to display the Permissions for *Share* dialog box, where *Share* is the share name you specified in step 5.

8. Select the Everyone group in the Group or User Names list, and then click Remove.

As the name implies, the Everyone user refers to every user. It's always best to remove this user so that you can apply permissions to specific users and groups.

9. Click Add to display the Select Users or Groups dialog box.

10. In the Enter the Object Names to Select text box, type the name of the user or users you want to give permission to access the shared resource (separate multiple user-names with semicolons). Click OK when you're done.

If you're not sure about the spelling of a user or group name, click Advanced to open an advanced version of the Select Users or Groups dialog box, and then click Find Now. Windows 7 displays a list of all the available users and groups. Click the name you want to use, and then click OK.

11. Select a user in the Group or User Names list.

12. Using the Permissions list (see Figure 19.4), you can allow or deny the following permissions:

> ▶ **Read**—Gives the group or user to ability only to read the contents of a folder or file. The user can't modify those contents in any way.

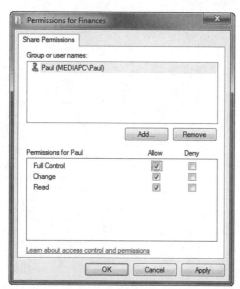

FIGURE 19.4   Use the Permissions dialog box to specify file permissions for the shared resource.

▶ **Change**—Gives the group or user Read permission and allows the group or user to modify the contents of the shared resource.

▶ **Full Control**—Gives the group or user Change permission and allows the group or user to take ownership of the shared resource.

13. Repeat steps 9–12 to add and configure other users or groups.

14. Click OK to return to the Advanced Sharing dialog box.

15. Click OK to return to the Sharing tab.

16. Click Close to share the resource with the network.

Setting Security Permissions on Shared Folders

If you want even more control over the use of your shared resources across the network, you should also set NTFS security permissions on the folder. Security permissions are similar to sharing permissions, except that you get a longer list of permissions for each group or user.

Here are the steps to follow to set security permissions on a shared folder:

1. In Windows Explorer, right-click the folder you want to work with, and then click Properties to open the folder's Properties dialog box.

2. Select the Security tab.

3. Click Edit to open the Permissions for *Folder* dialog box, where *Folder* is the name of the folder. As you can see in Figure 19.5, this dialog box is similar to the dialog box you saw earlier for sharing permissions (refer to Figure 19.4).

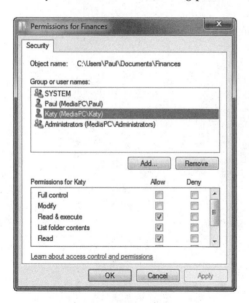

FIGURE 19.5   Use this version of the Permissions dialog box to specify security permissions for the shared resource.

4. To work with existing permissions, select the group or user you want to work with and skip to step 10.

5. To add new permissions, click Add to display the Select Users or Groups dialog box.

6. In the Enter the Object Names to Select text box, type the name of the user or users you want to give permission to access the shared resource (separate multiple usernames with semicolons).

7. Click OK to return to the Permissions dialog box.

8. Select a user in the Group or User Names list.

9. Using the Permissions list, use the check boxes in the Allow and Deny columns to allow or deny permissions.

   ▶**See** "Assigning Standard Permissions," **p. 363**.

10. Repeat steps 5–9 to add and configure other users or groups.

11. Click OK to return to the Security tab.

12. Click OK to put the new security settings into effect.

Hiding Your Shared Folders

Setting up user accounts with strong passwords and then applying shared-folder permissions on those accounts are the necessary network security tasks, and in most small networks they also suffice for achieving a decent level of security. However, when it comes to securing your network, a healthy dose of paranoia is another good "tool" to have at hand. For example, the properly paranoid network administrator doesn't assume that no one will ever infiltrate the network, just the opposite: The admin assumes that someday someone *will* get access, and then he or she wonders what can be done in that case to minimize the damage.

One of the first things these paranoid administrators do (or should do) is hide what's valuable, private, or sensitive. For example, if you have a shared folder named, say, `Confidential Documents`, you're simply *begging* a would-be thief to access that share. Yes, you could rename the share to something less inviting, but the thief may chance upon it anyway. To prevent this, it's possible to share a resource *and* hide it at the same time.

Even better, hiding a shared folder is also extremely easy to do: When you set up the shared resource, add a dollar sign ($) to the end of the share name. For example, if you're setting up drive L: for sharing, you could use `L$` as the share name. This prevents the resource from appearing in the list of resources when you open a remote computer from the Network window.

To show you how this works, check out Figure 19.6. In the Properties dialog box for the L: drive, you see that the drive is shared with the following path:

`\\Mediapc\l$`

Drive L: doesn't appear in the
computer's list of shared resources

Drive L: is set up as
a hidden share (L$)

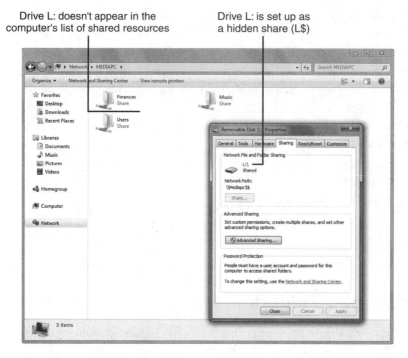

FIGURE 19.6 Hidden shared resources (such as drive L:, shown here) don't appear in the computer's list of shared resources.

That is, the drive is shared on the computer named MediaPC with the name L$. However, in the folder window, you can see that drive L: doesn't appear in the list of resources shared by MediaPC.

How do you connect to a hidden share? You need to know the name of the shared resource, of course, which enables you to use any of the following techniques:

► Select Windows Logo+R (or select Start, All Programs, Accessories, Run) to open the Run dialog box, type the network path for the hidden resource, and click OK. For example, to display the hidden share L$ on MediaPC, you would enter this:

```
\\mediapc\l$
```

► In a Command Prompt session, type **start**, a space, the network path, and then press the Enter key. For example, to launch the hidden share **L$** on MediaPC, you'd enter this:

```
start \\mediapc\l$
```

- ▶ Use the Map Network Drive command, as described in Chapter 26, "Accessing and Using Your Network." In the Map Network Drive dialog box, type the UNC path for the hidden share in the Folder text box.

- ▶ For the details on mapping a shared folder, **see** "Mapping a Network Folder to a Local Drive Letter," **p. 558.**

- ▶ For a hidden shared printer, follow the instructions for accessing a shared printer in Chapter 26 and, when Windows 7 begins searching for available printers, click The Printer That I Want Isn't Listed and click Next. In the dialog box that appears, type the network path to the hidden printer in the Printer text box.

- ▶ For information about using a network printer, **see** "Accessing a Shared Printer," **p. 563.**

Disabling the Hidden Administrative Shares

I mentioned in the preceding section that you can add $ to a share name to hide the share, and that it is a good idea to also modify the share name to something not easily guessable by some snoop. Note, however, that Windows 7 sets up certain hidden shares for administrative purposes, including one for drive C: (C$) and any other hard disk partitions you have on your system. Windows 7 also sets up the following hidden shares:

Share	Shared Path	Purpose
ADMIN$	%SystemRoot%	Remote administration
IPC$	N/A	Remote interprocess communication

To see these shares, select Start, All Programs, Accessories, Command Prompt to open a Command Prompt session, type **net share**, and press Enter. You see a listing similar to this:

```
Share name   Resource                         Remark
-------------------------------------------------------------------
C$           C:\                              Default share
D$           D:\                              Default share
ADMIN$       C:\Windows                       Remote Admin
IPC$                                          Remote IPC
```

So, although the C$, D$, and ADMIN$ shares are otherwise hidden, they're well known, and they represent a small security risk should an intruder get access to your network.

To close this hole, you can force Windows 7 to disable these shares. Here are the steps to follow:

1. Select Start, type **regedit**, and then press Enter. The User Account Control dialog box appears.

2. Enter your UAC credentials to continue. Windows 7 opens the Registry Editor.

19

CAUTION

Remember that the Registry contains many important settings that are crucial for the proper functioning of Windows 7 and your programs. Therefore, when you are working with the Registry Editor, don't make changes to any settings other than the ones I describe in this section.

---

3. Open the HKEY_LOCAL_MACHINE branch.
4. Open the SYSTEM branch.
5. Open the CurrentControlSet branch.
6. Open the Services branch.
7. Open the LanmanServer branch.
8. Select the Parameters branch.
9. Select Edit, New, DWORD (32-bit) Value. Windows 7 adds a new value to the Parameters key.
10. Type **AutoShareWks** and press Enter. (You can leave this setting with its default value of 0.)
11. Restart Windows 7 to put the new setting into effect.

Once again, select Start, All Programs, Accessories, Command Prompt to open a Command Prompt session, type **net share**, and press Enter. The output now looks like this:

```
Share name    Resource                            Remark
-------------------------------------------------------------------
IPC$                                              Remote IPC
```

CAUTION

Some programs expect the administrative shares to be present, so disabling those shares may cause those programs to fail or generate error messages. If that happens, enable the shares by opening the Registry Editor and either deleting the AutoShareWks setting or changing its value to 1.

Removing Stored Remote Desktop Credentials

When you log on to a network computer using Remote Desktop Connection (see Chapter 27, "Making Remote Network Connections"), the logon dialog box includes a check box named Remember My Credentials, as shown in Figure 19.7. If you activate this check box,

Windows 7 won't prompt you to enter a password when you connect to the computer in the future.

FIGURE 19.7   Remote Desktop Connection enables you to save your logon credentials.

▶ To learn how to log on with Remote Desktop Connection, **see** "Connecting to the Remote Desktop," **p. 592**.

That's certainly convenient, but it's a gaping security hole because it enables anyone who can access your computer to also access the remote computer's desktop. Therefore, it's never a good idea to activate the Remember My Credentials check box.

However, what if you activated that option earlier? Fortunately, you're not stuck because Windows 7 gives you a way to "unremember" those credentials.

CAUTION

The General tab of the Remote Desktop Connection dialog box (select Start, All Programs, Accessories, Remote Desktop Connection) has a check box named Always Ask for Credentials. (You may need to click the Options button to see it.) You might think that you can protect the connection by activating this check box. However, Windows 7 is still saving the credentials, and all someone has to do to use them is deactivate the Always Ask for Credentials check box.

19

Here are the steps to follow:

1. Select Start, type **credential**, and then press Enter. Windows 7 displays the Credential Manager window

2. Click the credentials you want to delete. Remote Desktop Connection credentials always begin with TERMSRV (Terminal Server). The Credential Manager displays the credential details, as shown in Figure 19.8.

FIGURE 19.8 You can use the Credential Manager to remove saved Remote Desktop Connection logon credentials.

3. Click Remove from Vault. Credential Manager asks you to confirm.

4. Click Yes.

5. Repeat steps 2–4 to remove any other saved Remote Desktop Connection credentials.

TIP

Another way to remove saved Remote Desktop Connection credentials is to select Start, All Programs, Accessories, Remote Desktop Connection. In the Remote Desktop Connection dialog box, click Options to expand the dialog box, select the General tab, and then click the Delete link in the Logon Settings group. Click Yes when Remote Desktop Connection asks you to confirm.

Preventing Users from Logging On at Certain Times

If you've set up user accounts so that other people on your network can access your computer, by default those users can view and use your shares any time of day. That's not usually a problem, but you may want to prevent users from logging on at certain times. For example, if you work with a particular shared folder each afternoon, you might not want users accessing that folder until you're done.

Windows 7 enables you to specify the days of the week and hours of the day that a particular user is allowed to log on to your system. When the user attempts to access your computer over the network outside of those hours, he or she sees a dialog box similar to the one shown in Figure 19.9.

The next couple of sections show you how to work with this feature.

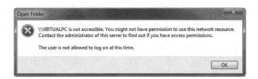

FIGURE 19.9   If you've set up logon hours for a user, that person sees a dialog box similar to this when attempting to log on outside of those hours.

Setting a User's Logon Hours

Unfortunately, Windows 7 doesn't have a dialog box or other interface that you can use to set logon hours for a user. Instead, you must use a Command Prompt session where you enter a command using the following general syntax:

```
net user username /times:day1,times1;day2,times2,...
```

username	The name of the user account you want to work with.
day1, day2	The day of the week that the user is allowed to log on. You can spell out the days, but it's quicker to use the following codes (case doesn't matter): Su, M, T, W, Th, F, and Sa. You can also specify a range of days, such as M-F (for Monday to Friday).
time1, time2	For a given day, the time range that the user is allowed to log on. The range syntax is *start-end,* where *start* is the beginning of the logon hours, and *end* is the end of the logon hours. You can either use 24-hour notation or 12-hour notation, although the latter means you must also specify AM and PM.

Here are some examples:

```
net user karen /times:M-F,9AM-5PM
net user steve /times:M,18-24
net user emily /times:Sa,10PM-6PM; Su,12PM-6PM
```

> **TIP**
>
> If you've previously set a user's logon hours, you may decide later to remove those restrictions. To give a user access at all times, use the all parameter:
>
> ```
> net user katy /times:all
> ```
>
> To give a user no access, use no parameters:
>
> ```
> net user jordan /times:
> ```

Follow these steps to specify logon hours for a user:

1. Select Start and type **command**.
2. In the search results, right-click Command Prompt, and then click Run as Administrator. The User Account Control dialog box appears.

19

3. Enter your UAC credentials to continue. Windows 7 opens an administrator Command Prompt session.

4. Type your **net user** /**times** command and press Enter. The NET USER command responds with The command completed successfully.

5. Repeat step 4 to specify all the logon hours you want to implement.

6. Type **exit** and press Enter to close the Command Prompt session.

Automatically Logging Off a User When the Logon Hours Expire

By default, Windows 7 does nothing if a user is currently logged on to your computer and that person's logon hours expire. In other words, there's nothing to prevent a teenager from hanging out online all night instead of doing homework! To fix this, you can configure Windows 7 to automatically log off the user when the account's logon hours are over. Here are the steps to follow:

> **NOTE**
>
> These steps require the Local Security Policy snap-in, which is available only with Windows 7 Professional, Enterprise, and Ultimate.

1. Select Start, type **secpol.msc**, and press Enter. The Local Security Policy window appears.

2. Open the Security Settings, Local Policies, Security Options branch.

3. Double-click the Network Security: Force Logoff When Logon Hours Expire policy.

4. Click the Enabled option, as shown in Figure 19.10.

5. Click OK.

FIGURE 19.10   Enable the Network Security: Force Logoff When Logon Hours Expire policy.

CHAPTER 20

Tightening Wireless Network Security

The wireless telegraph is not difficult to understand. The ordinary telegraph is like a very long cat. You pull the tail in New York, and it meows in Los Angeles. The wireless is the same, only without the cat.

—Albert Einstein

Computer veterans may be familiar with the term *wardialing*, a black-hat hacker technique that involves automatically calling thousands of telephone numbers to look for any that have a modem attached. (You might also know this term from 1983 movie *WarGames*, now a classic in computer cracking circles. In the movie, a young cracker, Matthew Broderick, uses wardialing to look for games and bulletin board systems. However, he inadvertently ends up with a direct connection to a high-level military computer that gives him control over the U.S. nuclear arsenal. Various things hit the fan after that.) Modems are becoming increasingly rare these days, so wardialing is less of a threat than it used to be.

That doesn't mean we're any safer, however. Our houses and offices may no longer have modems, but many of them have a relatively recent bit of technology: a wireless network. So now wardialing has given way to *wardriving*, where a cracker drives through various neighborhoods with a portable computer or another device set up to look for available wireless networks. If the miscreant finds a nonsecured network, he uses it for free Internet access (such a person is called a *piggybacker*) or to cause mischief with shared network resources. The hacker may then do a little *warchalking*, using chalk to place a special symbol on the sidewalk or other surface that indicates there's a nonsecure wireless network nearby.

Crackers engage in all these nefarious deeds for a simple reason: Wireless networks are less secure than wired ones. That's because the wireless connection that enables you to access the network from the kitchen or the conference room can also enable an intruder from outside your home or office to access the network.

Fortunately, you can secure your wireless network against these threats with a few simple tweaks and techniques, as you'll see in this chapter.

TIP

The most effective technique for securing your wireless access point is also the simplest: Turn it off if you won't be using it for an extended period. If you're going out of town for a few days, or if you're going on vacation for a week or two, shut down the access point and you're guaranteed that no wardriver will infiltrate your network.

Displaying the Router's Setup Pages

All routers come with a built-in configuration program. This program is a series of web pages that you access via a web browser on one of your network computers. These pages enable you to configure many different aspects of the router, particularly its wireless security settings if the router also doubles as a wireless access point (AP), which I'll be discussing throughout this chapter. To ensure that you can use the techniques I present here, the next two sections show you two methods you can use to access the router's setup pages.

Entering the Router's IP Address

Follow these steps to access the router's setup pages using the device's IP address:

1. Start Internet Explorer.
2. In the address bar, type the router address, and then press Enter. See your device documentation for the correct address, but in most cases, the address is either http://192.168.1.1 or http://192.168.0.1. One of two things will happen:

   ▶ You see a Connect dialog box like the one shown in Figure 20.1.

   ▶ You see a login page like the one shown in Figure 20.2.

NOTE

On Belkin routers, you see the Setup Utility right away. To make changes, you must click Login and then enter the router password. (The default password is blank.)

FIGURE 20.1   For some routers, Windows 7 displays the Connect dialog box for the login.

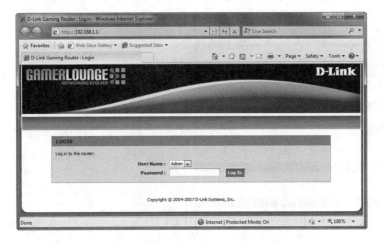

FIGURE 20.2   Other routers display their own login page.

3. Type the default username and password. Note that in most cases, you only need to enter the password; again, see the device documentation for the logon details.

TIP

If you're not sure which username and password to use, try **admin** for both. If that doesn't work, leave the username blank and try either **admin** or **password** for the password. If you still can't get in, see whether your device is listed in the default password list maintained at www.cirt.net/passwords and www.phenoelit-us.org/dpl/dpl.html.

---

4. If you see the Connect dialog box and you're the only person who uses your computer and your user account is protected by a password, activate the Remember

My Password check box so that you don't have to enter the logon information again in the future.

CAUTION

The only problem with telling Windows 7 to remember a password is that you open up a small security hole when you leave your desk for any length of time after you've logged on to your user account. Another person could sit down at your computer and easily access the protected feature. To plug this hole, be sure to lock your computer before you leave your desk unattended. To lock the computer, either press Windows Logo+L, or click Start and then click the Lock icon. This displays the Windows 7 logon screen. To unlock the PC, type your password and press Enter.

---

5. Click OK. The router's setup page appears. Figure 20.3 shows a sample setup page.

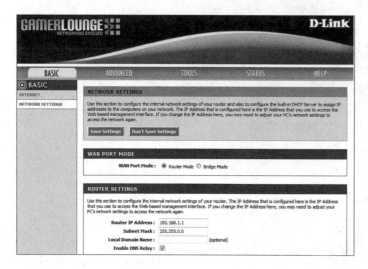

FIGURE 20.3   A typical router setup page.

Using the Network Window

For routers that support *Universal Plug and Play* (UPnP), follow these steps to access the setup pages:

1. On the computer connected to the router, select Start, Network. Windows 7 displays the Network window, which contains a list of devices on your network. If your router supports UPnP, you should see an icon for the router. The name of the icon is usually either the router's model number or model name. In Figure 20.4, for example, the router is the icon named GamerLounge Broadband Gigabit Gaming Router.

2. Right-click the router icon.

3. Click View Device Webpage (see Figure 20.4). The Connect dialog box or device login page appears.

FIGURE 20.4   If your router supports UPnP, you should see an icon for it in the Network window.

4. Type the default username and password. (See the device documentation for the logon details.)

5. If you are working with the Connect dialog box and you don't want to enter the logon information again in the future, activate the Remember My Password check box.

6. Click OK. The router's setup page appears.

TIP

If you forget your router's password, then your only option is to reset the router. All routers come with a reset feature that enables you to return the router to its factory configuration. In most cases, the device comes with a Reset button that you can push; it's usually a tiny switch or button that requires the end of a paper clip (or something similar) to activate. Once the reset is complete, you can access the router using its default user name and password.

Specifying a New Administrative Password

By far, the most important configuration chore for any new router is to change the default logon password (and username, if your router requires one). Note that I'm talking about the administrative password, which is the password you use to log on to the router's setup pages. This password has nothing to do with the password you use to log on to your Internet service provider (ISP) or to your wireless network.

Changing the default administrative password is particularly crucial if your router also includes a wireless AP because a nearby malicious hacker can see your router. This means that the intruder can easily access the setup pages just by navigating to one of the common router addresses—usually http://192.168.1.1 or http://192.168.0.1—and then entering the default password, which for most routers is well known or easy to guess.

Access your router's setup pages, as described in the previous section, locate the administrative password section (see Figure 20.5), and then modify the administrative password with a strong password.

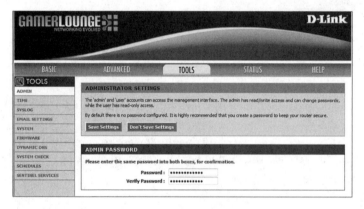

FIGURE 20.5   Access the administrative password section of your router's setup pages and type a strong password.

▶ For some pointers on building a strong password, see "Creating a Strong Password," p. 381.

Positioning the Access Point for Maximum Security

Almost all wireless network security problems stem from a single cause: wireless signals that extend outside of your home or office. This is called *signal leakage*, and if you can minimize the leakage, you're well on your way to having a secure wireless network. Of course, this assumes that a wardriver is using a standard antenna to look for wireless signals. That may be true in some cases, but many wardrivers use super-powerful antennas that offer many times the range of a regular antenna. There is, unfortunately, nothing you can do to hide your signal from such hackers. However, it's still worthwhile to reposition your AP to minimize signal leakage because this will help thwart those hackers using regular antennas.

NOTE

You might think that your wireless network signals extend at most just a few feet outside of your home or office. I thought so too, but then one day I was looking at Windows 7's list of available wireless networks, and I saw a network where the service set identifier (SSID) was the house address, and that house was *four* houses down from us!

Unfortunately, minimizing signal leakage isn't that easy because in most network setups, there are a couple of constraints on the position of the wireless AP:

▶ If you're using the wireless AP as your network router, you need the device relatively close to your broadband modem so that you can run ethernet cable from the modem's ethernet or LAN port to the router's Internet or WAN port.

▶ If you're using the wireless AP as your network switch, you need the device relatively close to your computers with ethernet network interface cards (NICs) so that you can run ethernet cable from the NICs to the switch's RJ-45 jacks.

However, even working within these constraints, in almost all cases, you can position the wireless AP away from a window. Glass doesn't obstruct radio frequency (RF) signals, so they're a prime source for wireless leakage. If your wireless AP must reside in a particular room, try to position it as far away as possible from any windows in that room.

In an ideal world, you should position the wireless AP close to the center of your house or building. This will ensure that the bulk of the signal stays in the building. If your only concern is connecting the router to a broadband modem, consider asking the phone or cable company to add a new jack to a central room (assuming the room doesn't have one already). Then, if it's feasible, you could used wired connections for the computers and devices in that room, and wireless connections for all your other devices. Of course, if your office (or, less likely, your home) has Ethernet wiring throughout, it should be easier to find a central location for the wireless AP.

TIP

If you find a more central location for your wireless AP, test for signal leakage. Unplug any wireless-enabled notebook and take it outside for a walk in the vicinity of your house. View the available wireless networks as you go, and see whether your network shows up in the list.

> **CAUTION**
>
> Many wireless APs come with an option to extend the range of the wireless signal. Unless you really need the range extended to ensure some distant device can connect to the AP, you should disable this option.

Encrypting Wireless Signals with WPA

Wardrivers usually look for leaking wireless signals so that they can piggyback on the Internet access. They may just be freeloading on your connection, but they may also have darker aims, such as using your Internet connection to send spam or download pornography.

However, some wardriving hackers are interested more in your data. They come equipped with *packet sniffers* that can pick up and read your network packets. Typically, these crackers are looking for sensitive data such as passwords and credit card numbers.

Therefore, it's absolutely crucial that you enable encryption for wireless data so that an outside user who picks up your network packets can't decipher them. Older wireless networks use a security protocol called Wired Equivalent Privacy, or WEP, that protects wireless communications with (usually) a 26-character security key. That sounds impregnable, but unfortunately there were serious weaknesses in the WEP encryption scheme, and now software exists that can crack any WEP key in minutes, if not seconds.

In newer wireless networks, WEP has been superseded by Wi-Fi Protected Access, or WPA, which is vastly more secure than WEP. WPA uses most of the IEEE 802.11i wireless security standard, and WPA2 implements the full standard. WPA2 Personal requires a simple pass phrase for access (so it's suitable for homes and small offices), and WPA2 Enterprise requires a dedicated authentication server.

Access your router's setup pages, as described earlier in this chapter, locate the wireless security section (see Figure 20.6), and then set up the encryption protocol and security key. Be sure to use the strongest encryption that your equipment supports.

> **CAUTION**
>
> Unfortunately, encryption is a "lowest common denominator" game. That is, if you want to use a strong encryption standard such as WPA2, *all* your wireless devices must support WPA2. If you have a device that only supports WEP, you either need to drop your encryption standard down to WEP, or you need to replace that device with one that supports the stronger standard. (You might also be able to upgrade the existing device; check with the manufacturer.) Note that some APs come with a setting that enables you to support both WPA and WPA2 devices.

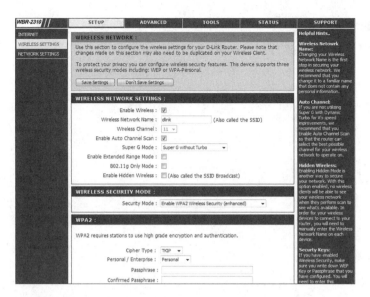

FIGURE 20.6   Access the wireless security settings on your router's setup pages to choose an encryption protocol and enter a security key.

NOTE

If you see the abbreviation PSK in the setup pages, it's short for *pre-shared key*, which refers in general to the sharing of some secret information with a person so that person can use the information later on (which is why this system is also sometimes called *shared secret*). In the case of WPA, the shared secret is the password or pass phrase that you give to your users so that they can connect to the wireless AP.

Changing the Wireless Connection Security Properties

If you change your wireless AP encryption method as described in the previous section, you also need to update each wireless Windows 7 computer to use the same form of encryption. Here are the steps to follow to modify the security properties for a wireless connection:

1. Click the Network icon in the taskbar's notification area, and then click Open Network and Sharing Center.

2. In the Network and Sharing Center's tasks list, click Manage Wireless Networks. Windows 7 displays the Manage Wireless Networks window.

3. Double-click the network for which you modified the encryption. Windows 7 opens the network's Wireless Network Properties dialog box.

4. Select the Security tab, shown in Figure 20.7.

5. Change the following three settings, as needed:

    ▶ **Security Type**—Select the encryption standard you're now using on the wireless AP.

20

- ▶ **Encryption Type**—Select the type of encryption used by the AP.

- ▶ **Network Security Key**—Type your security key.

6. Click OK.

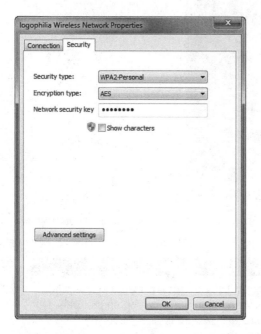

FIGURE 20.7 Use the Security tab to match the network connection's security properties with the new encryption settings on the wireless AP.

Disabling Network SSID Broadcasting

Windows 7 sees your wireless network because the AP broadcasts the network's SSID. However, Windows remembers the wireless networks that you have successfully connected to. Therefore, after all of your computers have accessed the wireless network at least once, you no longer need to broadcast the network's SSID. Therefore, you should use your AP setup program to disable broadcasting and prevent others from seeing your network.

However, you should know that when previously authorized devices attempt to connect to a nonbroadcasting network, they include the network's SSID as part of the probe requests they send out to see whether the network is within range. The SSID is sent in unencrypted text, so it is easy for a snoop with the right software (easily obtained from the Internet) to learn the SSID. If the SSID is not broadcasting to try to hide a network that is unsecure or uses an easily breakable encryption protocol, such as WEP, hiding the SSID in this way actually makes the network *less* secure.

Of course, *you* aren't trying to hide an unsecure network, right? From the previous section, you should now have WPA or WPA2 encryption enabled. So in your case, disabling SSID broadcasting either keeps your security the same or improves it:

▸ If a cracker detects your nonbroadcasting SSID, you're no worse off.

▸ If the snoop doesn't have the necessary software to detect your nonbroadcasting SSID, he won't see your network, so you're more secure.

So as long as your wireless signals are encrypted with WPA or WPA2, you should disable SSID broadcasting. Access your router's setup pages, as described earlier in this chapter, locate the wireless settings section (see Figure 20.8), and then activate the option to hide or disable SSID broadcasting.

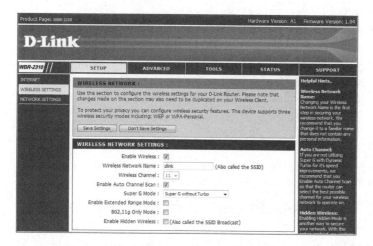

FIGURE 20.8   Access the wireless settings on your router's setup pages, and then disable SSID broadcasting.

CAUTION

Okay, there *is* one scenario where hiding your SSID can make your wireless network *less* secure. If a cracker detects that you've disabled SSID broadcasting, he might think you've done it because you've got something particularly important or sensitive to hide, so he might pull out all the stops to crack your network. How likely is this? Not very. Most crackers want easy targets, and most neighborhoods supply them, so unless a snoop *knows* that you're hiding something juicy, he'll almost certainly move on to a less-secure network.

20

Connecting to a Hidden Wireless Network

Each wireless network has a network name—the SSID—which identifies the network to wireless devices and computers with wireless network cards. By default, most wireless networks broadcast the network name so that you can see the network and connect to it. However, some wireless networks disable network name broadcasting as a security precaution. As I described in the previous section, the idea is that if unauthorized users can't see the network, they can't attempt to connect to it.

However, you can still connect to a hidden wireless network by entering the connection settings by hand. You need to know the network name, the network's security type and encryption type, and the network's security key or pass phrase.

Here are the steps to follow to connect to a nonbroadcasting wireless networking in Windows 7:

1. Click the Network icon in the taskbar's notification area, and then click Open Network and Sharing Center.

2. In the Network and Sharing Center window, click the Set Up a New Connection or Network link. The Choose a Connection Option dialog box appears.

3. Select Manually Connect to a Wireless Network, and then click Next. Windows 7 prompts you for the network connection data, as shown in Figure 20.9 (which shows a completed version of the dialog box).

4. Provide the following connection data:

   ▶ **Network Name**—The SSID of the hidden wireless network.

   ▶ **Security Type**—The security protocol used by the wireless network. Select No Authentication (Open) if the network is unsecured.

   ▶ **Encryption Type**—The method of encryption used by the wireless network's security protocol.

   ▶ **Security Key**—The key or password required for authorized access to the network.

   ▶ **Start This Connection Automatically**—Leave this check box activated to have Windows 7 connect to the network now (that is, when you click Next in step 5) and automatically the next time the network comes within range. If you always want to connect to the network manually, deactivate this option.

   ▶ **Connect Even If the Network Is Not Broadcasting**—If you activate this check box, Windows 7 will send probe requests to see whether the network is in range even if the network isn't broadcasting its SSID. Note, however, that this lessens security (because the SSID is sent in plain text in the probe request, as described in the previous tweak), so you should leave this check box deactivated.

5. Click Next. Windows 7 connects to the network and adds it to the list of wireless networks.

6. Click Close.

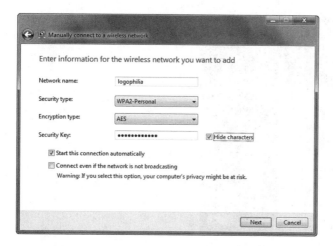

FIGURE 20.9   Use this dialog box to specify the connection settings for the hidden wireless network.

Changing the Default SSID

Even if you disable broadcasting of your network's SSID, users can still attempt to connect to your network by guessing the SSID. All wireless APs come with a predefined name, such as linksys, dlink, or default, and a would-be intruder will attempt these standard names first. Therefore, you can increase the security of your network by changing the SSID to a new name that is difficult to guess.

Even if you're broadcasting your wireless network's SSID, it's still a good idea to change the default SSID. Because in most cases the default SSID includes the name of the manufacturer, the SSID gives a would-be intruder valuable information on the type of AP you're using. In some cases, the default SSID offers not only the name of the manufacturer, but also information about the specific model (for example, belkin54g), which is of course even more useful to a cracker.

Finally, changing the default SSID is at the very least a small sign that you know what you're doing. One of the hallmarks of inexperienced users is that they don't change default settings because they're afraid of breaking something. If a wardriver sees a wireless network that's still using a default SSID, he's likely to think that he's dealing with an inexperienced user, so he'll be more likely to try to infiltrate the network.

Access your router's setup pages, as described earlier in this chapter, locate the wireless settings section (see Figure 20.10), and then edit the SSID value.

20

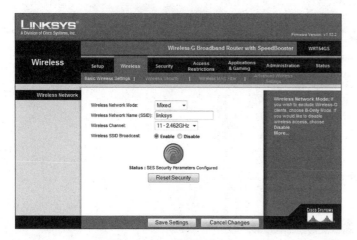

FIGURE 20.10   Access the wireless settings on your router's setup pages and then edit the network's SSID.

Another good reason to change the default SSID is to prevent confusion with other wireless networks in your area. If Windows 7's list of available wireless network includes two (or more) networks named, say, linksys, how will you know which one is yours?

Enabling MAC Address Filtering

The *MAC* (Media Access Control) *address* is the physical address of a network adapter. This is unique to each adapter, so you can enhance security by setting up your AP to use MAC address filtering. This feature means that the AP only accepts connections from a list of MAC addresses that you specify. If a hacker tries to connect to your network using a NIC that has a MAC address not on the list, the AP denies the connection.

Unfortunately, MAC address filtering isn't a particularly robust form of security. The problem is that wireless network packets use a nonencrypted header that includes the MAC address of the device sending the packet! So any reasonably sophisticated cracker can sniff your network packets, determine the MAC address of one of your wireless devices, and then use special software to spoof that address so that the AP thinks the hacker's packets are coming from an authorized device.

Does this mean you shouldn't bother configuring a MAC address filter? Not at all. For one thing, even if a savvy wardriver can fool your wireless AP into thinking his device is authorized, the hacker still has to get past your other security layers. For another, not every cracker out there uses sophisticated tools, such as packet sniffers and MAC address spoofing software, so your filter will at least thwart those would-be intruders.

Access your router's setup pages, as described earlier in this chapter, locate the Mac address filtering section (see Figure 20.11), turn on Mac address filtering, and then specify the MAC addresses that you want to allow on your network.

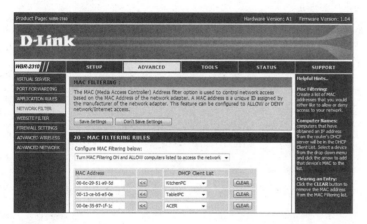

FIGURE 20.11   Access the MAC address filtering settings on your router's setup pages, and then activate and configure MAC address filtering.

Getting the MAC Address of Your Wireless NIC

The good news about MAC address filtering is that most modern APs come with a feature that displays a list of the devices currently connected to the AP and enables you to quickly add the MAC addresses of those devices to the AP's MAC address filter. Just in case your AP doesn't come with this feature, here are the steps to follow in Windows 7 to determine the MAC address of your wireless NIC:

1. Click the Network icon in the taskbar's notification area, and then click Open Network and Sharing Center.

2. In the Network and Sharing Center's tasks list, click Change Adapter Settings. Windows 7 displays the Network Connections window.

3. Double-click the wireless connection to open the Status dialog box.

20

4. Click Details to open the Network Connection Details dialog box.

5. Make a note of the Physical Address value (see Figure 20.12), which is the same as the MAC address.

6. Click Close.

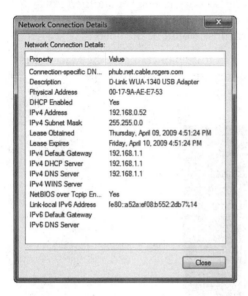

FIGURE 20.12   In the Network Connection Details dialog box, the wireless NIC's MAC address is given by the Physical Address value.

NOTE

Another way to find out the MAC address of your wireless network adapter is to select Start, type **command**, and then select Command Prompt to open a Command Prompt session. Type the following command and press Enter:

```
ipconfig /all
```

Find the data for the wireless adapter and look for the Physical Address value.

TIP

While we're on the subject of wireless NICs, this is as good a place as any to talk about security updates. Wireless NIC vendors occasionally find security vulnerabilities in their NIC device drivers, and they issue patches and driver upgrades to fix those security holes. You should check the manufacturer's website from time to time to see whether any updates are available for your NIC.

CHAPTER 21

Troubleshooting and Recovering from Problems

If it was so, it might be; and if it were so, it would be; but as it isn't, it ain't. That's logic.

—Lewis Carroll

A long time ago, somebody proved mathematically that it was impossible to make any reasonably complex software program problem-free. As the number of variables increase, as the interactions of subroutines and objects become more complex, and as the underlying logic of a program grows beyond the ability of a single person to grasp all at once, errors inevitably creep into the code. Given Windows 7's status as possibly the most complex software ever created, the bad news is that there are certainly problems lurking in the weeds. However, the good news is that the overwhelming majority of these problems are extremely obscure and appear only under the rarest circumstances.

This doesn't mean that you're guaranteed a glitch-free computing experience—far from it. Third-party programs and devices cause the majority of computer woes, either because they have inherent problems themselves or because they don't get along well with Windows 7. Using software, devices, and device drivers designed for Windows 7 can help tremendously, as can the maintenance program I outlined in Chapter 7, "Maintaining Your Windows 7 System." But computer problems, like the proverbial death and taxes, are certainties in life, so you need to know how to troubleshoot and resolve the problems that will inevitably come your way. In this chapter, I help you do just that by showing you my favorite techniques for determining problem sources, and by taking you through all of Windows 7's recovery tools.

The Origins of the Word *Bug*

Software glitches are traditionally called *bugs*, although many developers shun the term because it comes with too much negative baggage these days. Microsoft, for example, prefers the euphemistic term *issues*. There's a popular and appealing tale of how this sense of the word *bug* came about. As the story goes, in 1947 an early computer pioneer named Grace Hopper was working on a system called the Mark II. While investigating a problem, she found a moth among the machine's vacuum tubes, so from then on glitches were called bugs. A great story, to be sure, but this tale was *not* the source of the "computer glitch" sense of "bug." In fact, engineers had already been referring to mechanical defects as "bugs" for at least 60 years before Ms. Hopper's discovery. As proof, the *Oxford English Dictionary* offers the following quotation from an 1889 edition of the *Pall Mall Gazette*:

"Mr. Edison, I was informed, had been up the two previous nights discovering 'a bug' in his phonograph—an expression for solving a difficulty, and implying that some imaginary insect has secreted itself inside and is causing all the trouble."

Troubleshooting Strategies: Determining the Source of a Problem

One of the ongoing mysteries that all Windows users experience at one time or another is what might be called the "now you see it, now you don't" problem. This is a glitch that plagues you for a while and then mysteriously vanishes without any intervention on your part. (This also tends to occur when you ask a nearby user or someone from the IT department to look at the problem. Like the automotive problem that goes away when you take the car to a mechanic, computer problems will often resolve themselves as soon as a knowledgeable user sits down at the keyboard.) When this happens, most people just shake their heads and resume working, grateful to no longer have to deal with the problem.

Unfortunately, most computer ills aren't resolved so easily. For these more intractable problems, your first order of business is to track down the source of the glitch. This is, at best, a black art, but it can be done if you take a systematic approach. Over the years, I've found that the best approach is to ask a series of questions designed to gather the required information or to narrow down what might be the culprit. The next few sections take you through these questions.

Did You Get an Error Message?

Unfortunately, most computer error messages are obscure and do little to help you resolve a problem directly. However, error codes and error text can help you down the road, either by giving you something to search for in an online database (see "Troubleshooting Using Online Resources," later in this chapter) or by providing information to a tech support person. Therefore, you should always write down the full text of any error message that appears.

TIP

If the error message is lengthy and you can still use other programs on your computer, don't bother writing down the full message. Instead, while the message is displayed, press Print Screen to place an image of the current screen on the clipboard. Then open Paint or some other graphics program, paste the screen into a new image, and save the image. If you think you'll be sending the image via email to a tech support employee or someone else that can help with the problem, consider saving the image as a mono-chrome or 16-color bitmap or, if possible, a JPEG file, to keep the image size small.

TIP

If the error message appears before Windows 7 starts, but you don't have time to write it down, press the Pause Break key to pause the startup. After you record the error, press Ctrl+Pause Break to resume the startup.

Does an Error or Warning Appear in the Event Viewer Logs?

Launch the Event Viewer, open the Windows Logs branch, and then examine the Application and System logs. (Refer to Chapter 7 for more information on the Event Viewer.) In particular, look in the Level column for Error or Warning events. If you see any, double-click each one to read the event description. Figure 21.1 shows an example.

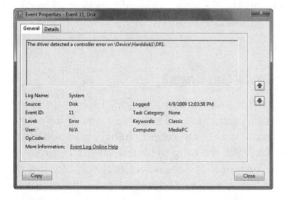

FIGURE 21.1   In the Event Viewer, look for Error and Warning events in the Application and System logs.

> ▶ See "Reviewing Event Viewer Logs," **p. 160.**

Does an Error Appear in System Information?

Select Start, type **msinfo32**, and press Enter to launch the System Information utility. In the Hardware Resources branch, check the Conflicts/Sharing sub-branch for device conflicts. Also, see whether the Components\Problem Devices category lists any devices, as shown in Figure 21.2.

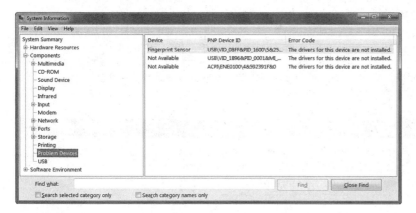

FIGURE 21.2   You can use the System Information utility to look for device conflicts and problems.

Did You Recently Edit the Registry?

Improper Registry modifications can cause all kinds of mischief. If the problem occurred after editing the Registry, try restoring the changed key or setting. Ideally, if you exported a backup of the offending key, you should import the backup. I showed you how to back up the Registry in Chapter 12, "Tweaking the Windows 7 Registry."

▶ See "Keeping the Registry Safe," **p. 233**.

Did You Recently Change Any Windows Settings?

If the problem started after you changed your Windows configuration, try reversing the change. Even something as seemingly innocent as activating a screensaver can cause problems, so don't rule anything out. If you've made a number of recent changes and you're not sure about everything you did, or if it would take too long to reverse all the changes individually, use System Restore to revert your system to the most recent checkpoint before you made the changes. See "Recovering Using System Restore," later in this chapter.

Did Windows 7 "Spontaneously" Reboot?

When certain errors occur, Windows 7 will reboot itself. This apparently random behavior is actually built in to the system in the event of a system failure (also called a *stop error* or a *blue screen of death*—BSOD). By default, Windows 7 writes an error event to the system log, dumps the contents of memory into a file, and then reboots the system. So, if your system reboots, check the Event Viewer to see what happened.

You can control how Windows 7 handles system failures by following these steps:

1. Select Start, type **systempropertiesadvanced**, and press Enter to open the System Properties dialog box with the Advanced tab displayed.

2. In the Startup and Recovery group, click Settings. Figure 21.3 shows the Startup and Recovery dialog box that appears.

FIGURE 21.3   Use the Startup and Recovery dialog box to configure how Windows 7 handles system failures.

3. Configure how Windows 7 handles system failures using the following controls in the System Failure group:

   ▶ **Write an Event to the System Log**—Leave this check box activated to have the system failure recorded in the system log. This enables you to view the event in the Event Viewer.

   ▶ **Automatically Restart**—This is the option that, when activated, causes your system to reboot when a stop error occurs. Deactivate this check box if you want to avoid the reboot. This is useful if an error message appears briefly before Windows 7 reboots. By disabling the automatic restart, you give yourself time to read and write down the error message.

TIP

If the BSOD problem occurs during startup, your computer winds up in an endless loop: You reboot, the problem occurs, the BSOD appears, and then your computer reboots. Unfortunately, the BSOD appears only fleetingly, so you never have enough time to read (much less record) the error message. If this happens, display the Windows Boot Manager menu (refer to Chapter 4, Customizing Startup and Shutdown"), press F8 to display the Advanced Boot Options menu, and then select the Disable Automatic Restart on System Failure item. This tells Windows 7 not to reboot after the BSOD appears, so you can then write down the error message and, hopefully, successfully troubleshoot the problem.

▶ **Write Debugging Information**—This list determines what information Windows 7 saves to disk (in the folder specified in the text box below the list) when a system failure occurs. This information—it's called a *memory dump*—contains data that can help a tech support employee determine the cause of the problem. You have four choices:

None—No debugging information is written.

Small Memory Dump (128 KB)—This option writes the minimum amount of useful information that could be used to identify what caused the stop error. This 128KB file includes the stop error number and its description, the list of running device drivers, and the processor state.

Kernel Memory Dump—This option writes the contents of the kernel memory to the disk. (The *kernel* is the Windows 7 component that manages low-level functions for processor-related activities such as scheduling and dispatching threads, handling interrupts and exceptions, and synchronizing multiple processors.) This dump includes memory allocated to the kernel, the hardware abstraction layer, and the drivers and programs used by the kernel. Unallocated memory and memory allocated to user programs are not included in the dump. This information is the most useful for troubleshooting, so I recommend using this option.

Complete Memory Dump—This option writes the entire contents of RAM to the disk.

CAUTION

Windows 7 first writes the debugging information to the paging file—`Pagefile.sys` in the root folder of the `%SystemDrive%`. When you restart the computer, Windows 7 then transfers the information to the dump file. Therefore, you must have a large enough paging file to handle the memory dump. This is particularly true for the Complete Memory Dump option, which requires the paging file to be as large as the physical RAM, plus 1 megabyte. The file size of the Kernel Memory Dump is typically about a third of physical RAM, although it may be as large as 800MB. If the paging file isn't large enough to handle the dump, Windows 7 writes only as much information as can fit into the paging file. I showed you how to check and adjust the size of the paging file in Chapter 6, "Tuning Windows 7's Performance."

> ▶ **See** "Changing the Paging File's Location and Size," **p. 132**.

> ▶ **Overwrite Any Existing File**—When this option is activated, Windows 7 overwrites any existing dump file with the new dump information. If you deactivate this check box, Windows 7 creates a new dump file with each system failure. Note that this option is enabled only for the Kernel Memory Dump and the Complete Memory Dump (which by default write to the same file: %SystemRoot%\Memory.dmp).

4. Click OK in all the open dialog boxes to put the new settings into effect.

Did You Recently Change Any Application Settings?

If so, try reversing the change to see whether doing so solves the problem. If that doesn't help, here are three other things to try:

▶ Check the developer's website to see whether an upgrade or patch is available.

▶ Run the application's Repair option (if it has one), which is often useful for fixing corrupted or missing files. To see whether a program as a Repair option, select Start, type **programs**, and then click Programs and Features to display a list of your installed applications. Click the problematic application, and then look for a Repair item in the taskbar (see Figure 21.4).

▶ Reinstall the program.

FIGURE 21.4   In the Programs and Features window, click the program and look for a Repair option in the taskbar.

NOTE

If a program freezes, you won't be able to shut it down using conventional methods. If you try, you might see a dialog box warning you that the program is not responding. If so, click End Now to force the program to close. If that doesn't work, right-click the taskbar, and then click Task Manager. When you display the Applications tab, you should see your stuck application listed, and the Status column will likely say Not responding. Click the program, and then click End Task.

Did You Recently Install a New Program?

If you suspect a new program is causing system instability, restart Windows 7 and try operating the system for a while without using the new program. (If the program has any components that load at startup, be sure to deactivate them, as I described in Chapter 4.) If the problem doesn't reoccur, the new program is likely the culprit. Try using the program without any other programs running.

▶ **See** "Custom Startups Using the Boot Configuration Data," **p. 63**.

You should also examine the program's readme file (if it has one) to look for known problems and possible workarounds. It's also a good idea to check for a Windows 7-compatible version of the program. Again, you can also try the program's Repair option or you can reinstall the program.

Similarly, if you recently upgraded an existing program, try uninstalling the upgrade.

TIP

One common cause of program errors is having one or more program files corrupted because of bad hard disk sectors. Before you reinstall a program, run a surface check on your hard disk to identify and block off bad sectors. I showed you how to do a hard disk surface scan in Chapter 7.

▶ **See** "Checking Your Hard Disk for Errors," **p. 135**.

TIP

When a program crashes, Windows 7 displays a dialog box asking if you want to see whether a solution to the problem is available. You can control the behavior of this prompt. See "Checking for Solutions to Problems," later in this chapter.

Did You Recently Install a New Device?

If you recently installed a new device or if you recently updated an existing device driver, the new device or driver might be causing the problem. Check Device Manager to see whether there's a problem with the device. Follow my troubleshooting suggestions in Chapter 22, "Troubleshooting Devices."

▶ **See** "Troubleshooting Device Problems," **p. 472**.

Did You Recently Install an Incompatible Device Driver?

As you see in Chapter 22, Windows 7 allows you to install drivers that aren't Windows 7 certified, but it also warns you that this is a bad idea. Incompatible drivers are one of the most common sources of system instability, so whenever possible, you should uninstall the driver and install one designed for Windows 7. If you can't uninstall the driver, Windows 7 automatically set a system restore point before it installed the driver, so you should use that to restore the system to its previous state. (See "Recovering Using System Restore," later in this chapter.)

Did You Recently Apply an Update from Windows Update?

It's an unfortunate fact of life that occasionally updates designed to fix one problem end up causing another problem. Fortunately, Windows 7 offers a couple of solutions for problems caused by updates:

- ▶ Select Start, type **updates**, and then click View Installed Updates. In the Installed Updates window, click the update you want to remove, and then click Uninstall.

- ▶ Before you install an update from the Windows Update site, Windows 7 creates a system restore point—usually named *Install: Windows Update*. If your system becomes unstable after installing the update, use System Restore to revert to the pre-update configuration.

TIP

If you have Windows 7 set up to perform automatic updating, you can keep tabs on the changes made to your system by select Start, type **updates**, and then click Windows Update. Click the View Update History link to see a list of the installed updates, which includes the update Name, Status (such as Successful), Type (such as Important or Optional), and Date Installed.

General Troubleshooting Tips

Figuring out the cause of a problem is often the hardest part of troubleshooting, but by itself it doesn't do you much good. When you know the source, you need to parlay that information into a fix for the problem. I discussed a few solutions in the previous section, but here are a few other general fixes you need to keep in mind:

- ▶ **Close all programs**—You can often fix flaky behavior by shutting down all your open programs and starting again. This is a particularly useful fix for problems caused by low memory or low system resources.

- ▶ **Log off Windows 7**—Logging off clears the RAM and so gives you a slightly cleaner slate than merely closing all your programs.

- ▶ **Reboot the computer**—If there are problems with some system files and devices, logging off won't help because these objects remain loaded. By rebooting the system, you reload the entire system, which is often enough to solve many computer problems.

▶ **Turn off the computer and restart**—You can often solve a hardware problem by first shutting your machine off. Wait for 30 seconds to give all devices time to spin down, and then restart.

▶ **Check connections, power switches, and so on**—Some of the most common (and some of the most embarrassing) causes of hardware problems are the simple physical things. So, make sure that a device is turned on, check that cable connections are secure, and ensure that insertable devices are properly inserted.

More Troubleshooting Tools

Windows 7 comes with diagnostic tools—together, they're called the *Windows Diagnostic Infrastructure (WDI)*—that not only do a better job of finding the source of many common disk, memory, and network problems, but can detect impending failures and alert you to take corrective or mitigating action (such as backing up your files). The next few sections describe these tools.

Running the Windows 7 Troubleshooters

NEW TO 7   Windows Vista introduced the idea of the *troubleshooter*, a Help system component that offered a series of solutions that led you deeper into a problem in an attempt to fix it. In Windows 7, the troubleshooters have been beefed up and given their own home within the Control Panel interface. To see the Windows 7 troubleshooters, select Start, type **trouble**, and then choose Troubleshooting in the search results. The Troubleshooting window (see Figure 21.5) is divided into several categories (Programs, Hardware and Sound, and so on), each of which offers a few links to general troubleshooting tasks.

Note, too, the Get the Most Up-to-Date Troubleshooters check box at the bottom of the window. If you leave that option activated, and then click a category, Windows 7 queries the Windows Online Troubleshooting service for the latest troubleshooting packs, and then displays the complete list for that category. For example, Figure 21.6 shows the troubleshooters that were available for the Programs category as I wrote this.

TIP

If you want to see all the available troubleshooters, click the View All link in the Troubleshooting window.

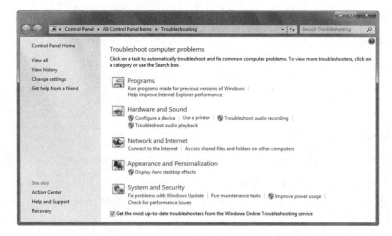

FIGURE 21.5   Windows 7's new Troubleshooting window offers links to various troubleshooting categories and tasks.

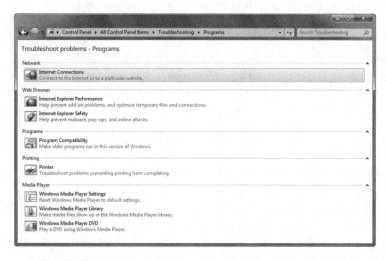

FIGURE 21.6   Click a category to see its available troubleshooters.

Understanding Disk Diagnostics

A hard disk can suddenly bite the dust thanks to a lightning strike, an accidental drop from a decent height, or an electronic component shorting out. However, most of the time hard disks die a slow death. Along the way, hard disks almost always show some signs of decay, such as the following:

▶ Spin-up time gradually slows.

▶ Drive temperature increases.

▶ The seek error rate increases.

▶ The read error rate increases.

▶ The write error rate increases.

▶ The number of reallocated sectors increases.

▶ The number of bad sectors increases.

▶ The cyclic redundancy check (CRC) produces an increasing number of errors.

Other factors that might indicate a potential failure are the number of times that the hard drive has been powered up, the number of hours in use, and the number of times the drive has started and stopped spinning.

Since about 1996, almost all hard disk manufacturers have built in to their drives a system called *Self-Monitoring, Analysis, and Reporting Technology*, or *SMART*. This system monitors the parameters just listed (and usually quite a few more highly technical hard disk attributes) and uses a sophisticated algorithm to combine these attributes into a value that represents the overall health of the disk. When that value goes beyond some predetermined threshold, SMART issues an alert that hard disk failure might be imminent.

Although SMART has been around for a while and is now standard, taking advantage of SMART diagnostics has, until now, required third-party programs. However, Windows 7 comes with a Diagnostic Policy Service (DPS) that includes a Disk Diagnostics component that can monitor SMART. If the SMART system reports an error, Windows 7 displays a message that your hard disk is at risk. It also guides you through a backup session to ensure that you don't lose any data before you can have the disk replaced.

Understanding Resource Exhaustion Detection

Your system can become unstable if it runs low on virtual memory, and there's a pretty good chance it will hang if it runs out of virtual memory. Older versions of Windows displayed one warning when they detected low virtual memory and another warning when the system ran out of virtual memory. However, in both cases, users were simply told to shut down some or all of their running programs. That often solved the problem, but shutting *everything* down is usually overkill because it's often the case that just one running program or process is causing the virtual memory shortage.

Windows 7 takes this more subtle point of view into account with its Windows Resource Exhaustion Detection and Resolution tool (RADAR), which is part of the Diagnostic Policy Service. This tool also monitors virtual memory and issues a warning when resources run low. However, RADAR also identifies which programs or processes are using the most virtual memory, and it includes a list of these resource hogs as part of the warning. This enables you to shut down just one or more of these offending processes to get your system in a more stable state.

Microsoft is also providing developers with programmatic access to the RADAR tool, thus enabling vendors to build resource exhaustion detection into their applications. When such a program detects that it is using excessive resources, or if it detects that the system as a whole is low on virtual memory, the program can free resources to improve overall system stability.

NOTE

The Resource Exhaustion Detection and Recovery tool divides the current amount of committed virtual memory by the *commit limit*, the maximum size of the virtual memory paging file. If this percentage approaches 100, RADAR issues its warning. If you want to track this yourself, run the Performance Monitor (see Chapter 6), and add the % Committed Bytes in Use counter in the Memory object. If you want to see the exact commit numbers, add the Committed Bytes and Commit Limit counters (also in the Memory object).

▶ **See** "Using the Performance Monitor," **p. 119.**

Running the Memory Diagnostics Tool

Few computer problems are as maddening as those related to physical memory defects because they tend to be intermittent and they tend to cause problems in secondary systems, forcing you to waste time on wild goose chases all over your system.

Therefore, it is welcome news that Windows 7 ships with a Windows Memory Diagnostics tool that works with Microsoft Online Crash Analysis to determine whether defective physical memory is the cause of program crashes. If so, Windows Memory Diagnostics lets you know about the problem and schedules a memory test for the next time you start your computer. If it detects actual problems, the system also marks the affected memory area as unusable to avoid future crashes.

Windows 7 also comes with a Memory Leak Diagnosis tool that's part of the Diagnostic Policy Service. If a program is leaking memory (using up increasing amounts of memory over time), this tool will diagnose the problem and take steps to fix it.

To run the Memory Diagnostics tool yourself, follow these steps:

1. Select Start, type **memory**, and then click Windows Memory Diagnostic in the search results. The Windows Memory Diagnostics Tool window appears, as shown in Figure 21.7.

2. Click one of the following options:

   ▶ **Restart Now and Check for Problems**—Click this option to force an immediate restart and schedule a memory test during startup. Be sure to save your work before clicking this option.

   ▶ **Check for Problems the Next Time I Start My Computer**—Click this option to schedule a memory test to run the next time you boot.

After the test runs (it takes 10 or 15 minutes, depending on how much RAM is in your system), Windows 7 restarts and you see (for a short time) the Windows Memory Diagnostic Tool icon in the taskbar's notification area. This icon displays the results of the memory text.

FIGURE 21.7   Use the Windows Memory Diagnostic tool to check for memory problems.

TIP

If you're having trouble starting Windows 7 and you suspect memory errors might be the culprit, boot your machine to the Windows Boot Manager menu (refer to Chapter 4). When the menu appears, press Tab to select the Windows Memory Diagnostic item, and then press Enter. If you can't get to the Windows Boot Manager, you can also run the Memory Diagnostic tool using Windows 7's System Recovery Options. See "Recovering Using the System Recovery Options" in Chapter 23, "Troubleshooting Startup."

Checking for Solutions to Problems

NEW TO **7**   Microsoft constantly collects information about Windows 7 from users. When a problem occurs, Windows 7 usually asks whether you want to send information about the problem to Microsoft and, if you do, it stores these tidbits in a massive database. Engineers then tackle the "issues" (as they euphemistically call them) and hopefully come up with solutions.

One of Windows 7's most promising features is called Problem Reporting (it was called Problem Reports and Solutions in Vista), and it's designed to make solutions available to anyone who goes looking for them. Windows 7 keeps a list of problems your computer is having, so you can tell it to go online and see whether a solution is available. If there's a solution waiting, Windows 7 will download it, install it, and fix your system.

Here are the steps to follow to check for solutions to problems:

1. Select Start, type **action**, and then click Action Center in the results. (You can also click the Action Center icon in the taskbar's notification area, and then click Open Action Center.) The Action Center window appears.

2. Click Maintenance to view the maintenance-related tools and messages.

3. Click the Check for Solutions link. Windows 7 begins checking for solutions.

4. If you see a dialog box asking whether you want to send more information about your problems, you can click View Problem Details to see information about the problems, as shown in Figure 21.8. When you're ready to move on, click Send Information.

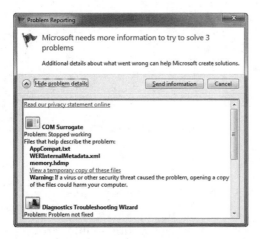

FIGURE 21.8   If Windows 7 tells you it need more information, click View Problem Details to see the problems.

5. If a solution exists for your computer, you see it listed in the Maintenance section of the Action Center window. Click the solution to install it.

By default, when a problem occurs, Windows 7 does two things:

▶ It automatically checks for a solution to the problem.

▶ It asks whether you want to send more information about the problem to Microsoft.

You can control this behavior by configuring a few settings:

1. Select Start, type **action**, and then click Action Center in the results. (You can also click the Action Center icon in the taskbar's notification area, and then click Open Action Center.) The Action Center window appears.

2. Click Maintenance to view the maintenance-related tools and messages.

3. Click Settings. The Problem Reporting Settings window appears.

4. In the Choose How to Check for Solutions to Computer Problems window, click Advanced Settings to display the Advanced Settings for Problem Reporting window shown in Figure 21.9.

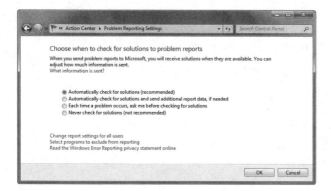

FIGURE 21.9   Use the Advanced Settings for Problem Reporting window to configure the Problem Reporting feature.

5. To configure problem reporting, click one of the following options:

  ▶ **Automatically Check for Solutions**—Activate this option (it's the default) to have Windows 7 automatically check online for an existing solution to a problem.

  ▶ **Automatically Check for Solutions and Send Additional Report Data, If Needed**—Activate this option to have Windows 7 automatically check online for an existing solution to a problem and to automatically send extra information about the problem.

  ▶ **Each Time a Problem Occurs, Ask Me Before Checking for Solutions**—Activate this option to have Windows 7 prompt you to check for solutions and to send additional information about the problem.

  ▶ **Never Check for Solutions**—Activate this option if you don't want to report problems at all.

6. By default, Windows 7 applies the setting from step 5 only to the current user. If you want to configure the same problem reporting option for every user, click the Change Report Settings for All Users link to open the Problem Reporting dialog box, choose the reporting option you want everyone to use, and then click OK.

NOTE

If you change your mind and prefer each user to choose his or her own reporting option, click the Change Report Settings for All Users link, activate the Allow Each User to Choose Settings option, and then click OK.

---

7. If you don't want Windows 7 to send information about a specific program, click the Select Programs to Exclude from Reporting link to open the Advanced Problem

Reporting Settings window. Click Add, locate and select the program's executable file, click Open, and then click OK.

8. Click OK to put the new settings into effect.

Troubleshooting Using Online Resources

The Internet is home to an astonishingly wide range of information, but its forte has always been computer knowledge. Whatever problem you have, there's a good chance that someone out there has run into the same thing, knows how to fix it, and has posted the solution on a website or newsgroup, or would be willing to share it with you if asked. True, finding what you need is sometimes difficult, and you often can't be sure how accurate some of the solutions are. However, if you stick to the more reputable sites and if you get second opinions on solutions offered by complete strangers, you'll find the online world an excellent troubleshooting resource. Here's my list of favorite online resources:

▶ **Microsoft Product Support Services**—This is Microsoft's main online technical support site. Through this site, you can access frequently asked questions about Windows 7, see a list of known problems, download files, and send questions to Microsoft support personnel: support.microsoft.com/.

▶ **Microsoft Knowledge Base**—The Microsoft Product Support Services site has links that enable you to search the Microsoft Knowledge Base, which is a database of articles related to all Microsoft products including, of course, Windows 7. These articles provide you with information about Windows 7 and instructions on using Windows 7 features. But the most useful aspect of the Knowledge Base is for troubleshooting problems. Many of the articles were written by Microsoft support personnel after helping customers overcome problems. By searching for error codes or keywords, you can often get specific solutions to your problems.

▶ **Microsoft TechNet**—This Microsoft site is designed for IT professionals and power users. It contains a huge number of articles on all Microsoft products. These articles give you technical content, program instructions, tips, scripts, downloads, and troubleshooting ideas: www.microsoft.com/technet/.

▶ **Windows Update**—Check this site for the latest device drivers, security patches, service packs, and other updates: windowsupdate.microsoft.com/.

▶ **Microsoft Security**—Check this site for the latest information on Microsoft security and privacy initiatives, particularly security patches: www.microsoft.com/security/.

▶ **Vendor websites**—All but the tiniest hardware and software vendors maintain websites with customer support sections that you can peruse for upgrades, patches, workarounds, frequently asked questions, and sometimes chat or bulletin board features.

▶ **Newsgroups**—There are computer-related newsgroups for hundreds of topics and products. Microsoft maintains its own newsgroups via the msnews.microsoft.com server (an account for which is automatically set up in Windows Mail), and Usenet has a huge list of groups in the alt and comp hierarchies. Before asking a question in a newsgroup, be sure to search Google Groups to see whether your question has been answered in the past: groups.google.com/.

TIP

You can also access Microsoft's Windows 7 newsgroups via the Web: http://answers.microsoft.com/en-us/windows/default.aspx.

Recovering from a Problem

Ideally, solving a problem will require a specific tweak to the system: a Registry setting change, a driver upgrade, a program uninstall. But sometimes you need to take more of a "big picture" approach to revert your system to some previous state in the hope that you'll leap past the problem and get your system working again. Windows 7 offers three ways to try such an approach: last known good configuration, System Restore, and System Recovery Options (which you should use in that order). The next two sections discuss the first two tools, and I talk about the System Recovery Options in Chapter 23.

▶ **See** "Recovering Using the System Recovery Options," **p. 485.**

Booting Using the Last Known Good Configuration

Each time Windows 7 starts successfully in Normal mode, the system makes a note of which *control set*—the system's drivers and hardware configuration—was used. Specifically, it enters a value in the following Registry key:

```
HKLM\SYSTEM\Select\LastKnownGood
```

For example, if this value is 1, it means that control set 1 was used to start Windows 7 successfully:

```
HKLM\SYSTEM\ControlSet001
```

If you make driver or hardware changes and then find that the system won't start, you can tell Windows 7 to load using the control set that worked the last time. (That is, the control set that doesn't include your most recent hardware changes.) This is the *last known good configuration*, and the theory is that by using the previous working configuration, your system should start because it's bypassing the changes that caused the problem. Here's how to start Windows 7 using the last known good configuration:

1. Restart your computer.
2. At the Windows Boot Manager menu (refer to Chapter 4), press F8 to display the Advanced Boot Options menu.
3. Select the Last Known Good Configuration option.

Recovering Using System Restore

The Last Known Good Configuration option is most useful when your computer won't start and you suspect that a hardware change is causing the problem. You might think that you can also use the last known good configuration if Windows 7 starts but is unstable, and you suspect a hardware change is causing the glitch. Unfortunately, that won't work because when you start Windows 7 successfully in Normal mode, the hardware change is added to the last known good configuration. To revert the system to a previous configuration when you can start Windows 7 successfully, you need to use the System Restore feature.

I showed you how to use System Restore to set restore points in Chapter 7. Remember, too, that Windows 7 creates automatic restore points each day and when you perform certain actions (such as installing an uncertified device driver).

> ► **See** "Setting System Restore Points," **p. 149**.

To revert your system to a restore point, follow these steps:

1. Select Start, type **restore**, and then select System Restore in the search results. Windows 7 displays the System Restore dialog box.

2. The first System Restore dialog box (see Figure 21.10) offers two options:

   > ► **Recommended Restore**—Activate this option to restore Windows 7 to the restore point shown (which is usually the most recent restore point). Skip to step 5.

   > ► **Choose a Different Restore Point**—Activate this option to select from a list of restore points. Click Next and continue with step 3.

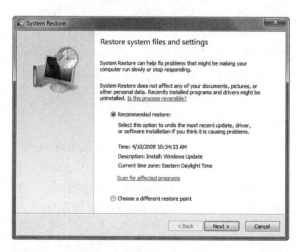

FIGURE 21.10   The initial System Restore window offers two restore options

3. If you don't see the restore point you want to use, click to activate the Show More Restore Points check box, which tells Windows 7 to display all the available restore points, as shown in Figure 21.11.

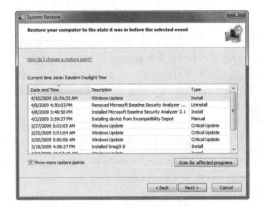

FIGURE 21.11   Use this dialog box to choose the restore point you want to revert to.

NOTE

By default, Windows 7 displays only the restore points from the previous 5 days. When you activate the Show More Restore Points check box, you tell Windows 7 to also show the restore points that are more than 5 days old.

4. Click the restore point you want to use. There are seven common types of restore points:

▶ **System**—A restore point that Windows 7 creates automatically. For example, the System Checkpoint is the restore point that Windows 7 creates each day or when you boot your computer.

▶ **Critical Update**—A restore point set prior to installing an important update.

▶ **Install**—A restore point set prior to installing a program or optional update.

▶ **Uninstall**—A restore point set prior to uninstalling a program or update.

▶ **Manual**—A restore point you create yourself.

▶ **Undo**—A restore point set prior to a previous use of System Restore to revert the system to an earlier state.

▶ **Unknown**—Any restore point that doesn't fit in the above categories.

5. Click Next. If other hard disks are available in the restore point, Windows 7 displays a list of the disks. Activate the check box beside each disk you want to include in the restore, and then click Next.

6. Click Finish. Windows 7 asks you to confirm that you want your system restored.

7. Click Yes. System Restore begins reverting to the restore point. When it's done, it restarts your computer and displays a message telling you the results of the restore.

8. Click Close.

TIP

System Restore is available in Safe mode. So, if Windows 7 won't start properly, and if using the last known good configuration doesn't work, perform a Safe mode startup and run System Restore from there. If you can't start Windows 7 at all, you can also run System Restore using the System Recovery Options, discussed in Chapter 23.

Troubleshooting Devices

Man is a shrewd inventor, and is ever taking the hint of a new machine from his own structure, adapting some secret of his own anatomy in iron, wood, and leather, to some required function in the work of the world.

—Ralph Waldo Emerson

Emerson's concept of a "machine" was decidedly low tech ("iron, wood, and leather"), but his basic idea is still apt in these high-tech times. Man has taken yet another "secret of his own anatomy" (the brain) and used it as the "hint of a new machine" (the computer). And although even the most advanced computer is still a mere toy compared to the breathtaking complexity of the human brain, some spectacular advancements have been made in the art of hardware in recent years.

One of the hats an operating system must wear is that of an intermediary between you and your hardware. Any OS worth its salt has to translate incomprehensible "devicespeak" into something you can make sense out of, and it must ensure that devices are ready, willing, and able to carry out your commands. Given the sophistication and diversity of today's hardware market, however, that's no easy task.

The good news is that Windows 7 brings to the PC world support for a broad range of hardware, from everyday devices such as keyboards, mice, printers, monitors, and video, sound, memory, and network cards, to more exotic hardware fare, such as multitouch input panels and the latest wireless standards. However, although this hardware support is broad, it's not all that deep, meaning that Windows 7 doesn't have built-in support for many older devices. So, even though lots of hardware vendors have taken at least some steps toward upgrading their devices and drivers, managing hardware is still one of Windows 7's trickier areas. This chapter should help as I take you through lots of practical techniques for installing, updating, and particularly troubleshooting devices in Windows 7.

Managing Your Hardware with Device Manager

Windows 7 stores all its hardware data in the Registry, but it provides Device Manager to give you a graphical view of the devices on your system. To display Device Manager, select Start, type **device**, and then click Device Manager in the search results.

TIP

To go directly to Device Manager without using the mouse, select Start, type **devmgmt.msc**, and press Enter.

Device Manager's default display is a tree-like outline that lists various hardware types. To see the specific devices, click the plus sign (+) to the left of a device type. For example, opening the Disk Drives branch displays all the hard drives, Flash drives, and memory card slots attached to your computer, as shown in Figure 22.1.

FIGURE 22.1   Device Manager organizes your computer's hardware in a tree-like hierarchy organized by hardware type.

Controlling the Device Display

Device Manager's default view is by hardware type, but it also offers several other views, all of which are available on the snap-in's View menu:

▶ **Devices by Connection**—This view displays devices according to what they are connected to within your computer. For example, to see which devices connect to the PCI bus, on most systems you'd open the ACPI branch, and then the Microsoft ACPI-Compliant System branch, and finally the PCI Bus branch.

▶ **Resources by Type**—This view displays devices according to the *hardware resources* they require. Your computer's resources are the communications channels by which devices communicate back and forth with software. There are four types: Interrupt Request (IRQ), Input/Output (IO), Direct Memory Access (DMA), and Memory (a portion of the computer's memory that's allocated to the device and is used to store device data).

▶ **Resources by Connection**—This view displays the computer's allocated resources according to how they're connected within the computer.

▶ **Show Hidden Devices**—When you activate this command, Device Manager displays those non–Plug and Play devices that you normally don't need to adjust or troubleshoot. It also displays *nonpresent devices*, which are those that have been installed but aren't currently attached to the computer. (However, see "Showing Nonpresent Devices in Device Manager" to be sure you're seeing all devices.)

Viewing Device Properties

Each device listed in Device Manager has its own properties sheet. You can use these properties not only to learn more about the device (such as the resources it's currently using), but also to make adjustments to the device's resources, change the device driver, alter the device's settings (if it has any), and make other changes.

To display the properties sheet for a device, double-click the device or click the device and then select Action, Properties. The number of tabs you see depends on the hardware, but most devices have at least the following:

▶ **General**—This tab gives you general information such as the name of the device, its hardware type, and the manufacturer's name. The Device Status group tells you whether the device is working properly, and gives you status information if it's not (see "Troubleshooting with Device Manager," later in this chapter).

▶ **Driver**—This tab gives you information about the device driver and offers several buttons to managing the driver. See "Working with Device Drivers."

▶ **Resources**—This tab tells you the hardware resources used by the device.

Showing Nonpresent Devices in Device Manager

I mentioned earlier that if you have any non-Plug and Play devices that you want to work with in Device Manager, you select View, Show Hidden Devices.

That works, but it doesn't mean that Device Manager is now showing all your devices. If you have any devices that you've installed in Windows, but that you regularly connect and then disconnect (such as a USB digital camera), Device Manager won't show them. (Windows describes such devices as *ghosted* devices.) That makes a bit of sense, because it might be confusing to see nonconnected hardware in Device Manager.

However, what if you're having a problem with a ghosted device? For example, suppose Windows hangs or crashes every time you connect such a device. Ideally, you'd like to use Device Manager to uninstall that device, but you can't because Windows goes belly-up whenever you connect the nasty thing. What do to?

The solution to this kind of problem is to force Device Manager to show ghosted devices. Here's how:

1. Select Start, type **command**, and then click Command Prompt. Windows 7 launches a new Command Prompt session.
2. Type the following command, and then press Enter:

   ```
   set devmgr_show_nonpresent_devices=1
   ```
3. Type the following command, and then press Enter to launch Device Manager:

   ```
   devmgmt.msc
   ```

NOTE

By setting the DEVMGR_SHOW_NONPRESENT_DEVICES environment variable in your Command Prompt session, you must launch Device Manager from that session. If you just launch Device Manager in the usual way, you won't see the ghosted devices.

---

4. In Device Manager, select View, Show Hidden Devices. Device Manager adds to the device list any ghosted devices that are installed on your PC.

Working with Device Drivers

For most users, device drivers exist in the nether regions of the PC world, shrouded in obscurity and the mysteries of assembly language programming. As the middlemen brokering the dialogue between Windows 7 and our hardware, however, these complex chunks of code perform a crucial task. After all, it's just not possible to unleash the full potential of your system unless the hardware and the operating system coexist harmoniously and optimally. To that end, you need to ensure that Windows 7 is using appropriate drivers for all your hardware. You do that by updating to the latest drivers and by rolling back drivers that aren't working properly.

Checking Windows Update for Drivers

Before getting to the driver tasks that Windows 7 offers, remember that if Windows 7 can't find drivers when you initially attach a device, it automatically checks Windows Update to see whether any drivers are available. If Windows 7 finds a driver, it installs the software automatically. In most cases, this is desirable behavior because it requires almost no input from you. However, lots of people don't like to use Windows on automatic pilot all the time because doing so can lead to problems. In this case, it could be that you've downloaded the driver you actually want to use from the manufacturer's website, so you don't want whatever is on Windows Update to be installed.

To gain control over Windows Update driver downloads, follow these steps:

1. Select Start, type **systempropertieshardware**, and then press Enter. Windows 7 opens the System Properties dialog box with the Hardware tab displayed.

2. Click Device Installation Settings. Windows 7 displays the Device Installation Settings dialog box.

3. Select the No, Let Me Choose What to Do option. Windows 7 displays the options shown in Figure 22.2.

FIGURE 22.2   Use the Device Installation Settings dialog box to control how Windows 7 uses Windows Update to locate and install device drivers.

4. You have three choices:

    ▶ **Always Install the Best Driver Software from Windows Update**—This is the default settings and it tells Windows 7 to go ahead and locate and install Windows Update drivers each time you attach a new device.

    ▶ **Install Driver Software from Windows Update If It Is Not Found On My Computer**—Activate this option to tell Windows 7 to only locate and install Windows Update drivers if it doesn't find a suitable driver on your system. If you want to control Windows Update driver installation, this is the ideal setting because it prevents those installs when a driver is available locally.

    ▶ **Never Install Driver Software from Windows Update**—Activate this option to tell Windows 7 to bypass Windows Update for all new devices. Use this option if you always use the manufacturer's device driver, whether it's on a disc that comes with the device or via the manufacturer's website.

5. Click Save Changes.

Updating a Device Driver

Follow these steps to update a device driver:

1. If you have a disc with the updated driver, insert it. If you downloaded the driver from the Internet, decompress the driver file, if necessary.

2. In Device Manager, click the device with which you want to work.

3. Select Action, Update Driver Software. (You can also click the Update Driver Software button in the toolbar or open the device's properties sheet, display the Driver tab, and click Update Driver.) The Update Driver Software Wizard appears.

4. You have two choices:

   ▸ **Search Automatically for Updated Driver Software**—Click this option to have Windows 7 check Windows Updates for the driver.

   ▸ **Browse My Computer for Driver Software**—Click this option if you have a local device driver, whether on a disc or in a downloaded file. In the dialog box that appears, click Browse, and then select the location of the device driver.

Rolling Back a Device Driver

If an updated device driver is giving you problems, you have two ways to fix things:

▸ If updating the driver was the last action you performed on the system, restore the system to most recent restore point.

▸ If you've updated other things on the system in the meantime, a restore point might restore more than you need. In that case, you need to roll back just the device driver that's causing problems.

Follow these steps to roll back a device driver:

1. In Device Manager, open the device's properties sheet.

2. Display the Driver tab.

3. Click Roll Back Driver.

Configuring Windows to Ignore Unsigned Device Drivers

Device drivers that meet the Designed for Windows 7 specifications have been tested for compatibility with Microsoft and are then given a digital signature. This signature tells you that the driver works properly with Windows and that it hasn't been changed since it was tested. (For example, the driver hasn't been infected by a virus or Trojan horse program.) When you're installing a device, if Windows 7 comes across a driver that has not been digitally signed, it displays a dialog box similar to the one shown in Figure 22.3.

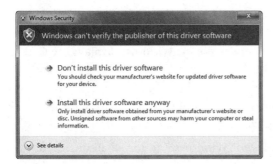

FIGURE 22.3   Windows 7 displays a dialog box similar to this one when it comes across a device driver that does not have a digital signature.

If you click Don't Install This Driver Software, Windows aborts the driver installation, and you won't be able to use the device. This is the most prudent choice in this situation because an unsigned driver can cause all kinds of havoc, including lock-ups, BSODs (blue screens of death), and other system instabilities. You should check the manufacturer's website for an updated driver that's compatible with your version of Windows, or you can upgrade to newer hardware that's supported by your version of Windows.

However, although not installing an unsigned driver is the *prudent* choice, it's not the most *convenient* choice because, in most cases, you probably want to use the device now rather than later. The truth is that *most* of the time these unsigned drivers cause no problems and work as advertised, so it's probably safe to continue with the installation. In any case, Windows always sets a restore point prior to the installation of an unsigned driver, so you can always restore your system to its previous state should anything go wrong.

NOTE

Test your system thoroughly after installing the driver: Use the device, open and use your most common applications, and run some disk utilities. If anything seems awry, roll back the driver, as described in the previous section. If that doesn't work, use the restore point to roll back the system to its previous configuration.

By default, Windows gives you the option of either continuing or aborting the installation of the unsigned driver. You can change this behavior to automatically accept or reject all unsigned drivers by following these steps:

1. In Windows 7, select Start, type `gpedit.msc`, and press Enter to launch the Local Group Policy Object Editor.

NOTE

If you're running a version of Windows 7 that doesn't come with the Group Policy Editor, I'll show you a bit later how to perform this tweak using the Registry.

2. Open the `User Configuration\Administrative Templates\System\Driver Installation` branch.

3. Double-click the Code Signing for Device Drivers policy. Windows displays the Code Signing for Device Drivers Properties dialog box.

4. Click Enable.

5. Use the When Windows Detects a Driver File Without a Digital Signature list to select one of the following items (see Figure 22.4):

   ▶ **Ignore**—Choose this option if you want Windows 7 to install all unsigned drivers.

   ▶ **Warn**—Choose this option if you want Windows 7 to warn you about an unsigned driver by displaying the dialog box shown earlier in Figure 22.3.

   ▶ **Block**—Choose this option if you do not want Windows 7 to install any unsigned drivers.

6. Click OK.

TIP

There are some device drivers that Windows 7 knows will cause system instabilities. Windows 7 will simply refuse to load these problematic drivers, no matter which action you choose in the Driver Signing Options dialog box. In this case, you'll see a dialog box similar to the one in Figure 22.3, except this one tells you that the driver will not be installed, and your only choice is to cancel the installation.

FIGURE 22.4　Enable the Code Signing for Device Drivers policy, and then choose what you want Windows 7 to do when it comes across an unsigned driver.

If your version of Windows 7 doesn't support the Local Group Policy Editor, follow these steps to set the driver signing options via the Registry:

1. Select Start, type **regedit**, press Enter, and then enter your User Account Control credentials. Windows 7 launches the Registry Editor.

2. Navigate to the following key:

   `HKCU\Software\Policies\Microsoft\`

3. If you don't see a `Windows NT` key, select Edit, New, Key, type **Windows NT**, and click OK.

4. Select Edit, New, Key, type **Driver Signing**, and click OK.

5. Select Edit, New, DWORD, type **BehaviorOnFailedVerify**, and click OK.

6. Double-click the `BehaviorOnFailedVerify` setting to open it for editing.

7. Type one of the following values:

   ▶ **1**—(Ignore) Use this value if you want Windows 7 to install all unsigned drivers.

   ▶ **2**—(Warn) Use this value if you want Windows 7 to warn you about an unsigned driver by displaying the dialog box shown earlier in Figure 22.3.

   ▶ **3**—(Block) Use this value if you do not want Windows 7 to install any unsigned drivers.

8. Click OK.

Writing a Complete List of Device Drivers to a Text File

There are times when you wish you had a list of all the drivers installed on your PC. For example, if your system crashes, it would be nice to have some kind of record of what drivers are in there. More likely, such a list would come in handy if you have to set up your PC from scratch and you want to know which drivers you have to update.

How do you get such a list? Oddly, Windows doesn't give you any straightforward way to do this. However, you can make your own list by using a script like the one shown in Listing 22.1.

NOTE

The file containing the script in Listing 22.1—WriteDeviceDrivers.vbs—is available from my website at http://mcfedries.com/Windows7Unleashed/. See Chapter 30, "Scripting Windows 7 with WSH," to learn how to run the script on your PC.

LISTING 22.1   Script That Writes a Complete List of a PC's Installed Device Drivers to a Text File

```
Option Explicit
Dim strComputer, objWMI, collDrivers, objDriver, intDrivers
Dim objFSO, strFolder, objFile
'
' Change the following value to the path of the folder
' where you want to store the text file
'
strFolder = "d:\backups\"
'
' Initialize the file system object
'
Set objFSO = CreateObject("Scripting.FileSystemObject")
'
' Create the text file
'
Set objFile = objFSO.CreateTextFile(strFolder & "drivers.txt", True)
'
' Get the WMI object
'
strComputer = "."
Set objWMI = GetObject("winmgmts:\\" & strComputer)
'
' Return the collection of device drivers on the computer
'
Set collDrivers = objWMI.ExecQuery _
    ("Select * from Win32_PnPSignedDriver")
'
' Run through each item in the collection
'
intDrivers = 0
For Each objDriver in collDrivers
    '
    ' Write the driver data to the text file
    '
    objFile.WriteLine(objDriver.DeviceName)
    objFile.WriteLine("=======================================")
    objFile.WriteLine("Device Class: " & objDriver.DeviceClass)
    objFile.WriteLine("Device Description: " & objDriver.Description)
    objFile.WriteLine("Device ID: " & objDriver.DeviceID)
    objFile.WriteLine("INF Filename: " & objDriver.InfName)
    objFile.WriteLine("Driver Provider: " & objDriver.DriverProviderName)
    objFile.WriteLine("Driver Version: " & objDriver.DriverVersion)
    objFile.WriteLine("Driver Date: " & ReturnDriverDate(objDriver.DriverDate))
```

```
        objFile.WriteLine("")
        intDrivers = intDrivers + 1
Next
'
' Close the text file
'
objFile.Close
WScript.Echo "Wrote " & intDrivers & " drivers to the text file."


'
' ReturnDriverDate()
' This function takes the driver datetime value and converts
' it to a friendlier date and time format
'
Function ReturnDriverDate(dDriverDate)
    Dim eventDay, eventMonth, eventYear
    Dim eventSecond, eventMinute, eventHour
    eventYear = Left(dDriverDate, 4)
    eventMonth = Mid(dDriverDate, 5, 2)
    eventDay = Mid(dDriverDate, 7, 2)
    eventHour = Mid(dDriverDate, 9, 2)
    eventMinute = Mid(dDriverDate, 11, 2)
    eventSecond = Mid(dDriverDate, 13, 2)
    ReturnDriverDate = DateSerial(eventYear, eventMonth, eventDay) & _
                " " & TimeSerial(eventHour, eventMinute, eventSecond)
End Function
```

The script uses VBScript's FileSystemObject to connect to the PC's file system. In this case, the script uses FileSystemObject to create a new text file in the folder specified by strFolder. The script then sets up the usual Windows Management Instrumentation (WMI) object, and then uses WMI to return the collection of installed device drivers. A For Each...Next loop goes through each device and writes various data to the text file, including the device name and description, and the driver version and date.

Uninstalling a Device

When you remove a Plug and Play device, the BIOS informs Windows 7 that the device is no longer present. Windows 7, in turn, updates its device list in the Registry, and the peripheral no longer appears in the Device Manager display.

If you're removing a legacy device, however, you need to tell Device Manager that the device no longer exists. To do that, follow these steps:

1. Click the device in the Device Manager tree.
2. Select Action, Uninstall. (Alternatively, click Uninstall in the toolbar or open the device's properties sheet, display the Driver tab, and click Uninstall.)
3. When Windows 7 warns you that you're about to remove the device, click OK.

Working with Device Security Policies

The Group Policy Editor offers several device-related policies. To see them, open the Group Policy Editor (select Start, type **gpedit.msc**, and press Enter) and select Local Computer Policy, Computer Configuration, Windows Settings, Security Settings, Local Policies, Security Options. Here are the policies in the Devices category:

▶ **Allow Undock Without Having to Log On**—When this policy is enabled, users can undock a notebook computer without having to log on to Windows 7. (That is, they can undock the computer by pressing the docking station's eject button.) If you want to restrict who can do this, disable this policy.

▶ **Allowed to Format and Eject Removable Media**—Use this policy to determine the groups allowed to format floppy disks and eject CDs and other removable media.

▶ **Prevent Users from Installing Printer Drivers**—Enable this policy to prevent users from installing a network printer. Note that this doesn't affect the installation of a local printer.

▶ **Restrict CD-ROM Access to Locally**—Enable this policy to prevent network users from operating the computer's CD-ROM or DVD drive at the same time as a local user. If no local user is accessing the drive, the network user can access it.

▶ **Restrict Floppy Access to Locally**—Enable this policy to prevent network users from operating the computer's floppy drive at the same time as a local user. If no local user is accessing the drive, the network user can access it.

Troubleshooting Device Problems

Windows 7 has excellent support for most newer devices, and most major hardware vendors have taken steps to update their devices and drivers to run properly with Windows 7. If you use only recent, Plug and Play–compliant devices that qualify for the Designed for Windows 7 logo, you should have a trouble-free computing experience (at least from a hardware perspective). Of course, putting *trouble-free* and *computing* next to each other is just asking for trouble. Hardware is not foolproof; far from it. Things still can, and will, go wrong, and, when they do, you'll need to perform some kind of troubleshooting. (Assuming, of course, that the device doesn't have a physical fault that requires a trip to the repair shop.) Fortunately, Windows 7 also has some handy tools to help you both identify and rectify hardware ills.

Troubleshooting with Device Manager

Device Manager not only provides you with a comprehensive summary of your system's hardware data, it also doubles as a decent troubleshooting tool. To see what I mean, check out the Device Manager tab shown in Figure 22.5. See how the icon for the Fingerprint Sensor device has an exclamation mark superimposed on it? This tells you that there's a problem with the device.

This device isn't functioning

FIGURE 22.5   The Device Manager uses icons to warn you there's a problem with a device.

If you examine the device's properties, as shown in Figure 22.6, the Device Status area tells you a bit more about what's wrong. As you can see in Figure 22.6, the problem here is that the device drivers aren't installed. Device Manager usually offers a suggested remedy (such as the Update Driver button shown in Figure 22.6).

Device Manager uses three different icons to give you an indication of the device's current status:

▶ A black exclamation mark (!) on a yellow field tells you that there's a problem with the device.

▶ A red *X* tells you that the device is disabled or missing.

▶ A blue *i* on a white field tells you that the device's Use Automatic Settings check box (on the Resources tab) is deactivated and that at least one of the device's resources was selected manually. Note that the device might be working just fine, so this icon doesn't indicate a problem. If the device isn't working properly, however, the manual setting might be the cause. (For example, the device might have a DIP switch or jumper set to a different resource.)

FIGURE 22.6   The Device Status area tells you if the device isn't working properly.

If your system flags a device, but you don't notice any problems, you can usually get away with just ignoring the flag. I've seen lots of systems that run perfectly well with flagged devices, so this falls under the "If it ain't broke..." school of troubleshooting. The danger here is that tweaking your system to try and get rid of the flag can cause other—usually more serious—problems.

Displaying a List of Nonworking Devices

Device Manager's icons (discussed in the previous section) are great, but it's not always convenient to fire up Device Manager to check for problems. To avoid that, use the script in Listing 22.2, which displays a list of all the problem devices on your system.

> **NOTE**
>
> The file containing the script in Listing 22.2—ListNonWorkingDevices.vbs—is avail-able from my website at http://mcfedries.com/Windows7Unleashed/. See Chapter 30 to learn how to run the script on your PC.

LISTING 22.2   Script That Displays a List of a PC's Nonworking Devices

```
Option Explicit
Dim strComputer, objWMI, collDevices, objDevice
Dim intDevices, strMessage
```

```
' Get the WMI object
'
strComputer = "."
Set objWMI = GetObject("winmgmts:\\" & _
            strComputer & "\root\cimv2")
'
' Return the collection of nonworking devices on the computer
'
Set collDevices = objWMI.ExecQuery _
    ("Select * from Win32_PnPEntity " _
        & "WHERE ConfigManagerErrorCode <> 0")
'
' Run through each item in the collection
'
intDevices = 0
strMessage = ""
For Each objDevice in collDevices
    strMessage = strMessage & "Device Name: " & objDevice.Name & vbCrLf
    strMessage = strMessage & "Manufacturer: " & objDevice.Manufacturer & vbCrLf
    strMessage = strMessage & "Device ID: " & objDevice.DeviceID & vbCrLf
    strMessage = strMessage & "Service: " & objDevice.Service & vbCrLf
    strMessage = strMessage & "Error Code: " & objDevice.ConfigManagerErrorCode &
➥vbCrLf
    strMessage = strMessage & vbCrLf & vbCrLf
    intDevices = intDevices + 1
Next
'
' Display the results
'
If intDevices = 0 Then
    WScript.Echo "No non-working devices found!"
Else
    WScript.Echo "Found " & intDevices & " non-working device(s):" & _
                vbCrLf & vbCrLf & _
                strMessage
End If
```

The script sets up the WMI object and then uses WMI to return the collection of nonworking devices (that is, where the device's ConfigManagerErrorCode property isn't 0). A For Each...Next loop goes through each device and stores various data about the device to a string variable, including the device name and ID, and the error code. The script then displays the results, and Figure 22.7 shows an example.

FIGURE 22.7   Sample output from the script in Listing 22.2.

Table 22.1 lists the various error codes and what they mean.

TABLE 22.1   Error Codes for Nonworking Devices

Code	Description
0	Device is working properly.
1	Device is not configured correctly.
2	Windows cannot load the driver for this device.
3	Driver for this device might be corrupted, or the system may be low on memory or other resources.
4	Device is not working properly. One of its drivers or the Registry might be corrupted.
5	Driver for the device requires a resource that Windows cannot manage.
6	Boot configuration for the device conflicts with other devices.
7	Cannot filter.
8	Driver loader for the device is missing.
9	Device is not working properly. The controlling firmware is incorrectly reporting the resources for the device.
10	Device cannot start.
11	Device failed.
12	Device cannot find enough free resources to use.
13	Windows cannot verify the device's resources.
14	Device cannot work properly until the computer is restarted.
15	Device is not working properly because of a possible reenumeration problem.
16	Windows cannot identify all the resources that the device uses.

TABLE 22.1   Continued

Code	Description
17	Device is requesting an unknown resource type.
18	Device drivers must be reinstalled.
19	Failure using the Vloader.
20	Registry might be corrupted.
21	System failure. If changing the device driver is ineffective, see the hardware documentation. Windows is removing the device.
22	Device is disabled.
23	System failure. If changing the device driver is ineffective, see the hardware documentation.
24	Device is not present, not working properly, or does not have all its drivers installed.
25	Windows is still setting up the device, but the installation is incomplete.
26	Windows is still setting up the device, but not all the devices drivers were installed or there's a problem with one of the device drivers.
27	Device does not have valid log configuration.
28	Device drivers are not installed.
29	Device is disabled. The device firmware did not provide the required resources.
30	Device is using an IRQ resource that another device is using.
31	Device is not working properly. Windows cannot load the required device drivers.

Troubleshooting Device Driver Problems

Other than problems with the hardware itself, device drivers are the cause of most device woes. This is true even if your device doesn't have one of the problem icons that I mentioned in the previous section. That is, if you open the device's properties sheet, Windows 7 may tell you that the device is "working properly," but all that means is that Windows 7 can establish a simple communications channel with the device. So if your device isn't working right, but Windows 7 says otherwise, suspect a driver problem. Here are a few tips and pointers for correcting device driver problems:

▶ **Reinstall the driver**—A driver might be malfunctioning because one or more of its files have become corrupted. You can usually solve this by reinstalling the driver. Just in case a disk fault caused the corruption, you should check the partition where the driver is installed for errors before reinstalling. (In Chapter 7, "Maintaining Your Windows 7 System," see the "Checking Your Hard Disk for Errors" section for instructions on checking a disk for errors.)

▶ **Upgrade to a signed driver**—Unsigned drivers are accidents waiting for a place to happen in Windows 7, so you should upgrade to a signed driver, if possible. How can you tell whether an installed driver is unsigned? Open the device's properties sheet, and display the Driver tab. Signed driver files display a name beside the Digital Signer label, whereas unsigned drivers display Not digitally signed instead. Refer to "Updating a Device Driver," earlier in this chapter.

▶ **Disable an unsigned driver**—If an unsigned driver is causing system instability and you can't upgrade the driver, try disabling it. In the Driver tab of the device's properties sheet, click Disable.

▶ **Use the Signature Verification Tool**—This program checks your entire system for unsigned drivers. To use it, select Start, type **sigverif**, and press Enter. In the File Signature Verification window, click Start. When the verification is complete, the program displays a list of the unsigned driver files (if any). The results for all the scanned files are written to the log file **Sigverif.txt**, which is copied to the %SystemRoot% folder when you close the window that shows the list of unsigned drivers. In the Status column of Sigverif.txt, look for files listed as Not Signed. If you find any, consider upgrading these drivers to signed versions.

▶ **Try the manufacturer's driver supplied with the device**—If the device came with its own driver, try either updating the driver to the manufacturer's or running the device's setup program.

▶ **Download the latest driver from the manufacturer**—Device manufacturers often update drivers to fix bugs, add new features, and tweak performance. Go to the manufacturer's website to see whether an updated driver is available. (See "Tips for Downloading Device Drivers," next.)

▶ **Try Windows Update**—The Windows Update website often has updated drivers for downloading. Select Start, All Programs, Windows Update and let the site scan your system. Then click the Driver Updates link to see which drivers are available for your system.

▶ **Roll back a driver**—If the device stops working properly after you update the driver, try rolling it back to the old driver. (Refer to "Rolling Back a Device Driver," earlier in this chapter.)

Tips for Downloading Device Drivers

Finding device drivers on the World Wide Web is an art in itself. I can't tell you how much of my life I've wasted rooting around manufacturer websites trying to locate a device driver. Most hardware vendor sites seem to be optimized for sales rather than service, so although you can purchase, say, a new printer with just a mouse click or two, downloading a new driver for that printer can take a frustratingly long time. To help you avoid such frustration, here are some tips from my hard-won experience:

► If the manufacturer offers different sites for different locations (such as different countries), always use the company's "home" site. Most mirror sites aren't true mirrors, and (Murphy's law still being in effect) it's usually the driver you're looking for that a mirror site is missing.

► The temptation when you first enter a site is to use the search feature to find what you want. This works only sporadically for drivers, and the site search engines almost always return marketing or sales material first.

► Instead of the search engine, look for an area of the site dedicated to driver downloads. The good sites will have links to areas called Downloads or Drivers, but it's far more common to have to go through a Support or Customer Service area first.

► Don't try to take any shortcuts to where you *think* the driver might be hiding. Trudge through each step the site provides. For example, it's common to have to select an overall driver category, and then a device category, and then a line category, and then the specific model you have. This is tedious, but it almost always gets you where you want to go.

► If the site is particularly ornery, the preceding method might not lead you to your device. In that case, try the search engine. Note that device drivers seem to be particularly poorly indexed, so you might have to try lots of search text variations. One thing that usually works is searching for the exact filename. How can you possibly know that? A method that often works for me is to use Google (www.google.com) or Google Groups (groups.google.com) or some other web search engine to search for your driver. Chances are someone else has looked for your file and will have the filename (or, if you're really lucky, a direct link to the driver on the manufacturer's site).

► When you get to the device's download page, be careful which file you choose. Make sure that it's a Windows 7 driver, and make sure that you're not downloading a utility program or some other nondriver file.

► When you finally get to download the file, be sure to save it to your computer rather than opening it. If you reformat your system or move the device to another computer, you'll be glad you have a local copy of the driver so that you don't have to wrestle with the whole download rigmarole all over again.

Troubleshooting Resource Conflicts

On modern computer systems that support the Advanced Configuration and Power Interface (ACPI), use PCI cards, and external Plug and Play–compliant devices, resource conflicts have become almost nonexistent. That's because the ACPI is capable of managing the system's resources to avoid conflicts. For example, if a system doesn't have enough IRQ lines, ACPI will assign two or more devices to the same IRQ line and manage the devices so that they can share the line without conflicting with each other. (To see which devices share an IRQ line, activate Device Manager's View, Resources by Connection command, and then double-click the Interrupt Request (IRQ) item.)

ACPI's success at allocating and managing resources is such that Windows 7 doesn't allow you to change a device's resources, even if you'd want to do such a thing. If you open a device's properties sheet and display the Resources tab, you'll see that none of the settings can be changed.

If you use legacy devices in your system, however, conflicts could arise because Windows 7 is unable to manage the device's resources properly. If that happens, Device Manager will let you know there's a problem. To solve it, first display the Resources tab on the device's properties sheet. The Resource Settings list shows you the resource type on the left and the resource setting on the right. If you suspect that the device has a resource conflict, check the Conflicting Device List box to see whether it lists any devices. If the list displays only No conflicts, the device's resources aren't conflicting with another device.

If there is a conflict, you need to change the appropriate resource. Some devices have multiple configurations, so one easy way to change resources is to select a different configuration. To try this, deactivate the Use Automatic Settings check box, and then use the Setting Based On drop-down list to select a different configuration. Otherwise, you need to play around with the resource settings by hand. Here are the steps to follow to change a resource setting:

1. In the Resource Type list, select the resource you want to change.

2. Deactivate the Use Automatic Settings check box, if it's activated.

3. For the setting you want to change, either double-click it or select it and then click the Change Setting button. (If Windows 7 tells you that you can't modify the resources in this configuration, select a different configuration from the Setting Based On list.) A dialog box appears that enables you to edit the resource setting.

4. Use the Value spin box to select a different resource. Watch the Conflict Information group to make sure that your new setting doesn't step on the toes of an existing setting.

5. Click OK to return to the Resources tab.

6. Click OK. If Windows 7 asks whether you want to restart your computer, click Yes.

TIP

An easy way to see which devices are either sharing resources or are conflicting is via the System Information utility. Select Start, type **msinfo32**, and press Enter. Open the Hardware Resources branch, and then click Conflicts/Sharing.

CHAPTER 23

Troubleshooting Startup

Never let a computer know you're in a hurry.

—Anonymous

Computers are often frustrating beasts, but few things in computerdom are as maddening as a computer that won't compute, or an operating system that won't operate. After all, if your PC won't even start Windows, then Windows can't start any programs, which means *you* can't get any work done.

What you've got on your hands is a rather expensive boat anchor, not to mention a hair-pullingly, teeth-gnashingly frustrating problem that you have to fix *now*. To help save some wear and tear on your hair and teeth, this chapter outlines a few common startup difficulties and their solutions.

First Things First: Some Things to Try Before Anything Else

Startup problems generally are either trivially easy to fix or are take-it-to-the-repair-shop difficult to solve. Fortunately, startup conundrums often fall into the former camp, and in many cases, one of the following solutions will get your PC back on its electronic feet:

▶ Some boot problems mercifully fall into the Temporary Glitch category of startup woes. That is, it could be that your PC has just gone momentarily and temporarily haywire. To find out, shut down the computer and leave it turned off for at least 30 seconds to give everything time to spin down and catch its breath. Turn your PC back on and cross whatever parts of your body you think might help.

▶ There may be a setting in your computer's BIOS options that's preventing a normal startup. For example, I once had a PC that wouldn't boot no matter what I did. When I decided to check the BIOS, I found that the hard drive wasn't listed as a boot device! When I configured the BIOS to boot from the hard drive, all was well. Restart your PC, and then press whatever key or key combination your BIOS requires to access the settings (usually the Delete key or a function key such as F2). If you don't see anything obvious (such as misconfigured boot options), try resetting all the options to the default state.

▶ Every now and then, a defective device will interfere with the boot process. To ensure that this isn't the case, disconnect every device that's disconnectable and then try booting your newly naked PC. If you get a successful launch, one of the devices was almost certainly the culprit. Attach the devices one by one and try rebooting each time until you find out which one is causing the boot failure. You could then reboot without the device, upgrade the device driver, and try again. If that still doesn't work, the device is probably defective and so should be repaired or replaced.

▶ If you get no power when you flick your PC's On switch, it's likely you've either got a defective power supply on your hands or one or more of the power supply connections have come loose. Check the connections or, if they're fine, replace the power supply.

NOTE

See my book *Build It. Fix It. Own It. A Beginner's Guide to Building and Upgrading a PC* for more info on PC power supplies and connections: http://mcfedries.com/cs/content/BuildItFixItOwnIt.aspx.

▶ Another useful startup solution is to boot your PC using the last known good configuration startup option, which I discussed in Chapter 21, "Troubleshooting and Recovering from Problems."

  ▶ **See** "Booting Using the Last Known Good Configuration," **p. 456**.

When to Use the Various Advanced Startup Options

You saw in Chapter 4, "Customizing Startup and Shutdown," that Windows 7 has some useful options on its Advanced Options menu. But under what circumstances should you use each option? Because there is some overlap in what each option brings to the table, there are no hard-and-fast rules. It is possible, however, to lay down some general guidelines.

Safe Mode

You should use the Safe mode option if one of the following conditions occurs:

- ▶ Windows 7 doesn't start after the POST ends.
- ▶ Windows 7 seems to stall for an extended period.
- ▶ You can't print to a local printer.
- ▶ Your video display is distorted and possibly unreadable.
- ▶ Your computer stalls repeatedly.
- ▶ Your computer suddenly slows down and doesn't return to normal without a reboot.
- ▶ You need to test an intermittent error condition.

Safe Mode with Networking

You should use the Safe Mode with Networking option if one of the following situations occurs:

- ▶ Windows 7 fails to start using any of the other Safe mode options.
- ▶ The drivers or programs you need to repair a problem exist on a shared network resource.
- ▶ You need access to email or other network-based communications for technical support.
- ▶ You need to access the Internet via a network gateway device to download device drivers or Windows 7 an online tech support site.
- ▶ Your computer is running a shared Windows 7 installation.

Safe Mode with Command Prompt

You should use the Safe Mode with Command Prompt option if one of the following situations occurs:

- ▶ Windows 7 fails to start using any of the other Safe mode options.
- ▶ The programs you need to repair a problem must be run from the Command Prompt.
- ▶ You can't load the Windows 7 GUI.

Enable Boot Logging

You should use the Enable Boot Logging option in the following situations:

- ▶ The Windows 7 startup hangs after switching to protected mode.
- ▶ You need a detailed record of the startup process.
- ▶ You suspect (after using one of the other Startup menu options) that a protected-mode driver is causing Windows 7 startup to fail.

After starting (or attempting to start) Windows 7 with this option, you end up with a file named `ntbtlog.txt` in the `%SystemRoot%` folder. This is a text file, so you can examine it with any text editor. For example, you could boot to the Command Prompt (using the Safe Mode with Command Prompt option) and then use Notepad to examine the file. Move to the end of the file and you might see a message telling you which device driver failed. You probably need to reinstall or roll back the driver.

Enable Low-Resolution Video (640×480)

You should use the Enable VGA Mode option in the following situations:

▶ Windows 7 fails to start using any of the Safe mode options.

▶ You recently installed a new video card device driver, and the screen is garbled or the driver is balking at a resolution or color depth setting that's too high.

▶ You can't load the Windows 7 GUI.

After Windows 7 has loaded, you can either reinstall or roll back the driver, or you can adjust the display settings to values that the driver can handle.

Last Known Good Configuration

Use the Last Known Good Configuration option under the following circumstances:

▶ You suspect the problem is hardware related, but you can't figure out the driver that's causing the problem.

▶ You don't have time to try out the other more detailed inspections.

Directory Services Restore Mode

The Directory Services Restore Mode option is only for domain controllers, so you should never need to use it.

Debugging Mode

Use the Debugging Mode option if you receive a stop error during startup and a remote technical support professional has asked you to send debugging data.

Disable Automatic Restart on System Failure

The Disable Automatic Restart on System Failure option prevents Windows 7 from restarting automatically when the system crashes. Choose this option if you want to prevent your system from restarting so that you can read an error message or deduce other information that can help you troubleshoot the problem.

Disable Driver Signature Enforcement

Use the Disable Driver Signature Enforcement option, which prevents Windows 7 from checking whether devices drivers have digital signatures, to ensure that Windows 7 loads an unsigned driver. It's possible that failing to load that driver is causing system problems.

What to Do If Windows 7 Won't Start in Safe Mode

If Windows 7 is so intractable that it won't even start in Safe mode, your system is likely afflicted with one of the following problems:

▶ Your system is infected with a virus. You need to run an antivirus program to cleanse your system.

▶ Your system has incorrect BIOS settings. Run the machine's BIOS setup program to see whether any of these settings needs to be changed or whether the CMOS battery needs to be replaced.

▶ Your system has a hardware conflict. See Chapter 22, "Troubleshooting Devices," for hardware troubleshooting procedures.

▶ There is a problem with a SCSI device. In this case, your system might hang during the SCSI BIOS initialization process. Try removing devices from the SCSI chain until your system starts normally.

Recovering Using the System Recovery Options

If Windows 7 won't start normally, your first troubleshooting step is almost always to start the system in Safe mode. When you make it to Windows 7, you can investigate the problem and make the necessary changes (such as disabling or rolling back a device driver). But what if your system won't even start in Safe mode?

Your next step should be booting with the last known good configuration. And if that doesn't work either? Don't worry, there's still hope in the form of the System Recovery Options, a utility that enables you to launch recovery tools or access the command line.

Here's how to use it:

1. Restart your computer.
2. At the Windows Boot Manager menu (refer to Chapter 4), press F8 to display the Advanced Boot Options menu.
3. Select the Repair Your Computer option. System Recovery Options prompts you to select a keyboard input method.
4. Click Next. System Recovery Options prompts you to log on to your computer.
5. Select the username and type a password for an Administrator account on your computer, and then click OK. The System Recovery Options window appears, as shown in Figure 23.1.

FIGURE 23.1   The System Recovery Options window offers several tools to help you get your system back on its feet.

The System Recovery Options window offers you the following five tools to help get your system back up and running:

▶ **Startup Repair**—This tool checks your system for problems that might be preventing it from starting. If it finds any, it attempts to fix them automatically.

▶ **System Restore**—This tool runs System Restore so that you can revert your system to a protection point (refer to "Recovering Using System Restore," earlier in this chapter).

▶ **System Image Recovery**—This tool restores your system using a system image backup, which you learned how to create in Chapter 7, "Maintaining Your Windows 7 System."

  ▶ **See** "Creating a System Image Backup," **p. 157**.

▶ **Windows Memory Diagnostic**—This tool checks your computer's memory chips for faults, as described earlier (see "Running the Memory Diagnostics Tool").

▶ **Command Prompt**—This tool takes you to the Windows 7 Command Prompt, where you can run commands such as CHKDSK. (See Chapter 13, "Controlling Windows 7 from the Command Line.")

All of this assumes that you can boot to your PC's hard drive. If that's not possible, you can still use the system recovery tools by booting to your Windows 7 DVD. Here's how it works:

1. Insert the Windows 7 DVD.

2. Restart your computer.

3. If your system prompts you to boot from the DVD, press the required key or key combination.

> **TIP**
>
> If your system won't boot from the Windows 7 DVD, you need to adjust the system's BIOS settings to allow this. Restart the computer and look for a startup message that prompts you to press a key or key combination to modify the BIOS settings (which might be called *Setup* or something similar). Find the boot options and either enable a DVD drive-based boot or make sure that the option to boot from the DVD drive comes before the option to boot from the hard disk. If you use a USB keyboard, you may also need to enable an option that lets the BIOS recognize keystrokes after the POST but before the OS starts.

4. In the initial Install Windows screen, click Next.

5. Click the Repair Your Computer link. System Recovery Options prompts you to select your operating system.

6. Click your Windows 7 operating system and click Next. System Recovery Options runs through the various tools, beginning with Startup Repair.

Troubleshooting Startup Using the System Configuration Utility

If Windows 7 won't start, troubleshooting the problem usually involves trying various advanced startup options. It's almost always a time-consuming and tedious business.

However, what if Windows 7 *will* start, but you encounter problems along the way? Or what if you want to try a few different configurations to see whether you can eliminate startup items or improve Windows 7's overall performance? For these scenarios, don't bother trying out different startup configurations by hand. Instead, take advantage of Windows 7's System Configuration utility, which, as you saw earlier in this book (Chapter 4), gives you a graphical front-end that offers precise control over how Windows 7 starts.

▶ See "Using the System Configuration Utility to Modify the BCD," **p. 66**.

Launch the System Configuration utility (select Start, type **msconfig**, and press Enter) and display the General tab, which has three startup options:

▶ **Normal Startup**—This option loads Windows 7 normally.

▶ **Diagnostic Startup**—This option loads only those device drivers and system services that are necessary for Windows 7 to boot. This is equivalent to deactivating all the check boxes associated with the Selective Startup option, discussed next.

▶ **Selective Startup**—When you activate this option, the following check boxes become available (see Figure 23.2): Load System Services, Load Startup Items, and Use Original Boot Configuration. I talk about this in more detail, but you use these check boxes to select which portions of the startup should be processed.

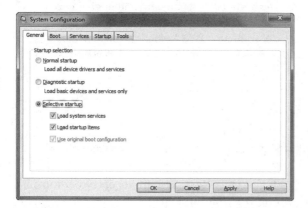

FIGURE 23.2   Use the System Configuration utility's General tab to troubleshoot the Windows 7 startup.

For a selective startup, you control how Windows 7 processes items using the following two categories (the Use Original Boot Configuration option is selected by default and can't be turned off):

▶ **Load System Services**—This category refers to the system services that Windows 7 loads at startup. The specific services loaded by Windows 7 are listed in the Services tab.

NOTE

A service is a program or process that performs a specific, low-level support function for the operating system or for an installed program. For example, Windows 7's Automatic Updates feature is a service. See Chapter 11, "Controlling Services," for more information.

▶ **Load Startup Items**—This category refers to the items in your Windows 7 Startup group and to the startup items listed in the Registry. For the latter, the settings are stored in one of the following keys:

```
HKEY_CURRENT_USER\SOFTWARE\Microsoft\Windows\CurrentVersion\Run
HKEY_LOCAL_MACHINE\SOFTWARE\Microsoft\Windows\CurrentVersion\Run
```

The specific items loaded from the Startup group or the Registry are listed in the Startup tab.

To control these startup items, the System Configuration utility gives you two choices:

▶ To prevent Windows 7 from loading every item in a particular category, activate Selective Startup in the General tab, and then deactivate the check box for the category you want. For example, to disable all the items in the Startup tab, deactivate the Load Startup Items check box.

▶ To prevent Windows 7 from loading only specific items in a category, display the category's tab, and then deactivate the check box beside the item or items you want to bypass at startup.

Here's a basic procedure you can follow to use the System Configuration utility to troubleshoot a startup problem (assuming that you can start Windows 7 by using some kind of Safe mode boot, as described earlier):

1. In the System Configuration utility, activate the Diagnostic Startup option, and then reboot the computer. If the problem did not occur during the restart, you know the cause lies in the system services or the startup items.

2. In the System Configuration utility, activate the Selective Startup option.

3. Activate Load System Services, deactivate Load Startup Items, and then reboot the computer.

4. Deactivate Load System Services, activate Load Startup Items, and then reboot the computer.

5. The problem will reoccur either during the step 3 reboot or the step 4 reboot. When this happens, you know that whatever item you activated before rebooting is the source of the problem. Display the tab of the item that is causing the problem. For example, if the problem reoccurred after you activated the Load Startup Items check box, display the Startup tab.

6. Click Disable All to clear all the check boxes.

7. Activate one of the check boxes to enable an item and then reboot the computer.

8. Repeat step 7 for each of the other check boxes until the problem reoccurs. When this happens, you know that whatever item you activated just before rebooting is the source of the problem.

Troubleshooting by Halves

If you have a large number of check boxes to test (such as in the Services tab), activating one check box at a time and rebooting can become very tedious very fast. A faster method is to begin by activating the first half of the check boxes and reboot. One of two things will happen:

▶ **The problem doesn't reoccur**—This means that one of the items represented by the deactivated check boxes is the culprit. Clear all the check boxes, activate half of the other check boxes, and then reboot.

▶ **The problem reoccurs**—This means that one of the activated check boxes is the problem. Activate only half of those check boxes and reboot.

Keep halving the number of activated check boxes until you isolate the offending item.

9. In the System Configuration utility's General tab, activate the Normal Startup option.

10. Fix or work around the problem:

   ▶ If the problem is a system service, you can disable the service. Select Start, Control Panel, click System and Security, Administrative Tools, Services. Double-click the problematic service to open its property sheet. In the Startup Type list, select Disabled, and then click OK.

   ▶ If the problem is a Startup item, either delete the item from the Startup group or delete the item from the appropriate Run key in the Registry. If the item is a program, consider uninstalling or reinstalling the program.

CHAPTER 24

Troubleshooting Networking

The greater the difficulty, the greater the glory.

—Cicero

As you've probably surmised through hard-won experience, networking can be a complex, arcane topic that taxes the patience of all but the most dedicated wireheads (an affectionate pet name often applied to network hackers and gurus). There are so many hardware components to deal with (from the network adapter to the cable to the switch to the router) and so many layers of software (from the device drivers to the protocols to the redirectors to the network providers) that networks often seem like accidents looking for a place to happen.

If your network has become a "notwork" (some wags also refer to a downed network as a *nyetwork*), this chapter offers a few solutions that might help. I don't make any claim to completeness here, however; after all, most network ills are a combination of several factors and therefore are relatively obscure and difficult to reproduce. Instead, I just go through a few general strategies for tracking down problems and pose solutions for some of the most common network afflictions.

Repairing a Network Connection

If you came to Windows 7 from Windows XP, you may have come across the latter's network repair tool that did an okay job of repairing connectivity problems because most networking problems can be resolved by running the repair tool's basic tasks: disconnecting, renewing the Dynamic Host Control Protocol (DHCP) lease, flushing various network caches, and then reconnecting.

Unfortunately, the repair tool would all too often report that it couldn't fix the problem, which usually meant that the trouble existed at a level deeper in the network stack than the repair tool could go. In an attempt to handle these more challenging connectivity issues, Windows 7 comes with a Network Diagnostics tool (borrowed from Windows Vista) that digs deep into all layers of the network stack to try to identify and resolve problems. Windows 7 gives you several methods of launching the Network Diagnostic tool:

▶ Right-click the notification area's Network icon, and then click Troubleshoot Problems.

▶ In the Network and Sharing Center, click the Troubleshoot Problems link.

▶ In the Network Connections window, click the broken connection, and then click Diagnose This Connection.

> **NOTE**
>
> To open the Network Connections window, select Start, type **connections,** and then click View Network Connections.

When you launch the diagnostics, Windows 7 invokes the new Network Diagnostics Framework (NDF), a collection of tools, technologies, algorithms, programming interfaces, services, and troubleshooters. The NDF passes the specifics of the problem to the Network Diagnostics Engine (NDE), which then generates a list of possible causes. For each potential cause, the NDE launches a specific troubleshooter, which determines whether the aspect of networking covered by the troubleshooter could be creating the problem. For example, there are troubleshooters related to wireless connectivity, Transport Control Protocol (TCP) connections, address acquisition, and many more. In the end, the troubleshooters end up creating a list of possible solutions to the problem. If only one solution can be performed automatically, the NDE attempts the solution. If there are multiple solutions (or a single solution that requires user input), you see a Windows Network Diagnostics dialog box similar to the one shown in Figure 24.1. Click the solution or follow the instructions that appear.

FIGURE 24.1   An example of a Windows Network Diagnostics dialog box.

Checking the Connection Status

The first thing you should check when you suspect a network problem is Windows 7's Network icon. There are four states:

▶ **Wired connection with Internet access**—This state (see Figure 24.2) means that you have access to both the network and to the Internet via a wired network connection.

FIGURE 24.2   The Network icon for a wired connection with Internet access.

▶ **Wireless connection with Internet access**—This state (see Figure 24.3) means that you have access to both the network and to the Internet via a wireless network connection.

FIGURE 24.3   The Network icon for a wireless connection with Internet access.

▶ **Connected, but with an error**—This state (see Figure 24.4) means that you have access to the network, but either your computer cannot access the Internet, or you have limited access to the network.

FIGURE 24.4   The Network icon for a connection that has either no Internet access or limited network access.

▶ **Not connected**—This state (see Figure 24.5) means that you are completely cut off from the network.

FIGURE 24.5   The Network icon for a broken network connection.

24

Remember, too, that the Network and Sharing Center (click the Network icon and then click Open Network and Sharing Center) also shows the connection status graphically. For example, you can see in Figure 24.6 that when you have a network connection but no Internet access, the Network and Sharing Center displays a red X on the Internet part of the network map.

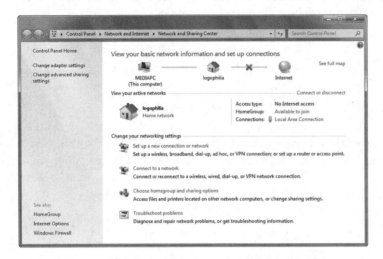

FIGURE 24.6   The network map for a network connection without Internet access.

General Solutions to Network Problems

Figuring out that a problem exists is one thing, but it's often quite another to come up with a fix for the problem. I discuss a few solutions in later sections, but here are a few other general fixes you need to keep in mind:

▶ **Enable network discovery**—If you can't access your network, by far the most common cause is that you have Windows 7's network discovery feature turned off. Make sure network discovery is turned on, as described later in this chapter (see "Turning On Network Discovery").

▶ **Close all programs**—You can often fix flaky behavior by shutting down all your open programs and starting again. This is a particularly useful fix for problems caused by low memory or low system resources.

▶ **Log off Windows 7**—Logging off clears the RAM and so gives you a slightly cleaner slate than merely closing all your programs.

▶ **Reboot the computer**—If there are problems with some system files and devices, logging off won't help because these objects remain loaded. By rebooting the system, you reload the entire system which is often enough to solve many computer problems.

▶ **Turn off the computer and restart**—You can often solve a hardware problem by first shutting your machine off. Wait for 30 seconds to give all devices time to spin down, and then restart. This is called *power cycling* the computer.

▶ **Power cycle the router**—If you're getting a network error or you can't access the Internet, the router may be at fault. Power off the router and then power it on again. Wait until the status lights stabilize and then try accessing the network.

▶ **Power cycle the modem**—If you can't get Internet access, it could be a problem with your broadband modem. Power off the modem, and then power it on again. Wait until the status lights stabilize and then try accessing the Internet.

▶ **Check connections, power switches, and so on**—Some of the most common (and some of the most embarrassing) causes of hardware problems are the simple physical things. So, you want to make sure that a device (for example, your router) is turned on, check that cable connections (particularly between the NIC and router) are secure, and ensure that insertable devices (such as a USB or PC Card NIC) are properly inserted.

▶ **Check for solutions to your problem**—Click the Action Center icon in the notification area, and then click Open Action Center. In the list of problems, check to see if your problem is listed and whether a solution exists.

▶ **Revert to a working configuration**—If you could access the network properly in the past, you may be able to solve the problem by reverting your system to that working state, as described in Chapter 21, "Troubleshooting and Recovering from Problems."

> ▶ **See** "Recovering from a Problem," **p. 456**.

▶ **Upgrade the router's firmware**—Some network problems are caused by router bugs. If the manufacturer has corrected these bugs, the fixes will appear in the latest version of the router firmware, so you should upgrade to the new version, as described later in this chapter (see "Updating the Router Firmware").

▶ **Reset the router**—Network problems may result if you misconfigure your router or if the router's internal settings become corrupted somehow. Almost all routers come with a reset feature that enables you to return the router to its factory settings. Ideally, the device comes with a Reset button that you can push; otherwise, you need access to the router's setup pages.

Turning On Network Discovery

Networking your computers is all about access. You may want to access another computer to view one of its files or use its printer, and you may want other computers to access your machine to play your digital media. In Windows 7, however, this access is not always automatic. Windows 7 comes with a feature called *network discovery* that, when turned on, means you can see (discover) the other computers on your network and that the other computers can see (discover) yours. In networking, it's generally true that if you can see something, you can access it. (I say that this is *generally* true because there may be security issues that prevent or restrict access to a computer.)

Whether you have discovery turned on for a network depends on the type of network you're connected to:

► In a private network such as the one in your home or office, you want to see other computers and have them see you, so network discovery should be turned on.

► In a public network, such as a wireless hot spot, network discovery should be turned off because you probably don't want other users in the coffee shop (or wherever) to see your computer.

These aren't hard-and-fast rules, however, and there might be times when you need to flaunt these rules. For example, there might be one computer on your home or office network that you don't want others to see because, for instance, it contains sensitive information. In this case, it makes sense to turn off network discovery for that computer. Similarly, you and a friend might want to see each other's computers in a public setting so that you can perform a quick file exchange. In such a scenario, you can turn on network discovery, if only temporarily.

Here are the steps to follow to change the current network discovery setting:

1. Click the taskbar's Network icon, and then click Open Network and Sharing Center. Windows 7 displays the Network and Sharing Center.

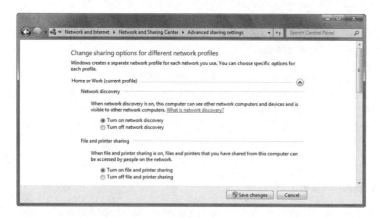

FIGURE 24.7   In the Advanced Sharing Settings window, open the Home or Work section.

2. Click the Change Advanced Sharing Settings link. The Advanced Sharing Settings window appears.

3. Open the Home or Work section, as shown in Figure 24.7.

4. Click either Turn On Network Discovery (which works only while you're connected to a network) or Turn Off Network Discovery.

5. Open the Public section.

6. Click either Turn On Network Discovery or Turn Off Network Discovery.

7. Click Save Changes to put the new settings into effect.

If you have network discovery turned off and you open the Network folder (in any Windows Explorer window, click Network in the Navigation pane), Windows 7 displays an

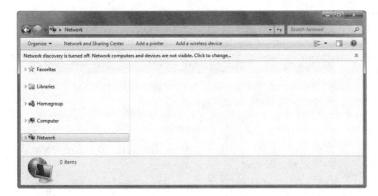

FIGURE 24.8   The Network window displays an information bar warning if network discovery is turned off.

information bar message warning you that network discovery is turned off (see Figure 24.8), which is why you don't see any icons in the window. If you want to turn network discovery on, click the information bar and then click Turn On Network Discovery and File Sharing.

Updating the Router Firmware

The *router firmware* is the internal program that your network router uses to perform its routing chores and to display the setup pages and process any configuration changes you make. Router manufacturers frequently update their firmware to fix bugs, to improve performance and to add new features. For all these reasons, it's a good idea to update the router's firmware to get the latest version. In case you're wondering, updating the firmware doesn't cause you to lose any of your settings.

> **TIP**
>
> The router's setup pages usually show you the current firmware version. However, if your router supports UPnP, you can usually get the router's firmware version through Windows 7. Select Start, Network to open the Network window, right-click the router's icon, and then click Properties. In the property sheet that appears, click the Network Device tab. The current firmware version usually appears as the Model Number value in the Device Details group.

The specifics of updating router firmware vary from device to device, so it's best to check either the manual that came with your router, or the manufacturer's website. However, here's the general procedure for finding out, downloading, and installing the latest firmware version:

1. Use Internet Explorer to navigate to the router manufacturer's website.
2. Navigate to the Support pages.
3. Navigate to the Download pages.
4. Use the interface to navigate to the download page for your router.

TIP

Most product support pages require the name and model number of the router. You can usually find this information on the underside of the router.

5. You should now see a list of firmware downloads. Examine the version numbers and compare them to your router's current firmware version.
6. If the latest version is later than the current version on your router, click the download link and save the firmware upgrade file on your computer.

TIP

A good place to save the firmware upgrade file is the Downloads folder, which is a sub-folder of your main Windows 7 user account folder.

CAUTION

Most router manufacturers require that you upgrade the firmware using a wired link to the router. Using a wireless link can damage the router.

7. Open and log in to the router's setup pages.
8. Navigate to the firmware upgrade page. Figure 24.9 shows a typical firmware upgrade page.
9. Locate the upload section, click Browse, and then select the firmware file that you downloaded.
10. Click Upload. The router uploads the file and then performs the upgrade.

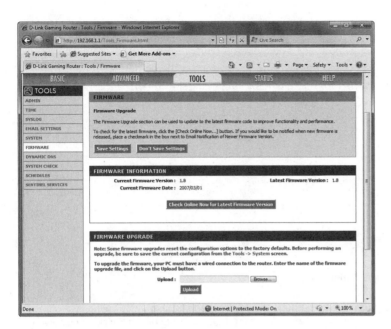

FIGURE 24.9   A typical firmware upgrade page for a router.

Troubleshooting from the Command Line

Windows 7 TCP/IP comes with a few command-line utilities that you can use to review your TCP/IP settings and troubleshoot problems. Here's a list of the available utilities:

ARP   This utility displays (or modifies) the IP-to-Ethernet or IP-to-Token Ring address trans-
           lation tables used by the Address Resolution Protocol (ARP) in TCP/IP. Enter the
           command arp -? for the syntax.

NBTSTAT   This utility displays the protocol statistics and the current TCP/IP connections using
           NBT (NetBIOS over TCP/IP). Enter nbtstat -? for the syntax.

NETSTAT   This utility displays the protocol statistics and current TCP/IP connections. The
           command netstat -? displays the syntax.

PING   This utility can check a network connection to a remote computer. This is one of the
           most commonly used TCP/IP diagnostic tools, so I describe it more detail in the next
           section.

ROUTE   This utility can manipulate a network routing table (LMHOSTS). Enter route -? for the
           syntax.

TRACERT   This utility can check the route taken to a remote host. I explain this valuable diag-
           nostic command in more detail later.

IPCONFIG This utility displays the current TCP/IP network configuration. If you run the
          command ipconfig without any switches, the utility returns your system's current IP
          address, subnet mask, and default gateway. If you run the command ipconfig
          /all, the utility returns more details information, as shown here:

```
Windows IP Configuration

  Host Name . . . . . . . . . . . . : MediaPC
  Primary Dns Suffix  . . . . . . . :
  Node Type . . . . . . . . . . . . : Hybrid
  IP Routing Enabled. . . . . . . . : No
  WINS Proxy Enabled. . . . . . . . : No
  DNS Suffix Search List. . . . . . : phub.net.cable.window.com

Ethernet adapter Local Area Connection:

  Connection-specific DNS Suffix  . : phub.net.cable.rogers.com
  Description . . . . . . . . . . . : Atheros L1 Gigabit Ethernet 10/100/1000Base-T
➥Controller
  Physical Address. . . . . . . . . : 00-1E-8C-7D-97-3A
  DHCP Enabled. . . . . . . . . . . : Yes
  Autoconfiguration Enabled . . . . : Yes
  Link-local IPv6 Address . . . . . : fe80::452f:6db7:eaf2:3112%11(Preferred)
  IPv4 Address. . . . . . . . . . . : 192.168.0.84(Preferred)
  Subnet Mask . . . . . . . . . . . : 255.255.0.0
  Lease Obtained. . . . . . . . . . : Wednesday, April 15, 2009 10:38:42 AM
  Lease Expires . . . . . . . . . . : Thursday, April 16, 2009 2:07:16 PM
  Default Gateway . . . . . . . . . : 192.168.1.1
  DHCP Server . . . . . . . . . . . : 192.168.1.1
  DHCPv6 IAID . . . . . . . . . . . : 234888844
  DHCPv6 Client DUID. . . . . . . . : 00-01-00-01-11-52-C4-05-00-1E-8C-7D-97-3A
  DNS Servers . . . . . . . . . . . : 192.168.1.1
  NetBIOS over Tcpip. . . . . . . . : Enabled

Tunnel adapter isatap.phub.net.cable.rogers.com:

  Media State . . . . . . . . . . . : Media disconnected
  Connection-specific DNS Suffix  . : phub.net.cable.rogers.com
  Description . . . . . . . . . . . : Microsoft ISATAP Adapter
  Physical Address. . . . . . . . . : 00-00-00-00-00-00-00-E0
  DHCP Enabled. . . . . . . . . . . : No
  Autoconfiguration Enabled . . . . : Yes

Tunnel adapter Teredo Tunneling Pseudo-Interface:

  Connection-specific DNS Suffix  . :
  Description . . . . . . . . . . . : Teredo Tunneling Pseudo-Interface
```

```
Physical Address. . . . . . . . . : 00-00-00-00-00-00-00-E0
DHCP Enabled. . . . . . . . . . . : No
Autoconfiguration Enabled . . . . : Yes
IPv6 Address. . . . . . . . . . . : 2001:0:4137:9e50:3032:38c1:3f57:ffab(Preferred)
Link-local IPv6 Address . . . . . : fe80::3032:38c1:3f57:ffab%13(Preferred)
Default Gateway . . . . . . . . . : ::
NetBIOS over Tcpip. . . . . . . . : Disabled

Tunnel adapter Reusable ISATAP Interface {D767BCA8-D27E-404C-9A50-CD680EF507C0}:

Media State . . . . . . . . . . . : Media disconnected
Connection-specific DNS Suffix  . :
Description . . . . . . . . . . . : Microsoft ISATAP Adapter #2
Physical Address. . . . . . . . . : 00-00-00-00-00-00-00-E0
DHCP Enabled. . . . . . . . . . . : No
Autoconfiguration Enabled . . . . : Yes
```

A Basic Command-Line Troubleshooting Procedure

Here's a basic procedure you can run through to troubleshoot networking problems using the command-line tools:

1. Release the current DHCP lease by running the following command:

   ```
   ipconfig /release
   ```

2. Renew the DNCP lease by running the following command:

   ```
   ipconfig /renew
   ```

> **NOTE**
>
> A *DHCP lease* is a guarantee that the Dynamic Host Control Protocol (DHCP) client computer will have the IP address supplied by the DHCP server for a specified period of time. To avoid lease expiration, the DHCP client usually sends a request—a DHCPREQUEST message—for lease renewal to the original DHCP server after 50% of the lease time has expired. If 87.5% of its lease time has expired, the DHCP client it sends a lease renewal request to all available DHCP servers.

3. Flush the ARP cache. The ARP handles the conversion of an IP address to a physical address of a network adapter. (To see the physical address of your adapter, open the connection's Status dialog box, display the Support tab, and click Details.) To improve performance, Windows 7 stores resolved addresses in the *ARP cache* for a short time. Some networking problems are caused by ARP cache entries that are obsolete or incomplete. The cache is normally flushed regularly, but to force a flush, run the following command:

   ```
   arp -d
   ```

TIP

To see the contents of the ARP cache, run the following command:

```
arp -a
```

You'll see output similar to the following:

```
Interface: 192.168.1.101  --- 0x2
  Internet Address        Physical Address      Type
  192.168.1.1             00-12-17-8c-48-88     dynamic
  192.168.1.100           00-11-24-1a-7a-fc     dynamic
  192.168.1.103           00-11-11-be-c7-78     dynamic
```

4. Flush the NetBIOS name cache. NetBIOS handles the conversion between the network names of computers and their IP addresses. To improve performance, Windows 7 stores resolved names in the *NetBIOS name cache*. To solve problems caused by NetBIOS name cache entries that are obsolete or bad, this step clears the cache. Run the following command:

```
nbtstat -r
```

5. Re-register the computer with the network's WINS server. That is, you ask the WINS server to release the computer's NetBIOS names that are registered with the server and then re-register them. This is useful if you're having problems connecting to other computers using their network names. Run the following command:

```
nbtstat -rr
```

6. Flush the DNS cache. DNS handles the conversion of domain names to IP addresses. To improve performance, Windows 7 stores resolved domain names in the *DNS cache*. To solve problems caused by DNS cache entries that are obsolete or bad, clear the cache by running the following command:

```
ipconfig /flushdns
```

7. Re-register the computer with the DNS server. This is useful if you're having trouble resolving domain names or if you're having trouble with a dynamic DNS server. Run the following command:

```
ipconfig /registerdns
```

Checking Connectivity with the PING Command

As you might know, a submarine can detect a nearby object by using sonar to send out a sound wave and then seeing whether the wave is reflected. This is called *pinging* an object.

Windows 7 has a PING command that performs a similar function. PING sends out a special type of IP packet—called an *Internet Control Message Protocol (ICMP) echo packet*—to a remote location. This packet requests that the remote location send back a response packet. PING then tells you whether the response was received. In this way, you can check your network configuration to see whether your computer can connect with a remote host.

To use PING, first open a command-line session by selecting Start, All Programs, Accessories, Command Prompt. Here's a simplified version of the PING syntax:

```
ping [-t] [-n count] target_name
```

-t   Pings the specified *target_name* until you interrupt the command.

-n *count* Sends the number of echo packets specified by *count*. The default is 4.

target_name Specifies either the IP address or the hostname (a fully qualified domain name) of the remote host you want to ping.

Here's an example that uses PING on the Google.com domain:

```
C:\Users\Paul>ping google.com


Pinging google.com [64.233.187.99] with 32 bytes of data:

Reply from 64.233.187.99: bytes=32 time=43ms TTL=240
Reply from 64.233.187.99: bytes=32 time=42ms TTL=239
Reply from 64.233.187.99: bytes=32 time=43ms TTL=239
Reply from 64.233.187.99: bytes=32 time=42ms TTL=240

Ping statistics for 64.233.187.99:
    Packets: Sent = 4, Received = 4, Lost = 0 (0% loss),A
Approximate round trip times in milli-seconds:
    Minimum = 42ms, Maximum = 43ms, Average = 42ms
```

Here, you see that each echo packet received a reply. If you can't connect to the remote host, PING returns a Request timed out message for each packet.

If you can't connect to a remote host, here are some notes on using PING to troubleshoot problems:

▶ First, check to see whether you can use PING successfully on the loopback address:

```
ping 127.0.0.1.
```

The only reason this PING would fail is if your computer doesn't have the Internet Protocol installed. However, all Windows 7 machines have IP installed, and the option to uninstall it is disabled, so pinging the loopback address will almost certainly work. The only reason to include it in your troubleshooting is that if it doesn't work, it means you have a serious problem with your machine. Either revert to a working configuration (see "Reverting to an Earlier Configuration," later in this chapter), reinstall Windows 7, or take your machine to a computer repair professional.

▶ Try using PING on your computer's IP address. (If you're using DHCP, run the IPCONFIG utility to get your current IP address.) If you don't get a successful echo, your NIC may not be inserted properly or the device drivers may not be installed. See "Troubleshooting the NIC," later in this chapter.

▶ Now PING another computer on your network. If PING fails, check your cable or wireless connections.

▶ The next test you should run is on your default gateway (that is, your router). If you can't successfully PING the router's internal IP address, you won't be able to access remote Internet sites. In this case, check the IP address you entered for the gateway, check the cable connections, and make sure the router is turned on. You may need to power cycle the router.

▶ If you get this far, try using PING on the remote host you're trying to contact. If you're unsuccessful, check to make sure that you're using the correct IP address for the host. Try power cycling your broadband modem.

Tracking Packets with the TRACERT Command

If you can't PING a remote host, it could be that your echo packets are getting held up along the way. To find out, you can use the TRACERT (trace route) command:

tracert [-d] [-h maximum_hops] [-j host-list] [-w timeout] target_name

-d	Specifies not to resolve IP addresses to hostnames.
-h maximum_hops	Specifies the maximum number of hops to search for the target_name. (The default is 30.)
-j host-list	Specifies loose source route along the host-list.
-w timeout	Waits the number of milliseconds specified by timeout for each reply.
target_name	Specifies the hostname of the destination computer.

TRACERT operates by sending ICMP echo packets with varying TTL values. Recall that TTL places a limit on the number of hops that a packet can take. Each host along the packet's route decrements the TTL value until, when the TTL value is 0, the packet is discarded (assuming that it hasn't reached its destination by then).

In TRACERT, the ICMP packets specify that whichever host decrements the echo packet to 0 should send back a response. So, the first packet has a TTL value of 1, the second has a TTL value of 2, and so on. TRACERT keeps sending packets with incrementally higher TTL values until either a response is received from the remote host or a packet receives no response. Here's an example of a TRACERT command in action:

```
C:\>tracert google.com


Tracing route to google.com [216.239.57.99]
over a maximum of 30 hops:

    1    <1 ms    <1 ms    <1 ms 192.168.1.1
    2     8 ms     8 ms     8 ms 64.230.197.178
    3     6 ms     6 ms     6 ms 64.230.221.201
    4     6 ms     6 ms     6 ms 64.230.234.249
    5     8 ms     6 ms     7 ms 64.230.233.93
    6    17 ms    17 ms    16 ms core1-chicago23-pos0-0.in.bellnexxia.net
➥[206.108.103.130]
    7    17 ms    17 ms    17 ms bx2-chicago23-pos11-0.in.bellnexxia.net
➥[206.108.103.138]
    8    17 ms    17 ms    17 ms so-4-3-3.cr1.ord2.us.above.net [208.184.233.185]
    9    18 ms    17 ms    18 ms so-0-0-0.cr2.ord2.us.above.net [64.125.29.186]
   10    36 ms    36 ms    36 ms so-5-2-0.cr1.dca2.us.above.net [64.125.30.225]
   11    47 ms    46 ms    46 ms so-4-1-0.mpr2.atl6.us.above.net [64.125.29.41]
   12    48 ms    48 ms    48 ms 64.124.229.173.google.com [64.124.229.173]
   13    48 ms    48 ms    48 ms 216.239.48.23
   14    49 ms    49 ms    49 ms 216.239.46.44
   15   100 ms   100 ms   100 ms 216.239.47.129
   16    99 ms    99 ms    99 ms 216.239.49.250
   17    99 ms    99 ms    99 ms 66.249.95.65
   18    99 ms    99 ms    99 ms 66.249.94.27
   19   102 ms   101 ms   101 ms 216.239.49.97
   20    99 ms   100 ms    99 ms 216.239.57.99

Trace complete.
```

The first column is the hop number (that is, the TTL value set in the packet). Notice that, in my case, it took 20 hops to get to Google.com. The next three columns contain round-trip times for an attempt to reach the destination with that TTL value. (Asterisks indicate that the attempt timed out.) The last column contains the hostname (if it was resolved) and the IP address of the responding system.

Changing the Default TTL Value

One of the reasons your packets might not be getting to their destination is that the default TTL value used by Windows 7 might be set too low. This is actually very unlikely because the default is 128, which should be more than enough. However, you *can* increase this value if you want. Start the Registry Editor and highlight the following key:

`HKLM\System\CurrentControlSet\Services\Tcpip\Parameters`

Select Edit, New, DWORD Value, type **DefaultTTL**, and press Enter. Change the value of this new setting to any decimal value between 0 and 255 (0 to FF in hexadecimal).

24

Troubleshooting Cables

If one of the problems discussed so far isn't the cause of your networking quandary, the next logical suspect is the cabling that connects the workstations. This section discusses cabling, gives you a few pointers for preventing cable problems, and discusses some common cable kinks that can crop up.

Although most large-scale cabling operations are performed by third-party cable installers, home setups are usually do-it-yourself jobs. You can prevent some cable problems and simplify your troubleshooting down the road by taking a few precautions and "ounce of prevention" measures in advance:

▶ First and foremost, always buy the highest-quality cable you can find (for example, Category 5e or Category 6 or higher for twisted-pair cable). With network cabling, you get what you pay for.

▶ Good-quality cable will be labeled. You should also add your own labels for things such as the source and destination of the cable.

▶ To avoid electromagnetic interference, don't run cable near electronic devices, power lines, air conditioners, fluorescent lights, motors, and other electromagnetic sources.

▶ Try to avoid phone lines because the ringer signal can disrupt network data carried over twisted-pair cable.

▶ To avoid the cable being stepped on accidentally, don't run it under carpet.

▶ To avoid people tripping over a cable (and possibly damaging the cable connector, the NIC port, or the person doing the tripping!), avoid high-traffic areas when laying the cable.

▶ If you plan to run cable outdoors, use conduit or another casing material to prevent moisture damage.

▶ Don't use excessive force to pull or push a cable into place. Rough handling can cause pinching or even breakage.

If you suspect cabling might be the cause of your network problems, here's a list of a few things to check:

▶ **Watch for electromagnetic interference**—If you see garbage on a workstation screen or experience random packet loss or temporarily missing nodes, the problem might be electromagnetic interference. Check your cables to make sure that they are at least 6 to 12 inches from any source of electromagnetic interference.

▶ **Check your connections**—Loose connections are a common source of cabling woes. Be sure to check every cable connection associated with the workstation that's experiencing network difficulty, including connections to the network adapter, router, switch, and so on.

▶ **Check the lay of the line**—Loops of cable could be generating an electrical field that interferes with network communication. Try not to leave your excess cable lying around in coils or loops.

▶ **Inspect the cable for pinching or breaks**—A badly pinched cable can cause a short in the wire, which could lead to intermittent connection problems. Make sure that no part of the cable is pinched, especially if the back of the computer is situated near a wall. A complete lack of connection with the network might mean that the cable's copper core has been severed completely and needs to be replaced.

Troubleshooting the NIC

After cabling, the NIC is next on the list of common sources of networking headaches. Here's a list of items to check if you suspect that Windows 7 and your NIC aren't getting along:

▶ **Make sure that Windows 7 installed the correct NIC**—Windows 7 usually does a pretty good job of detecting the network card. However, a slight error (such as choosing the wrong transceiver type) can wreak havoc. Double-check that the NIC listed in Device Manager is the same as the one installed in your computer. If it's not, click Remove to delete it, run the Add Hardware Wizard, and choose your NIC manually.

▶ **Perform a physical check of the NIC**—Open the case and make sure that the card is properly seated in its slot.

> **CAUTION**
>
> Before touching any component inside a computer case, ground yourself to prevent electrostatic discharge. To ground yourself, touch any metal surface, such as the metal of the computer case.

▶ **Disable the motherboard NIC**—If you added a new NIC to replace the motherboard NIC that came with your computer, it could be that the original NIC is interfering with the new one. To work around this problem, shut down Windows 7, restart your computer, and access your computer's BIOS configuration program. There should be an option that enables you to disable the motherboard NIC.

▶ **Try a new NIC**—Try swapping out the NIC for one that you know works properly. (If the existing NIC is on the computer's motherboard, insert the working NIC is an open bus slot.) If that fixes the problem, you'll have to remove the faulty interface card (if possible) and insert a new one.

▶ **Get the latest driver**—Check with the manufacturer of the NIC to see whether it has newer Windows 7 drivers for the card. If so, download and install them, as described in the next section.

24

Troubleshooting Wireless Network Problems

Wireless networking adds a whole new set of potential snags to your troubleshooting chores because of problems such as interference, compatibility, and device ranges. Here's a list of a few troubleshooting items that you should check to solve any wireless connectivity problems you're having:

▶ **Repair the connection**—Windows 7's network repair tool seems to work particularly well for solving wireless woes, so you should always start with that (see "Repairing a Network Connection," earlier in this chapter).

▶ **Reboot and power cycle devices**—Reset your hardware by performing the following tasks, in order: Log off Windows 7, restart your computer, power cycle your computer, power cycle the wireless access point, and then power cycle the broadband modem.

▶ **Check connections**—Make sure your wireless NIC is installed properly and that the antenna is attached securely.

▶ **Move the antenna**—If the wireless NIC antenna is on a cable, move the antenna to a higher position.

▶ **Check your notebook WLAN switch**—Many notebook computers come with a switch or program that turns the internal wireless NIC on and off. Make sure you haven't inadvertently turned the NIC off.

▶ **Look for interference**—Devices such as baby monitors and cordless phones that use the 2.4GHz radio frequency (RF) band can play havoc with wireless signals. Try either moving or turning off such devices if they're near your wireless NIC or wireless access point.

> **CAUTION**
>
> You should also keep your wireless NIC and access point well away from a microwave oven; microwaves can jam wireless signals.

▶ **Change the channel**—You can configure your wireless access to broadcast signals on a specific channel. Sometimes one channel gives a stronger signal than another, so try changing the channel. You do this by logging on to the access point's configuration pages and looking for a setting that determines the broadcast channel.

▶ **Check your range**—If you're getting no signal or a weak signal, it could be that your wireless NIC is too far away from the access point. You usually can't get much farther than about 115 feet away from an access point before the signal begins to degrade (230 feet if you're using 802.11n devices). Either move closer to the access point or turn on the access point's range booster feature, if it has one. You could also install a wireless range extender.

▶ **Check 802.11b/g/n compatibility**—For your wireless NIC to work properly with your wireless access point, both must use a compatible version of the wireless 802.11 standard. For example, if your NIC supports only 802.11n, but your access point supports only 802.11g, the two will not be able to connect.

▶ **Reset the router**—As a last resort, reset the router to its default factory settings. (Refer to the device documentation to learn how to do this.) Note that if you do this you'll need to set up your network from scratch.

CHAPTER 25

Setting Up a Small Network

Transport of the mails, transport of the human voice, transport of flickering pictures—in this century as in others our highest accomplishments still have the single aim of bringing men together.

—Antoine de Saint-Exupéry

For many years, networking was the private playground of IT panjandrums. Its obscure lingo and arcane hardware were familiar to only this small coterie of computer cognoscenti. Workers who needed access to network resources had to pay obeisance to these powers-that-be, genuflecting in just the right way, tossing in the odd salaam or two.

Lately, however, we've seen a democratization of networking. Thanks to the trend away from mainframes and toward client/server setups, thanks to the migration from dumb terminals to smarter PCs, and thanks to the advent of easy peer-to-peer setups, networking is no longer the sole province of the elite. Getting connected to an existing network, or setting up your own network in a small office or home office, has never been easier.

This chapter shows you how Windows 7 has helped take even more of the *work* out of networking. You'll learn how to set up your own simple network and how to perform some useful administrative tasks. (For the details on accessing network resources, see Chapter 26, "Accessing and Using Your Network.")

Setting Up a Peer-to-Peer Network

One of the biggest improvements in recent Windows versions is in networking setup. Specifically, if you have your computers connected correctly (more on that in a second), Windows sets up the appropriate networking settings automatically. It's true plug-and-play: You plug your machine into the network, and you can play with network resources within a few seconds. Note that this doesn't apply to wireless connections, which, for security reasons, require a few extra steps. Although, as you'll soon see, Windows 7 enables you to "save" a wireless connection so that the next time your computer comes within range of that network, Windows 7 makes the connection automatically.

So what is the "correct" network configuration required for this automatic networking setup to happen? For wired networks, it requires only the following:

- ▶ Each computer must have a network interface card (NIC), such as an internal network adapter, a USB network adapter, a motherboard-based network chip, or a network PC Card.

- ▶ You must have an external router or switch.

- ▶ You must activate Dynamic Host Control Protocol (DHCP) on the router. DHCP automatically assigns unique IP addresses to each computer on the network.

- ▶ Each computer must have a network cable running from the NIC to a port in the router (or switch).

- ▶ If you have a high-speed modem, you must run a network cable from the Internet (or WAN) port in the router to the network port in the modem. This ensures that every computer on the network can share the Internet connection.

- ▶ Each computer must have a unique name.

- ▶ Each computer must use the same workgroup name.

If you're not sure about the last two points, see "Changing the Computer and Workgroup Name," later in this chapter.

For wireless networks, the configuration is more or less the same (except, of course, you don't need to run a network cable from each computer to the router). Here are the differences for a wireless network:

NOTE

Networks don't have to be exclusively wired or wireless. In fact, it's quite common to have a mixture of the two connection types. Most wireless access points come with a few ports to accept wired connections.

- ▶ Each computer must have a NIC that supports wireless connections.

- ▶ You must have a wireless access point or gateway that also doubles as a router.

CAUTION

Some broadband providers are using "smart" modems that include routing and firewall features. That's fine, but these modems almost always have a static IP address, and that address is usually either http://192.168.1.1 or http://192.168.0.1, which might conflict with your wireless gateway's IP address. If you have connection problems after adding the wireless gateway, the likely culprit is an IP address conflict. Disconnect the broadband modem, access the gateway's configuration program, and change its IP address (to, say, http://192.168.1.2 or http://192.168.0.2).

▶ During the initial configuration, one computer must connect to the access point via a network cable. This enables you to configure the access point before the wireless connection is established.

See "Connecting to a Wireless Network," later in this chapter, to learn the extra few steps that you must run to make the wireless connection in Windows 7.

Changing the Computer and Workgroup Name

I mentioned earlier that to implement a flawless Windows 7 network, each computer must have a unique name, and every computer must use the same workgroup name. (I'm assuming here that you're setting up a small network in your home or small office. Larger networks are typically divided into multiple workgroups, where all the machines in each workgroup are related in some way—marketing, IT, sales, and so on.)

Here are the steps to follow to change the computer name and workgroup name in Windows 7:

1. Click Start, type `systempropertiescomputername`, and press Enter. The System Properties dialog box appears with the Computer Name tab displayed.

2. Click Change. The Computer Name/Domain Changes dialog box appears, as shown in Figure 25.1.

3. Type the computer name.

4. Select the Workgroup option and type the common workgroup name.

5. Click OK. Windows 7 tells you that you must restart the computer to put the changes into effect.

6. Click OK to return to the System Properties dialog box.

7. Click Close. Windows 7 prompts you to restart your computer.

8. Click Restart Now.

FIGURE 25.1   Use this dialog box to change your computer name and workgroup name.

Connecting to a Wireless Network

With your wireless network adapters installed and your wireless gateway or access point configured, you're ready to connect to your wireless network. This gives you access to the network's resources, as well as to the Internet, if you have a wireless gateway. Again, Windows 7 doesn't establish the initial connection to a wireless network automatically. This is mostly a security concern because a password or security key protects most wireless networks. However, it's also usually the case (particularly in dense urban neighborhoods) that Windows 7 might detect multiple wireless networks within range, so it's up to you to specify which network you want to connect to. Fortunately, you can configure Windows 7 to remember a wireless network's settings and automatically connect you the next time the network is in range. So, in most cases, you need to run through the connection procedure only once.

Here are the steps to follow to connect to a wireless network:

1. Click the Network icon in the taskbar's notification area. Windows 7 displays a list of the available wireless networks, as shown in Figure 25.2. Each network displays three pieces of information:

   ▶ The left column displays the network name (also called the *service set identifier* or *SSID*).

   ▶ The signal strength, as indicated by the five bars to the right (the more green bars you see, the stronger the signal). Note that the networks are in descending order of signal strength.

   ▶ Whether the network doesn't require a password or security key. An unsecure network is marked with a Caution icon above the signal strength.

FIGURE 25.2   Click the Network icon to see a list of the wireless networks that are in range.

25

> **NOTE**
>
> Some of the networks might be *wireless hot spots*, which are locations that allow wireless computers to use the location's Internet connection. You can find hot spots in many airports, hotels, and even businesses such as coffee shops, restaurants, and dental offices.

2. Select the network that you want to use.

3. If you want Windows 7 to connect to the network automatically the next time it comes within range, activate the Connect Automatically check box.

4. Click Connect. If the network that you want to use is unsecured—as are many public hot spots—Windows 7 connects to the network immediately (so skip to step 5). However, most private wireless networks are (or should be) secured against unauthorized access. In this case, Windows 7 prompts you to enter the required security key or password, as shown in Figure 25.3.

FIGURE 25.3   To access a secured wireless network, you must enter a security key or password.

NOTE

Older wireless networks use a security protocol called Wired Equivalent Privacy, or WEP, that protects wireless communications with (usually) a 26-character security key. That sounds impregnable, but unfortunately there were serious weaknesses in the WEP encryption scheme, and now software exists that can crack any WEP key in minutes, if not seconds. In newer wireless networks, WEP has been superseded by Wi-Fi Protected Access, or WPA, which is vastly more secure than WEP. WPA uses most of the IEEE 802.11i wireless security standard, and WPA2 implements the full standard. WPA2 Personal requires a simple pass phrase for access (so it's suitable for homes and small offices), whereas WPA2 Enterprise requires a dedicated authentication server.

5. Type the key or password, and then click OK. Windows 7 connects to the network.

Working with Windows 7's Basic Network Tools and Tasks

With your network hardware purchased, unpacked, plugged in, and connected, your network should be up and running. (If not, you might want to pay a visit to Chapter 24, "Troubleshooting Networking.") For the most part, you'll be using your network for useful tasks such as sharing files, streaming media, making backups, and accessing the Internet. However, it's inevitable that some of your network chores will be network related, because even the smallest networks demand a certain amount of administration and configuration. These network tasks range from simply viewing the current status of the network to viewing the computers and devices attached to the network to customizing settings, such as the network name.

These are all basic network chores, and if you're the person who's wearing the Network Administrator nametag in your home or office, you need to know how to perform these chores. Fortunately, none of this is at all complex, so it won't take much time away from your more useful or interesting pursuits. This section tells you everything you need to know.

Accessing the Network and Sharing Center

One of the things people often griped about with Windows XP (and earlier versions of Windows) was that the networking features were often scattered about the interface and it was hard to find what you needed. Windows XP's My Network Places folder helped a bit because it offered the Network Tasks section in the Tasks pane, but it only had a few useful commands.

Microsoft realized that more work needed to be done to make network administration easier, particularly for nonprofessionals. The result is the Network and Sharing Center, which debuted in Windows Vista, a window that acts as a kind of home base for networking. Proof that Microsoft is heading in the right direction here is the long list of network-related tasks that you can either perform or launch using the Network and Sharing Center:

▶ Switch between homegroup connections and user account connections.

▶ See a list of your current network connections.

▶ Visualize your network with a network map (see "Displaying a Network Map," later in this chapter).

▶ Customize the network name, type, and icon (see "Customizing Your Network," later in this chapter).

▶ Change your computer discovery options (see Chapter 24) and your sharing options (see Chapter 26).

> **See** "Turning On Network Discovery," **p. 495**.

> **See** "Sharing Resources with the Network," **p. 565**.

▶ View the status of each network connection (see "Viewing Network Status Details," later in this chapter).

▶ View the computers and devices on the network (see "Viewing Network Computers and Devices," later in this chapter).

▶ Connect to another network.

▶ Manage your network connections (see "Managing Network Connections," later in this chapter).

▶ Manage your wireless networks (see "Managing Wireless Network Connections," later in this chapter).

▶ Diagnose and repair a network connection (see Chapter 24).

> **See** "Repairing a Network Connection," **p. 491**.

The Network and Sharing Center is a handy networking tool that you'll probably use a great deal, particularly when you're first getting your new network configured the way you want. That might be why Microsoft offers so many ways to open it. Here are the two easiest methods:

▶ Click (or right-click) the Network icon in the notification area, and then click Open Network and Sharing Center.

▶ Select Start, type **net** in the Search box, and then select Network and Sharing Center in the search results.

Whichever method you use, the Network and Sharing Center window appears, and it will look similar to the window shown in Figure 25.4.

The Network and Sharing Center window comprises four main areas:

▶ **Map**—This section gives you a miniature version of the network map: a visual display of the current connection. See the "Displaying a Network Map" section, later in this chapter.

▶ **View Your Active Networks**—This section tells you the name of the network to which you're connected, the network category (such as Home or Public), whether you have Internet access via that connection, and which of your computer connections is in use. (This will usually be either Local Area Connection for a wired connection or Wireless Network Connection). If you're connected to multiple networks or have multiple connections to a single network (wired and wireless, for example), all the connections appear here.

▶ **Change Your Networking Settings**—This area offers four links to common networking tasks.

▶ **Tasks**—This pane on the left side of the Network Center window gives you one-click access to even more useful network tasks.

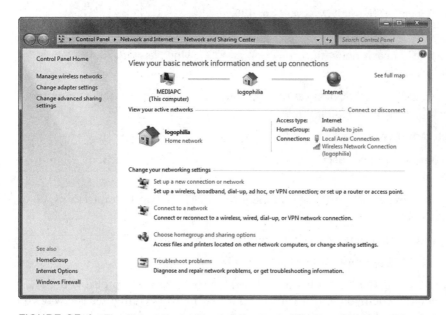

FIGURE 25.4   The Network and Sharing Center is Windows 7's networking hub.

The rest of this chapter takes you through a few of the most common network administration chores, all of which you initiate using the Network and Sharing Center. (Although if there are easier methods you can use to start a task, I'll let you know.)

Setting Up a Homegroup

NEW TO 7   One of the major innovations that Windows 7 brings to the networking table is the idea of a *homegroup*. This is a collection of computers on a peer-to-peer network that use a single password to share data between them. The idea is that once you join a homegroup by entering the homegroup password, you never need to worry about networking again because Windows 7 handles all the connections for you automatically. This is in contrast with the more traditional way of managing networking connections and sharing resources, which is by setting up user accounts and passwords and then assigning user permissions for each shared resource.

In other words, homegroups are designed to make networking easier and less problematic for new and inexperienced users. Of course, any Windows feature aimed at making life easier for novices is almost always *worse* for experienced or power users, because simpler always means fewer features, options, and settings.

Your purchase of this book tells me that you're in the experienced or power user camp, so I'm going to assume that homegroups are *not* for you, and the bulk of this chapter covers traditional small network tasks and settings. However, it's possible you may have to set up a simple network for someone (your parents or grandparents, for example), so it's worth knowing the homegroup basics, which you learn in the next few sections.

Activating Homegroup Connections

By default, homegroup networking is activated in new Windows 7 installations. To make sure, or to activate homegroup networking in an upgrade installation, follow these steps on each Windows 7 network computer:

1. In the Network and Sharing Center, click Change Advanced Sharing Settings.
2. Open the Home or Work profile.
3. In the Homegroup Connections section, click to activate the Allow Windows to Manage Homegroup Connections option, as shown in Figure 25.5.

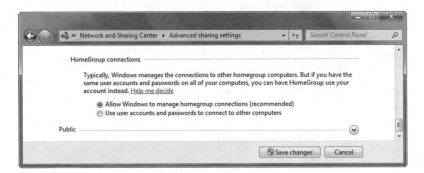

FIGURE 25.5   To use a Windows 7 homegroup on your network, activate the Allow Windows to Manage Homegroup Connections option.

4. Click Save Changes. Windows 7 tells you that you must log off to apply the changes.
5. Click Log Off Now. Windows 7 logs off your account.

When you log back on, you're ready to create a homegroup, as described next.

Creating a Homegroup

With all your home computers configured for homegroup networking, choose one of the Windows 7 computers to use to create the homegroup, and then follow these steps:

1. In the Network and Sharing Center, locate the Homegroup setting and click the Ready to Create link. (Alternatively, click Start, type **homegroup**, and press Enter.) The Homegroup window appears.

2. Click Create a Homegroup. The Create a Homegroup Wizard appears, and the first dialog box asks you to choose what you want to share (see Figure 25.6).

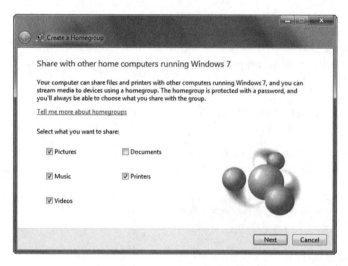

FIGURE 25.6   The Create a Homegroup Wizard takes you through the process of setting up your network's homegroup.

3. Activate the check box beside each type of file you want to share, and then click Next. The Create a Homegroup Wizard displays your homegroup password.

4. Make a note of the password (or click the Print Password and Instructions link, and then click Print This Page).

5. Click Finish. Windows 7 displays the Homegroup window, which I discuss a bit later (see "Changing Homegroup Settings").

Joining a Homegroup

After you've created your homegroup, you're next chore is to join all your other Windows 7 PCs to that homegroup. Here's how:

1. In the Network and Sharing Center, locate the Homegroup setting and click the Available to Join link. (Alternatively, click Start, type **homegroup**, and press Enter.) The Homegroup window appears.

2. Click Join Now. The Join a Homegroup Wizard appears, and the first dialog box asks you to choose what you want to share.

3. Activate the check box beside each type of file you want to share, and then click Next. The Create a Homegroup Wizard prompts your for the homegroup password.

4. Type the password and then click Next. The wizard joins the computer to the homegroup.

5. Click Finish. Windows 7 displays the Homegroup window, which I talk about later in this chapter (see "Changing Homegroup Settings").

Accessing the Homegroup

To view the other computers in your homegroup and access their shared resources, open any Windows Explorer window and click Homegroup in the navigation pane. This displays an icon for each homegroup computer, and opening an icon reveals the shared sources on that computer, as shown in Figure 25.7.

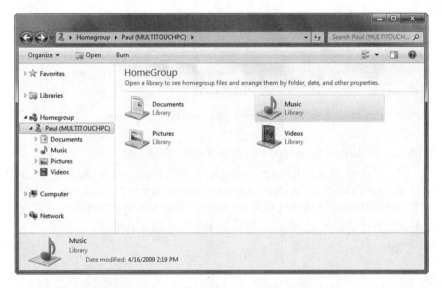

FIGURE 25.7   Click Homegroup in the navigation pane, and then open a Computer icon to see that computer's shared resources.

Changing Homegroup Settings

If you want to change the file types you share, just complete these steps:

1. In the Network and Sharing Center, click the Choose Homegroup and Sharing Options link. (Alternatively, click Start, type **homegroup**, and then click Choose Homegroup and Sharing Options.) The Homegroup window appears, as shown in Figure 25.8.

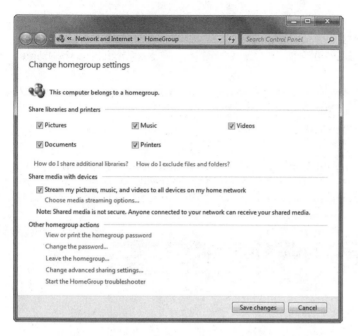

FIGURE 25.8   Use the Homegroup window to change your homegroup settings.

2. Activate the check box beside each type of file you want to share.

3. If you want to stream your media to other homegroup PCs, click to activate the Stream My Pictures, Music, and Video to All Devices On My Home Network check box. You can also click Choose Media Streaming Options to configure media streaming.

4. If you want to generate a new password, click Change the Password.

5. Click Save Changes.

NOTE

If you want to share specific folders and files with the homegroup, you need to activate the Sharing Wizard (which is activated by default, but I told you how to turn it off back in Chapter 19, "Implementing Network Security"). In any folder window, select Organize, Folder and Search Options, click the View tab, and then activate the Use Sharing Wizard check box. With that done, click the file or folder you want to share, click Share With, and then click either Homegroup (Read) for read-only sharing, or Homegroup (Read/Write) for read and write sharing.

Turning Off Homegroup Connections

NEW TO **7**   As I said earlier, my assumption here is that for your own networking needs, you're going to want the power and flexibility of traditional user account-based networking. If so, you must turn off homegroup networking by following these steps:

1. In the Network and Sharing Center, click Change Advanced Sharing Settings.
2. Open the Home or Work profile.
3. In the Homegroup Connections section, click to activate the Use User Accounts and Passwords to Connect to Other Computers option.
4. Click Save Changes. Windows 7 tells you that you must log off to apply the changes.
5. Click Log Off Now. Windows 7 logs off your account.

When you log back on, you're ready to use regular user account-based networking connections

Viewing Network Computers and Devices

If the Network icon is showing that you have a good connection to the network (see Chapter 24), you can go right ahead and see what's out there. One way to do this is to view Windows 7's network map (see "Displaying a Network Map," later in this chapter). However, Windows 7 offers a more straightforward method: the Network window.

▶ **See** "Checking the Connection Status," **p. 493.**

To open the Network window, open Windows Explorer and click Network in the navigation pane. Figure 25.9 shows the Network window for a typical small network, where you see the network's main resources, such as the computers and media devices. As you can see in Figure 25.10, Details view (select Views, Details) shows you the resource name, category, workgroup name, and the name of the network profile.

FIGURE 25.9   The Network window shows you the main resources on your network.

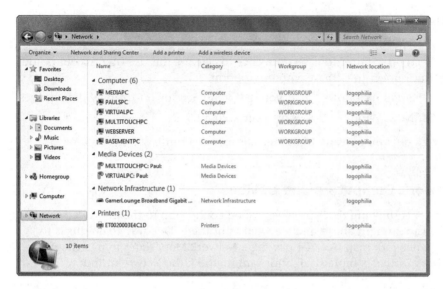

FIGURE 25.10   The Network window in Details view.

NOTE

To change the columns shown in Details view, right-click any column header, and then click a column name to toggle that column on and off.

You probably noticed in Figures 25.9 and 25.10 that some of the network resource names appear multiple times (for example, once in the Computer category and again in the Media Devices category). Multiple Network icons mean that the computer or device has other networking features, and these appear as "devices" in the Network window. The most common secondary icon is the Windows Media Connect device, which appears when the computer has configured Windows Media Player (in the case of a Windows 7 computer) to stream media to the network.

Displaying a Network Map

The Network window gives you a list of the network computers and devices, but it tells you nothing about how these devices connect to form your network. This bird's-eye view of your network is available via Windows 7's Network Map feature, which gives you a visual display of everything your computer is connected to: network connections (wired and wireless), ad hoc (computer-to-computer) connections, Internet connections, and the devices associated with these connections. Network Map also gives you a visual display of the connection status so that you can easily spot problems.

The Network and Sharing Center displays your local portion of the network map, and the layout depends on your current connections. You always see an icon for your computer on the left. If your computer is connected to a network (as shown earlier in Figure 25.4), a green line joins the Computer icon and the Network icon. If the network is connected to the Internet, another green line joins the Network icon and the Internet icon on the right. If there is no connection, you see a red *X* through the connection line.

The Network and Sharing Center also comes with a more detailed version of Network Map. To view it, click the See Full Map link. Figure 25.11 shows an example of the full network map. If you have multiple network connections, use the Network Map Of list to select a different connection and see its map.

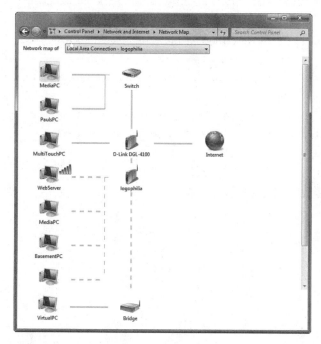

FIGURE 25.11   The full version of a network map.

NOTE

In the full network map, a double solid line indicates a wired connection, and double dashed line indicates a wireless connection.

Viewing Network Status Details

You saw in Chapter 24 that you can use the Network icon in Windows 7's notification area to get a quick visual read on the current network status. If the Network icon shows that your computer is connected to the network, you might find yourself wondering about some related status data: How long has the connection been running? How fast is the connection; that is, what is the connection's data transfer rate?

▶ See "Checking the Connection Status," **p. 493**.

NOTE

In this case, the data transfer rate is the theoretical maximum rate supported by the networking hardware. For example, if Windows 7 detects that at least one component of a wired connection (the NIC, the cable, or the switch/router) supports only Fast Ethernet, Windows 7 will report a connection speed of 100Mbps.

Windows 7 can supply you with these and other details about your network connection. Follow these steps to see them:

1. Open the Network and Sharing Center, as described earlier (see "Accessing the Network and Sharing Center").

2. In the View Your Active Networks section, click the link in the Connections area for the connection you want to work with:

   ▶ A wired connection is usually named Local Area Connection, so you'd click that link; Figure 25.12 shows the Status dialog box that appears for a wired connection.

FIGURE 25.12   The Status dialog box for a wired network connection.

   ▶ A wireless connection is usually named Wireless Network Connection, so you'd click that link for the wireless status; Figure 25.13 shows the Status dialog box for a wireless connection, which also shows the network's SSID and then the connection's current signal strength.

3. Click Details. Windows 7 displays the Network Connection Details dialog box, shown in Figure 25.14. This dialog box tells you, among other things, your NIC's

MAC address (the Physical Address value), your computer's IP address, and the addresses of your Internet service provider's (ISP) domain name system (DNS) servers.

FIGURE 25.13   The Status dialog box for a wireless network connection.

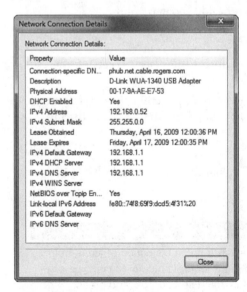

FIGURE 25.14   The Network Connection Details dialog box displays your computer's IP address, among other values.

4. Click Close to return to the Status dialog box.

5. Click Close.

25

Customizing Your Network

When you first open the Network Center, in most cases, you won't have a profile set up for the network, so Windows 7 configures the network with three default settings:

▶ A default name, usually either *Network* or the SSID of the wireless network.

▶ The network type, which depends on the network location you chose when you first connected to the network.

NOTE

Windows 7 supports three types of network categories: home, work, and public. Home networks are usually home or small office networks where you need to work with a few nearby computers. To that end, Windows 7 turns on network discovery and file and printer sharing. Public networks are usually wireless hot spot connections in airports, coffee shops, hotels, and other public places. When you designate a network as public, Windows 7 turns off network discovery and file and printer sharing. The work category applies to networks that are part of a corporate domain.

▶ A default Network icon, which depends on the network location you chose when you first connected to the network. (In the miniature network map shown in Figure 25.4, the default Home icon is the one shown beside logophilia.)

To change any of these default, follow these steps:

1. Open the Network and Sharing Center, as described earlier (see "Accessing the Network and Sharing Center").
2. To change the network name and icon, in the View Your Active Networks section, click the Network icon to open the Set Network Properties dialog box shown in Figure 25.15.
3. Type a name in the Network Name text box.
4. To change the icon, click Change to open the Change Network Icon dialog box, select an icon, and then click OK.

TIP

The Change Network Icon dialog box initially shows you a small collection of icons from the %SystemRoot%\system32\pnidui.dll file. To get a larger choice of icons, type any of the following pathnames into the Look for Icons in This File text box (and press Enter after you enter the pathname):

`%SystemRoot%\system32\shell32.dll`

`%SystemRoot%\system32\pifmgr.dll`

`%SystemRoot%\explorer.exe`

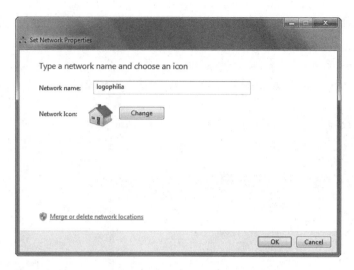

FIGURE 25.15   In the Network and Sharing Center, click the Network icon to display this dialog box so that you can change the network name and icon.

5. Click OK to return to the Network and Sharing Center window.

6. To change the network type, in the View Your Active Networks section, click the network type that appears under the network name.

7. Click the network type that applies to your network (Home Network, Work Network, or Public Network). Windows 7 changes the network type and its associated settings. (For example, it turns off network discovery if you choose the public network type.)

8. Click Close. Windows 7 updates the Network and Sharing Center window with the new settings.

Managing Network Connections

In Windows 7, you can link to many different types of remote resources, including dial-up and broadband Internet services, dial-up and Internet-based *virtual private networking* (VPN), and the ethernet and wireless networking that are the subject of this chapter. In Windows 7, all of these remote links are called *network connections*, and Windows 7 maintains a Network Connections window that lists all your network connections. Each *network interface card* (NIC) attached to your computer gets its own connection icon in the list, and you can use those icons to work with your network connections.

For example, you can rename a connection, disable an unused connection, switch a connection between using a dynamic and a static IP address, and find out a connection's Internet Protocol (IP) and Media Access Control (MAC) addresses. In this section, you learn about these and other tasks for wired connections. For more information about wireless connections, see "Managing Wireless Network Connections," later in this chapter.

Opening the Network Connections Window

You do most of your work in this chapter in Windows 7's Network Connections window, and Windows 7 gives you two main ways to access this window:

▶ In the Network and Sharing Center, click the Change Adapter Settings link in the Tasks list.

▶ Select Start, type **connections**, and then click View Network Connections.

Figure 25.16 shows an example of the Network Connections window.

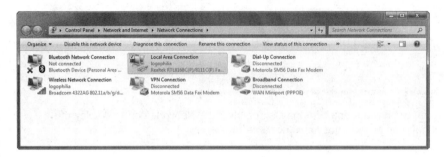

FIGURE 25.16   Windows 7's Network Connections window.

If you've previously created a direct broadband Internet connection, a dial-up Internet connection, or a connection to a VPN, you see icons for each connection. However, you always one or both of the following two types of icons:

▶ **Wired**—These Ethernet connections take the default name Local Area Connection, and you can recognize them by the RJ-45 jack shown with the icon. If you have more than one Ethernet NIC installed in your computer, you see a wired connection icon for each one (with subsequent connections named Local Area Connection 2, and so on).

▶ **Wireless**—These connections take the default name Wireless Network Connection, and you can recognize them by the green signal bars shown with the icon.

When you're in the default Tiles view, both wired and wireless icons show the name of the network to which they're connected (or the icon shows Disconnected if no current connection is present) and the name of the NIC through which each connection is made. (Details view shows you more data, such as the current connectivity setting—such as Access to Local Only or Access to Local and Internet—and the network category.) If the network connection currently has a problem, you see a red X added to the icon (see Figure 25.16), and the connection's Status field may display an error message (such as Network cable unplugged).

Renaming a Network Connection

The default network connection names—Local Area Connection and Wireless Network Connection—don't tell you much other than whether the connection is wired or wireless. Similarly, if your computer has two Ethernet NICs, having connections named Local Area

Connection and Local Area Connection 2 doesn't give you much to go on if you need to differentiate between them.

For these reasons, you might consider renaming your connections. For example, if you have Linksys and D-Link routers on your network, you could rename your connections as Linksys Connection and D-Link Connection. Here are the steps to follow:

1. Open the Network Connections window, as described earlier.
2. Click the icon of the network connection you want to rename.
3. Click Rename This Connection in the taskbar, or press F2. Windows 7 adds a text box around the connection name.
4. Type the new name and press Enter.

NOTE

You use the same rules for naming network connections as you use for naming files. That is, the maximum name length is about 255 characters, and you can include any letter, number, or symbol except the following: * | \ : 0 < > / and ?.

Enabling Automatic IP Addressing

Every computer on your network requires a unique designation so that packets can be routed to the correct location when information is transferred across the network. In a default Microsoft peer-to-peer network, the network protocol that handles these transfers is *Transport Control Protocol / Internet Protocol* (TCP/IP), and the unique designation assigned to each computer is the IP address.

▶ For the details on TCP/IP, **see** Appendix B, "Understanding TCP/IP," **p. 741**.

By default, Windows 7 computers obtain their IP addresses via the *Dynamic Host Configuration Protocol* (DHCP). In most small networks, the router's DHCP server provides each network computer at logon with an IP address from a range of addresses.

However, activating the router's DHCP server is only the first step toward automating the assignment of IP addresses on your network. The second step is to make sure that each of your Windows 7 machines is configured to accept automatic IP addressing. This feature is turned on by default in most Windows 7 installations, but it's worth checking, just to be sure.

NOTE

The instructions in this section work for both wired and wireless connections.

Confirming That Windows 7 Is Configured for Dynamic IP Addressing

Here are the steps to follow to check (and, if necessary, change) Windows 7's automatic IP addressing setting:

1. Open the Network Connections window, as described earlier.

2. Select the connection you want to work with.

3. In the taskbar, click Change Settings of This Connection. Windows 7 display's the connection's Properties dialog box.

TIP

If you don't see the Change Settings of This Connection command, either maximize the window or click the double arrow (>>) that appears on the right side of the taskbar to display the commands that won't fit. Note, too, that you can also right-click the connection and then click Properties.

---

4. In the Networking tab's list of items, select Internet Protocol Version 4 (TCP/IPv4).

5. Click Properties to display the Properties dialog box for Internet Protocol Version 4.

6. Select the Obtain an IP Address Automatically option, as shown in Figure 25.17.

FIGURE 25.17   Select the Obtain an IP Address Automatically option to configure Windows 7 to accept the dynamic IP addresses assigned by your network's router.

7. Select the Obtain DNS Server Address Automatically option.

8. Click OK to return to the connection's Properties dialog box.

9. Click Close.

10. Repeat steps 2 through 9 for your other network connections.

Displaying the Computer's Current IP Address

There may be times when you need to know the current IP address assigned to your Windows 7 machine. For example, one networking troubleshooting process is to see whether you can contact a computer over the connection, a process known as *pinging* the computer (because you use Windows 7's PING command). In some cases, you need to know the computer's IP address for this method to work.

▶ For the details on using PING as a troubleshooting tool, **see** "Checking Connectivity with the PING Command," **p. 502.**

To find out the current IP address of the Windows 7 machine, use any of the following methods:

▶ In the Network Connections window, click the Network icon, click the taskbar's View Status of This Connection command (or double-click the network connection) to open the connection's Status dialog box. Click Details to open the Network Connection Details dialog box. As shown in Figure 25.18, the computer's current IP address appears as the IPv4 IP Address value.

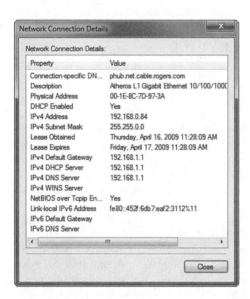

FIGURE 25.18   In the network connection's Status dialog box, the IPv4 IP Address value displays the Windows 7 computer's current IP address.

▶ Select Start, All Programs, Accessories, Command Prompt to open a command-line window. At the prompt, type **ipconfig | more** and press Enter. Windows 7 displays information about each network connection, including the IP address associated with each connection, as shown in the following (partial) example output:

NOTE

I've added the MORE command here to control the output of the IPCONFIG results. Windows 7 displays a screenful of data, and then displays -- More -- at the bottom of the screen. Press Enter to scroll through the rest of the results one line at a time, or press the spacebar to see the results one screen at a time.

```
Windows IP Configuration


Ethernet adapter Local Area Connection 2:


    Connection-specific DNS Suffix  . :
    Link-local IPv6 Address . . . . . : fe80::452f:6db7:eaf2:3112%11
    IPv4 Address. . . . . . . . . . . : 192.168.0.84
    Subnet Mask . . . . . . . . . . . : 255.255.0.0
    Default Gateway . . . . . . . . . : 192.168.1.1

Wireless LAN adapter Wireless Network Connection:


    Connection-specific DNS Suffix  . :
    Link-local IPv6 Address . . . . . : fe80::130:2a68:fde5:d668%8
    IPv4 Address. . . . . . . . . . . : 192.168.0.52
    Subnet Mask . . . . . . . . . . . : 255.255.0.0
    Default Gateway . . . . . . . . . : 192.168.1.1
```

Setting Up a Static IP Address

Your router's DHCP server offers each client a lease on the IP address, and in most cases, that lease expires after 24 hours. When the expiration time approaches, the client asks for a new IP address. In small networks, the DHCP server often assigns each client the same IP address each time, but that's not guaranteed. Because when you're working with Windows 7 you rarely need to know a connection's IP address, however, a changing IP address is no big deal the vast majority of the time.

However, there are times when a constantly changing IP address can be a big problem. For example, when you learn how to turn a Windows 7 machine into a lightweight web server in Chapter 28, "Turning Windows 7 into a Web Server," you see that a dynamic IP address makes it much harder for people to find and use the website. You can fix this problem by assigning a static IP address to a network connection.

TIP

Instead of assigning a static IP address to the Windows 7 computer, you might be able to get your router to handle this for you. Log on to your router's configuration pages and look for an option that enables you to map a static IP address to the computer MAC (see "Finding a Connection's MAC Address," later in this chapter) address. This means that whenever the computer requests a new DHCP lease, the router supplies the computer the same IP address each time. Note that not all routers offer this option.

NOTE

The instructions in this section work for both wired and wireless connections.

Displaying the Current DNS Addresses

When you use a dynamic IP address, in most cases, you also use dynamic DNS (*domain name system*) addresses, which are supplied by your *Internet service provider* (ISP). (The DNS enables computers and servers connected to the Internet to find resources using domain names rather than IP addresses.) When you switch your Windows 7 computer to a static IP address (as shown in the next section), Windows 7 also disables the feature that allows Windows 7 to obtain DNS addresses automatically. In other words, when you specify a static IP address, you must also specify static DNS addresses.

Therefore, before performing the procedure for converting Windows 7 to a static IP address, you need to determine your ISP's current DNS addresses. To find out the current DNS addresses for a network connection, use either of the following methods:

▶ In the Network Connections window, click the icon of the connection you want to work with, click the taskbar's View Status of This Connection command (or double-click the network connection) to open the connection's Status dialog box. Click Details to open the Network Connection Details dialog box. As shown earlier in Figure 25.18, the current DNS addresses appear as the IPv4 DNS Servers values.

▶ Select Start, All Programs, Accessories, Command Prompt to open a command-line window. At the prompt, type **ipconfig /all | more** and press Enter. Windows 7 displays information about each network connection, including the IP addresses of your ISP's DNS servers, as shown in the following (partial) example output:

25

NOTE

Remember that when using **MORE**, you control the output of the results by either pressing Enter (to scroll through the results one line at a time) or pressing the space-bar (to see the results one screen at a time).

```
Windows IP Configuration

    Host Name . . . . . . . . . . . . : OfficePC
    Primary Dns Suffix  . . . . . . . :
    Node Type . . . . . . . . . . . . : Hybrid
    IP Routing Enabled. . . . . . . . : No
    WINS Proxy Enabled. . . . . . . . : No

Ethernet adapter Local Area Connection 2:

    Connection-specific DNS Suffix  . :
    Description . . . . . . . . . . . : D-Link DGE-530T Gigabit Ethernet
➡Adapter
    Physical Address. . . . . . . . . : 00-13-46-95-84-28
    DHCP Enabled. . . . . . . . . . . : Yes
```

```
        Autoconfiguration Enabled . . . . : Yes
        Link-local IPv6 Address . . . . . : fe80::452f:6db7:eaf2:3112%11(Pre
➡ferred)
        IPv4 Address. . . . . . . . . . . : 192.168.1.84(Preferred)
        Subnet Mask . . . . . . . . . . . : 255.255.0.0
        Lease Obtained. . . . . . . . . . : Tuesday, August 28, 2009 10:01:41 AM
        Lease Expires . . . . . . . . . . : Wednesday, August 29, 2009 10:01:40 AM
        Default Gateway . . . . . . . . . : 192.168.1.1
        DHCP Server . . . . . . . . . . . : 192.168.1.1
        DHCPv6 IAID . . . . . . . . . . . : 301994822
        DNS Servers . . . . . . . . . . . : 207.164.234.193
                                            67.69.184.223
        NetBIOS over Tcpip. . . . . . . . : Enabled
```

Specifying the Static IP Address

You're now just about ready to assign a static IP address to your Windows 7 computer. The last bit of information you need to know is the IP address to use. This is important because you don't want to use an address that your router has already assigned to another computer. The easiest way to do this is to choose an address outside of the DHCP server's range. For example, if you configured the DHCP server to assign addresses from the range 192.168.0.100 to 192.168.0.150, an address such as 192.168.0.50 or 192.168.0.200 will work. (Remember, too, not to use the address assigned to your router.)

TIP

It's probably a good idea to check your router's DHCP table to see which addresses it has assigned. See your router documentation to learn how to do this.

With an IP address in hand, follow these steps to assign it to a network connection in Windows 7:

1. Open the Network Connections window, as described earlier.
2. Select the connection you want to work with.
3. In the taskbar, click Change Settings of This Connection. (You can also right-click the connection and then click Properties.) Windows 7 display's the connection's Properties dialog box.
4. In the Networking tab's list of items, select Internet Protocol Version 4 (TCP/IPv4).
5. Click Properties to display the Properties dialog box for Internet Protocol Version 4.
6. Click to activate the Use the Following IP Address option.
7. Use the IP Address box to type the IP address you want to use.
8. Use the Subnet Mask box to type the IP addresses for the subnet mask. (Windows 7 should fill this in for automatically; the most common value is 255.255.255.0.)

▶ To learn about subnet masks and other TCP/IP minutiae, **see** Appendix B, "Understanding TCP/IP," **p. 741**.

9. Use the Default Gateway box to type the IP address of your network's router.

10. Use the Preferred DNS Server and Alternate DNS Server boxes to type the IP addresses of your ISP's DNS servers. Figure 25.19 shows a completed version of the dialog box.

FIGURE 25.19   You can assign a static IP address to a network connection on a Windows 7 computer.

11. Click OK to return to the connection's Properties dialog box.

12. Click Close.

Finding a Connection's MAC Address

A NIC's MAC address seems like a pretty obscure value, but you'd be surprised how often it comes up. Here are two instances in this book:

▶ Later in this chapter, I show you how to wake up a remote computer that's in Windows 7's sleep mode, and the utility I mention requires the MAC address of a NIC on the remote computer.

▶ In Chapter 20, "Tightening Wireless Network Security," you learned that you can use wireless NIC MAC addresses to beef up the security of your wireless network.

▶ **See** "Enabling MAC Address Filtering," **p. 436**.

To find out the MAC address of the NIC associated with a network connection, use either of the following methods:

▶ In the Network Connections window, click the icon of the connection you want to work with, click the taskbar's View Status of This Connection command (or double-click the network connection) to open the connection's Status dialog box. Click

Details to open the Network Connection Details dialog box. As shown earlier in Figure 25.3, the connection's MAC address appears as the Physical Address value.

▶ Select Start, All Programs, Accessories, Command Prompt to open a command-line window. At the prompt, type **ipconfig /all | more** and press Enter. Windows 7 displays information about each network connection, including the MAC **addresses**, as shown in the following (partial) example output (see the Physical Address value):

```
Windows IP Configuration


    Host Name . . . . . . . . . . . . : OfficePC
    Primary Dns Suffix  . . . . . . . :
    Node Type . . . . . . . . . . . . : Hybrid
    IP Routing Enabled. . . . . . . . : No
    WINS Proxy Enabled. . . . . . . . : No


Ethernet adapter Local Area Connection 2:

    Connection-specific DNS Suffix  . :
    Description . . . . . . . . . . . : D-Link DGE-530T Gigabit Ethernet
➥Adapter
    Physical Address. . . . . . . . . : 00-13-46-95-84-28
    DHCP Enabled. . . . . . . . . . . : Yes
    Autoconfiguration Enabled . . . . : Yes
    Link-local IPv6 Address . . . . . : fe80::452f:6db7:eaf2:3112%11
➥(Preferred)
    IPv4 Address. . . . . . . . . . . : 192.168.1.84(Preferred)
    Subnet Mask . . . . . . . . . . . : 255.255.0.0
    Lease Obtained. . . . . . . . . . : Tuesday, August 28, 2009 10:01:41 AM
    Lease Expires . . . . . . . . . . : Wednesday, August 29, 2009 10:01:40 AM
    Default Gateway . . . . . . . . . : 192.168.1.1
    DHCP Server . . . . . . . . . . . : 192.168.1.1
    DHCPv6 IAID . . . . . . . . . . . : 301994822
    DNS Servers . . . . . . . . . . . : 207.164.234.193
                                        67.69.184.223
    NetBIOS over Tcpip. . . . . . . . : Enabled

Wireless LAN adapter Wireless Network Connection:

    Connection-specific DNS Suffix  . :
    Description . . . . . . . . . . . : D-Link AirPremier DWL-AG530 Wireless
➥PCI Adapter
    Physical Address. . . . . . . . . : 00-11-95-F5-BC-96
    DHCP Enabled. . . . . . . . . . . : Yes
    Autoconfiguration Enabled . . . . : Yes
    Link-local IPv6 Address . . . . . : fe80::130:2a68:fde5:d668%8(Preferred)
```

```
IPv4 Address. . . . . . . . . . . : 192.168.1.52(Preferred)
Subnet Mask . . . . . . . . . . . : 255.255.0.0
Lease Obtained. . . . . . . . . . : Tuesday, August 28, 2009 10:02:08 AM
Lease Expires . . . . . . . . . . : Wednesday, August 29, 2009 10:02:06 AM
Default Gateway . . . . . . . . . : 192.168.1.1
DHCP Server . . . . . . . . . . . : 192.168.1.1
DHCPv6 IAID . . . . . . . . . . . : 134222229
DNS Servers . . . . . . . . . . . : 207.164.234.193
                                    67.69.184.223
NetBIOS over Tcpip. . . . . . . . : Enabled
```

> **NOTE**
>
> The instructions in this section work for both wired and wireless connections.

Using a Network Connection to Wake Up a Sleeping Computer

Most Windows 7 computers are configured to go into sleep mode after a certain amount of idle time. If you're coming to Windows 7 from Windows XP, then sleep mode is the low-power state that Windows 7 uses to replace the confusing standby and hibernate modes from Windows XP. (Standby mode preserved your work and enabled you to restart quickly, but didn't entirely shut off the machine's power; hibernate mode preserved your work and completely shut off the machine, but also took a relatively long time to restart—faster than shutting down your computer entirely, but slower than standby.)

Windows 7's sleep state combines the best of the old standby and hibernate modes:

▶ As in standby, you enter sleep mode within just a few seconds.

▶ As in both standby and hibernate, sleep mode preserves all your open documents, windows, and programs.

▶ As in hibernate, sleep mode shuts down your computer, except it maintains power to the memory chips so that it can preserve the contents of RAM for when you restart.

▶ As in standby, you resume from sleep mode within just a few seconds.

To use sleep mode, you have two choices:

▶ To launch sleep mode by hand, open the Start menu, click the arrow beside the Shut Down button, and then click Sleep. Windows 7 saves the current state and shuts off the computer in a few seconds.

▶ To configure Windows 7 to go into sleep mode automatically, select Start, type **sleep**, and then click Change When the Computer Sleeps. Use the Put the Computer to Sleep list to select the number of minutes or hours of idle time after which Windows 7 automatically puts the computer to sleep. Click Save Changes.

Having a computer go to sleep when you're not using it is a good idea because it conserves power. However, it can be a pain if you need to access the computer remotely over your network because you have no way to wake up the sleeping computer (which normally requires a physical action such as jiggling the mouse or pressing the computer's power button).

Fortunately, most new NICs support a feature called *wake-on-LAN,* which enables the NIC to wake up the computer when the NIC receives a special Ethernet packet called a *magic packet* (usually the hexadecimal constant FF FF FF FF FF FF followed by several repetitions of the computer's MAC address).

For this to work, you must first configure the NIC to handle wake-on-LAN. Here are the steps to follow:

1. In the Network Connections window, right-click the connection that uses the NIC you want to configure, and then click Properties. The connection's Properties dialog box appears.
2. In the Networking tab, click Configure to open the NIC's Properties dialog box.
3. Display the Power Management tab.
4. Click to activate the Allow This Device to Wake the Computer check box.
5. Click to activate the Only Allow a Magic packet to Wake the Computer check box (see Figure 25.20).
6. Click OK.

FIGURE 25.20   To turn on a NIC's wake-on-LAN support, activate the Allow This Device to Wake the Computer check box.

NOTE

If the Allow This Device to Wake the Computer check box is disabled, it probably means your NIC doesn't support wake-on-LAN. However, it may also mean that this support has been disabled. In the NIC's Properties dialog box, display the Advanced tab and look for a property named Wake Up Capabilities. Click this property, and then choose an option in the Value list (such as Magic Packet or On). Click OK to put the new setting into effect, and then retry the steps in this section.

With the computer's NIC configured, you need to download a utility that can send a magic packet to the remote computer whenever you need to wake up the machine. I use MatCode Software's free Wake-on-LAN utility, available at www.matcode.com/wol.htm. (This utility requires the NIC's MAC address; see "Finding a Connection's MAC Address," earlier in this chapter.) You can also try Googling "wake-on-LAN utility."

TIP

When you use the wake-on-LAN feature, you probably don't want the remote computer to wake to the Windows 7 Welcome screen. Instead, it's almost always better to have the computer wake directly to the desktop. To disable the password requirement on wakeup, select Start, type **wake**, and then click the Require a Password When the Computer Wakes link to open the System Settings window. Click Change Settings That Are Currently Unavailable to enable the options. Activate the Don't Require a Password option, and then click Save Changes.

Disabling a Network Connection

It's possible that your Windows 7 computer has a network connection that it doesn't use. For example, if you upgraded to a Gigabit Ethernet NIC, you may no longer use your machine's old Fast Ethernet motherboard NIC. You can't detach a motherboard NIC from your computer (not easily, anyway), so the network connection icon remains, cluttering the Network Connections window and using up a few Windows 7 resources. If you don't plan on using such a connection, you're better off disabling it by following these steps:

1. In the Network Connections window, click the connection you want to work with, and then click the taskbar's Disable This Network Device command. (You can also right-click the connection and then click Disable.) The User Account Control dialog box appears.
2. Enter your UAC credentials to continue.

Windows 7 changes the connection's status to Disabled. If you want to use the connection again later on, click it, and then click the taskbar's Enable This Network Device command.

Managing Wireless Network Connections

Most small networks use just a single wireless connection—the connection to your network's wireless access point. However, it's no longer unusual to have multiple wireless networks configured on your computer. For example, you might have two or more wireless gateways in your home or office; you might have a wireless hot spot nearby; and as you see in this section, Windows 7 also enables you to set up computer-to-computer wireless connections to share files or an Internet connection without going through a wireless access point.

Windows 7 comes with a Manage Wireless Networks feature that lists your saved wireless networks and enables you to add new wireless connections, reorder the connections, and remove existing connections. This section shows you how to perform these and other wireless networking tasks.

Opening the Manage Wireless Networks Window

Most of the chores in this chapter take place in Windows 7's Manage Wireless Networks window. To get this window onscreen, open the Network and Sharing Center, and then click the Manage Wireless Networks link in the Tasks list. Figure 25.21 shows the Manage Wireless Networks window with a single network displayed.

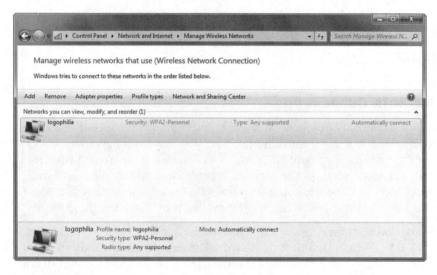

FIGURE 25.21   Windows 7's Manage Wireless Networks window.

By default, Windows 7 groups the wireless networks using the Extended Tiles view, and you can't change this view. The networks are listed in the order that Windows 7 uses to attempt connections (more on this later; see "Reordering Wireless Connections"). If your computer comes with multiple wireless NICs and you use those NICs to create separate connections, you can switch from one NIC to another by pulling down the Change Adapter list and selecting the NIC you want to work with.

Creating an Ad Hoc Wireless Network

If you don't have a wireless access point, Windows 7 enables you to set up a temporary network between two or more computers. This is an *ad hoc connection*, and it's useful if you need to share folders, devices, or an Internet connection temporarily. Note that the computers must be within 30 feet of each other for this type of connection to work.

Here are the steps to follow to create an ad hoc wireless network:

1. Open the Manage Wireless Networks window, as described earlier.
2. Click Add. Windows 7 displays the How Do You Want to Add a Network? dialog box.
3. Click Create an Ad Hoc Network. Windows 7 displays the Set Up a Wireless Ad Hoc Network dialog box.

NOTE

Another way to begin the process of creating an ad hoc wireless network is to open the Network and Sharing Center, click the Set Up a Connection or Network link to open the Choose a Connection Option dialog box, select Set Up a Wireless Ad Hoc (Computer-to-Computer) Network, and then click Next.

---

4. Click Next.
5. Provide the following data to set up the network (see Figure 25.22):

   ▶ **Network Name**—The name of the ad hoc network.

   ▶ **Security Type**—The security protocol used by the ad hoc wireless network. Select No Authentication (Open) if you want the network to be unsecured.

   ▶ **Security Key**—Type the key or password required for authorized access to the ad hoc network.

   ▶ **Save This Network**—Activate this check box to save the network in the Manage Wireless Networks list.

6. Click Next. Windows 7 sets up the ad hoc network.
7. If you want to share your computer's Internet connection, click Turn on Internet Connection Sharing.
8. Click Close. Windows 7 adds the ad hoc network to your list of networks in the Manage Wireless Networks window, as shown in Figure 25.23.

25

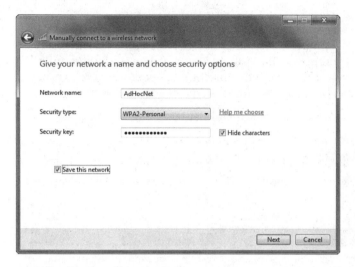

FIGURE 25.22   Use this dialog box to configure your ad hoc network's name and security type.

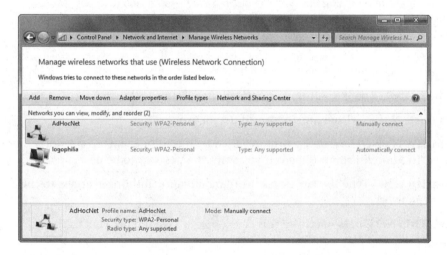

FIGURE 25.23   The new ad hoc network appears in the Manage Wireless Networks window.

Now, other people within 30 feet of your computer will see your ad hoc network in their list of available wireless networks, as shown in Figure 25.24. Note that the network remains available as long as at least one computer is connected to it, including the computer that created the network. The network is discarded when all computers (including the machine that created the network) have disconnected from it.

FIGURE 25.24   The ad hoc network is available to computers that are within 30 feet of the original computer.

Working with Wireless Connection Properties

When you connect to a wireless network, Windows 7 eases network management by doing two things:

▶ Windows 7 automatically stores the network in the Manage Wireless Networks window.

▶ If you tell Windows 7 to save the connection data (by activating the Connect Automatically check box), Windows 7 initiates the connection as soon as it detects the network when you log on. (In the Manage Wireless Networks window, Windows 7 displays the network's Mode value as Automatically Connect.)

These two features mean that, after running through the initial wireless network connection, you may never have to think about the connection again. However, if some aspect of the connection changes down the road, Windows 7 enables you to modify various connection properties, as described in the next two sections.

Before getting to the specifics, here are the techniques you can use to open a wireless network connection's Properties dialog box:

▶ Open the Manage Wireless Networks window, as described earlier, and then double-click the wireless network you want to work with.

▶ If the wireless network connection appears in the Network and Sharing Center, click the connection's link to open the Status dialog box, and then click Wireless Properties.

Modifying Connection Properties

In the wireless network connection's Properties dialog box, the Connection tab (see Figure 25.25) displays some basic information about the connection—the connection's local name, its SSID, the network type (Access Point or Ad Hoc Network), and the network availability (that is, which users can use the connection). You also get the following three check boxes:

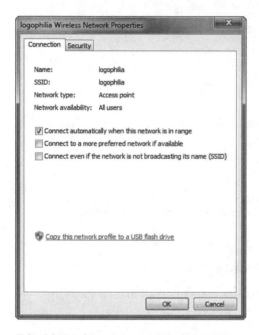

FIGURE 25.25   In the wireless network connection's Properties dialog box, the Connection tab enables you to configure a few connection-related properties.

▶ **Connect Automatically When This Network Is In Range**—Leave this check box activated to have Windows 7 connect to the network automatically whenever the network comes within range. If you prefer to connect to the network manually, deactivate this check box.

TIP

Connecting to a wireless network automatically is useful for those networks you use regularly. This applies to your home or office network, of course, but it may also be true of places you frequent, such as your local coffee shop or a hotel. However, if the network charges you for connection time, it's usually a good idea to connect manually.

▶ **Connect to a More Preferred Network If Available**—Leave this check box activated to have Windows 7 automatically disconnect from this network if a network that is listed higher in the Manage Wireless Networks list comes within range. (See "Reordering Wireless Connections" for more information about preferred networks.)

▶ **Connect Even If the Network Is Not Broadcasting Its Name (SSID)**—If you activate this check box, Windows 7 checks to see whether the network is within range even if the network isn't broadcasting its SSID. Leave this check box deactivated to improve security (see Chapter 20 for the details).

> ▶ See "Disabling Network SSID Broadcasting," **p. 432.**

Modifying Security Properties

After you make the initial connection to a wireless network, you may find that later on the network's security settings have changed. For example, an open network might decide to add encryption to improve security. Similarly, the person administering the network might upgrade to a more robust encryption setting or change the security key or password. You can adjust the security settings for an existing network using the settings in the Security tab of the wireless network connection's Properties dialog box. As shown in Figure 25.26, the Security tab offers the following controls:

▶ **Security Type**—The security protocol used by the wireless network. Select No Authentication (Open) if the network is unsecured.

▶ **Encryption Type**—The specific type of encryption used by the network's security protocol.

▶ **Network Security Key**—The key or password required for authorized access to the network.

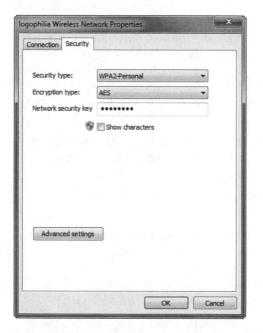

FIGURE 25.26   In the wireless network connection's Properties dialog box, the Security tab enables you to configure a few security-related properties.

▶ For more information about securing wireless networks with encryption, **see** "Encrypting Wireless Signals with WPA," **p. 430.**

Renaming Wireless Connections

By default, the local name that Windows 7 gives to a saved wireless network connection is the same as the network's SSID. Because SSIDs can sometimes be generic (for example, `default` is a common SSID on out-of-the-box access points) or obscure, you might want to change a network connection's local name to make it easier to work with. Here are the steps to follow to rename a connection:

1. Open the Manage Wireless Networks window, as described earlier.
2. Select the wireless network you want to rename.
3. Press F2. (You can also right-click the wireless network and then click Rename.)
4. Type the new name for the wireless network connection.
5. Press Enter.

NOTE

Note that renaming the wireless network connection means that you're only changing the local connection name used by Windows 7. The network's SSID is not affected.

Reordering Wireless Connections

Windows 7 configures a wireless network with an automatic connection so that you can get on the network as soon as Windows 7 detects it. (This is assuming that you activated the Connect Automatically check box when you made the initial connection.) If you have multiple wireless networks, Windows 7 maintains a priority list, and a network higher in that list connects before a network lower in that list. (A network higher in the list is said to be a *more preferred* network.) If you are not connecting to the wireless network you want, it might be that the network is lower on the network priority list. To work around this problem, you can move the network higher in the list.

Windows 7's wireless network priority list is none other than the list of networks in the Manage Wireless Networks window. Here are the steps to follow to use the Manage Wireless Networks window to reorder your wireless networks:

1. Open the Manage Wireless Networks window, as described earlier.
2. Select the network you want to move.
3. As you can see in Figure 25.27, the taskbar offers either the Move Up or Move Down command, and you use these commands to prioritize the networks:

   ▶ **Move Up**—Click this command to move the selected network to a higher priority. (You can also right-click the network and then click Move Up.)

   ▶ **Move Down**—Click this command to move the selected network to a lower priority. (You can also right-click the network and then click Move Down.)

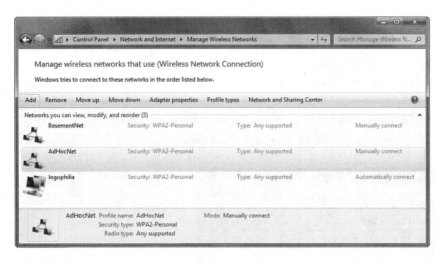

FIGURE 25.27   In the Manage Wireless Networks window, use the Move Up and Move Down commands to reorder your wireless networks.

NOTE

You don't see both Move Up and Move Down for every network. For example, if you select the network with the highest priority (that is, the network at the top of the list), you only see the Move Down command. Similarly, if you select the network with the lowest priority (that is, the network at the bottom of the list), you only see the Move Up command.

Creating User-Specific Wireless Connections

By default, when you connect to a wireless network and then elect to save the network (by activating the Save This Network check box after the connection has been made), Windows 7 makes the wireless connection available to all users of the computer. (That is, Windows 7 stores the wireless network connection in the computer's All Users profile, which is the profile that Windows 7 uses to make objects available to every user account on the computer.) This is usually the best way to go because it means you only have to make the connection to the wireless network once, and then the connection is set up for every user account.

Sometimes, however, you might not want other users to have access to a particular wireless network connection. For example, your neighbor might allow you to use his wireless network, but only on the condition that your kids not use the network.

For these kinds of situations, Windows 7 enables you to create user-specific wireless connections. This means that when a user connects to a wireless network, Windows 7 enables that user to save the wireless network connection in the user's profile. The other users on the computer will not see the connection.

Here are the steps to follow to activate Windows 7's user-specific profiles (or *per-user profiles*, as Windows 7 calls them) for wireless networks:

1. Open the Manage Wireless Networks window, as described earlier.

2. Select Profile Types in the taskbar. Windows 7 displays the Wireless Network Profile Type dialog box.

3. Select the Use All-User and Per-User Profiles option, as shown in Figure 25.28.

4. Click Save. Windows 7 puts the new setting into effect.

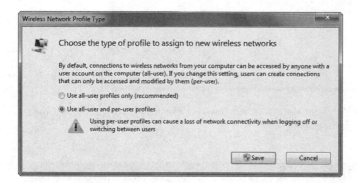

FIGURE 25.28   Use this dialog box to activate per-user wireless network profiles.

Now, when a user creates a wireless network connection, Windows 7 displays the dialog box shown in Figure 25.29, which gives the user three options:

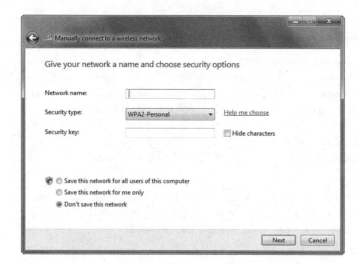

FIGURE 25.29   With per-user profiles activated, users can save wireless network connections in their own user profiles.

▶ **Save This Network for All Users of This Computer**—The user selects this option to save the wireless network connection in the All Users profile, which means that every user account will have access to the wireless network.

▶ **Save This Network for Me Only**—The user selects this option to save the wireless network connection in the user's profile only. Other user accounts will not have access to the wireless network.

▶ **Don't Save This Network**—The user selects this option to bypass saving the network connection.

Removing Wireless Connections

If you no longer use a wireless network, or if an existing wireless network has changed and you'd like to create a fresh connection for it, you can remove the wireless network from the Manage Wireless Networks window. Here are the steps to follow:

1. Open the Manage Wireless Networks window, as described earlier.
2. Select the wireless network you want to remove.
3. Click Remove or press Delete. Windows 7 warns you that you'll no longer be able to connect to the network automatically.
4. Click OK. Windows 7 removes the wireless network.

25

CHAPTER 26

Accessing and Using Your Network

I always get back to the question, is it really necessary that men should consume so much of their bodily and mental energies in the machinery of civilized life?
—William Allingham

Many home and small office networks exist for no other reason than to share a broadband Internet connection. The administrators of those networks attach a broadband modem to a router, configure the router, run some Ethernet cable (or set up wireless connections), and then they never think about the network again.

There's nothing wrong with this scenario, of course, but there's something that just feels, well, *incomplete* about such a network. Sharing an Internet connection is a must for any modern network, but networking should be about sharing so much more: disk drives, folders, documents, music, photos, videos, recorded TV shows, printers, scanners, CD and DVD burners, projectors, and more.

This expanded view of networking is about working, playing, and connecting with your fellow network users. It is, in short, about *sharing*, and sharing is the subject of this chapter. You learn how to access those network resources that others have shared, you learn how to share your own resources with the network, and you learn how to work with shared resources even when you're not connected to the network.

Accessing Shared Network Resources

After you connect to the network, the first thing you'll likely want to do is see what's on the network and access the available resources. Windows 7 gives you three ways to get started:

▶ Select Start, type **network**, and then click Network in the results.

▶ In any Windows Explorer window, click Network in the navigation pane.

▶ In the Network and Sharing Center, click the Network icon in the mini network map.

Either way, you see the Network window, which lists the main network resources, such as the computers and media devices in your workgroup. As you can see in Figure 26.1, Details view shows you the resource name, category, workgroup or domain name, and the name of the network profile.

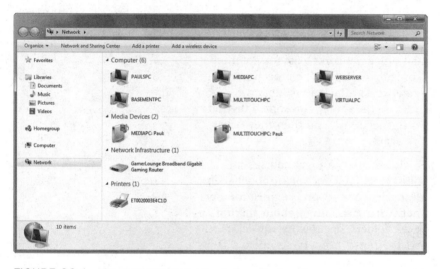

FIGURE 26.1   Windows 7's Network window displays the main resources on your network.

▶ For a more detailed look at the types of items you see in the Network window, **see** "Viewing Network Computers and Devices," **p. 523**.

Viewing a Computer's Shared Resources

Your Network window will likely show mostly computers, and those are the network items you'll work with most often. (The computers display an icon that shows a monitor and mini tower computer; if you're not sure, select View, Details and look for the objects that have Computer in the Category column.) If you don't see a particular computer, it likely means that the machine is either turned off or is currently in sleep mode. You need to either turn on or wake up the computer.

▶ You may be able to remotely wake up a computer that's in sleep mode; **see** "Using a Network Connection to Wake Up a Sleeping Computer," **p. 539**.

If you see the computer you want to work with, double-click the computer's icon. One of two things will happen:

▶ If your user account is also a user account on the remote computer, and that account has permission to view the view the remote computer, Windows 7 displays the computer's shared resources.

▶ If your user account is not a user account on the remote computer, and the remote computer has activated password-protected sharing (see "Setting Sharing Options," later in this chapter), Windows 7 displays the Enter Network Password dialog box. You need to type the username and password of an account on the remote computer, as shown in Figure 26.2.

FIGURE 26.2   You may need to log on to the remote computer to see its shared resources.

Figure 26.3 shows a typical collection of shared resources for a computer.

CAUTION

Double-clicking a network computer to see its shared resources works because the default action (which you initiate by double-clicking) for a network computer is to run the Open command, which opens the computer's shared resources in a folder window. However, not all the devices you see in the Network window have Open as the default action. For example, with media devices, the default action is either Open Media Player or Open Media Sharing. Other devices have more dangerous default actions. On some routers, for example, the default action is Disable, which disconnects the router's Internet connection! So, instead of just double-clicking any device to see what happens, it's better to right-click the device and examine the list of commands. In particular, make note of the command shown in bold type, which is the default action.

The computer shown in Figure 26.3 is sharing folders named Downloads, Paul, and Writing; two hard drives (c and d), a DVD drive, and a printer. The computer is also sharing the Public folder, which is open to everyone on the network and usually provides users with full read/write access. However, it's also possible to protect this folder by giving users read-only access, or by not displaying the Public folder at all. See "Sharing the Public Folder," later in this chapter.

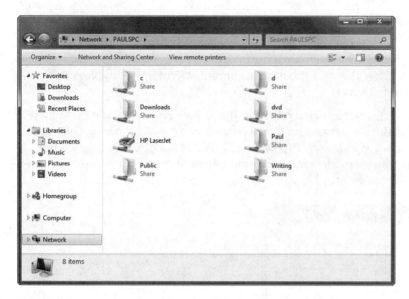

FIGURE 26.3   Double-click a network computer to see its shared resources.

Double-click a shared folder to see its contents. For example, Figure 26.4 displays the contents of the Paul folder shown in Figure 26.3. What you can do with the shared folder's contents depends on the permissions the computer owner has applied to the folder. See "Sharing a Resource with the Sharing Wizard" and "Sharing a Resource with Advanced Permissions," later in this chapter.

Working with Network Addresses

In Figure 26.4, the address bar shows the breadcrumb path to the shared folder:

Network > PAULSPC > Paul

Clicking an empty section of the address bar (or the icon that appears on the left side of the address bar) changes the breadcrumb path to the following network address, as shown in Figure 26.5:

\\PAULSPC\Paul

As you can see, a network address uses the following format:

\\ComputerName\ShareName

Here, ComputerName is the name of the network computer, and ShareName is the name of the shared resource on that computer. This format for network addresses is known as the

FIGURE 26.4   Double-click a shared folder to see its contents.

Network address

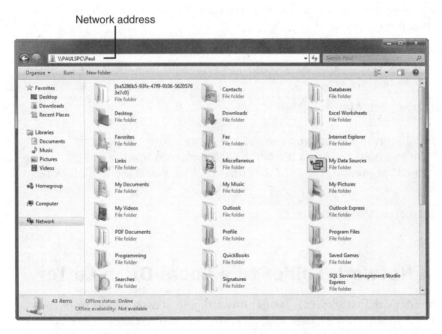

FIGURE 26.5   Click an empty section of the address bar to see the network address.

Universal Naming Convention (UNC). If the UNC refers to a drive or folder, you can use the regular Windows path conventions to access folders and subfolders on that resource. For example, the resource `Paul` on PAULSPC has a `Databases` folder, and the network address of that folder would be as follows:

```
\\PAULSPC\Paul\Databases
```

Similarly, if that `Databases` folder has an `Access` subfolder, here's the network address of that subfolder:

```
\\PAULSPC\Paul\Databases\Access
```

So, although you'll most often use icons in folder windows to navigate through a computer's shared resources, network addresses give you an alternative way to specify the resource you want to work with. Here are some examples:

▶ In the Network Explorer, click an empty section of the address bar, type the network address for a shared resource, and then press Enter.

▶ Press Windows Logo+R (or select Start, All Programs, Accessories, Run) to open the Run dialog box. Type the network address for a shared resource, and then click OK to open the resource in a folder window.

▶ In a program's Open or Save As dialog box, you can type a network address in the File Name text box.

▶ In a Command Prompt session (select Start, All Programs, Accessories, Command Prompt), type **start**, then a space, then the network address of the resource you want to open. Here's an example:

```
start \\paulspc\paul\databases
```

▶ In a Command Prompt session, you can use a network address as part of a command. For example, to copy a file named `projects.mdb` from `\\PAULSPC\Paul\Databases\Access` to the current folder, you'd use the following command:

```
copy "\\paulspc\paul\databases\access\projects.mdb"
```

Mapping a Network Folder to a Local Drive Letter

Navigating a computer's shared folders is straightforward, and is no different from navigating the folders on your own computer. However, you might find that you need to access a particular folder on a shared resource quite often. That's not a problem if the folder is shared directly—see, for example, the shared `Paul` folder in Figure 26.3. However, the folder you want might be buried several layers down. For example, you may need to open the `Paul` folder, then the `Databases` folder, then `Access`, and so on. That's a lot of double-clicking. You could use the network address, instead, but even that could get long and unwieldy. (And, with Murphy's law still in force, the longer the address, the greater the chance of a typo slipping in.)

You can avoid the hassle of navigating innumerable network folders and typing lengthy network addresses by *mapping* the network folder to your own computer. Mapping means that Windows assigns a drive letter to the network folder, such as G: or Z:. The advantage here is that now the network folder shows up as just another disk drive on your machine, enabling you to access the resource quickly by selecting Start, Computer.

NOTE

You might also find that mapping a network folder to a local drive letter helps with some older programs that aren't meant to operate over a network connection. For example, I have a screen-capture program that I need to use from time to time. If I capture a screen on another computer and then try to save the image over the network to my own computer, the program throws up an error message telling me that the destination drive is out of disk space (despite having, in fact, hundreds of gigabytes of free space on the drive). I solve this problem by mapping the folder on my computer to a drive letter on the other computer, which fools the program into thinking it's dealing with a local drive instead of a network folder.

Creating the Mapped Network Folder

To map a network folder to a local drive letter, follow these steps:

1. Select Start, right-click Computer, and then click Map Network Drive. (In any folder window, you can also click Map Network Drive in the toolbar.) Windows 7 displays the Map Network Drive dialog box.

2. The Drive drop-down list displays the last available drive letter on your system, but you can pull down the list and select any available letter.

CAUTION

If you use a removable drive, such as a memory card or Flash drive, Windows 7 assigns the first available drive letter to that drive. This can cause problems if you have a mapped network drive that uses a lower drive letter. Therefore, it's good practice to use higher drive letters (such as *X*, *Y*, and *Z*) for your mapped resources.

---

3. Use the Folder text box to type the network address of the folder, as shown in Figure 26.6. (Alternatively, click Browse, select the shared folder in the Browse for Folder dialog box, and then click OK.)

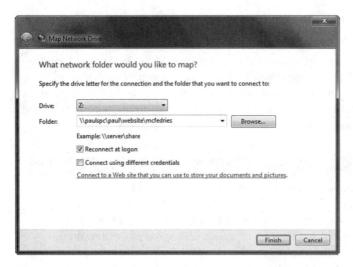

FIGURE 26.6   Use the Map Network Drive dialog box to assign a drive letter to a network resource.

4. If you want Windows 7 to map the network folder to this drive letter each time you log on to the system, leave the Reconnect at Logon check box activated.

TIP

By default, Windows 7 connects you to the network folder using your current username and password. If the network folder requires a different username and password, click the Different User Name link to open the Connect As dialog box. Type the account data in the User Name and Password text boxes, and then click OK.

5. Click Finish. Windows 7 adds the new drive letter to your system and opens the new drive in a folder window.

To open the mapped network folder later, select Start, Computer, and then double-click the drive in the Network Location group (see Figure 26.7).

Mapped network drive

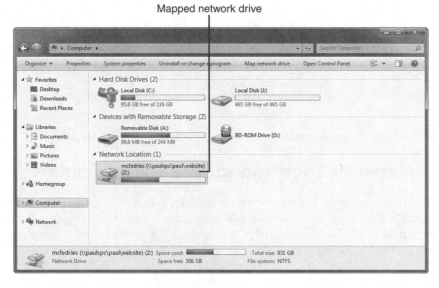

FIGURE 26.7   After you map a network folder to a local drive letter, the mapped drive appears in the Computer window for easier access.

Mapping Folders at the Command Line

You can also map a network folder to a local drive letter by using a Command Prompt session and the NET USE command. Although you probably won't use this method very often, it's handy to know how it works, just in case. Here's the basic syntax:

```
NET USE [drive] [share] [password] [/USER:user] [/PERSISTENT:[YES | NO]] | /DELETE]
```

drive	The drive letter (following by a colon) of the local drive to which you want the network folder mapped.
share	The network address of the folder.
password	The password required to connect to the shared folder (that is, the password associated with the username, specified next).
/USER:*user*	The username you want to use to connect to the shared folder.
/PERSISTENT:	Add YES to reconnect the mapped network drive the next time you log on.
/DELETE	Deletes the existing mapping that's associated with *drive*.

For example, the following command maps the shared folder \\PAULSPC\Paul\Writing\Books to the Z: drive:

```
net use z: \\paulspc\paul\writing\books \persistent:yes
```

Disconnecting a Mapped Network Folder

If you no longer need to map a network resource, disconnect it by following these steps:

1. Select Start, Computer to open the Computer window.
2. Right-click the mapped drive, and then click Disconnect.
3. If there are files open from the resource, Windows 7 displays a warning to let you know that it's unsafe to disconnect the resource. You have two choices:

   ▶ Click No, close all open files from the mapped resource, and then repeat steps 1 and 2.

   ▶ If you're sure there are no open files, click Yes to disconnect the resource.

Creating a Network Location for a Remote Folder

When you map a network folder to a drive on your computer, Windows 7 creates an icon for the mapped drive in the Computer folder's Network Location group. However, you may find that the supply of available drive letters is getting low if your computer has multiple hard drives, multiple CD or DVD drives, a memory card reader, a Flash drive or two, and so on.

To work around this problem, you can add your own icons to the Computer folder's Network Location group. These icons are called, appropriately enough, *network locations*, and each one is associated with a particular network folder. That is, after you create a network location, you can access the network folder associated with that location by double-clicking the icon. This is usually a lot faster than drilling down through several layers of folders on the network computer, so create network locations for those network folders you access most often.

Follow these steps to create a network location:

1. Select Start, Computer to open the Computer folder.
2. Right-click an empty section of the Computer folder, and then click Add a Network Location. Windows 7 launches the Add Network Location Wizard.
3. Click Next in the initial wizard dialog box.
4. Select Choose a Custom Network Location, and then click Next.
5. Type the network address of the folder you want to work with. Notice that as you enter the address, the Add Network Location Wizard displays a list of objects that match what you've typed; so, you can save some typing by selecting items from the lists as they appear (see Figure 26.8). You can also click Browse to use the Browse for Folder dialog box to select the network folder.
6. Click Next.
7. Type a name for the network location and click Next.
8. Click Finish. The Add Network Location Wizard adds an icon for the network folder to the Computer window, as shown in Figure 26.9.

FIGURE 26.8   As you enter the network address, the Add Network Location Wizard displays a list of objects that match what you've typed.

Network location

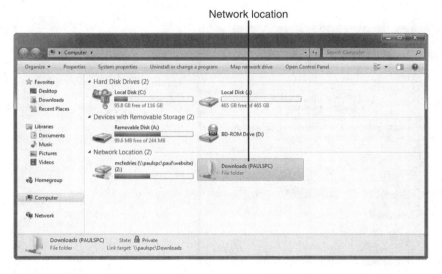

FIGURE 26.9   After you associate a network folder with a network location, an icon for the new location appears in the Computer window.

Accessing a Shared Printer

Except for perhaps disk drives, the most commonly shared device on small networks is almost certainly the printer. This makes sense because almost everyone needs to print something sometime, and those print jobs vary: One day it's a letter to send to the laser printer, and the next it's a photo to send to the inkjet. Of course, it's wasteful (and decidedly impractical) to attach both a laser printer and an inkjet printer to every computer. It's just so much easier (and cheaper) to share one of each type of printer on the network so that everyone can use them.

To access a shared printer, you must connect to it. Here are the steps to follow:

1. Open the network computer or print server that has the printer you want to use.
2. Right-click the shared printer.
3. Click Connect. If a Windows 7 driver for the shared printer isn't already installed on your computer, Windows 7 warns you that it must install the driver to use the shared printer.
4. Click Install Driver. Windows 7 installs the printer driver.

You can also add a shared network printer using Windows 7's Add Printer Wizard. Follow these steps:

1. Select Start, Devices and Printers to open the Devices and Printers window.
2. Click Add a Printer in the Task bar to open the Add Printer Wizard.
3. Click Add a Network, Wireless or Bluetooth Printer. Windows 7 searches for shared printers on the network and then displays a list of the printer it found, as shown in Figure 26.10.

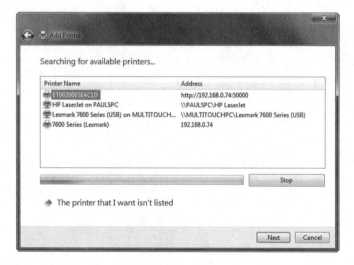

FIGURE 26.10   The Add Printer Wizard displays a list of the shared printers that it found on your network.

4. Select the network printer you want to use.
5. Click Next. If a Windows 7 driver for the shared printer isn't already installed on your computer, Windows 7 warns you that it must install the driver to use the shared printer.
6. Click Install Driver. Windows 7 installs the printer driver.
7. Click Finish.

After you connect to a shared printer, Windows 7 adds it to the Devices and Printers window. The name of the icon you see takes the following general form:

PrinterName on *ComputerName*

Here, *PrinterName* is the name of the printer as given by its device driver, and *ComputerName* is the name of the computer or print server to which the printer is attached. For example, Figure 26.11 shows a connected shared printer that uses the following name:

`Lexmark 7600 Series (USB) on MULTITOUCHPC`

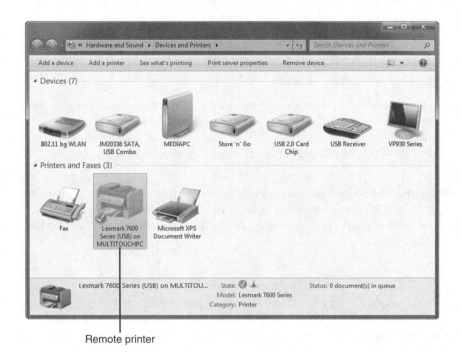

Remote printer

FIGURE 26.11   When you connect to a remote shared printer, Windows 7 adds an icon for the printer to your Printers window.

Sharing Resources with the Network

Small networks are normally egalitarian affairs because no computer is in any significant sense more important than the others. One of the ways that this digital equality manifests itself is via the universal sharing of at least some resources on each computer. People rarely make their entire computer available to their fellow network users, but it's a rare machine that doesn't have at least a drive or folder to share.

Setting Sharing Options

Fortunately, when it comes to sharing resources on the network, Windows 7 comes with options that enable you to share what resources you want to share for controlling how others can access those resources. Network sharing in Windows 7 begins by configuring the basic sharing options, of which there are five in all:

- ▸ **File and Printer Sharing**—You use this option to turn file and printer sharing on or off.

- ▸ **Public Folder Sharing**—You use this option to turn sharing of the Public folder on or off.

- ▸ **Media Streaming**—You use this option to turn media sharing on or off. Note that this sharing option is only available for Homegroup-based networks (see Chapter 25).

  - ▸ **See** "Setting Up a Homegroup," **p. 518**.

- ▸ **File-Sharing Connections**—You use this option to set the encryption level of your network connections. By default, Windows 7 uses strong 128-bit encryption to protect connections from network snoops. If you have network equipment that doesn't support this level of encryption, you can switch to a lower level of encryption.

- ▸ **Password-Protected Sharing**—You use this option to turn sharing with password protection on or off. When you turn on password-protected sharing, only people who know the username and password of an account on your computer can access your shared resources.

Follow these steps to set these options:

1. Select Start, type **sharing**, and then select Manage Advanced Sharing Settings in the search results. (Alternatively, open the Network and Sharing Center and click the Advanced Sharing Settings link.) The Advanced Sharing Settings window appears, as shown in Figure 26.12.
2. Click the downward-pointing arrow to the right of the Home or Work profile to expand it.
3. Select the option you want in the File and Printer Sharing section.
4. Select the option you want in the Public Folder Sharing section.
5. To turn on media sharing for your homegroup (if you have one), click Choose Media Streaming Options and then click Turn On Media Streaming.
6. Select the option you want in the File Sharing Connections section.
7. Select the option you want in the Password Protected Sharing section.
8. Click Save Changes to put the new settings into effect.

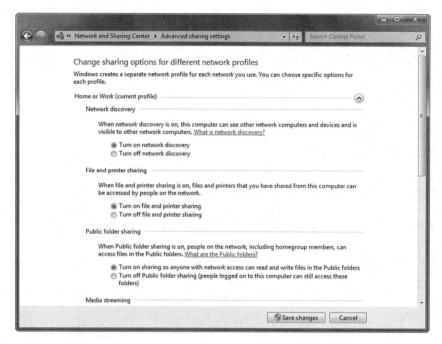

FIGURE 26.12   In the Advanced Sharing Settings window, expand the Home or Work profile to see the profile's sharing options.

Creating User Accounts for Sharing

If you activated the Password Protected Sharing option (see the previous section), you have to do one of the following:

▶ **Set up separate accounts for each user that you want to access a shared resource**—Do this if you want to assign each user a different set of permissions, or if you want the usernames and passwords to match each user's local username and password.

▶ **Set up a single account for all remote users to use**—Do this if you want to assign the same set of permissions for all users.

Here are some notes to bear in mind for creating users who will access your computer over a network:

▶ Windows 7 does *not* allow users without passwords to access network resources. Therefore, you must set up your network user accounts with passwords.

▶ The usernames you create don't have to correspond with the names that users have on their local machines. You're free to set up your own usernames, if you like.

▶ If you create a user account that has the same name and password as an account of a user on his or her local machine, that user will be able to access your shared resources directly. Otherwise, as you saw earlier (see Figure 26.2), a Windows Security dialog box appears so that the user can enter the username and password that you established when setting up the account on your computer.

See Chapter 18, "Setting Up User Security," to learn the details of creating user accounts.

▶ **See** "Creating and Managing User Accounts," **p. 384**.

▶ To learn how to share a folder using advanced permissions, **see** "Setting Sharing Permissions on Shared Folders," **p. 411**.

Monitoring Your Shared Resources

After a while, you might lose track of which folders you've shared. You could look through all your folders to look for those that have the Shared icon attached, but that's too much work, and you could easily miss some shared folder. Fortunately, Windows 7 comes with a snap-in tool called Shared Folders that enables you to monitor various aspects of the folders that you've shared with the network. For example, for each shared folder, you can find out the users who are connected to the folder, how long they've been connected, and the files they have open. You can also disconnect users from a shared folder or close files that have been opened on a shared folder. The next few sections provide the details.

To get started, you need to open the Shared Folders snap-in: select Start, type `fsmgmt.msc`, and press Enter.

Viewing the Current Connections

To see a list of the users connected to any Windows 7 shared folder, select Shared Folders, Sessions. Figure 26.13 shows an example. For each user, you get the following data:

User	The name of the user.
Computer	The name of the user's computer. If Windows 7 doesn't recognize the computer, it shows the machine's IP address, instead.
Type	The type of network connection. Windows 7 always shows this as Windows (even if the user is connected from a Mac or from Linux).
Open Files	The number of open files in the shared folders.
Connected Time	The amount of time that the user has been connected to the remote computer.
Idle Time	The amount of time that the user has not been actively working on the open files.
Guest	Whether the user logged on using the Guest account.

NOTE

To ensure that you're always viewing the most up-to-date information, regularly select the Action, Refresh command or click the Refresh toolbar button (pointed out in Figure 26.13).

Remote printer

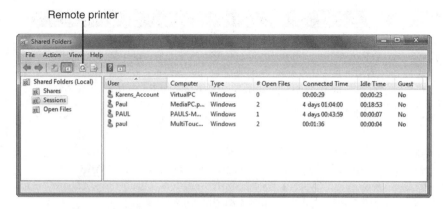

FIGURE 26.13   The Sessions folder shows the users currently connected to shared folders on the remote computer.

Viewing Connections to Shared Folders

The Shared Folders snap-in also makes it possible for you to view the connections to Windows 7 by its shared folders. To get this display, select Shared Folders, Shares. As you can see in Figure 26.14, this view provides the following information:

Share Name	The name of the shared folder. Note that the list includes the Windows 7 hidden shares.
Folder Path	The drive or folder associated with the share.
Type	The type of network connection, which Windows 7 always shows as Windows.
# Client Connections	The number of computers connected to the share.
Description	The description of the share.

26

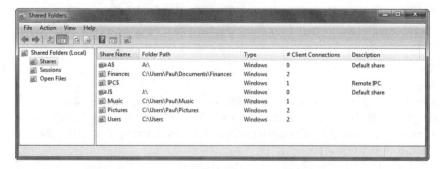

FIGURE 26.14   The Shared Folders snap-in can display a server's connections by its shared folders.

TIP

You can also use the Shares branch to work with the shared folders. For example, select a share and then select Action, Open to display the folder. You can also select Action, Properties to modify the share name, description, and permissions of the selected share. Finally, you can also select Action, Stop Sharing to turn off sharing on the selected folder.

Viewing Open Files

The Shared Folders snap-in can also display the files that are open on the Windows 7 shares. To switch to this view, select System Tools, Shared Folders, Open Files. Figure 26.15 shows the result. Here's a summary of the columns in this view:

Open File   The full pathname of the file.

Accessed By   The name of the user who has the file open.

Type   The type of network connection, which Windows 7 always shows as `Windows`.

Locks   The number of locks on the file.

Open Mode   The permissions the user has over the file.

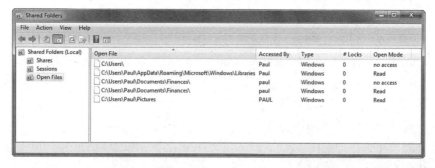

FIGURE 26.15   The Shared Folders snap-in can also display a remote computer's open files in its shared resources.

Closing a User's Session or File

Although, in the interest of network harmony, you'll want to let users connect and disconnect as they please, at times you might need to boot someone off a machine. For example, you might see that someone has obtained unauthorized access to a share. To disconnect that user, follow these steps:

1. In the Shared Folders snap-in, select Shared Folders, Sessions.
2. Right-click the name of the user you want to disconnect.
3. Click Close Session. Windows 7 asks you to confirm.
4. Click Yes.

Similarly, you'll usually want to let users open and close files themselves so that they don't lose information. However, you might find that a user has a particular file open and you would prefer that the user not view that file (for example, because you want to work on the file yourself or because the file contains information you don't want the user to see). To close a file opened by a user, follow these steps:

1. In the Shared Folders snap-in, select Shared Folders, Open Files.
2. Right-click the name of the file you want to close.
3. Click Close Open File. Windows 7 asks you to confirm.
4. Click Yes.

CAUTION

If you have a file in a shared folder and you don't want other users to see that file, it makes more sense to either move the file to a protected folder or change the permissions on the file's current folder.

NOTE

The remote user doesn't see a warning or any other indication that you're closing the file. For example, if the user is playing a music file, that file just stops playing and can't be started again (except by closing all open shared files and folders and starting a new session).

Working with Network Files Offline

In Chapter 27, "Making Remote Network Connections," you learn how to connect to computers on your network using an Internet connection. This is very useful if you're away from your network and need to grab a file or two or just check a fact in some document. However, what do you do if there's no Internet connection available? In that case, there's nothing you can do to get connected to your network. Still, with a bit of advance planning on your part, you can do the next best thing: You can take a bit of the network with you.

This is possible using a Windows 7 feature known as *offline files*. These are network files or folders that Windows 7 has copied to a special folder on your computer. When you disconnect from the network—that is, when you go *offline*—the files and folders remain on your computer, so you can view and even edit the files any time you like. When you reconnect to the network—that is, when you go online—you can synchronize your offline files with the network originals.

The rest of this chapter shows you how to enable offline files, work with files offline, and synchronize the files to keep everything up-to-date. Note, however, that not all versions of Windows 7 come with the Offline Files feature. You only see this feature if you have Windows 7 Business, Enterprise, or Ultimate.

▶ For the details on making remote connections to your network, **see** "Connecting to a Remote Desktop via the Internet," **p. 599**.

Activating the Offline Files Feature

Most Windows 7 systems should have offline files enabled by default. However, it's a good idea to check to make sure that your system has them enabled. Here are the steps to follow:

    1. Select Start, type **offline**, and then select Manage Offline Files in the search results. Windows 7 opens the Offline Files dialog box, shown in Figure 26.16.

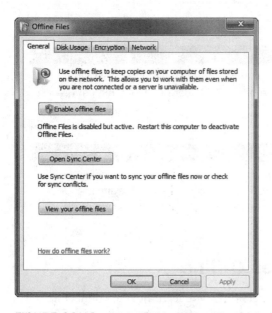

FIGURE 26.16   Click Enable Offline Files to activate the Offline Files feature.

    2. Click the Enable Offline Files button. (If you see the Disable Offline Files button instead, offline files are enabled, so click Cancel.)

    3. Click OK. Windows 7 prompts you to restart your computer to put the new setting into effect.

    4. Click Yes. Windows 7 restarts your computer.

Making a File or Folder Available for Offline Use

With the Offline Files feature turned on, you're ready to make network files or folders available offline. First, decide what data you need to take with you. Remember that the more files you make available offline, the longer it will take to synchronize everything later, and the more disk space the files will take up on your system. (Note, however, that Windows 7 places a ceiling the amount of disk space that offline files can use; see "Changing the Amount of Disk Space Used By Offline Files," next.)

When you've decided which files and folders you want to use offline, follow these steps to set them up for offline use:

1. Use Windows Explorer to open the folder that contains the shared network files or folders that you want to use offline.
2. Select the files or folders you want to use offline.
3. Right-click any selected item, and click Always Available Offline.

TIP

If your right mouse button doesn't work, press Alt to display the menu bar, and then select File, Always Available Offline.

4. Windows 7 synchronizes the files or folders for offline use. While the initial synchronization occurs, Windows 7 displays the Always Available Offline dialog box. If you're using quite a few files offline, the synchronization might take a long time. If so, click Close to hide the Always Available Offline dialog box.

When you make a file or folder available offline, Windows 7 changes the object's Offline Availability property to `Always Available`, and it adds the Sync Center icon to the object's regular icon, as shown in Figure 26.17. Note, too, the Sync button in the Task pane, which enables you to quick synchronize an offline file or folder; see "Synchronizing Your Offline Files," later in this chapter.

26

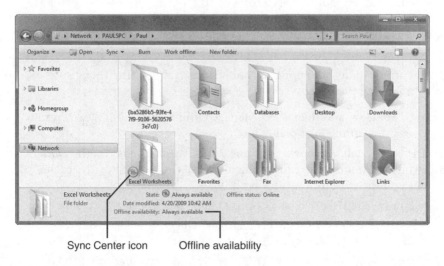

Sync Center icon   Offline availability

FIGURE 26.17   An offline file or folder shows `Always Available` in the Offline Availability property, and the Sync Center icon on its regular icon.

When the initial synchronization finishes, you can disconnect from the network and work with the files offline.

Changing the Amount of Disk Space Used by Offline Files

I mentioned earlier that you want to be a bit careful about the amount of data you choose to work with offline because synchronizing large amounts of data can take quite a while, and each offline file and folder takes up some disk space on your own computer. Fortunately, just in case you go overboard, Windows 7 puts a limit on the amount of disk space that it uses for both the offline files themselves and for temporary offline files. (Temporary offline files are local copies of network files that you've used recently. Windows 7 keeps these files cached automatically so that you can use them offline if you need them.)

The default limits on the disk space used by offline files and temporary offline files imposed by Windows 7 depend on the size of your hard drive and the amount of free space on that drive. (More specifically, it depends on the size and free space of the hard drive where Windows 7 is installed.) In general, the larger the hard drive and the more free space it has, the greater the percentage of disk space that Windows 7 sets aside for offline data. The usual limits are between 10% and 24% of the total disk space. For example, on a 15GB drive, if Windows 7 sets a limit of 10% of total disk space, you have 1.5GB available for both types of offline files. Similarly, on a 190GB drive, if Windows 7 sets a limit of about 24% of total disk space, you have 50GB available for both types of offline files.

You can check your current limits, and optionally adjust them if you find them to be too high or too low, by following these steps:

1. Select Start, type **offline**, and then select Manage Offline Files in the search results. Windows 7 opens the Offline Files dialog box.
2. Display the Disk Usage tab. As shown in Figure 26.18, this tab tells you the amount of disk space you're currently using for offline files and for the offline files cache, and it also tells you the current limits for both types.
3. Click Change Limits. The User Account Control dialog box appears.
4. Enter your User Account Control (UAC) credentials. The Offline Files Disk Usage Limits dialog box appears, as shown in Figure 26.19.
5. Use the Maximum Amount of Space All Offline Files Can Use slider to set the limit for offline files.
6. Use the Maximum Amount of Space Temporary Offline Files Can Use slider to set the limit for the offline files cache.

FIGURE 26.18   The Disk Usage tab shows you the disk space used by your offline files as well as the disk space limits.

FIGURE 26.19   Use the Offline Files Disk Usage Limits dialog box to adjust the maximum disk space used by offline and temporary offline files.

7. Click OK to return to the Offline Files dialog box.

8. Click OK.

Prohibiting a Network Folder from Being Made Available Offline

You may occasionally come across a network folder or file that you don't want some users on your network to make available offline:

▶ You might want to prohibit people from making a recorded TV folder available offline because the synchronization would take too long and use up too many network resources.

▶ You might have a network folder or file that contains private or sensitive data, and you don't want that data leaving the office.

▶ You might want to do extensive work on the files in a particular folder, and so you don't want other making changes to those files while offline.

For these and similar reasons, Windows 7 enables you to prohibit a user from making a particular network folder available offline. This means that when the user navigates to the network folder or file, Windows 7 doesn't display the Always Available Offline command, so the user can't make the object available offline.

Here are the steps to follow:

1. Log on to the computer of the user for whom you want to set up the restriction. Ideally, you should log on with an Administrator-level account.

2. Select Start, type **gpedit.msc** and press Enter. The Local Group Policy Object Editor appears.

3. Select User Configuration, Administrative Templates, Network, Offline Files.

4. Double-click the Prohibit 'Make Available Offline' for These Files and Folders option.

5. Click the Enabled option.

6. Click Show to open the Show Contents dialog box.

7. In the Value Name column, type the network address of the folder or file you want to prohibit (see Figure 26.20).

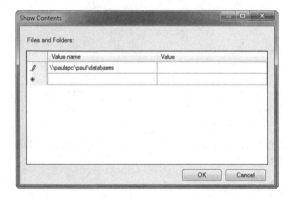

FIGURE 26.20   Specify the network address of the file or folder that you don't want to be made available offline.

8. Press Enter.

9. Repeat steps 7 and 8 to add any other files or folders that you want to prohibit.

10. Click OK to return to the Prohibit 'Make Available Offline' for These Files and Folders dialog box.

11. Click OK.

Encrypting Offline Files

In the previous section, I mentioned that one of the reasons you might want to prohibit a file or folder from being made available offline is that it may contain private or sensitive data that you don't want leaving your home or office. That's sensible because a thief could easily steal your notebook and might be able to access the sensitive data. However, it's a problem if you really need to work with that data while you're offline.

To work around this problem, you can encrypt your offline files, which scrambles the file contents so that no snoop can read them unless he can log on to your computer using your Windows 7 account. Because that's unlikely (I'm assuming here that your account is protected by a strong password, which it should be if you're working with sensitive data), your data is safe.

> **CAUTION**
>
> Of course, when you're logged in to Windows 7, you should never leave your notebook unattended. Not only does this make it easy for someone to make off with your computer, it also defeats the purpose of encryption because the thief will already be logged on.

Follow these steps to encrypt your offline files:

1. Select Start, type **offline**, and then select Manage Offline Files in the search results. Windows 7 opens the Offline Files dialog box.
2. Display the Encryption tab.
3. Click Encrypt. Windows 7 encrypts the offline files.
4. Click OK.

> **NOTE**
>
> After Windows 7 encrypts the offline files, it displays the Encrypting File System icon in the taskbar. You should back up your encryption key to a removable media, such as a USB thumb drive, external hard drive, or memory card, as soon as possible. To do this, click the Back Up Your File Encryption Key message to open the Encrypting File System dialog box, and then click Back Up Now to launch the Certificate Export Wizard.

Working with Network Files While You're Offline

After you disconnect from your network, you can start working with your offline files just as though you were still connected to the network. Windows 7 gives you two ways to go about this:

- ▶ You can access the offline files via the Sync Center.

- ▶ You can access the offline files by leaving the remote computer's folder window open.

The next couple of sections provide the details.

26

Working with Offline Files via the Sync Center

The Sync Center is Windows 7's home base for information that you want to keep synchronized, particularly offline files. To open the Sync Center and view your offline files, follow these steps:

1. Select Start, type **sync**, and press Enter. Windows 7 opens the Sync Center window.

2. Click View Sync Partnerships (although this is selected by default). You see the Offline Files folder.

3. Double-click Offline Files. The Sync Center displays your sync partnership details, as shown in Figure 26.21.

4. Double-click a sync partnership to open the offline files in a folder window.

Now you can open and edit the files just as though you were connected to the network.

FIGURE 26.21   Double-click a sync partnership to see your offline files.

Working with Offline Files via the Remote Computer

If you leave the remote computer's folder open when you disconnect, you can use that folder to navigate the offline files directly. Figure 26.22 shows a folder for a network PC, but the computer itself is disconnected from the network (as shown by the Network icon in the notification area). As you saw earlier, the objects available offline display the Offline Files icon superimposed on their regular icon and, when you select an offline object, the Details pane shows Offline (not connected) as the Offline Status (see Figure 26.22).

> **TIP**
>
> After you disconnect, you can't navigate to a remote computer's folder via Start, Network because Windows 7 will tell you that you aren't connected to a network. Besides leaving the remote computer's folder window open when you disconnect, you can also type the remote computer's network address into the Start menu's Search box, the Run dialog box, or the Windows Explorer address bar.

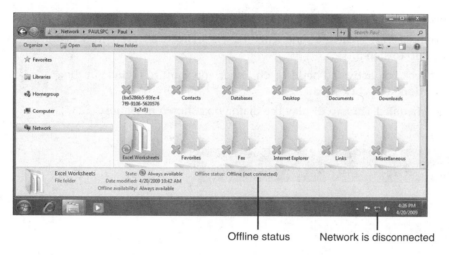

Offline status   Network is disconnected

FIGURE 26.22   A shared network folder displayed offline.

Synchronizing Your Offline Files

When you reconnect to the network, Windows 7 automatically synchronizes the files.
This means that Windows 7 does two things: First, it updates your local copy of an offline
folder by creating copies of any new or changed files in the shared network folder. Second,
it updates the shared network folder with the files you changed while you were offline.
This synchronization occurs automatically when you log on to the network and when you
log off the network. You can also synchronize the offline files yourself. You have four
choices:

▶ Open the shared network folder and select Sync, Sync Offline Files in This Folder in
  the Task pane.

▶ Open the Sync Center, click View Sync Partnerships, double-click Offline Files, select
  the offline folder, and click Sync.

▶ Open the Sync Center, click View Sync Partnerships, double-click Offline Files, and
  click Sync All.

▶ Right-click the Sync Center icon in the notification area, and click Sync All.

You can also set up a synchronization schedule, either based on a time or on one or more
events, as described in the next two sections.

Scheduling a Synchronization by Time

If you want synchronization to occur automatically, and you know when you want it to
occur, follow these steps to set up a time-based sync schedule:

1. In the Sync Center, click View Sync Partnerships.

2. Select Offline Files.

3. Click Schedule. The Offline Files Sync Schedule dialog box appears.

4. If you haven't already created a sync schedule, click Create a New Sync Schedule; otherwise, skip to step 5.

5. Leave the check box activated beside each folder you want to include in the synchronization, and click Next.

6. Click At a Scheduled Time to display the dialog box shown in Figure 26.23.

FIGURE 26.23   Use this dialog box to set up a basic sync schedule.

7. Use the Start On controls to specify the date and time when you want synchronization to begin.

8. Use the Repeat Every controls to specify the numbers of minutes, hours, days, weeks, or months you want to occur between synchronizations.

9. Click More Options to see the More Scheduling Options dialog box with the following options):

   ▶ **Start Sync Only If: The Computer Is Awake**—Leave this check box activated to ensure that the synchronization occurs only if the computer isn't in Standby or Hibernate mode.

   ▶ **Start Sync Only If: The Computer Has Been Idle for at Least *X* Minutes/Hours**—Activate this check box to tell Windows 7 to synchronize only when you're not using your computer. Use the spin box to set the amount of idle time that must occur before the sync begins.

   ▶ **Start Sync Only If: The Computer Is Running on External Power**—Activate this check box to avoid running the synchronization when your portable computer is running on batteries.

- ▶ **Stop Sync If: The Computer Wakes Up from Being Idle**—Activate this check box to have Windows 7 abandon the sync if you start using your computer.

- ▶ **Stop Sync If: The Computer Is No Longer Running on External Power**—Activate this check box to have Windows 7 stop the sync if you switch your portable computer to battery power.

10. Click OK.

11. Click Next.

12. Type a name for the schedule.

13. Click Save Schedule.

Scheduling a Synchronization by Event

If you want the synchronization to occur automatically, and you know when you want the synchronization to occur, follow these steps to set up a time-based sync schedule:

1. In the Sync Center, click View Sync Partnerships.

2. Select Offline Files.

3. Click Schedule. The Offline Files Sync Schedule dialog box appears.

4. If you haven't already created a sync schedule, click Create a New Sync Schedule; otherwise, skip to step 5.

5. Leave the check box activated beside each folder you want to include in the synchronization, and click Next.

6. Click When an Event Occurs to display the dialog box shown in Figure 26.24.

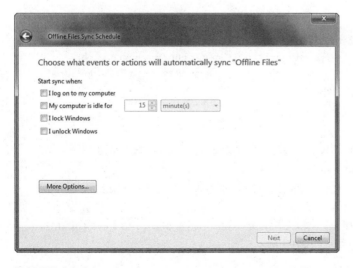

FIGURE 26.24   Use this dialog box to synchronize offline files based on one or more events.

7. Specify the events or actions that trigger the sync by activating one or more of the following check boxes:

   ▶ **I Log On to My Computer**—Activate this check box to start the sync when you log on.

   ▶ **My Computer Is Idle for *X* Minutes/Hours**—Activate this check box to start the sync when your computer has been idle for the number of minutes or hours that you specify.

   ▶ **I Lock Windows**—Activate this check box to start the sync when you lock your computer.

   ▶ **I Unlock Windows**—Activate this check box to start the sync when you unlock your computer.

8. Click More Options to see the More Scheduling Options dialog box (described in the previous section), select your options, and then click OK.

9. Click Next.

10. Type a name for the schedule.

11. Click Save Schedule.

Dealing with Synchronization Conflicts

When Windows 7 synchronizes your offline files, it might find that a file has changed both on the network share and on your offline computer. In that case, the Sync Center icon displays a `Sync Conflicts Have Occurred` message. Here's what you do:

1. Click the `Sync Conflicts Have Occurred` message to open the Sync Center.

NOTE

If the `Sync Conflicts Have Occurred` message no longer appears, you can either right-click the Sync Center icon and then click View Sync Conflicts, or you can open the Sync Center and click the View Sync Conflicts link.

---

2. Click View Sync Conflicts. The Sync Center displays a list of the conflicts.

3. Select the conflict you want to work with.

4. Click Resolve. Windows 7 displays a Resolve Conflict dialog box similar to the one shown in Figure 26.25.

5. Click the version you want to keep, or click Keep Both Versions to have the offline version saved under a modified filename.

FIGURE 26.25   Use the Resolve Conflict dialog box to tell Windows 7 how you want it to handle a file that has been changed both locally and offline.

26

Making Remote Network Connections

Far folks fare well.
—English proverb

One of the big advantages to having a network is that you can set up shared folders for other people to access, and you can access the shared folders that other people have set up. This is so much easier than trying to share data using less-direct means, such as the old "sneakernet" solution. (That is, place the files on a memory card or other removable media, walk the card over the other computer—sneakers are optional—and then insert the card in the other computer.)

Shared folders are great, but there are plenty of problems they can't solve:

▶ A program you need is installed on a remote computer, but not on your computer. For example, you might want to open or edit a document in a shared folder, but only the remote computer has a program that's capable of opening that document.

▶ A remote computer has data that's impossible or difficult to share. For example, you may need to read or respond to an email message that you received on the remote computer, or you might need to visit an Internet site that you've set up as a favorite in Internet Explorer on the remote computer.

▶ A remote computer contains data you need, but that data resides in a folder that hasn't been shared.

To solve these and similar problems, you need to go beyond shared folders and establish a more powerful connection to the remote computer. That is, you need to connect to the remote machine's desktop, which enables you to open folders, run programs, edit documents, and tweak settings. In short, anything you can do while physically sitting in front of the other computer you can do remotely from your own computer. As you see in this chapter, Windows 7's Remote Desktop feature enables you to connect to a computer's desktop over the network. It's also possible to configure your network to allow you to make a Remote Desktop connection over the Internet. This is a great way to give yourself access to your home computer while you're traveling with a laptop.

You might think that operating another computer remotely would be too slow to be useful. However, the responsiveness of the remote session depends a great deal on the speed of the connection. For a LAN connection, an ethernet (10Mbps) connection or 802.11b (11Mbps) wireless connection is just too slow, whereas a Fast Ethernet (100Mbps) or 802.11g (54Mbps) connection will give you adequate performance for most tasks. If you want to play games or perform other graphics-intensive tasks, you really need a Gigabit Ethernet (1Gbps) connection or an 802.11n (248Mbps) wireless connection. Over the Internet, don't even bother connecting with dial-up; instead, you need a cable or Digital Subscriber Line (DSL) broadband (1Mbps or better) link, and even then you'll want to avoid large files and heavy-duty graphic tasks.

Setting Up the Remote Computer as a Host

Remote Desktop is easy to configure and use, but it does require a small amount of prep work to ensure trouble-free operation. Let's begin with the remote computer, also called the *host* computer. The next few sections tell you how to set up a machine to act as a Remote Desktop host.

Windows Versions That Can Act as Hosts

The first thing you need to know is that not all versions of Windows can act as Remote Desktop hosts:

▶ With Windows 7 and Windows Vista, the only versions that support Remote Desktop are Professional, Enterprise, and Ultimate.

▶ If you want to use a Windows XP computer as the host, you can use any version except XP Home.

Setting Up User Accounts on the Host

For security reasons, not just anyone can connect to a remote computer's desktop. By default, Windows gives permission to connect remotely to the host to the following:

▶ The user who is currently logged on to the host machine

▶ Members of the host's Administrators and Remote Desktop Users groups

Note, however, that all of these users must have password-protected accounts to use Remote Desktop.

For anyone else, if you want to give a person permission to connect to the host remotely, you first need to set up an account for the username with which you want that person to connect from the client, and you must assign a password to this account.

▶ To learn how to set up a user account in Windows 7, **see** "Creating and Managing User Accounts," **p. 384**.

Configuring Windows 7 or Vista to Act as a Remote Desktop Host

If the host machine is running the Business, Enterprise, or Ultimate version of Windows 7 or Windows Vista, you have to do three things to prepare the computer for its Remote Desktop hosting duties:

▶ Disable automatic sleep mode.

▶ Allow Remote Desktop through the Windows Firewall.

▶ Activate the Remote Desktop service.

Disabling Automatic Sleep Mode

By default, most Windows 7 and Vista machines are configured to go into sleep mode after 1 hour of inactivity. Sleep is a low-power mode that turns everything off except power to the memory chips, which store the current desktop configuration. When you turn the machine back on, the desktop and your open programs and documents appear within a few seconds. However, remote clients won't be able to connect to the host if it's in sleep mode, so you have to disable this feature.

> **NOTE**
>
> All we're doing here is disabling the feature that puts your computer into sleep mode automatically after a period of inactivity. If need be, you can still put the computer into sleep mode manually by selecting Start and clicking the Sleep button.

Here are the steps to follow:

1. Select Start, type **power**, and then click Power Options in the search results. The Power Options window appears.
2. Click the Change When the Computer Sleeps link. Windows opens the Edit Plan Settings window.
3. In the Put the Computer to Sleep list, select Never, as shown in Figure 27.1.
4. Click Save Changes.

27

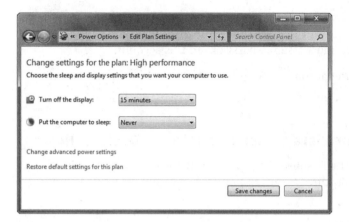

FIGURE 27.1   On the Remote Desktop host, turn off the feature that automatically puts the computer into sleep mode.

Configuring a Windows Firewall Exception for Remote Desktop

By default, Windows Firewall doesn't allow Remote Desktop connections. This is a sensible security precaution because connecting to someone's desktop gives you nearly complete control over that PC. To enable remote connections, you must configure a Windows Firewall exception for Remote Desktop.

Here are the steps you need to follow:

1. Select Start, type **firewall**, and then select Windows Firewall in the search results. The Windows Firewall window appears.
2. Click the Allow a Program or Feature Through Windows Firewall link.
3. In Windows 7, click the Change Settings button; in Windows Vista, enter your User Account Control (UAC) credentials to continue.
4. Activate the check box beside Remote Desktop, as shown in Figure 27.2.
5. Click OK. Windows enables the firewall exception for Remote Desktop.

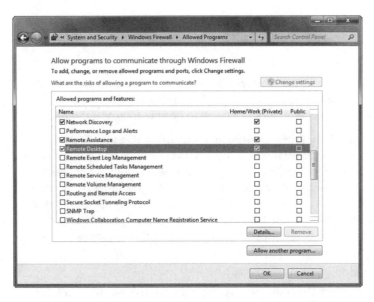

FIGURE 27.2   On the host, activate the Remote Desktop firewall exception.

Activating the Remote Desktop Service

Now follow these steps to activate the Remote Desktop service:

1. Select Start, type **systempropertiesremote**, and then press Enter. In Windows Vista, enter your UAC credentials to continue. Windows 7 opens the System Properties dialog box with the Remote tab displayed, as shown in Figure 27.3.

FIGURE 27.3   On the remote host, select an option in the Remote Desktop group to enable remote connections to the computer's desktop.

2. In the Remote Desktop group, you have three choices:

   ▶ **Don't Allow Connections to This Computer**—This option turns off Remote Desktop hosting.

   ▶ **Allow Connections from Computers Running Any Version of Remote Desktop**—Select this option if you want people running previous versions (that is, Windows XP and earlier) of Remote Desktop to be able to access the host.

   ▶ **Allow Connections Only from Computers Running Remote Desktop with Network Level Authentication**—Select this option if you only want the most secure form of Remote Desktop access. In this case, Windows 7 checks the client computer to see whether its version of Remote Desktop supports Network Level Authentication (NLA). NLA is an authentication protocol that authenticates the user before making the Remote Desktop connection. NLA is built in to every version of Windows 7, but is not supported on older Windows systems.

3. If you didn't add more users earlier, skip to step 6. Otherwise, click Select Users to display the Remote Desktop Users dialog box.

4. Click Add to display the Select Users dialog box, type the username, and click OK. (Repeat this step to add other users.)

5. Click OK to return to the System Properties dialog box.

6. Click OK.

Configuring XP to Act as a Remote Desktop Host

You may want to connect your Windows 7 computer to the desktop of a remote XP machine. If the host machine is running any version of XP except XP Home, here are the steps to follow to set it up to host Remote Desktop sessions:

1. Log on to the XP computer as an administrator.

2. Select Start, Control Panel to open the Control Panel window.

3. Double click the System icon to open the System Properties dialog box.

4. Display the Remote tab.

TIP

Another way to get to the System Properties dialog box in Windows XP and its Remote tab is to select Start, right-click My Computer, click Properties, and then select the Remote tab. Alternatively, you can display the Remote tab directly by pressing Windows Logo+R (or selecting Start, Run) to open the Run dialog box, typing `control sysdm.cpl,,6,` and clicking OK. (For what it's worth, the equivalent command in Windows 7 is `control sysdm.cpl,,5.`)

---

5. In the Remote Desktop group, activate the Allow Users to Connect Remotely to This Computer check box, as shown in Figure 27.4.

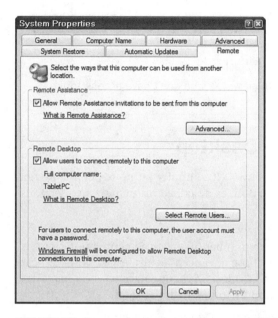

FIGURE 27.4   In XP, the Allow Users to Connect Remotely to This Computer check box must be activated to enable Remote Desktop sessions on the computer.

6. If you didn't add more users earlier, skip to step 9. Otherwise, click Select Remote Users to display the Remote Desktop Users dialog box.

7. Click Add to display the Select Users dialog box, type the username, and click OK. (Repeat this step to add other users.)

8. Click OK to return to the System Properties dialog box.

9. Click OK.

Installing Remote Desktop on an XP Client Computer

A computer that connects to a remote computer's desktop is said to be a Remote Desktop *client*. To act as a client, the computer must have the Remote Desktop Connection software installed. Remote Desktop Connection is installed by default in all versions of Windows 7, but some versions of XP don't come with the program installed. However, you can install the Remote Desktop Connection software from the Windows XP CD (if you have one):

1. Insert the Windows XP CD and wait for the Welcome to Microsoft Windows XP screen to appear.

2. Click Perform Additional Tasks.

3. Click Set Up Remote Desktop Connection.

27

> **NOTE**
>
> You can also download the latest client software from Microsoft:
>
> www.microsoft.com/windowsxp/downloads/tools/rdclientdl.mspx
>
> You can also use this client if you're running Windows XP and don't have access to the XP install disc.

Connecting to the Remote Desktop

With your Windows 7, Windows Vista, or Windows XP computer set up to act as a Remote Desktop host, you've ready to make the connection, as described in the next two sections.

Making a Basic Connection

Remote Desktop Connection comes with a large number of advanced connection options and settings. If you don't want to bother with those advanced features right now, you can connect to the host in just a few steps. On the Windows 7 client computer, you make a basic connection to the host computer's desktop by following these steps:

1. Select Start, type **remote**, and then select Remote Desktop Connection in the search results.

2. In the Computer text box, type the name or the IP address of the host computer, as shown in Figure 27.5.

3. Click Connect. Windows 7 prompts you to enter your security credentials.

4. In Windows 7, type the username and password of the host account you want to use for the logon, and then click OK. (Note that in subsequent logons, you only need to type the password.)

FIGURE 27.5   In the Remote Desktop Connection dialog box, type the name or the IP address of the remote host computer.

NOTE

If you're using Windows XP to connect to a Windows 7 host, select Start, All Programs, Accessories, Communications, Remote Desktop Connection to open the Remote Desktop Connection window. Type the host computer name or IP address, and then click Connect. When the Windows 7 logon screen appears, click the icon of the user account with which you want to connect, type the account's password, and press Enter to complete the connection.

NEW TO **7**   In Windows 7, the Remote Desktop Connection program supports jump lists, and its jump list consists of recent connections you've made. For example, in Figure 27.6 you can see that the MEDIAPC connection I just made now appears in the Remote Desktop Connection jump list. I can reconnect to t6hat PC quickly by selecting if from the jump list.

FIGURE 27.6   In the Windows 7 version of Remote Desktop Connection, the jump list shows you recent connections.

Making an Advanced Connection

The basic remote connection from the previous section may be all you need to use for your remote sessions. However, Remote Desktop Connection comes with many settings that enable you to configure options such as the size of the remote desktop screen, whether your Windows keyboard shortcuts (such as Alt+Tab) apply to the remote computer or your computer, and much more.

Here are the steps to follow to use these settings to make an advanced connection to the host computer's desktop:

1. Select Start, type **remote**, and then select Remote Desktop Connection in the search results.
2. In the Computer text box, type the name or the IP address of the host computer.
3. Click Options to expand the dialog box to the version shown in Figure 27.7.

FIGURE 27.7   Click the Options button to expand the dialog box so that you can customize Remote Desktop.

4. The General tab offers the following additional options:

   ▶ **Computer**—The name or IP address of the remote computer.

   ▶ **User Name**—(Windows XP only) The username you want to use to log in to the host computer.

   ▶ **Password**—(Windows XP only) The password to use to log on to the host computer.

   ▶ **Domain**—(Windows XP only) Leave this text box blank.

   ▶ **Save**—(Windows 7/Vista only) Click this button to have Windows remember your current settings so that you don't have to type them again the next time you connect. This is useful if you only connect to one remote host.

   ▶ **Save As**—Click this button to save your connection settings to a Remote Desktop (.rdp) file for later use. This is convenient if you regularly connect to multiple hosts.

▶ **Open**—Click this button to open a saved .rdp file.

5. The Display tab offers three options for controlling the look of the Remote Desktop window:

▶ **Remote Desktop Size**—Drag this slider to set the resolution of Remote Desktop. Drag the slider all the way to the left for a 640×480 screen size. Drag the slider all the way to the right to have Remote Desktop take up the entire client screen, no matter what resolution the host is currently using.

▶ **Colors**—Use this list to set the number of colors used for the Remote Desktop display. Note that if the number of colors on either the host or the client is fewer than the value you select in the Colors list, Windows uses the lesser value.

▶ **Display the Connection Bar When I Use the Full Screen**—When this check box is activated, the Remote Desktop Connection client displays a connection bar at the top of the Remote Desktop window, provided you selected Full Screen for the Remote Desktop Size setting. You use the connection bar to minimize, restore, and close the Remote Desktop window. If you find that the connection bar just gets in the way, deactivate this check box to prevent it from appearing.

CAUTION

You may need to be a bit careful if the remote host is currently using a higher resolution than the one you select using the Remote Desktop Size slider. When you make the connection, Windows 7 will change the host's screen resolution to the lower setting, and then when you disconnect from the host Windows 7 will return the resolution to the higher setting. However, some video cards don't react well to these resolution switches, and they cause the running programs to think they're still operating at the lower resolution. To work around this, try to use the same resolution both locally and remotely. If you can't do that, minimize all the open windows before making the connection (if possible).

---

6. The Local Resources tab offers three options for controlling certain interactions between the client and host:

▶ **Remote Audio**—Use this list to determine where Windows plays the sounds generated by the host. You can play them on the client (if you want to hear what's happening on the host), on the host (if you want a user sitting at the host to hear the sounds), or not at all (if you have a slow connection).

▶ **Keyboard**—Use this list to determine which computer is sent special Windows key combinations—such as Alt+Tab and Ctrl+Esc—that you press on the client keyboard. You can have the key combos sent to the client, to the host, or to the host only when you're running the Remote Desktop window in full-screen mode. What happens if you're sending key combos to one computer and you need to use a particular key combo on the other computer? For such situations, Remote Desktop offers several keyboard equivalents, outlined in the following table:

Windows Key Combo	Remote Desktop Equivalent
Alt+Tab	Alt+Page Up
Alt+Shift+Tab	Alt+Page Down
Alt+Esc	Alt+Insert
Ctrl+Esc or Windows Logo	Alt+Home
Print Screen	Ctrl+Alt+– (numeric keypad)
Alt+Print Screen	Ctrl+Alt++ (numeric keypad)

TIP

Here are three other useful keyboard shortcuts that you can press on the client computer and have Windows send to the host:

Ctrl+Alt+End	Displays the Windows Security dialog box. This is equivalent to pressing Ctrl+Alt+Delete, which Windows always applies to the client computer.
Alt+Delete	Displays the active window's Control menu.
Ctrl+Alt+Break	Toggles the Remote Desktop window between full-screen mode and a regular window.

▶ **Local Devices and Resources**—Leave the Printers check box activated to display the client's printers in the host's Printers and Faxes window. The client's printers appear with the syntax *Printer (from COMPUTER), where Printer* is the printer name and *COMPUTER* is the network name of the client computer. In Windows 7 and Vista, leave the Clipboard check box activated to use the client's Clipboard during the remote session. In XP, you can also connect disk drives and serial ports, which I describe in the next step.

7. In Windows 7 and Vista, click More to see the Remote Desktop Connection dialog box. Use the following check boxes to configure more client devices and resources on the host. (Click OK when you've finished.)

▶ **Smart Cards**—Leave this check box activated to access the client's smart cards on the host.

▶ **Ports**—Activate this check box to make any devices attached to the client's ports (such as a barcode scanner) available while you're working with the host.

▶ **Drives**—Activate this check box to display the client's hard disk partitions and mapped network drives in the hosts Computer (or My Computer) window. (You can also open the branch to activate the check boxes of specific drives.)

The client's drives appear in the window's Other group with the syntax *D on Computer,* where *D* is the drive letter and *Computer* is the network name of the client computer.

▶ **Other Supported Plug and Play (PnP) Devices**—Activate this check box to make some of the client's Plug and Play devices, such as media players and digital cameras, available to the host. (You can also open the branch to activate the check boxes of specific devices.)

8. Use the Programs tab to specify a program to run on connection. Activate the Start the Following Program on Connection check box, and then use the Program Path and File Name text box to specify the program to run. After connecting, the user can work with only this program, and when he quits the program, the session also ends.

9. Use the Experience tab (the Windows 7 version is shown in Figure 27.8) to set performance options for the connection. Use the Choose Your Connection Speed to Optimize Performance drop-down list to set the appropriate connection speed. Because you're connecting over a network, you should choose the LAN (10Mbps or higher) option. Depending on the connection speed you choose, one or more of the following check boxes will be activated. (The faster the speed, the more check boxes Windows activates.)

FIGURE 27.8   Use the Experience tab to set performance options for the connection.

▶ **Desktop Background**—Toggles the host's desktop background on and off.

▶ **Font Smoothing**—(Windows 7/Vista only) Toggles the host's font smoothing on and off.

> ▶ **Desktop Composition**—(Windows 7/Vista only) Toggles the host's desktop composition engine on and off.

> ▶ **Show Contents of Window While Dragging**—Toggles the display of window contents when you drag a host window with your mouse.

> ▶ **Menu and Windows Animation**—Toggles on and off the animations that Windows normally uses when you pull down menus or minimize and maximize windows.

> ▶ **Themes**—Toggles the host's current visual theme on and off.

> ▶ **Bitmap Caching**—Improves performance by not storing frequently used host images on the client computer.

10. Click Connect. Windows 7 prompts you to enter your security credentials.

11. In Windows 7, type the username and password of the host account you want to use for the logon, and then click OK. (Note that in subsequent logons, you only need to type the password.) In Windows XP, click the icon of the user account with which you want to connect, type the account's password, and press Enter to complete the connection.

12. If you activated the Disk Drives or Serial Ports check boxes in the Local Resources tab, a security warning dialog box appears. If you're sure that making these resources available to the remote computer is safe, activate the Don't Prompt Me Again for Connections to This Remote Computer check box. Click OK.

Working with the Connection Bar

The remote computer's desktop then appears on your computer. If you chose to work in full-screen mode, move the cursor to the top of the screen to see the connection bar, shown in Figure 27.9.

If you want the connection bar to appear all the time, click to activate the Pin button. If you need to work with your own desktop, you have two choices:

> ▶ Click the connection bar's Minimize button to minimize the Remote Desktop window.

> ▶ Click the connection bar's Restore button to display the Remote Desktop window.

Connection bar   Restor

Pin   Minimize   Close

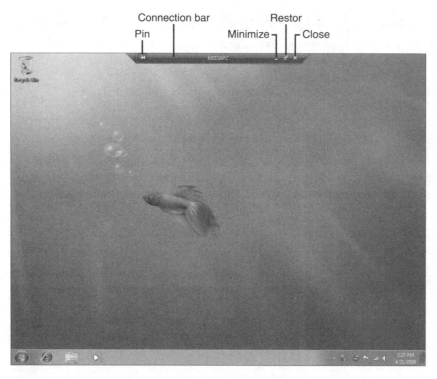

FIGURE 27.9   After you've connected and the remote computer's desktop appears on your screen, move the cursor to the top of the screen to see the connection bar.

Disconnecting from the Remote Desktop

When you finish with the Remote Desktop session, you have two choices for disconnecting:

▶ To shut down the host's running programs and windows, use the host desktop to select Start, Log Off.

▶ To leave the programs and windows open on the host, click the Close button in the connection bar. Windows displays a dialog box to let you know that your remote session will be disconnected. Click OK.

Connecting to a Remote Desktop via the Internet

Connecting to a Remote Desktop host over your network is easy to set up and fast, but your local area network might not always be so local. If you're traveling, what do you do if you want to connect to your desktop or to the desktop of some computer on your network? This is possible, but it requires some care to ensure that you don't open up your computer or your network to Internet-based hackers.

27

> **CAUTION**
>
> Besides the security precautions I present in this section, you should also set up your accounts with robust passwords, as described in Chapter 18, "Setting Up User Security." Using Remote Desktop over the Internet means that you open up a small window on your network that is at least visible to others on the Net. To ensure that other Internet users cannot exploit this hole, a strong password is a must.

> ▶ To learn more about what constitutes a strong password, **see** "Creating and Enforcing Bulletproof Passwords," **p. 380.**

To configure your system to allow Remote Desktop connections via the Internet, you need to perform these general steps. (I explain each step in more detail in the sections that follow.)

1. Configure Remote Desktop to use a listening port other than the default port.
2. Configure Windows Firewall to allow TCP connections through the port you specified in step 1.
3. Determine the IP address of the Remote Desktop host or your network's router.
4. Configure your network router (if you have one) to forward data sent to the port specified in step 1 to the Remote Desktop host computer.
5. Use the IP address from step 3 and the port number from step 1 to connect to the Remote Desktop host via the Internet.

Changing the Listening Port

Your first task is to modify the Remote Desktop software on the host computer to use a listening port other than 3389, which is the default port. This is a good idea because there are hackers on the Internet who use port scanners to examine Internet connections (particularly broadband connections) for open ports. If the hackers see that port 3389 is open, they could assume that it's for a Remote Desktop connection, so they try to make a Remote Desktop connection to the host. They still have to log on with an authorized username and password, but knowing the connection type means they've cleared a very large hurdle.

To change the Remote Desktop listening port, follow these steps:

1. Select Start, type **regedit**, and then press Enter. The User Account Control dialog box appears.
2. Enter your UAC credentials to continue. Windows 7 opens the Registry Editor.

> **CAUTION**
>
> I would be remiss if I didn't remind you the Windows 7's Registry contains settings that are vitally important for both Windows 7 and your installed programs. Therefore, when you're working with the Registry Editor, don't make changes to any keys or settings other than the ones I describe in this section, and make a backup of the Registry before you make *any* changes.

3. Open the following branch:

   `HKLM\SYSTEM\CurrentControlSet\Control\TerminalServer\WinStations\RDP-Tcp`

4. Double-click the `PortNumber` setting to open the Edit DWORD (32-bit) Value dialog box.

5. Select the Decimal option.

6. Replace the existing value (3389) with some other number between 1024 and 65536, as shown in Figure 27.10.

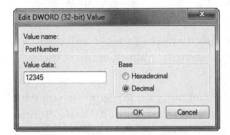

FIGURE 27.10   Replace port 3389 with another number between 1024 and 65536.

7. Click OK.

8. Reboot the computer to put the new port setting into effect.

Configuring Windows Firewall

Now you have to configure Windows Firewall to allow data to pass through the port you specified in the previous section. Here are the steps to follow:

1. Select Start, type **wf.msc**, and then press Enter. The Windows Firewall with Advanced Security window appears.

2. Click Inbound Rules.

3. In the Actions pane, click New Rule to launch the New Inbound Rule Wizard.

4. Click Port and then click Next. The Protocol and Ports dialog box appears.

5. Make sure the TCP is selected.

6. Activate the Specific Local Ports option and use the text box to type the port number you specified in the previous section.

7. Click Next. The Action dialog box appears.

8. Click Allow the Connection and then click Next. The Profile dialog box appears.

9. Activate the check box beside each profile you use (Domain, Private, or Public), and then click Next. The Name dialog box appears.

27

10. Use the Name text box to make up a name for this exception. This is the name that appears in the Exceptions tab, so make it reasonably descriptive (for example, `Remote Desktop Alternate`).

11. Click Finish to put the exception into effect.

Determining the Host IP Address

To connect to a remote desktop via the Internet, you need to specify an IP address rather than a computer name. (See "Using Dynamic DNS to Access Your Network," later in this chapter, for a way to avoid using IP addresses.) The IP address you use depends on your Internet setup:

▶ If the Remote Desktop host computer connects directly to the Internet and your Internet service provider (ISP) supplied you with a static IP address, connect using that address.

▶ If the host computer connects directly to the Internet but your ISP supplies you with a dynamic IP address each time you connect, use the IPCONFIG utility to determine your current IP address. (That is, select Start, type **command**, and then select Command Prompt to get to the command line, type **ipconfig**, and press Enter.) Make note of the `IPv4 Address` value returned by IPCONFIG (you might need to scroll the output up to see it) and use that address to connect to the Remote Desktop host.

▶ If your network uses a router, determine that router's external IP address by examining the router's status page. When you set up your Remote Desktop connection, you connect to the router, which will then forward your connection (thanks to your efforts in the next section) to the Remote Desktop host.

   ▶ To learn how to get to your router's setup pages, **see** "Displaying the Router's Setup Pages," **p. 424.**

TIP

Another way to determine your router's external IP address is to navigate to any of the free services for determining your current IP. Here are two:

WhatISMyIP (www.whatismyip.com)

DynDNS (http://checkip.dyndns.org)

Setting Up Port Forwarding

If your network uses a router, you need to configure it to forward data sent to the port specified in step 1 to the Remote Desktop host computer. This is *port forwarding*, and the steps you follow depend on the device.

Figure 27.11 shows the Port Forwarding screen of the router on my system. In this case, the firewall forwards data that comes in to port 12345 to the computer at the address

192.168.0.56, which is the Remote Desktop host. Consult your device documentation to learn how to set up port forwarding.

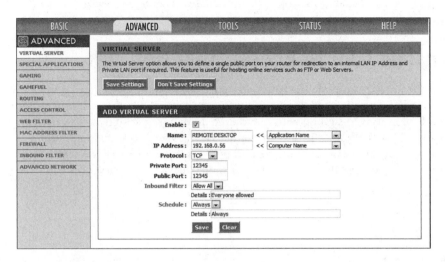

FIGURE 27.11   On your router, forward the new Remote Desktop listening port (12345, in this case) to the Remote Desktop host computer (192.168.0.56 in this case).

Connecting Using the IP Address and New Port

You're now ready to make the connection to the Remote Desktop host via the Internet. Here are the steps to follow:

1. Connect to the Internet.
2. Select Start, type **remote**, and then select Remote Desktop Connection in the search results.
3. In the Computer text box, type the external IP address of the router or remote computer and the alternative port you specified in step 1, separated by a colon. Figure 27.12 shows an example.

FIGURE 27.12   In the Remote Desktop Connection dialog box, type the external IP address, a colon, and then the new Remote Desktop listening port.

4. Set up your other Remote Desktop options as needed. For example, click Options, display the Experience tab, and then select the appropriate connection speed, such as Modem (28.8Kbps), Modem (56Kbps), or Broadband (128Kbps–1.5Mbps).

5. Click Connect.

Using Dynamic DNS to Access Your Network

If you want to use Remote Desktop via the Internet regularly, constantly monitoring your dynamic IP address can be a pain, particularly if you forget to check it before heading out of the office. A useful solution is to sign up with a dynamic domain name system DNS (DDNS) service, which supplies you with a static domain name. The service also installs a program on your computer that monitors your IP address and updates the service's DDNS servers to point your domain name to your IP address. Here are some DDNS services to check out:

DynDNS (www.dyndns.org)

TZO (www.tzo.com)

No-IP.com (www.no-ip.com)

D-Link (www.dlinkddns.com)

However, you may not want to rely on a program to keep your network external IP address and your domain name synchronized. For example, you may want to turn off the computer when you're away from home or the office. In that case, most routers offer a DDNS feature that will handle this for you. You specify your DDNS provider, your domain name, and your logon data, and the router does the rest. Figure 27.13 shows an example.

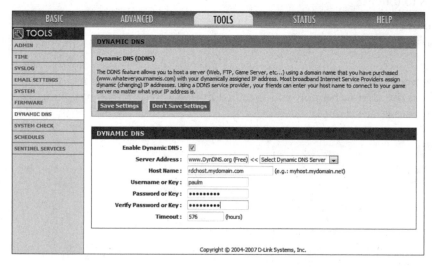

FIGURE 27.13   In your router's setup pages, configure dynamic DNS.

Configuring a Network Computer for Remote Administration

You can use Windows' remote administration tools to work with remote computers from the comfort of your own PC. Remote administration tools mostly use the Remote Procedure Call (RPC) protocol to communicate with the remote computer. RPC enables a local computer to run a program on a remote computer. For this to happen successfully, you must configure an exception in the remote computer's firewall that allows RPC traffic.

Here are the steps to follow:

1. In Windows 7, select Start and type **command.**
2. Right-click Command Prompt, and then click Run as Administrator. The User Account Control dialog box appears.
3. Enter your UAC credentials to open the Administrator command line.
4. At the prompt, enter the following command:

```
netsh firewall set service type=remoteadmin mode=enable
```

Using Virtual Private Network Connections

In the remote connections you've seen so far, the security exists mostly at the connection point. That is, you set up usernames with strong passwords, and no one can access your dial-up or Remote Desktop connection without entering the correct logon data. This works well, but it doesn't do much for the actual data that's passed between the host and client. A malicious hacker might not be able to access your system directly, but he certainly can use a packet sniffer or similar technology to access your incoming and outgoing data. Because that data isn't encrypted, the hacker can easily read the contents of the packets.

What do you do, then, if you want to transfer secure data such as financial information or personnel files, but you love the simplicity of a dial-up connection? The answer is a tried-and-true technology called *virtual private networking* (VPN), which offers secure access to a private network over a public connection, such as the Internet or a phone line. VPN is secure because it uses a technique called *tunneling*, which establishes a connection between two computers—a *VPN server* and a *VPN client*—using a specific port (such as port 1723). Control-connection packets are sent back and forth to maintain the connection between the two computers (to, in a sense, keep the tunnel open).

When it comes to sending the actual network data—sometimes called the *payload*—each network packet is encrypted and then encapsulated within a regular IP packet, which is then routed through the tunnel. Any hacker can see this IP packet traveling across the Internet, but even if he intercepts the packet and examines it, no harm is done because the content of the packet—the actual data—is encrypted. When the IP packet arrives on the other end of the tunnel, VPN *decapsulates* the network packet and then decrypts it to reveal the payload. (Which is part of the reason why VPN connections tend to be quite slow.)

27

Windows 7 comes with VPN client support built in and it uses two tunneling protocols:

▶ **Point-to-Point Tunneling Protocol (PPTP)**—This protocol is the most widely used in VPN setups. It was developed by Microsoft and is related to the *Point-to-Point Protocol* (PPP) that's commonly used to transport IP packets over the Internet. A separate protocol—*Microsoft Point-to-Point Encryption* (MPPE)—encrypts the network packets (IP, IPX, NetBEUI, or whatever). PPTP sets up the tunnel and encapsulates the encrypted network packets in an IP packet for transport across the tunnel.

▶ **IP Security (IPSec)**—This protocol encrypts the payload (IP packets only), sets up the tunnel, and encapsulates the encrypted network packets in an IP packet for transport across the tunnel.

NOTE

A third popular VPN protocol is *Layer 2 Tunneling Protocol* (L2TP), which goes beyond PPTP by allowing VPN connections over networks other than just the Internet (such as networks based on X.25, ATM, or Frame Relay). L2TP uses the encryption portion of IPSec to encrypt the network packets.

There are two main ways to use VPN:

▶ **Via the Internet**—In this case, you first connect to the Internet using any PPP-based dial-up or broadband connection. Then you connect to the VPN server to establish the VPN tunnel over the Internet.

▶ **Via a dial-up connection**—In this case, you first connect to the host computer using a regular dial-up connection. Then you connect to the VPN server to establish the VPN tunnel over the telephone network.

Configuring a Network Gateway for VPN

The best way to use VPN is when the client has a broadband Internet connection and the server has a public IP address or domain name. This enables you to access the server directly using your fast Internet connection. What happens, however, if the Windows 7 machine you set up as the VPN server sits behind a gateway or firewall and so uses only an internal IP address?

You can often get around this problem by setting up a network gateway to pass through VPN packets and forward them to the VPN server. (Note that some broadband routers come with VPN capabilities built in, so they can handle an incoming VPN connection automatically.)

The details depend on the device, but the usual first step is to enable the gateway's support for *VPN passthrough*, which allows network computers to communicate via one or more VPN protocols (such as PPTP and IPSec). Figure 27.14 shows a sample page in a gateway setup application that that lets you enable passthrough for the PPTP and IPSec protocols.

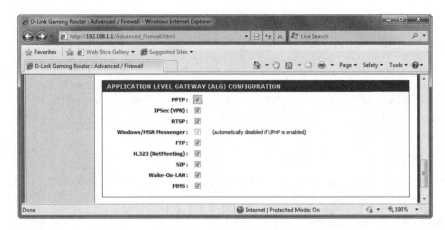

FIGURE 27.14   In your gateway setup application, enable VPN passthrough for the protocols you use.

In some cases, just enabling VPN passthrough is all you need to do to get VPN up and running through your gateway. If your VPN connection doesn't work or if your gateway doesn't support VPN passthrough, you have to open a port for the VPN protocol you're using and then have data to that port forwarded to the VPN server. (This is similar to the port forwarding described earlier for Remote Desktop connections.) The forwarded ports depend on the protocol:

PPTP   Forward TCP to port 1723

IPSec   Forward UPD to port 500

Figure 27.15 shows an example of port forwarding.

FIGURE 27.15   In your gateway setup application, forward the ports of the VPN protocols you use to the IP address of your network's VPN server.

Configuring the VPN Client

Now you have to configure the remote computer as a VPN client. Here are the steps to follow:

1. Select Start, type `connect`, and then select Set Up a Network or Connection in the search results. Windows 7 displays the Choose a Connection Option dialog box.

2. Click Connect to a Workplace and then click Next. The How Do You Want to Connect? dialog box appears.

3. Click one of the following two choices:

   ▶ **Use My Internet Connection**—Click this option if you want to make the VPN connection over the Internet.

   ▶ **Dial Directly**—Click this option to use a dial-up VPN connection.

4. In the next dialog box (Figure 27.16 shows the Internet connection version), configure the following controls (click Next when you're done):

   ▶ **Internet Address**—If you're using an Internet connection, type the domain name or IP address of the VPN server (or the network gateway that forwards your connection to the VPN server).

   ▶ **Telephone Number**—If you're using a dial-up connection, type the phone number used by the VPN server.

   ▶ **Destination Name**—Type a name for the VPN connection.

   ▶ **Use a Smart Card**—Activate this check box if your VPN server requires you to have a smart card security device inserted in your system as part of the server's authentication process.

   ▶ **Allow Other People to Use This Connection**—Activate this check box to make this connection available to other user accounts on your computer.

   ▶ **Don't Connect Now**—Activate this check box to prevent Windows 7 from connecting to the VPN server right away. This is useful if you're just setting up the connection for later use.

5. Type your VPN logon data: your username, your password, and your network domain (if any).

6. Click Create. Windows 7 creates the connection and launches it (unless you activated the Don't Connect Now check box in step 5).

7. Click Close.

Windows 7 adds a Virtual Private Network group to the Network Connections folder, and places in that group an icon with the name you specified in step 5.

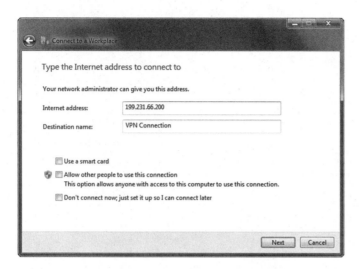

FIGURE 27.16   Use this dialog box to specify the location of your network's VPN server and other connection options.

Making the VPN Connection

With the VPN client configured, you can now use the client to make the VPN connection. Follow these steps on the VPN client computer:

1. If you need to establish a dial-up connection to the Internet before connecting to the VPN server, make that connection now.

TIP

You can configure the VPN connection to make the dial-up connection to the Internet automatically. Click Start, type **connections**, and then select View Network Connections in the search results. Right-click the VPN connection icon, and then click Properties to open its properties sheet. In the General tab. activate the Dial Another Connection First check box, and then use the associated list box to select the dial-up connection you want dialed. Click OK.

2. Click the Network icon in the taskbar's notification area.
3. Click the VPN connection and then click Connect. The Connect dialog box appears for the VPN connection. Type your username, password, and domain (if applicable).
4. If you want Windows 7 to remember your logon data, activate the Save This User Name and Password for the Following Users, and then activate either Me Only or Anyone Who Uses this Computer.
5. Click Connect. Windows 7 sets up the VPN connection.

27

Turning Windows 7 into a Web Server

A man may know the world without leaving his own home.
—Lao-Tzu

Windows 7 is definitely a client operating system, but it does have its server moments. For example, you've seen that Windows 7 acts as a kind of server when you set up a folder to be shared with the network. Similarly, Windows 7 also acts as a kind of server when you use it to host an ad hoc wireless network and when you create a meeting using Windows Meeting Space.

However, these are only "server-like" applications. Surprisingly, there is a way that Windows 7 can act as a full-fledged server: by running the built-in service called Internet Information Services (IIS) that enables Windows 7 to serve web pages. Why bother? Here are just a few good reasons:

▶ You're running a home office or small office and you want to set up an internal website for your employees (that is called an *intranet*).

▶ You want to set up a simple site with photos and updates for friends and family to access.

▶ You don't want to pay a web hosting company to store your site.

▶ You want to learn web programming and need a server to practice on.

▶ You're already a web developer and you need a full-fledged server to test your applications.

Yes, for at least some of these scenarios it's easier to use one of the many thousands of web hosting companies to put up your site. However, if you want complete control over the site, you need to roll up your sleeves and get hands on with IIS. Fortunately, as you see in this chapter, although IIS itself is tremendously complex, the basic features of IIS (which are all you need) aren't hard to grasp.

Understanding Internet Information Services

A *web server* is a computer that accepts and responds to remote requests for pages and other web content that are stored on the server. Most of these requests come from remote users running Internet Explorer, Firefox, Safari, or some other web browser. IIS is Microsoft's web server and, amazingly, they've made it available on some versions of Windows 7. IIS runs the World Wide Web Publishing Service, which makes a default website available to anyone on your network (or, with a bit of tweaking, anyone on the Internet) who uses a web browser. You can add your own pages and folders to the default website, so you can serve almost any type of World Wide Web content from your Windows 7 computer. IIS also comes with the IIS Management Console, which enables you to customize your website to get it set up the way you want.

I mentioned earlier that some versions of Windows 7 come with IIS. Specifically, you get IIS on Windows 7 Home Premium, Professional, Enterprise, and Ultimate. However, the Home Premium version doesn't implement IIS in the same way as the other versions:

▶ Home Premium doesn't come with some high-end features, such as advanced authentication.

▶ Home Premium doesn't offer remote administration of IIS.

▶ Home Premium doesn't include the FTP server.

▶ Home Premium is restricted to a maximum of three simultaneous data requests (compared to the limit of 10 simultaneous requests in the Business, Enterprise, and Ultimate versions).

If you used IIS 5.1 on Windows XP, note that two major restrictions have been lifted from Windows 7's IIS 7.5: First, there is no maximum connection limit. XP IIS 5.1 had a connection limit of 10 users, but there is no such limit in Windows 7's IIS 7.5. Second, there is no website limit. XP IIS 5.1 allowed you to create just one website, but Windows 7's IIS 7.5 lets you create as many sites as you want.

NOTE

Windows 7 IIS 7.5's simultaneous data request limit is different than XP IIS 5.1's connection limit. With the connection limit of 10, when an eleventh user tried to access your site, he or she received a `Server Too Busy` error. With the simultaneous data request limit of 10 (3 in Home Premium), if an eleventh (or fourth) request comes in at the same time, that request is simply placed in a queue and is handled when the server is ready for it.

Installing Internet Information Services

IIS 7.5 is a feature in the Home Premium, Business, Enterprise, and Ultimate versions of Windows 7, but it's not installed by default on any of them. To install it, you need to work through the following steps:

1. Select Start, type **features**, and then select Turn Windows Features On or Off in the search results. Windows 7 displays the Windows Features dialog box, which takes a few moments to populate.

2. Click to activate the check box beside Internet Information Services. Windows 7 selects the most commonly used IIS features.

3. Open the Internet Information Services branch, and then activate the check boxes beside each component you want to work with. Here are some suggestions (see Figure 28.1):

FIGURE 28.1   Open the Internet Information Services branch to customize the IIS install.

▶ **Web Management Tools, IIS Management Service**—Install this component to configure your web server from any other computer on your network.

▶ **World Wide Web Services, Application Development Features**—The components in this branch represent the IIS programming features. If you're running IIS to build and test web applications, be sure to activate the check box for each development technology you require.

▶ **World Wide Web Services, Security, Basic Authentication**—Install this component if you want to restrict website access to users who have a valid Windows username and password.

4. Click OK. Windows 7 installs IIS 7.5.

Accessing Your Website

Although there's not much to see, the default website is ready for action as soon as you install IIS. To access the website from the computer running IIS, you can enter any of the following addresses into your web browser:

```
http://127.0.0.1/
http://localhost/
http://IPAddress/ (replace IPAddress with the IP address of the computer)
http://ComputerName/ (replace ComputerName with name of the computer)
```

Figure 28.2 shows the home page of the default IIS website that appears.

FIGURE 28.2   The default IIS 7.5 website home page.

Creating a Windows Firewall Exception for the Web Server

As things stand now, your new website will only work properly when you access it using a web browser running on the Windows 7 PC that's running IIS. If you try to access the site on any other computer (or from a location outside your network), you get an error message, as shown in Figure 28.3.

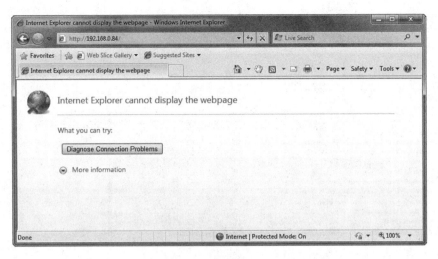

FIGURE 28.3   Other computers on your network can't access your web server.

The problem is that the Windows Firewall on the Windows 7 machine hasn't been configured to allow data traffic through the World Wide Web Services used by IIS. For your website to work from any remote location, you need to set up an exception for the World Wide Web Services in Windows Firewall. Here are the steps to follow:

1. Select Start, type **firewall**, and then click Allow a Program through Windows Firewall in the search results. The Allowed Programs window appears.

2. Click Change Settings to enable the window controls.

3. Click to activate the check box beside the World Wide Web Services (HTTP) item, as shown in Figure 28.4.

> **NOTE**
>
> HTTP is short for Hypertext Transport Protocol, the protocol used to exchange information on the World Wide Web.

4. Click OK to put the exception into effect.

Accessing Your Website over the Network

With the Windows Firewall exception for the World Wide Web Services in place, you can now access the website from any remote computer on your network. You do this by launching your web browser and entering one of the following addresses:

```
http://IPAddress/ (replace IPAddress with the IP address of the IIS computer)
http://ComputerName/ (replace ComputerName with name of the IIS computer)
```

28

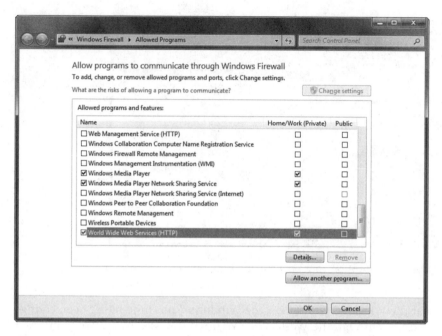

FIGURE 28.4   You need to configure Windows Firewall on the Windows 7 machine running IIS to allow traffic over the World Wide Web Services.

For example, Figure 28.5 shows Internet Explorer accessing the same IP address as shown earlier in Figure 28.3, but now instead of an error the user sees the default IIS site.

FIGURE 28.5   With the firewall exception in place, other computers on your network can now access your Web server.

Accessing Your Website over the Internet

People on your network can now access your website, but you may also want to allow website access to people from outside your network (that is, from the Internet). To set this up, you must do three things:

1. Set up the Windows 7 machine that's hosting the website with a permanent IP address, as described in Chapter 25, "Setting Up a Small Network."

   ▶ **See** *"Setting Up a Static IP Address,"* **p. 534**.

2. Configure your router to forward TCP traffic on port 80 to the IP address you specified in step 1. See Chapter 27, "Making Remote Network Connections," for the details.

   ▶ **See** *"Setting Up Port Forwarding,"* **p. 602**.

3. (Optional) If you want people to access your website using a domain name, you need to sign up for and configure a dynamic domain name system (DDNS) service, as described in Chapter 27.

   ▶ **See** *"Using Dynamic DNS to Access Your Network,"* **p. 604**.

An Internet user can now access your website by entering the following addresses into a web browser:

```
http://IPAddress/ (replace IPAddress with your router's external IP address)
http://DomainName/ (replace DomainName with your Dynamic DNS domain name)
```

   ▶ To learn how to find out your router's external IP address, **see** "Determining the Host IP Address," **p. 602**.

For this chapter, I set up a DDNS service to map the domain paulmcfedries.com to my local network, and then configured my router to forward web traffic to my Windows 7 machine running IIS. As you can see in Figure 28.6, entering the address http://www.paulmcfedries.com/ brings up the default IIS website.

NOTE

No, I don't currently run my own website, although I did for many years. Chances are if you try http://www.paulmcfedries.com/, you won't get very far.

28

FIGURE 28.6   With dynamic DNS and port forwarding in place, Internet users can access your Windows 7 web server using your domain name.

Understanding the Default Website

As you've seen, the default website set up by IIS isn't much to look at. That's okay because a bit later you'll be adding plenty of your own content to the site. For now, the simplicity of the site is an advantage because it makes it easy for you to look around and see how the default site is constructed. This will help you down the road to customize the site and to add your own content.

Viewing the Default Website Folder

Let's begin by examining the folder that holds the website content:

1. Select Start, Computer to open the computer window.
2. Double-click the hard drive on which Windows 7 is installed.

TIP

The Windows 7 hard drive is usually the C: drive. If you're not sure, look for the drive icon that has the Windows flag superimposed on it. You may need to pull down the Views menu and select Large Icons or Tiles to see the flag.

---

3. Open the inetpub folder.
4. Open the wwwroot subfolder.

The wwwroot folder holds the IIS default website files, as shown in Figure 28.7.

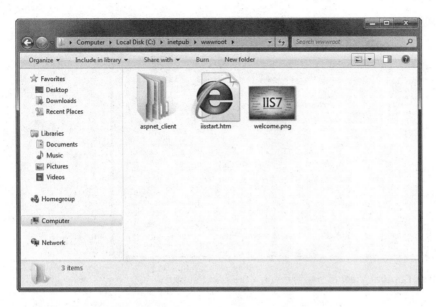

FIGURE 28.7   The contents of the IIS **wwwroot** folder.

The wwwroot folder has one subfolder (`aspnet_client`, which you can ignore) and two files:

`iisstart.htm`   This file contains the code that is used to display the home page you saw earlier in Figures 28.2, 28.5, and 28.6.

`welcome.png`   This file is the IIS7 image that you see in the home page.

Viewing the Default Website with IIS Manager

The wwwroot folder enables you to examine the physical files and subfolders associated with the IIS default website. However, you probably won't often deal with the wwwroot folder (or any folder) directly when creating and configuring your own web pages and websites. Instead, you'll most often use a Microsoft Management Console snap-in called the IIS Manager.

To display this snap-in and the default IIS website, follow these steps:

1. Select Start, type **iis**, and then select IIS Manager in the search results. The Internet Information Services (IIS) Manager window appears.

2. Open the *Computer* branch (where *Computer* is the name of your Windows 7 PC).

3. Open the Sites branch.

4. Select the Default Web Site branch.

IIS Manager gives you two ways to view the website files:

▶ Click the Content View button to see the site contents. As you can see in Figure 28.8, you see the same subfolder and files as you saw earlier (see Figure 28.7) when you examined the contents of the wwwroot folder.

28

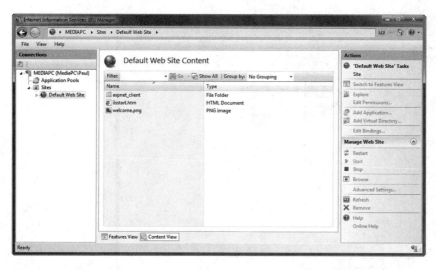

FIGURE 28.8   Click Content View to see the site's files and subfolders.

▶ Click Features View to see a collection of icons associated with the site's features, as shown in Figure 28.9. Most of these are advanced features, so you'll be using only a small subset of them.

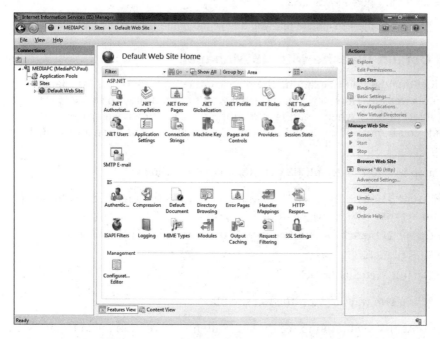

FIGURE 28.9   Click Features View to see icons associated with the site's features.

> **TIP**
>
> You can also use IIS Manager to open the website in your default web browser. In IIS Manager, open the *Computer*, Sites branch (where *Computer* is the name of the computer running IIS), select Default Web Site, and then click Browse in the Actions pane. (You can also right-click Default Web Site, and then select Manage Web Site, Browse in the shortcut menu.)

Much of the rest of this chapter shows you how to use IIS Manager to create and configure Windows 7 website content.

Adding Folders and Files to the Default Website

By far, the easiest way to set up your own web content in Windows 7 is to add that content to the existing default website. This requires no reconfiguration of the server, of IIS, of the Windows 7 Firewall, of the client computers, or of the router. You simply add the content, and it's ready for browsing.

Setting Permissions on the Default Website Folder

Somewhat annoyingly, Windows 7 makes it difficult for you to modify the contents of the wwwroot folder. For example, if you copy a file to the folder, you need to enter your User Account Control (UAC) credentials to allow the copy. Even worse, you get read-only access to the files, so if you edit a file you can't save your changes.

To avoid these hassles, you need to adjust the Security permissions on the wwwroot folder to give your Windows 7 user account Full Control. Here are the steps to follow:

1. Select Start, Computer, and navigate to the inetpub folder on your system drive.
2. Right-click the wwwroot folder, and then click Properties to open the folder's Properties dialog box.
3. Select the Security tab.
4. Click Edit. Windows 7 displays the Permissions for wwwroot dialog box.
5. Click Add to display the Select Users or Groups dialog box.
6. In the Enter the Object Names to Select text box, type your username, and then click OK to return to the Permissions dialog box.
7. Select your username in the Group or User Names list.
8. In the Permissions list, under the Allow column, click to activate the Full Control check box, as shown in Figure 28.10.

28

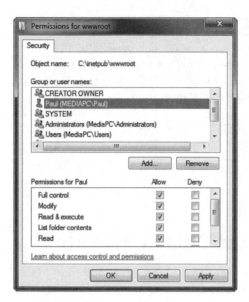

FIGURE 28.10   For hassle-free editing in the `wwwroot` folder, give your user account Full Control permission.

9. Click OK to return to the Security tab.

10. Click OK to put the new security settings into effect.

Adding a File to the Default Website

If you have just a few web content files that you want to add to the Windows 7 website, you can add them directly to the default website folder. First, create your web content file (HTML, ASP, or whatever). Here's a sample HTML file—which I've named `HelloWorld.htm`—that I'll use as an example:

```
<html>
<head>
<title>Hello World!</title>
</head>

<body>

<div style="font-size: 36pt;
            font-family: Verdana;
            color: DarkBlue">
Hello Windows 7 World!!
</div>

</body>
</html>
```

NOTE

For a primer on Hypertext Markup Language (HTML) and Cascading Style Sheets (CSS), check out my book *The Complete Idiot's Guide to Creating a Website*. You can find out more about it at my own site at www.mcfedries.com/.

CAUTION

Don't use spaces in the names of files (or folders) that you add to your website. Although Internet Explorer may display such pages successfully, other browsers may not.

Next, save the file to the wwwroot folder.

CAUTION

If your web content file references other files—for example, an HTML file that uses the <img> tag to reference an image file—be sure to copy those files to the wwwroot folder. You can either put the files in the root, or you can store them in a subfolder. For example, you might want to create a subfolder named images and use it to store your image files. If you store the files in subfolders, make sure you adjust the path in your code, as required. For example, if you place a file named HelloWorld.jpg in the images subfolder, you need to add the subfolder to the <img> tag, like so:

```
<img src="images\HelloWorld.jpg" />
```

TIP

A quick way to navigate to the wwwroot folder from IIS Manager is to open the *Computer*, Sites branch (where *Computer* is the name of the computer running IIS), select Default Web Site, and then click Explore in the Actions pane. (You can also right-click Default Web Site, and then click Explore in the shortcut menu.)

Figure 28.11 shows the HelloWorld.htm file copied to the wwwroot folder, and Figure 28.12 shows the file displayed with Internet Explorer.

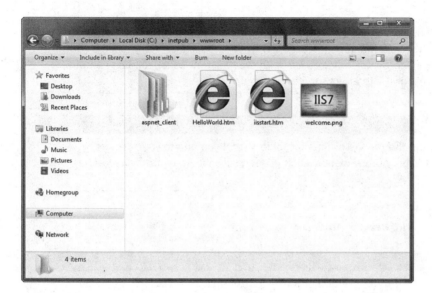

FIGURE 28.11   You can add individual files directly to the wwwroot folder.

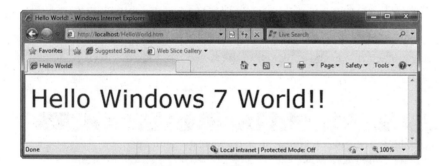

FIGURE 28.12   The HelloWorld.htm file displayed with Internet Explorer.

Changing the Default Website Home Page

One of the first things you'll probably want to do with your new website is change the home page. To do that, you need to create a new HTML (or other web content) file in the wwwroot folder and give the file one of the following names:

```
default.htm
default.asp
index.htm
index.html
```

See "Setting the Default Content Page," to learn more about these special filenames. For example, here's some bare-bones HTML code that I've put in a file named default.htm:

```
<html>
<head>
```

```
<title>Home Page</title>
</head>

<body>

<div style="text-align: center;
            font-size: 24pt;
            font-family: Verdana;
            color: Navy">
Welcome to Our Website!
</div>

</body>
</html>
```

Figure 28.13 shows `default.htm` added to the Default Web Site in IIS Manager, and Figure 28.14 shows the site's new home page in a web browser.

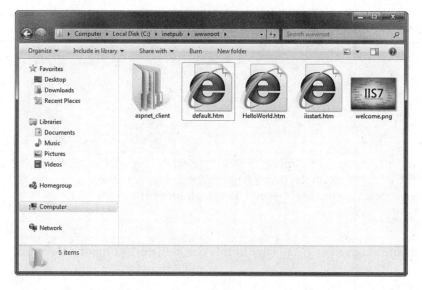

FIGURE 28.13   The `default.htm` file added to the default website.

FIGURE 28.14   The `default.htm` file now appears as the website's home page.

Adding a Folder to the Default Website

To add a folder to the Windows 7 default website, you have two choices:

▶ Add the folder manually.

▶ Add the folder as a new virtual directory.

The next two sections provide you with the details.

Adding a Folder Manually

Adding a folder to the Windows 7 default website is not all that different from adding a file. That is, you can create a new subfolder within the wwwroot folder, or copy or move an existing folder and paste it within wwwroot. To access web content within the new folder, tack the folder name and filename to the default website address. For example, if you create a subfolder named photos within the wwwroot folder, and the main page is named photos.htm, you access the content by entering the following address into the browser:

http://localhost/photos/photos.htm

Note that you can save some wear and tear on your typing fingers by changing the name of the main content file to one of the following:

```
default.htm
default.asp
index.htm
index.html
default.aspx
```

When you use one of these names, IIS displays the file by default if you don't specify a filename as part of the URL. For example, if you rename the photos.htm file to default.htm, you can access the file just by specifying the folder path in the URL:

```
http://localhost/photos/
```

I discuss default content files in more detail later in this chapter (see "Setting the Default Content Page").

Adding a Folder as a New Virtual Directory

When you add a folder manually, IIS Manager detects the new folder and adds it to the folder content. (If you don't see the folder right away, switch to Content View, right-click Default Web Site, and then click Refresh.) However, you can also use IIS Manager to create a new folder within the default website. Here are the steps to follow:

1. In IIS Manager, open the *Computer*, Sites, Default Web Site branch (where *Computer* is the name of your Windows 7 PC).

2. Right-click Default Web Site, and then click Add Virtual Directory. IIS Manager displays the Add Virtual Directory dialog box. Figure 28.15 shows a completed version of the dialog box.

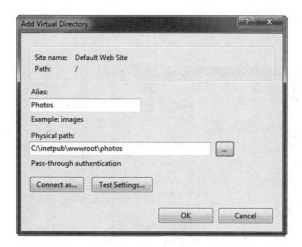

FIGURE 28.15   Use the Add Virtual Directory dialog box to add a folder to your website using IIS Manager.

3. Use the Alias text box to enter an alias for the virtual directory. The alias is the name that will appear in IIS Manager as a sub-branch of the default website.

NOTE

The alias doesn't have to be the same as the name of the virtual directory itself. For example, if you give the name photos to the new virtual directory, you could use something like Photos Virtual Directory as the alias.

4. To specify the location of the virtual directory, you have three choices:

   ▶ If the folder exists and you know the full pathname (drive and folders), type it in the Physical Path text box.

   ▶ If the folder exists and you're not sure of the full pathname (or it's too long to type), click the Browse (...) button, use the Browse for Folder dialog box to select the folder, and then click OK.

   ▶ If the folder doesn't exist, click Browse (...), use the Browse for Folder dialog box to select the folder within which you want the new folder to appear (for example, wwwroot), click Make New Folder, type the folder name, press Enter, and then click OK.

5. Click OK.

28

Figure 28.16 shows the Default Web Site in IIS Manager with the new virtual directory added.

FIGURE 28.16   The new virtual directory appears as part of the default website in IIS Manager.

Controlling and Customizing Your Website

At this point, you could use your website as is and just continue adding web pages, folders, and other content. However, IIS Manager offers a number of features and settings that enable you control your website and to customize its look and feel. For example, you can stop and start the website, change the default name of the site, and specify the default content page. The rest of this chapter takes you through the most useful of these IIS Manager features.

Stopping Your Website

By default, when you start Windows 7, the World Wide Web Publishing Service starts automatically, and that service automatically starts your website. This is reasonable behavior because in most cases you'll want your website available full time (that is, as long as the Windows 7 computer is running). However, there might be occasions when you don't want your site to be available:

▶ If you plan on making major edits to the content, you might prefer to take the site offline while you make the changes.

▶ You might only want your website available at certain times of the day.

▶ If you're developing a web application, certain changes may require that you stop and then restart the website.

For these and similar situations, you can stop the website. Here are the steps to follow:

   1. Open IIS Manager.

2. Select *Computer*, Sites, Default Web Site (where *Computer* is the name of the computer running IIS).

3. In the Actions pane, click Stop. (You can also right-click Default Web Site and then select Manage Web Site, Stop.) IIS Manager stops the website.

> **TIP**
>
> If you'd prefer that your website not start automatically when you log on to Windows 7, select Default Web Site, and then click Advanced Settings in the Actions pane. (You can also right-click Default Web Site, and then click Advanced Settings.) In the Start Automatically setting, select False, and then click OK.
>
> If you only want your website to not start the next time you launch Windows 7, stop the site and then shut down Windows 7. When you next log on to Windows 7, your website won't start. Note, however, that if you then restart the website during the Windows 7 session, the website will start automatically the next time you start Windows 7.

Restarting Your Website

When you're ready to get your website back online, follow these steps to restart it:

1. Open IIS Manager.

2. Select *Computer*, Sites, Default Web Site (where *Computer* is the name of the computer running IIS).

3. In the Actions pane, click Start. (You can also right-click Default Web Site and then select Manage Web Site, Start.) IIS Manager starts the website.

> **TIP**
>
> If your website is stuck or behaving erratically, you can often solve the problem by stopping and restarting the site. However, instead of performing two separate operations— clicking Stop and then clicking Start—IIS Manager lets you perform both actions in one shot by clicking Restart.

Renaming the Default Website

The name Default Web Site is innocuous enough, I suppose, but it's a bit on the bland side. If you prefer to use a more interesting name, follow these steps to change it:

1. Open IIS Manager.

2. Open the *Computer*, Sites branch (where *Computer* is the name of the computer running IIS).

3. Right-click Default Web Site, and then click Rename in the shortcut menu. IIS Manager adds a text box around the name.

4. Type the new name for the website.

5. Press Enter.

28

CAUTION

When you rename the site, the new name can be up to 259 characters long, but you must be sure to not use any of the following illegal characters:

@ $ & = + | \ ; : " ' , < > / ?

Changing the Website Location

By default, your website's home folder is the wwwroot folder, but that isn't necessarily permanent. You may decide to move the website to a different home folder, or you may decide to rename the existing folder. In either case, you must use IIS Manager to specify the new home folder. Here are the steps to follow:

1. Open IIS Manager.

2. Open the *Computer*, Sites branch (where *Computer* is the name of the computer running IIS).

3. Select Default Web Site.

4. Click Features View.

5. In the Actions pane, click Basic Settings to open the Edit Web Site dialog box, shown in Figure 28.17.

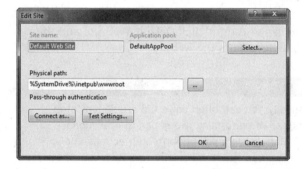

FIGURE 28.17   Use the Edit Web Site dialog box to change the site's home folder.

6. To specify the website's new home folder, you have three choices:

   ▶ If the folder exists and you know the full pathname (drive and folders), type it in the Physical Path text box.

   ▶ If the folder exists and you're not sure of the full pathname (or it's too long to type), click the Browse (...) button, use the Browse for Folder dialog box to select the folder, and then click OK.

► If the folder doesn't exist, click Browse (...), use the Browse for Folder dialog box to select the folder within which you want the new folder to appear, click Make New Folder, type the folder name, press Enter, and then click OK.

7. Click OK.

Setting the Website's Default Document

A normal website URL looks like the following:

```
http://name/folder/file
```

Here, *name* is a domain name or hostname, *folder* is a folder path, and *file* is the filename of the web page or other resource. Here's an example:

```
http://localhost/photos/default.htm
```

Intriguingly, you can view the same web page by entering the following address into the browser:

```
http://localhost/photos/
```

This works because IIS defines default.htm as one of its default document filenames. Here are the others:

```
default.asp
index.htm
index.html
iisstart.htm
default.aspx
```

This means that as long as a folder contains a file that uses one of these names, you can view the corresponding page without specifying the filename in the URL.

Note, too, that these default documents have an assigned priority, with default.htm having the highest priority, followed by default.asp, then index.htm, then index.html, then iisstart.htm, and finally default.aspx. This priority defines the order in which IIS looks for and displays the default document pages. That is, IIS first looks for default.htm; if that file doesn't exist in a folder, IIS next looks for default.asp, and so on.

For your own websites, you can add new default documents (for example, default.html and index.asp), remove existing default documents, and change the priority of the default documents. Here are the steps to follow:

1. Open IIS Manager.

2. Open the *Computer*, Sites branch (where *Computer* is the name of the computer running IIS).

3. Select Default Web Site.

4. Click Features View.

28

5. Double-click the Default Document icon. IIS Manager displays the Default Document page, shown in Figure 28.18.

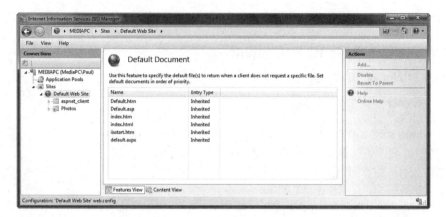

FIGURE 28.18   Use the Default Document page to add, remove, and reorder a site's default content pages.

6. To specify a new default document, click Add, type the filename in the Name text box, and then click OK.

7. To change the default document priority order, select a default document and then use the Move Up and Move Down buttons to set the order.

8. To delete a default document, select it and then click Remove.

9. Click the Back button to return to the website's main page in IIS Manager.

Working Without a Default Document

Using a default document is usually a good idea because it enables users to access your site without knowing the name of any file. However, for security reasons, you might want to allow access to the site only to users who know a specific filename on the site (for example, through a URL that you've provided). In that case, you have two choices:

▶ Don't include a file that uses one of the default document names.

▶ Disable the default documents.

Here are the steps to follow to disable default documents for your website:

1. Open IIS Manager.

2. Open the *Computer*, Sites branch (where *Computer* is the name of the computer running IIS).

3. Select Default Web Site.

4. Click Features View.

5. Double-click the Default Document icon to display the Default Document page.

6. In the Actions pane, click Disable. IIS Manager disables the default documents.

7. Click the Back button to return to the website's main page in IIS Manager.

At this point, you may still have a security risk because it's possible that any anonymous user who surfs to the site without specifying a filename will see a listing of all the files and subfolders in the website's home folders! An example is shown in Figure 28.19.

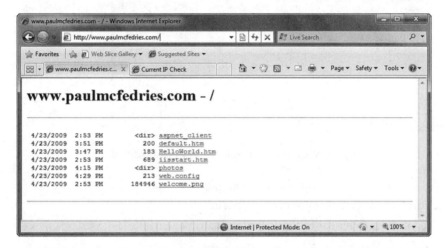

FIGURE 28.19   If you've disabled the default documents but directory browsing is enabled, anonymous users who don't specify a filename see a listing of the contents of the home folder.

> **NOTE**
>
> In the directory listing shown in Figure 28.19, you see a file named `web.config`. This is a file created by IIS Manager to store some of the settings you've been working with so far, including the name and order the default documents and whether default documents are enabled.

This is called *directory browsing*, and it's normally disabled in IIS 7.5, but just to make sure, follow these steps:

1. Open IIS Manager.

2. Open the *Computer*, Sites branch (where *Computer* is the name of the computer running IIS).

3. Select Default Web Site.

4. Click Features View.

5. Double-click the Directory Browsing icon to display the Directory Browsing page.

6. In the Actions pane, look for the message `Directory browsing has been disabled`, as shown in Figure 28.20. If you see the message, skip to step 8.

Look for this message

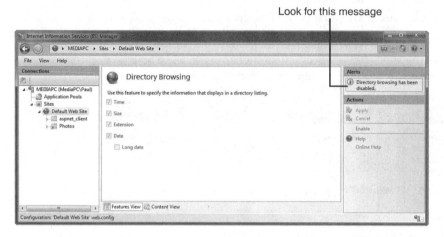

FIGURE 28.20   Make sure that your website has directory browsing disabled.

7. If you do not see the message, click the Disable link to disable directory browsing. IIS Manager disables directory browsing for the site.

8. Click the Back button to return to the website's main page in IIS Manager.

Now when an anonymous user surfs to your website without specifying a filename (and assuming you still have default documents disabled), that person sees the error message shown in Figure 28.21.

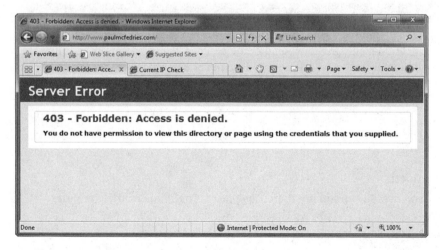

FIGURE 28.21   If you've disabled default documents and directory browsing, anonymous users who don't specify a filename see the error message shown here.

Disabling Anonymous Access

Earlier in this chapter, I showed you how to give yourself Full Control permission on the wwwroot folder to make it easier (and in some cases possible) to add and edit content in that folder. When you access your website on the IIS computer using the `http://localhost/`, `http://127.0.0.1/`, or `http://Computer/` addresses (where `Computer` is the name of the IIS computer), you access the site using your own user account. Everyone else on your network, and anyone who surfs to your site from the Internet (including you if you navigate to the site using `http://IPAddress/`, where `IPAddress` is your router's external IP address) accesses the site as an anonymous user. This means that IIS gives the person read-only access to the site without requiring a username and password, a technique called *anonymous authentication*.

However, you may have content that you want to restrict to people who have user accounts on Windows 7. In that case, you need to disable anonymous access for the website and switch to *basic authentication*, which means IIS prompts each user for a username and password before allowing access to the site.

Follow these steps to disable anonymous access:

1. Open IIS Manager.
2. Open the *Computer*, Sites branch (where *Computer* is the name of the computer running IIS).
3. If you want to disable anonymous authentication on the entire site, select Default Web Site; if you want to disable anonymous authentication only on a specific folder within the site, open the Default Web Site branch and select the folder.
4. Click Features View.
5. Double-click the Authentication icon to display the Authentication page.
6. Select Anonymous Authentication.
7. In the Actions pane, click the Disable link.
8. Select Basic Authentication.
9. In the Actions pane, click the Enable link. The Authentication page should now appear as shown in Figure 28.22.
10. Click the Back button to return to the website's main page in IIS Manager.

28

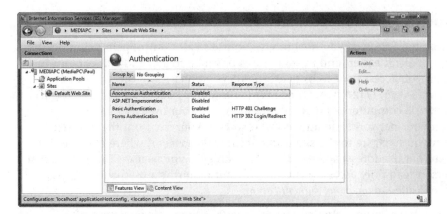

FIGURE 28.22   To secure your website or a folder within the website, disable anonymous authentication and enable basic authentication.

When an anonymous user attempts to access your website or website folder, he sees a Connect dialog box similar to the one shown in Figure 28.23. The user must enter a username and password for an account that exists on the Windows 7 machine that's running IIS.

FIGURE 28.23   With basic authentication enabled, users must enter a valid Windows 7 username and password to access the website or folder.

> **TIP**
>
> Switching to basic authentication means that any user with a valid account on Windows 7 can access the website. What if there are one or more users with Windows 7 accounts that you do *not* want to view the website? In that case, you must adjust the security of the website's home folder directly. Use Windows Explorer to display the website's home folder, right-click the folder, and then click Properties. In the Security tab, click Edit, click Add, type the name of the user, and then click OK. Select the user, and then activate the Full Control check box in the Deny column. This tells Windows 7 not to allow that user to view the folder, thus barring the user from viewing the website.

Viewing the Server Logs

After your web server is chugging along and serving pages to all and sundry, you might start to wonder which pages are popular with surfers and which ones are languishing. You might also want to know whether users are getting errors when they try to access your site.

You can tell all of this and more by working with the IIS logs. A log is a text file that records all the activity on your website, including the IP address and computer name (if applicable) of the surfer, the file that was served, the date and time the file was shipped to the browser, and the server return code (see the next Note box). For each server request, the log file writes a sequence of space-separated values, which makes it easy to import the file into a database or spreadsheet program for analysis.

The log files are stored in the \inetpub\logs\LogFiles\W3SVC1 folder of your Windows 7 system drive. (As you navigate to this folder, you may see one or two dialog boxes telling you that you don't have permission to open a particular folder. In each case, click Continue and enter your UAC credentials.)

Each filename takes the form u_ex*yymmdd*.log, where *yy* is the two-digit year, *mm* is the two-digit month, and *dd* is the two-digit day. For example, the log for August 23, 2008 would be stored in u_ex080823.log. Figure 28.24 shows a typical log file.

At first glance, an IIS log file appears to be nothing but a jumble of letters, numbers, and symbols. However, there's a bit of method in the apparent madness. First, know that each line (that is, each line that doesn't begin with #) represents an object that IIS served. This could be a file, and image, or some other content on the website. Second, remember that each field is separated by a space. Third, notice the #Fields line, which appears from time to time in the log:

```
#Fields: date time s-ip cs-method cs-uri-stem cs-uri-query s-port cs-username
➥c-ip cs(User-Agent) sc-status sc-substatus sc-win32-status
```

This line tells you the name of each log field. To help you make sense of what you're looking at, Table 28.1 gives you a summary of what you see in each field.

28

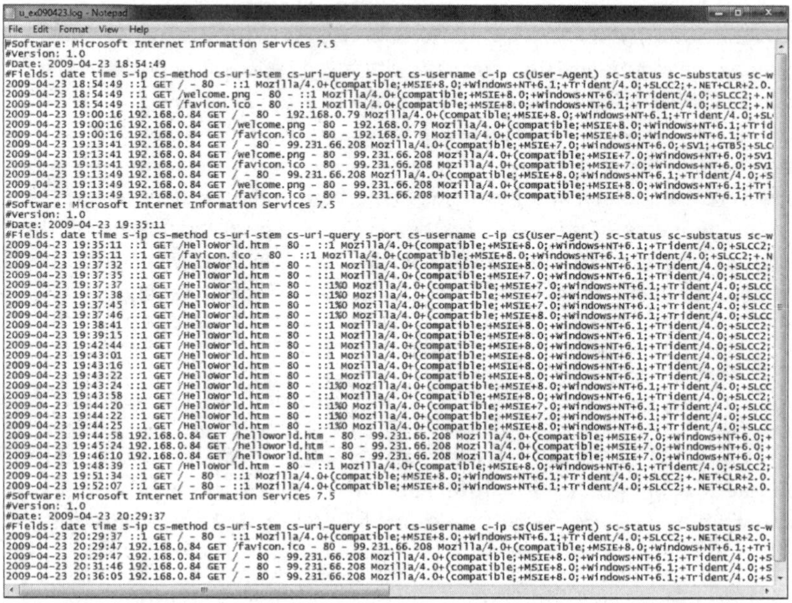

FIGURE 28.24   A typical IIS log file.

TABLE 28.1   Description of the Fields Found in an IIS Log File

Field	Description
date	The date on which the item (file or folder) was served.
time	The time at which the item was served.
s-ip	The IP address of the computer that's running the web server.
cs-method	The method used to request the item. (This is almost always GET.)
cs-uri-stem	The name of the requested item.
cs-uri-query	The query used to generate the item request. (This will usually be blank, represented by a dash.)
s-port	The port used to exchange the data. (This will always be 80.)
cs-username	The name—and sometimes the computer name—of the authenticated user. You only see values in this field if you turn on basic authentication for the website or a folder.
c-ip	The IP address of the user who requested the item.
cs(User-Agent)	A string that identifies the user's web browser.
sc-status	A code that specifies whether the request was handled successfully and, if not, what the error was.
sc-substatus	A secondary error code if the request failed.
sc-win32-status	The Windows status during the request.

Server Return Codes

A `sc-status` code of 200 means the document was sent successfully to the browser. For unsuccessful operations, here's a summary of some of the return codes you'll find in the log:

Return Code	What It Means
204	File contains no content
301	File moved permanently
302	File moved temporarily
304	File not modified
400	Bad request
401	Unauthorized access
402	Payment required
403	Access forbidden
404	File not found
500	Internal server error
501	Service not implemented
502	Bad gateway
503	Service unavailable

28

Adding Macs to Your Windows 7 Network

Mac users swear by their computers. PC users swear at their computers.
—Anonymous

The so-called *iPod halo effect* refers to the increase in the sales and perceived prestige of Apple products based on the massive popularity of Apple's iPod digital music player. (The iPhone is almost as popular as the iPod, so, yes, there's an iPhone halo effect, as well.) On the Mac front, this halo effect has translated into a steadily increasing market share for Mac computers over the past few years. Not that Macs are taking over the market, mind you. Recent stats give Macs between 8% and 9% of the PC market in the United States (depending on whose numbers you're looking at), which is up from a measly 3% not all that long ago. However, even that big increase still pales in comparison to the roughly 88% of the market owned by Windows PCs.

Still, with nearly 1 in 10 computers sporting the Apple logo, chances are you'll eventually end up with 1 or 2 on your Windows network, if you haven't already. Or, I should say, you might end up with 1 or 2 that *want* access to your Windows network. As you see in this chapter, although it's not hard to get Mac and Windows PC networking together, it's not out-of-the-box easy, either.

Making Sure That SMB Support Is Activated in Mac OS X Tiger

One of the important networking layers used by all Microsoft networks—including, of course, your Windows network—is called Server Message Block (SMB). It's via SMB that Windows PCs can share folders on the network and access folders that other Windows PCs have shared. In a very real sense, SMB *is* the network.

SMB's central role in Windows networking is good news if you have a Mac in your household or small office. That's because all versions of Mac OS X support SMB natively, so you can use your Mac not only to view the Windows 7 shares, but also to open and work with files on those shares (provided, of course, that you have permission to access the share and that Mac OS X has an application that's compatible with whatever file you want to work with). You can even switch things around and view your Mac shares from within Windows. The next few sections provide you with the details.

Mac OS X Leopard (10.5) and later support SMB natively by default. However, if you're running Mac OS X Tiger (10.4) or earlier, before going any further it's worthwhile to take a second now and ensure that SMB support is activated on your Mac. Here are the steps to follow:

1. On your Mac, click the Finder icon in the Dock.

2. Select Applications, Utilities to open the Utilities folder. (You can also select Go, Utilities or press Shift+Command+U.)

3. Double-click Directory Access to open the Directory Access window.

4. Select the Services tab.

5. Check to see if the SMB/CIFS check box is activated.

6. If the check box is activated, skip to step 8. Otherwise, click the Lock icon, and then enter your system's administrative password to make the settings available.

7. Activate the SMB/CIFS check box, as shown in Figure 29.1.

FIGURE 29.1   In Mac OS X Tiger and earlier, make sure the SMB/CIFS check box is activated.

8. Select Directory Access, Quit Directory Access.

Connecting to the Windows Network

Now you're ready to connect your Mac to the Windows network. If the Mac is near your network's router (or switch, depending on your configuration), and your Mac has an Ethernet port (the MacBook Air, for example, doesn't come with built-in Ethernet), run a network cable from the Mac to the device.

If you're using a wireless connection, follow these steps to connect your Mac to the wireless portion of your Windows network:

1. Click the System Preferences icon in the Dock. (Or pull down the Apple menu and select System Preferences.)

2. Click Network to open the Network preferences.

3. Click AirPort.

4. If the AirPort status is currently Off, click Turn AirPort On.

5. Use the Network Name pop-up menu to select your wireless network ID.

TIP

Mac OS X normally shows the AirPort status icon in the menu bar. If you see that icon, a faster way to initiate a wireless connection is to click the icon and then click the name of the network you want to join.

---

6. If your network requires a password, Mac OS X prompts you to enter the password, as shown in Figure 29.2.

FIGURE 29.2   If your wireless network is secure, you need to enter the password to access it.

7. Type the security key in the Password text box.

8. If you want Mac OS X to automatically connect to the network the next time it comes within range, click to activate the Remember This Network check box.

29

9. Click OK to return to the Network preferences. As shown in Figure 29.3, the AirPort Status now shows as Connected.

10. Close the Network preferences window.

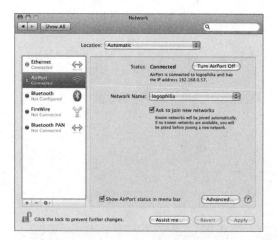

FIGURE 29.3   When you connect your Mac to the Windows network via wireless, the AirPort tab shows the connection status.

TIP

To configure Mac OS X to display the AirPort icon in the menu bar, click to activate the Show AirPort Status in Menu Bar check box.

Connecting to a Windows Shared Folder

Mac OS X support for connecting to shared Windows folders is turned on by default, so connecting your Mac to a Windows PC on your network and selecting a shared folder requires no prep work on your part.

How you go about making the connection depends on whether your Mac "sees" the Windows PC. To check this, switch to Finder, and then do one of the following:

▶ In the Sidebar, open the Shared section and look for an icon for the Windows PC.

▶ Choose Go, Network (or press Shift+Command+K) and use the Network window to look for an icon for the Windows PC.

Connecting to a Seen Windows PC

If you see an icon for the Windows PC, follow these steps to connect to it:

1. Open the Windows PC icon.

2. Click Connect As. Mac OS X displays the dialog box shown in Figure 29.4.

FIGURE 29.4   When you connect to the Windows PC, you need to provide a username and password for an account on the PC.

NOTE

If you don't know the username and password of an account on the Windows PC, select the Guest option instead. This gives you read-only access to the Windows PC's shared folders.

3. Select the Registered User option.
4. Type a username and password for an account on the Windows PC.
5. Click to activate the Remember This Password in My Keychain check box.
6. Click Connect. Mac OS X presents a list of the shared folders on the Windows PC, as shown in Figure 29.5.

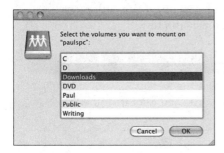

FIGURE 29.5   After you connect to the Windows PC, choose the shared folder you want to mount in Finder.

7. Select the folder you want to mount, and then click OK. Mac OS X mounts the shared folder in Finder and displays the folder's contents.

Connecting to an Unseen Windows PC

If your Windows PC doesn't show up in the Sidebar or the Network window, first make sure it's turned on and not in sleep mode. If you still don't see it, follow these steps to make the connection:

1. In Finder, choose Go, Connect to Server (or press Command+K). The Connect to Server dialog box appears.

TIP

You can also right-click (or Control+click if you have a one-button mouse) the Finder icon in the Dock and then click Connect to Server.

2. In the Server Address text box, type **smb://WindowsPC,** where *WindowsPC* is either the name of the Windows computer you want to connect to or its IP address. See Figure 29.6 for an example.

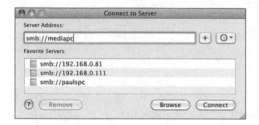

FIGURE 29.6   If you don't see the Windows PC in Finder, use the Connect to Server command to connect to the PC directly.

3. If you want to save this address as a favorite (for example, if you plan on connecting to the Windows PC regularly), click the Add icon (+) to insert the address in the Favorite Servers list (again, see Figure 29.6 for some examples).

TIP

Rather than saving the address as a favorite, you can click the Recent Servers icon (it's the one to the right of the Add icon) and then click the server you want from the list that appears.

4. Click Connect. Your Mac prompts you for the credentials of a user account on the Windows PC.

5. Select the Registered User option.

6. Type a username and password for an account on the Windows PC.

7. Click to activate the Remember This Password in My Keychain check box.

8. Click Connect. Your Mac displays a list of the Windows PC's shared folders.

9. Select the folder you want to mount, and then click OK. Mac OS X mounts the shared folder in Finder and displays the folder's contents.

Working with the Windows PC's Shared Folders

When you first connect to a Windows share, Mac OS X mounts the shared folder in Finder and displays the folder's contents, as shown in Figure 29.7. You can then work with the folder's contents just like any other shared network folder (assuming, of course, that your Mac has compatible applications installed).

Mounted Windows PC

FIGURE 29.7   After you mount the Windows PC's shared folder, the folder contents appear in a Finder window.

To switch to a different shared folder on the Windows PC, you have two choices:

▶ In the Finder's Sidebar, click the icon for the Windows PC.

▶ In Finder, select Go, Network (or press Shift+Command+K) to open the Network window, and then double-click the icon for the Windows PC.

Either way, Mac OS X displays the PC's shared folders, as shown in Figure 29.8. Open the folder you want to work with.

Eject icon

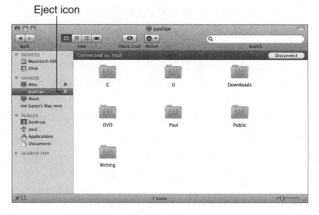

FIGURE 29.8   Open the Windows PC in Finder to see the PC's shared folders.

Unmounting a Windows Shared Folder

When you've completed your work with the Windows PC, you can unmount the PC by using either of the following techniques:

▶ In the Finder's Sidebar, click the Eject icon that appears to the right of the icon for the Windows PC (see Figure 29.8).

▶ In Finder, select Go, Network (or press Shift+Command+K) to open the Network window, double-click the icon for the Windows PC, and then click the Disconnect button.

Backing Up Mac Data to a Windows Shared Folder

Besides working with the files on a Windows share in a Mac OS X application, you can use a Windows 7 share to store Mac OS X backups. This is handy if you don't have a second hard drive attached to your Mac, or if your backups are too big to burn to a DVD. The easiest way to do this in Mac OS X is to use the Disk Utility to archive a folder or the entire system to an image file on a Windows 7 share. Here's how it's done:

1. In Windows 7, create a share to store the Mac OS X backup.

   ▶ For the details on setting up a new share in Windows 7, **see** "Sharing Resources with the Network," **p. 565**.

2. Follow the steps given earlier in this chapter to mount the new share in Mac OS X.

3. Click the Finder icon in the Dock.

4. Select Applications, Utilities, and then double-click Disk Utility. Mac OS X launches the Disk Utility application.

5. If you want to back up your entire system, click Macintosh HD in the Disk Utility window.

6. Select File, New, and then select either Disk Image from Folder or Disk Image from *disk* (Macintosh HD), where *disk* is the name of your Mac's hard disk.

7. If you selected Disk Image from Folder, the Select Folder to Image dialog box appears. Select the folder you want to back up, and then click Image.

8. In the New Image dialog box, use the Save As text box to edit the filename, if desired.

9. Select the Windows share that you mounted in step 2. Figure 29.9 shows an example that will save the image to the Backups folder on the mounted share named D on PAULSPC.

10. Click Save. Mac OS X creates the disk image on the Windows 7 share. (Depending on the amount of data you're archiving, this may take several hours.)

11. When the image creation is done, select Disk Utility, Quit Disk Utility.

FIGURE 29.9   Select a shared folder on the mounted Windows PC to store the disk image.

Using a Mac to Make a Remote Desktop Connection to Windows 7

You learned in Chapter 27, "Making Remote Network Connections," how to use the Windows Remote Desktop Connection program to connect to the desktop of another computer on your network. However, it's also possible to make Remote Desktop connections to Windows computers from your Mac.

▶ For the details on connecting via Remote Desktop, **see** "Connecting to the Remote Desktop," **p. 592**.

To do this, you need to install on your Mac an application called Remote Desktop Connection Client for Mac 2, which is available from Microsoft. Go to www.microsoft.com/downloads and search for "Remote Desktop Mac." (Figure 29.10 shows the download page.)

After you have the Remote Desktop Connection Client installed on your Mac, follow these steps:

1. Ensure that the Windows PC to which you'll be connecting is configured to accept Remote Desktop connections.

   ▶   To learn how to get a computer set up for Remote Desktop connections, **see** "Setting Up the Remote Computer as a Host," **p. 586**.

2. In Finder, open the Applications folder, and then launch the Remote Desktop Connection icon.

3. In the Computer text box, type the name or IP address of the host computer, as shown in Figure 29.11.

29

FIGURE 29.10   Download and install Remote Desktop Connection Client for Mac 2.

FIGURE 29.11   In the Remote Desktop Connection window, type the name or IP address of the Windows host computer.

NOTE

In my experience, Mac-based Remote Desktop connections work best when you use the IP address of the Windows host PC.

4. If you don't want to customize Remote Desktop, skip to step 7. Otherwise, select Remote Desktop Connection, Preferences to open the Remote Desktop Connection preferences dialog box.

5. The Login tab offers the following options:

   ▶ **User Name**—This is the username you want to use to log in to the host computer.

   ▶ **Password**—This is the password to use to log in to the host computer.

   ▶ **Domain**—Leave this text box blank.

   ▶ **Add User Information to Your Keychain**—Activate this check box to have Mac OS X remember your login data.

▶ **Reconnect Automatically If Disconnected**—Leave this check box activated to have Remote Desktop Connection automatically reestablish a connect to the host if you get disconnected.

6. Fill in the options in the other tabs, as required. Note that most of these tabs provide a similar set of options that the Windows version of Remote Desktop Connection provides. For example, the Display tab, shown in Figure 29.12, combines many of the options that you see in the Display and Experience tabs in the Windows version.

> ▶ For a complete look at the various Remote Desktop Connection options, **see** "Making an Advanced Connection," **p. 593**.

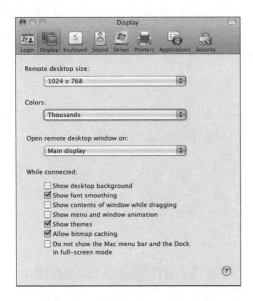

FIGURE 29.12   The Mac version of Remote Desktop Connection, the preferences are similar to the options in the Windows version of the program.

TIP

The default Colors setting that Remote Desktop Connection Client for Mac 2 uses is Thousands, which can make most Windows screens look awful. In the Display tab, use the Colors pop-up menu to select Millions.

---

7. Click Connect. If you didn't specify the login data for the Windows PC in the Remote Desktop Connection preferences, the programs prompts you to enter them now.

29

8. Type the username and password for an account on the Windows PC, activate the
   Add User Information to Your Keychain check box to save the login data, and
   then click OK.

Remote Desktop Connection Client for Mac 2 connects to the Windows PC. Figure 29.13
shows Mac OS X with a connection to a Windows 7 computer.

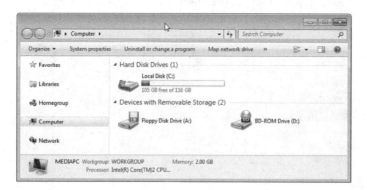

FIGURE 29.13   A Mac connected to a Windows 7 PC using the Remote Desktop Connection
Client for Mac software.

When you're done, select RDC, Quit RDC, and then click Disconnect when the program
warns you that you're about to disconnect from the Windows PC.

Letting Windows Computers See Your Mac Shares

The techniques you've seen so far have assumed that you want to access a Windows
shared network folder from your Mac. However, if your Mac has data of interest to
Windows users, you'll need to set things up so that those Windows users can see that
data. You do that by sharing one or more folders on your Mac in such a way that
Windows PCs can see and access them.

This feature isn't turned on by default on your Mac, so you need to follow these steps to
turn it on:

1. Click the System Preferences icon in the Dock (or select Apple, System Preferences).
   The System preferences appear.

2. Click the Sharing icon. The Sharing preferences appear.

3. In the list of services, activate the File Sharing check box.

4. Click Options.

5. Activate the Share Files and Folders Using SMB (Windows) check box, as shown in Figure 29.14.

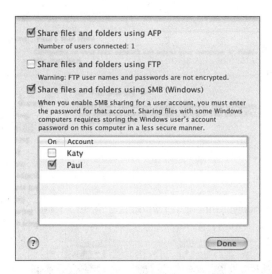

FIGURE 29.14   To share your Mac with Windows PCs, select SMB sharing.

6. Select the check box for each user account to which you want to give access.

7. Click Done.

8. To share a folder, click the + icon under Shared Folders in the Sharing preferences, select the folder, and then click Add.

9. Click the folder in the Shared Folders list, click + under Users, select a user, and then click Add.

10. Click a user in the Users list, and then click the permission level you want to assign from the drop-down menu. You have four choices:

   ▶ **Read & Write**—The user can read the folder contents and make changes to the data.

   ▶ **Read Only**—The user can only read the folder contents.

   ▶ **Write Only (Drop Box)**—The user can only add new data to the folder.

   ▶ **No Access**—The user can't open the folder.

11. Repeat steps 8–10 to share other folders and set other user permissions.

12. Select System Preferences, Quit System Preferences.

Figure 29.15 shows the Sharing preferences with several folders and users.

29

Computer name

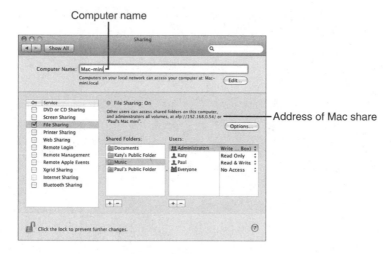

Address of Mac share

FIGURE 29.15   The Sharing preferences with Windows Sharing activated and several folders shared and permissions assigned.

TIP

Macs often end up with long-winded computer names, such as Paul McFedries' MacBook Pro. Because you need to use the computer name to log on to the share, consider editing the `Computer Name` field to something shorter.

One way to access the Mac shares from a Windows PC is to enter the share address directly, using the Start menu's Search box, the Run dialog box, or Windows Explorer's address bar. You have two choices:

```
\\IP\folder
\\Computer\folder
```

Here, *IP* is the IP address shown in the Sharing window (shown in Figure 29.15 as //192.168.0.54), *Computer* is the Mac's computer name (shown in Figure 29.15 as Mac-mini), and in both cases, *folder* is the name of a shared folder on the Mac. If you prefer to see all the shares, you can leave off the folder name. Here are some examples:

```
\\192.168.0.54\
\\192.168.0.54\paul
\\Mac-mini\Music
```

NOTE

Again, just as IP addresses are the most reliable way to may Mac connections to Windows shares, I also find that IP addresses are the best way for Windows PCs to connect to shared Macs.

You're then prompted for the username and password of the Mac account that you enabled for Windows Sharing. Figure 29.16 shows an example, and Figure 29.17 shows a Mac opened in Windows 7 to reveal its shared resources.

FIGURE 29.16   When you connect to the Mac, you'll most likely have to log in to an account on the Mac.

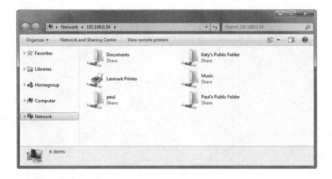

FIGURE 29.17   A shared Mac opened in Windows 7.

CHAPTER 30

Scripting Windows 7 with WSH

Most of you are familiar with the virtues of a programmer. There are three, of course: laziness, impatience, and hubris."
—Larry Wall

In Chapter 13, "Controlling Windows 7 from the Command Line," you learned how to tame the Command Prompt by creating *batch files*—small, executable text files that run one or more commands. You'll see that with a little ingenuity and a dash of guile, it's possible to make batch files perform some interesting and useful tasks. Indeed, for many years, batch files were the only way to automate certain kinds of tasks. Unfortunately, the batch file world is relentlessly command line oriented. So, with the exception of being able to launch Windows programs, batch files remain ignorant of the larger Windows universe.

If you're looking to automate a wider variety of tasks in Windows, you need to supplement your batch file knowledge with scripts that can deal with the Registry, shortcuts, files, and network drives, and that can even interact with Windows programs via automation. The secret to these powerful scripts is the *Windows Script Host* (WSH). This chapter introduces you to the Windows Script Host, shows you how to execute scripts, and runs through the various elements in the WHS object model.

Understanding Windows Script Host

As you might know, Internet Explorer is really just an empty container application that's designed to host different data formats, including ActiveX controls, various file formats (such as Microsoft Word documents and Microsoft Excel worksheets), and several ActiveX scripting engines. A *scripting engine* is a dynamic link library (DLL) that provides programmatic support for a particular scripting language. Internet Explorer supports two such scripting engines: VBScript (VBScript.dll) and JavaScript (JSscript.dll). This enables web programmers to write small programs—*scripts*—that interact with the user, control the browser, set cookies, open and close windows, and more. Although these scripting engines don't offer full-blown programmability (you can't compile scripts, for example), they do offer modern programming structures such as loops, conditionals, variables, objects, and more. In other words, they're a huge leap beyond what a mere batch file can do.

The Windows Script Host is also a container application, albeit a scaled-down application in that its only purpose in life is to host scripting engines. Right out of the box, the Windows Script Host supports both the VBScript and JavaScript engines. However, Microsoft designed the Windows Script Host to be a universal host that can support any ActiveX-based scripting engine. Therefore, there are also third-party vendors offering scripting engines for languages such as Perl, Tcl, and Rexx.

The key difference between Internet Explorer's script hosting and the Windows Script Host is the environment in which the scripts run. Internet Explorer scripts are web page based, so they control and interact with either the web page or the web browser. The Windows Script Host runs scripts within the Windows 7 shell or from the Command Prompt, so you use these scripts to control various aspects of Windows. Here's a sampling of the things you can do:

- ▶ Execute Windows programs

- ▶ Create and modify shortcuts

- ▶ Use automation to connect and interact with automation-enabled applications, such as Microsoft Word, Outlook, and Internet Explorer

- ▶ Read, add, and delete Registry keys and items

- ▶ Access the VBScript and JavaScript object models, which give access to the file system, runtime error messages, and more

- ▶ Use pop-up dialog boxes to display information to the user, and determine which button the user clicked to dismiss the dialog box

- ▶ Read environment variables, which are system values that Windows 7 keeps in memory, such as the folder into which Windows 7 is installed—the %SystemRoot% environment variable—and the name of the computer—the %ComputerName% environment variable

- ▶ Deal with network resources, including mapping and unmapping network drives, accessing user data (such as the username and user domain), and connecting and disconnecting network printers

- ▶ Use the Windows Management Instrumentation service to manage applications, systems, devices, networks, and more, either locally or remotely

Clearly, we've gone *way* beyond batch files!

What about speed? After all, you wouldn't want to load something that's the size of Internet Explorer each time you need to run a simple script. That's not a problem because, as I've said, the Windows Script Host does nothing but host scripting engines, so it has much less memory overhead than Internet Explorer. That means that your scripts run quickly. For power users looking for a Windows-based batch language, the Windows Script Host is a welcome tool.

> **NOTE**
>
> This chapter does not teach you how to program in either VBScript or JavaScript and, in fact, assumes that you're already proficient in one or both of these languages. If you're looking for a programming tutorial, my *VBA for the 2007 Microsoft Office System* (Que, 2007) is a good place to start (VBScript is a subset of VBA—Visual Basic for Applications). For JavaScript, try my *Special Edition Using JavaScript* (Que, 2001). Another good choice is *Windows 7 and Vista Guide to Scripting, Automation, and Command Line Tools*, by Brian Knittel (Que, 2009)

Scripts and Script Execution

Scripts are simple text files that you create using Notepad or some other text editor. You can use a word processor such as WordPad to create scripts, but you must make sure that you save these files using the program's Text Only document type. For VBScript, a good alternative to Notepad is the editor that comes with either Visual Basic or any program that supports VBA (such as the Office suite). Just remember that VBScript is a subset of VBA (which is, in turn, a subset of Visual Basic), so it does not support all objects and features.

In a web page, you use the `<script>` tag to specify the scripting language you're using, as in this example:

```
<SCRIPT LANGUAGE="VBScript">
```

With the Windows Script Host, the script file's extension specifies the scripting language:

- ▶ For VBScript, save your text files using the `.vbs` extension (which is registered as the following file type: VBScript Script File).

- ▶ For JavaScript, use the `.js` extension (which is registered as the following file type: JScript Script File).

As described in the next three sections, you have three ways to run your scripts: by launching the script files directly, by using `WSscript.exe`, or by using `CScript.exe`.

30

Running Script Files Directly

The easiest way to run a script from within Windows is to launch the .vbs or .js file directly. That is, you either double-click the file in Windows Explorer or type the file's path and name in the Run dialog box. Note, however, that this technique does not work at the Command Prompt. For that, you need to use the CScript program described a bit later.

Using WScript for Windows-Based Scripts

The .vbs and .js file types have an open method that's associated with WScript (WScript.exe), which is the Windows-based front end for the Windows Script Host. In other words, launching a script file named MyScript.vbs is equivalent to entering the following command in the Run dialog box:

```
wscript myscript.vbs
```

The WScript host also defines several parameters that you can use to control how the script executes. Here's the full syntax:

WSCRIPT *filename arguments* //B //D //E:*engine* //H:*host* //I //Job:*xxxx* //S //T:*ss* //X

filename	Specifies the filename, including the path of the script file, if necessary.
arguments	Specifies optional arguments required by the script. An *argument* is a data value that the script uses as part of its procedures or calculations.
//B	Runs the script in batch mode, which means script errors and Echo method output lines are suppressed. (I discuss the Echo method later in this chapter.)
//D	Enables Active Debugging. If an error occurs, the script is loaded into the Microsoft Script Debugger (if it's installed) and the offending statement is high-lighted.
//E:*engine*	Executes the script using the specified scripting *engine*, which is the scripting language to use when running the script.
//H:*host*	Specifies the default scripting host. For *host*, use either CScript or WScript.
//I	Runs the script in interactive mode, which displays script errors and Echo method output lines.
//Job:*xxxx*	In a script file that contains multiple jobs, executes only the job with id attribute equal to *xxxx*.
//S	Saves the specified WScript arguments as the default for the current user; uses the following Registry key to save the settings: HKCU\Software\Microsoft\Windows Script Host\Settings
//TT:*ss*	Specifies the maximum time in seconds (*ss*) that the script can run before it shuts down automatically.
//X	Executes the entire script in the Microsoft Script Debugger (if it's installed).

For example, the following command runs `MyScript.vbs` in batch mode with a 60-second maximum execution time:

```
wscript myscript.vbs //B //TT:60
```

Creating Script Jobs

A script *job* is a section of code that performs a specific task or set of tasks. Most script files contain a single job. However, it's possible to create a script file with multiple jobs. To do this, first surround the code for each job with the `<script>` and `</script>` tags, and then surround those with the `<job>` and `</job>` tags. In the `<job>` tag, include the `id` attribute and set it to a unique value that identifies the job. Finally, surround all the jobs with the `<package>` and `</package>` tags. Here's an example:

```
<package>
<job id="A">
<script language="VBScript">
    WScript.Echo "This is Job A."
</script>
</job>

<job id="B">
<script language="VBScript">
    WScript.Echo "This is Job B."
</script>
</job>
</package>
```

Save the file using the `.wsf` (Windows Script File) extension.

NOTE

If you write a lot of scripts, the Microsoft Script Debugger is an excellent programming tool. If there's a problem with a script, the debugger can help you pinpoint its location. For example, the debugger enables you to step through the script's execution one statement at a time. If you don't have the Microsoft Script Debugger, you can download a copy from http://msdn.microsoft.com/en-us/library/ms950396.aspx.

30

Using CScript for Command-Line Scripts

The Windows Script Host has a second host front-end application called CScript (`CScript.exe`), which enables you to run scripts from the command line. In its simplest form, you launch CScript and use the name of the script file (and its path, if required) as a parameter, as in this example:

```
cscript myscript.vbs
```

The Windows Script Host displays the following banner and then executes the script:

```
Microsoft (R) Windows Script Host Version 5.8 for Windows
Copyright (C) Microsoft Corporation. All rights reserved.
```

As with WScript, the CScript host has an extensive set of parameters you can specify:

```
CSCRIPT filename arguments //B //D //E:engine //H:host //I //Job:xxxx //S //T:ss
➡//X //U //LOGO //NOLOGO
```

This syntax is almost identical to that of WScript, but adds the following three parameters:

//LOGO   Displays the Windows Script Host banner at startup

//NOLOGO   Hides the Windows Script Host banner at startup

//U   Uses Unicode for redirected input/output from the console

Script Properties and .wsh Files

In the preceding two sections, you saw that the WScript and CScript hosts have a number of parameters you can specify when you execute a script. It's also possible to set some of these options by using the properties associated with each script file. To see these properties, right-click a script file and then click Properties. In the properties sheet that appears, display the Script tab, shown in Figure 30.1. You have two options:

▶ **Stop Script After Specified Number of Seconds**—If you activate this check box, Windows shuts down the script after it has run for the number of seconds specified in the associated spin box. This is useful for scripts that might hang during execution. For example, a script that attempts to enumerate all the mapped network drives at startup might hang if the network is unavailable.

▶ **Display Logo When Script Executed in Command Console**—As you saw in the previous section, the CScript host displays some banner text when you run a script at the Command Prompt. If you deactivate this check box, the Windows Script Host suppresses this banner (unless you use the //LOGO parameter).

When you make changes to these properties, the Windows Script Host saves your settings in a new file that has the same name as the script file, except with the .wsh (Windows Script Host Settings) extension. For example, if the script file is MyScript.vbs, the settings are stored in MyScript.wsh. These .wsh files are text files organized into sections, much like .ini files. Here's an example:

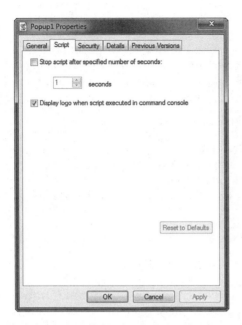

FIGURE 30.1   In a script file's properties sheet, use the Script tab to set some default options for the script.

```
[ScriptFile]
Path=C:\Users\Paul\Documents\Scripts\Popup1.vbs
[Options]
Timeout=0
DisplayLogo=1
```

To use these settings when running the script, use either WScript or CScript and specify the name of the .wsh file:

```
wscript myscript.wsh
```

NOTE

Rather than setting properties for individual scripts, you might prefer to set global properties that apply to the WScript host itself. Those global settings then apply to every script that runs using the WScript host. To do this, run WScript.exe without any parameters. This displays the properties sheet for WScript, which contains only the Script tab shown in Figure 30.1. The settings you choose in the properties sheet are stored in the following Registry key:

HKLM\Software\Microsoft\Windows Script Host\Settings

Running a Script as the Administrator

When you run scripts in Windows 7, you may on occasion need to run those scripts under the auspices of the Administrator account. For example, in Chapter 12, "Tweaking the Windows 7 Registry," I show you a script that toggles the Registry Editor between disabled and enabled, and that script must be run under the Administrator account.

▶ **See** "Preventing Other Folks from Messing with the Registry," **p. 233**.

When you need to run a script under the Administrator account, one solution is to first launch an elevated Command Prompt session, as described in Chapter 13. From the elevated command line, you could then use CScript to launch the script, as described earlier. That would work, but it's a bit of a hassle. If you run a lot of administrator scripts, you'd probably prefer something a lot more direct.

▶ **See** "Running Command Prompt as the Administrator," **p. 246**.

I'm happy to report that a much more direct method is available. You can tweak the Windows 7 file system to display a Run as Administrator command when you right-click a VBScript file. Click that command, enter your UAC credentials, and your script runs with administrator privileges.

Here's what you do:

> **NOTE**
>
> If you don't feel like modifying the Registry by hand, there's a file containing the necessary changes—VBSFile_RunAsAdminisrator.reg—on my website at http://mcfedries.com/Windows7Unleashed/.

1. Select Start, type **regedit**, and press Enter. The User Account Control dialog box appears.
2. Enter your UAC credentials to open the Registry Editor.
3. Navigate to the following key:

   HKEY_CLASSES_ROOT\VBSFile\Shell
4. Select Edit, New, Key, type **RunAs**, and press Enter.
5. With the new runas key selected, select Edit, New, Key, type **Command**, and press Enter.
6. In the Command key, double-click the (Default) to open the Edit String dialog box.
7. Type the following value and click OK (modify the Windows location if yours is installed somewhere other than C:\Windows):

   "C:\Windows\System32\WScript.exe" "%1" %*
8. Select Edit, New, String Value. The Registry Editor creates a new value in the Layers key.
9. Type **IsolatedCommand** and press Enter.
10. Double-click the entry you just created. The Edit String dialog box appears.

11. Type the following value and click OK (again, modify the Windows location if yours is installed somewhere other than C:\Windows):

```
"C:\Windows\System32\WScript.exe" "%1" %*
```

Figure 30.2 shows the modified Registry. With these tweaks in place, right-click a VBScript file and you see the Run as Administrator command, as shown in Figure 30.3.

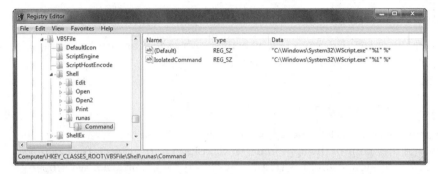

FIGURE 30.2   The dialog box that's displayed when you run the script.

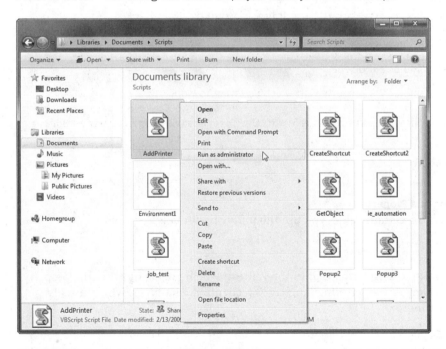

FIGURE 30.3   Tweaking the Windows 7 Registry to add the Run as Administrator command to the shortcut menu of any VBScript file.

Programming Objects

Although this chapter isn't a programming primer per se, I'd like to take some time now to run through a few quick notes about programming objects. This will serve you well throughout the rest of the chapter as I take you on a tour of the Windows Script Host object model.

The dictionary definition of an object is "anything perceptible by one or more of the senses, especially something that can be seen and felt." In scripting, an *object* is an application element that exposes an interface to the programmer, who can then perform the programming equivalent of seeing and feeling:

▶ You can make changes to the object's *properties* (this is the seeing part).

▶ You can make the object perform a task by activating a *method* associated with the object (this is the feeling part).

Working with Object Properties

Every programmable object has a defining set of characteristics. These characteristics are the object's *properties*, and they control the appearance and position of the object. For example, the WScript object (the top-level Windows Script Host object) has an Interactive property that determines whether the script runs in interactive mode or batch mode.

When you refer to a property, you use the following syntax:

`Object.Property`

`Object`   The name of the object

`Property`   The name of the property with which you want to work

For example, the following expression refers to the Interactive property of the WScript object:

`WScript.Interactive`

Setting the Value of a Property

To set a property to a certain value, you use the following syntax:

`Object.Property = value`

Here, `value` is an expression that specifies the value to which you want to set the property. As such, it can be any of the scripting language's recognized data types, which usually include the following:

▶ A numeric value

▶ A string value, enclosed in double quotation marks (such as `"My Script Application"`)

▶ A logical value (in VBScript: `True` or `False`; in JavaScript: `true` or `false`)

For example, the following VBScript statement tells the Windows Script Host to run the script using interactive mode:

`WScript.Interactive = True`

Returning the Value of a Property

Sometimes, you need to know the current setting of a property before changing the property or performing some other action. You can find out the current value of a property by using the following syntax:

```
variable = Object.Property
```

Here, *variable* is a variable name or another property. For example, the following statement stores the current script mode (batch or interactive) in a variable named currentMode:

```
currentMode = WScript.Interactive
```

Working with Object Methods

An object's properties describe what the object is, whereas its *methods* describe what the object *does*. For example, the WScript object has a Quit method that enables you to stop the execution of a script.

How you refer to a method depends on whether the method requires any arguments. If it doesn't, the syntax is similar to that of properties:

```
Object.Method
```

Object   The name of the object

Method   The name of the method you want to run

For example, the following statement shuts down a script:

```
WScript.Quit
```

If the method requires arguments, you use the following syntax:

```
Object.Method(Argument1, Argument2, ...)
```

> **NOTE**
>
> In VBScript, the parentheses around the argument list are necessary only if you'll be storing the result of the method in a variable or object property. In JavaScript, the parentheses are always required.

For example, the WshShell object has a RegWrite method that you use to write a key or value to the Registry. (I discuss this object and method in detail later in this chapter; see "Working with Registry Entries.") Here's the syntax:

```
WshShell.RegWrite strName, anyValue[, strType]
```

strName   The name of the Registry key or value

anyValue   The value to write, if *strName* is a Registry value

strType   The data type of the value

30

Argument Naming Conventions

When presenting method arguments in this chapter, I'll follow Microsoft's naming conventions, including the use of the following prefixes for the argument names:

Prefix	Data Type
any	Any type
b	Boolean
int	Integer
nat	Natural numbers
obj	Object
str	String

For many object methods, not all the arguments are required. In the RegWrite method, for example, the *strName* and *anyValue* arguments are required, but the *strType* argument is not. Throughout this chapter, I differentiate between required and optional arguments by surrounding the optional arguments with square brackets—for example [, *strType*].

For example, the following statement creates a new value named Test and sets it equal to Foo:

```
WshShell.RegWrite "HKCU\Software\Microsoft\Windows Script Host\Test", "Foo", "REG_SZ"
```

Assigning an Object to a Variable

If you're using JavaScript, you assign an object to a variable using a standard variable assignment:

```
var variableName = ObjectName
```

variableName   The name of the variable

ObjectName   The object you want to assign to the variable

In VBScript, you assign an object to a variable by using the Set statement. Set has the following syntax:

```
Set variableName = ObjectName
```

variableName   The name of the variable

ObjectName   The object you want to assign to the variable

You'll see later on that you must often use automation to access external objects. For example, if you want to work with files and folders in your script, you must access the scripting engine object named `FileSystemObject`. To get this access, you use the `CreateObject` method and store the resulting object in a variable, like so:

```
Set fs = CreateObject("Scripting.FileSystemObject")
```

Working with Object Collections

A *collection* is a set of similar objects. For example, `WScript.Arguments` is the set of all the arguments specified on the script's command line. Collections are objects, too, so they have their own properties and methods, and you can use these properties and methods to manipulate one or more objects in the collection.

The members of a collection are *elements*. You can refer to individual elements by using an *index*. For example, the following statement refers to the first command-line argument (collection indexes always begin at 0):

```
WScript.Arguments(0)
```

If you don't specify an element, the Windows Script Host assumes that you want to work with the entire collection.

VBScript: Using For Each...Next Loops for Collections

As you might know, VBScript provides the `For...Next` loop that enables you to cycle through a chunk of code a specified number of times. For example, the following code loops 10 times:

```
For counter = 1 To 10
    Code entered here is repeated 10 times
Next counter
```

A useful variation on this theme is the `For Each...Next` loop, which operates on a collection of objects. You don't need a loop counter because VBScript loops through the individual elements in the collection and performs on each element whatever operations are inside the loop. Here's the structure of the basic `For Each...Next` loop:

```
For Each element In collection
    [statements]
Next
```

`element`	A variable used to hold the name of each element in the collection
`collection`	The name of the collection
`statements`	The statements to execute for each element in the collection

The following code loops through all the arguments specified on the script's command line and displays each one:

```
For Each arg In WScript.Arguments
    WScript.Echo arg
Next
```

JavaScript: Using Enumerators and for Loops for Collections

To iterate through a collection in JavaScript, you must do two things: create a new Enumerator object and use a for loop to cycle through the enumerated collection.

To create a new Enumerator object, use the new keyword to set up an object variable (where *collection* is the name of the collection you want to work with):

```
var enum = new Enumerator(collection)
```

Then set up a special for loop:

```
for (; !enumerator.atEnd(); enumerator.moveNext())
{
    [statements];
}
```

enumerator   The Enumerator object you created

statements   The statements to execute for each element in the collection

The Enumerator object's moveNext method runs through the elements in the collection, whereas the atEnd method shuts down the loop after the last item has been processed. The following code loops through all the arguments specified on the script's command line and displays each one:

```
var args = new Enumerator(WScript.Arguments);
for (; !args.atEnd(); args.moveNext())
{
   WScript.Echo(args.item());
}
```

Programming the WScript Object

The WScript object represents the Windows Script Host applications (WScript.exe and CScript.exe). You use this object to get and set certain properties of the scripting host, as well as to access two other objects: WshArguments (the WScript object's Arguments property) and WshScriptEngine (accessed via the WScript object's GetScriptEngine method). WScript also contains the powerful CreateObject and GetObject methods, which enable you to work with automation-enabled applications.

Displaying Text to the User

The WScript object method that you'll use most often is the Echo method, which displays text to the user. Here's the syntax:

```
WScript.Echo [Argument1, Argument2,...]
```

Here, *Argument1, Argument2,* and so on, are any number of text or numeric values that represent the information you want to display to the user. In the Windows-based host (WScript.exe), the information displays in a dialog box. In the command-line host (CScript.exe), the information displays at the Command Prompt (much like the command-line ECHO utility).

Shutting Down a Script

You use the WScript object's Quit method to shut down the script. You can also use Quit to have your script return an error code by using the following syntax:

```
WScript.Quit [intErrorCode]
```

intErrorCode   An integer value that represents the error code you want to return

You could then call the script from a batch file and use the ERRORLEVEL environment variable to deal with the return code in some way. (See Chapter 13, "Controlling Windows 7 from the Command Line," for more information on ERRORLEVEL.)

Scripting and Automation

Applications such as Internet Explorer and Word come with (or *expose*, in the jargon) a set of objects that define various aspects of the program. For example, Internet Explorer has an Application object that represents the program as a whole. Similarly, Word has a Document object that represents a Word document. By using the properties and methods that come with these objects, it's possible to programmatically query and manipulate the applications. With Internet Explorer, for example, you can use the Application object's Navigate method to send the browser to a specified web page. With Word, you can read a Document object's Saved property to see whether the document has unsaved changes.

This is powerful stuff, but how do you get at the objects that these applications expose? You do that by using a technology called *automation*. Applications that support automation implement object libraries that expose the application's native objects to automation-aware programming languages. Such applications are *automation servers*, and the applications that manipulate the server's objects are *automation controllers*. The Windows Script Host is an automation controller that enables you to write script code to control any server's objects.

This means that you can use an application's exposed objects more or less as you use the Windows Script Host objects. With just a minimum of preparation, your script code can refer to and work with the Internet Explorer Application object, or the Microsoft Word

30

Document object, or any of the hundreds of other objects exposed by the applications on your system. (Note, however, that not all applications expose objects. Windows Live Mail and most of the built-in Windows 7 programs—such as WordPad and Paint—do not expose objects.)

Creating an Automation Object with the `CreateObject` Method

The `WScript` object's `CreateObject` method creates an automation object (specifically, what programmers call an *instance* of the object). Here's the syntax:

```
WScript.CreateObject(strProgID)
```

strProgID   A string that specifies the automation server application and the type of object to create. This string is a *programmatic identifier*, which is a label that uniquely specifies an application and one of its objects. The programmatic identifier always takes the following form:

AppName.ObjectType

Here, *AppName* is the automation name of the application and *ObjectType* is the object class type (as defined in the Registry's HKEY_CLASSES_ROOT key). For example, here's the programmatic ID for Word:

Word.Application

Note that you normally use `CreateObject` within a `Set` statement, and that the function serves to create a new instance of the specified automation object. For example, you could use the following statement to create a new instance of Word's `Application` object:

```
Set objWord = CreateObject("Word.Application")
```

You need to do nothing else to use the automation object. With your variable declared and an instance of the object created, you can use that object's properties and methods directly. Listing 30.1 shows a VBScript example (you must have Word installed for this to work).

LISTING 30.1   VBScript Example That Creates and Manipulates a Word `Application` Object

```
' Create the Word Application object
'
Set objWord = WScript.CreateObject("Word.Application")
'
' Create a new document
'
objWord.Documents.Add
'
' Add some text
'
objWord.ActiveDocument.Paragraphs(1).Range.InsertBefore "automation test."
```

LISTING 30.1   Continued

```
'
' Save the document
'
objWord.ActiveDocument.Save
'
' We're done, so quit Word
'
objWord.Quit
```

This script creates and saves a new Word document by working with Word's Application object via automation. The script begins by using the CreateObject method to create a new Word Application object, and the object is stored in the objWord variable. From there, you can wield the objWord variable just as though it were the Word Application object.

For example, the objWord.Documents.Add statement uses the Documents collection's Add method to create a new Word document, and the InsertBefore method adds some text to the document. The Save method then displays the Save As dialog box so that you can save the new file. With the Word-related chores complete, the Application object's Quit method runs to shut down Word. For comparison, Listing 30.2 shows a JavaScript procedure that performs the same tasks.

LISTING 30.2   JavaScript Example That Creates and Manipulates a Word Application Object

```
// Create the Word Application object
//
var objWord = WScript.CreateObject("Word.Application");
//
// Create a new document
//
objWord.Documents.Add();
//
// Add some text
//
objWord.ActiveDocument.Paragraphs(1).Range.InsertBefore("automation test.");
//
// Save the document
//
objWord.ActiveDocument.Save();
//
// We're done, so quit Word
//
objWord.Quit();
```

Making the Automation Server Visible

The `CreateObject` method loads the object, but doesn't display the automation server unless user interaction is required. For example, you see Word's Save As dialog box when you run the `Save` method on a new document (as in Listings 30.1 and 30.2). Not seeing the automation server is the desired behavior in most automation situations. However, if you *do* want to see what the automation server is up to, set the `Application` object's `Visible` property to `True`, as in this example:

```
objWord.Visible = True
```

Working with an Existing Object Using the GetObject Method

If you know that the object you want to work with already exists or is already open, the `CreateObject` method isn't the best choice. In the example in the previous section, if Word is already running, the code will start a second copy of Word, which is a waste of resources. For these situations, it's better to work directly with the existing object. To do that, use the `GetObject` method:

```
WScript.GetObject(strPathname [, strProgID])
```

strPathname	The pathname (drive, folder, and filename) of the file you want to work with (or the file that contains the object you want to work with). If you omit this argument, you have to specify the *strProgID* argument.
strProgID	The programmatic identifier that specifies the automation server application and the type of object to work with (that is, the *AppName.ObjectType* class syntax).

Listing 30.3 shows a VBScript procedure that puts the `GetObject` method to work.

LISTING 30.3   VBScript Example That Uses the `GetObject` Method to Work with an Existing Instance of a Word `Document` Object

```
' Get the Word Document object
'
Set objDoc = WScript.GetObject("C:\GetObject.doc", "Word.Document")
'
' Get the word count
'
WScript.Echo objDoc.Name & " has " & objDoc.Words.Count & " words."
'
' We're done, so quit Word
'
objDoc.Application.Quit
```

The `GetObject` method assigns the Word `Document` object named `GetObject.doc` to the `objDoc` variable. After you've set up this reference, you can use the object's properties and methods directly. For example, the Echo method uses objDoc.Name to return the filename and objDoc.Words.Count to determine the number of words in the document.

Note that although you're working with a Document object, you still have access to Word's Application object. That's because most objects have an Application property that refers to the Application object. In the script in Listing 30.3, for example, the following statement uses the Application property to quit Word:

```
objDoc.Application.Quit
```

Exposing VBScript and JavaScript Objects

One of the most powerful uses for scripted automation is accessing the object models exposed by the VBScript and JavaScript engines. These models expose a number of objects, including the local file system. This enables you to create scripts that work with files, folders, and disk drives, read and write text files, and more. You use the following syntax to refer to these objects:

```
Scripting.ObjectType
```

Scripting is the automation name of the scripting engine, and *ObjectType* is the class type of the object.

> **NOTE**
>
> This section just gives you a brief explanation of the objects associated with the VBScript and JavaScript engines. For the complete list of object properties and methods, refer to http://msdn.microsoft.com/en-us/library/ms950396.aspx.

Programming the FileSystemObject

FileSystemObject is the top-level file system object. For all your file system scripts, you begin by creating a new instance of FileSystemObject:

In VBScript

```
Set fs = WScript.CreateObject("Scripting.FileSystemObject")
```

In JavaScript

```
var fs = WScript.CreateObject("Scripting.FileSystemObject");
```

Here's a summary of the file system objects you can access via automation and the top-level FileSystemObject:

▶ **Drive**—This object enables you to access the properties of a specified disk drive or UNC network path. To reference a Drive object, use either the Drives collection (discussed next) or the FileSystemObject object's GetDrive method. For example, the following VBScript statement references the C: drive:

```
Set objFS = WScript.CreateObject("Scripting.FileSystemObject")
Set objDrive = objFS.GetDrive("C:")
```

▶ **Drives**—This object is the collection of all available drives. To reference this collection, use the `FileSystemObject` object's `Drives` property:

```
Set objFS = WScript.CreateObject("Scripting.FileSystemObject")
Set objDrives = objFS.Drives
```

▶ **Folder**—This object enables you to access the properties of a specified folder. To reference a `Folder` object, use either the `Folders` collection (discussed next) or the `FileSystemObject` object's `GetFolder` method:

```
Set objFS = WScript.CreateObject("Scripting.FileSystemObject")
Set objFolder = objFS.GetFolder("C:\My Documents")
```

▶ **Folders**—This object is the collection of subfolders within a specified folder. To reference this collection, use the `Folder` object's `Subfolders` property:

```
Set objFS = WScript.CreateObject("Scripting.FileSystemObject")
Set objFolder = objFS.GetFolder("C:\Windows")
Set objSubfolders = objFolder.Subfolders
```

▶ **File**—This object enables you to access the properties of a specified file. To reference a `File` object, use either the `Files` collection (discussed next) or the `FileSystemObject` object's `GetFile` method:

```
Set objFS = WScript.CreateObject("Scripting.FileSystemObject")
Set objFile = objFS.GetFile("c:\autoexec.bat")
```

▶ **Files**—This object is the collection of files within a specified folder. To reference this collection, use the `Folder` object's `Files` property:

```
Set objFS = WScript.CreateObject("Scripting.FileSystemObject")
Set objFolder = objFS.GetFolder("C:\Windows")
Set objFiles = objFolder.Files
```

▶ **TextStream**—This object enables you to use sequential access to work with a text file. To open a text file, use the `FileSystemObject` object's `OpenTextFile` method:

```
Set objFS = WScript.CreateObject("Scripting.FileSystemObject")
Set objTS= objFS.OpenTextFile("C:\Boot.ini")
```

Alternatively, you can create a new text file by using the `FileSystemObject` object's `CreateTextFile` method:

```
Set objFS = WScript.CreateObject("Scripting.FileSystemObject")
Set objTS= objFS.CreateTextFile("C:\Boot.ini")
```

Either way, you end up with a `TextStream` object, which has various methods for reading data from the file and writing data to the file. For example, the following script reads and displays the text from `C:\Boot.ini`:

```
Set objFS = WScript.CreateObject("Scripting.FileSystemObject")
Set objTS = objFS.OpenTextFile("C:\Boot.ini")
strContents = objTS.ReadAll
WScript.Echo strContents
objTS.Close
```

Programming the `WshShell` Object

`WshShell` is a generic name for a powerful object that enables you to query and interact with various aspects of the Windows shell. You can display information to the user, run applications, create shortcuts, work with the Registry, and control Windows environment variables. The next few sections discuss each of those useful tasks.

Referencing the `WshShell` Object

`WshShell` refers to the `Shell` object exposed via the automation interface of WScript. Therefore, you must use `CreateObject` to return this object:

```
Set objWshShell = WScript.CreateObject("WScript.Shell")
```

From here, you can use the `objWshShell` variable to access the object's properties and methods.

Displaying Information to the User

You saw earlier that the `WScript` object's `Echo` method is useful for displaying simple text messages to the user. You can gain more control over the displayed message by using the `WshShell` object's `Popup` method. This method is similar to the `MsgBox` function used in Visual Basic and VBA in that it enables you to control both the dialog box title and the buttons displayed, and to determine which of those buttons the user pressed. Here's the syntax:

WshShell.Popup(*strText* [, *nSecondsToWait*] [, *strTitle*] [, *intType*])

WshShell	The WshShell object.
strText	The message you want to display in the dialog box. You can enter a string up to 1,024 characters long.
nSecondsToWait	The maximum number of seconds the dialog box will be displayed.
strTitle	The text that appears in the dialog box title bar. If you omit this value, Windows Script Host appears in the title bar.

30

intType   A number or constant that specifies, among other things, the command
                   buttons that appear in the dialog box (see the next section). The default value
                   is 0.

For example, the following statements display the dialog box shown in Figure 30.4:

```
Set objWshShell = WScript.CreateObject("WScript.Shell")
objWshShell.Popup "Couldn't find Memo.doc!", , "Warning"
```

FIGURE 30.4   A simple message dialog box produced by the Popup method.

TIP

For long messages, VBScript wraps the text inside the dialog box. If you prefer to
create your own line breaks, use VBScript's Chr function and the carriage return character (ASCII 13) between each line:

```
WshShell.Popup "First line" & Chr(13) & "Second line"
```

For JavaScript, use \n instead:

```
WshShell.Popup("First line" + "\n" + "Second line");
```

Setting the Style of the Message

The default Popup dialog box displays only an OK button. You can include other buttons
and icons in the dialog box by using different values for the *intType* parameter. Table 30.1
lists the available options.

TABLE 30.1   Popup Method's *intType Parameter Options*

VBScript Constant	Value	Description
Buttons		
vbOKOnly	0	Displays only an OK button. This is the default.
vbOKCancel	1	Displays the OK and Cancel buttons.
vbAbortRetryIgnore	2	Displays the Abort, Retry, and Ignore buttons.
vbYesNoCancel	3	Displays the Yes, No, and Cancel buttons.
vbYesNo	4	Displays the Yes and No buttons.

TABLE 30.1   Continued

VBScript Constant	Value	Description
vbRetryCancel	5	Displays the Retry and Cancel buttons.
Icons		
vbCritical	16	Displays the Critical Message icon.
vbQuestion	32	Displays the Warning Query icon.
vbExclamation	48	Displays the Warning Message icon.
vbInformation	64	Displays the Information Message icon.
Default Buttons		
vbDefaultButton1	0	The first button is the default (that is, the button selected when the user presses Enter).
vbDefaultButton2	256	The second button is the default.
vbDefaultButton3	512	The third button is the default.

You derive the *intType* argument in one of two ways:

▶ By adding the values for each option

▶ By using the VBScript constants separated by plus signs (+)

The script in Listing 30.4 shows an example and Figure 30.5 shows the resulting dialog box.

LISTING 30.4   VBScript Example That Uses the **Popup** Method to Display the Dialog Box Shown in Figure 30.3

```
' First, set up the message
'
strText = "Are you sure you want to copy" & Chr(13)
strText = strText & "the selected files to drive G?"
strTitle = "Copy Files"
intType = vbYesNoCancel + vbQuestion + vbDefaultButton2
'
' Now display it
'
Set objWshShell = WScript.CreateObject("WScript.Shell")
intResult = objWshShell.Popup(strText, ,strTitle, intType)
```

Here, three variables—strText, strTitle, and intType—store the values for the Popup method's *strText, strTitle,* and *intType* arguments, respectively. In particular, the following statement derives the *intType* argument:

```
intType = vbYesNoCancel + vbQuestion + vbDefaultButton2
```

30

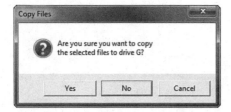

FIGURE 30.5   Right-clicking a VBScript file reveals the new Run as Administrator command.

You also could derive the *intType* argument by adding up the values that these constants represent *(3, 32, and 256, respectively)*, but the script becomes less readable that way.

Getting Return Values from the Message Dialog Box

A dialog box that displays only an OK button is straightforward. The user either clicks OK or presses Enter to remove the dialog from the screen. The multibutton styles are a little different, however; the user has a choice of buttons to select, and your script should have a way to find out which button the user chose, which enables it to decide what to do next, based on the user's selection. You do this by storing the Popup method's return value in a variable. Table 30.2 lists the seven possible return values.

TABLE 30.2   Popup Method's Return Values

VBScript Constant	Value	Button Selected
vbOK	1	OK
vbCancel	2	Cancel
vbAbort	3	Abort
vbRetry	4	Retry
vbIgnore	5	Ignore
vbYes	6	Yes
vbNo	7	No

To process the return value, you can use an If...Then...Else or Select Case structure to test for the appropriate values. For example, the script shown earlier used a variable called intResult to store the return value of the Popup method. Listing 30.5 shows a revised version of the script that uses a VBScript Select Case statement to test for the three possible return values.

LISTING 30.5   Script That Uses a Select Case Statement to Process the Popup Method's Return Value

```
' First, set up the message
'
strText = "Are you sure you want to copy" & Chr(13)
strText = strText & "the selected files to drive A?"
strTitle = "Copy Files"
intType = vbYesNoCancel + vbQuestion + vbDefaultButton2
'
' Now display it
'
Set objWshShell = WScript.CreateObject("WScript.Shell")
intResult = objWshShell.Popup(strText, ,strTitle, intType)
'
' Process the result
'
Select Case intResult
    Case vbYes
        WScript.Echo "You clicked ""Yes""!"
    Case vbNo
        WScript.Echo "You clicked ""No""!"
    Case vbCancel
        WScript.Echo "You clicked ""Cancel""!"
End Select
```

Running Applications

When you need your script to launch another application, use the Run method:

WshShell.Run *strCommand* [, *intWindowStyle*] [, *bWaitOnReturn*]

WshShell   The WshShell object.

strCommand   The name of the file that starts the application. Unless the file is in the
                 Windows folder, you should include the drive and folder to make sure that the
                 script can find the file.

intWindowStyle A constant or number that specifies how the application window will appear:

intWindowStyle	Window Appearance
0	Hidden
1	Normal size with focus
2	Minimized with focus (this is the default)
3	Maximized with focus
4	Normal without focus
6	Minimized without focus

bWaitOnReturn A logical value that determines whether the application runs asynchronously. If this value is True, the script halts execution until the user exits the launched application. If this value is False, the script continues running after it has launched the application.

Here's an example:

```
Set objWshShell = WScript.CreateObject("WScript.Shell")
objWshShell.Run "Control.exe Inetcpl.cpl", 1, True
```

This Run method launches Control Panel's Internet Properties dialog box.

▶ To learn more about launching individual Control Panel icons using Control.exe, **see** "Understanding Control Panel Files," **p. 172**.

Working with Shortcuts

The Windows Script Host enables your scripts to create and modify shortcut files. When writing scripts for other users, you might want to take advantage of this capability to display shortcuts for new network shares, Internet sites, instruction files, and so on.

Creating a Shortcut

To create a shortcut, use the CreateShortcut method:

WshShell.CreateShortcut(*strPathname*)

WshShell The WshShell object.

strPathname The full path and filename of the shortcut file you want to create. Use the .lnk extension for a file system (program, document, folder, and so on) shortcut; use the .url extension for an Internet shortcut.

The following example creates and saves a shortcut on a user's desktop:

```
Set WshShell = objWScript.CreateObject("WScript.Shell")
Set objShortcut = objWshShell.CreateShortcut("C:\Users\Paul\Desktop\test.lnk")
objShortcut.Save
```

Programming the WshShortcut Object

The `CreateShortcut` method returns a `WshShortcut` object. You can use this object to manipulate various properties and methods associated with shortcut files.

This object contains the following properties:

▶ **Arguments**—Returns or sets a string that specifies the arguments used when launching the shortcut. For example, suppose that the shortcut's target is the following:

```
C:\Windows\Notepad.exe C:\Users\Paul\Documents\todolist.txt
```

In other words, this shortcut launches Notepad and loads the `Boot.ini` file. In this case, the `Arguments` property would return the following string:

```
C:\Users\Paul\Documents\todolist.txt
```

▶ **Description**—Returns or sets a string description of the shortcut.

▶ **FullName**—Returns the full path and filename of the shortcut's target. This will be the same as the *strPathname value used in the CreateShortcut* method.

▶ **Hotkey**—Returns or sets the hotkey associated with the shortcut. To set this value, use the following syntax:

```
WshShortcut.Hotkey = strHotKey
```

WshShortcut   The WshShortcut object.

strHotKey   A string value of the form *Modifier+Keyname*, where *Modifier* is any combination of Alt, Ctrl, and Shift, and *Keyname* is one of A through Z or 0 through 12.

For example, the following statement sets the hotkey to Ctrl+Alt+7:

```
objShortcut.Hotkey = "Ctrl+Alt+7"
```

▶ **IconLocation**—Returns or sets the icon used to display the shortcut. To set this value, use the following syntax:

```
WshShortcut.IconLocation = strIconLocation
```

WshShortcut   The WshShortcut object.

strIconLocation A string value of the form *Path,Index*, where *Path* is the full pathname of the icon file and *Index* is the position of the icon within the file (where the first icon is 0).

Here's an example:

```
objShortcut.IconLocation = "C:\Windows\System32\Shell32.dll,21"
```

30

▶ **TargetPath**—Returns or sets the path of the shortcut's target.

▶ **WindowStyle**—Returns or sets the window style used by the shortcut's target. Use the same values outlined earlier for the Run method's *intWindowStyle* argument.

▶ **WorkingDirectory**—Returns or sets the path of the shortcut's working directory.

NOTE

If you're working with Internet shortcuts, bear in mind that they support only two properties: FullName and TargetPath (the URL target).

The WshShortcut object also supports two methods:

▶ **Save**—Saves the shortcut file to disk.

▶ **Resolve**—Uses the shortcut's TargetPath property to look up the target file. Here's the syntax:

```
WshShortcut.Resolve = intFlag
```

WshShortcut   The WshShortcut object.

intFlag   Determines what happens of the target file is not found:

intFlag	**What Happens**
1	Nothing
2	Windows continues to search subfolders for the target file
4	Updates the TargetPath property if the target file is found in a new location

Listing 30.6 shows a complete example of a script that creates a shortcut.

LISTING 30.6   Script That Creates a Shortcut File
_____

```
Set objWshShell = WScript.CreateObject("WScript.Shell")
'
' Create the shortcut
'
Set objShortcut = objWshShell.CreateShortcut(strUserProfile & _
                "\Desktop\Edit To Do List.lnk")
'
' Set some shortcut properties and then save it
'
With objShortcut
    .TargetPath = "C:\Windows\Notepad.exe"
```

LISTING 30.6   Continued

```
    .Arguments = "C:\Users\Paul\Documents\todolist.txt"
    .WorkingDirectory = "C:\Users\Paul\Desktop"
    .Description = "Opens ToDoList.txt in Notepad"
    .Hotkey = "Ctrl+Alt+7"
    .IconLocation = "C:\Windows\System32\Shell32.dll,21"
    .WindowStyle = 3
    .Save
End With
```

Working with Registry Entries

You've seen throughout this book that the Registry is one the most crucial data structures in Windows. However, the Registry isn't a tool that only Windows yields. Most 32-bit applications make use of the Registry as a place to store setup options, customization values the user selected, and much more. Interestingly, your scripts can get in on the act, too. Not only can your scripts read the current value of any Registry setting, but they can also use the Registry as a storage area. This enables you to keep track of user settings, recently used files, and any other configuration data that you'd like to save between sessions. This section shows you how to use the WshShell object to manipulate the Registry from within your scripts.

Reading Settings from the Registry

To read any value from the Registry, use the WshShell object's RegRead method:

WshShell.RegRead(*strName*)

WshShell   The WshShell object.

strName   The name of the Registry value or key that you want to read. If *strName* ends with a backslash (\), RegRead returns the default value for the key; otherwise, RegRead returns the data stored in the value. Note, too, that *strName* must begin with one of the following root key names:

Short Name	Long Name
HKCR	HKEY_CLASSES_ROOT
HKCU	HKEY_CURRENT_USER
HKLM	HKEY_LOCAL_MACHINE
N/A	HKEY_USERS
N/A	HKEY_CURRENT_CONFIG

The script in Listing 30.7 displays the name of the registered owner of this copy of Windows 7.

LISTING 30.7   Script That Reads the `RegisteredOwner` Setting from the Registry

```
Set objWshShell = WScript.CreateObject("WScript.Shell")
strSetting = "HKLM\SOFTWARE\Microsoft\Windows NT\CurrentVersion\RegisteredOwner"
strRegisteredUser = objWshShell.RegRead(strSetting)
WScript.Echo strRegisteredUser
```

Storing Settings in the Registry

To store a setting in the Registry, use the `WshShell` object's `RegWrite` method:

WshShell.RegWrite *strName*, *anyValue* [, *strType*]

WshShell	The WshShell object.
strName	The name of the Registry value or key that you want to set. If *strName* ends with a backslash (\), RegWrite sets the default value for the key; otherwise, RegWrite sets the data for the value. *strName* must begin with one of the root key names detailed in the RegRead method.
anyValue	The value to be stored.
strType	The data type of the value, which must be one of the following: REG_SZ (the default), REG_EXPAND_SZ, REG_DWORD, or REG_BINARY.

The following statements create a new key named `ScriptSettings` in the `HKEY_CURRENT_USER` root:

```
Set objWshShell = WScript.CreateObject("WScript.Shell")
objWshShell.RegWrite "HKCU\ScriptSettings\", ""
```

The following statements create a new value named `NumberOfReboots` in the `HKEY_CURRENT_USER\ScriptSettings` key, and set this value to 1:

```
Set objWshShell = WScript.CreateObject("WScript.Shell")
objWshShell.RegWrite "HKCU\ScriptSettings\NumberOfReboots", 1, "REG_DWORD"
```

Deleting Settings from the Registry

If you no longer need to track a particular key or value setting, use the `RegDelete` method to remove the setting from the Registry:

WshShell.RegDelete(*strName*)

WshShell   The WshShell object.

strName   The name of the Registry value or key that you want to delete. If *strName* ends with a backslash (\), RegDelete deletes the key; otherwise, RegDelete deletes the value. *strName* must begin with one of the root key names detailed in the RegRead method.

To delete the NumberOfReboots value used in the previous example, you would use the following statements:

```
Set objWshShell = WScript.CreateObject("WScript.Shell")
objWshShell.RegDelete "HKCU\ScriptSettings\NumberOfReboots"
```

Working with Environment Variables

Windows 7 keeps track of a number of *environment variables* that hold data such as the location of the Windows folder, the location of the temporary files folder, the command path, the primary drive, and much more. Why would you need such data? One example would be for accessing files or folders within the main Windows folder. Rather than guessing that this folder is C:\Windows, it is much easier to just query the %SystemRoot% environment variable. Similarly, if you have a script that accesses files in a user's My Documents folder, hard-coding the username in the file path is inconvenient because it means creating custom scripts for every possible user. Instead, it is much easier to create just a single script that references the %UserProfile% environment variable. This section shows you how to read environment variable data within your scripts.

The defined environment variables are stored in the Environment collection, which is a property of the WshShell object. Windows 7 environment variables are stored in the "Process" environment, so you reference this collection as follows:

WshShell.Environment("Process")

Listing 30.8 shows a script that runs through this collection, adds each variable to a string, and then displays the string.

LISTING 30.8   Script That Displays the System's Environment Variables

```
Set objWshShell = WScript.CreateObject("WScript.Shell")
'
' Run through the environment variables
'
strVariables = ""
For Each objEnvVar In objWshShell.Environment("Process")
    strVariables = strVariables & objEnvVar & Chr(13)
Next
WScript.Echo strVariables
```

30

Figure 30.6 shows the dialog box that appears. (Your mileage may vary.)

FIGURE 30.6   A complete inventory of a system's environment variables.

If you want to use the value of a particular environment variable, use the following syntax:

WshShell.Environment("Process")("*strName*")

WshShell	The WshShell object
strName	The name of the environment variable

Listing 30.9 shows a revised version of the script from Listing 30.6 to create a shortcut. In this version, the Environment collection is used to return the value of the %UserProfile% variable, which is used to contrast the path to the current user's Desktop folder.

LISTING 30.9   Script That Creates a Shortcut File Using Environment Variables

```
Set objWshShell = WScript.CreateObject("WScript.Shell")
'
' Get the %UserProfile% and %SystemRoot% environment variables
'
strUserProfile = objWshShell.Environment("Process")("UserProfile")
strSystemRoot = objWshShell.Environment("Process")("SystemRoot")
'
' Create the shortcut
'
Set objShortcut = objWshShell.CreateShortcut(strUserProfile & _
```

LISTING 30.9   Continued

```
                    "\Desktop\Edit To Do List.lnk")
'
' Set some shortcut properties and then save it
'
With objShortcut
    .TargetPath = strSystemRoot & "\Notepad.exe"
    .Arguments = strUserProfile & "\Documents\todolist.txt"
    .WorkingDirectory = strUserProfile & "\Desktop"
    .Description = "Opens ToDoList.txt in Notepad"
    .Hotkey = "Ctrl+Alt+7"
    .IconLocation = strSystemRoot & "\System32\Shell32.dll,21"
    .WindowStyle = 3
    .Save
End With
```

Programming the WshNetwork Object

WshNetwork is a generic name for an object that enables you to work with various aspects of the Windows network environment. You can determine the computer name and user-name, you can enumerate the mapped network drives, you can map new network drives, and more. The next couple of sections show you how to work with this object.

Referencing the WshNetwork Object

WshNetwork refers to the Network object exposed via the automation interface of WScript. This means you use CreateObject to return this object, as shown here:

```
Set objWshNetwork = WScript.CreateObject("WScript.Network")
```

From here, you use the WshNetwork variable to access the object's properties and methods.

WshNetwork Object Properties

The WshNetwork object supports three properties:

ComputerName   Returns the network name of the computer

UserDomain   Returns the network domain name of the current user

UserName   Returns the username of the current user

Mapping Network Printers

The WshNetwork object supports several methods for working with remote printers. For example, to map a network printer to a local printer resource, use the WshNetwork object's AddWindowsPrinterConnection method:

WshNetwork.AddPrinterConnection *strPrinterPath*

30

WshNetwork   The WshNetwork object

strPrinterPath   The UNC path to the network printer

Here's an example:

```
Set objWshNetwork = WScript.CreateObject("WScript.Network")
objWshNetwork.AddWindowsPrinterConnection "\\ZEUS\printer"
```

To remove a remote printer mapping, use the WshNetwork object's
RemovePrinterConnection method:

WshNetwork.RemovePrinterConnection *strPrinterPath* [, *bForce*] [, *bUpdateProfile*]

WshNetwork   The WshNetwork object

strPrinterPath   The UNC path to the network printer

bForce   If True, the resource is removed even if it is currently being used

bUpdateProfile   If True, the printer mapping is removed from the user's profile

Here's an example:

```
Set objWshNetwork = WScript.CreateObject("WScript.Network")
objWshNetwork.RemovePrinterConnection "\\ZEUS\inkjet"
```

Mapping Network Drives

The WshNetwork object supports several methods for mapping network drives. To map a
shared network folder to a local drive letter, use the WshNetwork object's MapNetworkDrive
method:

WshNetwork.MapNetworkDrive *strLocalName*, *strRemoteName*, [*bUpdateProfile*]
➥[, *strUser*] [, *strPassword*]

WshNetwork   The WshNetwork object.

strLocalName   The local drive letter to which the remote share will be mapped (for example,
                    F:).

strRemoteName   The UNC path for the remote share.

bUpdateProfile   If True, the drive mapping is stored in the user's profile.

strUser   Use this value to enter a username that might be required to map the
                    remote share (if you're logged on as a user who doesn't have the proper
                    permissions, for example).

strPassword   Use this value to enter a password that might be required to map the remote
                    drive.

Here's an example:

```
Set objWshNetwork = WScript.CreateObject("WScript.Network")
objWshNetwork.MapNetworkDrive "Z:", "\\ZEUS\SharedDocs"
```

To remove a mapped network drive, use the WshNetwork object's RemoveNetworkDrive:

WshNetwork.RemoveNetworkDrive *strName* [, *bForce*] [, *bUpdateProfile*]

WshNetwork	The WshNetwork object.
strName	The name of the mapped network drive you want removed. If you use a network path, all mappings to that path are removed. If you use a local drive letter, only that mapping is removed.
bForce	If True, the resource is removed even if it is currently being used.
bUpdateProfile	If True, the network drive mapping is removed from the user's profile.

Here's an example:

```
Set objWshNetwork = WScript.CreateObject("WScript.Network")
objWshNetwork.RemoveNetworkDrive "Z:"
```

Example: Scripting Internet Explorer

To give you a taste of the power and flexibility of scripting—particularly automation programming—I close this chapter by showing you how to program a specific automation server: Internet Explorer. You'll see that your scripts can control just about everything associated with Internet Explorer:

- ▶ The position and dimensions of the window
- ▶ Whether the menu bar, toolbar, and status bar are displayed
- ▶ The current URL
- ▶ Sending the browser backward and forward between navigated URLs

Displaying a Web Page

To get started, I show you how to use the InternetExplorer object to display a specified URL. You use the Navigate method to do this, and this method uses the following syntax:

InternetExplorer.Navigate *URL* [, *Flags*,] [*TargetFramename*] [, *PostData*] [,*Headers*]

InternetExplorer	A reference to the InternetExplorer object with which you're working.
URL	The address of the web page you want to display.
Flags	One of (or the sum of two or more of) the following integers that control various aspects of the navigation:

30

1	Opens the *URL* in a new window
2	Prevents the *URL* from being added to the history list
4	Prevents the browser from reading the page from the disk cache
8	Prevents the *URL* from being added to the disk cache

TargetFrameName	The name of the frame in which to display the *URL*.
PostData	Specifies additional POST information that HTTP requires to resolve the hyperlink. The most common uses for this argument are to send a web server the contents of a form, the coordinates of an image map, or a search parameter for an ASP file. If you leave this argument blank, this method issues a GET call.
Headers	Specifies header data for the HTTP header.

Here's an example:

```
Set objIE = CreateObject("InternetExplorer.Application")
objIE.Navigate "http://www.microsoft.com/"
```

Navigating Pages

Displaying a specified web page isn't the only thing the InternetExplorer object can do. It also has quite a few methods that enable you to navigate backward and forward through visited web pages, refresh the current page, stop the current download, and more. Here's a summary of these methods:

GoBack	Navigates backward to a previously visited page
GoForward	Navigates forward to a previously visited page
GoHome	Navigates to Internet Explorer's default Home page
GoSearch	Navigates to Internet Explorer's default Search page
Refresh	Refreshes the current page
Refresh2	Refreshes the current page using the following syntax: Refresh2(*Level*)

	Level	A constant that determines how the page is refreshed:

	0	Refreshes the page with a cached copy
	1	Refreshes the page with a cached copy only if the page has expired
	3	Performs a full refresh (doesn't use a cached copy)

Stop	Cancels the current download or shuts down dynamic page objects, such as background sounds and animations

Using the `InternetExplorer` Object's Properties

Here's a summary of many of the properties associated with the `InternetExplorer` object:

Busy	Returns `True` if the `InternetExplorer` object is in the process of downloading text or graphics. This property returns `False` when a download of the complete document has finished.
FullScreen	A Boolean value that toggles Internet Explorer between the normal window and a full-screen window in which the title bar, menu bar, toolbar, and status bar are hidden.
Height	Returns or sets the window height.
Left	Returns or sets the position of the left edge of the window.
LocationName	Returns the title of the current document.
LocationURL	Returns the URL of the current document.
MenuBar	A Boolean value that toggles the menu bar on and off.
StatusBar	A Boolean value that toggles the status bar on and off.
StatusText	Returns or sets the status bar text.
ToolBar	A Boolean value that toggles the toolbar on and off.
Top	Returns or sets the position of the top edge of the window.
Type	Returns the type of document currently loaded in the browser.
Visible	A Boolean value that toggles the object between hidden and visible.
Width	Returns or sets the window width.

Running Through a Sample Script

To put some of the properties and methods into practice, Listing 30.10 shows a sample script.

LISTING 30.10   Script That Puts the `InternetExplorer` Object Through Its Paces

```
Option Explicit
Dim objIE, objWshShell, strMessage, intResult

' Set up the automation objects
Set objIE = WScript.CreateObject("InternetExplorer.Application")
Set objWshShell = WScript.CreateObject("WScript.Shell")
```

LISTING 30.10   Continued

```
' Navigate to a page and customize the browser window
objIE.Navigate "http://www.wordspy.com/"
objIE.Toolbar = False
objIE.StatusBar = False
objIE.MenuBar = False

' Twiddle thumbs while the page loads
Do While objIE.Busy
Loop

' Get the page info
strMessage = "Current URL: " & objIE.LocationURL & vbCrLf & _
    "Current Title: " & objIE.LocationName & vbCrLf & _
    "Document Type: " & objIE.Type & vbCrLf & vbCrLf & _
    "Would you like to view this document?"

' Display the info
intResult = objWshShell.Popup(strMessage, , "Scripting IE", vbYesNo + vbQuestion)

' Check the result
If intResult = vbYes Then

    ' If Yes, make browser visible
    objIE.Visible = True
Else

    ' If no, bail out
    objIE.Quit
End If
Set objIE = Nothing
Set objWshShell = Nothing
```

The script begins by creating instances of the InternetExplorer and WScript Shell objects. The Navigate method displays a page, and then turns off the toolbar, status bar, and menu bar. A Do...Loop checks the Busy property and loops while it's True. In other words, this loop won't exit until the page is fully loaded. A string variable is used to store the URL, the title, and type of the page, and this string is then displayed in a Popup box, which also asks whether the user wants to see the page. If the user clicks the Yes button, the browser is made visible. If the user clicks the No button, the Quit method shuts down the browser.

Programming the Windows Management Instrumentation Service

Windows Management Instrumentation (WMI) is a powerful tool that gives you access to just about every aspect of Windows Home Server and of remote computers. With WMI, your scripts can manage applications, systems, devices, networks, and much more. WMI consists of a series of classes that implement various properties and methods that you can access using your scripts. For example, the Win32_OperatingSystem class represents the computer's operating system. Its properties include InstallDate, the date and time the OS was installed, and LastBootUpTime, the date and time when the OS was last started; its methods include Reboot for restarting the computer and SetDateTime for setting the system's date and time.

> **NOTE**
>
> WMI is massive. It has hundreds of classes that you can use, although you'll mostly use the Win32 classes, which enable you to manage the operating system, hardware, and applications, and to monitor performance. For the complete WMI reference, see http://msdn.microsoft.com/en-us/library/aa394582.aspx.

Referencing the WMI Service Object

Your WMI scripts will always begin by setting up a variable for the WMI service object. One way to do that is to create the SWbemLocator object and use it to connect to the WMI service. Here's the code:

```
strComputer = "localhost"
Set objLocator = CreateObject("WbemScripting.SWbemLocator")
Set objWMI = objLocator.ConnectServer(strComputer, "root\cimv2")
objWMI.Security.ImpersonationLevel = 3
```

That works fine, but most scripts use a shortcut method that reduces to just a couple of statements:

```
strComputer = "localhost"
Set objWMI = GetObject("winmgmts:{impersonationLevel=impersonate}!\\" & _
        strComputer & "\root\cimv2")
```

> **TIP**
>
> I like to use localhost to reference the local computer because it's straightforward and easy to read. However, you can also use just dot (.) to refer to the local machine:

```
    strComputer = "."
    Set objWMI = GetObject("winmgmts:{impersonationLevel=impersonate}!\\" & _
                    strComputer & "\root\cimv2")
```

Returning Class Instances

After you have your WMI service object, you can use it to access a class. Each class is really a collection of instances, or actual implementations of the class. For example, the Win32_UserAccount class consists of all the user accounts defined on the computer. Each user account is an instance of the Win32_UserAccount class. To access the instances of a class, you can use either of the following WMI object methods: ExecQuery or InstancesOf.

The ExecQuery method executes a SELECT query using the WMI Query Language (WQL). In general, this method uses the following form:

object.ExecQuery("SELECT * FROM *class*")

object   A variable that references the WMI object.

class   The WMI class you want to work with.

For example, the following method assumes the WMI object is referenced by the objWMI variable, and the query returns all the instances of the Win32_UserAccount class:

objWMI.ExecQuery("SELECT * FROM Win32_UserAccount")

The InstancesOf method uses the following syntax:

object.InstancesOf("*class*")

object   A variable that references the WMI object.

class   The WMI class you want to work with.

For example, the following method assumes the WMI object is referenced by the objWMI variable, and the code returns all the instances of the Win32_UserAccount class:

objWMI.InstancesOf("Win32_UserAccount")

Which method should you use? If you want to work with all instances of a particular class, either method is fine, and you may gravitate to the InstancesOf method only because it's slightly shorter. However, if you want to work with only a subset of the instances, the ExecQuery method is better because you can add a WHERE clause to the WQL statement. For example, if you just want to work with the account named Administrator, the following code returns just that instance from the Win32_UserAccounts class:

objWMI.ExecQuery("SELECT * FROM Win32_UserAccount " & _
                "WHERE Name = 'Administrator'")

Both ExecQuery and InstancesOf return a collection object that contains the class instances. You usually store that collection in a variable, as in this example:

```
Set objUsers = objWMI.ExecQuery("SELECT * FROM Win32_UserAccount")
```

You could then use a For Each...Next loop to run through the collection and perform some action on each instance. For example, Listing 30.11 presents a script that runs through all the instances of the Win32_UserAccount class, stores the Name and Fullname properties for each user in a string, and then displays the string.

LISTING 30.11   Script That Runs Through the Instances of the Win32_UserAccount Class

```
Option Explicit
Dim strComputer, strUserInfo
Dim objWMI, objUsers, objUser
'
' Work with the local computer
'
strComputer = "localhost"
'
' Get the WMI service
'
Set objWMI = GetObject("winmgmts:{impersonationLevel=impersonate}!\\" & _
                    strComputer & "\root\cimv2")
'
' Store the instances of the Win32_UserAccount class
'
Set objUsers = objWMI.ExecQuery("SELECT * FROM Win32_UserAccount")
'
' Initialize the display string
'
strUserInfo = ""
'
' Loop through the instances
'
For each objUser in objUsers
    strUserInfo = strUserInfo & objUser.Name & " (" & _
                            objUser.FullName & ")" & vbCrLf
Next
'
' Display the string
'
WScript.Echo strUserInfo
'
```

30

LISTING 30.11   Continued

```
' Release the objects
'
Set objWMI = Nothing
Set objUsers = Nothing
Set objUsers = Nothing
```

In many cases, the class only returns a single instance, either because the class only has one instance or because you used the WQL WHERE clause to restrict the class to a particular instance. Either way, you still need to use a For Each...Next loop to extract the data from the instance.

As an example, consider the script in Listing 30.12.

LISTING 30.12   Script That Displays BIOS Data

```
Option Explicit
Dim strComputer, strBIOS
Dim objWMI, objBIOS, objItem
'
' Get the WMI service
'
strComputer = "mediapcrver"
Set objWMI = GetObject("winmgmts:{impersonationLevel=impersonate}!\\" & _
            strComputer & "\root\cimv2")
'
' Get the BIOS instance
'
Set objBIOS = objWMI.ExecQuery("SELECT * FROM Win32_BIOS " & _
                        "WHERE PrimaryBIOS = true")
'
' Initialize the display string
'
strBIOS = "BIOS Data for " & UCase(strComputer) & ":" & vbCrLf & vbCrLf
'
' Collect the BIOS data
'
For Each objItem in objBIOS
        strBIOS = strBIOS & _
            "BIOS Name:" & vbTab & objItem.Name & vbCrLf & _
            "Manufacturer:" & vbTab & objItem.Manufacturer & vbCrLf & _
            "BIOS Version:" & vbTab & objItem.Version & vbCrLf & _
            "SMBIOS Version:" & vbTab & objItem.SMBIOSBIOSVersion & vbCrLf & _
            "BIOS Date:" & vbTab & ConvertToDate(objItem.ReleaseDate)
```

LISTING 30.12   Continued

```
Next
'
' Display the string
'
WScript.Echo strBIOS
'
' Release the objects
'
Set objWMI = Nothing
Set objBIOS = Nothing
Set objItem = Nothing
'
' This function takes a datetime string and
' converts it to a real date object
'
Function ConvertToDate(strDate)
    Dim strYear, strMonth, strDay
    strYear = Left(strDate, 4)
    strMonth = Mid(strDate, 5, 2)
    strDay = Mid(strDate, 7, 2)
    ConvertToDate = DateSerial(strYear, strMonth, strDay)
End Function
```

This script uses ExecQuery to return the instance of the Win32_BIOS class that represents the computer's primary BIOS (that is, where the PrimaryBIOS property equals true). Then a For Each...Next loop runs through the single instance and uses a string variable to store the values of five properties: Name, Manufacturer, Version, SMBBIOSBIOSVersion, and ReleaseDate. The last of these is converted to a proper date object using the ConvertToDate function. The script then uses the Echo method to display the results, as shown in Figure 30.7.

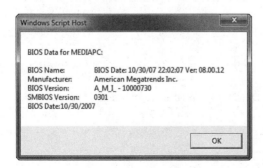

FIGURE 30.7   A computer's BIOS data displayed by the script in Listing 30.12.

30

Scripting a Remote Computer

In the WMI examples you've seen so far, I've used localhost as the value of the strComputer variable, which connects to the local computer's WMI service:

```
strComputer = "localhost"
Set objWMI = GetObject("winmgmts:{impersonationLevel=impersonate}!\\" & _
             strComputer & "\root\cimv2")
```

You may have noticed that in Listing 30.11, I did something a bit different:

```
strComputer = "mediapc"
Set objWMI = GetObject("winmgmts:{impersonationLevel=impersonate}!\\" & _
             strComputer & "\root\cimv2")
```

In this case, I used the name of the local computer—mediapc—instead of localhost. However, WMI scripting doesn't restrict you to working only with the local machine. In fact, WMI was created so that IT types and network admins could manage remote computers on the network. This means that it's almost trivial to configure a script to run on a network client:

▶ You change the value of the strComputer variable to the name of the remote computer you want to manage.

▶ You configure the network client's firewall to accept remote administration traffic.

> ▶ For the details on configuring the remote administration firewall exception, **see** "Configure a Network Computer for Remote Administration," **p. 605**.

> **NOTE**
>
> Unfortunately, scripting remote Windows Vista and Windows 7 computers only works if those PCs have User Account Control turned off. When UAC is activated on a remote computer, your script will always generate "Access Denied" errors (even if you run the script under the Administrator account). Because UAC is such an important part of the Windows 7 and Windows Vista security models, turning UAC off just to access remote machines in scripts isn't worth it.

Listing 30.13 shows a script that returns disk drive information from a remote computer.

LISTING 30.13   Script That Displays Disk Drive Data for a Remote Computer on the Network

```
Option Explicit
Dim strComputer, strDriveData
Dim objWMI, objDrives, objDrive
'
' Get the WMI service
'
strComputer = "officepc"
```

LISTING 30.13 Continued

```vbnet
Set objWMI = GetObject("winmgmts:{impersonationLevel=impersonate}!\\" & _
    strComputer & "\root\cimv2")
'
' Get the instances of hard disk drives (MediaType = 12)
'
Set objDrives = objWMI.ExecQuery("SELECT * FROM Win32_LogicalDisk " & _
                                 "WHERE MediaType = 12")
'
' Initialize the display string
'
strDriveData = "Disk Drive Data for " & UCase(strComputer) & ":" & vbCrLf & vbCrLf
    strDriveData = strDriveData & _
        "Letter:" & vbTab & _
        "Name:" & vbTab & _
        "System:" & vbTab & _
        "Size:" & vbTab & _
        "Free:" & vbTab & _
        "% Free:" & vbTab & vbCrLf & _
        "=====" & vbTab & _
        "=====" & vbTab & _
        "=====" & vbTab & _
        "=====" & vbTab & _
        "=====" & vbTab & _
        "=====" & vbTab & vbCrLf
'
' Collect the drive data
'
For Each objDrive In objDrives
    strDriveData = strDriveData & _
        objDrive.Name & vbTab & _
        objDrive.VolumeName & vbTab & _
        objDrive.FileSystem & vbTab & _
        FormatNumber(objDrive.Size / 1073741824, 1) & " GB" & vbTab & _
        FormatNumber(objDrive.FreeSpace / 1073741824, 1) & " GB" & vbTab & _
        FormatPercent(objDrive.FreeSpace / objDrive.Size, 1) & vbTab & vbCrLf

Next
'
' Display the string
'
WScript.Echo strDriveData
'
' Release the objects
'
Set objWMI = Nothing
Set objDrives = Nothing
Set objDrive = Nothing
```

30

The script begins by setting the strComputer variable to officepc, which is the name of the client computer on my network. The script then gets the remote computer's WMI service and uses it to return the instances of the remote computer's Win32LogicalDisk class, which represents a computer's logical disk drives. In this case, I'm only interested in the hard drives, so I use the WHERE clause to return only those disks where the MediaType property equals 12.

> **NOTE**
>
> If you want to examine a computer's removable media drives (except its floppy drives), use WHERE MediaType = 11. Floppy drives use various values for the MediaType property, depending on the floppy format (3.5 inch versus 5.25 inch), the size (for example, 1.2MB or 1.44MB), and the number of bytes per sector (for example, 512 or 1024).

The script initializes the strDriveData display variable, and then it uses For Each...Next to loop through the hard drive instances. In each case, six values are added to the strDriveData string: the Name (drive letter), VolumeName, FileSystem, Size, and FreeSpace properties, and a calculation of the percentage of free space available. The strDriveData string is then displayed using the Echo method. Figure 30.8 shows an example.

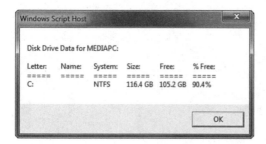

FIGURE 30.8   A remote computer's disk drive data displayed by the script in Listing 30.12.

CHAPTER 31

Scripting Windows with PowerShell

Rock is all about writing your own script; it's all about pioneering.
—Courtney Love

Back in Chapter 13, "Controlling Windows 7 from the Command Line," I went on and on about Command Prompt and the various features it offered to tweak and twiddle Windows 7. Command Prompt is powerful and useful, for sure, but its days are probably numbered because Microsoft has developed what appears to be its replacement: Windows PowerShell. This is another command-line tool, but while Command Prompt exudes a distinct 20th-century odor, PowerShell is as modern as anything else that comes with the Windows 7 package. That's because although PowerShell is happy to perform most of the same techniques as Command Prompt, PowerShell is much more sophisticated. That sophistication mostly comes in two forms:

▶ PowerShell has hooks to the Windows 7 .NET Framework, which is a massive library of classes that provide access to many aspects of Windows 7, such as files, services, processes, and much more.

▶ You can combine multiple PowerShell commands into an executable script. This sounds like just a fancy batch file, but PowerShell scripts are closer to real programs because they support true programming constructs such as objects, variables, and loops.

In this chapter, I introduce you to what I think are the most useful and most important PowerShell features, commands, and techniques. PowerShell is actually a huge topic that would require an entire book to investigate fully, so I'm really only scratching the surface here. My goal is to give you a taste of how powerful and how useful PowerShell is so that you may find yourself motivated to investigate further.

> **NOTE**
>
> If you want to get knee-deep in PowerShell, check out *PowerShell Unleashed*, Second Edition, by Tyson Kopczynski, Pete Handley, and Marco Shaw (Sams, 2008).

Getting Started with PowerShell

NEW TO 7   Windows 7 ships with PowerShell 2.0 installed and ready for action, so you can start scripting right away. Before getting to that, however, I should make a quick note about my use of the word *scripting* in this chapter. Although that term generally means something like "entering multiple statements or commands in a file that you can then execute all at once," things are a bit different in the PowerShell world. What I mean is that when you're at the PowerShell command line, you can execute single commands, as you can using Command Prompt, but you can also run through an entire script by executing multiple, consecutive commands. For example, you can run one command that stores data in a variable, and then you can run another command later on that includes that variable.

So when you're executing commands in a PowerShell session, you're essentially always executing a script, even if it's a script that contains only a single command.

Starting a PowerShell Session

To get PowerShell up and running, select Start, type **power**, and then select Windows PowerShell in the search results. Windows 7 starts a new PowerShell console session, and displays it in the Windows PowerShell window, as shown in Figure 31.1.

FIGURE 31.1   Windows PowerShell is eerily similar to Command Prompt.

As you can see, on the surface PowerShell looks like a Command Prompt clone with its character-based console and command-line prompt. In fact, not only does PowerShell *look*

31

like Command Prompt, it also *works* like Command Prompt. That is, almost anything you can do in a Command Prompt session you can also do in exactly the same way in a PowerShell session:

▶ PowerShell supports the standard Command Prompt commands, including `cd`, `del`, `dir`, `echo`, `md`, `move`, `ren`, `rm`, `rmdir`, `set`, `sort`, and `start`.

▶ PowerShell supports the standard DOSKEY techniques for recalling command lines and running multiple commands at once.

▶ You can use PowerShell to start batch files, script, and programs.

▶ PowerShell supports redirection (such as >) and piping (|).

▶ You can use PowerShell's system menu (click the icon in the upper-left corner of the window) to select, copy, and paste text, just as with the Command Prompt window.

All this means that if you're comfortable working with Command Prompt, you won't have much of a learning curve when it comes to PowerShell (at least as far as the above techniques are concerned).

Understanding PowerShell Cmdlets

What truly separates PowerShell from Command Prompt is the concept of the *cmdlet* (pronounced "commandlet"), which is a PowerShell component that encapsulates some larger functionality into a single item. (If you're familiar with Excel, a cmdlet is analogous to an Excel worksheet function.) The name of each PowerShell cmdlet takes the following general form:

verb-subject

Here, *subject* refers to some kind of object, *and verb* is some action that the cmdlet performs on that object. For example, you can use the `Get-Host` cmdlet to return information about the current PowerShell hosting environment, or you can use the `Out-File` cmdlet to output data to a file.

> **NOTE**
>
> The names of PowerShell cmdlets aren't case sensitive, so `Stop-Service` is the same as `stop-service`. In this chapter, I generally use the first-letter caps in the regular text to help the names stick out a bit, but I use all-lowercase letters in the code because it's easier to type.

Although you can run most cmdlets with no other text, most of the time you'll augment a cmdlet name with various parameters, depending on the cmdlet syntax. For example, you use the `Write-Host` cmdlet to write text to the hosting environment (which means the command line in a PowerShell console session), so you need to specify the text you want to write, as in this example:

```
write-host "Hello PowerShell World!"
```

I should also mention here that many cmdlets have alternate names called *aliases* that you can use. For example, the `Get-Service` cmdlet returns the current status of whatever service you specify, as in this example:

```
get-service w32time
```

However, `Get-Service` also uses the alias gsv, the following command is equivalent:

```
gsv w32time
```

Table 31.1 lists the PowerShell aliases

TABLE 31.1   Cmdlet Aliases Used By PowerShell

Alias	Cmdlet	Alias	Cmdlet
%	ForEach-Object	ise	powershell_ise.exe
?	Where-Object	iwmi	Invoke-WMIMethod
ac	Add-Content	kill	Stop-Process
asnp	Add-PSSnapIn	lp	Out-Printer
cat	Get-Content	ls	Get-ChildItem
cd	Set-Location	man	help
chdir	Set-Location	md	mkdir
clc	Clear-Content	measure	Measure-Object
clear	Clear-Host	mi	Move-Item
clhy	Clear-History	mount	New-PSDrive
cli	Clear-Item	move	Move-Item
clp	Clear-ItemProperty	mp	Move-ItemProperty
cls	Clear-Host	mv	Move-Item
clv	Clear-Variable	nal	New-Alias
compare	Compare-Object	ndr	New-PSDrive
copy	Copy-Item	ni	New-Item
cp	Copy-Item	nmo	New-Module
cpi	Copy-Item	nsn	New-PSSession
cpp	Copy-ItemProperty	nv	New-Variable

TABLE 31.1 Continued

Alias	Cmdlet	Alias	Cmdlet
cvpa	Convert-Path	ogv	Out-GridView
dbp	Disable-PSBreakpoint	oh	Out-Host
del	Remove-Item	popd	Pop-Location
diff	Compare-Object	ps	Get-Process
dir	Get-ChildItem	pushd	Push-Location
ebp	Enable-PSBreakpoint	pwd	Get-Location
echo	Write-Output	r	Invoke-History
epal	Export-Alias	rbp	Remove-PSBreakpoint
epcsv	Export-Csv	rcjb	Receive-Job
epsn	Export-PSSession	rd	Remove-Item
erase	Remove-Item	rdr	Remove-PSDrive
etsn	Enter-PSSession	ren	Rename-Item
exsn	Exit-PSSession	ri	Remove-Item
fc	Format-Custom	rjb	Remove-Job
fl	Format-List	rm	Remove-Item
foreach	ForEach-Object	rmdir	Remove-Item
ft	Format-Table	rmo	Remove-Module
fw	Format-Wide	rni	Rename-Item
gal	Get-Alias	rnp	Rename-ItemProperty
gbp	Get-PSBreakpoint	rp	Remove-ItemProperty
gc	Get-Content	rsn	Remove-PSSession
gci	Get-ChildItem	rsnp	Remove-PSSnapin
gcm	Get-Command	rv	Remove-Variable
gcs	Get-PSCallStack	rvpa	Resolve-Path
gdr	Get-PSDrive	rwmi	Remove-WMIObject
ghy	Get-History	sajb	Start-Job

31

TABLE 31.1   Continued

Alias	Cmdlet	Alias	Cmdlet
gi	Get-Item	sal	Set-Alias
gjb	Get-Job	saps	Start-Process
gl	Get-Location	sasv	Start-Service
gm	Get-Member	sbp	Set-PSBreakpoint
gmo	Get-Module	sc	Set-Content
gp	Get-ItemProperty	select	Select-Object
gps	Get-Process	set	Set-Variable
group	Group-Object	si	Set-Item
gsn	Get-PSSession	sl	Set-Location
gsnp	Get-PSSnapIn	sleep	Start-Sleep
gsv	Get-Service	sort	Sort-Object
gu	Get-Unique	sp	Set-ItemProperty
gv	Get-Variable	spjb	Stop-Job
gwmi	Get-WmiObject	spps	Stop-Process
h	Get-History	spsv	Stop-Service
history	Get-History	start	Start-Process
icm	Invoke-Command	sv	Set-Variable
iex	Invoke-Expression	swmi	Set-WMIInstance
ihy	Invoke-History	tee	Tee-Object
ii	Invoke-Item	type	Get-Content
ipal	Import-Alias	where	Where-Object
ipcsv	Import-Csv	wjb	Wait-Job
ipmo	Import-Module	write	Write-Output
ipsn	Import-PSSession		

31

> **NOTE**
>
> Notice that all the standard Command Prompt commands—including cd, del, dir, echo, md, move, ren, rm, rmdir, set, sort, and start—are actually aliases of PowerShell cmdlets (Set-Location, Remove_Item, Get-ChildItem, and so on).

Running PowerShell Cmdlets

PowerShell 2.0 is positively bursting at the seams with well over 200 cmdlets. However, the fact is that most of those cmdlets are quite obscure and are unlikely to be of interest to most of us. So, my goal in this section is to introduce you to a few cmdlets that *are* useful or interesting, so not only can you can use them to learn how PowerShell works, but I hope you'll also make use of these techniques to help you control and tweak Windows 7.

Before getting to all that, it might help to get an overview of all the PowerShell cmdlets. To that end, Table 31.2 presents a complete list of the 236 cmdlets, organized by category. I don't have room to describe them all, but if you're curious about anything in this list that I don't cover later in the chapter, you can take advantage of the decent Help system that comes with PowerShell. You can view the Help text for any command by entering a command at the PowerShell prompt using the following syntax:

```
get-help cmdlet [-detailed | -examples | -full]
```

Here, replace *cmdlet* with the name of the cmdlet you want to investigate. Add the -detailed switch to get extra-geeky data about the cmdlet, or add the -examples switch to see how you use the cmdlet in action; if you want both, add the -full switch, instead.

TABLE 31.2   PowerShell's Cmdlets, Organized by Category

Aliases		
Get-Alias	Import-Alias	Set-Alias
Export-Alias	New-Alias	
Content		
Add-Content	Get-Content	
Clear-Content	Set-Content	
Debugging		
Debug-Process	Get-TraceSource	Set-StrictMode
Disable-PSBreakpoint	Remove-PSBreakpoint	Write-Debug
Enable-PSBreakpoint	Set-PSBreakpoint	Write-Error
Get-PSBreakpoint	Set-PSDebug	
Drives		
Get-PSDrive	New-PSDrive	

TABLE 31.2   Continued

Get-PSProvider	Remove-PSDrive	
Events		
Clear-EventLog	New-Event	Set-TraceSource
Get-Event	New-EventLog	Show-EventLog
Get-EventLog	Register-EngineEvent	Trace-Command
Get-EventSubscriber	Register-ObjectEvent	Unregister-Event
Get-WinEvent	Remove-Event	Wait-Event
Limit-EventLog	Remove-EventLog	Write-EventLog
Executing		
Get-Job	Measure-Command	Start-Job
Invoke-Command	Receive-Job	Stop-Job
Invoke-Expression	Remove-Job	Wait-Job
Export/Import		
Export-Clixml	Export-Csv	Import-Counter
Export-Counter	Import-Clixml	Import-Csv
Formats		
ConvertFrom-Csv	ConvertTo-Html	Format-List
ConvertFrom-SecureString	ConvertTo-SecureString	Format-Table
ConvertFrom-StringData	ConvertTo-Xml	Format-Wide
ConvertTo-Csv	Format-Custom	
Items		
Clear-Item	Get-ItemProperty	Remove-ItemProperty
Clear-ItemProperty	Invoke-Item	Rename-Item

TABLE 31.2   Continued

Copy-Item	Move-Item	Rename-ItemProperty
Copy-ItemProperty	Move-ItemProperty	Set-Acl
Get-Acl	New-Item	Set-Item
Get-ChildItem	New-ItemProperty	Set-ItemProperty
Get-Item	Remove-Item	

Management

Connect-WSMan	Get-WSManInstance	Set-WSManInstance
Disable-WSManCredSSP	Invoke-WSManAction	Set-WSManQuickConfig
Disconnect-WSMan	New-WSManInstance	Test-WSMan
Enable-WSManCredSSP	New-WSManSessionOption	
Get-WSManCredSSP	Remove-WSManInstance	

Miscellaneous

Get-Date	Read-Host	Send-MailMessage
Import-LocalizedData	Select-String	Set-Date
New-TimeSpan	Select-Xml	

Operating System

Add-Computer	New-Service	Start-Process
Checkpoint-Computer	New-WebServiceProxy	Start-Service
Disable-ComputerRestore	Remove-Computer	Start-Sleep
Enable-ComputerRestore	Reset-ComputerMachinePassword	Stop-Computer
Get-ComputerRestorePoint	Restart-Computer	Stop-Process
Get-Counter	Restart-Service	Stop-Service
Get-HotFix	Restore-Computer	Suspend-Service
Get-Process	Resume-Service	Test-Connection
Get-Service	Set-Service	Wait-Process

31

TABLE 31.2   Continued

Objects

Add-Member	Group-Object	Tee-Object
Compare-Object	Measure-Object	Update-List
ForEach-Object	New-Object	Where-Object
Get-Member	Select-Object	
Get-Random	Sort-Object	

Output

Out-Default	Out-Null	Write-Output
Out-File	Out-Printer	Write-Progress
Out-GridView	Out-String	Write-Verbose
Out-Host	Write-Host	Write-Warning

Paths

Convert-Path	Pop-Location	Set-Location
Get-Location	Push-Location	Split-Path
Join-Path	Resolve-Path	Test-Path

PowerShell System

Get-Command	Get-Help	Get-UICulture
Get-Culture	Get-Host	

PowerShell Session

Add-History	Get-ExecutionPolicy	New-PSSession
Add-PSSnapin	Get-FormatData	New-PSSessionOption
Add-Type	Get-History	Register-PSSessionConfiguration

TABLE 31.2   Continued

Clear-History	Get-Module	Remove-Module
Disable-PSSessionConfiguration	Get-PSCallStack	Remove-PSSession
Enable-PSRemoting	Get-PSSession	Remove-PSSnapin
Enable-PSRemoting	Get-PSSession	Remove-PSSnapin
Enable-PSSessionConfiguration	Get-PSSessionConfiguration	Set-PSSessionConfiguration
Enable-PSSessionConfiguration	Get-PSSessionConfiguration	Set-PSSessionConfiguration
Enter-PSSession	Get-PSSnapin	Start-Transcript
Exit-PSSession	Import-Module	Stop-Transcript
Export-Console	Import-PSSession	Test-ModuleManifest
Export-PSSession	New-ModuleManifest	

Security

Get-AuthenticodeSignature	Get-PfxCertificate	Set-ExecutionPolicy
Get-Credential	Set-AuthenticodeSignature	Test-ComputerSecureChannel

Transactions

Complete-Transaction	Start-Transaction	Use-Transaction
Get-Transaction	Undo-Transaction	

Variables

Clear-Variable	New-Variable	Set-Variable
Get-Variable	Remove-Variable	Update-TypeData

WMI

Invoke-WmiMethod	Remove-WmiObject	

31

TIP

In Table 31.2, you'll see lots of cmdlets that use the verb Get (such as Get-Alias and Get-Content). Get is PowerShell's default verb, so you can save a bit of time and typing by leaving off the get- part when entering commands. For example, the following two commands are identical:

```
get-alias
alias
```

Scripting Objects

Scripting with PowerShell is really about scripting objects, so the most fundamental skills you need to master PowerShell scripting are those that enable you to work with and use objects.

In programming, an *object* is an element that exposes an interface to the programmer, who can then use that interface to work with the object in two ways:

▶ Make changes to the object's *properties*, which are the elements that describe or configure the object.

▶ Make the object perform a task by activating one of the object's *methods*, which are the elements that enable the object to perform actions.

In PowerShell, an object's properties and methods are part of the collection known as the object's *members*. Other items in an object's member collection includes *events* (occurrences that trigger object actions) and property aliases (alternate names for certain properties).

Returning Object Members

When you need to work with an object in PowerShell, you usually begin by listing all the members associated with that object, which tells you which properties you can read or change, and which methods you can invoke. To return an object's members, you use the Get-Member cmdlet:

```
object | get-member
```

NOTE

PowerShell's pipe operator (|) works just like it does in a Command Prompt session. That is, it combines both input and output redirection, so that the output of one cmdlet is captured and sent as input to another cmdlet.

▶ See "Piping Commands," **p. 259**.

Replace *object* with the object you want to interrogate. For example, the following command returns the members associated with the current location (folder) in the PowerShell session:

```
get-location | get-member
```

Here's the output you see:

```
Name           MemberType Definition
----           ---------- ----------
Equals         Method     bool Equals(System.Object obj)
GetHashCode    Method     int GetHashCode()
GetType        Method     type GetType()
ToString       Method     string ToString()
Drive          Property   System.Management.Automation.PSDriveInfo Drive {get;}
Path           Property   System.String Path {get;}
Provider       Property   System.Management.Automation.ProviderInfo Provider {get;}
ProviderPath   Property   System.String ProviderPath {get;}
```

Some member collections are quite large and may displays dozens of properties, methods, and other member types. If you're only interested in a particular type of member, you can restrict the output of Get-Member by adding the -MemberType switch:

```
object | get-member -membertype type1, type2, ...
```

Here, replace *type1, type2,* and so on with one or more of the following member type keywords: AliasProperty, CodeProperty, Property, NoteProperty, ScriptProperty, Properties, PropertySet, Method, CodeMethod, ScriptMethod, Methods, ParameterizedProperty, MemberSet, Event, or All.

For example, if you only want to see the properties and methods associated with the Get-Process object (which returns a handle to a running process), enter the following command:

```
get-process | get-member -membertype property, method
```

Selecting Object Members

When you work with an object, PowerShell usually defines a default subset of the object's members. For example, if you want to see a list of the running processes on your system, you use the Get-Process cmdlet, which sends to the console output similar to the following:

```
Handles  NPM(K)   PM(K)     WS(K) VM(M)   CPU(s)     Id ProcessName
-------  ------   -----     ----- -----   ------     -- -----------
     50       3     960      4120    47     0.02   3308 conhost
     52       3    1844      5216    48     4.60   3860 conhost
    475       5    1264      2808    33             344 csrss
```

310	10	1784	6208	69		412	csrss
105	7	36520	31568	109	49.31	2324	dwm
1139	38	51544	75488	316	95.78	2348	explorer
0	0	0	24	0		0	Idle
741	14	3028	8032	33		468	lsass
187	5	1696	3996	26		476	lsm
64	3	1016	2824	40		1552	lxdwcoms
434	10	85840	88124	219	7.24	2300	powershell
279	15	76000	66380	287	1.56	684	powershell_ise
154	7	14628	13572	124		2304	PresentationFontCache
764	26	39980	22148	123		2684	SearchIndexer
206	7	4096	5692	38		452	services
29	1	264	648	4		256	smss
461	21	15936	34336	221	17.61	2464	SnagIt32
407	12	7920	11464	79		1368	spoolsv
143	4	1820	6672	28		2192	sppsvc
351	7	3020	5928	39		588	svchost
272	9	3304	5928	30		708	svchost
579	14	14832	14336	82		764	svchost
1254	17	34740	37652	129		864	svchost
1331	28	17232	27928	128		908	svchost
662	20	8116	14136	67		1056	svchost
601	18	11352	13080	88		1232	svchost
315	24	11024	10896	52		1404	svchost
91	9	2748	4244	30		1496	svchost
126	9	4804	4472	33		1680	svchost
401	17	6240	11872	73		2920	svchost
261	7	2864	8268	54		3228	svchost
350	17	45248	11416	122		3936	svchost
709	0	52	4092	6		4	System
195	10	7416	7572	66	0.30	1216	taskhost
108	6	1892	7544	91	2.81	2520	taskmgr
53	3	920	3720	55	0.06	2576	TscHelp
77	5	924	2752	30		404	wininit
113	4	1708	3976	36		636	winlogon
441	16	10372	12764	128		2832	wmpnetwk
331	6	1716	4188	33		352	WUDFHost

These columns represent (from left to right) the number of open handles, the amount of nonpaged memory, the amount of paged memory, the size of the working set, the amount of virtual memory, the amount of CPU time, the process ID, and the process name. This is all useful information, but it might not be what you want to see. For example, you might not need to see the number of file handles each process is using, or you may be interested in not only the current working set for each process, but also the peak working set (the most memory the process has used in the current session).

▶ To learn about the working set, **see** "Using the Resource Monitor," **p. 117.**

In other words, there may be default properties that you don't want to see, and other properties (such as `PeakWorkingSet`) that you do want to see. You can customize the members you work with by using the `Select-Object` cmdlet:

```
object | select-object member1[, member2, ...]
```

Here, `object` is the object you're working with, and *member1, member2,* and so on are the members you want to use. Here's an example:

```
get-process | select-object processname, workingset, peakworkingset
```

If you only want to see the first few results, add the `-First` *n switch, where n* is the number of results you want to see. For example, the following command returns the first five results:

```
    get-process | select-object processname, workingset, peakworkingset -first 5
```

Similarly, if you only want to see the last few results, add the `-Last` *n switch, where n* is the number of results you want to see. For example, the following command returns the last 10 results:

```
    get-process | select-object processname, workingset, peakworkingset -last 10
```

A Brief Aside About Formatting Output

If you run the command `show` at the end of the previous section, the console displays the name, working set, and peak working set for each running process. However, the two memory values are displayed in bytes, rather than an easier-to-read value such as kilobytes (as you get when you run `Get-Process` by itself). To fix this, you need to define a statement that defines how you want the output to look. In this case, the statement you want takes the following general form:

```
@{Label="Label"; Expression={expression}}
```

Here, `Label` is the text you want to appear at the top of the output column, and *expression* is an expression that defines how you want the values in that column to appears. For example, to convert a memory value in bytes to kilobytes, you need to divide it by 1,024:

```
[int]($_.workingset/1024)
```

We add `[int]` because we only want an integer result displayed. The symbols `$_` are a PowerShell shorthand that refers to whatever object is currently being piped, so `$_.workingset` refers to the `WorkingSet` property of the current object. If we want the column name to be, say, `WS (KB)`, the full statement looks like this:

```
@{Label="WS (KB)";Expression={[int]($_.workingset/1024)}}
```

We can do the same for the `PeakWorkingSet` property:

```
@{Label="Peak WS (KB)";Expression={[int]($_.peakworkingset/1024)}}
```

We then pipe everything through the `Format-Table` cmdlet using its `-auto` switch, which makes each column only wide enough to hold the widest item in the column:

```
get-process | select-object name, @{Label="WS (KB)";Expression={[int]
➥($_.workingset/1024)}}, @{Label="Peak WS (KB)";Expression={[int]
➥($_.peakworkingset/1024)}} | format-table -auto
```

Here's the resulting output:

```
Name                   WS (KB) Peak WS (KB)
----                   ------- ------------
conhost                   4120         4148
conhost                   5464         7724
csrss                     2812         2844
csrss                     6208        11428
dwm                      31568        44884
explorer                 75492        95140
Idle                        24            0
lsass                     8044         8292
lsm                       4036         4316
lxdwcoms                  2824         6256
powershell               89676        91252
powershell_ise           66380        68040
PresentationFontCache    13572        13600
SearchIndexer            22172        26588
services                  5688        11280
smss                       648          780
SnagIt32                 34336        45548
spoolsv                  11464        13620
sppsvc                    6728         6748
svchost                   5964         6552
svchost                   5964         5988
svchost                  14348        15448
svchost                  37068        47276
svchost                  27900        30128
svchost                  14004        14420
svchost                  13080        13228
svchost                  10920        26924
svchost                   4216         6196
svchost                   4472         7576
svchost                  11876        12252
svchost                   8296         9608
```

```
svchost                 16056         66828
System                   4092          8032
taskhost                 7584          8016
taskhost                10404         10424
taskmgr                  7584          7592
TscHelp                  3720          3720
wininit                  2752          3172
winlogon                 3976          6276
wmpnetwk                12760         24908
WUDFHost                 4188          5128
```

Filtering Object Instances

By default, PowerShell returns all the instances of an object. If you want to work with only some subset of the object, you can use the Where-Object cmdlet to filter the instances and return just the ones you want. Here's the general syntax:

object | where-object { *expression* }

Here, *expression* is a logical expression that defines the filter, and this expression usually takes the following general form:

property operator value

In this statement, *property* is the name of the object property you want to use as the filter, *value* is the text or numeric value you want to use as the comparison, and *operator* is one of the following PowerShell conditional operators:

-eq	Equals
-ne	Not equal
-gt	Greater than
-lt	Less than
-ge	Greater than or equal to
-le	Less than or equal to
-like	Match with wildcards
-notlike	No match with wildcards
-match	Match with regular expression
-notmatch	No match with regular expression

For example, suppose you want to work with processes via Get-Process, but you're only interested in the PowerShell process. In that case, you'd filter the Get-Process output as follows:

```
get-process | where-object { $_.processname -eq "powershell" }
```

Here's the result:

```
Handles NPM(K)    PM(K)     WS(K) VM(M)   CPU(s)     Id ProcessName
------- ------    -----     ----- -----   ------     -- -----------
    474     10    87924     90356   219     7.94   2300 powershell
```

Here's another example that returns just those processes where the working set is greater than 20MB:

```
get-process | where-object { $_.workingset -gt 20*1024*1024 }
```

Here's the result:

```
Handles NPM(K)    PM(K)     WS(K) VM(M)   CPU(s)     Id ProcessName
------- ------    -----     ----- -----   ------     -- -----------
    105      8    36532     31576   112    51.34   2324 dwm
   1208     41    56712     76460   325    97.13   2348 explorer
    439     10    88440     90900   219     8.19   2300 powershell
    265     15    75240     65624   287     1.58    684 powershell_ise
    775     26    40412     23260   131            2684 SearchIndexer
    459     21    15892     34012   220    17.61   2464 SnagIt32
   1254     17    34764     37412   129             864 svchost
   1321     28    17196     27888   128             908 svchost
```

You'll probably find that the two wildcard operators are particularly useful. You use the standard wildcard characters: ? for a single characters, and * for any number of characters. For example, to work with any process that contains the string "powershell", you'd use the following command:

```
get-process | where-object { $_.processname -like "*powershell*" }
```

Here's the output:

```
Handles NPM(K)    PM(K)     WS(K) VM(M)   CPU(s)     Id ProcessName
------- ------    -----     ----- -----   ------     -- -----------
    478     10    88700     91168   219     8.25   2300 powershell
    265     15    75240     65624   287     1.58    684 powershell_ise
```

Sorting Object Instances

When you work with the instances of an object in PowerShell, those instances are sorted on the object's default property. For example, the instances returned by Get-Process are

31

sorted on the ProcessName property. If you'd prefer to use the instances in some other order, you can use the Sort-Object cmdlet, which uses the following (partial) syntax:

```
object | sort-object -Property property [-Descending]
```

Here, *property* is the name of the property you want to use for the sort. For example, the following command sorts the output of the Get-Process cmdlet on the WorkingSet property values:

```
get-process | sort-object -property workingset
```

Here's the result:

Handles	NPM(K)	PM(K)	WS(K)	VM(M)	CPU(s)	Id	ProcessName
0	0	0	24	0		0	Idle
29	1	264	648	4		256	smss
77	5	924	2752	30		404	wininit
478	5	1264	2808	33		344	csrss
64	3	1016	2824	40		1552	lxdwcoms
53	3	920	3720	55	0.06	2576	TscHelp
113	4	1708	3976	36		636	winlogon
189	5	1740	4008	26		476	lsm
710	0	52	4092	6		4	System
50	3	960	4120	47	0.02	3308	conhost
331	6	1716	4188	33		352	WUDFHost
91	9	2748	4240	30		1496	svchost
126	9	4804	4476	33		1680	svchost
52	3	1864	5468	48	6.52	3860	conhost
208	7	4096	5692	38		452	services
353	7	3020	5928	39		588	svchost
274	9	3308	5944	30		708	svchost
311	10	1784	6192	70		412	csrss
143	4	1820	6672	28		2192	sppsvc
195	10	7416	7572	66	0.31	1216	taskhost
106	6	1964	7772	92	2.81	2520	taskmgr
741	14	3028	8032	33		468	lsass
261	7	2864	8268	54		3228	svchost
315	24	11024	10896	52		1404	svchost
407	12	7920	11464	79		1368	spoolsv
399	17	6240	11868	73		2920	svchost
439	16	10372	12764	128		2832	wmpnetwk
601	18	11352	13080	88		1232	svchost
154	7	14628	13572	124		2304	PresentationFontCache
647	20	8088	13996	66		1056	svchost
594	15	14912	14352	82		764	svchost
349	17	45248	15992	122		3936	svchost

763	26	39996	22212	123		2684	SearchIndexer
1329	28	17208	27932	128		908	svchost
105	8	36532	31576	112	52.24	2324	dwm
459	21	15892	34012	220	17.61	2464	SnagIt32
1254	17	33848	36808	129		864	svchost
265	15	75240	65624	287	1.58	684	powershell_ise
1208	41	56712	76460	325	97.13	2348	explorer
424	10	90108	92584	219	9.05	2300	powershell

Here's a command that sorts Get-Process on the WorkingSet property in descending order and displays the top 10 results:

```
get-process | sort-object -property ws -descending | select-object -first 10
```

Here's the output:

Handles	NPM(K)	PM(K)	WS(K)	VM(M)	CPU(s)	Id	ProcessName
443	10	91072	93552	219	9.06	2300	powershell
1208	41	56720	76468	325	97.13	2348	explorer
265	15	75240	65624	287	1.58	684	powershell_ise
1254	17	33920	36872	129		864	svchost
459	21	15892	34012	220	17.61	2464	SnagIt32
105	8	36540	31584	112	52.43	2324	dwm
1324	28	17204	27916	128		908	svchost
773	26	40416	23332	131		2684	SearchIndexer
579	14	14856	14316	82		764	svchost
640	20	8056	13968	66		1056	svchost

Assigning an Object to a Variable

In PowerShell, if you want to work with an object's properties or methods, you must first use cmdlets to define your object, as described in the past few sections, and then assign the result to a variable. Here's the general syntax:

```
$variable = object
```

For example, you saw earlier that the following command returns the PowerShell process:

```
get-process | where-object { $_.processname -eq "powershell" }
```

To access the properties and methods for this process, you need to assign the result to a variable, like so:

```
$ps = get-process | where-object { $_.processname -eq "powershell" }
```

In PowerShell, you always start a variable name with a dollar sign ($).

Working with Object Properties

Every programmable object has a defining set of characteristics. These characteristics are the object's *properties*, and they control the appearance and position of the object. When you refer to a property, you use the following syntax:

```
Object.Property
```

Object   A variable containing the object instance

Property The name of the property you want to work with

For example, suppose you want to reference the current working set value for the PowerShell process. In that case, you'd use cmdlets to filter Get-Process to just that instance, assign it to a variable, and then use that variable to access the WorkingSet property:

```
$ps = get-process | where-object { $_.processname -eq "powershell" }
$wset = $ps.workingset
```

Returning the Value of a Property

Sometimes you need to know the current setting of a property before changing the property or performing some other action. You can find out the current value of a property by using the following syntax:

```
$variable = Object.Property
```

Here, *$variable* is a variable name. For example, if you have a process stored in a variable, you can use that variable to return the value of the WorkingSet property. Here's a sequence of commands that does this:

```
$ps = get-process | where-object { $_.processname -eq "powershell" }
$wset = $ps.workingset
write-host "The PowerShell working set is $wset bytes."
The PowerShell working set is 96444416 bytes.
```

Setting the Value of a Property

When you pipe an object into Get-Members, the resulting output includes a Definition column, and for Property members the definition includes braces ({}) at the end, and within those braces you see get if you can read the value of the property, and set if you can change the value of the property.

To set a property to a certain value, you use the following syntax:

```
Object.Property = value
```

Here, *value* is an expression that specifies the value to which you want to set the property. As such, it can be any of the scripting language's recognized data types, which usually include the following:

- ▶ A numeric value

- ▶ A string value, enclosed in double quotation marks (such as `"My Script Application"`)

- ▶ A logical value (`$True` or `$False`)

For example, each running process has a `MaxWorkingSet` property that determines the maximum amount of memory the process can use. Here's a sequence of commands that sets the `MaxWorkingSet` property for a process to 20MB:

```
$ps = get-process | where-object { $_.processname -eq "myapp" }
$ps.maxworkingset = 20*1024*1024
```

Working with Object Methods

An object's properties describe what the object is, whereas its *methods* describe what the object *does*. For example, the `WScript` object has a `Quit` method that enables you to stop the execution of a script.

How you refer to a method depends on whether the method requires any arguments. If it doesn't, the syntax is similar to that of properties:

Object.Method()

Object	The name of the object
Method	The name of the method you want to run

For example, each process has a `Kill()` method that shuts down the process. Here's an example that runs this method:

```
$ps = get-process | where-object { $_.processname -eq "myapp" }
$ps.kill()
```

Working with Object Collections

A *collection* is a set of similar objects. For example, when you run `Get-Process` by itself, the return value is a collection of process objects. Collections are objects, too, so they have their own properties and methods, and you can use these properties and methods to manipulate one or more objects in the collection.

To assign a collection to a variable, you use the following general syntax:

$variable = @(*collection*)

For example, the following command stores the collection of Get-Process instances in a variable:

```
$p = @(get-process)
```

The members of a collection are *elements*. You can refer to individual elements by using an *index*. For example, the following statement returns the name of the first process (collection indexes always begin at 0):

```
$p[0].name
```

Each collection has a Length property that tells you how many items are in the collection, which means that the expression Length-1 always refers to the last element in the collection:

```
$p[$_.length-1].workingset
```

If you don't specify an element, PowerShell assumes that you want to work with the entire collection.

You often have to loop through the individual elements in a collection and perform some action on each element using one or more commands inside the loop. You use a foreach loop to do this:

```
foreach ($element in $collection) {
    [statements]
}
```

$element   A variable used to hold the name of each element in the collection

$collection A variable that stores the collection

statements   The statements to execute for each element in the collection

The multiline structure of a foreach loop makes it better suited to a PowerShell script, but it's possible to run short loops at the console by putting everything on one line:

```
foreach ($element in $collection) {statement1; statement2;...}
```

Here's an example:

```
foreach ($pitem in $p) { write-host $pitem.name; write-host $pitem.id }
```

NOTE

You use the Write-Host cmdlet to write text to the console.

Creating PowerShell Scripts

Running individual command at the PowerShell console is fine, but if you have commands you run regularly, or if you want to combine multiple commands into a single package, you need to create PowerShell scripts.

Setting the Script Execution Policy

By default, PowerShell is configured to not allow any unsigned scripts to run. That's a sensible precaution on systems that don't have a PowerShell programmer, but that's not the case on your system. So, you need to configure PowerShell to allow your own scripts to run, and you do that by changing the PowerShell execution policy.

However, only the system Administrator account can change the PowerShell execution policy. That is, it's not enough that your user account is a member of the Administrators group: It must be the Administrator account itself. Because you change the execution policy at the PowerShell prompt, you need to open a new PowerShell using the Administrator account:

1. Select Start.
2. Type **powershell**.
3. Right-click Windows PowerShell in the search results, and then click Run as Administrator. The User Account Control dialog box appears.
4. Enter your UAC credentials to continue. The Administrator: Windows PowerShell window appears.

With your Administrator PowerShell session loaded, enter the following command at the PowerShell prompt:

```
set-executionpolicy remotesigned
```

PowerShell displays the following message:

```
Execution Policy Change
The execution policy helps protect you from scripts that you do not trust. Changing
the execution policy might expose you to the security risks described in the
about_Execution_Policies help topic. Do you want to change the execution policy?
[Y] Yes [N] No [S] Suspend [?] Help (default is "Y"):
```

Type **y** and press Enter (or just press Enter) to put the new policy into effect. You can now run your own scripts.

Working with the PowerShell Integrated Scripting Environment

Although you could easily use Notepad or some other text editor to create your scripts, you're much better off using the PowerShell Integrated Scripting Environment (ISE), which includes programmer-friendly goodies such as color-coded syntax, breakpoints, stepping through scripts, and more.

To launch PowerShell ISE, select Start, type **power**, and then select PowerShell ISE in the search results. Figure 31.2 shows PowerShell ISE with a script loaded.

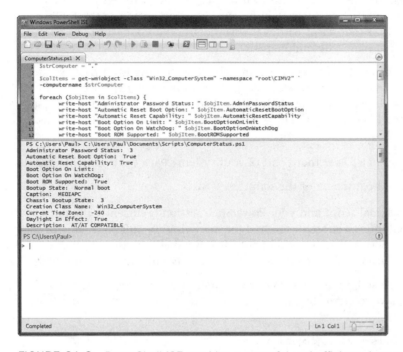

FIGURE 31.2   PowerShell ISE provides a powerful and efficient place to build your scripts.

The PowerShell ISE window is divided into three panes:

- ▶ **Script pane**—This is the top pane, and it's where you type your script code. PowerShell ISE automatically color-codes your text to make it easier to read the code and to help you find errors. For example, cmdlets appear in blue; variables appear in red; comments appear in dark green; and strings appear in dark red.

- ▶ **Command pane**—This is the bottom pane, and it works pretty much like the PowerShell console. That is, you can use the prompt top enter PowerShell commands, which saves you having to open a separate PowerShell command-line session.

- ▶ **Output pane**—This is the middle pane, and it's where PowerShell ISE displays the output from your script or from the commands you enter into the Command pane.

TIP

You can switch from one pane to the other using keyboard shortcuts: Press Ctrl+I to switch to the Script pane; press Ctrl+D to switch to the command pane; and press Shift+Ctrl+O to switch to the Output pane.

Running PowerShell Scripts

If you're using the PowerShell ISE to compose your scripts, you don't have to leave the application to run the current script. Instead, either click the Run button in the toolbar or press F5. PowerShell ISE runs that script within the window, and if your script has output, it's displayed in the Output pane (the middle pane).

If you're running a script from the PowerShell command line, you might think you can change to the folder where your script resides (using the command cd *path, where path* is the full pathname of the folder), type the name of the script, and then press Enter. That would be nice, but it isn't likely to work. That's because PowerShell is configured to run scripts only under the following circumstances:

▶ If the script is stored in a folder that's part of your system's Path environment variable

▶ If you specify the full pathname of the script

If you only run the occasional script and your PowerShell session is currently in your scripts folder, PowerShell offers a shortcut method for specifying the full pathname of the script. If you precede the script filename with a dot (.), PowerShell interprets that dot as the parent folder of the current folder, so it's just the same as typing out the entire path.

For example, if you have a script named RegAdd.ps1 stored in the Documents\Scripts folder, you'd normally have to enter the following to run the script (where *account* is your user account name):

```
c:\users\account\documents\scripts\regadd.ps1
```

However, if you've got PowerShell in the Scripts folder, you can run the same script using the following command:

```
.\regadd.ps1
```

On the other hand, if you run lots of scripts, or if you want to be able to run your scripts from any folder, you need to add your Scripts folder to the Path variable. Here's how it's done:

1. Select Start, type **systempropertiesadvanced**, and then press Enter. Windows 7 displays the System Properties dialog box with the Advanced tab displayed.

2. Click Environment Variables. Windows 7 opens the Environment Variables dialog box.

3. In the System Variables list, select Path, and then click Edit. The Edit System Variable dialog box appears.

4. In the Variable Value text box, move the cursor to the end of the existing value, type a semicolon (;), and then type the full path to the folder where you store your scripts. Figure 31.3 shows an example.

Edit System Variable   X

Variable name: Path

Variable value: hell\v1.0\;c:\users\paul\documents\scripts

                              OK   Cancel

FIGURE 31.3   Add your script folder to the `Path` environment variable to run your scripts from any folder.

5. Click OK in all open dialog boxes.

6. If you have a PowerShell session running, shut it, and then restart PowerShell to put the new `Path` variable into effect.

Windows 7 Keyboard Shortcuts

Windows 7 was made with the mouse in mind, so most day-to-day tasks are designed to be performed using the standard mouse moves. However, this doesn't mean you should ignore your keyboard when you're not typing. Windows 7 is loaded with keyboard shortcuts and techniques that you can use as replacements or enhancements for mouse clicks and drags. These shortcuts (as shown in Tables A.1 through A.13) are often a faster way to work because you don't have to move your hand from the keyboard to the mouse and back. Also, the Windows 7 keyboard techniques are useful to know just in case you have problems with your mouse and must rely on the keyboard to get your work done.

TABLE A.1   General Windows 7 Shortcut Keys

Press	To Do This
Ctrl+Esc	Open the Start menu.
Windows Logo	Open the Start menu.
Ctrl+Alt+Delete	Display the Windows Security window.
Print Screen	Copy the entire screen image to the Windows Clipboard.
Alt+Print Screen	Copy the active window's image to the Windows Clipboard.
Alt+Double-click	Display the property sheet for the selected object.
Alt+Enter	Display the property sheet for the selected object.
Shift	Prevent an inserted disc from running its AutoPlay application. (Hold Shift while inserting the disc.)
Shift+F10	Display the shortcut menu for the selected object. (This is the same as right-clicking the object.)
Shift+Right-click	Display the shortcut menu with alternative commands for the selected object.

TABLE A.2   Shortcut Keys for Working with Program Windows

Press	To Do This
Alt	Activate or deactivate the program's menu bar.
Alt+Esc	Cycle through the open program windows.
Alt+F4	Close the active program window.
Alt+Spacebar	Display the system menu for the active program window.
Alt+Tab	Cycle through icons for each of the running programs.
Windows Logo+Tab	Launch Flip 3D to cycle through a 3D stack of running program windows.
F1	Display context-sensitive help.
F10	Activate the application's menu bar.

TABLE A.3   Shortcut Keys for Working with Documents

Press	To Do This
Alt+ - (hyphen)	Display the system menu for the active document window.
Alt+Print Screen	Copy the active window's image to the Clipboard.
Ctrl+F4	Close the active document window.
Ctrl+F6	Cycle through the open documents within an application.
Ctrl+N	Create a new document.
Ctrl+O	Display the Open dialog box.
Ctrl+P	Display the Print dialog box.
Ctrl+S	Save the current file. If the file is new, display the Save As dialog box.

TABLE A.4   Shortcut Keys for Working with Data

Press	To Do This
Backspace	Delete the character to the left of the insertion point.
Ctrl+C	Copy the selected data to memory.
Ctrl+F	Display the Find dialog box.
Ctrl+H	Display the Replace dialog box.
Ctrl+X	Cut the selected data to memory.
Ctrl+V	Paste the most recently cut or copied data from memory.
Ctrl+Z	Undo the most recent action.
Delete	Delete the selected data.
F3	Repeat the most recent Find operation.

TABLE A.5   Shortcut Keys for Moving the Insertion Point

Press	To Do This
Ctrl+End	Move the insertion point to the end of the document.
Ctrl+Home	Move the insertion point to the beginning of the document.
Ctrl+left arrow	Move the insertion point to the next word to the left.
Ctrl+right arrow	Move the insertion point to the next word to the right.
Ctrl+down arrow	Move the insertion point to the beginning of the next paragraph.
Ctrl+up arrow	Move the insertion point to the beginning of the paragraph.

TABLE A.6   Shortcut Keys for Selecting Text

Press	To Do This
Ctrl+A	Select all the text in the current document.
Ctrl+Shift+End	Select from the insertion point to the end of the document.
Ctrl+Shift+Home	Select from the insertion point to the beginning of the document.
Ctrl+Shift+left arrow	Select the next word to the left.
Ctrl+Shift+right arrow	Select the next word to the right.
Ctrl+Shift+down arrow	Select from the insertion point to the end of the paragraph.
Ctrl+Shift+up arrow	Select from the insertion point to the beginning of the paragraph.
Shift+End	Select from the insertion point to the end of the line.
Shift+Home	Select from the insertion point to the beginning of the line.
Shift+left arrow	Select the next character to the left.
Shift+right arrow	Select the next character to the right.
Shift+down arrow	Select the next line down.
Shift+up arrow	Select the next line up.

TABLE A.7   Shortcut Keys for Working with Dialog Boxes

Press	To Do This
Alt+down arrow	Display the list in a drop-down list box.
Alt+*Underlined letter*	Select a control.
Ctrl+Shift+Tab	Move backward through the dialog box tabs.
Ctrl+Tab	Move forward through the dialog box tabs.
Enter	Select the default command button or the active command button.
Spacebar	Toggle a check box on and off; select the active option button or command button.
Esc	Close the dialog box without making any changes.
F1	Display help text for the control that has the focus.
F4	Display the list in a drop-down list box.
Backspace	In the Open and Save As dialog boxes, move up to the parent folder when the folder list has the focus.
Shift+Tab	Move backward through the dialog box controls.
Tab	Move forward through the dialog box controls.

TABLE A.8   Shortcut Keys for Drag-and-Drop Operations

Press	To Do This
Ctrl	Copy the dragged object.
Ctrl+Shift	Display a shortcut menu after dropping a left-dragged object.
Esc	Cancel the current drag.
Shift	Move the dragged object.

TABLE A.9   Shortcut Keys for Working in a Folder Window

Press	To Do This
Alt	Display Classic menus.
Alt+D	Display the pathname of the current folder in the address bar.
Alt+left arrow	Navigate backward to a previously displayed folder.
Alt+right arrow	Navigate forward to a previously displayed folder.
Backspace	Navigate to the parent folder of the current folder.
Ctrl+A	Select all the objects in the current folder.
Ctrl+C	Copy the selected objects.
Ctrl+V	Paste the most recently cut or copied objects.
Ctrl+X	Cut the selected objects.
Ctrl+Z	Undo the most recent action.
Ctrl+E	Activate the Instant Search box.
Delete	Delete the selected objects.
F2	Rename the selected object.
F3	Display a Search window.
F5	Refresh the folder contents.
Shift+Delete	Delete the currently selected objects without sending them to the Recycle Bin.

TABLE A.10   Shortcut Keys for Working with Internet Explorer

Press	To Do This
Alt	Display Classic menus.
Alt+Home	Go to the home page.
Alt+left arrow	Navigate backward to a previously displayed web page.
Alt+right arrow	Navigate forward to a previously displayed web page.
Ctrl+A	Select the entire web page.
Alt+C	Display the Favorites Center.
Ctrl+B	Display the Organize Favorites dialog box.
Ctrl+D	Add the current page to the Favorites list.
Ctrl+E	Activate the Instant Search box.
Ctrl+F	Display the Find dialog box.
Ctrl+H	Display the History list.
Ctrl+Shift+H	Pin the History list.
Ctrl+I	Display the Favorites list.
Ctrl+Shift+I	Pin the Favorites list.
Ctrl+J	Display the Feeds list.
Ctrl+Shift+J	Pin the Feeds list.
Ctrl+N	Open a new window.
Ctrl+T	Open a new tab.
Ctrl+W	Close the current tab.
Ctrl+Q	Display the Quick Tabs.
Ctrl+O	Display the Open dialog box.
Ctrl+P	Display the Print dialog box.
Ctrl+Tab	Cycle forward through the open tabs.
Ctrl+Shift+Tab	Cycle backward through the open tabs.
Ctrl++	Zoom in on the current web page.
Ctrl+−	Zoom out of the current web page.
Esc	Stop downloading the web page.

TABLE A.10   Continued

Press	To Do This
F4	Open the Address toolbar's drop-down list.
F5	Refresh the web page.
F11	Toggle between Full Screen mode and the regular window.
Spacebar	Scroll down one screen.
Shift+Spacebar	Scroll up one screen.
Shift+Tab	Cycle backward through the Address toolbar and the web page links.
Tab	Cycle forward through the web page links and the Address toolbar.

TABLE A.11   Shortcut Keys for Working with Windows Media Player

Press	To Do This
Ctrl+O	Open a media file.
Ctrl+U	Open a media URL.
Ctrl+P	Play or pause the current media.
Ctrl+S	Stop the current media.
Ctrl+B	Go to the previous track.
Ctrl+Shift+B	Rewind to the beginning of the media.
Ctrl+F	Go to the next track.
Ctrl+Shift+F	Fast-forward to the end of the media.
Ctrl+H	Toggle Shuffle playback.
Ctrl+T	Toggle Repeat playback.
Ctrl+M	Show the menu bar.
Ctrl+Shift+M	Auto-hide the menu bar.
Ctrl+N	Create a new playlist.
Ctrl+1	Switch to Full mode.
Ctrl+2	Switch to Skin mode.
Alt+1	Display video size at 50%.
Alt+2	Display video size at 100%.
Alt+3	Display video size at 200%.
Alt+Enter	Toggle Full Screen mode.

TABLE A.11   Continued

Press	To Do This
F3	Display the Add to Library dialog box.
F7	Mute sound.
F8	Decrease volume.
F9	Increase volume.

TABLE A.12   Shortcut Keys for DOSKEY

Press	To Do This
Command Recall Keys	
Alt+F7	Delete all the commands from the recall list.
Arrow keys	Cycle through the commands in the recall list.
F7	Display the entire recall list.
F8	Recall a command that begins with the letter or letters you've typed on the command line.
F9	Display the Line number: prompt. You then enter the number of the command (as displayed by F7) that you want.
Page Down	Recall the newest command in the list.
Page Up	Recall the oldest command in the list.
Command-Line Editing Keys	
Backspace	Delete the character to the left of the cursor.
Ctrl+End	Delete from the cursor to the end of the line.
Ctrl+Home	Delete from the cursor to the beginning of the line.
Ctrl+left arrow	Move the cursor one word to the left.
Ctrl+right arrow	Move the cursor one word to the right.
Delete	Delete the character over the cursor.
End	Move the cursor to the end of the line.
Home	Move the cursor to the beginning of the line.
Insert	Toggle DOSKEY between Insert mode (your typing is inserted between existing letters on the command line) and Overstrike mode (your typing replaces existing letters on the command line).
Left arrow	Move the cursor one character to the left.

TABLE A.12   Continued

Press	To Do This
Right arrow	Move the cursor one character to the right.

TABLE A.13   Windows Logo Key Shortcut Keys

Press	To Do This
Windows Logo	Open the Start menu.
Windows Logo+D	Minimize all open windows. Press Windows Logo+D again to restore the windows.
Windows Logo+E	Open Windows Explorer (Computer folder).
Windows Logo+F	Display a Search window.
Windows Logo+Ctrl+F	Find a computer.
Windows Logo+L	Lock the computer.
Windows Logo+M	Minimize all open windows, except those with open modal windows.
Windows Logo+Shift+M	Undo minimize all.
Windows Logo+R	Display the Run dialog box.
Windows Logo+U	Display the Ease of Access Center.
Windows Logo+F1	Display Windows Help.
Windows Logo+Break	Display the System window.
Windows Logo+Spacebar	Scroll down one page (supported only in certain applications, such as Internet Explorer).
Windows Logo+Shift+Spacebar	Scroll up one page (supported only in certain applications, such as Internet Explorer).
Windows Logo+Tab	Cycle through a 3D stack of running program windows.

TIP

If your keyboard doesn't have a Windows Logo key, you can remap an existing key to act as a Windows Logo key. The trick here is to tell Windows 7 to take the built-in scancode of an existing key and convert it to the scancode associated with the Windows Logo key. For example, when you press the right Alt key, the hexadecimal scancode E038 is generated. The scancode associated with the right Windows Logo key is E05C. Therefore, you need to tell Windows 7 that whenever it detects the scancode E038 after a right Alt keypress, that it should send to the system the code E05C instead. This means that pressing the right Alt key will be the same thing as pressing the Windows Logo key.

To do this, open the Registry Editor and navigate to the following key:

`HKLM\SYSTEM\CurrentControlSet\Control\Keyboard Layout`

Select, Edit, New, Binary Value, type **Scancode Map**, and press Enter. Open the Scancode Map setting and set its value to the following:

`00 00 00 00 00 00 00 00 01 00 00 00 5C E0 38 E0`

Reboot your computer to put the new key mapping into effect.

Understanding TCP/IP

They want to deliver vast amounts of information over the Internet. And again, the Internet is not something you just dump something on. It's not a truck. It's a series of tubes.
—Senator Ted Stevens

One of Windows 7's major goals is to simplify networking, a topic that's all too often complex, arcane, even incomprehensible. Indeed, for many users, the only "networking" chore they have to perform on the Windows 7 machine is connecting it to their network's router or switch. That's as it should be, because most small network users don't want to become network administrators; they just want Windows 7 to do its job and let them share files, stream media, and perhaps make remote connections, all of which I covered in Part VI, "Unleashing Windows 7 Networking."

One of this book's major goals is to show you the power that lurks under Windows 7's gentle façcade. Some of that power comes in the form of the world-class networking infrastructure that Microsoft has been building ever since Windows for Workgroups appeared in 1992. This means that Windows 7 networks with the best of them, but—and here's the good news—you don't need to know very much about all the available network layers, protocols, and whatnot.

However, as you saw in Part VI, if you want to unleash Windows 7's networking potential, things like IP addresses, subnet masks, DNS servers, and other networking arcane will bubble up from the depths. To understand these ideas, you don't need a degree in electrical engineering. Instead, you mostly just need to know a bit about a protocol named TCP/IP, which is the default protocol used not only by

Windows 7, but also by Windows Vista, Windows XP, Windows Home Server, and Mac OS X. In other words, all the computers on your small network talk to each other using TCP/IP, so to a very large extent your home network *is* TCP/IP. Therefore, to get the most out of Windows 7 networking—even on your relatively humble network—you need to understand what TCP/IP is, how it works, and how you use it.

If there's a downside to TCP/IP, it's that compared to other protocols, TCP/IP is much more complex to implement and manage. However, we're still not talking about brain surgery here. With just a smattering of background info, the mysteries of TCP/IP will become clear, and your configuration chores will become downright comprehensible. That's my goal in this appendix: to give you enough knowledge about TCP/IP plumbing to stand you in good stead when you get down to the brass tacks of actually setting up, using, and if necessary, troubleshooting TCP/IP.

What Is TCP/IP?

Although people often speak of TCP/IP as being a protocol, it is in fact a suite of protocols (more than 100 in all!) housed under one roof. Here's a summary of the most important protocols:

Internet Protocol (IP)	This is a connectionless protocol that defines the Internet's basic packet structure and its addressing scheme, and that also handles routing of packets between hosts.
Transmission Control Protocol (TCP)	This is a connection-oriented protocol that sets up a connection between two hosts and ensures that data is passed between them reliably. If packets are lost or damaged during transmission, TCP takes care of retransmitting the packets.
File Transfer Protocol (FTP)	This protocol defines file transfers among computers on the Internet.
Simple Mail Transport Protocol (SMTP)	This protocol describes the format of Internet email messages and how messages are delivered.
Post Office Protocol (POP)	This protocol specifies how an email client connects to and downloads messages from a mail server.
Internet Message Access Protocol (IMAP)	This protocol defines how to manage received messages on a remote server, including viewing headers, creating folders, and searching message data.
Hypertext Transport Protocol (HTTP)	This protocol defines the format of Uniform Resource Locator (URL) addresses and how World Wide Web data is transmitted between a server and a browser.
Remote Desktop Protocol (RDP)	This protocol defines the secure communication channel between a host PC and a client running Remote Desktop Connection.

Network News Transport   This protocol defines how Usenet newsgroups and postings are
Protocol (NNTP)   transmitted.

Of these, IP and TCP are the most important for our purposes, so the next two sections look at these protocols in greater detail.

THE TCP/IP STACK

You'll often see references to the TCP/IP stack. Networks are always implemented in a layered model that begins with the application and presentation layers at the top (these layers determine how programs interact with the operating system and user, respectively) and the data link and physical layers at the bottom (these layers govern the network drivers and network adapters, respectively). In between, you have a three-layer stack of protocols:

Session layer—These protocols let applications communicate across the network. This is where protocols such as FTP and SMTP reside.

Transport layer—These connection-oriented protocols ensure that data is transmitted correctly. This is where TCP resides.

Network layer—These connectionless protocols handle the creation and routing of packets. This is where IP resides.

Understanding IP

As the name *Internet Protocol* implies, the Internet, in a basic sense, *is* IP. That's because IP has a hand in everything that goes on in the Internet:

▶ The structure of all the data being transferred around the Internet is defined by IP.

▶ The structure of the address assigned to every host computer and router on the Internet is defined by IP.

▶ The process by which data gets from one address to another (this is called *routing*) is defined by IP.

Clearly, to understand the Internet (or, on a smaller scale, an *intranet*: the implementation of Internet technologies for use within a corporate organization), you must understand IP. In turn, this understanding will make your life a lot easier when it comes time to implement TCP/IP in your Windows 7 network.

The Structure of an IP Datagram

Network data is broken down into small chunks called *packets*. These packets include not only the data (such as part of a file), but also *header information* that specifies items, such as the destination address and the address of the sender. On the Internet, data is transmitted in a packet format defined by IP. These IP packets are known as *datagrams*.

The datagram header can be anywhere from 160 to 512 bits in length, and it includes information, such as the address of the host that sent the datagram and the address of the host that is supposed to receive the datagram. Although you don't need to know the exact format of a datagram header to implement TCP/IP, Table B.1 spells it out in case you're interested.

TABLE B.1   Structure of a Datagram Header

Field	Bits	Description
Version	0 to 3	The format of the header.
Internet Header Length	4 to 7	The length of the header, in words (32 bits).
Type of Service	8 to 15	The quality of service desired. (For example, this field can be used to set precedence levels for the datagram.)
Total Length	16 to 31	The length of the datagram, including the header and data. Because this is a 16-bit value, datagrams can be as large as 65,536 bytes.
Identification	32 to 47	An identifying value that lets the destination reassemble a fragmented datagram. (Some systems can't handle packets larger than a particular size, so they'll fragment datagrams as needed. The header is copied to each fragment, and the next two fields are altered as necessary.)
Flags	48 to 50	One flag specifies whether a datagram can be fragmented. If it can't, and the host can't handle the datagram, it discards the datagram. If the datagram can be fragmented, another flag indicates whether this is the last fragment.
Fragment Offset	51 to 63	A field that specifies the position in the datagram of this fragment if the datagram is fragmented.
Time to Live	64 to 71	The maximum number of hosts through which the datagram can be routed. Each host decrements this value by 1, and if the value reaches 0 before arriving at its destination, the datagram is discarded. This prevents runaway datagrams from traversing the Internet endlessly.
Protocol	72 to 79	The session layer protocol being used (such as FTP or SMTP).
Header Checksum	80 to 95	A check of the integrity of the header (not the data).
Source Address	96 to 127	The IP address of the host that sent the datagram.
Destination Address	128 to 159	The IP address of the host that is supposed to receive the datagram.
Options	160 and over	A field that can contain anywhere from 0 to 352 bits. It specifies extra options such as security.

The rest of the datagram is taken up by the data that is to be transmitted to the destination host.

The Structure of an IP Address

You saw in the preceding section that the addresses of both the source and the destination hosts form an integral part of every IP datagram. This section looks at the structure of these IP addresses. When working with TCP/IP in your Windows 7 network, you might have to specify the server's static IP address, use an IP address to connect to another computer, or enter the IP address of your network router to perform a remote network connection. In other words, IP addresses come up a lot these days, so you need to know how they work.

An *IP address* is a 32-bit value assigned to a computer by a network administrator or, if you've signed up for an Internet account, by your *Internet service provider* (ISP). As you'll see in a minute, these addresses are designed so that every host and router on the Internet or within a TCP/IP network has a unique address. That way, when an application needs to send data to a particular locale, it knows that the destination address it plops into the datagram header will make sure that everything ends up where it's supposed to.

Dotted-Decimal Notation

The problem with IP addresses is their "32-bitness." Here's an example:

11001101110100000111000100000010

Not very inviting, is it? To make these numbers easier to work with, the TCP/IP powers that be came up with the *dotted-decimal notation* (also known in the trade as *dotted-quad notation*). This notation divides the 32 bits of an IP address into four groups of 8 bits each (each of these groups is called a *quad*), converts each group into its decimal equivalent, and then separates these numbers with dots.

Let's look at an example. Here's the previous IP address grouped into four 8-bit quads:

11001101 11010000 01110001 00000010

Now you convert each quad into its decimal equivalent. When you do, you end up with this:

```
11001101 11010000 01110001 00000010
   205      208      113       2
```

TIP

You can convert a value from binary to decimal using Windows' Calculator. Select Start, type **calc**, and then select Calculator in the results. In the Calculator window, select View, Programmer. Activate the Bin option, use the text box to type the 1s and 0s of the binary value you want to convert, and activate the Dec option.

Now you shoehorn dots between each decimal number to get the dotted-decimal form of the address:

`205.208.113.2`

IP Address Classes

So, how is it possible, with millions of hosts on the Internet the world over, to ensure that each computer has a unique IP address? The secret is that each network that wants on the Internet must sign up with a domain registrar (such as VeriSign.com or Register.com). In turn, the registrar assigns that network a block of IP addresses that the administrator can then dole out to each computer (or, in the case of an ISP, to each customer). These blocks come in three classes: A, B, and C.

In a *Class A network*, the registrar assigns the first (that is, the leftmost) 8 bits of the address: The first bit is 0, and the remaining 7 bits are an assigned number. Two to the power of 7 is 128, so 128 Class A networks are possible. The dotted-decimal versions of these IP addresses begin with the numbers 0 (that is, 00000000) through 127 (that is, 01111111). However, 0 isn't used, and 127 is used for other purposes, so there are really only 126 possibilities.

> **NOTE**
>
> The numbers assigned by the registrar are called *network IDs*, and the numbers assigned by the network administrator are called *host IDs*. For example, consider the following address from a Class A network: 115.123.234.1. The network ID is 115 (or it's sometimes written as 115.0.0.0), and the host ID is 123.234.1.

The number 126 might seem small, but consider that the remaining 24 address bits are available for the network to assign locally. In each quad, you have 254 possible numbers (0 and 255 aren't used), so you have 254×254×254 possible addresses to assign, which comes out to a little more than 16 million. In other words, you need to have a large system to rate a Class A network. (If you do have such a system, don't bother petitioning the registrar for a block of IP addresses because all the Class A networks were snapped up long ago by behemoths such as IBM.) Figure B.1 shows the layout of the IP addresses used by Class A networks.

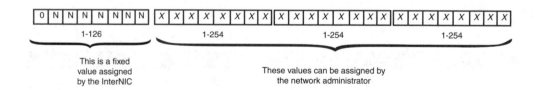

FIGURE B.1   The IP address structure for Class A networks.

> **NOTE**
>
> Bear in mind that you need to register your network with the registrar only if you require Internet access. If you're just creating an internal TCP/IP network, you can create your own block of IP addresses—usually in the range 192.168.1.x or 192.168.0.x, where x is a number between 1 and 254—and assign them at will.

In a *Class B network*, the registrar assigns the first 16 bits of the address: The first 2 bits are 10, and the remaining 14 bits are an assigned number. This allows for a total of 16,384 (2 to the power of 14) Class B networks, all of which have a first quad dotted-decimal value between 128 (that is, 10000000) and 191 (that is, 10111111). Note that, as with Class A networks, all the possible Class B numbers have been assigned.

Again, the network administrator can dole out the remaining 16 bits to the network hosts. Given 254 possible values in each of the two quads, that produces a total of 64,516 possible IP addresses. Figure B.2 shows the layout of Class B network IP addresses.

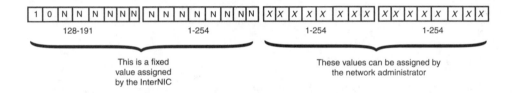

FIGURE B.2   The IP address structure for Class B networks.

In a *Class C network*, the registrar assigns the first 24 bits of the address: The first 3 bits are 110, and the remaining 21 bits are an assigned number. So, the total number of Class C networks available is 2,097,152 (2 to the power of 21), all of which have a first quad dotted-decimal value between 192 (that is, 11000000) and 223 (that is, 11011111).

This leaves only the remaining 8 bits in the fourth quad for network administrators to assign addresses to local computers. Again, 0 and 255 aren't used, so a Class C network has a total of 254 possible IP addresses. The layout of Class C network IP addresses is shown in Figure B.3.

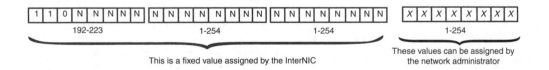

FIGURE B.3   The IP address structure for Class C networks.

> **NOTE**
>
> Because the first quad of an IP address is 8 bits, the range of possible values should be between 0 and 255, but Class A, B, and C networks usurp only 0 through 223. What happened to 224 through 255? Well, the values between 224 and 239 are used for special multicast protocols (these are *Class D addresses*), and the values between 240 and 255 are used for experimental purposes (these are *Class E addresses*).

> **NOTE**
>
> I already mentioned that the address blocks for Class A and Class B networks are long gone, but with more than two million Class C blocks available, there's plenty to go around, right? Wrong! These blocks are being gobbled up quickly, and it's predicted that they'll run out before too long. To overcome this problem with the current version of IP—called *IP version 4* or *IPv4*—, the *Internet Engineering Task Force* (IETF) and other industry mavens have come up with a 128-bit replacement—usually known as *IPv6* (IP version 6), but also sometimes called *IPng* (next generation). IPv6 is gradually being phased in to the Internet. Windows 7 supports IPv6, but it uses IPv4 by default, which is why I haven't covered IPv6 in this appendix.

IP Routing

So far, you've seen that IP datagrams include the source and destination IP addresses in their headers and that these addresses use the dotted-decimal notation. The next question is, how do the datagrams get from the source to the destination? The answer is that IP also defines how datagrams travel from host to host in a process called *routing*. (Each leap from one host to the next is called a *hop*.)

When IP is ready to send data, it compares the addresses in the datagram header to see whether the source and destination reside on the same network. If they do, IP just hands the packets over to the LAN for delivery, and the data is sent directly to the destination. If the addresses are on different networks, however, the packets must be routed outside of the network.

Subnet Masks

At first blush, deciding whether the source and destination hosts are on the same network sounds easy: Just compare the network IDs of the two addresses. For example, consider the following two addresses:

Source   200.100.55.101

Destination   200.100.66.72

These are Class C networks, so the source address has a network ID of 200.100.55, and the destination has a network ID of 200.100.66. Therefore, they're on different networks. Or are they? One of the consequences of having no more Class A and Class B address blocks is that many large corporations can handle their addressing needs only by obtaining multiple blocks of Class C addresses. So, it's entirely possible that the 200.100.55 and 200.100.66 network IDs belong to the same company and could therefore be part of the same network! If so, IP should look at only the first two quads (200.100) to determine whether the addresses are on the same network.

So, how does IP know to compare the first one, two, or three quads? By using a *subnet mask*. A *subnet* is a subsection of a network that uses related IP addresses. On a Class C network, for example, you could define the first 127 addresses to be on one subnet and the second 127 addresses to be on another subnet. On a larger scale, from the point of view of the Internet—which you can think of as being *the* network—each Class A, B, and C network is a subnet.

The subnet mask is a 32-bit value that is usually expressed in the same dotted-decimal notation used by IP addresses. The purpose of the subnet mask is to let IP separate the network ID (or, as you saw in the preceding example, part of the network ID) from the full IP address and thus determine whether the source and destination are on the same network. Table B.2 spells out the default subnet masks used for each type of network class.

TABLE B.2   Normal Subnet Masks Used for Each Network Class

Network	Subnet Mask	Bit Values
Class A	255.0.0.0	11111111 00000000 00000000 00000000
Class B	255.255.0.0	11111111 11111111 00000000 00000000
Class C	255.255.255.0	11111111 11111111 11111111 00000000

When IP applies the subnet mask to an IP address, the part of the mask that is all 0s strips off the corresponding section of the address. Consider the following example:

	IP Address	Mask	Result
Source	200.100.55.101	255.255.0.0	200.100.0.0
Destination	200.100.66.72	255.255.0.0	200.100.0.0

The mask produces the same result, so these two addresses are on the same network. Now consider the example I used earlier. In this case, we need to use a nonstandard mask of 255.255.0.0:

	IP Address	Mask	Result
Source	205.208.113.2	255.255.255.0	205.208.113.0
Destination	205.208.113.50	255.255.255.0	205.208.113.0

NOTE

The operation of the subnet mask is a bit more complex than I've let on. It's actually a two-step process. In the first step, the IP addresses are compared bit by bit with the subnet mask using a Boolean AND operation—if both bits are 1, a 1 is returned; otherwise, a 0 is returned:

Source:

205.208.113.2	11001101 11010000 01110001 00000010
255.255.255.0	11111111 11111111 11111111 00000000
Result of AND	11001101 11010000 01110001 00000000

Destination:

205.208.113.50	11001101 11010000 01110001 00110010
255.255.255.0	11111111 11111111 11111111 00000000
Result of AND	11001101 11010000 01110001 00000000

Now the two results are compared bit by bit using a *Boolean Exclusive Or* (XOR) operation—if both bits are 0 or both bits are 1, a 0 is returned; otherwise, a 1 is returned:

Source Result	11001101 11010000 01110001 00000000
Destination Result	11001101 11010000 01110001 00000000
Result of XOR	00000000 00000000 00000000 00000000

If the result of the XOR operation is all 0s, the source and destination are on the same network.

Routing and the Default Gateway

As I said, if IP determines that the source and destination exist on the same network, it hands the datagrams over to the LAN for immediate delivery. If the destination is outside the network, however, IP's routing capabilities come into play.

Routing is the process by which a datagram travels from the source host to a destination host on another network. The first part of the routing process involves defining a default gateway. This is the IP address of a computer or dedicated router on the same network as the source computer. When IP sees that the destination is on a different network, it sends the datagrams to the default gateway.

When the gateway gets the datagrams, it checks the IP header for the destination address and compares that address to its internal list of other gateways and network addresses on the Internet. In some cases, the gateway will be able to send the datagrams directly to the destination. More likely, though, the gateway will only be able to forward the packet to another system that's en route to the destination. This system repeats the procedure: It checks the destination and forwards the datagrams accordingly. Although many hops might be involved, the datagrams will eventually arrive at their destination.

NOTE

Actually, if the datagram has to perform too many hops, it might never reach its destination. That's because each datagram is supplied with a Time to Live (TTL) value in its header (as described earlier). If the TTL value is 64, for example, and if the datagram has made 64 hops before getting to its destination, it's discarded without a second thought. The TTL is useful for preventing datagrams from running amok and wandering the Internet's highways and byways endlessly.

TIP

If you're curious about how many hops it takes to get from here to there (wherever *there* might be), TCP/IP provides a way to find out. You use a utility called TRACERT. I showed you how it works in Chapter 24, "Troubleshooting Networking."

▶ **See** "Tracking Packets with the TRACERT Command," **p. 504.**

Dynamic IP Addressing

If your network has just a few computers and if the organization of the network is static (the computers attached to the network remain attached at all times), it's easiest to assign an IP address to every computer from the block of addresses supplied by the registrar.

Managing IP addresses, however, can become quite cumbersome if the network has many computers or if the network configuration changes constantly, thanks to users logging on to the network remotely or computers being moved from one subnet to another. One way to solve this problem is to assign IP addresses to network computers dynamically. In other words, when a computer logs on to the network, it is assigned an IP address from a pool of available addresses. When the computer logs off, the address it was using is returned to the pool.

The system that manages this dynamic allocation of addresses is called *Dynamic Host Configuration Protocol* (DHCP), and the computers or devices that implement DHCP are called *DHCP servers*. In most home networks, the router acts as a DHCP server.

Domain Name Resolution

Of course, when you're accessing an Internet resource such as a website or FTP site, you don't use IP addresses. Instead, you use friendlier names such as www.mcfedries.com and ftp.domain.net. That's because TCP/IP, bless its heart, lets us mere humans use English-language equivalents of IP addresses. So, in the same way that IP addresses can be seen as network IDs and host IDs, these English-language alternatives are broken down into *domain names* and *hostnames*.

When you sign up with a registrar, what you're really doing is registering a domain name that is associated with your network. For example, the domain name mcfedries.com might point to the network ID of 205.208.113. The computers—or hosts—on the network have their own hostnames. For example, there might by one machine with the hostname hermes, so its full Internet name is hermes.mcfedries.com and this machine's IP address might be 205.208.113.4); similarly, the web server's hostname is probably www, so its full Internet name is www.mcfedries.com and its IP address might by 205.208.113.2.

Even though domain names and hostnames look sort of like IP addresses (a bunch of characters separated by dots), there's no formula that translates one into the other. Instead, a process called *name resolution* is used to look up hostnames and domain names to find their underlying IP addresses (and vice versa). Three mechanisms are used to perform this task: the LMHOSTS file, the Domain Name System, and the Windows Internet Name System.

The LMHOSTS File

The simplest method of mapping a hostname to an IP address is to use an LMHOSTS file. This is a simple text file that implements a two-column table with IP addresses in one column and their corresponding hostnames in the other, like so:

```
127.0.0.1 localhost
205.208.113.2 www.mcfedries.com
205.208.113.4 hermes.mcfedries.com
```

The address 127.0.0.1 is a special IP address that refers to your computer. If you send a packet to 127.0.0.1, it comes back to your machine. For this reason, 127.0.0.1 is called a *loopback* address. You just add an entry for every host on your network.

For a sample LMHOSTS file—named LMHOSTS.SAM—see the following folder on your computer:

```
%SystemRoot%\System32\drivers\etc
```

You can use this file as a start by copying it to a file in the same folder named LMHOSTS (no extension). Note, however, that after you have the LMHOSTS file set up for your network, you must copy it to *every* machine on the network.

The Domain Name System

The LMHOSTS system is fine for resolving hostnames within a network, but with millions of hosts worldwide, it's obviously impractical for resolving the names of computers that reside outside of your subnet.

You might think that because the registrar handles all the registration duties for domains, your TCP/IP applications could just query some kind of central database at the registrar to resolve hostnames. This approach has two problems: The number of queries this database would have to handle would be astronomical (and thus extremely slow), and you'd have to contact the registrar every time you added a host to your network.

Instead of one central database of hostnames and IP addresses, the Internet uses a distributed database system called the *Domain Name System* (DNS). The DNS databases use a hierarchical structure to organize domains. The *generic top-level domains* (gTLDs) in this hierarchy consist of 19 categories, as described in Table B.3.

TABLE B.3   Generic Top-Level Domains in the DNS

Domain	What It Represents
com	Commercial businesses
edu	Educational institutions
gov	Governments
int	International organizations
mil	Military organizations
net	Networking organizations
org	Nonprofit organizations
aero	The aviation industry
biz	Businesses or firms
cat	Catalan language and culture
coop	Cooperatives
info	Organizations providing information services
jobs	Employment-related websites
mobi	Websites designed for mobile devices
museum	Museums and museum professionals
name	Individual or personal Internet
pro	Registered professionals such as accountants, doctors, lawyers, and engineers
tel	Internet communication services.
travel	The travel industry

Top-level domains also exist for various countries. Table B.4 lists a few of these *country code top-level domains* (ccTLDs).

TABLE B.4   Some Country Code Top-Level Domains in the DNS

Domain	Country It Represents
at	Austria
au	Australia
ca	Canada
ch	Switzerland
cn	China
de	Germany
dk	Denmark
es	Spain
fi	Finland
fr	France
hk	Hong Kong
ie	Ireland
il	Israel
jp	Japan
mx	Mexico
nl	Netherlands
no	Norway
nz	New Zealand
ru	Russia
se	Sweden
uk	United Kingdom
us	United States

Below these top-level domains are the domain names, such as whitehouse.gov and microsoft.com. From there, you can have subdomains (subnetworks), and then hostnames at the bottom of the hierarchy. The database maintains a record of the corresponding IP address for each domain and host.

To handle name resolution, the DNS database is distributed around the Internet to various computers called *DNS servers*, or simply *name servers*. When you set up TCP/IP, you specify one of the DNS servers, and your TCP/IP software uses this server to resolve all hostnames into their appropriate IP addresses.

The Windows Internet Name Service

Earlier, I told you about how DHCP can be used to assign IP addresses to hosts dynamically. On a Microsoft TCP/IP network, how are these addresses coordinated with hostnames? By using a name resolution feature called the *Windows Internet Name Service* (WINS). WINS maps *NetBIOS names* (the names you assign to computers in the Identification tab of the Network properties sheet) to the IP addresses assigned via DHCP.

Understanding TCP

IP is a connectionless protocol, so it doesn't care whether datagrams ever reach their eventual destinations. It just routes the datagrams according to the destination address and then forgets about them. This is why IP is also called an *unreliable* protocol.

We know from experience, however, that the Internet is reliable—most of the time! Where does this reliability come from if not from IP? It comes from the rest of the TCP/IP equation: TCP. You can think of TCP as IP's better half because through TCP, applications can make sure that their data gets where it's supposed to go and that it arrives there intact.

To help you visualize the difference between IP and TCP, imagine IP as analogous to sending a letter through the mail. You put the letter in an envelope, address the envelope, and drop it in a mailbox. You don't know when the letter gets picked up, how it gets to its destination, or even *whether* it gets there.

Suppose, however, that after mailing the letter you were to call up the recipient and say that a letter was on its way. You could give the recipient your phone number and have that person call you when she receives the letter. If the letter doesn't arrive after a preset length of time, the recipient could let you know so that you could resend it.

That phone link between you and the recipient is analogous to what TCP does for data transfers. TCP is a connection-oriented protocol that sets up a two-way communications channel between the source and the destination to monitor the IP routing.

TCP Sockets

In the TCP scheme of things, this communications channel is called a *socket*, and it has two components on each end:

IP address   You've already seen that each IP datagram header includes both the source and the destination IP address. For a TCP socket, these addresses are analogous to the sender and receiver having each other's phone number.

Port number   Having a phone number might not be enough to get in touch with someone. If the person works in an office, you might also have to specify his extension. Similarly, knowing the IP address of a host isn't enough information for TCP. It also must know which application sent the datagram. After all, in a multitasking environment such as Windows, you could be running a web browser, an email client, and an FTP program at the same time. To differentiate between programs, TCP uses a 16-bit number called a *port* that uniquely identifies each running process.

> **NOTE**
>
> On the source host, the port number usually specifies an application. On the destination host, the port can also specify an application, but it's more likely that the port is a fixed number that is used by an Internet service. For example, FTP uses port 21, SMTP uses port 25, and HTTP uses port 80.

The Structure of a TCP Segment

When a TCP/IP application sends data, it divides the data into a number of *TCP segments*. These segments include part of the data along with a header that defines various parameters used in the TCP communication between the source and the destination. These TCP segments are then encapsulated within the data portion of an IP datagram and sent on their way.

Wait a minute. If TCP segments are sent inside IP datagrams, and I just said that IP is unreliable, how can TCP possibly be reliable? The trick is that, unlike straight IP, TCP expects a response from its TCP counterpart on the receiving end. Think of it this way: Imagine mailing a letter to someone and including a Post-it Note on the letter that specifies your phone number and tells the recipient to call you when he receives the letter. If you don't hear back, you know he didn't get the letter. To ensure reliable communications, TCP includes an electronic "Post-it Note" in its header that does two things:

- ▶ When the application requests that data be sent to a remote location, TCP constructs an initial segment that attempts to set up the socket interface between the two systems. No data is sent until TCP hears back from the receiving system that the sockets are in place and that it's ready to receive the data.

- ▶ When the sockets are ready to go, TCP starts sending the data within its segments and always asks the receiving TCP to acknowledge that these data segments have arrived. If no acknowledgment is received, the sending TCP retransmits the segment.

As with IP, you don't need to know the exact format of a TCP header. In case you're curious, however, I've laid it all out in Table B.5.

TABLE B.5   Structure of a TCP Segment Header

Field	Bits	Description
Source Port	0 to 15	This is the source port number.
Destination Port	16 to 31	This is the destination port number.
Sequence Number	32 to 63	In the overall sequence of bytes being sent, this field specifies the position in this sequence of the segment's first data byte.
Acknowledgment Number	64 to 95	If the ACK control bit is set (see the Control Bits entry), this field contains the value of the next sequence number that the sender of the segment is expecting the receiver to acknowledge.
Data Offset	96 to 99	This is the length of the TCP segment header, in 32-bit words. It tells the receiving socket where the data starts.
Reserved	100 to 105	This field is reserved for future use.
Control Bits	106 to 111	These codes specify various aspects of the communication. When set to 1, each bit controls a particular code, as listed here:
	106	URG: Urgent Pointer field significant.
	107	ACK: Acknowledgment Number field is to be used.
	108	PSH: Push function.
	109	RST: Reset the connection.
	110	SYN: Synchronize sequence numbers. This bit is set when the connection is opened.
	111	FIN: No more data from sender, so close the connection.
Window	112 to 127	This is the number of data bytes that the sender can currently accept. This sliding window lets the sender and receiver vary the number of bytes sent and thus increase efficiency.
Checksum	128 to 143	This value lets the receiver determine the integrity of the data.
Urgent Pointer	144 to 159	If the URG control bit is set, this field indicates the location in the data where urgent data resides.
Options	160 and over	This variable-length field specifies extra TCP options such as the maximum segment size.

TCP Features

To ensure that IP datagrams are transferred in an orderly, efficient, and reliable manner, TCP implements the following six features:

Connection opening
On the sending host, a process (such as a web browser) issues a request to send data (such as a URL) to a destination host (such as a web server). TCP creates an initial segment designed to open the connection between the sender and the receiver (the browser and server). In this initial contact, the two systems exchange IP addresses and port numbers (to create the socket interface) and set up the flow control and sequencing (discussed next).

Flow control
One of the parameters that the sending and receiving hosts exchange is the number of bytes each is willing to accept at one time. That way, one system doesn't end up sending more data than the other system can handle. This value can move up or down as circumstances change on each machine, so the systems exchange this information constantly to ensure efficient data transfers.

Sequencing
Every segment is assigned a sequence number. (Or, technically, the first data byte in every segment is assigned a sequence number.) This technique lets the receiving host reassemble any segments that arrive out of order.

Acknowledgment
When TCP transmits a segment, it holds the segment in a queue until the receiving TCP issues an acknowledgment that it has received the segment. If the sending TCP doesn't receive this acknowledgment, it retransmits the segment.

Error detection
A checksum value in the header lets the receiver test the integrity of an incoming segment. If the segment is corrupted, the receiver fires back an error message to the sender, which then immediately retransmits the segment.

Connection closing
When the process on the sending host indicates that the connection should be terminated, the sending TCP sends a segment that tells the receiver that no more data will be sent and that the socket should be closed.

These features illustrate why Internet communications are generally reliable. They show that TCP acts as a sort of chaperone for the IP datagrams traveling from host to host.

Index

Symbols & Numerics

A

B

C

How can we make this index more useful? Email us at indexes@samspublishing.com

How can we make this index more useful? Email us at indexes@samspublishing.com

F

N

How can we make this index more useful? Email us at indexes@samspublishing.com

How can we make this index more useful? Email us at indexes@samspublishing.com

How can we make this index more useful? Email us at indexes@samspublishing.com

X-Y-Z

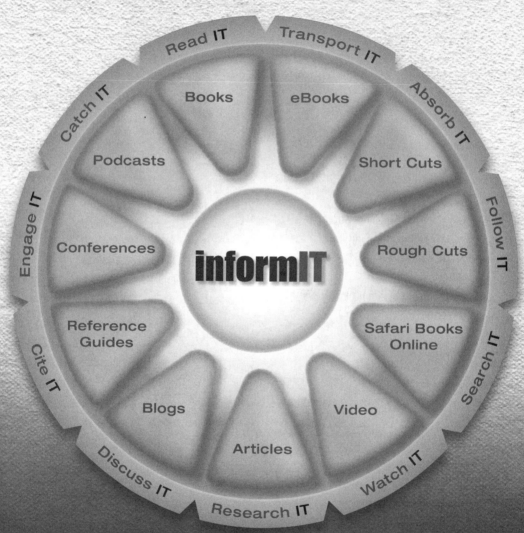